THE STATE OF THE WORLD'S REFUGEES 2000

Fifty years of humanitarian action

D0138970

UNHCR

OXFORD
UNIVERSITY PRESS

OXFORD
UNIVERSITY PRESS

Great Clarendon Street, Oxford OX2 6DP

Oxford University Press is a department of the University of Oxford. It furthers
the University's objective of excellence in research, scholarship, and education by publishing
worldwide in Oxford New York Athens Auckland Bangkok Bogotá Buenos Aires Calcutta Cape Town
Chennai Dar es Salaam Delhi Florence Hong Kong Istanbul Karachi Kuala Lumpur Madrid
Melbourne Mexico City Mumbai Nairobi Paris São Paulo Shanghai Singapore Taipei
Tokyo Toronto Warsaw and associated companies in Berlin Ibadan

Oxford is a registered trade mark of Oxford University Press in the UK and certain other countries

Published in the United States by Oxford University Press Inc., New York

The opinions expressed in this book do not necessarily represent official UNHCR policy
nor are they necessarily endorsed by members of the academic advisory group. Unless otherwise
stated, the book does not refer to events occurring after 31 December 1999. The maps do not
imply the expression of any opinion on the part of UNHCR, concerning the legal status of
any country, territory, city or area, or the delimitation of frontiers or boundaries.

Unless otherwise stated, all maps are produced by the UNHCR Geographic Information Unit
(geographic data from Global Insight—1998 © Europa Technologies Ltd).
Unless otherwise stated, all statistics are provided by the UNHCR Statistical Unit.

This book is available in other languages. For details, contact:
Centre for Documentation and Research
UNHCR, CP 2500
CH-1211 Geneva 2
Switzerland
Fax: (+41 22) 739 7367
E-mail: cdr@unhcr.ch

British Library Cataloguing in Publication Data
Data available

ISBN 0-19-924104-X
ISBN 0-19-924106-6
1 3 5 7 9 10 8 6 4 2

Designed and typeset by Epps Ransom Associates, London
Printed in Great Britain on acid-free paper by The Bath Press Ltd, Bath, Avon

Editorial team

Managing editor and
principal author
Mark Cutts

Editors and analysts
Sean Loughna
Frances Nicholson

Special advisors
Jeff Crisp
Irene Khan

Production editors
Udo Janz
Raymond Wilkinson

Statisticians
Bela Hovy
Tarek Abou Chabake

Cartographers
Jean-Yves Bouchardy
Yvon Orand

Assistants
Claire Bessette
Elena Bovay
Maureen Gumbe

Produced by UNHCR's Division of
Communication and Information,
under the direction of
John Horekens

Main contributing authors:

**Joel Boutroue, Sarah Collinson,
Filippo Grandi, Jane Hoverd Chanaa,
Judith Kumin, Bohdan Nahajlo,
Kathleen Newland, Gérard Prunier,
W. Courtland Robinson, Philip
Rudge, Hiram Ruiz, Sumit Sen,
Hugo Slim, Patricia Weiss Fagen
and Michael Williams.**

Acknowledgements

The editorial team wishes to thank all those who contributed to the preparation of this book. For contributions to boxes: Erin Baines, Carol Batchelor, Jon Bennett, Jo Boyden, Walter Brill, Peter Carey, Roberta Cohen, Nicola Cozza, Bryan Deschamp, David Griffiths, Karen Jacobsen, Kris Janowski, Mahendra P. Lama, Milton Moreno, Terence Ranger, Paul Richards, Ronald Skeldon, Claudena Skran, Samia Tabari, Rick Towle, Nicholas Van Hear and Peter van der Vaart.

For other editorial assistance and support: Marilyn Achiron, Daniel Bellamy, Axel Bisschop, Emery Brusset, Gervaise Coles, Maureen Connelly, Steven Corliss, Damtew Dessalegne, Khassim Diagne, Jiddo van Drunen, Jean-François Durieux, Ragnhild Ek, Kemlin Furley, Mireille Girard, Oldrich Haselman, Otto Hieronymi, Anneliese Hollmann, Susan Hopper, Arafat Jamal, Mitch Januska, Stéphane Jaquemet, Anne Kellner, Sanda Kimbimbi, Pirkko Kourula, Wei Meng Lim-Kabaa, Marion Lindsay, Christina Linner, Serge Malé, Michael McBride, Nicholas Morris, Ilunga Ngandu, Bernadette Passade Cissé, Trudy Peterson, Françoise Peyroux, Ron Redmond, José Riera, John Ryle, Stacy Sullivan, Hans Thoolen, Volker Türk, Neill Wright, Kirsten Young and Philippa Youngman.

The editorial team also wishes to thank the members of the academic advisory group for their assistance and support, and would like to acknowledge the important role played by the late Myron Weiner in encouraging and inspiring UNHCR's research activities.

Academic advisory group

B.S. Chimni, Jawaharlal Nehru University, New Delhi, India
Shahram Chubin, Geneva Centre for Security Policy, Geneva, Switzerland
Leonardo Franco, Lanus University, Buenos Aires, Argentina
Bill Frelick, US Committee for Refugees, Washington DC, United States
Marrack Goulding, St Antony's College, Oxford, United Kingdom
Ivor C. Jackson, UNHCR (retd.), Geneva, Switzerland
Monica Juma, Moi University, Nairobi, Kenya
Kemal Kirisci, Bogazici University, Istanbul, Turkey
Gil Loescher, Notre Dame University, Indiana, United States
Thandika Mkandawire, UN Research Institute for Social Development, Geneva, Switzerland
Yves Sandoz, International Committee of the Red Cross, Geneva, Switzerland
Astri Suhrke, Chr. Michelsen Institute, Bergen, Norway
Valery Tishkov, Institute of Ethnology and Anthropology, Moscow, Russian Federation
Catherine Wihtol de Wenden, Centre National de la Recherche Scientifique, Paris, France

Contents

Page

Preface
by the UN Secretary-General   ix

Foreword
by the UN High Commissioner for Refugees   x

Introduction   1
- International approaches to
  refugee protection
- History of forced displacement

1 The early years   13
- The UN Relief and Rehabilitation
  Administration
- The International Refugee Organization
- The establishment of UNHCR
- The drafting of the 1951 UN
  Refugee Convention
- The Hungarian crisis of 1956
1.1 High Commissioners Nansen and
     McDonald   15
1.2 United Nations assistance to
     Palestinian refugees   20
1.3 The 1951 UN Refugee Convention   23
1.4 Germany's refugee compensation scheme   28
1.5 Chinese refugees in Hong Kong   33

2 Decolonization in Africa   37
- The Algerian war of independence
- Decolonization south of the Sahara
- Rwanda and the Great Lakes region
- Expanding the international
  refugee regime
2.1 Flight from Rhodesia, return to
     Zimbabwe   45
2.2 The 1967 Protocol to the 1951
     UN Refugee Convention   53
2.3 The 1969 OAU Refugee Convention   55

3 Rupture in South Asia   59
- The birth of the state of Bangladesh
- Repatriation and population exchanges
- UNHCR's expanding role in Asia

3.1 The Tibetan refugee community in India   63
3.2 The expulsion of South Asians from
     Uganda   69
3.3 The plight of the Rohingyas   75

4 Flight from Indochina   79
- War and exodus from Viet Nam
- Cambodian refugees in Thailand
- Laotian refugees in Thailand
- Indochina as a turning point
4.1 International conferences on
     Indochinese refugees   84
4.2 Piracy in the South China Sea   87
4.3 Vietnamese refugees in the United States   90
4.4 Indochina's unaccompanied minors   94

**5 Proxy wars in Africa, Asia and
   Central America**   105
- War and famine in the Horn of Africa
- Afghan refugees in Pakistan and Iran
- Mass displacement in Central America
- Conflict resolution and repatriation
5.1 Refugee camps and settlements   108
5.2 Mozambican refugees in Malawi   112
5.3 The 1984 Cartagena Declaration   123
5.4 Chile under General Pinochet   126

**6 Repatriation and peacebuilding
   in the early 1990s**   133
- The Namibian repatriation
- Repatriation in Central America
- The Cambodian repatriation
- The Mozambican repatriation
- Changing approaches to repatriation
  and reintegration
6.1 Protecting refugee children   138
6.2 Linking relief and development   142
6.3 Human rights and refugees   150

**7 Asylum in the
   industrialized world**   155
- The evolution of asylum policy
  in Europe

Contents

Page

• Resettlement and asylum
  in North America
• Asylum policies in Australia,
  New Zealand and Japan
• Preserving the right to seek asylum

7.1   European Union asylum policy   159
7.2   Non-state agents of persecution   163
7.3   Funding trends   166
7.4   Haitian asylum seekers   176

**8   Displacement in the former
      Soviet region   185**
• The Soviet legacy
• Conflicts in the South Caucasus
  and Tajikistan
• New challenges in CIS countries
• Conflict in the North Caucasus
• The challenges ahead

8.1   Statelessness and disputed citizenship 189
8.2   Non-governmental organizations   194
8.3   Armed attacks on humanitarian
      personnel   206

**9   War and humanitarian action:
      Iraq and the Balkans   211**
• The Kurdish crisis in northern Iraq
• War in Croatia and in Bosnia
  and Herzegovina
• The Kosovo crisis
• Limits of humanitarian action
  in times of war

9.1   Internally displaced persons   214
9.2   East Timor: the cost of independence 236
9.3   International criminal justice   240

**10   The Rwandan genocide
      and its aftermath   245**
• The mass exodus from Rwanda
• Flight from the refugee camps
• Searching for lost refugees in Zaire
• A new phase in the Congolese war

10.1 The problem of militarized refugee camps 248
10.2 Refugees and the AIDS pandemic   253
10.3 Somalia: from exodus to diaspora   256
10.4 War and displacement in West Africa   260
10.5 Western Sahara: refugees in the desert 266

**11   The changing dynamics of
      displacement   275**

Endnotes   288

Page

Annexes
Technical notes
on statistical information   301

1   States party to the 1951 UN
     Refugee Convention, the 1967
     Protocol, the 1969 OAU Refugee
     Convention and members of UNHCR's
     Executive Committee (EXCOM),
     as on 31 December 1999   302

2   Number of refugees and others of
     concern to UNHCR,
     31 December 1999   306

3   Estimated number of refugees by
     region, 1950–99   310

4   Refugee populations by main
     country of asylum, 1980–99   311

5   Largest refugee populations by
     origin, 1980–99   314

6   Refugee populations by origin
     and country/territory of asylum,
     31 December 1999   316

7   Refugees per 1,000 inhabitants:
     top 40 countries as on
     31 December 1999   319

8   Number of refugees in the Great
     Lakes region of Africa, 1960–99   320

9   Asylum applications and refugee
     admissions to selected industrialized
     states, 1990–99   321

10   Main country/territory of origin of
     asylum seekers in Western Europe,
     1990–99   325

11   UN High Commissioners
     for Refugees, 1951–2000   326

Further reading   328

Index   334

Page

Maps

1.1 States party to the 1951 UN Refugee Convention and/or the 1967 Protocol, 30 June 2000   25

2.1 Colonial rule and independence in Africa   46

3.1 Location of main refugee camps in India, November 1971   61

3.2 UNHCR airlift operation in South Asia, 1973–74   70

4.1 Exodus from Indochina, 1975–95   80

4.2 UNHCR-assisted Cambodian, Laotian and Vietnamese refugee camps in Thailand, 1980s and 1990s   100

5.1 Main refugee flows in northeast Africa during the 1980s   107

5.2 Main Afghan refugee flows, 1979–90   117

5.3 Main refugee flows within Central America during the 1980s   122

6.1 Repatriation to Mozambique, 1992–94   149

7.1 Political map of Europe, 1999   172

8.1 The Commonwealth of Independent States and neighbouring countries, 1999   190

8.2 Main population displacements in the Caucasus region during the 1990s   204

9.1 Areas of control in Croatia and Bosnia and Herzegovina, April 1995   223

9.2 Main displaced populations from the former Yugoslavia, December 1995   229

9.3 The 1995 Dayton Agreement for Bosnia and Herzegovina   232

9.4 Displaced populations from Kosovo in neighbouring countries/territories, mid-June 1999   235

9.5 East Timor and region, 1999   237

10.1 Populations of refugees and internally displaced persons in West Africa, 1994   261

10.2 Western Sahara, 1999   267

10.3 Rwandan and Burundian refugee movements, 1994–99   270

11.1 Major refugee populations worldwide, 1999   278

Figures

0.1 Total population of concern to UNHCR, 31 December 1999   10

2.1 Number of refugees in the Great Lakes region, 1960–2000   51

3.1 Bangladeshi refugees in India as on 1 December 1971   65

4.1 Indochina: resettlement and repatriation, 1975–97   85

Page

4.2 Arrivals of Vietnamese boat people by country or territory of first asylum, 1975–95   89

4.3 Indochinese arrivals by country or territory of first asylum, 1975–95   98

4.4 Resettlement of Indochinese refugees by destination, 1975–95   99

5.1 Refugee populations in Ethiopia, Kenya, Somalia and Sudan, 1982–99   106

5.2 Afghan refugee population by country of asylum, 1979–99   119

5.3 Main registered refugee populations in Central America and Mexico, 1980–99   124

5.4 Refugees by main region of asylum, 1975–2000   125

6.1 Estimated annual refugee returns worldwide, 1975–99   151

7.1 Asylum applications submitted in Europe, North America, Australia and New Zealand 1980–2000   157

7.2 Main country/territory of origin of asylum seekers in Western Europe, 1990–99   160

7.3 Central European asylum applications, 1990–99   164

7.4 Annual number of asylum seekers granted asylum in Europe, 1990–99   165

7.5 Contributions to UNHCR as a percentage of GDP by major donors, 1999   166

7.6 Top 15 contributors to UNHCR, 1980–99   166

7.7 UNHCR expenditure, 1950–2000   167

7.8 UNHCR expenditure by region, 1990–2000   167

7.9 Asylum applications submitted in main receiving industrialized states, 1980–99   170

7.10 Number of asylum applications per 1,000 inhabitants submitted in main receiving industrialized states, 1999   171

7.11 Proportion of asylum seekers recognized as refugees or granted humanitarian status,1990–2000   175

7.12 Refugees resettled in industrialized states, 1981–99   181

8.1 Soviet mass deportations of the 1940s   187

8.2 'Forced migrants' registered in the Russian Federation by previous place of residence, 1993–98   199

8.3 Refugees and IDPs in the Commonwealth of Independent States, 1999   208

9.1 Largest IDP populations, 1999   215

10.1 Rwandan and Burundian refugee populations, 1993–99   250

10.2 Rwandan refugees in the Great Lakes region, end-August 1994   251

Preface

by the United Nations Secretary-General

The problem of forced displacement has been one of the most pressing issues facing the United Nations throughout its history. Among the most vulnerable groups of people in the world are those who are displaced, whether as a result of conflict, persecution or other human rights violations. In the 50 years since its creation, the Office of the United Nations High Commissioner for Refugees (UNHCR) has been at the forefront of efforts to protect these people.

UNHCR began as a small organization, with a three-year mandate to help resettle European refugees who were still homeless in the aftermath of the Second World War. Since that time, the organization has continually expanded to meet the growing needs of refugees and other displaced people. Today it assists some 22 million people in every corner of the world.

The State of the World's Refugees 2000 is a timely and important book. It provides a detailed history of half a century of international humanitarian action on behalf of refugees and other displaced people, covering all the major refugee emergencies of the last 50 years. It examines the way in which each succeeding crisis has helped shape an expanding body of refugee law, and it analyses the international community's changing response to the problem of forced migration. Above all, it places humanitarian action in the broader political context and examines the fundamental link between displacement and international peace and security.

As a former UNHCR staff member myself, I have personally witnessed the desperate plight of uprooted people in many situations. This book is a tribute both to the courage demonstrated by millions of displaced people and to the dedication and commitment of all those who have worked to protect and assist them over the last half century.

Kofi Annan

Foreword

by the United Nations High Commissioner for Refugees

It takes only a glance at some of the chapter titles of this book to understand why UNHCR's 50th anniversary is not a cause for celebration. Decade by decade, the book provides a stark chronicle of the major upheavals of the past half century—a seemingly unending string of conflicts and crises that have resulted in the displacement of tens of millions of people.

As we enter the new millennium, the fact that the world still finds a need for UNHCR should serve as a sobering reminder of the international community's continuing failure to prevent prejudice, persecution, poverty and other root causes of conflict and displacement. With over a million people forced to flee their homes in Kosovo, East Timor and Chechnya in the last year of the 20th century alone, it is clear that the problem of forced displacement has not gone away, and is likely to remain a major concern of the international community in the 21st century.

But if the longevity of UNHCR as an organization is nothing to celebrate, the courage of the tens of millions of refugees and displaced people who have survived over the past 50 years certainly is. Often losing everything but hope, they are amongst the great survivors of the 20th century and they deserve our respect. That is why in this anniversary year, UNHCR is honouring them for their countless individual and collective accomplishments.

As the number of people of concern to UNHCR has grown, so has the complexity of the problem of forced displacement. Today, policy is set against a backdrop of radical geopolitical shifts; the enormous growth in numbers of the internally displaced; the prevalence of humanitarian emergencies in conflict situations where civilians are the main targets and where humanitarian workers often come under fire; the process of globalization which simultaneously offers opportunities to some but denies them to others; the rise in human trafficking; declining opportunities for asylum; and open criticism of the 1951 UN Refugee Convention which lies at the heart of UNHCR's work.

States have often shown great hospitality and generosity in hosting refugees and other displaced people. Likewise, UNHCR—together with its partners—has on many occasions played an important role in protecting and assisting these people, and in helping them to restart their lives. But, as the chapters of this book illustrate all too clearly, humanitarian action is of limited value if it does not form part of a wider strategic and political framework aimed at addressing the root causes of conflict. Experience has shown time and time again that humanitarian action alone cannot solve problems which are fundamentally political in nature. Yet all too often, humanitarian organizations like UNHCR have found themselves isolated and alone in dangerous and difficult situations, where they have had to operate without adequate financial and political support.

Unfortunately, the kind of international political commitment that states have shown in dealing with human displacement in some regions has been absent in other regions considered to be of lesser strategic importance. Although the international community has responded quickly to some of the major refugee emergencies in Africa, such as the Rwandan refugee crisis which began in 1994, donors have been slow to provide support in other situations. In 1999, for example, donors were quick to provide funds and resources for those displaced by the conflict in Kosovo. But little attention was paid to the situation in West Africa, where hundreds of thousands of people were uprooted by crises in Sierra Leone and Guinea-Bissau.

States have also often demonstrated a lack of political commitment to solving refugee problems during the post-conflict phase, when the spotlight of the international media has moved away. Refugees and other displaced people often return to places where a fragile peace needs to be consolidated through reconciliation, rehabilitation and reconstruction. Unfortunately, political uncertainty often discourages the involvement of development organizations and investment by financial institutions, with the result that the gap between emergency humanitarian assistance and longer-term development aid remains largely unaddressed.

This book provides a critical analysis of many of these important issues. It attempts to offer an objective account of the difficult situations in which displaced people have found themselves, and of the changing international political environment in which UNHCR and other humanitarian organizations have operated. The aim of the book is not to be judgemental, nor is it to provide an official history of UNHCR and the refugee problem. Rather, it is to present a historical overview of the many dilemmas which have been faced by governments, humanitarian organizations and other actors in dealing with the problem of human displacement.

I have had the privilege of leading UNHCR and its dedicated staff throughout most of the 1990s. During my time as High Commissioner, I have repeatedly attempted to highlight the link between human displacement and international peace and security. It is vital that the international community continue to seek lasting solutions to problems of human displacement. Those who would ignore them do so at their peril. History has shown that displacement is not only a consequence of conflicts; it can also cause conflict. Without human security, there can be no peace and stability.

Sadako Ogata

Sadako Ogata

Introduction

Much has been written in recent years on the subject of humanitarian action. A wealth of specialist literature also exists on the legal aspects of refugee protection. But few historians have focused specifically on the issue of forced human displacement and on the development of international approaches to the problem. As the historian Eric Hobsbawm has noted in his book *On History*, why some historical experiences become part of a wider historical memory, but so many others do not, is a disquieting phenomenon.[1] This book attempts to address this issue by looking at the history of forced displacement in the second half of the 20th century.

During the last decade of the 20th century, governments, international organizations and the public became increasingly aware of the problems faced by refugees and internally displaced people. This was largely a result of live television reports, which provided dramatic images of desperate people fleeing from places such as Bosnia and Herzegovina, Chechnya, Iraq, Kosovo and Rwanda. It also resulted from the increased scope, in the post-Cold War era, for involvement in situations of mass displacement by humanitarian organizations, human rights organizations, multinational military forces, peace negotiators, war crimes investigators, journalists and a range of other external actors. The problem of forced displacement, however, is not new, and neither are international efforts to alleviate the suffering of uprooted people.

International approaches to refugee protection

Throughout history, people have had to abandon their homes and seek safety elsewhere to escape persecution, armed conflict or political violence. This has happened in every region of the world. Most religions incorporate concepts such as asylum, refuge, sanctuary and hospitality for people who are in distress. But until the 20th century there were no universal standards for the protection of such people. Efforts to protect and assist them were essentially localized and *ad hoc* in nature.

It was not until the period after the First World War, when the League of Nations came into being, that the refugee issue came to be regarded as an international problem that had to be tackled at the international level. Even then, the growth of an international system to respond to and manage refugee problems was slow and intermittent. The League of Nations appointed a number of High Commissioners

Refugees crossing from the Soviet to the British zone of occupation in Germany in 1949. (GERMIN/BPK/1949)

and envoys to deal with specific refugee groups such as Russians, Armenians and Germans, but none of these developed into long-standing arrangements. Similarly, after the Second World War, separate bodies were established to deal with European, Palestinian and Korean refugees.

By 1950, the international community had still not established a network of institutions, systems and laws to deal with the refugee problem in a global manner. The turning-point came in 1950–51, with the establishment of the office of the United Nations High Commissioner for Refugees (UNHCR) and the adoption of the United Nations Convention Relating to the Status of Refugees. Together they provided, for the first time, a formal structure for responding to the needs of refugees and standards for the protection of refugees under inter-national law.

The 1951 UN Refugee Convention is significant in two respects. First, although it was initially limited to refugees from Europe, it provides a general definition of a refugee as someone outside his or her own country and unable to return as a result of a well-founded fear of persecution on grounds of race, religion, nationality, political opinion or membership of a social group. This means that people displaced within their own borders do not come under the international legal definition of 'refugees'. Second, it recognizes that people who fall within the refugee definition should benefit from certain rights, and that helping refugees should not simply be a question of international charity and political advantage. The Convention places obligations upon states which are party to it, the most fundamental of which is the principle of 'non-refoulement'. This concerns the oblig-ation of countries of asylum not to return people forcibly to situations where they have a well-founded fear of persecution.

Primary responsibility for protecting and assisting refugees lies with states, particularly the countries of asylum to which refugees flee. But UNHCR also has an important role in promoting and monitoring states' adherence to the Convention and in enabling them to offer adequate protection to the refugees on their territory.

UNHCR has a mandate to provide both international protection and solutions for refugees. Solutions to refugee problems have traditionally been divided by UNHCR into three categories: voluntary repatriation, local integration in the country of asylum, and resettlement from the country of asylum to a third country. As the chapters of the book illustrate, over the years varying emphasis has been placed on each of these solutions at different times.

While the international community has addressed the refugee problem in a more consistent and global manner since 1950, there has always been tension between different actors involved in responding to the problem of forced displacement. That tension is particularly evident in UNHCR's relationship with states. On the one hand, states are UNHCR's partners. They established the framework of international refugee law that guides UNHCR's work, they are represented on UNHCR's Executive Committee, they donate the funds without which UNHCR cannot operate, and they provide UNHCR with permission to operate on their territory. On the other hand, UNHCR's role is often to challenge states either for causing refugee movements or for failing to provide adequate protection and assistance to refugees and asylum seekers.

UNHCR's mandate and activities

UNHCR's core mandate has not changed since 1950. The protection of refugees and the search for solutions to the problems of refugees remain the central objectives of the organization. But the environment in which UNHCR works and the types of activity undertaken by the organization have changed significantly over the past 50 years.

First, the scale of UNHCR operations has greatly increased. The organization initially focused on finding solutions for some 400,000 refugees who were still homeless in the aftermath of the Second World War. By 1996, it was assisting some 26 million people. The organization's budget and staffing levels have also risen greatly. In 1951, UNHCR had a budget of US$300,000 and 33 staff members; by 1999, the budget had reached over US$1 billion and the organization was employing over 5,000 staff. UNHCR has also continually expanded the geographic scope of its activites. Initially, it operated only in Europe; by 1999, it had offices in 120 countries across the world.

Second, the range of activities carried out by UNHCR has grown. In its early days, UNHCR focused mainly on facilitating the resettlement of refugees. As the organization became involved in other parts of the world, it was drawn into a wide range of other activities. This included the provision of material assistance such as food and shelter, as well as the provision of healthcare, education and other social services. In an attempt to avoid treating refugee populations as an undifferentiated mass, UNHCR also developed special programmes to assist specific groups of people, such as women and children, adolescents, the elderly, those suffering from the effects of trauma and people with physical disabilities.

Third, the range of UNHCR's beneficiaries has steadily increased. Throughout its history, UNHCR has functioned primarily as an organization for the protection of refugees. Yet refugees are not its only beneficiaries. Over the years, the organization has developed programmes to assist other categories of people, including those displaced within the borders of their own countries, returnees (refugees or internally displaced people who have returned), asylum seekers (whose formal status has not yet been assessed), stateless people, war-affected populations and others.

The expansion of UNHCR's role to cover categories of people other than refugees is consistent with the Statute of the organization. Article 1 directs UNHCR to seek 'permanent solutions for the problem of refugees', while Article 9 provides that the organization 'shall engage in such additional activities . . . as the General Assembly may determine'. A series of General Assembly resolutions has since then provided the legal basis for many of UNHCR's activities with non-refugee populations.

Fourth, the number of international actors involved in programmes aimed at protecting and assisting refugees and other displaced people has grown significantly. In the early 1950s, UNHCR's partners were small in number. By 1999, its implementing partners included over 500 non-governmental organizations (NGOs). UNHCR has also increasingly been called upon by the UN Secretary-General to act as the lead UN humanitarian agency in emergency situations. In addition, UNHCR has found itself working side by side with other UN agencies, UN peacekeepers, other multinational military forces, regional organizations, human rights organizations, and a range of other international and local actors.

Fifth, the organization has become increasingly involved in volatile and unstable places, as well as in situations of ongoing armed conflict. Initially, UNHCR worked only in countries of asylum which were safe and unaffected by armed conflict. UNHCR staff are now often present in the midst of war. This has exposed them to new dangers and has presented the organization with a whole set of new challenges.

UNHCR's activities during its early years are sometimes described as having been reactive, exile-oriented and refugee-specific.[2] Reactive, because UNHCR dealt with refugee problems primarily in the country of asylum. Exile-oriented, because efforts were focused on activities in the country of asylum, and responsibility for solving refugee problems was seen as resting with countries receiving refugees rather than with those producing them. Refugee-specific, because UNHCR generally did not concern itself with other forms of forced displacement.

By contrast, UNHCR's activities in later years—particularly in the post-Cold War period—have been described as proactive, homeland-oriented and holistic. Proactive, because the organization has been much more willing to engage in activities aimed at preventing the human rights abuses and situations which give rise to the displacement in the first place. Homeland-oriented, because UNHCR's strategy has increasingly emphasized not only the duties of host countries but also the obligations of countries from which refugees flee. Holistic, because the organization has sought to promote a more comprehensive approach to the problem of forced displacement. This approach is more long-term and takes into consideration the needs not only of refugees but also of internally displaced people, returnees, asylum seekers, stateless people and others.

History of forced displacement

This book does not set out to provide an institutional history of UNHCR but rather a general history of forced displacement in the 50 years since UNHCR's inception. Much of the book deals with crises in which UNHCR has played a central role in responding to the needs of refugees and other displaced people. But it also examines other groups such as Palestinians (most of whom fall under the mandate of the United Nations Relief and Works Agency for Palestine Refugees in the Near East) and Tibetan refugees in India, where UNHCR's role in providing protection and assistance has been marginal. Throughout the book, an attempt is made to describe not only the plight of those forced to flee their homes, but the political context leading to their displacement, the politics of the international response, and the evolution in the policies and practices of governments, humanitarian organizations and other actors.

The book does not attempt to provide an exhaustive account of all movements of refugees and displaced people in the last 50 years. Instead, it comprises a series of case studies. Each case study highlights certain aspects of forced displacement and shows how different experiences have influenced the development of organizations such as UNHCR. The advantage of this approach is that it allows for particular situations of forced displacement to be analyzed in some depth. The disadvantage is that a number of important cases and some thematic issues are covered only briefly or not at all.

The book covers the period up to 31 December 1999. Unless otherwise explicitly stated, no events after this date are discussed or referred to. The structure of the book is largely chronological, though certain chapters focus on particular regions or thematic issues. It is based on first-hand accounts from UNHCR staff members, extensive use of the UNHCR archives, a series of interviews with people outside the organization and a wealth of literature—much of which is cited in the endnotes and in the list of further reading. For the early years, the book has made extensive use of Louise Holborn's important two-volume work, *Refugees: A Problem of our Time: The Work of the United Nations High Commissioner for Refugees, 1951–1972*.[3]

Early focus on Europe

Chapter 1 begins by assessing briefly the antecedents of UNHCR, including the first High Commissioner for refugees during the League of Nations period, Fridtjof Nansen, the UN Relief and Rehabilitation Administration (UNRRA, 1943–47) and the International Refugee Organization (IRO, 1947–52). It examines the establishment of UNHCR and the conflicting views on the purpose of the organization, as well as the July 1951 Conference of Plenipotentiaries which led to the adoption of the UN Refugee Convention.

Throughout the 1950s, UNHCR focused on refugees in Europe. Since UNHCR's establishment coincided with the onset of the Cold War, the solution generally envisaged for refugee problems at the time was resettlement. Clearly, what Western governments had in mind when UNHCR was created and the UN Refugee Convention was drawn up were refugees fleeing communist regimes. Given the tense East–West relations of the period, UNHCR's early steps were cautious. They were confined mainly to Western Europe and to work of a legal nature, such as helping European governments to adopt laws and procedures to implement the 1951 UN Refugee Convention.

UNHCR's first major challenge was the exodus of some 200,000 refugees from Hungary in 1956, following the Soviet suppression of the Hungarian uprising. This refugee crisis was resolved by the resettlement of most of the refugees in Western countries. At this time, UNHCR was an overwhelmingly Eurocentric organization doing little, for example, for the hundreds of thousands of Chinese refugees who arrived in Hong Kong or for the Tibetan refugees who fled to India in the same decade. In its first years, UNHCR barely touched the world outside Europe, with the exception of the assistance it provided to European refugees stranded in Shanghai by the Chinese revolution.

The 1960s and 1970s

Chapter 2 discusses the decolonization process in Africa which gained momentum in the 1960s. This process ushered in a new era for UNHCR in which the focus moved away from Europe. In particular, the organization became involved in assisting the refugees from the war of independence in Algeria who fled to Morocco and Tunisia. When Algeria achieved independence from France in 1962, some 250,000 refugees returned to their country. This was the first mass repatriation operation in which UNHCR was involved. The chapter goes on to examine other cases of forced displacement in sub-Saharan Africa. In particular, it focuses on UNHCR's role in assisting Rwandan refugees in the Congo and elsewhere.

These refugees were different in many ways from those envisaged in the 1951 UN Refugee Convention. In most cases, they were people who had fled their homes not because of a fear of persecution but because of war and violence related to the process of decolonization. Most of them did not seek to integrate in the country of asylum, but wanted to repatriate when their own countries became independent or when the environment became more secure. Rather than dealing with individual refugees on a case by case basis, UNHCR now found itself dealing with mass flows of refugees.

The chapter describes how in 1967 the geographical and temporal limits of the 1951 UN Refugee Convention were removed by a new Protocol, which made it universally applicable. In 1969, the Organization of African Unity adopted a regional refugee convention of its own, expanding the definition of a refugee to include not only people fleeing persecution but also those fleeing war and communal violence.

Turning to South Asia, chapter 3 examines the Bangladesh refugee crisis which led to UNHCR's first involvement on the Indian sub-continent. In 1971, the war which led to the independence of Bangladesh caused an estimated 10 million Bangladeshi refugees to flee to India in what became the largest single displacement of refugees in the second half of the 20th century. This involved UNHCR in its largest humanitarian emergency to date. During the crisis, the UN Secretary-General called upon UNHCR to act as the 'Focal Point' for coordinating UN and other international humanitarian assistance. This was the precursor of the 'lead agency' concept used in later years. After hostilities ended, UNHCR assisted in organizing a mass repatriation of refugees to Bangladesh. Most refugees returned by the end of February 1972. In 1973, UNHCR was also instrumental in organizing the movement of large numbers of people between Bangladesh and Pakistan—one of the largest population exchanges in history.

While the chapter focuses primarily on the Bangladesh refugee crisis, there is also a brief description of Tibetan refugees in India, UNHCR's involvement with

Rohingyas from Burma who fled to Bangladesh, and UNHCR's role in assisting Asians expelled from Uganda by President Idi Amin in 1972.

Expanding refugee protection

Chapter 4 describes the flight of refugees from Cambodia, Laos and Viet Nam which followed the political upheavals there in the mid-1970s. The exodus from Indochina continued for more than two decades, during which time over three million people fled their countries. Unlike the refugee crises in Algeria and Bangladesh—which had been followed by large-scale repatriation operations—resettlement was seen as the preferred option for most of the Indochinese refugees, as had been the case with refugees in Europe in the 1950s. Altogether, with UNHCR's assistance, some two million people from Indochina were resettled in other countries—around 1.3 million of them in the United States alone.

UNHCR played a lead role in assisting refugees throughout this massive and sustained crisis. The organization greatly expanded the scope of its activities during this period, becoming involved in the construction and management of refugee camps for Cambodians, Laotians and Vietnamese, and in helping to set up innovative anti-piracy and rescue-at-sea measures to protect Vietnamese 'boat people'. Between 1975 and 1980, UNHCR's budget increased from US$76 million to US$510 million and the number of staff more than doubled.

During the 1980s, Western governments became concerned about the large number of Indochinese people arriving in their countries. They came to view them increasingly as economic migrants rather than refugees. Under pressure from these governments, new measures were eventually adopted by states in the region to control departures and to facilitate repatriation. The Indochinese exodus tested the limits of Western states' willingess to provide asylum, even to people fleeing communist regimes.

Chapter 5 focuses on the 1980s, when the Cold War intensified and superpower involvement in civil wars in different parts of the world turned these into intractable proxy wars. These conflicts produced new waves of refugees and displaced people, particularly in the Horn of Africa, Asia and Central America. The country to produce the largest number of refugees during this period was Afghanistan. Following the Soviet invasion of the country in 1979, war eventually caused over six million Afghans to seek refuge in Iran and Pakistan.

This was the decade of large refugee camps. States had clear strategic interests in granting asylum, but they showed little interest in finding long-term, durable solutions for the refugees. On the contrary, the refugees were used as pawns in geopolitical games to destabilize regimes and to encourage insurgency in their countries of origin. This was the case with Afghan *mujahedin* in Pakistan, the Cambodian Khmer Rouge in Thailand, Eritrean and Ethiopian opposition movements with bases in Sudan, and rebels in Central America. It was in this decade that the term 'refugee warrior' became commonplace.

UNHCR continued to grow rapidly during the 1980s, as it responded for the first time to major emergencies on three continents at the same time. In the tense atmosphere of the Cold War, UNHCR found itself working in highly politicized situations. During this period, UNHCR also became involved to a greater extent than before in providing assistance to local people in refugee-affected areas.

This chapter also looks at UNHCR's first significant involvement in South America. The overthrow of the democratically elected government of Salvador Allende in Chile in 1973 and the installation of a military junta in Argentina in 1974 produced thousands of refugees. In both cases, considerable numbers were resettled in Europe, North America and elsewhere.

Chapter 6 goes on to describe the optimism which surrounded the end of the Cold War. A number of large repatriation operations took place and there was hope that lasting solutions might be found for many of the world's refugee problems. From 1989, a series of United Nations peacebuilding operations were established in Namibia, Cambodia, El Salvador, Guatemala and Mozambique. In each of these cases, UNHCR played a major role in facilitating voluntary repatriation. Unlike previous repatriations, where UNHCR's involvement ended soon after the refugees returned to their countries, the chapter describes how in Cambodia, Mozambique and El Salvador UNHCR expanded its role and became involved in a wide range of protection and assistance activities to help returnees and others to reintegrate and rebuild their lives.

The challenge to asylum

Chapter 7 examines the evolution of asylum policies in the industrialized world, focusing primarily on countries in Europe and North America. In the 1980s and 1990s, large numbers of asylum seekers began to arrive in these countries, and suspicions about the motives of many of these people led governments to adopt increasingly restrictive measures to deter arrivals. Much of the chapter focuses on the impact on asylum seekers of measures taken by countries in Europe to harmonize their asylum policies and procedures. The chapter then goes on to examine the development of asylum policies in countries such as Australia, New Zealand and Japan.

Legislative changes which have been introduced in industrialized countries have seriously affected the ability of asylum seekers to gain access to asylum procedures and safety. A number of issues are addressed in the chapter, including the illegal trafficking and smuggling of people, the way in which asylum seekers—including unaccompanied children and family groups—are often kept for prolonged periods in detention centres, and the difficulties which refugees often face in achieving family reunification. Policies to deter irregular migrants from reaching industrialized countries have in many cases led to a blurring of the already problematic distinction between refugees and economic migrants. Such policies have often contributed to the stigmatization of refugees as people trying to circumvent the law.

While acknowledging that states have legitimate interests in controlling access to their territory, the chapter emphasizes that states also have international obligations to provide protection to those fleeing persecution in their own countries. It insists that the fundamental right to seek asylum—as enshrined in the 1951 UN Refugee Convention—needs to be preserved.

After the Cold War

Chapter 8 examines the massive population movements which took place following the dissolution of the Soviet Union in 1991 and some of the complex interconnections between migration and forced displacement. Up to nine million people found themselves on the move in the 1990s. These movements included the repatriation of people who found themselves outside their 'homelands' following the erection of new national boundaries, and the return of thousands of people who had been deported by Josef Stalin in the 1940s.

Inter-ethnic and separatist armed conflicts in the South Caucasus and Central Asia also created waves of displaced people and refugees in the first half of the decade, leading UNHCR to set up large relief operations. The chapter describes the Armenian–Azerbaijani conflict over Nagorno-Karabakh, the conflicts in the Georgian autonomous territories of Abkhazia and South Ossetia and the civil war in Tajikistan. It also describes the displacement caused by conflict in Chechnya in the latter part of the decade, which involved UNHCR in dangerous and complex relief operations in the North Caucasus.

The upheavals of the 1990s saw a rapid expansion of UNHCR's functions and operations, as the international community frequently looked to it to address some of its most acute dilemmas. The organization became involved in situations of ongoing armed conflict and started working side by side with UN peacekeepers and other multinational military forces to a greater extent than ever before. UNHCR also became increasingly involved in assisting internally displaced people and other war-affected populations.

Chapter 9 focuses on two major refugee emergencies in the 1990s in which UNHCR coordinated large-scale relief operations while working closely with multi-national military forces. The first involved the mass flight of Kurds from northern Iraq in 1991, following the Iraqi government's suppression of a rebellion which took place at the end of the Gulf war. The Turkish government's refusal to grant asylum to the Iraqi Kurds caused US-led coalition forces to mount a huge relief operation for people stranded on the mountain passes on the Iraqi–Turkish border. Subsequently, the coalition forces set up a 'safe haven' for them in northern Iraq. The relief operation, which was then taken over by UNHCR, proved to be a watershed for the organization. It marked the beginning of a trend towards greater involvement in 'countries of origin' as compared with 'countries of asylum'.

The other major emergency was in the Balkans. The violent break-up of Yugoslavia, which began in 1991, led to the largest refugee crisis in Europe since the Second World War. The chapter describes the dilemmas faced by UNHCR and other

Total population of concern to UNHCR, 31 December 1999* (Total = 22.3 million)

Figure 0.1

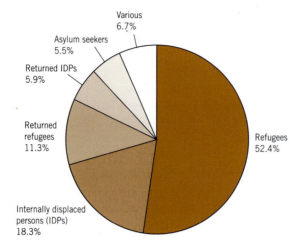

Various
6.7%

Asylum seekers
5.5%

Returned IDPs
5.9%

Returned refugees
11.3%

Returned refugees
11.3%

Refugees
52.4%

Internally displaced persons (IDPs)
18.3%

* For details and explanations, see Annex 2.

humanitarian organizations in confronting 'ethnic cleansing', the difficulties of protecting vulnerable civilians in an active war zone, and the decision by the international community to establish 'safe areas' in Bosnia and Herzegovina—which eventually ended in tragedy with the fall of Srebrenica and Zepa in 1995.

Throughout the Bosnian war, UNHCR coordinated a massive emergency relief operation. Numerous obstacles were faced by humanitarian organizations in gaining access to vulnerable populations. Staff were exposed to extreme dangers and many were injured or killed. To a large extent, the UNHCR-led humanitarian operation became a substitute for other forms of political or military action. The chapter then describes the first four years after the signing of the Dayton Peace Agreement in December 1995, during which time repatriation made little progress in reversing the process of ethnic separation.

Chapter 9 also describes the refugee crisis which took place in the southern Balkans in 1999, when some 800,000 Kosovo Albanians fled to Albania and the former Yugoslav Republic of Macedonia (FYR Macedonia). It examines UNHCR's attempts to coordinate international assistance to the refugees, the trend of increasing bilateral assistance, the role of the NATO-led military force in constructing refugee camps and in providing other support for the humanitarian operation, and the 'humanitarian evacuation programme' which was set up to take refugees from FYR Macedonia to third countries. It then assesses the situation in Kosovo since June 1999, when the Federal Republic of Yugoslavia formally accepted a peace plan under which all its military, police and paramilitary forces withdrew from the province, leading to the deployment of a NATO-led force in Kosovo. Within three months, some 200,000 Serbs and other minorities left Kosovo in a process which became known as 'reverse ethnic cleansing'.

Turning to refugee emergencies in Africa during the 1990s, chapter 10 describes the exodus of over two million Rwandans to Zaire, Tanzania, Burundi and Uganda following the Rwandan genocide in 1994. It focuses mainly on the situation in Zaire (renamed the Democratic Republic of the Congo in 1997) and Tanzania, describing the many dilemmas faced by UNHCR and other humanitarian organizations as they attempted to assist refugees in camps largely controlled by members of the former Rwandan government and its army, which had been responsible for organizing the genocide in the first place. The chapter explains how many of the refugees in the camps were effectively held as political hostages, and how they were used as a 'human shield' by those who had carried out the genocide. Various attempts were made by UNHCR to improve security for the refugees and to ensure the civilian and humanitarian nature of the camps. The chapter illustrates how the politicization or militarization of refugee camps and settlements can result in armed attacks and incursions into neighbouring countries, which can destabilize entire regions in the process.

Chapters 9 and 10 also provide brief descriptions of other major emergencies of the 1990s, including the conflict in Somalia which led to mass displacement and a large diaspora, the refugee crisis in East Timor in 1999, and refugee emergencies in West Africa. These chapters also examine policies towards internally displaced people, the subject of international criminal justice, the problem of militarized refugee camps, and the issue of refugees and the AIDS pandemic.

Finally, chapter 11 looks at some of the challenges of the 21st century. It considers the process of globalization, the changing nature of conflict, the growing complexity of population movements and new forms of humanitarian action. In particular, it analyzes UNHCR's evolving role in responding to the needs of refugees, internally displaced people and others. The chapter stresses the continuing need to find lasting solutions to problems of forced displacement, emphasizing that international peace and stability are dependent on human security.

1 The early years

The Second World War and the immediate post-war period produced the largest population displacement in modern history. In May 1945, over 40 million people were estimated to be displaced in Europe, excluding Germans who fled the advancing Soviet armies in the east and foreign forced labourers in Germany itself. There were also some 13 million ethnic Germans (*Volksdeutsche*) who were expelled from the Soviet Union, Poland, Czechoslovakia and other east European countries in the following months and who became known as expellees (*Vertriebene*). Another 11.3 million forced labourers and displaced persons were found by the Allies to be working on the territory of the former German Reich.[1]

In addition to these people, over a million Russians, Ukrainians, Belorussians, Poles, Estonians, Latvians, Lithuanians and others fled from communist domination as it became clear that a new totalitarianism was being imposed by the Soviet leader, Josef Stalin. Meanwhile, civil war in Greece and other conflicts in southeastern Europe unleashed after the Nazi withdrawal began to generate tens of thousands of refugees. There had also been massive displacements outside Europe during the war. These included millions of Chinese people who had been displaced in areas controlled by Japanese forces in China.[2]

It was the movements of people across the European continent, which had been so devastated by war, that most concerned the Allied powers. Well before the war ended, they recognized that the liberation of Europe would bring with it the need to tackle this massive upheaval. The United Nations Relief and Rehabilitation Administration was therefore set up in 1943, and this was replaced in 1947 by the International Refugee Organization. This chapter examines the work of these organizations, which were the direct predecessors of UNHCR. It then describes the processes which led to the establishment in 1950 of UNHCR and to the adoption in 1951 of the UN Convention Relating to the Status of Refugees, which has since become the cornerstone of international refugee protection. Finally, the chapter examines UNHCR's response to its first major challenge—the flight of 200,000 people from Hungary following the suppression by Soviet forces of the 1956 uprising.

The UN Relief and Rehabilitation Administration

In November 1943, even before the end of the Second World War and the formal establishment of the United Nations itself in June 1945, the Allies (including the Soviet Union) set up the United Nations Relief and Rehabilitation Administration

This woman in Germany was one of millions of people who had to search for new homes at the end of the Second World War. (ASSOCIATED PRESS-SANDERS/1945)

Among the millions of people left homeless at the end of the Second World War were these refugees from eastern Europe in a camp in Germany. (UNHCR/1953)

(UNRRA). With a broad mandate to assist in the relief and rehabilitation of devastated areas, UNRRA was not created specifically as a refugee agency. It assisted all who had been displaced by the war and not only refugees who had fled their countries. In 1944–45, UNRRA provided emergency assistance to thousands of refugees and displaced persons in areas under Allied control, although the Soviet Union did not permit UNRRA to operate in the Soviet zone. Until the end of the war in Europe in May 1945, UNRRA worked closely with the Allied forces, which provided logistics and material support. By mid-1945, UNRRA had more than 300 teams on the ground.

Once the war ended, UNRRA focused largely on repatriation. Most of those who had been uprooted by the war were anxious to return to their homes. Countries providing asylum to large numbers of refugees, such as Germany, Austria and Italy, also wanted to see these people repatriate quickly. In addition, agreements made at the Yalta and Potsdam conferences in 1945 had provided for a speedy repatriation of Soviet citizens to the Soviet Union.

From May to September 1945, UNRRA assisted with the repatriation of some seven million people.[3] As one historian has noted, however, UNRRA was constantly frustrated by its subordination to the Allied forces:

UNRRA found its prestige drained and its capacity for independent action stripped away . . . In the vacuum opened at an early stage by UNRRA's manifest lack of preparation for an enormous task, the military men took charge of a substantial amount of refugee activity. But the soldiers seemed equally ill-equipped to deal with displaced persons, particularly the steadily increasing proportion that could not or would not be repatriated. Gruff and impatient with their charges, military administrators often saw the refugees as a bother to be overcome.[4]

The repatriation operation became increasingly controversial, in particular as opposition to repatriation grew. Among those speedily repatriated during this period were some two million Soviet citizens of whom many, particularly Ukrainians and those from the Baltic states, had not wanted to return. Many of these people eventually ended up in Stalin's labour camps. East Europeans were repatriated less quickly. Many of them, likewise, did not wish to return to countries which were now under communist rule. But many were sent back, with

Box 1.1   High Commissioners Nansen & McDonald

UNHCR began its work after the Second World War, but concerted international efforts to assist refugees actually began in the inter-war years. Between 1919 and 1939, violent conflicts and political turmoil uprooted over five million people in Europe alone, including Russians, Greeks, Turks, Armenians, Jews and Spanish Republicans.

Two of the most important pioneers of international work on behalf of refugees in the inter-war period were the first two High Commissioners for refugees appointed by the League of Nations, Fridtjof Nansen of Norway (1921–30) and James McDonald of the United States (1933–35). These two men held different views on how to approach refugee problems, but they both made their mark on subsequent international refugee protection efforts.

Fridtjof Nansen

Formal international efforts to assist refugees first began in August 1921 when the International Committee of the Red Cross appealed to the League of Nations to assist the over one million Russian refugees displaced during the Russian civil war, many of them affected by famine. The League responded by appointing Fridtjof Nansen, a famous polar explorer, as 'High Commissioner on behalf of the League in connection with the problems of Russian refugees in Europe'. His responsibilities were later extended to include Greek, Bulgarian, Armenian and certain other groups of refugees.

Nansen took up the huge task of defining the legal status of Russian refugees and organizing either their employment in host countries or their repatriation. The League gave him £4,000 sterling to accomplish this enormous task and he moved quickly to set up his staff. He established what would eventually become the basic structure of UNHCR—an office of the High Commissioner in Geneva with local representatives in host countries. To find suitable employment for refugees, he worked closely with the International Labour

Organization, helping around 60,000 refugees to find work.

Nansen devoted particular attention to the legal protection of refugees. He organized an international conference which resulted in the creation of travel and identity documents for refugees, commonly called 'Nansen passports'. When negotiations with the Soviet Union about the repatriation of Russian refugees failed, Nansen spearheaded the adoption of additional measures to provide a secure legal status for refugees in their host countries. These early legal agreements later became the basis for both the 1933 and 1951 refugee conventions.

In 1922, Nansen had to address another refugee crisis—the flight of nearly two million refugees from the Graeco-Turkish war. He immediately travelled to the region to help coordinate international relief efforts. While in Greece, Nansen stressed that the High Commissioner must remain neutral in political disputes. Although he personally blamed Turkey for the crisis, he delivered aid to both Greek and Turkish refugees and met with officials on both sides. The League of Nations eventually assigned him responsibility for settling ethnic Greek refugees from Turkey in western Thrace. He spent much of his later life trying to arrange a loan to resettle Armenian refugees in the Soviet Union. Strong anti-communist opposition, however, prevented him from achieving this goal.

In 1922, Nansen was awarded the Nobel Peace Prize for his work. After his death in 1930, this work was continued by the Nansen International Office. Since 1954, UNHCR has presented a Nansen medal annually to individuals or groups of people who have given exceptional service to refugees.

James McDonald

In the 1930s, the international community faced the challenge posed by the flight of refugees from Nazi Germany. Although the League of Nations refused to finance refugee

assistance directly, it did appoint James McDonald, a US professor and journalist, to be an independent 'High Commissioner for refugees (Jewish and other) coming from Germany'. From 1933 until 1935, McDonald fought immigration restrictions around the world in order to arrange resettlement for Jewish refugees. He was particularly useful in coordinating the work of voluntary agencies, which provided most of the funding for refugee assistance. In his two years as High Commissioner, he helped to resettle 80,000 refugees in Palestine and elsewhere.

In September 1935, McDonald faced his greatest challenge, when the Nazis adopted the Nuremberg laws. These deprived Jews of citizenship and the right to vote. The Nazis also encouraged Germans to dismiss Jewish employees and to boycott Jewish businesses. As persecution increased, a flood of refugees left the country. Frustrated that the League would not take stronger action, McDonald resigned on 27 December 1935. In a letter widely published in the international press at the time, he warned:

> When domestic policies threaten the demoralization of human beings, considerations of diplomatic correctness must yield to those of common humanity. I should be recreant if I did not call attention to the actual situation, and plead that world opinion, acting through the League and its Member States and other countries, move to avert the existing and impending tragedies.[i]

Despite McDonald's efforts, his plea for direct intervention in Germany went unheeded. The League of Nations continued to regard Germany's treatment of Jews as a purely domestic matter. Although McDonald's efforts failed, he stands out as an early advocate of the need for decisive political action to deal with the root causes of refugee movements.

little attention paid to their individual wishes. Although Western countries did not initially appreciate what was happening to many of those who were forcibly returned, the United States government in particular became increasingly critical of such returns.

By 1946, an acrimonious debate had arisen over whether or not UNRRA should provide assistance to people who did not wish to be repatriated. Eastern bloc countries asserted that assistance should be given only to displaced persons who returned home. Western bloc countries insisted that individuals should be free to decide whether or not to return, and that this choice should not prejudice their right to assistance. For its part, the US government denounced UNRRA's repatriation policies and its rehabilitation programmes in Eastern bloc countries as serving only to strengthen Soviet political control over eastern Europe.[5]

The reluctance of refugees to return to their countries of origin remained a major problem that would dominate the post-war years. Within the United Nations itself, the subject of repatriation became a major political issue. It was one of the most contentious issues before the UN Security Council during the first few years of its existence. The debate went to the heart of the fundamental ideological conflicts dividing East and West at the time. This concerned the issue of whether or not people should have the right to choose their country of residence, to flee oppression and to express their own opinions.

Eventually the US government, which provided 70 per cent of UNRRA's funding and much of its leadership, refused to extend the organization's mandate beyond 1947 or to grant further financial support. In its place and in the face of adamant opposition from Eastern bloc countries, the United States pressed hard for the creation of a new refugee organization with a different orientation.

The International Refugee Organization

The International Refugee Organization (IRO) was created in July 1947 as a non-permanent United Nations specialized agency. When it was set up, the expectation was that its three-year programme would be completed by 30 June 1950.

Although the IRO's work was limited to assisting European refugees, it was the first international body to deal comprehensively with every aspect of the refugee issue. Its functions were defined as encompassing repatriation, identification, registration and classification, care and assistance, legal and political protection, transport, resettlement and re-establishment. These multiple functions nevertheless masked a clear shift in priorities from a policy of repatriation, as carried out by UNRRA, to one of resettlement from countries of asylum to third countries.

The IRO Constitution included the assertion that the principal objective of the organization was that of 'encouraging and assisting in every way possible [refugees'] early return to their country of nationality, or former habitual residence'.[6] This was put into perspective, however, by the General Assembly resolution establishing the IRO, which declared that that 'no refugees or displaced persons [with valid objections] shall be compelled to return to their country of origin'.[7]

Displaced people in Germany line up at the offices of the International Refugee Organization in 1950, hoping to be resettled in a new country. (IRO/1950)

This shift of emphasis from repatriation to resettlement prompted criticism by Eastern bloc countries. They argued that resettlement was a means of acquiring a ready source of labour, and of offering shelter to subversive groups which might threaten international peace. In the event, the IRO assisted with the repatriation of a mere 73,000 people, compared with over a million people whom it assisted in resettling. The majority went overseas to the United States, which took over 30 per cent of the total, to Australia, Israel, Canada, and various Latin American countries.

It became clear that the 1950s had ushered in a new era of emigration. One of the motivations for taking in refugees was the economic benefits that they could bring, fuelling economies by providing a ready labour force. Western governments argued that the scattering of refugees around the world would promote a more favourable distribution of population by decongesting Europe and benefiting the under-populated, less developed 'overseas democracies'.[8]

The IRO was not able, however, to bring the refugee problem to a conclusion. Around 400,000 people remained displaced in Europe at the end of 1951 and the organization officially closed down in February 1952.[9] There was general agreement on the need for continued international cooperation in dealing with the refugee problem, but fundamental disagreement as to the objectives that such cooperation

Displaced people from camps in Austria, Germany and Italy board a ship chartered by the International Refugee Organization to start a new life in the United States. (UNHCR/1951)

should seek to fulfil. Eastern bloc countries were full of recriminations for the way in which the IRO had, in their view, been used as a tool by Western bloc countries. The United States, for its part, had become increasingly disillusioned with providing nearly two thirds of the funding for an organization which was costing more than the combined operating budget of the rest of the United Nations.

The establishment of UNHCR

The end of the 1940s saw a hardening of the Cold War stand-off that was to dominate international relations for the next 40 years. The Berlin blockade of 1948–49 was followed in quick succession by the explosion of the first Soviet atomic bomb, the formation of two separate German states, the creation of the North Atlantic Treaty Organization, Mao Zedong's victory in China, and the start of the Korean War in 1950. It became increasingly apparent that the refugee issue was not a temporary post-war phenomenon. New crises were generating new outflows of refugees, as had happened following the communist seizure of power in countries from Czechoslovakia to China. At the same time, the Iron Curtain between Eastern and Western Europe was restricting movement between the two blocs.

Cold War ideological tensions permeated negotiations within the United Nations on the formation of a new UN refugee body. The formation of such a body had been proposed by various actors, including the International Committee of the Red Cross (ICRC). The Soviet Union boycotted many of the negotiations altogether, along with its satellite states. There were also widespread divergences amongst the Western powers themselves. The United States sought a strictly defined, temporary agency, requiring little financing and with limited objectives, notably the protection of the remaining IRO refugees until they were permanently settled. In particular, it sought to deny the new body a role in relief operations by depriving it of General Assembly assistance for operations and by denying it the right to seek voluntary contributions. By contrast, Western European states, which bore the brunt of the refugee burden, together with Pakistan and India, which were each hosting millions of refugees following the partition of India in 1947, favoured a strong, permanent, multipurpose refugee agency. They argued for an independent High Commissioner with the power to raise funds and disperse them to refugees.

The result of this debate was a compromise. In December 1949, the UN General Assembly decided, by 36 votes to five with 11 abstentions, to establish the Office of the United Nations High Commissioner for Refugees (UNHCR) for an initial period of three years, from 1 January 1951.[10] It was to be a subsidiary organ of the General Assembly under Article 22 of the UN Charter. The UNHCR Statute, adopted by the General Assembly on 14 December 1950, reflected both the consensus of the United States and other Western states vis-à-vis their counterparts in the Eastern bloc and the differences between the United States and Western European states in their immediate priorities. According to one analyst: 'The severe limitations on UNHCR's functional scope and authority were principally the result of the desire of the United States and its Western allies to create an international refugee agency that would neither pose any threat to the national sovereignty of the Western powers nor impose any new financial obligations on them.'[11]

Article 2 of the UNHCR Statute states that the work of the High Commissioner 'shall be of an entirely non-political character; it shall be humanitarian and social and shall relate, as a rule, to groups and categories of refugees'. The distinction made here between political and humanitarian concerns was crucial. Many UNHCR officials maintain that the emphasis on the non-political nature of the High Commissioner's work has been largely responsible for enabling the organization to operate both during the tense Cold War era and in subsequent situations of armed conflict. Other observers argue that while the distinction was to prove useful in many ways, it was in fact a somewhat misleading one from the start, having been designed primarily to mitigate the severe effects of bipolarization in the early 1950s and to prevent a total paralysis of the United Nations in dealing with the refugee issue at that time.[12] Some analysts have also argued that since UNHCR is a subsidiary UN body, which is subject to the formal control of the General Assembly, it can never be entirely independent of the political organs of the United Nations.[13] The continuing

Box 1.2

United Nations assistance to Palestinian refugees

In November 1947, the United Nations General Assembly approved the partition of Palestine into a Jewish state and an Arab state. Five-and-a-half months later, the United Kingdom, which had a mandate for the administration of the territory throughout the period of the League of Nations, withdrew. The Arab population of Palestine and the Arab states rejected the partition plan which gave the Jewish population over half the territory, in spite of the fact that the Arab population at the time was larger. In the ensuing conflict between the Jews and the Palestinians, the Jews seized more territory. An Israeli state was declared on 14 May 1948 and, by the time an armistice was agreed in 1949, Israel controlled three quarters of the territory of the former British mandate.

In the period leading up to the declaration of the state of Israel and immediately following further clashes between the Arabs and the Jews, some 750,000 Palestinians were expelled or were forced to flee from areas under Jewish control. The United Nations tried to negotiate their return home, but this was blocked by Israel.

New Jewish settlements were quickly established on large tracts of land belonging to the Palestinians and newly arriving Jewish immigrants were settled in Palestinians' houses. The majority of the Palestinian refugees settled in urban areas in Arab countries or repatriated, but roughly one third of the refugees remained in camps in the region. Ever since then, these camps have remained symbolic of the plight of the Palestinian refugees.

The creation of UNRWA

Assistance to the Palestinian refugees was first provided by non-governmental organizations under the umbrella of the United Nations Relief for Palestine Refugees (UNRPR). Then, in December 1949, the UN General Assembly decided to establish the United Nations Relief and Works Agency for Palestine Refugees in the Near East (UNRWA).

The decision to establish UNRWA was primarily an initiative of the United States government, which was chairing the United Nations Conciliation Commission for Palestine. The decision was taken when it became clear that the government of the new state of Israel was unlikely to agree to any substantial return of refugees to its territory.

The US government proposed that the General Assembly establish a special agency which would continue to provide relief to the refugees, but which would primarily be responsible for initiating large-scale development projects—hence the 'works' in UNRWA's name. The Arab states only accepted this proposal after they were assured that the establishment of UNRWA would not jeopardize the right of the refugees to return to their original homes as stipulated in General Assembly Resolution 194(III) of 11 December 1948. This was clearly stated in UNRWA's founding mandate, UN General Assembly Resolution 302(IV) of 8 December 1949.

At the same time, negotiations were taking place at the United Nations on the formation of what was to become UNHCR. Once UNRWA was established, however, Arab states insisted that Palestinian refugees receiving UNRWA assistance should be excluded from UNHCR's mandate and from the 1951 UN Refugee Convention. Arab states were concerned lest the individual refugee definition under discussion in the draft convention undermine the position of Palestinians, whose rights as a group to return had been recognized in General Assembly resolutions. Other parties also feared that the non-political character of the work envisaged for the nascent UNHCR was not compatible with the highly politicized nature of the Palestinian question.

For these reasons, both the 1950 UNHCR Statute and the 1951 UN Refugee Convention exclude 'persons who are at present receiving . . . protection or assistance' from other UN organs or agencies. The geographical field of UNRWA's operations is restricted to Lebanon, Syria, Jordan, the West Bank and the Gaza Strip. It is only once a Palestinian leaves the UNRWA field of operations that this person falls within the UNHCR mandate and the 1951 Convention.

Unlike UNHCR, UNRWA did not have a detailed statute and over time developed its own operational refugee definition in its *Consolidated Registration Instructions*. These define a Palestinian refugee as including people whose normal place of residence was Palestine for a minimum of two years preceding the 1948 conflict and who, as result of this conflict, lost both their home and means of livelihood and took refuge in 1948 in the areas where UNRWA operates. Also eligible for services are the descendants of such refugees.

Unlike the work of UNHCR, the scope of UNRWA's work does not include the search for permanent solutions for the refugees under its care. Also, UNRWA's mandate extends primarily to the delivery of essential services and not to the provision of international protection, which by contrast lies at the core of UNHCR's work.

UNRWA's early years

UNRWA was established as a temporary agency with a mandate that was to be renewed periodically. In the early 1950s, when the United States was still refusing to fund UNHCR, it was UNRWA's principal donor. Since then the United States has remained UNRWA's main donor.

In 1950, UNRWA was responsible for almost one million refugees in Jordan, Lebanon, Syria, the West Bank and the Gaza Strip. UNRWA's first task was to continue the ongoing emergency relief started by its predecessors and to help the refugees move from tents to more permanent shelters. From 1950 to 1957, UNRWA supported regional economic development plans designed to expand agriculture, foster international cooperation, and thus absorb the Palestinians into the regional economy. In the mid-1950s, UNRWA tried to implement two major resettlement schemes. In both cases, it was both the host countries and the refugees themselves who rejected them and insisted on their right to return.

The failure of such initiatives led to a re-evaluation of the purpose of UNRWA. From 1957 to 1967, the agency abandoned grandiose regional development schemes and focused on relief, education and health programmes in the refugee camps.

As a result of the Arab–Israeli Six-Day War in 1967, large numbers of Palestinians fled or were expelled and a new group of Palestinian refugees was created. These refugees included those who fled from the West Bank to Jordan and Syria, or from the Gaza Strip to Egypt or Jordan. As in 1948, once they had fled, the Israeli government prevented their return to what became known as the Occupied Territories.

Of the 350,000 Palestinians who fled the 1967 war, about half were categorized as 'internally displaced'. They had not been displaced in 1948 and so did not fall under the UNRWA mandate, making them even more vulnerable. Although no formal adjustment to UNRWA's mandate was made to include this new category, the organization nevertheless provided some emergency services to these Palestinians with the support of the UN General Assembly. The others were fleeing for the second time in 20 years. In the West Bank and Gaza, Israel's occupation created a new and highly sensitive relationship between UNRWA, the Palestinian refugees and the Israeli government.

Later developments

It was 20 years before Palestinians took to the streets of the Occupied Territories in open and spontaneous revolt in December 1987. A month after the outbreak of what became known as the *intifada* (uprising), the UN Secretary-General proposed a limited expansion of UNRWA's work to include 'passive protection' functions in the Israeli Occupied Territories of the West Bank and the Gaza Strip. General Assembly resolutions subsequently supported this approach and as a result a legal aid scheme was set up, additional local and international staff were recruited, and human rights monitors were deployed.

The September 1993 Declaration of Principles on Palestinian self-rule in the Occupied Territories, signed by the Palestinian leader Yasser Arafat and the Israeli Prime Minister Yitzak Rabin, was designed to effect a gradual transfer of powers to the Palestinian National Authority. A month later, in order to support the peace process, UNRWA launched a 'peace implementation programme'. This has included projects to improve education and health facilities, to construct emergency housing and other infrastructure, and to provide small business loans.

The refugees are now in their third and even fourth generation. In 1999, there were some 3.6 million in the region, out of a total of some six million Palestinians worldwide. Around 1.5 million refugees are in Jordan and 1.3 million in the West Bank and the Gaza Strip. About a third of the refugees live in 59 refugee camps and the rest live in villages, towns and cities in the UNRWA areas of operation. Despite funding difficulties, over the years UNRWA has set up some 650 schools, which today have more than 450,000 pupils, eight vocational training centres, 122 health centres and many other projects serving different community needs. But the needs of the refugees remain great, and until a long-term and comprehensive political solution to the Palestinian problem is found and implemented, the status and future of the majority of Palestinian refugees will remain uncertain.

debate on this issue revolves largely around the fact that there has been a failure to define clearly what constitutes 'humanitarian action' and 'political action'.

The debate over the extent to which an organization can protect and assist refugees and remain non-political was not a new one. It had been an issue even during the League of Nations period, when Fridtjof Nansen and James McDonald, two High Commissioners with responsibilities for particular groups of refugees, adopted different approaches [see Box 1.1].

UNHCR's primary functions were defined as being twofold: first, to provide international protection for refugees; and second, to seek permanent solutions to the problem of refugees by assisting governments to facilitate their voluntary repatriation or their assimilation within new national communities. While the new organization was granted the right to seek voluntary contributions, the United States succeeded in making General Assembly approval a precondition for all such appeals. As a result, UNHCR became dependent on a small administrative budget from the General Assembly and on a small 'emergency fund'.

The US government initially refused to make any contributions to this fund, as it did not at that stage view UNHCR as the most appropriate body through which to channel funds. Instead, it chose to fund the United States Escapee Program and the Intergovernmental Committee for European Migration. The latter was founded in 1952 to help move migrants and refugees in Europe to overseas immigration countries; it later became the International Organization for Migration. Within the UN system, the United States also funded the United Nations Relief and Works Agency for Palestine Refugees in the Near East (UNRWA) [see Box 1.2] and the United Nations Korean Reconstruction Agency (UNKRA), which provided assistance to the millions of people displaced by the Korean War.

UNHCR was constrained by inadequate funding from the start. Each project to aid refugees had to be financed through voluntary contributions, mostly from states. It was not given the resources to implement a repatriation programme such as the one carried out by UNRRA or a resettlement programme such as that carried out by the IRO. Rather, it was required to provide international protection and to promote solutions for refugee problems with only a small budget. As the first UN High Commissioner for Refugees, Gerrit Jan van Heuven Goedhart, expressed it, there was a real danger his office would simply 'administer misery'.[14]

With an annual budget of no more than US$300,000, the expectation that UNHCR would be able to effect a final settlement of the European refugee problem within a few years proved false. Despite High Commissioner van Heuven Goedhart's efforts to persuade governments of the extent of the refugee problem, they provided only minimal funding. UNHCR nevertheless developed an increasingly effective partnership with voluntary agencies. The first substantial amount of money placed at the disposal of UNHCR came not from governments but from the Ford Foundation in the United States which granted the organization US$3.1 million in 1951. This money was used for a pilot project, which for the first time put emphasis on local integration in European countries as a solution to refugee problems. Eventually, in 1954, a new United Nations Refugee Fund (UNREF) was set up to carry out projects in countries such as Austria, the Federal Republic of Germany, Greece and Italy. The United States contributed to this fund, having previously refused to fund UNHCR due to a decision

Box 1.3

The 1951 UN Refugee Convention

The 1951 Convention Relating to the Status of Refugees was adopted by the United Nations Conference on the Status of Refugees and Stateless Persons held in Geneva on 2–25 July 1951. It was opened for signature on 28 July and entered into force on 22 April 1954.

The Convention spells out the obligations and rights of refugees, and the obligations of states towards refugees. It also sets out international standards for the treatment of refugees. It embodies principles that promote and safeguard refugees' rights in the fields of employment, education, residence, freedom of movement, access to courts, naturalization and, above all, the security against return to a country where they may risk persecution. Two of the most important provisions are found in Articles 1 and 33:

Article 1—Definition of the term 'refugee'

A(2) [Any person who] . . . owing to well-founded fear of being persecuted for reasons of race, religion, nationality, membership of a particular social group or political opinion, is outside the country of his nationality and is unable or, owing to such fear, is unwilling to avail himself of the protection of that country; or who, not having a nationality and being outside the country of his former habitual residence . . . is unable or, owing to such fear, is unwilling to return to it . . .

Article 33—Prohibition of expulsion or return ('*refoulement*')

1. No Contracting State shall expel or return ('*refouler*') a refugee in any manner whatsoever to the frontiers of territories where his life or freedom would be threatened on account of his race, religion, nationality, membership of a particular social group or political opinion . . .

The refugee definition contained in the 1951 Convention was limited to persons who became refugees 'as a result of events occurring before 1 January 1951'. The time limitation, however, was subsequently removed by Article I(2) of the 1967 Protocol to the Convention [see box 2.2]. When becoming a party to the 1951 Convention, states also had the possibility of making a declaration limiting their obligations under the Convention to refugees from events occurring in Europe.

The 1951 UN Refugee Convention—along with its 1967 Protocol—is still the most important, and the only universal, instrument of international refugee law. By 31 December 1999, 131 states had acceded to both the 1951 Convention and its 1967 Protocol, and 138 states had ratified either one or both of these instruments.

by the US Congress in 1950 to veto the use of US funds for any international organization working in countries behind the Iron Curtain.

The Soviet Union's initial rigid opposition to UNHCR also began to shift in the mid-1950s. By then, the Cold War had spread well beyond the borders of Europe and new countries were influencing the work of the United Nations. The Soviet Union had helped to facilitate the admission of several developing countries to the United Nations and these countries now recognized the potential usefulness of UNHCR to their own refugee problems.

The drafting of the 1951 UN Refugee Convention

The rights and obligations set out in the 1951 UN Convention Relating to the Status of Refugees lie at the heart of UNHCR's work. Negotiations on the Convention took place in parallel with those concerning the establishment of UNHCR. The Convention was adopted by an international conference over seven months later, on 28 July 1951.

It was the definition of the term 'refugee' that provoked particular controversy. Since the Convention created new obligations which would be binding under international law, states participating in the drafting process aimed to restrict the definition to categories of refugees towards whom they would be willing to assume legal obligations. The United States favoured a narrow definition, in view of the resulting legal obligations that a broader definition would impose. Western European states, on the other hand, argued for a broad definition, although there were also divisions among these states as to what the definition should be.

In the end a compromise formula was reached. Governments agreed on a general, universally applicable definition of the term 'refugee' centred on the concept of a 'well-founded fear of persecution'. At the same time, they applied two important limitations on the Convention's scope. First, the benefits of the Convention were not to apply to people who became refugees as a result of events occurring after 1 January 1951, even if they otherwise corresponded to the definition. Second, when becoming a party to the Convention, states had the possibility of making a declaration limiting their obligations under the Convention to European refugees.

The adoption of this definition of the term 'refugee' marked a significant change in policy, as it meant that refugees would now be identified not only on a group basis, as had been the case in preceding years, but also on an individual case-by-case basis. The definition was also now a general one and not one which was tied to specific national groups, such as Russians from the Soviet Union or Greeks from Turkey, as had been the case in the inter-war years.

Although the 1948 Universal Declaration of Human Rights had affirmed an individual's right to seek and enjoy asylum, the importance for states of preserving their sovereign right to grant admission to their territory meant that the states which drew up the UN Refugee Convention were not prepared to recognize an unconditional right of asylum in this new legally binding Convention. The new Convention therefore contains no mention of a 'right to asylum'. However, one of the key provisions of the Convention is the obligation of states which are party to it not to expel or return a refugee to a state where he or she would face persecution. This is known as the principle of *non-refoulement*, using the French word used in Article 33 of the Convention. Other provisions contained in the Convention outline refugees' rights in relation to issues such as employment, housing, education, social security, documentation and freedom of movement [see Box 1.3].

Similar rights had been set out in the 1933 Convention Relating to the International Status of Refugees, which was the first international instrument to refer to the principle that refugees should not forcibly be returned to their country of origin.[15] This convention was, however, only ratified by eight states. Another relevant international instrument was the 1938 Convention Concerning the Status of Refugees from Germany,

States party to the 1951 UN Refugee Convention and/or the 1967 Protocol, 30 June 2000 — Map 1.1

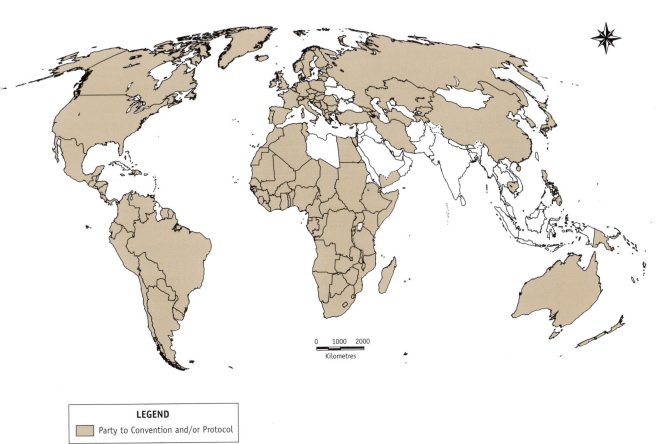

LEGEND

▇ Party to Convention and/or Protocol

Note:
The boundaries shown on this map are those used by the UN Cartographic Section, New York.
The boundaries and names shown and the designations used on this map do not imply official endorsement or acceptance by the United Nations.

but this was overtaken by the outbreak of the Second World War and received only three ratifications. By contrast, the strength of the 1951 UN Refugee Convention lies in the large number of ratifications it has secured across the globe [see Map 1.1].

The Hungarian crisis of 1956

UNHCR's first major test was the exodus of refugees from Hungary after the Soviet suppression of the uprising in 1956. Many of these refugees followed the same route to Austria that Hungarians fleeing the Red Army had taken in 1944–45. While the vast majority of the refugees—some 180,000—fled to Austria, some 20,000 escaped to socialist Yugoslavia, which had broken with the Soviet Union in 1948. This exodus provided UNHCR with its first experience of working with a mass influx of refugees fleeing political repression. It also gave UNHCR its first experience of working with the International Committee of the Red Cross (in Hungary) and the League of Red Cross Societies (in Austria).

During 1956–57, UNHCR carried out a major relief operation, looking after Hungarian refugees in Austria and Yugoslavia, assisting with their resettlement in 35 countries around the world, and with the voluntary repatriation of some to Hungary. The crisis was handled by Auguste Lindt, who replaced van Heuven Goedhart as High Commissioner on 10 December 1956. This operation marked the beginning of UNHCR's transformation from a small UN body dealing with a residual caseload of refugees remaining from the Second World War to a much larger organization with broader responsibilities. UNHCR was to emerge from the crisis, which became one of the important landmarks of the Cold War, much strengthened and with its international prestige considerably enhanced.

The roots of the Hungarian crisis lay in the thaw in Eastern Europe and the Soviet Union following Stalin's death in March 1953. The communist regime which had taken power in Hungary in 1947–48 had been led by one of Stalin's closest followers in Eastern Europe. In 1949, it had staged a series of show trials, mirroring those in Moscow in 1936, and resulting in the execution of many leading communists. Then, in 1954, the year after Stalin's death, the chief of the security police and the first secretary of the ruling communist party were themselves arrested and tried on charges of exceeding their authority and carrying out unwarranted detentions.

Nikita Khrushchev's famous speech to the 20th congress of the Communist Party of the Soviet Union in February 1956, in which he acknowledged that Stalin had made serious mistakes, sent shock waves not only through the Soviet Union but throughout the communist world. His specific undertaking to reassess the Soviet Union's relations with its satellite neighbours had dramatic consequences in Eastern Europe, especially in Poland and Hungary. In Poland, demonstrations and strikes in June led to a change of government and a carefully calibrated liberalization of the regime, which was reluctantly accepted by Moscow.

Hungarians fleeing the Soviet suppression of the 1956 uprising cross the border into Austria. (RDZ/1956)

In Hungary, by contrast, the attempt at reform was to have a tragic outcome. At first the regime appeared to recognize the need for reform. It endorsed concessions to the peasantry and a relaxation of the terror, while reluctantly appointing Imre Nagy, a critic of collectivization and forced industrialization, as Prime Minister. But popular demonstrations in October 1956 nevertheless revealed widespread disapproval of the regime itself and hatred of its secret police. The movement culminated in a wholesale revolt on 23 October, when some 300,000 people protested on the streets and clashed with Hungarian and Soviet troops. Responding to popular demands, on 27 October Nagy formed a coalition government excluding communist hardliners and promised free elections. On 1 November he fatefully proposed to withdraw Hungary from the Warsaw Pact and to declare the country neutral.

Having initially removed its troops from the Hungarian capital, Budapest, the Soviet Army attacked the capital in force on 4 November. In the widespread street fighting which followed, resistance to the Red Army—with 200,000 troops and more than 2,000 tanks at its disposal—was decisively crushed. Thousands of Hungarians were deported or, like Nagy, executed. More than 3,000 people died on the streets of Budapest in 10 days of what turned out to be the most violent confrontation in Europe between the Second World War and the wars in Yugoslavia in the 1990s.

Box 1.4

Germany's refugee compensation scheme

Soon after the Federal Republic of Germany was founded in 1949, discussions began on the issue of compensation for victims of Nazi persecution. The word 'reparation' or *Wiedergutmachung* in German (literally, 'to make good again') was rarely used, since it was generally agreed that no financial payment could compensate for the horrors of the Holocaust.

The early laws of the Federal Republic of Germany defined as 'persecuted' for the purposes of indemnification and compensation those people who had suffered because of their race, religion or political opinion. Others, even if they had been in a concentration camp or forced to work as slave labourers, did not qualify as 'persecutees', but rather as persons 'injured for reasons of nationality' (*Nationalgeschädigte*, in German).

There were tens of thousands of these 'national persecutees'—Poles, Ukrainians, Belarussians, Serbs, Czechs, Slovaks and others who had been interned or deported to work as slave labourers in German factories. The lives of these survivors had been shattered in most cases: their health ruined, their families uprooted and dispersed, their homes damaged or destroyed. After the war, many went to North or South America, South Africa or Australia. However, their new countries of residence did not take up their claims, since they were not citizens of those countries when the persecution occurred.

The first negotiations on indemnification focused on those persecuted for religious reasons. The Conference on Jewish Material Claims against Germany (the 'Claims Conference'), founded in 1951, brought together numerous Jewish organizations and, over the next half-century, intervened energetically on behalf of Nazism's Jewish victims. Others—Roma (gypsies) or communists, for example—had no similar organization, nor did the 'national persecutees'.

The Federal Republic of Germany's first Indemnification Act, adopted in 1953, provided for some limited payments to certain 'national persecutees' whose health was seriously damaged and who became refugees by specified cut-off dates. Further legislation in 1956 did not provide this group with any additional help.

In 1957, Western governments started negotiations with the German government in Bonn about compensation for their citizens. There was talk of a global fund to include the 'national persecutees', but it was decided that the question of compensation should await a formal peace treaty. Mean- while, Germany would hold talks with UNHCR about the refugees who suffered because of their nationality.

In 1960, Germany and UNHCR concluded a first agreement. UNHCR would administer a 'hardship fund' worth DM 45 million provided by the government for 'national persecutees' who became refugees before 1 October 1953. Over the next five years, UNHCR made payments of between DM 3,000 and DM 8,000 to some 10,000 people.

Meanwhile, other potential beneficiaries fled to the West. By 1965, the Fund was exhausted. One year later, UNHCR and Germany concluded a supplementary agreement advancing the cut-off date to 31 December 1965 and providing an additional DM 3.5 million. Demand for compensation continued to outstrip the money available, however, and this additional sum was rapidly spent.

It was a difficult task deciding who should receive the modest amounts put at UNHCR's disposal. UNHCR staff sifted through applications from survivors around the globe. Many had enclosed snapshots of themselves before they were deported and put to work as slave labourers in Germany. Others had enclosed medical certificates, hand-written household budgets or unpaid bills. The relatively small amounts available for distribution were in no way commensurate with the persecution which they had suffered. It was nonetheless considered to be of great importance to show the victims that they had not been forgotten.

In 1980, the Claims Conference started negotiations with the Federal Republic of Germany concerning the establishment of a new fund for Jewish persecutees who only fled to the West after 1965. UNHCR also sought further funds for 'national persecutees' who became refugees after 1965.

The negotiations led by the Claims Conference resulted in three new funds worth a total of DM 500 million for victims as defined in German law, excluding the 'national persecutees'. For the latter group, a new UNHCR-administered fund of DM 5 million was established. It rapidly became clear that this would not suffice. Emigration from Eastern Europe, especially from Poland, was on the rise, and the new wave of refugees included many eligible for compensation. In 1984, Germany increased the UNHCR-administered fund by a further DM 3.5 million. By May of that year, over 1,100 new applications had been received and more were expected, all from survivors who became refugees after 1965.

The letters received by UNHCR demonstrated that the applicants still suffered the effects of persecution. Many were in such bad health that they were unable to work. No sum of money could repair the damage done, but the victims wanted their suffering to be recognized, even if they were already beyond retirement age. UNHCR's assistance to refugees through the hardship fund ended in 1993. By this time, the Federal German government had paid DM 59 million through the UNHCR-administered fund to refugees and former refugees who had been victims of Nazi persecution.

The refugee exodus

Even before the suppression of the Hungarian uprising, refugees had begun arriving in Austria. By 5 November, this was serious enough for the Austrian government to appeal to UNHCR for help. Offers of permanent or temporary asylum soon came from Canada, Chile, France, Denmark, Norway Sweden and the United Kingdom. On 8 November, President Dwight D. Eisenhower announced that the United States was willing to take 5,000 refugees immediately. This number was subsequently raised to 6,000 and in December the US government announced that an additional 16,500 Hungarians could be processed in Austria for admission to the United States.[16]

In the end, some 200,000 Hungarian refugees were to flee their homeland. By the end of November, 115,851 had been recorded as having arrived in Austria. Men, women and children fled, frightened and desperate, dragging behind them suitcases and wheelbarrows. They followed the same road to the border town of Hegyeshalom that tens of thousands of Hungarian Jews who had been deported by the Nazis had trodden 12 years previously. One refugee explained: 'We left everything behind, like you would if your house were on fire.'[17] Between December 1956 and January 1957 a further 56,800 arrived in Austria. Thereafter, arrivals in Austria tapered off dramatically, principally as a result of the tightening of border controls by the new Soviet-installed regime in Budapest led by János Kádár.

Faced with this influx, the Austrian government addressed an urgent appeal to UNHCR for financial assistance and for the resettlement of as many refugees in third countries as possible. Austria was still recovering from the hardships of the Second World War, in the closing stages of which the country had been the scene of bitter fighting between the Nazis and advancing Soviet forces. The Allied occupation of Austria, which like Germany had been divided into four zones, had formally ended in May 1955. The occupying forces had left four months later and in early 1956 the Hungarian authorities had removed many of the barbed wire barriers between the two countries. Austria had thus only recently regained its sovereignty and during the crisis it stressed its neutral position between the two Cold War blocs.

The relief operation to assist the refugees was led by the Red Cross, which worked closely with UNHCR. This was to be the first of many emergency operations in which the two organizations would work alongside each other in the field. The basis for UNHCR's involvement was provided by UN General Assembly Resolution 1006 of 9 November 1956. In December, within days of his election as High Commissioner, Auguste Lindt travelled to the Austrian capital, Vienna, to assess for himself the urgent needs of the Hungarian refugees who at that time were arriving at a rate of 3,000 a night across the Austrian border.[18]

Some refugees also found an alternative to asylum in Austria by fleeing to Yugoslavia, itself a communist state but one whose leader, Josip Broz Tito, had broken with Stalin in 1948. After Stalin's death, relations had improved and his successors, Nikita Khrushchev and Nikolai Bulganin, had visited Belgrade in May 1955, signalling Soviet acceptance of Yugoslavia's independent path. In this context, Tito's act in admitting the Hungarian refugees was a courageous move.[19]

Yugoslavia had been the only communist country to participate in the international conference in Geneva which drafted the 1951 UN Refugee Convention. The first UN High Commissioner for Refugees, van Heuven Goedhart, had himself visited Yugoslavia in April 1953 to introduce the work of UNHCR to the Yugoslav government. It was the first such visit to a communist country.[20] This bridge-building exercise between UNHCR and Yugoslavia was to prove very useful during the Hungarian crisis. In December 1956, Tito appealed directly to UNHCR to assist in handling the refugee influx.

At first, the Yugoslav government insisted that all the refugees had to be resettled and that the government had to be compensated for all its expenses. These conditions were, however, eventually dropped. Between November and December 1956 some 1,500 Hungarians arrived in Yugoslavia. By contrast, in January 1957 over 13,000 arrived.[21] Tens of thousands of ethnic Hungarians already lived in Yugoslavia, principally in the Vojvodina region, making acceptance of the refugees easier. Ironically, in the 1990s, with the break-up of Yugoslavia, many ethnic Hungarians were to make the journey in the opposite direction.

In Yugoslavia, a coordinating committee to deal with the emergency was established on 21 February 1957 with representatives of the Yugoslav government, UNHCR, the League of Red Cross Societies, Cooperative Action for American Relief Everywhere (CARE), Church World Service, and the British Voluntary Society for Aid to Hungarians. By March 1957, when High Commissioner Lindt visited Belgrade and commended the government on its treatment of Hungarian refugees, UNHCR had already dispersed US$50,000 to the Yugoslav Red Cross and a further US$124,000 had been allocated to the UNHCR office in Belgrade.[22]

The applicability of the 1951 UN Refugee Convention

While the Hungarians who left their country in 1956 were generally considered by governments of Western countries to be 'refugees', it was not immediately clear that the rights and responsibilities set out in the 1951 UN Refugee Convention would apply to the Hungarian crisis, since the Convention stated clearly that it applied only to 'events occurring before 1 January 1951'. Irrespective of their legal position, however, all those who left after 23 October 1956, the date of the general uprising in Budapest, were in practice considered by UNHCR and Western governments to be refugees, provided that individual screening did not provide evidence to exclude them from this category. In this respect, there was a similarity with the practice followed during the League of Nations period, when the status of an individual was determined on the basis of his or her identification as a part of a particular refugee group.

For the legal justification of this matter, as on so many other issues in the first two decades of UNHCR's existence, the defining voice was that of Paul Weis, a refugee from Vienna and Legal Adviser to the High Commissioner at the time. At the request of the High Commissioner, Weis defined UNHCR's position in a key memorandum in January 1957.[23] He did so, not simply because of the necessity for clarification on the matter, but also because there had been some misgivings even amongst friendly countries, such as Sweden, over the extension of UNHCR's role to include contemporary events.

Weis's obvious starting point was the definition of the term 'refugee' contained in Article 1A(2) of the 1951 UN Refugee Convention and especially its problematic linking of the definition to 'events occurring before 1 January 1951'. He pointed out that the Ad Hoc Committee on Statelessness and Related Problems, which drew up the draft convention, argued in the report on its first session on 17 February 1950, that this expression was 'intended to apply to happenings of major importance involving territorial or profound political changes, as well as systematic programmes of persecution'. He declared that this interpretation and the discussions which took place in the various bodies which drew up the definition in the Convention made it clear that the date on which a person became a refugee was irrelevant. Weis also argued that in Hungary it was clear that there had been 'profound political changes', namely the establishment of a people's republic dominated by the Communist Party in 1947–48. The October 1956 uprising and the consequent exodus of refugees were in that sense 'an after-effect of this earlier political change'. Provided they fulfilled the conditions of Article 1A(2), they were therefore definitely refugees.

As regards the UNHCR Statute itself, Weis said it was clear that refugees from Hungary who fulfilled the conditions of Article 6B must be considered as falling within the mandate of UNHCR. This Article extends UNHCR's competence to 'any other person, who is outside the country of his nationality . . . because he has or had well-founded fear of persecution by reason of his race, religion, nationality or political opinion and is unable . . . to return to the country of his former habitual residence'. Weis granted that it seemed 'baffling' that the UNHCR Statute contains two definitions of refugees who fall within UNHCR's competence in Articles 6A(ii) and 6B which are almost identical apart from the fact that Article 6A(ii) contains the dateline of 1 January 1951. He attributed this to the fact that, in the deliberating bodies which framed the Convention and the Statute, there were two opposing views as to the definition of the term 'refugee', namely the universalist one advocating a broad general definition and the more conservative one advocating a definition by the enumeration of categories of refugees. In the end, the definition which emerged was a compromise drawn up by an informal working party.

Finally, for Weis, the history of these deliberations made it clear that, while those who became refugees as a result of events after 1 January 1951 also came within the mandate of UNHCR, the High Commissioner could in addition consult its Advisory Committee (which later became the Executive Committee) or bring the question to the General Assembly. This much was clear from Articles 1 and 3 of the Statute. In the case of Hungary, the UN General Assembly had clearly established the competence of the High Commissioner as regards the Hungarian refugees.[24]

Resettlement of Hungarian refugees

Resources from the United Nations Refugee Fund, which had been established in 1954, made possible the UNHCR emergency operation for the refugees who fled the suppression of the Hungarian uprising. The High Commissioner also appealed for special contributions and the response was generous. In November 1956 a joint committee was established, composed of UNHCR, the Intergovernmental Committee for European Migration, the Austrian government, the United States Escapee Program and voluntary agencies. In the winter of 1956 and throughout 1957, voluntary agencies played a key role in assisting in the relief and resettlement of the Hungarian refugees.

From the beginning, a premium was placed on resettling the refugees in third countries as the main solution to the problem. Austria, which had initially carried an overwhelming burden, needed prompt relief. Also, there was a feeling of revulsion throughout the Western world at the turn of events in Hungary and considerable guilt that more had not been done to assist the Hungarian people in their struggle for democracy.

To a degree perhaps not easy to imagine at the end of the 20th century, there was a great deal of popular pressure upon Western governments to grant immediate access to the refugees. No central agency for the registration of the refugees arriving in Austria was established because of the perceived need to resettle them as soon as possible. In a memorandum of 20 November 1956, for example, the UNHCR branch office in Vienna informed the High Commissioner that it was simply not possible to carry out the normal screening and eligibility procedures.[25] It was therefore agreed with the Austrian authorities that detailed screening should take place in the country of resettlement.

The speed with which the refugees were resettled can be gauged from the figures relating to arrivals in the United States. The first group of 60 Hungarian refugees arrived by aeroplane on 21 November 1956.[26] A large army base, Camp Kilmer in New Jersey, was turned over for the temporary accommodation of the refugees. By the end of February 1957, a further 9,000 refugees had been flown across the Atlantic by the US Air Force and another 7,000 arrived on US Navy ships. By mid-1958, the United States had resettled some 38,000 Hungarian refugees. Other major countries of resettlement included Canada (35,000), the United Kingdom (16,000), the Federal Republic of Germany (15,000), Australia (13,000), Switzerland (11,500), and France (10,000). Smaller numbers were resettled in places as diverse as Chile, the Dominican Republic, Iceland, Ireland, New Caledonia, Paraguay and South Africa.

Repatriation to Hungary

Even in the context of the Cold War stand-off, resettlement was not the only solution available for the refugees. A number of refugees, including in particular those divided from their immediate families, opted for repatriation. Such repatriation was encouraged by the Hungarian government. The Kádár regime, installed on the back of the Soviet military intervention, began cautiously to display signs of modest independence from 1957 onwards. This was tacitly tolerated by the Soviet Union. In this sense, there was a considerable difference between post-1956 Hungary and post-1968 Czechoslovakia, the object of an even more repressive Soviet military intervention.

As early as late November 1956, the new Hungarian government had offered a limited amnesty to those who had fled as a result of the uprising.[27] The acute political tensions notwithstanding, High Commissioner Lindt established contact with the new government. As a subsequent legal adviser to the High Commissioner noted:

Box 1.5 — Chinese refugees in Hong Kong

As a city on the southern coast of China under British colonial administration from 1842, Hong Kong became a refuge during periods of unrest on the Chinese mainland. Its population was swollen by people seeking sanctuary from the Taiping Rebellion in the 1850s, the Boxer Rebellion around 1900, the revolution that resulted in the foundation of the Republic of China in 1912, and the Sino-Japanese War of 1937–45. Following the Japanese defeat of British forces in December 1941, Hong Kong's population declined by over a million to about 650,000, but most of those who fled during the Japanese occupation returned when British control was re-established in 1945.

In 1949–50, these returnees were joined by hundreds of thousands of new arrivals fleeing from the triumph of the communist forces in China. Many of these new arrivals subsequently returned to their homes on the mainland once peaceful conditions returned. Hong Kong's population began to stabilize at around 2.25 million in 1953–54. This more than threefold increase in population in just eight years put a severe strain on the local infrastructure.

The representative of China to the UN raised the issue of these new arrivals in the UN General Assembly in 1951 and 1952. In response, in 1954, High Commissioner van Heuven Goedhart dispatched a 'survey mission' funded by the Ford Foundation to investigate the case of the Chinese refugees in Hong Kong. According to the mission's report, submitted in 1954, not all of the new arrivals could be considered refugees with a 'well-founded fear of persecution'.[ii] It identified some 285,000 people who had come to Hong Kong for 'political reasons', amounting to 53 per cent of the immigrants who had arrived between 1945 and 1952. This figure rose to 385,000 including 'refugees *sur place*' (those who had initially come for other reasons but who were unwilling to return for political reasons). The figure rose even higher when taking into account all members of refugee households, such as spouses and Hong Kong-born children. By including all these categories, almost 30 per cent of the total population of Hong Kong at the time of the mission survey could be classified as 'refugees'. This appeared to reaffirm the common assumption in Europe and North America at the time that virtually anyone leaving a communist state was a refugee.

This relatively straightforward picture was complicated by two main factors. First, the British did not recognize that a refugee situation, as such, existed in Hong Kong. The vast majority of the new arrivals, regardless of their motives for entering the colony, had integrated and were able to move around freely. Less than one third of the heads of household of the new arrivals were registered with a refugee organization. The British considered that while there were problems of overcrowding and a lack of basic services, the Chinese population was not discriminated against. The one exception to the new arrivals entering the community at large was the settlement at Rennie's Mill, which was inhabited mainly by Guomindang sympathizers from northern China, who remained separate from the majority of Hong Kong Cantonese.

The second factor was the curious legal position of the new arrivals in Hong Kong. While hundreds of thousands left China for political reasons, there was theoretically nothing to prevent them from returning safely to China, in the sense that they could go to Taiwan. This was where the government of the Republic of China (as recognized by the United Nations until 1971) was based. Strictly, therefore, it could be argued that the new arrivals in Hong Kong were not refugees as they had the protection of, and could return to, their state of origin. In practice, however, the number of new arrivals from mainland China who were accepted by nationalist Taiwan was relatively small, even though the mission survey had shown that well over half of the new arrivals in Hong Kong had expressed a willingness to be resettled in Taiwan. This may have been due to Taiwanese fears that the new arrivals might try to subvert the nationalist government. In the end, the nationalist regime in Taiwan admitted over 150,000 refugees from Hong Kong and Macau between 1949 and 1954.

The United Kingdom, meanwhile, recognized the government of the People's Republic of China in Beijing and dealt with it directly in attempting to control the movement of people to Hong Kong from mainland China. Thus, the attitude of the colonial government, and the curious situation of people in Hong Kong belonging to the two Chinas of the time, prevented more vigorous intervention by UNHCR. Nevertheless, in 1957, the UN General Assembly requested UNHCR to use its 'good offices' to seek contributions to assist the Chinese refugees in Hong Kong, marking a first step towards UNHCR's involvement with refugees outside Europe.[iii] Funds raised by UNHCR during World Refugee Year in 1959/60 were channelled in particular to housing projects being undertaken by voluntary organizations in Hong Kong.

'The humanity and courage of this action did much to break the almost complete isolation of his Office from the Socialist countries and to facilitate family reunion and the large return movement which took place in the succeeding months and years.'[28]

Lindt went to considerable lengths to see that UNHCR played a positive role in the voluntary repatriation of refugees. Specific procedures were established in both Austria and Yugoslavia to this end. Hungarian repatriation missions were always accompanied by Hungarian-speaking staff members, and refugees wishing to go home were accompanied to the border by UNHCR staff. In January 1958, when Lindt visited Budapest at the invitation of the Hungarian government, he met with a number of the refugees who had returned home.[29] Altogether, some 18,200 refugees returned to Hungary, representing more than nine per cent of the total.

The problem of unaccompanied minors

A particularly vexed question was raised by the problem of 'unaccompanied minors', now often referred to as 'separated children'. When refugee children flee on their own or become separated from their families during flight, they are highly vulnerable. Determination of refugee status for such children is difficult but important, since only in so far as a minor can be regarded as a refugee does he or she come within the mandate of UNHCR.

In November 1956, the Hungarian authorities requested that the Austrian government return unaccompanied children under the age of 18. The matter was discussed at an urgent meeting between UNHCR and ICRC in Geneva on 13 December. It was agreed that children under 14 would have to be repatriated if both parents were in Hungary and if they asked for the child's return. The age distinction was later dropped. Requests had to be made in writing to ICRC which, unlike UNHCR, was represented in both Austria and Hungary.

From the start, it was foreseen that problems might arise if the parents could not be traced, if only one parent were alive, or indeed if the child were an orphan. In these cases, the best interest of the child had to be taken into consideration. It was the legal authority of the country concerned which was judged to be competent in this matter.[30] There remained a substantial problem, however, where both parents demanded the return of the child to Hungary, but the child objected to such a return. UNHCR was to confront similar problems relating to unaccompanied minors many times in the years ahead.

Bridging the East–West divide

In April 1961, Lindt reported to the UNHCR Executive Committee that the progress achieved towards a solution of the Hungarian refugees meant that 'it was no longer necessary to treat these refugees as a special group'.[31] UNHCR's international profile had been substantially raised as a result of its emergency operation to assist the Hungarian refugees. If there was a defining moment for UNHCR in the 1950s, it was the Hungarian refugee crisis.

In particular, the attitude of the US government towards UNHCR changed for the better after 1956. Indeed, what was most remarkable about the crisis was the passive acquiescence of Western states in what they deemed a Soviet *fait accompli*. In that sense, as with many of the high profile crises in which UNHCR was to be involved in the years to come, governments in London, Paris, Washington and elsewhere were relieved that 'something was being done'.

The Hungarian refugee crisis was important to UNHCR because, for the first time, it opened doors for the organization in the communist world, both in Yugoslavia and in Hungary itself. This came about largely as a result of High Commissioner Lindt's political and diplomatic handling of the crisis. One of Lindt's main achievements was that of extending support to countries in the communist world, whilst securing the support of the Western world in general and the United States in particular. Earlier US scepticism towards UNHCR gave way to a recognition of the need for an international body with specific responsibilities for refugees.

The Hungarian crisis was the first big emergency in which UNHCR was involved. It highlighted the need for maintaining an international system for handling refugee emergencies as they arose. During the crisis, UNHCR had played a critical role as a coordinating body, linking up not only with governments, but also with non-governmental organizations and inter-governmental agencies. The crisis had also demonstrated in a remarkably clear way the close connections between UNHCR's various functions—providing not only international protection and material assistance but also searching for permanent solutions to refugee problems.

UNHCR's handling of the Hungarian emergency played a major role in influencing the passage of a General Assembly resolution the following year which recognized that the refugee problem was global.[32] This resolution provided for the establishment of an emergency fund. It also established the Executive Committee of the High Commissioner's Programme (EXCOM), to approve the High Commissioner's annual material assistance programme and to advise the High Commissioner, when called upon, on matters concerning the Office's protection and assistance functions. Both organizational changes marked a wider acceptance of the ongoing role of UNHCR, which was further consolidated by World Refugee Year in 1959/60. Amongst other things, this publicized not only UNHCR's work in Europe but also its work on behalf of Chinese refugees who had fled to Hong Kong [see Box 1.5] and on behalf of Algerian refugees in Morocco and Tunisia.

UNHCR's involvement with Chinese refugees in Hong Kong represented an important breakthrough in the evolution of the organization's work. It was on behalf of this specific group that in November 1957 the UN General Assembly first asked UNHCR to use its 'good offices' to seek funds to assist a group of refugees who were outside Europe.[33] Although relatively little support was eventually needed, as the refugees were soon absorbed into the expanding Hong Kong economy, the request set an important precedent for UNHCR's involvement in the developing world. For the first time, the organization was becoming equipped to handle major refugee crises not only in Europe but also beyond.

2 Decolonization in Africa

During the 1960s, UNHCR's focus shifted increasingly away from Europe. Since the end of the Second World War, demands for independence by countries in the colonized world had increased dramatically. By 1960, it was apparent that the end of European colonial rule on the African continent was imminent. In many cases, relatively peaceful transfers of power took place. In other instances, colonial powers refused to yield, resulting in major wars which in turn caused refugee crises.

The precursor to the wars which broke out in Africa in the 1960s and 1970s was the Algerian war of 1954–62. It was one of the bloodiest 'wars of national liberation'. UNHCR's involvement in assisting Algerian refugees in Morocco and Tunisia, and in helping them repatriate at the end of the war, marked the beginning of a much wider involvement in Africa.

UNHCR's experiences in Africa were to transform the organization. In the early 1960s, UNHCR was exposed to many new challenges and dangers as it attempted to provide protection and assistance to Rwandan refugees in the Great Lakes region of central Africa. The Rwandan refugee problem proved very different from the first two major crises in which UNHCR had been involved in Hungary and Algeria. In both those cases, lasting solutions had been found: resettlement for the vast majority of Hungarians and repatriation for the overwhelming majority of the Algerians. Addressing the problems of the Rwandan refugees was to prove far more difficult. Durable solutions had worked for Hungarian and Algerian refugees in no small part because the countries of first asylum, Austria and Yugoslavia in the first case and Morocco and Tunisia in the second, were politically stable. By contrast, in the Great Lakes region, the countries of first asylum for the Rwandan refugees were highly volatile politically, with the solitary exception of Tanzania.

By the end of the 1960s, UNHCR was involved in assisting a number of African states in dealing with refugee problems in sub-Saharan Africa. By 1969, some two-thirds of UNHCR's global programme funds were being spent in African countries, illustrating the enormous shift which had taken place in the organization's focus in the space of a decade. Reflecting the international community's increasing awareness of the global nature of refugee problems, a new Protocol was drawn up in 1967 extending the scope of the 1951 UN Refugee Convention. In another significant development, in 1969 the Organization of African Unity, in consultation with UNHCR, drew up its own regional refugee convention.

This Algerian refugee in Tunisia was amongst some 250,000 refugees who fled to either Tunisia or Morocco during the Algerian war of independence (1954–62). (UNHCR/S. WRIGHT/1961)

The Algerian war of independence

The Algerian war of independence was a savage colonial war in which an estimated 300,000 Algerians were killed and over a million European settlers were forced to flee the country. The French army lost over 24,000 men and around 6,000 French settlers were killed. The war was to cause the fall, directly or indirectly, of six French prime ministers and the collapse of the Fourth Republic. It came close to bringing down President Charles de Gaulle and plunging France into civil war. It was a guerrilla struggle, pitting an indigenous, lightly armed force against a largely foreign intervention force. It was made all the more bitter by the fact that over one million French settlers, or *pieds noirs*, some of whose families had lived in Algeria for over a century, considered the country to be their home and were viscerally opposed to independence.

France had invaded Algeria in 1830 and had declared it a part of metropolitan France in 1848. By the early 20th century, neighbouring Morocco and Tunisia had also come under French domination, but, unlike Algeria, these countries were declared protectorates.

The Algerian war of independence began in November 1954 in the Aurès mountains, 400 kilometres southeast of the capital, Algiers. Within a few years, France had deployed some 500,000 soldiers in the field, roughly the same number that the United States was to send to Viet Nam in the 1960s. The French army was caught between the settler community and an increasingly militant insurgency, led by the *Front de libération nationale* (FLN). The French government focused on counter-insurgency operations, but in spite of some temporary military successes, the armed insurgency continued. Even with the return of General de Gaulle to power in 1958 and the proclamation of the Fifth Republic the following year, it was to be many years before a political solution to the conflict was found.

The widespread use of torture by French forces prompted many Algerians to flee the country.[1] This was of deep concern to the International Committee of the Red Cross (ICRC) which, after some hesitation on the part of the French authorities, was allowed to begin prison visits in 1955. In a leaked report which was published in *Le Monde* on 5 January 1960, the ICRC cited devastating evidence of torture in Algeria. Publication of the report led to much political controversy in France. The visits of the ICRC were suspended for a year. When they resumed, there was some improvement in the situation.

French strategies of counter-revolutionary warfare, which were later to become models to be used in other wars in Indochina, Latin America and Africa, increasingly involved the forced relocation of tens of thousands of peasants thought to be sympathetic to the insurgents. Resettlement, or *regroupement*, cut communities off from the FLN and denied the latter refuge and supplies. More than a million peasants were resettled in barbed wire encampments where privations were often excessive. *Regroupement* undoubtedly made life much more difficult for the militants of the FLN's armed wing, the *Armée de libération nationale* (ALN), but while the French policy was militarily successful, it was politically disastrous. By March 1960, there were more than 1.2 million people displaced and living in camps in Algeria. A UNHCR representative travelling in eastern Algeria after the end of the war described the conditions in these camps:

We went far into the mountains escorted by an ALN patrol to visit two camps of *regroupés*. Both camps were very similar in that each contained several hundred persons whose houses had been destroyed by military action, and who had been concentrated on the side of a hill for the past few years; they had built huts for shelter, and the whole camp had been encircled with barbed wire and closely overlooked by a fortress. Up to the ceasefire they had not been allowed to leave the camp except once a day, under armed escort, to collect water. They had been confined to the immediate camp area, encircled by barbed wire, and were not permitted access to agricultural land. Food had been distributed irregularly and on an inadequate scale.[2]

Flight to Tunisia and Morocco

To avoid these grim French encampments, thousands of Algerians fled over the border to Tunisia and Morocco. As the *regroupement* programme got under way in 1957, the number of Algerians leaving the country increased. In August 1957, the UNHCR Legal Adviser, Paul Weis, noted that in two years, some 30,000 people had fled the country. All of them appeared to be in need of emergency assistance. Moreover, Weis argued that many were *prima facie* refugees whom UNHCR had a mandate to protect and assist under Article 6B of the Statute on the grounds that 'they had been exposed to measures on the part of the French authorities taken against civilians because of their race or their national and political sympathies or who had reason to believe that such measures might be applied to them in the course of so-called "*ratissage*" operations'.[3]

The governments in Tunisia and Morocco, which had only obtained independence from France in March 1956, were unable to provide adequate assistance. In May 1957, President Habib Bourguiba of Tunisia appealed to the High Commissioner, Auguste Lindt, for assistance.[4] Lindt responded by sending one of his most experienced officers, Arnold Rørholt, to Tunisia. Having established that the French government had no objection to a UNHCR relief operation that was confined to material assistance, Lindt appealed for initial funds to the Swiss government.

There was inevitably great delicacy with regard to the position of France. Not only was France a member of the UN Security Council and a supporter of UNHCR from its inception, but Algeria was regarded by the French government as part of metropolitan France, and the French government was loathe to recognize those who had fled to Tunisia as being 'refugees'. As the Deputy High Commissioner at the time, James Read, noted: 'To declare the Algerians in Tunisia refugees would mean that they had well-founded fear of persecution by the French authorities in Algeria and would be a slap in the face of the French Government.'[5]

At the United Nations, France had fought a hard struggle to maintain that the conflict in Algeria was an internal affair, and that therefore the United Nations was not competent to deal with it. Lindt himself went to Paris to see the foreign minister to try to allay French suspicions about a UNHCR relief operation. The High Commissioner

Many of the Algerians who took refuge in Morocco and Tunisia in the late 1950s and early 1960s lived in conditions of extreme poverty. (UNHCR/1961)

was also aware, however, that US policy on Algeria was beginning to come under pressure. In September, Lindt wrote to John Foster Dulles, the US Secretary of State, to inform him of his intentions concerning the refugees in Tunisia and to seek Washington's political and financial support. Throughout the Algerian operation, Lindt and his successor, Félix Schnyder, went to considerable lengths to ensure the continuing support of the US administration.[6]

By 1958, tent cities had been erected amongst the dunes in Morocco and Tunisia. They were home to thousands of refugees, who were given assistance by the League of Red Cross Societies (through local Red Crescent societies) and UNHCR. With funding from the Swiss government and material assistance from the United States, the League and UNHCR began the daunting task of providing food, clothing and medical assistance to the refugees. The situation in Tunisia deteriorated further and more people fled Algeria when the French military created an extensive 'no man's land', the 'Morice Line', during the first half of 1958.

The first three years of UNHCR's experience with the Algerian crisis were devoted to helping the League of Red Cross Societies carry out its relief operation. On 5 December 1958, the UN General Assembly had passed Resolution 1286(XIII) requesting the High Commissioner 'to continue his action on behalf of the refugees in Tunisia on a substantial scale and to undertake similar action in Morocco'. The Resolution represented the second time (after Hong Kong in 1957) that UNHCR had been asked to use its 'good offices' on behalf of refugees outside Europe.

The League of Red Cross Societies became UNHCR's formal operational partner in February 1959 and between 1959 and 1962 UNHCR raised US$2 million annually in cash contributions for the relief operation. In September 1959, UNHCR appointed representatives in Tunis and Rabat to liaise with the Tunisian and Moroccan governments respectively and to coordinate international efforts to bring aid to the refugees. By December 1959, there were 110,245 refugees in Morocco and 151,903 in Tunisia.[7]

There were also, however, militants of the FLN's armed wing amongst the refugees.[8] Shooting incidents along the Tunisian–Algerian border were common. In February 1958, in response to FLN artillery firing into Algerian territory, French aircraft attacked Sakiet in Tunisia. Seventy-five civilians were killed in the incident, most of them refugees.[9] The raid was widely condemned internationally. Such incidents contributed to a permanent climate of insecurity in the camps and made the refugees even more sympathetic to the FLN. It also produced a problem that was to haunt UNHCR for a long time, that of differentiating between genuine refugees and armed groups interspersed amongst the refugees.

In Morocco and Tunisia, the problem of fighters within the refugee camps increased as the war escalated. In February 1961, the UNHCR Representative for Morocco wrote that many of those in the camps were either ALN guerrillas or were being drafted into its forces.[10] In a subsequent memorandum he noted:

The mobilisation is openly in progress and appears to have been going on for some weeks. The press-gang method is used for reluctant persons. A small green truck known as the 'salad basket' circulates in the streets of Oujda City and young men are suddenly knocked on the head and popped into the bus. In some cases of reluctance extreme measures have been used and I have been informed of three persons found with their throats cut. The extent of the mobilisation in actual numbers is quite impossible for me to judge, but I am convinced that the new recruits must run into thousands.[11]

Ceasefire and repatriation

Following the opening of the first round of peace talks between France and the FLN at Evian, France, in May 1961, the High Commissioner, now Félix Schnyder, went to Morocco and Tunisia to hold talks with the two governments on repatriation and related issues. It was a significant token of the trust and confidence that UNHCR now enjoyed that he was received by both King Hassan II of Morocco and President Bourguiba of Tunisia.

It was to be almost a year, however, before a ceasefire agreement was signed between France and the provisional Algerian authorities on 18 March 1962. Among the provisions of the agreement were measures concerning the repatriation of the refugees from Morocco and Tunisia in time for a referendum on independence to be held on 1 July 1962. As far as UNHCR was concerned, a formal basis for its involvement had already been established by a General Assembly resolution in December 1961. This requested the High Commissioner to 'use the means at his disposal to assist in the orderly return of Algerian refugees in Morocco and Tunisia to their homes and [to] consider the possibility, when necessary, of facilitating their resettlement in their homeland'.[12]

In April 1962, a joint UNHCR–ICRC mission arrived at the French administrative headquarters at Rocher Noir, outside Algiers, to begin preparations for the repatriation of the refugees. At the same time, Deputy High Commissioner Sadruddin Aga Khan visited Morocco, where he met two members of the Executive Committee of the Popular Revolutionary Government of Algeria as well as the Moroccan authorities. He was concerned that neither the French nor the Algerians had yet appointed their representatives to the tripartite repatriation commissions and events were not moving as fast as they might.[13] It was important for the Algerian authorities that as many of the refugees as possible were repatriated in time for the referendum on self-determination on 1 July 1962.

UNHCR made an urgent appeal to donors for funds. The repatriation proceeded relatively smoothly, though in some areas refugees were reluctant to return to the countryside, as war and displacement had accelerated a process of social change and urbanization. In the eastern part of the country, repatriation was slower and more problematic than in the west. This was because of the degree of destruction caused by the war, and also because of the sudden withdrawal of the French administration. A particular problem, which was to be a recurrent feature of conflicts in the latter part of the century, was the dangers posed by landmines. Nevertheless, a target date of 20 July was set for repatriation of all refugees from Tunisia, and one of 25 July for those from Morocco. The joint Red Cross–UNHCR relief operation in the two countries was to be terminated on 31 July 1962. Relief for the repatriated refugees in Algeria was organized and carried out by the League of Red Cross Societies with financial support from UNHCR.

Between 4 May and 25 July, more than 61,400 refugees were repatriated from Morocco.[14] In Tunisia, 120,000 refugees were repatriated between 30 May and 20 July. Transport was provided from the Moroccan and Tunisian centres and 12 medical teams examined the refugees before their return home. Some 15,000 tents were distributed to those without shelter. The numbers were much lower than the number of UNHCR-registered refugees. In some instances, refugees had returned spontaneously without assistance, while others had integrated into Moroccan or Tunisian society. The figures had also undoubtedly been somewhat inflated due to double registration by refugees— a phenomenon which UNHCR would often find itself dealing with in subsequent relief operations. The total cost of the repatriation operation was US$1,241,000.

The referendum on independence was held as scheduled on 1 July 1962. Of those who voted, 99.7 per cent (representing 91.2 per cent of the registered electorate) voted in favour of independence, French voters in metropolitan France having given their approval to the agreement reached in Evian in a referendum on 8 April 1962. General de Gaulle duly declared Algeria to be independent on 3 July 1962.

Integration of returnees in Algeria and new arrivals in France

Within six months, well over a million colonists left Algeria for France. Many left after an outbreak of fighting in late August 1962 between factions within the ALN which contributed to a further haemorrhage of the European population and to deepening economic problems. This was the single largest migration to take place in Europe between the population upheavals at the end of the Second World War and the movements which took place as a result of the dissolution of the Soviet Union and the break-up of Yugoslavia in the 1990s. In addition to those who went to France, some 50,000 *pieds noirs* left for Spain, 12,000 went to Canada and 10,000 to Israel.

Among those who went to France were Algerians who had fought alongside the French forces in the war or who had worked for the French colonial authorities. They were known as *harkis*. Over 160,000 were relocated to France by the French armed forces between 1962 and 1967. They were given French citizenship but many faced and indeed continue to face problems of integration and discrimination. In Algeria, *harkis* were viewed as traitors and faced persecution and death. More than 100,000 are estimated to have been killed in the aftermath of the war.[15]

The problems of reintegration of returnees in Algeria were substantial. They were exacerbated by the widespread destruction caused by the war. In addition, the sudden and abrupt departure of the entire European community, the *pieds noirs*, had gutted the infrastructure of Algerian society. For UNHCR, it was to be the first of many involvements in post-conflict situations. In Algeria, as would so often be the case in subsequent years, peace had come but the commitment of the international community to consolidate that peace with economic and institutional reconstruction was limited. In October, High Commissioner Schnyder wrote to UN Secretary-General U Thant urging widespread international cooperation with the new Algerian government and offering UNHCR's services to the new authorities. He noted, in words which have often been echoed by later holders of his post, 'the fate of the repatriated ex-refugees can no longer be dissociated from that of the Algerian population as a whole without seriously endangering the country's social stability'.[16]

UNHCR's involvement in the Algerian crisis had by no means been axiomatic. Lindt's original decision to become involved in 1957 had not been without controversy. Some senior UNHCR officials had been of the opinion that such a move would risk incurring the wrath of the French government. Lindt had been very clear, however, that the mandate of the organization had universal application and that UNHCR could not concern itself solely with refugees fleeing communism.[17] UNHCR's activities in the Algerian crisis underlined not only the global nature of the refugee problem but also the potential for coordinated and effective international action to protect and assist refugees. Beginning with its involvement in Algeria during the 1960s, UNHCR's work began to take on a much more global character. In succeeding years, as Africa south of the Sahara went through similar types of conflict and upheaval, the 'good offices' function which had been conferred upon UNHCR by the General Assembly for the first time in 1957 was invoked time and time again.

Decolonization south of the Sahara

At the time of the outbreak of the Algerian war in 1954, the only independent African states were Egypt, Ethiopia, Liberia and South Africa. By the time the war ended in 1962, virtually all the British, French and Belgian colonies had either obtained independence or would do so in the next few years. After 1965, all of Africa was independent with the exception of the Portuguese-governed territories and what was then known as Spanish Sahara. The white minority regimes in Rhodesia (later Zimbabwe), the Republic of South Africa and South West Africa (later Namibia) represented a form of local colonization which was much slower to disappear, majority rule in South Africa only being achieved in 1994. Dozens of new states were formed during the decolonization process, and as the number of UN member states grew, so the balance within the United Nations began to change.

While independence was attained peacefully in some countries, in other cases challenges to new governments took the form of armed conflict, driving people from their homes and often across borders. Political domination of one ethnic group over another and upheavals that followed coups and attempted coups in the new African states also caused refugee flight.

At the beginning of the 1960s, the violence which followed the independence of the Congo, Rwanda and Burundi in the Great Lakes region of central Africa led to widespread slaughter and massive displacement. Elsewhere during the 1960s, thousands of refugees fled from Portuguese-administered Angola, Mozambique and Guinea-Bissau and lesser numbers left the minority-controlled Republic of South Africa, South West Africa and Rhodesia. The largest group were those from the Portuguese territories who fled into neighbouring countries to escape the impact of armed struggles for independence. Those from northern Angola moved into the Republic of the Congo where most settled permanently.[18] Those from the east and south of Angola fled into Zambia and Botswana. Refugees from Guinea-Bissau entered Senegal, where they integrated with their ethnic kin in the south of the country. Refugees from Mozambique flooded into both southern Tanzania and Zambia. The smaller numbers that fled from the Republic of South Africa arrived in Botswana, Zambia and Tanzania. Some moved even further afield to other African states, Europe and the United States.

Other significant refugee movements resulting from internal armed conflict during the 1960s are numerous. Ewe refugees from Ghana entered Togo following the defeat of their efforts to reunite Ewes in Togo and Ghana. In the years following independence, the Republic of the Congo suffered a prolonged civil war which forced people to flee to safety in all nine neighbouring countries, most notably the Central African Republic, Sudan, Uganda, Burundi and Tanzania. The civil war in Sudan caused successive waves of refugees from the south to flood into Uganda, the

Box 2.1 Flight from Rhodesia, return to Zimbabwe

By the mid-1960s, almost all of the United Kingdom's former African colonies were independent. Rhodesia remained an exception. The white minority government there refused to extend the right to vote to the majority of its citizens and in November 1965 Rhodesian Prime Minister Ian Smith issued a Unilateral Declaration of Independence. The lack of a military response from the United Kingdom, the ineffectiveness of externally negotiated settlements, and the brutal suppression of African political activities led the black nationalist movement to resort to armed struggle.

The two opposition parties, the Zimbabwe African National Union (ZANU) and the Zimbabwe African People's Union (ZAPU), formed military wings and began a guerrilla war. The Rhodesian police and army responded ruthlessly. Earlier that decade, white refugees from the Congo had poured into Rhodesia; now white Rhodesians were determined not to become refugees themselves.

At first, prospects for a negotiated settlement were bleak. Rhodesian security forces were able to contain the insurgency, while the small numbers who left for neighbouring countries were primarily people who wanted to join the national liberation struggle. But by the late 1960s, people were fleeing Rhodesia because of government-sanctioned brutality. From 1973, harsh Rhodesian legislation targeted black people accused of supporting the guerrilla war. Thousands of villagers were forced to relocate to fenced 'protected villages' under the watch of special security forces. Violence and abuses by the Rhodesian security forces were rife. In 1975, Rhodesia passed an Indemnity and Compensation Act, with retrospective effect from December 1972, to protect the security forces from liability for killing, torture or destruction of property in the war. In response, the insurgency intensified and many more people joined the guerrillas. Throughout the 1970s, the guerrillas became better trained and equipped, and they began operating from bases in Mozambique and Zambia.

Flight to Mozambique, Botswana and Zambia

The main refugee flows began in the mid-1970s, as the fighting intensified. By the end of 1975, UNHCR estimated that there were some 14,500 refugees from Rhodesia in Mozambique. This number increased rapidly over the next few years and by 1979 there were estimated to be over 210,000 such refugees in Mozambique, Botswana and Zambia.

Along the eastern border with Mozambique, many fled only a short distance, crossing the frontier but remaining among kinsfolk. Many others went to large camps deeper inside Mozambique, in places like Chimoio and Nyadzonia, which were run by ZANU. These camps held not only large numbers of refugees, but also trainee guerrillas. As a result, the camps became vulnerable to raids by Rhodesian armed forces. For example, on 9 August 1976 in an attack on the Nyadzonia camp, hundreds of refugees were killed. Camps in Zambia also accommodated both refugees and guerrillas, and there were transit camps in Botswana for people on their way to Zambia. In Rhodesia itself, thousands of people fled their homes in the countryside to live in makeshift encampments around bigger towns and cities.

With camps in neighbouring countries so blatantly militarized, relief organizations and governments had difficulty providing assistance to refugees without simultaneously aiding the combatants. The medical aid and food sent into Mozambique to assist refugees inevitably also found its way to the guerrillas. Church groups attempting to trace abducted children found that many were now well-trained fighters. UNHCR provided assistance to refugees and operated in some of the camps, but found it increasingly difficult to distinguish between refugees and guerrilla fighters. In 1978, UNHCR stopped assisting ZAPU-affiliated camps, though it did provide emergency aid. The many political and security problems associated with these camps meant that international assistance to refugees in all three of the refugee-hosting countries was minimal. Many of the camps suffered chronic food shortages.

Repatriation and reconstruction

In 1976, ZANU and ZAPU merged, forming the Patriotic Front alliance and putting further pressure on the Rhodesian security forces. Weak-ening Rhodesian resolve brought the parties to the negotiating table in 1978 and at the Lancaster House talks in London in September-December 1979 an agreement was reached. This included provisions for the early repatriation of refugees to take part in elections. UNHCR participated in the US$140 million repatriation programme on condition that repatriation was voluntary, that there was agreement between the country of origin and the countries of asylum on modalities of movement and reception, and that refugees were allowed to return to their former homes and villages.

A ceasefire came into effect at the end of 1979, the country's first full elections were held in February 1980, and the formal independence of the Republic of Zimbabwe was declared in April 1980. By the early 1980s, three-quarters of the Zimbabwean refugees had returned home. With the country no longer run by a white minority government, the returnees were eager not just to rebuild their own lives but to participate in building a new nation. Communities were rebuilt rapidly and UNHCR and other international relief organizations provided reintegration assistance. Then, from the early 1980s, Zimbabwe itself became host to increasing numbers of refugees fleeing the civil war in Mozambique. By 1992, there were over 230,000 Mozambican refugees in the country.

Colonial rule and independence in Africa

Map 2.1

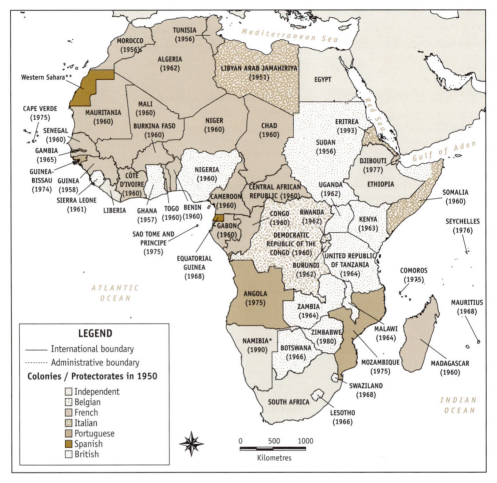

Notes:

The year given indicates when the country first gained independence for those countries that did so after 1950.

The colonial power indicated refers to the power which ruled in 1950.

The country names and borders are those as of 31 Dec. 1999.

* Namibia, formerly known as South West Africa, was administered by South Africa between 1920 and 1990, when it achieved independence.

** Spain relinquished control of Spanish Sahara in 1975. Since then the status of what has become known as Western Sahara has been in dispute and a UN-sponsored referendum on the issue has yet to be held.

Sources: UNHCR; Global Insight Digital Mapping, Europa Technologies Ltd, 1998; J. Scott, *The World Since 1914*, Heinemann Educational, Oxford, 1989; *The Europa World Yearbook 1999*, Europa Publications, London, 1999.

Congo, the Central African Republic and Ethiopia. Armed conflict between Ethiopian forces and separatists in the province of Eritrea resulted in a refugee flow into Sudan. After armed assertion of their religious separatism, members of the Lumpa sect fled Zambia to become refugees in the Congo.

Perhaps the most devastating of all was the Biafran war which began in 1967. This war erupted when the predominantly Ibo region of eastern Nigeria proclaimed the independent republic of Biafra in June that year. Civil war broke out the following month as the federal government sought to keep Nigeria united as one country. Two-and-a-half years later, federal forces eventually prevailed, but during the course of the war at least 600,000 people died, mostly as a result of famine, and some two million people were uprooted from their homes. The famine in Biafra received unprecedented television coverage. Dramatic images of emaciated children were successfully employed by the Biafran leadership to galvanize the international community into action. ICRC, the UN Children's Fund (UNICEF) and a small number of international non-governmental, mainly church-based organizations worked directly with the Biafrans and set up an airlift to the encircled rebel territory. At its peak, the airlift was bringing in 500 tonnes of humanitarian assistance in 40 flights each night. Interestingly, the person the ICRC appointed as their 'High Commissioner for Nigeria' during the crisis was Auguste Lindt, who had been the UN High Commissioner for Refugees in 1957–60.[19]

During the Biafran war, more than 50,000 Nigerians fled to neighbouring countries. UNHCR did not become involved in assisting those displaced inside Nigeria, although it did provide assistance to some 40,000 Ibo refugees in Equatorial Guinea after the latter requested UNHCR's help in March 1969. After the end of the war in January 1970, UNHCR also assisted in repatriations from several countries, including that of over 5,000 children from Gabon and Côte d'Ivoire.

Rwanda and the Great Lakes region

The displacement which took place in the Great Lakes region during the 1960s and the role of UNHCR at that time is of particular significance in view of the crisis which unfolded there some 30 years later [see Chapter 10]. The independence of the Belgian colony of the Congo in 1960, and of the Belgian-administered trusteeship territory of Ruanda–Urundi (which became the two states of Rwanda and Burundi) two years later, was accompanied by widespread bloodletting and a full-blown international crisis. In the 1960s, as in the 1990s, the epicentre of the political violence that spawned refugee movements throughout the region was Rwanda.[20]

Like its southern neighbour Burundi, Rwanda had been a German colony until 1918. After the First World War, Belgium administered the two countries as trusteeship territories on behalf of first the League of Nations and then the United Nations. The root causes of ethnic violence in both Rwanda and Burundi can be found in the extent to which communal identities were activated, mythologized and manipulated for political advantage by international and local actors.

The origins of the 1994 genocide of some 800,000 Rwandan Tutsi go back many years. Colonial rule had rigidified and polarized the two main communities in many ways. Belgian authorities had simplified the complex local system of chiefdoms, giving the Tutsi almost total control over the Hutu peasantry. As early as 1930, they had also introduced identity cards that included an ethnic categorization. In addition, the Roman Catholic church had destroyed many pre-colonial religious customs which had served as a bond between the two ethnic groups. As pressure from the United Nations grew in the 1950s to accelerate moves towards independence, the Belgian

These Rwandan refugees at Kalonge refugee centre, Kivu province, Congo, were among some 150,000 Rwandans who fled to neighbouring countries in the early 1960s. (UNHCR/S. WRIGHT/1961)

authorities abruptly shifted their long-held support for the Tutsi minority to the Hutu majority. This prompted rioting in November 1959 and the overthrow of the Tutsi monarchy. In January 1961, a Belgian-supported *coup d'état* proclaimed what in effect was a Hutu republic. Tutsi were displaced from entrenched political positions and, as a result, the first large displacement of around 120,000 Tutsi into neighbouring countries took place. Some refugees, who had returned to participate in the elections of September 1961, became the victims of widespread reprisals and many fled anew. Nevertheless, the refugees expected they could return *en masse* in July 1962 when Rwanda attained independence and the Belgians withdrew. Many of the refugees, however, saw return as only possible if Tutsi political hegemony and the monarchy were restored. Repatriation, for most, was only to come three decades later. The failure to address the problems of the Rwandan refugees in the 1960s contributed substantially to the cataclysmic violence of the 1990s.

General Assembly Resolution 1743(XVI) of 27 February 1962, anticipating independence a few months hence, had indeed called for the return and resettlement of refugees. UN officials tried to put pressure on the government in the Rwandan capital Kigali to allow the refugees to return, but to little avail. A UN report of the period came to a pessimistic conclusion: 'The developments of these last eighteen months have brought about the racial dictatorship of one party. . . An oppressive system has been replaced by another one. . . It is quite possible that some day we will witness violent reactions on the part of the Tutsi.'[21]

In neighbouring Burundi, a UNHCR representative noted a 'psychosis of fear on the part of refugees as far as a safe return to Rwanda is concerned'.[22] Acting on requests from the Belgian and Burundi governments, the High Commissioner was anxious to see if something could be done before independence. In June, the Director of Operations, Thomas Jamieson, visited Burundi and neighbouring countries to make an assessment of the Rwandan refugee problem. The Burundi authorities agreed to settle only 15,000 of the approximately 40,000 Rwandan refugees on their territory and asked that Tanganyika, which became the United Republic of Tanzania in October 1964, and the Republic of the Congo, take the rest. From the beginning, Tanganyika was generous and provided the best example of resettlement of the refugees. The head of state, President Julius Nyerere, took a personal interest in the matter.[23] By this time, some 150,000 Rwandan refugees had taken refuge in neighbouring countries. In addition to the 40,000 in Burundi, there were some 60,000 in the Kivu in eastern Congo, 35,000 in Uganda and 15,000 in Tanganyika.[24]

In the short term, it was the refugees in Burundi who had the most marked political impact. As a result of the influx of the Rwandan Tutsi refugees, the Burundian Tutsi became hardened in their resolve to maintain control of the political system. Above all, they kept tight control of the army. Rwandan refugees wanted a restoration of the former regime in their country. Armed elements among the Rwandan refugees, who were for the most part in two camps close to the Rwandan border, carried out raids into Rwanda itself. These armed groups, known as *inyenzi* (the cockroaches), had the effect of hardening anti-Tutsi sentiment within Rwanda and confirming the Hutu ethnic mythology. Tutsi remaining in Rwanda were frequently the subject of murderous attacks.[25] This was especially the case after the *inyenzi* organized what amounted to an invasion of Rwanda in December 1963. The attempt failed within days. In its aftermath, at least 10,000 Tutsi were killed and a new exodus of Tutsi refugees took place: some 7,500 left for Uganda and another 10,000 for Burundi.

Nor was Burundi itself immune to political upheavals. After the assassination of Hutu Prime Minister Pierre Ngendandumwe in January 1965, a failed Hutu uprising led to an army coup and to the abolition of the monarchy. The new hardline military regime led by Tutsi extremists later organized a massacre of over 100,000 Hutu in 1972, causing the flight of several hundred thousand survivors to Tanzania.[26]

In response to the Rwandan crisis, UNHCR launched a major programme for the Rwandan refugees throughout the central African states where they had taken refuge. Such programmes provided for the distribution of food for at least an initial period so as to give the refugees time to clear and cultivate the land placed at their disposal, so that they could eventually become self-sufficient. Rural settlements were not always successful, however, as they required a degree of social and political stability in the host country which could not be taken for granted. Another recurring problem was the exploitation of refugees in some camps by political leaders who wanted to return the refugees by force to Rwanda. In the 1960s, Rwandan refugees settled most easily in Tanzania, one of the most stable countries in the region. In many other countries to which the Rwandans had fled, however, local settlement was far more difficult. Even Uganda, which at the time enjoyed considerable stability, was plunged into internal turmoil after Prime Minister Obote overthrew President Mutesa in 1966.

Refugees in the Kivu provinces of the Congo

In the 1960s, the government in Leopoldville struggled to keep the country together against strong secessionist tendencies, most notably in Katanga (later Shaba) province in the south. It also had to cope with large numbers of internally displaced people.[27] Most of the Rwandan refugees who had fled their homeland were living in the provinces of North Kivu and South Kivu in the east of the country. By early 1962, there were already 60,000 Rwandan refugees in the Kivu area. They were principally concentrated around Goma, Bukavu, Nyangezi and Luvungi.[28] Initially well-received by the provincial government, internal political divisions within the Congo produced growing uncertainty for the refugees during 1963. Violence became commonplace and was increasingly directed at the refugees. A UNHCR official working in the Rwandan refugee camps in the Congo, François Preziosi, wrote to the High Commissioner in October 1963 in terms which were to find a chilling echo 30 years later:

I found that the authorities of North Kivu are using this term [Tutsi] as a propaganda stunt. Everything evil in their area is caused by 'Tutsi'. This word seems to be the depository of a blend of subjective fear, hate and frustration, very much like the term 'Jew' in Hitler's Germany. Therefore, anyone looking like a Tutsi is liable to be beaten, killed or imprisoned, likewise anyone who helps them. I saw in Sake a cable emanating from the North Kivu government addressed to the central government in Leopoldville in which all disorders and atrocities in North Kivu were ascribed to the Tutsis.[29]

In November 1963, High Commissioner Schnyder cabled Prime Minister Cyrille Adoula in Leopoldville, urging the central government's intervention to protect the refugees. At the suggestion of Ralph Bunche, the senior political assistant of UN Secretary-General U Thant, a joint UN–Congolese commission was set up to investigate the situation and to try to reduce political tensions. But the rebellion led by Pierre Mulele in the eastern Congo added a new dimension to the problem. The provincial government, supported this time by the central authorities in Leopoldville,

Number of refugees in the Great Lakes region, 1960–2000*

Figure 2.1

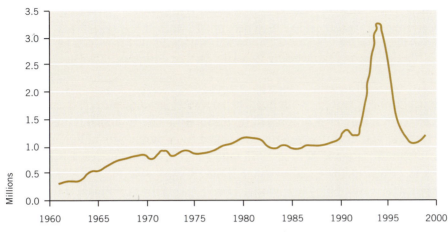

*This comprises Burundi, Rwanda, Tanzania, Uganda and Zaire/Democratic Republic of the Congo

used the threat posed by the rebels to seek the expulsion of the refugees on the grounds that some of them had assisted the rebels.[30] In August 1964, while attempting to assist refugees who were being intimidated by the insurgents at a camp near Kalonge, François Preziosi and an official working for the International Labour Organization (ILO) were brutally murdered [see Box 8.3]. As a result, UNHCR and the ILO temporarily suspended all operations in the Kivu area.

Almost simultaneously, the government in Leopoldville ordered the expulsion of all refugees. Although the decree was never systematically applied, it was used henceforth by local authorities to harass Rwandan refugees.[31] The central government now wanted the refugees expelled to Uganda or Tanzania. In November 1964, Rwandan refugees began moving from Goma to Tanzania. It was an arduous journey. Eventually, with assistance from UNHCR, some 5,000 refugees were moved by boat from Bukavu to Goma, from where they were flown in chartered aircraft to Tabora in Tanzania. There they were accommodated by UNHCR in a transit centre. Thence they travelled by train to Mpanda, some 20 hours away. From Mpanda, they proceeded by truck to the Mwezi Highlands where they settled. Over 10,000 other refugees fled of their own volition to Uganda and another 10,000 to Burundi. Although the airlift itself was financed almost entirely by two German religious organizations, UNHCR decided to assist with this operation because it considered that the refugees could no longer be protected in the Congo itself, at least as far as Kivu was concerned.[32] Later, in 1996, a very similar decision was made by UNHCR in the same region.

The refugees who remained in the Congo continued to be assisted by UNHCR. These Kinyarwanda-speakers were assimilated into the wider Congolese Kinyarwanda-speaking community, although they were not granted Congolese citizenship. This community faced considerable hostility, particularly after President Mobutu Sese Seko came to power in 1965. President Mobutu had an antagonistic relationship with the Kinyarwanda-speakers and it was difficult for the refugees to distance themselves from the rest of this community. As a result, they were drawn into the local politics. Preziosi noted at the time:

The refugees cannot remain neutral. They have to take sides. If they do not take sides they attract upon themselves the enmity of the chiefs and populations where they are. If they do take sides, they are accused of meddling in politics by their adversaries. They stand to lose in either case.[33]

Inevitably, one is forced to ask how the course of subsequent events might have been different if a durable solution had been found for the Rwandan refugees in the 1960s. That the vast majority of refugees wanted to go home was in little doubt. An inquiry into the situation in Kivu in 1963 found an overwhelming desire amongst the refugees to return to their homeland if UNHCR were able to give a 'watertight' guarantee for their well-being in Rwanda.[34] Had repatriation taken place at that time, a new accommodation might have been found between the Tutsi and Hutu, thus avoiding the genocide that occurred 30 years later. Or, it may be argued, if the international community had been more generous in providing the necessary funds, then local settlement in a politically stable environment like Tanzania might have worked. More, too, could no doubt have been done to find regional solutions.

At the time, however, the attention of the international community had been diverted by the war over the mineral-rich, secessionist southern province of Katanga in the Congo. With Belgian forces supporting the secessionists, the United Nations had become involved at the request of the Congolese government and had deployed troops in the United Nations Operation in the Congo (*Opération des Nations Unies pour le Congo*, or ONUC) from 1960 to 1964—a complex peace enforcement operation which faced many problems. Cold War tensions and states' preoccupation with other events—particularly the Cuban missile crisis of 1962—also help to put into context their lack of willingness at the time to address the Rwandan refugee crisis in a more comprehensive and thorough way.

Expanding the international refugee regime

By 1965 there were some 850,000 refugees in Africa. Although many of those who fled during the independence struggles were able to return within a relatively short period, new conflicts created further outflows, and by the end of the decade the number of refugees in Africa had risen to around one million. In size, character and needs, these successive refugee groups were very different from those in Europe and they called for a new approach to the question of how to determine refugee status.

UNHCR had to act with flexibility to assist these new refugees. The large numbers of people involved meant that it was impracticable to screen each individual in order to establish whether or not the person had a well-founded fear of persecution. UNHCR therefore resorted to a *prima facie* group determination of

Box 2.2

The 1967 Protocol to the 1951 UN Refugee Convention

The 1967 Protocol Relating to the Status of Refugees removed the time limitation of 'events occurring before 1 January 1951' which had been written into the 1951 UN Refugee Convention's definition of a refugee [see box 1.3]. The Protocol entered into force on 4 October 1967.

The 1967 Protocol is an independent legal instrument, though it is integrally related to the 1951 Convention. In acceding to it, states agree to apply Articles 2–34 of the 1951 Convention to all persons covered by the refugee definition without reference to time or geographical limitations. Acceding to the Protocol alone is sufficient to render most of the Convention's provisions applicable to the acceding state. Most states, however, have preferred to ratify both the Convention and the Protocol, thus reinforcing the two instruments' authority as the basis of international refugee law.

By 31 December 1999, 134 states had acceded to the 1967 Protocol. At that time, the only states which had acceded to the 1951 Convention but not to the 1967 Protocol were Madagascar, Monaco, Namibia, and St Vincent and the Grenadines. The only states which had acceded to the 1967 Protocol but not to the 1951 Convention were Cape Verde, Swaziland, the United States and Venezuela.

refugee status whereby, in the light of circumstances that led to departure from the country of origin, refugees could be identified on a group basis. These refugees were generously received in neighbouring countries, but often required urgent material assistance. In many cases, UNHCR used its 'good offices' to provide emergency relief to support such refugees.

Refugees in Africa, however, did not benefit from the framework of international legal protection applicable to those refugees whom UNHCR had assisted in Europe. The scope of the 1951 UN Refugee Convention remained confined to people who had become refugees as a result of events that took place before 1 January 1951, and signatory states were given the option of limiting its geographical application to Europe. By contrast, UNHCR was given a general competence under its Statute to deal with refugee problems wherever they might arise. In Africa, the Convention's limitations, including in particular the dateline, proved an increasing obstacle. By the mid-1960s, the UN Refugee Convention did not apply to the majority of refugees being assisted by UNHCR.

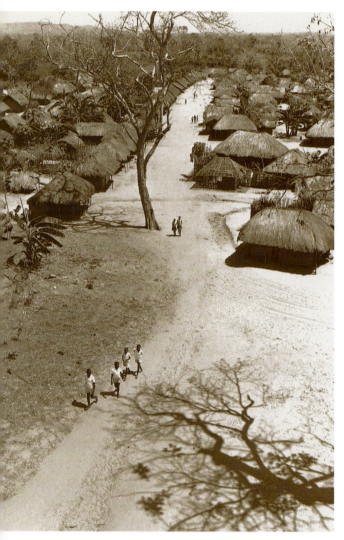

During the 1960s, UNHCR assisted with the integration of African refugees in countries of asylum, as in the case of these Mozambicans in Rutamba, Tanzania.
(UNHCR/J. MOHR 1968)

African governments, which were concerned about the security problems that refugee movements could create, also had their own interests in drawing up a regional convention on refugees. They feared that refugees might use countries of asylum as bases from which to seek the overthrow of the regimes from which they had fled. UNHCR and African states both decided, therefore, that there was a need for new international legal instruments to be drawn up regarding the treatment of refugees.

The drafting of the 1967 Protocol to the 1951 UN Refugee Convention

When the 1951 UN Convention Relating to the Status of Refugees was adopted, those drafting it were aware of its limitations and expressed the hope that nations would extend the treatment provided by the Convention to those 'who would not be covered by the terms of the Convention'.[35] In 1964, this hope materialized when UNHCR's Executive Committee asked the High Commissioner what steps might be taken to expand the temporal scope of the 1951 Convention. The High Commissioner proposed a variety of ways in which the time limitation might be narrowed rather than removed. However, the legal experts from Africa, Europe, and North and South America who had gathered to discuss such proposals recommended that the time was ripe for its complete removal. Moreover, they urged that this be accomplished by means of a new international agreement. Instead of simply amending the Convention by removing the time limitation, this new protocol would also restate it in broader terms so that a state party to the protocol would in effect be bound by the Convention.

The legal experts suggested ways in which the protocol might be made more acceptable to states hesitant to accept responsibility for future refugees. The optional geographic restriction of the Convention would be retained, but only for those states that had invoked it when signing the 1951 Convention. Furthermore, parties to the protocol would be allowed to make a reservation refusing the compulsory jurisdiction of the International Court of Justice over disputes arising out of the protocol. Although only

Box 2.3	# The 1969 OAU Refugee Convention

In 1969, the Organization of African Unity (OAU) adopted the Convention Governing the Specific Aspects of Refugee Problems in Africa. While acknowledging the 1951 UN Refugee Convention as 'the basic and universal instrument relating to the status of refugees', and reiterating the UN Convention's definition of a refugee, the OAU Refugee Convention broadens that definition and contains other important provisions which are not explicit in the UN Convention. These include provisions relating to non-rejection at the frontier, asylum, the location of refugee settlements, the prohibition of subversive activities by refugees, and voluntary repatriation.

Article I—Definition of the term 'refugee'

1. [Definition as in Article 1 A(2) of the 1951 Convention]
2. The term 'refugee' shall also apply to every person who, owing to external aggression, occupation, foreign domination or events seriously disturbing public order in either part or the whole of his country of origin or nationality, is compelled to leave his place of habitual residence in order to seek refuge in another place outside his country of origin or nationality . . .

Article II—Asylum

1. Member States of the OAU shall use their best endeavours consistent with their respective legislations to receive refugees and to secure the settlement of those refugees who, for well-founded reasons, are unable or unwilling to return to their country of origin or nationality.
2. The grant of asylum to refugees is a peaceful and humanitarian act and shall not be regarded as an unfriendly act by any Member State.
3. No person shall be subjected by a Member State to measures such as rejection at the frontier, return or expulsion, which would compel him to return to or remain in a territory where his life, physical integrity or liberty would be threatened for the reasons set out in Article I, paragraphs 1 and 2.
4. Where a Member State finds difficulty in continuing to grant asylum to refugees, such Member State may appeal directly to other Member States and through the OAU, and such other Member States shall in the spirit of African solidarity and international cooperation take appropriate measures to lighten the burden on the Member State granting asylum . . .
6. For reasons of security, countries of asylum shall, as far as possible, settle refugees at a reasonable distance from the frontier of their country of origin.

Article III—Prohibition of subversive activities

1. Every refugee . . . shall also abstain from any subversive activities against any Member State of the OAU.
2. Signatory States undertake to prohibit refugees residing in their respective territories from attacking any State Member of the OAU, by any activity likely to cause tension between Member States, and in particular by use of arms, through the press, or by radio . . .

Article V—Voluntary repatriation

1. The essentially voluntary character of repatriation shall be respected in all cases and no refugee shall be repatriated against his will . . .

The OAU Refugee Convention entered into force on 20 June 1974. By 31 December 1999, a total of 45 out of the 53 states in Africa were party to the Convention.

opened for accession in January 1967, by September the necessary six states had accepted the Protocol, thereby bringing it into force on 4 October 1967.

The procedure used to move the 1967 Protocol so quickly from idea to reality involved innovations in international law and strong personal direction by High Commissioner Sadruddin Aga Khan. It avoided the traditional amendment process which would have required calling an international conference of representatives of every government that was a party to the Convention—a process that would have taken a long time. The resulting 1967 Protocol to the 1951 UN Refugee Convention was short and direct and as an independent international instrument came into effect after accession by only a small number of states. The most important innovation, however, was opening the Protocol for acceptance by states which had not thus far ratified the Convention. This move resulted in the accession of the United States, which had not signed or ratified the 1951 Convention.

The steadily increasing acceptance of the 1967 Protocol has been of great importance to UNHCR. The Protocol expands the scope of obligations undertaken by states and has reaffirmed the obligation of states to cooperate with UNHCR [see Box 2.2].

The drafting of the 1969 OAU Refugee Convention

The High Commissioner's interest in seeking the rapid adoption of the Protocol was partly stimulated by the efforts of the member states of the Organization of African Unity (OAU) to draft their own regional convention on refugees.[36] As early as 1963, the OAU had decided that a regional treaty was needed to take account of the special characteristics of the refugee situation in Africa. While OAU member states were quick to welcome the 1967 Protocol, they still felt that a regional convention was necessary. The decision of the OAU to draft a separate instrument initially posed a problem for UNHCR. The emergence of an instrument that in any sense competed with the 1951 Convention would impair the universal character of the Convention that UNHCR had been working to achieve since its inception. Moreover, if an OAU refugee convention did not also set the high standards of the 1951 Convention, refugees in Africa would not receive the same standards of protection.

Such concerns were allayed as UNHCR was invited to be part of the drafting process. The OAU Secretariat agreed with UNHCR that the African instrument should be a regional complement to the 1951 Convention. The Preamble to the 1969 OAU Convention Governing the Specific Aspects of Refuge Problems in Africa therefore recognizes the 1951 Convention as constituting 'the basic and universal instrument relating to the status of refugees'. As such, the OAU Refugee Convention, like the UN Refugee Convention, defines a refugee as someone who has 'a well-founded fear of persecution'. It also includes those who have fled as a result of external aggression, foreign occupation or domination, or events disturbing public order in their country of origin. Persons fleeing civil disturbances, violence and war were now entitled to claim the status of refugees in states party to the OAU Refugee Convention, irrespective of whether or not they could establish a well-founded fear of persecution.

Further important additions were made. First, although no international convention had recognized an individual right to asylum, the OAU Refugee Convention affirms that states shall use their 'best endeavours . . . to receive refugees and to secure [their] settlement'. Second, it expands on the guarantee of *non-refoulement* contained in the 1951 Convention. It mentions an absolute and unqualified requirement that no refugee shall be subjected 'to measures such as rejection at the frontier, return or expulsion, which would compel him to return or remain in a territory where his life, physical integrity or liberty would be threatened'. Third, it gives unqualified expression to the principle of voluntary repatriation in an international legal context for the first time. Fourth, it defines the duties of the countries of asylum and origin, stipulating that refugees shall not be penalized for having fled and that they shall be given every possible assistance to facilitate their return. Fifth, in cases where large numbers of refugees are involved, states are encouraged to adopt a system of burden-sharing.

African governments were also determined to ensure that the security concerns of both countries of asylum and of origin were taken into account. The OAU Refugee Convention therefore states that 'the grant of asylum . . . shall not be regarded as an unfriendly act by any Member State'. The Preamble of the Convention discusses the need to 'make a distinction between a refugee who seeks a peaceful and normal life and a person fleeing his country for the sole purpose of fomenting subversion from outside'. It also contains a pledge by state parties 'to prohibit refugees residing in their respective territories from attacking any Member State of the OAU'. A further provision requires that refugees be settled 'at a reasonable distance from the frontier of their country of origin' and that they 'abstain from any subversive activities against any Member State of the OAU' [see Box 2.3].

The OAU Refugee Convention came into effect in June 1974. Since then, it has, together with the 1951 UN Refugee Convention and its 1967 Protocol, provided an important legal framework for all UNHCR activities in Africa. Although it was inspired by events in Africa, the norms and principles contained in the OAU Refugee Convention have set important standards for the protection of refugees in general and have often been applied in other parts of the world. With only a few exceptions, and in marked contrast to some other parts of the world, African countries have been extremely generous in receiving and hosting large refugee populations throughout the latter half of the 20th century.

3 Rupture in South Asia

While the 1950s had seen UNHCR preoccupied with events in Europe and the 1960s with events in Africa following decolonization, the 1970s saw a further expansion of UNHCR's activities as refugee problems arose in the newly independent states. Although UNHCR had briefly been engaged in assisting Chinese refugees in Hong Kong in the 1950s, it was not until the 1970s that UNHCR became involved in a large-scale relief operation in Asia.

In the quarter of a century after the end of the Second World War, virtually all the previously colonized countries of Asia obtained independence. In some states this occurred peacefully, but for others—including Indonesia and to a lesser extent Malaysia and the Philippines—the struggle for independence involved violence. The most dramatic upheaval, however, was on the Indian sub-continent where communal violence resulted in partition and the creation of two separate states—India and Pakistan—in 1947. An estimated 14 million people were displaced at the time, as Muslims in India fled to Pakistan and Hindus in Pakistan fled to India. Similar movements took place on a smaller scale in succeeding years. Inevitably, such a momentous process produced strains and stresses in the newly decolonized states. Many newly independent countries found it difficult to maintain democratic political systems, given the economic problems which they faced, political challenges from the left and the right, and the overarching pressures of the Cold War.

In several countries in Asia, the army seized political power in a wave of coups which began a decade or so after independence. Beginning in Pakistan in 1958 and spreading to Burma in 1962 and Indonesia in 1965, military regimes replaced democratic governments. The new regimes, with rare exceptions, suppressed democratic political parties. In many cases, they were harsh in their treatment of ethnic minorities. In some instances, the seizure of political power by the military was accompanied by considerable bloodshed, as in Indonesia in 1965–66, when more than 500,000 people are estimated to have been killed. In this case, many of the victims of the coup came from the ethnic Chinese minority. Similarly, in Burma, minority groups were subjected to harsh military repression.

In Pakistan, the drift to militarism had calamitous effects and resulted in civil war, the dismemberment of Pakistan as a state, war between India and Pakistan and a massive refugee exodus, the likes of which the world had not seen since the 1947 partition of India. With an estimated 10 million people leaving what was then East Pakistan for India between April and December 1971, this became the largest single displacement of refugees in the second half of the century. Remarkably, traumatic though these events were, the vast majority of these people returned within a year to what became the independent state of Bangladesh, in the largest repatriation operation of the post-Second World War era. In a further large-scale repatriation

Bengali refugees arriving in India in 1971. Altogether some 10 million Bengalis from East Pakistan fled to India during the crisis which led to the independence of Bangladesh. (USIS/1971)

operation in 1973–74, UNHCR was instrumental in organizing an airlift of large numbers of displaced people between Bangladesh and Pakistan.

The birth of the state of Bangladesh

When Pakistan gained independence in 1947, it was not only an ethnically mixed—though predominantly Muslim—country, but was physically separated by India into eastern and western wings. Politically, the new country was dominated by West Pakistan, which caused resentment in the Bengali East. After the military regime of General Ayub Khan took power in 1958, relations between the two halves of the country steadily worsened and East Pakistan had limited representation in Pakistani politics, despite containing the majority of the population. In the civil service, Bengalis held a small fraction of positions and the representation of Bengalis in the army was believed to be less than 10 per cent. In addition, the economic interests of East Pakistan were subordinated to those of West Pakistan.

Bengali demands for autonomy increased in the 1960s and coincided with unrest in West Pakistan, culminating in demonstrations and strikes which led to the fall of General Ayub Khan's government in 1969. The subsequent military administration headed by General Yahya Khan announced early on that it was to be a transitional government that would endeavour to transfer power to civilian authority. In January 1970 the ban on political parties and political activity was lifted. Elections for a new National Assembly were duly held on 7 December that year. To the surprise of virtually all observers, the regionally based Awami League, led by Sheikh Mujibur Rahman, was elected with an absolute majority of seats nationally, all its seats being in East Pakistan. In West Pakistan, the majority of seats were won by the Pakistan People's Party led by Zulfiqar Ali Bhutto. Initially, the Awami League sought autonomy for the East, in a loose union with the West. It proved impossible, however, to reach a political consensus between the Awami League, the Pakistan People's Party and the army.[1]

As discontent rose in the east, negotiations on a constitutional compromise collapsed. President Yahya Khan postponed indefinitely the inauguration of the National Assembly, scheduled for 3 March 1971, prompting violent protests in East Pakistan. On 26 March, following a crackdown by the Pakistani armed forces and the imposition of military rule, the independence of the People's Republic of Bangladesh was declared. The Awami League was outlawed and the Pakistani army launched a massive counterinsurgency operation. Wholesale attacks on those suspected of supporting the Awami League and widespread repression, accompanied by severe human rights violations, resulted in thousands of civilian deaths and soon led to a refugee exodus on a colossal scale.[2]

The exodus of 10 million refugees

On 29 March 1971, the UNHCR Representative in India, F.L. Pijnacker Hordijk, warned the High Commissioner of an impending refugee influx into India.[3] As with so many other refugee crises, however, the scale of the exodus was underestimated. Within a month, nearly a million refugees had entered India, fleeing the military repression in East Pakistan. By the end of May, the average daily influx into India was over 100,000 and had reached a total of almost four million. By the end of 1971, figures provided by the Indian government to the United Nations indicated that this total had reached 10 million.

Such an exodus of refugees inevitably produced extraordinary problems for the host country, India. From the beginning, the Indian government made it clear that there were no circumstances under which it would allow the refugees to settle in India.

Location of main refugee camps in India, November 1971   Map 3.1

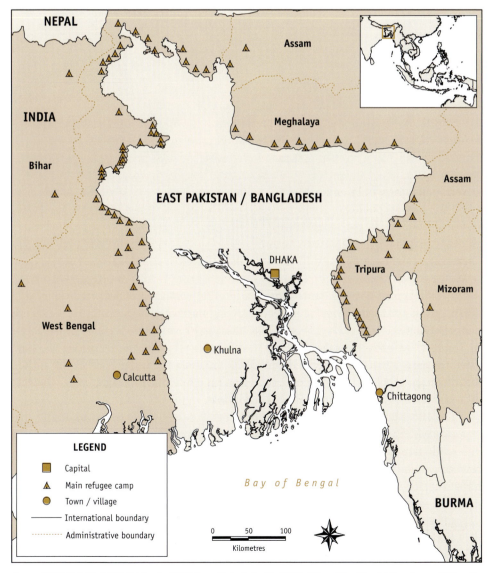

Sources: UNHCR; Global Insight Digital Mapping ©1998, Europa Technologies Ltd; UNHCR, *A Story of Anguish and Actions*, Geneva, 1972, p. 43.

The millions of Bengali refugees who fled to India in 1971 were accommodated in some 800 camps. There were serious outbreaks of cholera in some camps due to the crowded conditions. (WFP/T. PAGE/1971)

Increasingly, the government realized that it would need international assistance to cope with the massive refugee influx. On 23 April 1971, the Permanent Representative of India at the United Nations, Samar Sen, in a meeting with the UN Secretary-General, U Thant, requested international aid.[4] With growing international demands for assistance for the refugees, High Commissioner Sadruddin Aga Khan met with Secretary-General U Thant in the Swiss capital, Bern, on 26–27 April to discuss the situation. Two days later, the Secretary-General decided that UNHCR should act as the 'Focal Point' for the coordination of all UN assistance. For the first time in a humanitarian crisis, UNHCR was entrusted with the role of general coordinator.

The Focal Point was an innovative concept. It was distinct from the traditional responsibilities of the Office of the High Commissioner. It involved mobilization of international support and funds, procurement and delivery of relief supplies to India, and coordination with the Indian government, which organized the distribution of these supplies. In early May, High Commissioner Sadruddin Aga Khan sent a high-level UNHCR mission to India which consisted of the Deputy High Commissioner, Charles Mace, the Director of Operations, Thomas Jamieson, and Legal Consultant, Paul Weis. The mission was required to make a direct assessment of the situation, to achieve a measure of coordination among the UN agencies seeking to help the refugees and to discuss with the Indian authorities the ways and means to provide international assistance.[5]

Box 3.1   The Tibetan refugee community in India

The Tibetan refugees who have lived in India since the late 1950s are often overlooked. This is largely due to the fact that they have survived with relatively little international assistance. Large numbers of Tibetan refugees first arrived in India in March 1959 after the Chinese suppression of an uprising and the flight of the Dalai Lama, the spiritual and political leader of the Tibetan people. Most of the tens of thousands of Tibetans who have fled Chinese rule since that time have escaped on foot on a perilous weeks-long journey across the Himalayas. Although the Chinese side of the border was sealed in 1960, Tibetans have continued to flee since then. Most arrive via Nepal, where there is a reception centre in the capital Kathmandu. More than 40 years after the exodus from Tibet began, the refugee community in India now numbers around 100,000.

When the refugees first began arriving in India, they were accommodated in transit camps at Missamari in Assam, and Buxa in West Bengal. An unofficial 'central relief committee' supervised their affairs. It received some assistance from abroad but international organizations, including UNHCR, were not involved at this stage. The 1962 Sino-Indian border war marked a turning point. It was then that it was recognized that the Tibetans would not soon be returning to their homeland.

It was also at this time that the Indian authorities first requested international help for the refugees. UNHCR began providing assistance to the Tibetans in India from 1964, even though it did not formally establish a presence in the Indian capital, New Delhi, until 1969. Official international assistance remained limited, however. Since the 1960s, most international assistance for Tibetan refugees has been channelled through the Tibet Bureau of the Dalai Lama. Both governments and international organizations have been wary of providing assistance to the Tibetans, aware that such action would be viewed by the Chinese authorities as interference in their domestic affairs.

Since 1962, assistance programmes for the refugees have included the establishment of agricultural settlements and vocational training schemes. State governments in India have allocated refugee families an average of three acres of land each and have assisted them in constructing houses. They have also given Tibetan communities assistance in establishing water supplies, civic amenities, handicraft centres and schools. There are currently some 85 Tibetan schools across India catering for some 25,000 students.

The Indian authorities have also provided ration cards, identity papers, residence permits and travel documents for registered Tibetan refugees, who are officially viewed as having come to India on pilgrimage. Although they are considered as foreigners under the 1946 Foreigners Act, they have been accorded the basic rights of most citizens but are not allowed to contest or vote in Indian elections. Those who migrated to India before March 1959 and who have been ordinarily resident in India since then are considered for Indian citizenship on an individual basis. Those married to Indian nationals may apply for Indian citizenship.

The Indian government has consciously promoted a policy which enables the Tibetan community to maintain its distinct identity and cultural values, together with a political and administrative system of its own. From the start, separate settlements were identified and established in geographically suitable areas so as to provide them with economic, social and religious autonomy. A separate Tibetan government-in-exile has been established in Dharamsala, Himachal Pradesh.

In a relatively short period of time, Tibetan refugees settled in communities in Indian states such as Himachal Pradesh, Sikkim, Uttar Pradesh, Orissa, Arunachal Pradesh, Karnataka, Madhya Pradesh, West Bengal and Maharashtra. In certain areas, such as Darjeeling, Sikkim and Arunachal Pradesh, where cultural practices were not dissimilar to those in Tibet, the Tibetans adjusted quickly. In other places, such as Karnataka and Himachal Pradesh, there was occasionally local resistance to the Tibetans' visible presence and economic success.

Many Tibetans initially experienced problems in moving from what was a strongly traditional and almost closed society to the culturally diverse one of democratic India. In general, however, they have successfully maintained their cultural and religious practices. One author has written that the ability of the Tibetan refugees 'to build and fund in foreign lands numerous monasteries of a remarkably high architectural standard and their success in developing viable monastic communities similar to those of Tibet is one of the miracles of the twentieth century.'[i]

Despite these positive achievements, the majority of the Tibetan refugees in India still want to return to Tibet. While the conditions under which many of these refugees live are relatively good, the unresolved nature of the refugee problem is illustrated by the fact that each year Tibetan refugees not only in India, but also in Nepal and Bhutan, continue to seek asylum in Western countries. More than four decades after the initial flight of this group of refugees, permanent solutions for them still appear to be a long way off.

Between 6 and 19 May, the UNHCR mission visited numerous refugee camps in West Bengal, Tripura and Assam, the Indian states most affected by the refugee influx, and held discussions with high-level Indian officials, UN agencies and non-governmental organizations (NGOs). In a cable to the High Commissioner, the mission declared itself 'depressed by situation and reign of terror which is obvious in faces of people which are stunned and in some cases almost expressionless . . . Saw many bullet wounded men, women and children . . . Arson, rape and dispersal is the common topic [of discussion]'.[6] Mace said: 'Words fail me to describe the human plight we have just seen.'[7]

The UNHCR mission coincided with a visit by the Indian Prime Minister, Indira Gandhi, to the same states of West Bengal, Tripura and Assam. In some districts in these states, refugees already outnumbered local residents. By mid-May, Indira Gandhi noted in the Lok Sabha, the lower house of the Indian parliament, that some 330 camps had been established to accommodate the refugees who by now numbered four million. By the end of that month, there were 900,000 refugees in the hill state of Tripura alone, set against an indigenous population of 1.5 million.[8] As two scholars of the 1971 war have noted, the 'problem for India was not just the "existence" of refugees, but where they existed'.[9]

Cholera in the camps

The general sense of crisis created by such an enormous influx of refugees was heightened by severe health problems in the camps. The UN Children's Fund (UNICEF) reported that children in particular were suffering severely, many of them being considerably under-nourished.[10] Sanitation was extremely rudimentary and dysentery soon became a problem, especially amongst the children. At the end of May, a correspondent for the *Hindustan Standard* reported:

Many of the refugees are suffering from infectious diseases. Some 626 doctors and 60 refugee doctors are trying to cope with this overwhelming situation, aided by some 800 paramedical personnel. Over 2,700 beds have been added to the existing 42 hospitals, but what will the situation be tomorrow? On this day a further 100,000 refugees have arrived in the Nadia district alone.[11]

In May and June, cholera began to spread through the camps. In no time at all, medical stocks in West Bengal were exhausted, leading to an urgent appeal to the World Health Organization for vaccines and dehydration fluid, which were brought from Geneva in an emergency airlift. At the beginning of June, the number of cholera cases was estimated at 9,500. By the end of September, this figure had risen to over 46,000. A British journalist described the scene in one hospital in the London newspaper the *Observer*:

Cholera is a horrible and humiliating way to die. The only mercy is that it is comparatively quick. The cholera wards are two buildings behind the main hospital block. There are no beds. The patients lie on metal sheets covering a concrete floor. The disease produces uncontrollable diarrhoea and vomiting, the results of which are everywhere. Those who still can fan themselves weakly; those who are too far gone to do so are black with flies. There are men and women of all ages.[12]

With the spread of disease amongst the refugees the pressures on the Indian authorities increased. The health crisis could have been far worse were it not for the fact that India had

Bangladeshi refugees in India as on 1 December 1971

Figure 3.1

State	Number of camps	Refugees in camps	Refugees with host families	Total number of refugees
West Bengal	492	4,849,786	2,386,130	7,235,916
Tripura	276	834,098	547,551	1,381,649
Meghalaya	17	591,520	76,466	667,986
Assam	28	255,642	91,913	347,555
Bihar	8	36,732	–	36,732
Madhya Pradesh	3	219,298	–	219,298
Uttar Pradesh	1	10,169	–	10,169
Total	**825**	**6,797,245**	**3,102,060**	**9,899,305**

Source: 'Report of the Secretary-General Concerning the Implementation of General Assembly Resolution 2790(XXVI) and Security Council Resolution 307(1971)', UN Doc. A/8662/Add.3, 11 Aug. 1972.

sufficient food stocks which the authorities could draw upon to feed the refugees. The history of past famine disasters, like that of 1943 when over 1.5 million people died in Bengal, is sufficiently harrowing to suggest how much worse the calamity of 1971 might have been.

The relief operation

In spite of India's food reserves, the refugees placed a severe economic burden on the country. The government in New Delhi expected the international community to refund a major part of the expenses it was now incurring in looking after the refugees. In May, a visiting UNHCR mission had to stress that it would be unrealistic for the United Nations to bear full responsibility for the financial burden, given the voluntary nature of contributions to the UN budget. Nevertheless, on 19 May 1971, UN Secretary-General U Thant launched a global appeal for emergency assistance to refugees in India and appealed to the international community to respond generously.[13] U Thant also issued an appeal the following month for humanitarian assistance for the people in East Pakistan. Within weeks of the Secretary-General's initial global appeal on 19 May, some US$17 million had been pledged.[14] By 22 June, when High Commissioner Sadruddin Aga Khan went to New York to brief the Secretary-General about a 12-day visit to the sub-continent, the total had reached US$70 million.

From the outset of the crisis in East Pakistan, Indira Gandhi had made it clear that India would do its utmost to assist the refugees, but that the refugees could not remain on a permanent basis. India's firm position that refugees would have to return to their country of origin had implications for the range of measures taken by Delhi. By mid-April 1971, the Indian Ministry of Labour and Rehabilitation, which was coordinating the relief operation, decided to establish 50 camps, each equipped to accommodate 50,000 refugees, to be run by officials from the central government.

The Indian authorities registered the refugees on their arrival at the border, where they were given an entry document, a special food ration for their inland journey and anti-cholera and smallpox injections. Those who did not register at the border were presumed to be living with friends, relatives or other host families. At the beginning of December 1971, Indian government figures showed 6.8 million refugees living in camps and a further 3.1 million living with host families [see Figure 3.1].

The complexities arising from this massive population influx required extensive consultations between UNHCR and the numerous branches of the Indian government. A Central Coordinating Committee was therefore established under the aegis of the Indian Ministry of Labour and Rehabilitation, with representatives of various other ministries, the Indian Red Cross and UNHCR. From June 1971 until the end of the monsoon, the main worry, apart from adequate health facilities and shelter for the refugees, was the maintenance of the vital supply lines linking Calcutta and the outlying states in northeast India. The monsoon created more operational problems for the administration of relief and the incessant rain caused more disease.

UNHCR, which had recently established an office in New Delhi, played a major role in fundraising and in liaising with governments and NGOs. But it was the Indian government which assumed overall responsibility for handling the crisis on the ground. In Geneva, High Commissioner Sadruddin Aga Khan established and chaired a UN Standing Inter-Agency Consultative Unit to assist communication between the components of the UN system most directly concerned with the refugee problem. This body facilitated inter-agency cooperation and the framing of a common UN position on issues of assistance, and took up offers of assistance by governments, inter-governmental and non-governmental organizations.[15]

Growing tensions between India and Pakistan

At the outset of the crisis, India had taken the position that refugees would have to return within a six-month period and referred to them as 'evacuees' to emphasize their temporary status. This was a major policy constraint in planning the assistance programme, as it meant that there were no formal contingency plans for a longer period. The six-month period was supposed to have begun at the start of the first refugee influx in March 1971, and was therefore supposed to cease in September. While generosity was extended to the millions who came across the border, the Indian government was never disposed to accept the permanent settlement of refugees from East Pakistan in India.

As time went by, it became clear that the refugees would not be able to return within the six-month time frame because of the continuation of the persecution that had caused them to flee to India in the first place. The Indian authorities claimed that Pakistan was attempting to resolve the political impasse in East Pakistan through the mass expulsion of a considerable proportion of its population, most of whom were Bengali Hindus. Increasingly, India considered imposing its own political solution in East Pakistan. As early as April, the Indian government had effectively sanctioned the functioning of a government-in-exile on Indian soil and the training of Bangladeshi military forces.

For its part, from 21 May Pakistan several times stated its willingness to accept the refugees back. On 28 June, President Yahya Khan even appointed a Bengali, A.M. Malik, as special assistant for displaced persons. But the human rights situation in East Pakistan did not improve and the outflow of refugees to India continued. The Pakistani authorities remained unwilling to remove the ban on the Awami League and were determined to proceed with the trial of Awami League leader Sheikh Mujibur Rahman for sedition.

The Indian government considered the international response to the crisis to be inadequate, and its relations with the United Nations—including UNHCR—became increasingly strained. UN-sponsored efforts to settle the dispute and even to offer humanitarian aid were sometimes viewed with scepticism by the Indian authorities. The Indian government was particularly critical of High Commissioner Sadruddin Aga Khan for making a visit in June to the sub-continent at the invitation of President Yahya Khan of Pakistan, who allowed the High Commissioner to travel extensively in East Pakistan itself. The Indian government viewed the visit as an endorsement of Pakistani efforts to persuade the refugees to return. It also considered the visit to be premature, given the need for a political settlement before the refugees could return safely. At the end of the trip, the High Commissioner went to New Delhi for talks with Prime Minister Indira Gandhi. To many in the Indian government, the Delhi leg of the visit looked too much like an afterthought.[16]

Efforts by UNHCR to establish a presence in the refugee camps in India were firmly rebuffed by the Indian government, which also objected to UNHCR's efforts to establish a presence in reception centres in East Pakistan. Even the presence of NGOs in the camps was becoming unacceptable, as New Delhi stepped up its assistance to the Mukhti Bahini, the Bangladeshi guerrilla force which it had tolerated from the start of the crisis. Moreover, as tensions between India and Pakistan and the likelihood of war increased, efforts by the United Nations to mediate in the conflict became increasingly irksome to Delhi. Secretary-General U Thant offered in late September to mediate between India and Pakistan in the midst of the rising tension and mobilization of their respective military forces. While Pakistan responded favourably, India interpreted the move as trying to save the military regime in Pakistan which it saw as responsible for the massive refugee exodus. India urged the Secretary-General to find a political solution, which would take into consideration the wishes of the people of East Pakistan.[17]

War between India and Pakistan

India's fundamental objectives from the beginning of the crisis in March 1971 had been, first, the repatriation of all the refugees who had fled East Pakistan and, second, the transfer of political power within East Pakistan itself to the Awami League. Thus, any solution to the crisis which did not include provisions for the return of the refugees was plainly unacceptable.[18] From the outset, however, it was difficult to see how this could happen without the military defeat of Pakistan and its ousting from East Pakistan.

Direct military intervention was considered by Indian leaders as early as April 1971. However, the Indian Chief of Staff, General Manekshaw, dismissed this proposal as premature, since the Indian Army was not ready for any offensive operation and would require six to seven months to prepare for a conflict on both fronts. When the Indian government later discovered that both the United States and China were providing the Pakistan government with arms to maintain the unity of the country, its position hardened. By late July, the Indian government had reached a consensus on the issue of East Pakistan, which included the direct supervision of the Bangladeshi government-in-exile and military training for the Mukhti Bahini and other Bangladeshi 'liberation forces'. In August 1971, India concluded a 20-year Treaty of Peace and Friendship with the Soviet Union, while Prime Minister Indira Gandhi travelled to Western Europe and the United States to promote the cause of an independent Bangladesh.

Despite efforts by UN Secretary-General U Thant to mediate, the situation continued to deteriorate, with reports of cross-border skirmishes and incursions along the Indian border with East Pakistan. On a visit to India on 6–8 November 1971, High Commissioner Sadruddin Aga Khan expressed his anxiety at the growing tensions and the effects this would have on the delivery of assistance to the refugees. Throughout November the situation deteriorated further along the Indian borders with both East and West Pakistan. On 3 December, Pakistan launched air attacks against Indian bases on India's western front. Indian forces subsequently entered East Pakistan in force. The UN Security Council discussed the issue at length, but was paralysed by the use of the veto by one or other of its permanent members. On 5 December, Indira Gandhi recognized Bangladesh's independence and on 16 December Dhaka fell to the Indian forces.[19] The UNHCR head of office there, John Kelly, played a critical intermediary role in ensuring a ceasefire between the two opposing armies.[20] With the surrender of the Pakistani army, the war ended, paving the way for the independence of Bangladesh.

Repatriation and population exchanges

The way was now open for the return of the refugees. India quickly announced that all refugees who had entered the country after 25 March 1971 would need to return to Bangladesh by the end of February 1972. This time frame seemed optimistic, and the provision of necessary transportation for most of the 10 million refugees raised huge operational difficulties. Nevertheless, within days of the conclusion of hostilities, the refugees began returning home of their own accord. Indeed, some had even begun returning while the fighting was still going

Box 3.2

The expulsion of South Asians from Uganda

The decree in 1972 by Ugandan President Idi Amin ordering the departure of Uganda's population of South Asian origin sparked a mass exodus. As thousands of Ugandan Asians sought to find countries to accept them, UNHCR and other organizations played an important part in assisting those who were expelled.

The South Asians in East Africa were long-settled and of diverse backgrounds. They included Hindus, Muslims, Sikhs and Christians from various parts of the Indian sub-continent. Their origins varied from pre-colonial merchants, to labourers and artisans imported by the British to build the railways, small traders, people brought in to staff the colonial civil service, and cotton ginners and traders who later moved into other areas of the economy.

When Uganda became independent in 1962, Asians living there were offered the option of becoming Ugandan citizens. While some did so, many others chose to retain their British passports and the option of future settlement in the United Kingdom. By the early 1970s, there were about 75,000 South Asians in Uganda. About half held British passports, one-third were Ugandan citizens or had applications for citizenship pending, and the rest were Indian, Pakistani or Kenyan nationals. During the colonial period, Asians had been targets of periodic outbursts of hostility, largely because they controlled significant parts of the economy. After independence, this gathered momentum as African nationalism fuelled demands for 'indigenization', an attempt to redress the exclusion of Africans from economic and political power structures. Such moves were seen first in neighbouring Kenya, and coincided with restrictive admission measures introduced in the United Kingdom in 1968 against the background of increasing anxiety about immigration from the former colonies.

In Uganda, efforts in the 1960s by the regime of Amin's predecessor,

Milton Obote, to shift control of trade from Asians to Africans, heightened inter-communal tensions. It was partly in reaction to those efforts that most Asians welcomed Amin's seizure of power early in 1971. However, as the economy lurched from bad to worse, discontent among the urban population and within the armed forces drove Amin to seek a scapegoat for the country's economic ills. Late in 1971, Amin called a meeting of prominent members of the Asian community and berated them for dominating sections of the economy and failing to integrate.

In August 1972, Amin abruptly announced that all non-citizens of South Asian origin should leave the country within three months. He later ordered that all Asians should leave, even if they had Ugandan citizenship. Subsequently he withdrew this edict, but many of those who had applied for citizenship were refused and they became effectively stateless. Various exemptions were made, notably for professionals, but the atmosphere of insecurity and harassment that prevailed provoked a mass exodus as the deadline approached.

More than 50,000 Asians left Uganda between the expulsion order and the November deadline. Others had fled earlier. After the deadline, only about 200 Asian families were left in Uganda. The Departed Asians' Property Custodian Board was established to oversee the disposal of the assets of those expelled. Unless they had managed to transfer money or assets abroad before they left, those who fled Uganda arrived in their new host countries with little to start anew.

As the crisis unfolded, the United Kingdom reluctantly agreed to waive its annual immigration quota, and admitted in all about 29,000 Ugandan Asians, most of whom held British passports. At the same time, the UK government appealed to other countries to accept expelled Asians. Eventually, some 6,000 Ugandan

Asians, many of them holders of British passports, were settled in Canada, and about 1,500, including some of undetermined nationality, were settled in the United States.

To leave Uganda, Asians needed a valid travel document, a country of temporary or permanent asylum, and the means to travel. For those Asians still lacking any of these necessities when the deadline approached, a UN mission, which included a UNHCR representative, flew to the Ugandan capital Kampala and negotiated an emergency evacuation. The International Committee of the Red Cross agreed to deliver travel documents to those needing them, and the Inter-governmental Committee for European Migration (precursor to the International Organization for Migration) arranged transport to temporary or permanent resettlement countries.

UNHCR appealed to the international community for assistance in the form of offers of permanent resettlement, and funds to transport and assist those in transit. The response was positive and, in less than two weeks, some 3,600 people were flown to transit accommodation in Austria, Belgium, Italy, Malta and Spain. In addition to the United Kingdom, Canada and the United States, permanent resettlement places were offered by Australia, Austria, Belgium, Denmark, the Netherlands, New Zealand, Norway, Sweden and Switzerland. India and Pakistan took some 10,000 of the expellees, though many did not settle there permanently. Governments and non-governmental organizations provided accommodation, food and medical care for people in transit, with UNHCR meeting the costs.

It was not until the 1980s that some redress was won in Uganda itself. This was slow at first, but eventually several thousand Asians went back on a short-or longer-term basis to reclaim or sell many of the properties confiscated in the wake of the expulsion.

UNHCR airlift operation in South Asia, 1973–74   Map 3.2

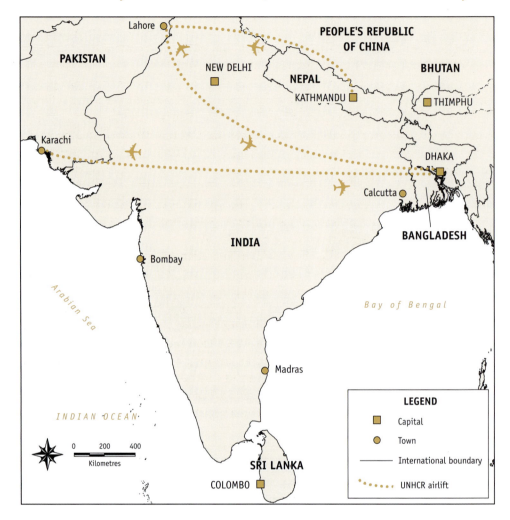

Source: UNHCR, 'Airlift: The Sub-Continent Repatriation Operation September 1973–June 1974', Geneva, 1975.

on. On 6 January, UNHCR Director of Operations Thomas Jamieson cabled UNHCR headquarters in Geneva to report that one million refugees had already left India: 'Prodigious and coordinated efforts are made on both sides of the border . . . Special trains are leaving every day and more are planned for the coming weeks.'[21]

By the end of January some six million refugees had returned home. A UNHCR report noted:

Visitors to the camp areas during the same period marvelled at the unending streams of people on the trek, walking, riding bicycles and rickshaws, standing on truck platforms, with the single purpose in mind of reaching as soon as possible their native places in East Bengal. In January, a daily average of 210,000 persons crossed the Bangladesh border.[22]

During the return, refugees were given food for the journey, medical assistance, and two weeks' basic rations. Remarkably, by the end of February 1972, over nine million refugees had gone back to Bangladesh. The desire to return home had outweighed practical problems. On 25 March, the Indian government estimated that only 60,000 refugees remained in the country.

By the end of May 1972, contributions for the repatriation operation, pledged to UNHCR as a result of an appeal launched that January, amounted to US$14.2 million, of which US$6.3 million was transferred to the Bangladesh government to finance relief and rehabilitation projects for the returnees. UNHCR endorsed an agreement between the Indian Red Cross and the Bangladesh Red Cross, under which the equipment and supplies of the nutritional centres operating in India would be trans- ferred to the Bangladesh Red Cross. The latter would, in turn, be able to carry out preventive health programmes among the returned refugees. UNHCR also agreed to the Indian proposal of transferring 800 trucks, 300 jeeps and 136 ambulances to Bangladesh, which India had received from UNHCR.

The independence of Bangladesh facilitated conditions for a mass return of the refugees. While there were no major disputes as a result of their return, the refugees had no immediate means of supporting themselves. Once in Bangladesh, refugees could pass through any of the 271 transit camps that were set up. Medical services, food rations and free transport were provided in these camps. The vast majority of the refugees went directly to their communities, however, without calling at the registration offices in Indian camps or at the Bangladeshi transit camps. The UNHCR liaison office in Dhaka had functioned throughout the crisis. It worked closely with the United Nations East Pakistan Relief Operation, which had been established to coordinate international assistance following the disastrous cyclone of November 1970.

Even though the Bangladesh repatriation operation was by far the largest, it was but one of many repatriations which took place during the 1970s. As one UNHCR official noted several years later, earlier predictions that repatriation was 'a minor, even negligible solution' were proven to be wrong. Instead, 'in respect of the political realities of the Third World, the post-war Western emphasis on integration in new communities as the normal solution no longer corresponded with the predominant realities elsewhere'.[23] Among the other repatriations in Asia were some 300,000 refugees who returned to Cambodia mainly from Thailand in 1979, and some 200,000 Rohingyas in Bangladesh who returned to Burma in a more contro- versial operation in 1978–79 [see Box 3.3]. In Africa, major voluntary repatriations involving nearly two million people in total took place in Nigeria (1970–71), Sudan (1972), Angola, Mozambique and Guinea-Bissau (1975–77), and Zaire (1978).

The 1973–74 population exchanges

The break-up of Pakistan, the independence of Bangladesh, and the war between India and Pakistan left thousands of individuals stranded in states of which they no longer wanted to be a part. In March 1973, more than a year after the end of the war, Sheikh

In 1973–74, some 230,000 people on the Indian sub-continent were repatriated in a UNHCR-organized airlift.
(UNHCR/1973)

Mujibur Rahman, by then Prime Minister of Bangladesh, wrote to UN Secretary-General Kurt Waldheim requesting UN assistance in what was referred to as a 'repatriation' operation. Some of those repatriated were people who had been stranded in one or other half of the country during the conflict, while others chose to move from Bangladesh to Pakistan or *vice versa* as a result of the changed political circumstances. In April, India and Bangladesh made a joint statement calling for the simultaneous repatriation of prisoners of war and of civilian internees and their families. The statement also called for the repatriation of Bengalis in Pakistan and of Pakistanis in Bangladesh. This proved to be a major step forward in breaking the deadlock resulting from Pakistan's continuing refusal to recognize Bangladesh's independence. The following month, the High Commissioner visited Pakistan and Bangladesh at the request of the Secretary-General to discuss the possibility of a mass repatriation with the governments.

On 28 August 1973, the governments of Bangladesh, India and Pakistan signed the New Delhi Agreement, which included provisions for the simultaneous repatriation of three primary groups. These comprised Pakistani prisoners of war and civilian internees in India, all Bengalis in Pakistan, and 'a substantial number of non-Bengalis' present in Bangladesh who had 'opted for repatriation to Pakistan'. The 'non-Bengalis' were commonly referred to as Biharis, since a majority of them were Indian Muslims originally from the state of Bihar in India who had come to East Pakistan at the time of partition in 1947. The United Nations was requested to provide assistance to facilitate the repatriation. Given its recent involvement as the Focal Point, the Secretary-General asked UNHCR to coordinate all activities relating to the humanitarian effort. In so doing, UNHCR worked closely with the International Committee of the Red Cross.

Under the terms of the New Delhi Agreement, the return of Pakistani prisoners of war and civilian internees was to be conducted bilaterally between India and Pakistan. UNHCR was to assist other categories of people in their repatriation. High Commissioner Sadruddin Aga Khan therefore launched another humanitarian appeal for US$14.3 million on 13 September 1973, stressing 'the role this large-scale repatriation operation may play in creating conditions conducive to peace and stability in the sub-continent'.[24] In November, the High Commissioner visited both Bangladesh and Pakistan again to assess for himself how the operation was proceeding.

By the end of October 1973, a huge air repatriation operation was under way with aircraft loaned by East Germany, the Soviet Union and the United Kingdom. During November, there were six planes on mission duty, carrying an average of 1,200 people per day. By late January 1974, some 90,000 people had been transported from Pakistan to Bangladesh, and over 44,000 from Bangladesh to Pakistan.[25]

In the absence of diplomatic relations and communications facilities between Bangladesh and Pakistan, the air operation was fraught with difficulties. UNHCR had to negotiate clearances for overflying rights over India and provisions for technical landing.[26] It had to liaise constantly with governments, airlines and other partners to carry out the operation. In effect, UNHCR became the *de facto* implementing agency for the 1973 New Delhi Agreement.

By mid-February 1974, over 200,000 people had been repatriated under the terms of the New Delhi Agreement. The successful implementation of the agreement played no small part in Pakistan's decision on 22 February 1974 to recognize Bangladesh. On 1 July 1974, in agreement with the governments concerned, UNHCR phased out the repatriation operation which had begun the previous September. By that time, some 9,000 people had been transported by sea between Bangladesh and Pakistan, and some 231,000 people had been airlifted across the sub-continent. Those airlifted included some 116,000 Bengalis who went from Pakistan to Bangladesh, some 104,000 non-Bengalis who went from Bangladesh to Pakistan, and some 11,000 Pakistanis who were airlifted from Nepal to Pakistan, having previously fled there overland from Bangladesh.[27] It was, at the time, the largest emergency airlift of civilians ever organized.

The Biharis in Bangladesh

One of the unresolved issues at this time was the status and citizenship of the Biharis, which in many cases still remains unresolved. At the time of partition in 1947, around a million Muslims from the Indian state of Bihar moved to what became East Pakistan. Most spoke Urdu, which bound them to West Pakistan, but they fared relatively well in East Pakistan. As tensions between West and East Pakistan increased, however, the Biharis were perceived as being on the side of West Pakistan. During 1971, many Biharis joined Pakistani militias or collaborated with the Pakistani army. As a result, after the surrender of the Pakistani army in mid-December 1971, the entire Bihari community faced the wrath of Bengali nationalism and Biharis were viewed as collaborators of the Pakistani administration and troops. Many Biharis were killed and much of their property was seized.

Although Biharis were among those accepted by Pakistan under the August 1973 repatriation accord, Pakistan was slow in giving clearances.[28] At a further meeting of the three countries' foreign ministers in New Delhi in April 1974, a new tripartite agreement on a second phase of repatriations was reached. More than 170,000 Biharis moved to Pakistan under the terms of these agreements.[29] But Pakistan interpreted the categories of 'non-Bengalis' set out in the agreement restrictively and did not take back all Biharis. In addition to this earlier movement, between 1977 and 1979 nearly 9,900 Biharis repatriated to Pakistan followed by another 4,800 Biharis in 1982. Finally, in 1993, 53 Bihari families were accepted by Pakistan before protests there stopped the process.

Observers attribute Pakistan's reluctance to accept the Biharis, who have always regarded themselves as Pakistani nationals, to the fear that their presence might exacerbate already existing ethnic and political tensions in Pakistan. In Bangladesh, the Biharis have encountered problems acquiring citizenship, as Bangladeshi citizenship provisions dating from 1972 deny citizenship to someone who 'owes, affirms or acknowledges, expressly or by conduct, allegiance to a foreign state'.[30] Although many Biharis have in practice been accepted in Bangladesh, in 1999 over 200,000 Biharis were still living in 66 camps with poor facilities scattered around Bangladesh. Their

Box 3.3 The plight of the Rohingyas

At the end of the 1970s, UNHCR became involved in a complex and controversial repatriation operation on Bangladesh's eastern border. This involved the Rohingyas, a Muslim minority from Arakan state in largely Buddhist Burma, who had taken refuge in Bangladesh.

Burma had a long history of conflict and migration amongst its diverse peoples. Almost immediately after Burma gained independence from the United Kingdom in 1948, tension increased between the Rohingyas and the local Rakhine population in Arakan. The Burmese government claimed that the Rohingyas were relatively recent migrants from the Indian sub-continent and the Burmese constitution therefore did not include them among the indigenous groups qualifying for citizenship. This marginalized the Rohingyas and made it extremely difficult for them to gain access to basic social, educational and health services.

In March 1978, the Burmese immigration authorities launched operation *Nagamin Sit Sin Yay* (King Dragon Operation), the stated aim of which was to scrutinize systematically the status of individuals living in border areas and to 'take actions against foreigners' who had 'filtered into the country illegally'. The effect was to target the Rohingyas, who were not regarded as citizens. Widespread arrests and expulsions followed and by July 1978, large numbers of Rohingyas had fled into Bangladesh.

Estimates as to the actual numbers varied. The Bangladesh government claimed that more than 250,000 Rohingyas had sought refuge, while the Burmese authorities put the figure at less than 150,000. The arrival of so many refugees put considerable pressure on densely populated, impoverished Bangladesh and strained relations between the two countries.

These pressures and other Muslim countries' concerns over the Rohingyas' treatment led the Bangladesh government to appeal to the United Nations for assistance. Many of these refugees lived in pitiful conditions, and the government insisted that the country could not continue to shelter them indefinitely. As a result, a large UN relief programme was launched and coordinated by UNHCR from May 1978. In all, 13 refugee camps were established. As the crisis eased, Burma and Bangladesh sought a permanent solution to the refugee problem. Neither country was at that time (or has since become) party to the 1951 UN Refugee Convention.

A bilateral agreement between the two countries, to which UNHCR was not a party, was concluded in July 1978, providing for the Rohingyas' repatriation. There was much opposition to return among the refugees, and serious clashes between the refugees and Bangladesh officials were reported, resulting in hundreds of deaths. Deteriorating conditions in the camps, the arrest of a number of Rohingya leaders, and a reduction in food rations were other factors which led refugees to return. By the end of 1979, more than 180,000 had returned to Burma.

In an attempt to improve the conditions of the returnees, UNHCR spent US$7 million on projects to assist their reintegration. With only a limited presence, UNHCR could not, however, monitor the situation closely or ensure the returning Rohingyas were treated fairly by the authorities. Discrimination against them continued. In 1982, a new citizenship law created three classes of citizenship but it remained extremely difficult for Rohingyas to obtain citizenship.

In 1991–92, Rohingyas fled once more from northern Rakhine state (as Arakan had been renamed). Some 250,000 people were registered and given shelter in 20 camps in Bangladesh. The repatriation of these refugees to Myanmar, as the country was renamed in 1989, was again controversial. Returns in 1992–93 were carried out under another bilateral Bangladesh–Myanmar agreement, from which UNHCR was again excluded. In 1993, the Myanmar government finally agreed to allow UNHCR to have a presence in Rakhine state. In April 1994, once this was established, UNHCR facilitated the voluntary repatriation of refugees from Bangladesh. At the time, human rights organizations strongly criticized UNHCR, questioning whether the repatriation was truly voluntary and arguing that the situation had not improved sufficiently to allow for the Rohingyas' safe return.[ii] While acknowledging the vulnerability of the Rohingyas on both sides of the border, UNHCR's assessment was that in most cases they were better off in their homes in Myanmar than in camps in Bangladesh.

Thousands of Rohingyas again fled to Bangladesh in 1996 and 1997. At first, Bangladeshi forces forcibly repatriated hundreds of them, but this was largely stopped after intervention by UNHCR. Since establishing a presence in northern Rakhine state, UNHCR has carried out a number of projects aimed at facilitating reintegration and improving basic infrastructure. It has established a dialogue with all levels of the Myanmar government, pressing them to address the question of citizenship for the Rohingyas and to put an end to forced labour practices. Of those who fled to Bangladesh in the early 1990s, around 200,000 had returned by December 1999, leaving some 22,000 in Bangladesh. But even though many of the causes which prompted mass departures in earlier years may have diminished, the plight of the Rohingyas in Myanmar remains a matter of international concern.

unclear citizenship status has created innumerable problems for them. Since neither country is prepared to accept full responsibility for them, the Biharis are potentially stateless. After so many years of a refugee-like existence, there are now indications that some Biharis would prefer to obtain Bangladeshi nationality.[31]

UNHCR's expanding role in Asia

The relief operation for Bangladeshi refugees exposed UNHCR to many of the problems which the organization was to face with increasing regularity in the following decades. These included the management of sudden mass refugee influxes involving millions of refugees, the use of large and hastily constructed refugee camps, and the difficulties of procuring and distributing food and other basic relief supplies. It also exposed UNHCR to the devastating impact which cholera can have in crowded refugee camps.

UNHCR's assumption of the role of Focal Point was an important element in the handling of the Bangladeshi refugee crisis. Although the term 'Focal Point' was not used again, the concept was considered to be a useful one in emergency situations, where the overall needs exceeded the mandate of any one UN agency. This operation became but the first of many refugee crises in which UNHCR was called upon by the Secretary-General to act as the lead UN agency for the coordination of international humanitarian assistance.

One of the most notable aspects of this relief operation was the highly politicized environment in which it was carried out. The crisis increased awareness within the United Nations that mass movements of refugees do not only result from conflict but can in themselves create serious threats to regional peace and security. The role played by the Head of the UNHCR office in Dhaka, in arranging a ceasefire between the Indian and Pakistani armies in the last hours of the war, illustrates how closely the organization was involved on the ground as the crisis unfolded. Both the Indian and Pakistan governments were often suspicious of UNHCR's motives and, as a result, relations with them were often strained. High Commissioner Sadruddin Aga Khan liaised closely with the UN Secretary-General throughout the crisis.

The solutions which were applied to the upheavals on the Indian sub-continent in the early 1970s had their roots in approaches which predate the Second World War. The repatriation agreements concluded by the governments of Bangladesh, India and Pakistan after 1973 were based on a view that population exchanges were an effective way of resolving problems concerning minority groups within independent states. Given the vast distances between Pakistan and Bangladesh, these repatriations were carried out largely by air, but they were in fact similar to previous population exchanges, such as those which had taken place in Europe in the 1920s between Greece and Turkey and between Greece and Bulgaria.

UNHCR's involvement in South Asia continued after the Bangladeshi refugee crisis was over. By the end of the 1970s, the organization was engaged in the repatriation of

Rohingya Muslim refugees from Bangladesh to Burma. Outside the region, UNHCR was also involved in the early 1970s in assisting South Asians expelled from Uganda by the regime of President Idi Amin [see Box 3.2]. Another refugee population in South Asia, which has often been overlooked, and with which UNHCR has had only minimal involvement, is the Tibetan refugee population in India, which has been there since 1959 [see Box 3.1]. Although UNHCR became involved in assisting various new groups of refugees in South Asia in the years which followed the Bangladeshi refugee crisis, from the mid-1970s the focus of UNHCR's work in Asia moved to Indochina.

4 Flight from Indochina

The upheavals which followed the communist victories in 1975 in the former French colonies of Indochina—Viet Nam, Cambodia and Laos—caused more than three million people to flee these countries over the next two decades. The sustained mass exodus from the region and the massive international response to the crisis thrust UNHCR into a leading role in a complex, expensive and high-profile humanitarian operation. When the first refugees fled Viet Nam, Cambodia and Laos in 1975, UNHCR's total annual expenditure stood at less than US$80 million worldwide. By 1980, this had increased to over US$500 million.[1]

The displacement caused by the conflicts in Indochina, which were exacerbated by rivalries between the United States and the Soviet Union as well as China, tested to breaking point the capacity of states in the region to absorb the refugees. It also tested the commitment of Western states to resettle refugees fleeing communism. Eventually, it brought the affected states together in a search for solutions. In the case of Viet Nam, an Orderly Departure Programme was devised, whereby the Vietnamese authorities agreed to permit the orderly departure of individuals to resettlement countries, to avoid the clandestine and dangerous departures by sea. The programme marked the first occasion in which UNHCR became involved in efforts to pre-empt a refugee problem rather than simply dealing with its aftermath. Other innovative programmes included anti-piracy and rescue-at-sea measures to protect the Vietnamese 'boat people'.

During the early stages of the crisis, the resettlement of refugees in countries outside the region offered a solution which reduced the pressure on countries of first asylum. As the 1980s continued, however, Western governments became increasingly concerned about the large numbers of refugees arriving in their countries. They also became more suspicious of their motives for leaving, regarding many of them as economic migrants rather than refugees. The argument was increasingly heard that open-ended resettlement was perpetuating an open-ended need for asylum. After 1989, new measures were therefore taken, under what was known as the Comprehensive Plan of Action, to control the departures and to encourage and facilitate the repatriation of asylum seekers from the region. This marked a crossroads in Western attitudes towards refugee issues. As the coming crises of the 1990s were to demonstrate all too clearly, Western countries, while upholding the principle of asylum, were no longer prepared to envisage the resettlement of massive refugee populations.

The exodus of Vietnamese 'boat people' after 1975 resulted in thousands of deaths as people fell victim to pirate attacks or drowned at sea. (G. KLIJN/1980)

Exodus from Indochina, 1975–95 Map 4.1

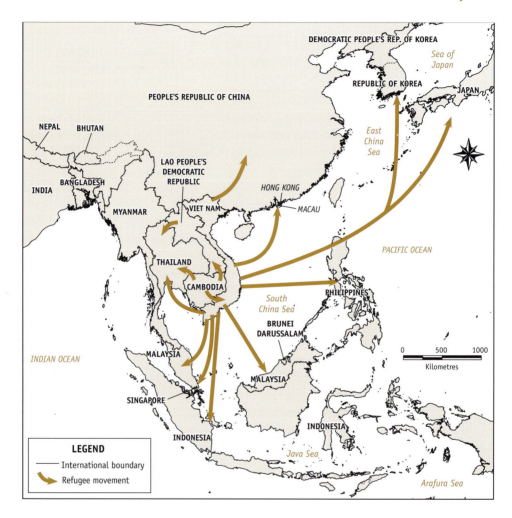

War and exodus from Viet Nam

The 30 years of almost continuous war that beset Viet Nam from 1945 to 1975 were marked by immense suffering and massive displacement of people. Following the French defeat at Dien Bien Phu in May 1954, the first Indochina war concluded with the establishment of a communist state in the north (the Democratic Republic of Viet Nam—also known as North Viet Nam) and a separate state in the south (the Republic of Viet Nam—also known as South Viet Nam). With the founding of a communist government in the north, more than a million people moved south in the years 1954–56. Their numbers included nearly 800,000 Roman Catholics, an estimated two-thirds of the total Roman Catholic population in the north. There was a smaller movement in the opposite direction, as some 130,000 supporters of the communist Viet Minh movement were transported north by Polish and Soviet ships.[2]

In 1960, there was renewed conflict in South Viet Nam. Anti-communist forces, supported by the United States, which eventually sent in over 500,000 troops, sought to halt the spread of Soviet and Chinese-backed communism in Southeast Asia. The war in Viet Nam lead to greater and greater waves of displacement in all three Indochinese countries. Most of the displacement was internal, but in some cases it spilled across borders, as in the case of the 'delta Khmer' who fled into Cambodia to escape the fighting in Viet Nam.[3] By the late 1960s, when the war was at its height, an estimated half of South Viet Nam's 20 million people had been internally displaced.[4]

The Paris Peace Agreement of 27 January 1973 brought a temporary end to the Viet Nam conflict and opened the door for a greater role for UNHCR, which launched a programme to assist displaced people in Viet Nam and Laos. This included US$12 million which was used for reconstruction projects. The programme was soon eclipsed, however, by the renewal of hostilities in early 1975 and the fall of Saigon to the revolutionary forces on 30 April. The same year, communist governments came to power in neighbouring Laos and Cambodia.

Unlike the ultra-radical Khmer Rouge movement, which took control of Cambodia in April 1975, more conventional, pro-Soviet leaderships assumed power in Viet Nam and Laos. Through its prior involvement in these two countries before April 1975, UNHCR was able to maintain contact with the governments in Hanoi and Vientiane respectively. Indeed, High Commissioner Sadruddin Aga Khan visited both countries in September 1975, inspecting projects where UNHCR was engaged in assisting war-displaced people to return to their homes.

In the north of Viet Nam, UNHCR provided agriculture, health and reconstruction aid to some of the 2.7 million displaced people. Many of these people had fled the fighting in the south, while others had been displaced by US bombing of the north between 1965 and 1972. In the south, UNHCR made available over 20,000 tonnes of food and other relief supplies for millions of displaced people, who were seeking to rebuild their lives after the war.

The fall of Saigon

Increasingly, UNHCR's focus shifted from helping the displaced within Viet Nam to helping those who fled the country. In the final days before the fall of Saigon in April 1975, some 140,000 Vietnamese who were closely associated with the former South Vietnamese government were evacuated from the country and resettled in the United States. The US-organized evacuation was followed by a smaller exodus of Vietnamese who found their own way by boat to neighbouring Southeast Asian countries. By the end of 1975, some 5,000 Vietnamese had arrived in Thailand, along with 4,000 in Hong Kong, 1,800 in Singapore, and 1,250 in the Philippines.

UNHCR's initial reaction was to treat these movements as the aftermath of war rather than as the beginning of a new refugee crisis. In a November 1975 funding appeal, High Commissioner Sadruddin Aga Khan emphasized that programmes for Vietnamese and Laotians inside or outside their country were 'interrelated humanitarian actions, designed to assist those who had been most seriously uprooted by war and its consequences'.[5]

As discontent with the new communist regime increased, however, so did the number of people fleeing the country. In July 1976, the government in Hanoi stripped the Provisional Revolutionary Government which had been established in the south after the fall of Saigon of any remaining autonomy it possessed, and unified the country as the Socialist Republic of Viet Nam. It also embarked on a programme of resettling urban dwellers in the countryside in so-called 'new economic zones'. More than a million people were placed in 're-education camps'. Many died, while tens of thousands were to languish in detention until the late 1980s. As time went by, it also became clear that the prominence of the ethnic Chinese population in the private economic sector was contrary to the socialist vision of the new authorities.

By early 1978, formal measures were being taken to expropriate businesses of private entrepreneurs, most of whom were ethnic Chinese. These actions coincided with a marked deterioration in relations between Viet Nam and China, itself a reflection of Viet Nam's increasingly bitter relationship with China's ally, Cambodia. Official Vietnamese attitudes towards the ethnic Chinese (or Hoa) became increasingly hostile and, in February 1979, Chinese forces attacked Vietnamese border regions and normal relations were not resumed until more than a decade later.

In 1977, about 15,000 Vietnamese sought asylum in Southeast Asian countries. By the end of 1978, the numbers fleeing by boat had quadrupled and 70 per cent of these asylum seekers were Vietnamese of Chinese origin. Many more ethnic Chinese fled to China itself. They were mainly from northern Viet Nam, where they had lived for decades, and they were mostly poor fishermen, artisans and peasants. China subsequently established a project to settle the refugees on state farms in southern China. UNHCR assisted by donating US$8.5 million to the Chinese authorities and opening an office in Beijing. By the end of 1979, more than 250,000 people from Viet Nam had taken refuge in China.[6] China was virtually alone in the east Asia region in granting not only asylum, but also local settlement for refugees fleeing Viet Nam.

The boat people

By the end of 1978, there were nearly 62,000 Vietnamese 'boat people' in camps throughout Southeast Asia. As the numbers grew, so too did local hostility. Adding to the tension was the fact that several of the boats arriving on the shores of countries in Southeast Asia were not small wooden fishing craft but steel-hulled freighters chartered by regional smuggling syndicates and carrying over 2,000 people at a time. In November 1978, for example, a 1,500-tonne freighter, the *Hai Hong*, anchored at Port Klang, Malaysia, and requested permission to unload its human cargo of 2,500 Vietnamese. When the Malaysian authorities demanded that the boat be turned back

Part of a group of 162 Vietnamese refugees who arrived in Malaysia on a small fishing boat which sank a few metres from the shore. (UNHCR/K. GAUGLER/1978)

to sea, the local UNHCR representative argued that the Vietnamese on board were considered to be 'of concern to the Office of the UNHCR'.[7] This position was reinforced by a cable from UNHCR headquarters suggesting that 'in the future, unless there are clear indications to the contrary, boat cases from Viet Nam be considered *prima facie* of concern to UNHCR'.[8] For more than a decade, Vietnamese who reached a UNHCR-administered camp were accorded *prima facie* refugee status and were given the opportunity of eventual resettlement overseas.

At the beginning of the Indochinese exodus in 1975, not a single country in the region had acceded to the 1951 UN Refugee Convention or the 1967 Protocol. None of the countries receiving Vietnamese boat people gave them permission to stay permanently and some would not even permit temporary refuge. Singapore refused to disembark any refugees who did not have guarantees of resettlement within 90 days. Malaysia and Thailand frequently resorted to pushing boats away from their coastlines. When Vietnamese boat arrivals escalated dramatically in 1979, with more than 54,000 arrivals in June alone, boat 'pushbacks' became routine and thousands of Vietnamese may have perished at sea as a result.

At the end of June 1979, the then five members of the Association of Southeast Asian Nations (ASEAN)—Indonesia, Malaysia, the Philippines, Singapore, and Thailand—issued a warning that they had 'reached the limit of their endurance and [had] decided that they would not accept any new arrivals'.[9] With the principle of

Box 4.1

International conferences on Indochinese refugees

The 1979 Geneva conference

By mid-1979, of the more than 550,000 Indochinese who had sought asylum in Southeast Asia since 1975, some 200,000 had been resettled and some 350,000 remained in first-asylum countries in the region. Over the previous six months, for every individual who moved on to resettlement, three more had arrived in the camps. At the end of June 1979, the member states of the Association of Southeast Asian Nations (ASEAN) announced that they would not accept any new arrivals. 'Pushbacks' were in full spate and asylum was in jeopardy. 'The problem', said High Commissioner Poul Hartling, 'has clearly run ahead of the solutions.'[i]

On 20–21 July 1979, 65 governments responded to an invitation from the UN Secretary-General to attend an international conference on Indochinese refugees. The international commitments they made were several and significant. Worldwide resettlement pledges increased from 125,000 to 260,000. Viet Nam agreed to try to halt illegal departures and, instead, to promote orderly and direct departures from Viet Nam. Indonesia and the Philippines pledged to establish regional processing centres to speed resettlement and new pledges to UNHCR totalled about US$160 million in cash and in kind, more than doubling the total of the previous four years.

Although no formal commitments were made regarding asylum, the meeting endorsed the general principles of asylum and *non-refoulement*. As the Secretary-General had said in his opening remarks, countries of first asylum expected that no refugees would stay in their countries for more than a specified period. Thus was formalized a *quid pro quo*—temporary or 'first' asylum in the region for permanent resettlement elsewhere— or, as some came to describe it, 'an open shore for an open door'.

The 'pushbacks' of Vietnamese boats seeking to flee were largely halted. Regional arrival rates fell dramatically

as Viet Nam placed heavy penalties on clandestine departures and a small trickle of direct departures began from Viet Nam. More than 450,000 Indochinese refugees were resettled from Southeast Asian camps in the space of 18 months. From 1980 to 1986, as resettlement out-paced declining arrivals, refugee officials began to speak with growing optimism about solving the regional crisis.

In 1987–88, however, Vietnamese arrivals surged again and it became apparent that the old consensus would no longer hold. Western countries, faced with a rising tide of asylum seekers at their own doors and persuaded that the Indochinese arrivals no longer warranted automatic refugee status, had gradually been reducing resettlement numbers and had introduced more selective criteria. The agreement of 1979—temporary asylum to be followed by resettlement in a third country—no longer held. As High Commissioner Jean-Pierre Hocké remarked: 'The passage of time [has] progressively eroded the consensus on which our approach to the Indo-Chinese refugee question has been based.'[ii]

The 1989 Geneva conference and the Comprehensive Plan of Action

In June 1989, 10 years after the first Indochinese refugee conference, another was held in Geneva. On this occasion, the 70 governments present adopted a new regional approach, which became known as the Comprehensive Plan of Action (CPA). The CPA represented a major multi-lateral effort to resolve the Vietnamese refugee problem. It was one of the first examples of a situation where the country of origin became a key player, together with other countries and actors from both within and outside the region, in helping to resolve a major refugee crisis.

The CPA had five main objectives: first, to reduce clandestine departures through official measures against those organizing boat departures and

through mass information campaigns, and to promote increased opportunities for legal migration under the Orderly Departure Programme; second, to provide temporary asylum to all asylum seekers until their status was established and a durable solution found; third, to determine the refugee status of all asylum seekers in accordance with international standards and criteria; fourth, to resettle in third countries those recognized as refugees, as well as all Vietnamese who were in camps prior to the regional cut-off dates; and fifth, to return those found not to be refugees and to reintegrate them in their home countries.[iii]

The task of implementing the CPA fell to UNHCR, with financial support coming from the donor community. A Steering Committee was established, chaired by UNHCR and comprising representatives of all governments making commitments under the CPA, whether for asylum, resettlement or repatriation.

Where the 1979 commitments on asylum were general, those made a decade later were more specific. They stated: 'Temporary refuge will be given to all asylum seekers who will be treated identically regardless of their mode of arrival until the status determination process is completed.' These commitments were honoured throughout most of the region, though there were exceptions. Thailand, amongst others, halted its pushbacks, but Singapore no longer permitted rescue-at-sea cases or direct arrivals to disembark. In Malaysia, throughout much of 1989–90, local authorities had orders to redirect boat arrivals back into international waters.

Through the combined effect of disincentives in the camps (including the termination of repatriation assistance for new arrivals after September 1991) and UNHCR media campaigns inside Viet Nam, the CPA finally brought an end to the flow of Vietnamese asylum seekers. In 1989, roughly 70,000 Vietnamese sought asylum in

Southeast Asia. In 1992, only 41 Vietnamese did so and the numbers have remained negligible ever since.

At the time of the CPA conference in 1989, a total of 50,670 pre-cut-off-date Vietnamese refugees were in Southeast Asian camps. Of these, nearly a quarter had already been rejected by at least one resettlement country and another quarter were low priority cases under increasingly restrictive resettlement criteria. By the end of 1991, virtually all of these people were resettled. Of the post-cut-off-date Vietnamese, a total of some 32,300 were recognized as refugees and resettled, as against 83,300 whose claims were rejected and who returned home. Overall, during the eight years of the CPA, more than 530,000 Vietnamese and Laotians were resettled in other countries.

None of the countries which agreed to implement the refugee status determination procedures were parties to the 1951 Refugee Convention except the Philippines, and none had previous legislative or administrative experience in determining refugee status. Never-theless, all of the five principal places of first asylum—Hong Kong, Indonesia, Malaysia, the Philippines and Thailand—adopted procedures giving asylum seekers access to UNHCR, a full refugee status determination interview, the services of an interpreter, and the possibility of review by a second authority. Additionally, in Hong Kong, applicants had access to the courts for judicial review.

Overall, about 28 per cent of Vietnamese asylum seekers who applied for refugee status under CPA procedures were successful. Hong Kong, which interviewed the highest number of applicants (60,275), also had the lowest approval rate (18.8 per cent). UNHCR's authority to recognize refugees under its mandate provided an important safety net for ensuring that no person with a valid claim was rejected and returned to Viet Nam.

In order to reach a consensus on repatriation to Viet Nam, the governments that were party to the CPA had agreed in 1989 that 'in the first instance, every effort will be made to encourage the voluntary return of [those whose applications are rejected] . . . If, after the passage of reasonable time, it becomes clear that voluntary repatriation is not making sufficient progress toward the desired objective, alternatives recognized as being acceptable under international practices would be examined.'[iv] Although no one would say so directly, most people acknowledged at the time that this meant involuntary return.

Hong Kong had begun screening arrivals one year earlier than the rest of the region and, by March 1989, had already organized the first voluntary repatriation to Viet Nam in more than a decade. Over the following months, however, the government decided that insufficient numbers were returning voluntarily and resorted to more extreme measures. On 12 December 1989, under cover of darkness, more than 100 Hong Kong police escorted a group of 51 Vietnamese men, women

and children to a waiting aeroplane and flew them to Hanoi. The ensuing international protests persuaded Hong Kong to postpone further involuntary repatriation but, in a new development, the United Kingdom, Hong Kong and Viet Nam signed an agreement in October 1991 to implement an 'Orderly Return Programme'.

The ASEAN countries of asylum eventually signed their own Orderly Return Programme agreements, under which UNHCR agreed to cover transportation costs and to provide some logistical support, while insisting that it would not participate in movements that involved force. In the end, however, the distinction between voluntary and involuntary return became blurred with rising tensions in the Vietnamese camps and frequent outbreaks of violence in the Hong Kong camps. From 1992, the pace of repatriation quickened and the task fell to UNHCR to coordinate reintegration assistance and to monitor the more than 109,000 Vietnamese who ultimately returned home under the CPA arrangements.

Indochina: resettlement and repatriation, 1975–97*   Figure 4.1

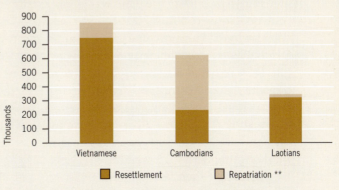

* The table shows resettlement or repatriation from countries or territories of first asylum.
** Includes 367,040 Cambodians who were not counted as arrivals in UNHCR camps in Thailand but returned under UNHCR auspices in 1992–93 as well as screened-out Vietnamese asylum seekers.

asylum under direct threat, the UN Secretary-General convened an international conference on 'refugees and displaced persons in Southeast Asia' in Geneva that July [see Box 4.1].[10] 'A grave crisis exists in Southeast Asia', said High Commissioner Poul Hartling in a background note prepared for the conference, for 'hundreds of thousands of refugees and displaced persons . . . [the] fundamental right to life and security is at risk'.[11]

As a result of the 1979 conference, the immediate crisis was averted. In what amounted to a three-way agreement between the countries of origin, the countries of first asylum and the countries of resettlement, the ASEAN countries promised to uphold commitments to provide temporary asylum as long as Viet Nam endeavoured to prevent illegal exits and to promote orderly departures, and as long as third countries accelerated the rate of resettlement. Indonesia and the Philippines agreed to establish regional processing centres to help resettle refugees more quickly and, with notable exceptions, pushbacks were halted. International resettlement, which had been taking place at the rate of around 9,000 per month in the first half of 1979, increased to around 25,000 per month in the latter half of the year. Between July 1979 and July 1982, more than 20 countries—led by the United States, Australia, France, and Canada—together resettled 623,800 Indochinese refugees.[12]

For its part, Viet Nam agreed to make every effort to halt illegal departures and to follow through on a Memorandum of Understanding it had signed with UNHCR in May 1979 on the establishment of the Orderly Departure Programme.[13] Under the terms of that arrangement, the Vietnamese authorities undertook to authorize the exit of those Vietnamese wishing to leave the country for family reunion and other humanitarian reasons, while UNHCR coordinated with resettlement countries to obtain entry visas. Although the programme started slowly, it gradually gathered momentum. By 1984, annual departures under the programme had risen to 29,100, exceeding the regional boat arrival total of 24,865.

Throughout much of the 1980s, although regional arrivals declined and resettlement commitments were sustained, the Vietnamese boat exodus continued and the human cost was immense. One writer has estimated that around 10 per cent of the boat people were lost at sea, fell victims to pirate attacks, drowned, or died of dehydration.[14] The anti-piracy programme and rescue-at-sea efforts [see Box 4.2] had their successes, but every failure was a tragedy. A boat reaching the Philippines in July 1984 reported that during 32 days at sea, some 40 vessels had passed by without providing any assistance. In November 1983, UNHCR's Director of the Division of International Protection, Michel Moussalli, spoke of 'scenes that surpass normal imagination . . . Eighteen persons leave in a small craft and in crossing the Gulf of Thailand are attacked by pirates, one girl who resists being raped is killed and another young girl of 15 is abducted. The remaining 16 persons who are of no use to the pirates have their boat rammed repeatedly and all perish at sea'.[15]

As the years passed, there was increasing fatigue in Western countries towards the Vietnamese boat people, and suspicions grew about the motives of some of these people for leaving. The task fell to UNHCR to make sure that governments maintained their resettlement commitments, both in order to preserve the principle

Box 4.2   Piracy in the South China Sea

Piracy in Southeast Asia is as old as seafaring itself. For the Vietnamese 'boat people' it posed an unexpected terror and for those seeking to protect them it was a vexing problem. In 1981 alone, when 452 boats arrived in Thailand carrying 15,479 refugees, UNHCR's statistics were a study in horror: 349 boats had been attacked an average of three times each; 578 women had been raped; 228 women had been abducted; and 881 people were dead or missing.

The anti-piracy programme

Responding to mounting international outrage and a demand for action, UNHCR launched a fund-raising appeal at the end of 1981. By June 1982, an anti-piracy programme was officially begun with US$3.6 million in funding from 12 countries.

In Thailand, anti-piracy efforts initially focused on sea and air patrols, which produced a gradual decline in the number of attacks. However, as High Commissioner Poul Hartling noted at the time: 'Even if the quantity has gone down, the quality of the attacks, if you can say that, is going up . . . What we hear is even more horrifying than in the past.' The reports 'tell of cruelty, brutality and inhumanity that go beyond my imagination. The refugees are attacked with knives and clubs. There is murder, robbery and rape, everything in this world.'[v]

From 1984, the UNHCR anti-piracy programme shifted increasingly toward land-based operations. Thai police units and harbour officials registered fishing boats, photographed crews, and conducted public awareness campaigns on the penalties for piracy. UNHCR helped to link piracy victims with police and prosecutors, monitored court trials, arranged witness transfers from abroad, and provided interpretation

services for investigations, arrests and trials. By 1987, only eight per cent of all boats arriving in Thailand were attacked. There were abductions and rape but no reported deaths due to piracy.

In 1988, however, the violence of the attacks began to rise alarmingly again, with more than 500 people reported dead or missing. In 1989, this number exceeded 750. Rapes and abductions spiralled upward. In August 1989, one UNHCR official who debriefed the survivors of one attack, described how the pirates brought up men singly from the hold, clubbed them and then killed them with axes. Vietnamese in the water were then rammed, sunk and killed, leaving 71 people dead, including 15 women and 11 children. The rise in violence at sea, anti-piracy experts suggested, was due in part to the success of the land-based efforts. More sophisticated investigations were leading to higher rates of arrest and conviction. This was scaring off the occasional opportunists but leaving behind a hard core of professional criminals who, in turn, wished to leave behind no witnesses.

Eventually, it seems that even they tired of the chase. After mid-1990, there were no more reports of pirate attacks on Vietnamese boats, and in December 1991 the UNHCR anti-piracy programme was discontinued. 'The war on the pirates is not over', said the final assessment report, 'but it has reached the stage where it can be effectively managed' by local agencies.

Rescue at sea

From 1975 to late 1978, 110,000 Vietnamese boat people arrived in first-asylum countries. At first, ship captains seemed eager to aid boats in distress and during these three years ships from 31 different countries

rescued refugees from a total of 186 boats. In the first seven months of 1979, however, when Vietnamese arrivals climbed to more than 177,000 in the region and 'push-backs' of these boats were at their peak, only 47 boats were rescued. Half the rescues, moreover, were by ships from only three countries.

In August 1979, UNHCR convened a meeting in Geneva on the subject of rescue at sea. Out of these discussions came a programme known as DISERO (Disembarkation Resettlement Offers). Under this programme, eight Western states including the United States jointly agreed to guarantee resettlement for any Vietnamese refugee rescued at sea by merchant ships flying the flags of states that did not resettle refugees. The new commitments appeared to have an almost immediate effect. In the last five months of 1979, 81 boats carrying 4,031 people were rescued at sea. In May 1980, UNHCR donated an unarmed speedboat to the Thai government in a token effort to bolster sea patrolling. Meanwhile, some of the private international mercy ships, including most prominently the *Kap Anamur* and the *Ile de Lumière*, shifted their operations from resupply of island camps to boat rescue. Altogether, 67,000 Vietnamese were rescued at sea between 1975 and 1990.

The problem with this programme was that the guarantee that any Vietnamese rescued at sea would be resettled within 90 days did not square with the 1989 Comprehensive Plan of Action guidelines, which required that all new arrivals undergo screening to determine their status. Eventually, both DISERO and a later companion programme known as RASRO (Rescue at Sea Resettlement Offers) were terminated as countries in the region proved unwilling to disembark rescued boat people.

of asylum itself and to ensure that the especially vulnerable were not left behind in camps throughout Southeast Asia. It was of course beyond UNHCR's scope to grant or deny permanent admission to another country. That authority lay with governments. By the late 1980s, however, international willingness to resettle all Vietnamese asylum seekers was waning and resettlement numbers were scarcely keeping pace with the rate of arrivals in first asylum countries.

Then, in mid-1987, Vietnamese arrivals began to climb again. Encouraged by the relaxation of internal travel restrictions and the prospect of resettlement in Western countries, thousands of southern Vietnamese had discovered a new route that took them through Cambodia then, via a short boat ride, to Thailand's east coast. At the turn of the year, Thai authorities began interdicting boats and sending them back to sea.

Tens of thousands of others from the north took another new route via southern China to Hong Kong. In 1988, more than 18,000 boat people poured into Hong Kong. This was by far the highest number since the crisis of 1979. Most were from northern Viet Nam—a population that had proved to be of little interest to most resettlement countries. Consequently, on 15 June 1988, the Hong Kong administration announced that any Vietnamese arriving after that date would be placed in detention centres to await a 'screening' interview to determine their status. In May 1989, the Malaysian authorities again began to redirect boat arrivals toward Indonesia, as they had done a decade earlier.

A new formula

By the late 1980s, it had become apparent to virtually all concerned with the Indochinese refugee crisis that the regional and international consensus reached in 1979 had collapsed. A new formula was needed, one that preserved asylum but decoupled its link to guarantees of resettlement. In June 1989 therefore, a second international conference on Indochinese refugees was held in Geneva and a new consensus was reached. The Comprehensive Plan of Action, as it came to be called, reaffirmed some of the elements of the 1979 agreement, namely the commitments to preserve first asylum, to reduce clandestine departures and promote legal migration, and to resettle refugees in third countries. It also contained some new elements, including in particular a commitment to institute regional refugee status determination procedures and to return those whose applications were rejected [see Box 4.1].

The new commitments on asylum successfully ended pushbacks in Thailand, although Malaysia did not relent on its policy of redirecting boats away from its waters. With the exception of Singapore, all of the first asylum countries dropped their demands for guarantees of resettlement. The 50,000 Vietnamese who had arrived in camps before the cut-off date (14 March 1989 in most countries) were resettled overseas. Those arriving after that date were expected to undergo screening to determine their status. Viet Nam enforced penalties against clandestine departures and UNHCR launched a media campaign designed to acquaint would-be asylum seekers with the new regional arrangements, which now included the return of asylum seekers whose applications were rejected.

The Comprehensive Plan of Action has generally been credited with restoring the principle of asylum in the region. But some analysts have seen such measures as running counter to the right to leave one's country, and have questioned whether UNHCR should—even tacitly—have effectively condoned such operations by Viet Nam.[16] The Comprehensive Plan of Action also represented an early instance of the application of a cut-off date. Those who fled before this date were automatically accepted for resettlement abroad, while those who arrived afterwards had to be screened first to determine their status.

If the success of the 1979 conference depended on the commitments of the countries of resettlement, that of the Comprehensive Plan of Action depended on the commitments of the countries of first asylum and the countries of origin. In December 1988, seven months before the Geneva conference, UNHCR and Viet Nam signed a Memorandum of Understanding, whereby Viet Nam would allow for the voluntary return of its citizens without penalizing them for having fled, it would expand and accelerate the Orderly Departure Programme, and it would permit UNHCR to monitor returnees and facilitate reintegration.

It has been argued that the Orderly Departure Programme created a 'pull factor' which effectively encouraged departure. While this may often have been the case, it nevertheless enabled those seeking to leave to do so by legal means rather than in illegal and dangerous departures. Even if this did create a 'pull factor', it was but one

Arrivals of Vietnamese boat people by country or territory of first asylum, 1975–95

Figure 4.2

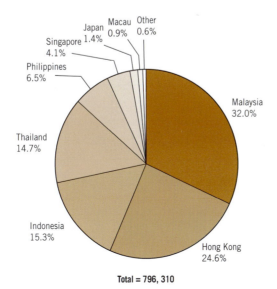

Total = 796, 310

Box 4.3 — Vietnamese refugees in the United States

From 1975, the United States opened its doors to over a million Vietnamese people. Although the largest number now live in California, these people have made their way to every state and almost every major US city.

The Vietnamese arrived in several waves. More than 175,000 Vietnamese refugees fled to the United States during the first two years following the fall of Saigon in 1975. A large majority arrived within a few weeks and were sheltered in four makeshift refugee camps on US military bases. A dozen private, mostly religious organizations were given responsibility for resettling the Vietnamese in cities and towns across the United States. They arranged housing and English-language classes, found schools for the children, and helped the adults to find jobs.

Americans responded positively to this first wave of Vietnamese. Many felt a sense of guilt over the US involvement in Viet Nam and welcomed the opportunity to help the refugees. Churches and community groups across the country served as local sponsors, helping orient the refugees in their new communities. This first group of refugees fared remarkably well in the United States. Most of them came from the urban middle class in the south of Viet Nam. Of household heads, more than a quarter had university education and over 40 per cent more had some secondary education. Overall, this group was relatively skilled, urbanized and flexible.[vi]

Despite having arrived in the United States at a time of serious economic recession, by 1982 their rate of employment was higher than that of the general US population. Vietnamese communities sprang up in California, Texas and Washington, DC. Soon, Vietnamese businesses were catering to the new communities. A second wave of Vietnamese refugees began arriving in the United States in 1978. These were the 'boat people', who fled increasing political repression in Viet Nam, especially against ethnic Chinese Vietnamese. Although exact figures are difficult to assess, the total number of Vietnamese boat people who entered between 1978 and 1997 is estimated to be in excess of 400,000.[vii] The boat people were less well equipped for life in the United States. In general, they were less well educated and had a more rural background than the refugees who arrived in 1975; far fewer spoke English. Many had experienced persecution in Viet Nam, trauma on the high seas, and harsh conditions in refugee camps in Southeast Asian countries that only reluctantly accepted their temporary presence. Also, unlike the first wave of Vietnamese, many of whom fled in family groups, a large number of boat people were single men.

By the time this group of Vietnamese arrived, many Americans were growing weary of refugees. Anti-immigrant sentiment fuelled by a declining economy led to attacks on Vietnamese in several communities. US government support for the refugee programme was also waning. In 1982, the US government reduced the period of time during which it assisted newly arrived refugees and, despite the economy being in an even worse state than in 1975, instituted a number of measures aimed at moving refugees into the workforce as soon as possible. Many of the boat people ended up in poorly paid jobs, often without having had an opportunity to learn English or acclimatize to their new environment. Nevertheless, according to a 1985 US-government commissioned study on self-sufficiency among Southeast Asian refugees, within three years of their arrival, their economic status was comparable to that of other US minority groups.

The Orderly Departure Programme, established in 1979, made it possible for Vietnamese to migrate directly from Viet Nam to the United States. Initially intended to benefit relatives of Vietnamese refugees already in the United States and South Vietnamese who had ties to the US government, the US government later extended the Orderly Departure Programme to Amerasians (Vietnamese children of US servicemen), and former political prisoners and re-education camp detainees. Between 1979 and 1999, more than 500,000 Vietnamese entered the United States under this programme.

Many of these arrivals found making a new start in the United States particularly difficult. Former political prisoners and re-education camp detainees arrived traumatized by their experiences in Viet Nam.

They were also older than most boat people or those who had arrived in 1975. It was more difficult for them to find work, and what jobs they could find were often not commensurate with their previous social position. Together, these factors have made both their economic and psychological adjustment harder. Overall, however, most of the million-plus Vietnamese who resettled in the United States—and more particularly the second-generation Vietnamese Americans—have adapted well and today form an integral part of US society.

of many factors encouraging people to leave. Indeed, it has been argued by some analysts that ever since 1975 the US and other Western governments showed an interest in encouraging departures, not least to demonstrate to the world that the people in the southern half of Viet Nam were 'voting with their feet' by leaving in the wake of the communist victory.[17]

On 30 July 1989, the US and Vietnamese governments issued a joint statement that they had reached agreement on the emigration of former political prisoners and their families. With that agreement, departures under the Orderly Departure Programme increased dramatically, reaching a high point of 86,451 in 1991. This included 21,500 former re-education camp detainees and family members, and nearly 18,000 Amerasian children. The latter were children of US troops who had served in Viet Nam. The United States eventually resettled a total of over a million Vietnamese people [see Box 4.3].

During the eight-year period of the Comprehensive Plan of Action, more than 109,000 Vietnamese returned home. To assist them in their reintegration, UNHCR offered each returnee a cash grant of between US$240 and US$360, which was paid in instalments by the government's Ministry of Labour, War Invalids, and Social Affairs. UNHCR also spent more than US$6 million on 300 micro-projects around the country, focusing on water, education, and community infrastructure. In the area of employment and job development, UNHCR looked to the European Community International Programme which made more than 56,000 loans of between US$300 and US$20,000 to returnees and local residents alike. The loans greatly facilitated the development of small businesses and 88 per cent were repaid.

Although 80 per cent of the returnees went primarily to eight coastal provinces, they returned to all of Viet Nam's 53 provinces from north to south. To make UNHCR's monitoring responsibilities even more challenging, an estimated 25 per cent of returnees moved at least once after returning from the camps, mostly to cities and towns to look for work. UNHCR officials monitoring the reintegration of the returnees reported that the great majority of requests from returnees dealt with matters of economic assistance and that 'monitoring has revealed no indication that returnees have been persecuted'.[18]

Cambodian refugees in Thailand

Among the countries of asylum in Southeast Asia, Thailand was alone in bearing the burden of all three Indochinese refugee populations, of whom the largest number were Cambodian. Thailand had not acceded to the 1951 UN Refugee Convention, but it was willing to sign an agreement with UNHCR in July 1975 pledging to cooperate in providing temporary humanitarian aid to those forcibly displaced, and in seeking durable solutions including voluntary repatriation or resettlement in third countries. A Thai cabinet decision a month earlier had established that the new arrivals should be housed in camps run by the Ministry of the Interior. This decision captured the ambivalent and even contradictory attitude which would be reflected in much of the country's subsequent policies and practices towards the displaced population on Thai territory. It stated: 'Should any displaced persons attempt to enter the Kingdom, measures will be taken to drive them out of the Kingdom as fast as possible. If it is impossible to repel them, such persons will be detained in camps.'[19]

On 17 April 1975, communist revolutionaries who had been carrying out their own armed struggle in Cambodia for years, marched triumphantly into the capital, Phnom Penh, and proceeded systematically to empty it of its inhabitants. Although the new Khmer Rouge regime of what was renamed Democratic Kampuchea never revealed itself fully to the world or even to the Cambodian people, its shadowy leader, Pol Pot, directed a brutal campaign to rid the country of foreign influences and establish an agrarian autarky.[20] During the four-year rule of the Khmer Rouge in Cambodia, the regime evacuated major cities and towns, abolished markets and currency, prevented Buddhist monks from practising their religion, expelled foreign residents, and established collectivized labour camps throughout the country.[21] By the time of the Vietnamese invasion in early 1979, more than one million Cambodians had been executed or had died of starvation, disease or overwork, while hundreds of thousands were internally displaced.

Although a substantial number of Cambodians did manage to flee the country, this was small compared with the widespread internal displacement that occurred under the brutal Khmer Rouge regime. UNHCR estimates that only 34,000 Cambodians managed to escape into Thailand from 1975 to 1978, another 20,000 going to Laos and 170,000 to Viet Nam.[22] When the Indochinese refugee exodus exploded in early 1979, Thailand received a relatively small flow of Vietnamese refugees, but by the middle of the year it was playing reluctant host to 164,000 Cambodian and Laotian refugees in camps managed by UNHCR. As a result of the Vietnamese invasion that ousted the Khmer Rouge regime, tens of thousands more Cambodians fled to Thailand's eastern border. This invasion installed another communist regime in what was then renamed the People's Republic of Kampuchea.

In June 1979, Thai soldiers rounded up more than 42,000 Cambodian refugees in border camps and pushed them down the steep mountainside at Preah Vihear into Cambodia. At least several hundred people, and possibly several thousand, were killed in the minefields below. One day after the pushbacks began, the representative of the International Committee of the Red Cross issued an urgent, public appeal that they cease; he was ordered to leave Thailand. Fearing an adverse Thai reaction, UNHCR effectively kept silent, despite the fact that this was the single largest instance of forced return (refoulement) the organization had encountered since it was established. As a senior protection official commented later, 'UNHCR's remarkable failure to formally or publicly protest the mass expulsions of Cambodians from Thailand during 1979 must be seen as one of the low points of its protection history'.[23]

Against this backdrop, the July 1979 conference in Geneva sought reset-tlement commitments from third countries to relieve pressures on Thailand. Of the 452,000 Indochinese resettled in 1979–80, nearly 195,000 came from the camps in Thailand. In October 1979, Thailand announced an 'open-door' policy towards the Cambodians who had continued to gather at the border in search of food and security. UNHCR was invited to establish 'holding centres' for these new arrivals, which would be supervised not by the Interior Ministry but by the armed forces. The reason for this, the Thai government argued, was that 'among the Kampucheans fleeing to Thailand, a number of them are combatants. So to put them under control in safe areas, the Thai military has to get involved.'[24]

UNHCR pledged nearly US$60 million to meet the needs of up to 300,000 Cambodian refugees and created a special Kampuchean Unit in its regional office in Bangkok to coordinate the building and administration of the holding centres. Never before had UNHCR been so involved in the actual construction and maintenance of refugee camps. Among the many outcomes of its operational role on the Cambodian border was the creation within UNHCR of an Emergency Unit, which has played a central role in every major refugee emergency since that time.

By the beginning of 1980, the principal holding centre, Khao-I-Dang, was home to more than 100,000 Cambodians. Among these refugees were many unaccompanied minors, who were of particular concern to UNHCR and other agencies [see Box 4.4]. Enjoying the sometimes mixed blessing of extraordinary media exposure, Khao-I-Dang became, for a time at least, what one observer called 'probably . . . the most elaborately serviced refugee camp in the world'.[25] At the time, it had a larger population than any city in Cambodia. By March 1980, when the camp population reached a peak of 140,000, 37 non-governmental organizations (NGOs) were working in Khao-I-Dang. This reflected the global proliferation of NGO activity which was taking place at the time.

Thailand's door for Cambodians was not to remain open for very long. In January 1980, only three months after announcing its 'open-door' policy, the Thai government backtracked and declared the holding centres closed to new arrivals. Henceforth, the government declared, Cambodian arrivals would be kept in border encampments without access to third-country resettlement.

The border camps

From 1979 to 1981, relief aid to the Cambodian border camps was coordinated by a Joint Mission, headed by the UN Children's Fund (UNICEF) and the International Committee of the Red Cross. At the end of 1981, UNICEF officially withdrew as the lead UN agency for the border relief programme—partly to focus its attention on development aid inside Cambodia and partly in protest at the increased militarization of the border camps, especially by the resurgent Khmer Rouge forces.

Since 1979, UNHCR had been responsible for Khao-I-Dang and other 'holding centres' for Cambodian refugees, but it had avoided seeking a role in the border camps. At one point in late 1979, UNHCR had offered to be the lead UN agency on the border. However, the terms it set—including the removal of all soldiers and weapons from the camps and the relocation of the camps away from the border—were considered to be unrealistic at the time. Moreover, at least some

Box 4.4

Indochina's unaccompanied minors

When Cambodian refugees began to spill across the Thai border in 1979, they included a high proportion of children and adolescents under the age of 18, who appeared to have no relatives. Such children were known as 'unaccompanied minors' or 'separated children'. From the beginning, there were urgent international appeals for their resettlement abroad. But their situation was complex, and finding solutions for them became highly controversial.

Many of these children had been forcibly recruited years earlier to serve in the Khmer Rouge youth brigades. Some had lost their families; others had become separated by the disruptions that followed the Vietnamese invasion of Cambodia in 1978. Still others were true orphans, having lost both parents. But a significant number of children turned out, after more detailed enquiry, to have close relatives living in Cambodia, somewhere along the border, or even in the same camp. Here lay the crux of the controversy. In December 1979, therefore, UNHCR cautioned against any precipitous moves toward third-country resettlement and permanent adoption until exhaustive efforts had been made to reunite unaccompanied or separated children with their surviving relatives in Cambodia or in the border camps.

A study the following year sponsored by the Norwegian Redd Barna and other non-governmental organizations (NGOs) found evidence that parents of many of the children were alive. After examining more than 2,000 files, Redd Barna concluded that more than half the children in the camps had been separated from their parents by circumstance, not death. Some children presumed their parents were dead on the basis of long separation or unfounded rumours. Others falsely claimed their parents were dead in the belief that their 'unaccompanied' status would facilitate their resettlement in third countries. 'The evidence suggests', the Redd Barna report concluded, 'that the majority of the unaccom-

panied minors' parents are still alive inside Kampuchea, therefore the potential for eventual reunification is considerable.'[viii]

The report proved correct on the first point, but it was wrong on the second. For the next decade, Cold War politics defeated all efforts at family reunification inside Cambodia. While hundreds of unaccompanied or separated Cambodian children were eventually reunited with family members in border camps, the great majority were indeed resettled in third countries, whether or not they had relatives there.

The best interests of the child

The framework of family and child welfare law upon which policies for unaccompanied or separated children are based accords parents the presumptive right and obligation to care for their children until they reach the age of majority. In the case of a child whose parents are dead or unavailable, the unifying international principle is to promote 'the best interests of the child' by providing temporary safety and care while seeking reunification with a family member or fostering by another responsible adult.

The question is, what happens when the principle of 'family unity' clashes with the 'best interests of the child', as so frequently happened in Indochina? Some seven per cent of all Vietnamese who reached first asylum countries were unaccompanied minors. Some had been separated from family members during the chaotic war years or had lost their parents at sea on the journey out. But for many of the children, the separation from parents was an intentional act. As many as a third were fleeing not so much from political oppression as from dysfunctional households. In other cases, the parents were sending their children out in the hope that they would secure an education and a better life in the West. In the 1970s and 1980s, when *prima facie* refugee status applied to virtu-

ally all Vietnamese boat people, the debate about unaccompanied minors centred on how they could best be protected in the first asylum camps and on how to resettle them successfully thereafter. But with the establishment of regional status determination procedures under UNHCR's Comprehensive Plan of Action, the question of repatriation and the return of minors to their families in Viet Nam became a central issue.

In 1989, UNHCR set up special committees in each country of first asylum to decide on a case-by-case basis what solution would be in the best interests of each unaccompanied minor. Members of these committees included representatives of the host government, UNHCR, and other agencies with child welfare expertise. UNHCR insisted that speed was of the essence, since prolonged residence in camps was potentially harmful to unaccompanied minors, even more so than to adults or children accompanied by other family members. By November 1990, there were 5,000 unaccompanied minors in the region awaiting a decision, and the special procedures were attracting intense criticism. More than one NGO accused UNHCR of a bias in favour of repatriation and of creating unwarranted delays as a means of achieving this objective.

Those unaccompanied minors who were recommended for resettlement during the status determination process—nearly a third of those concerned—moved on to start new lives. Those recommended for repatriation mostly remained in the camps. In reality, the special procedures meant that many minors were kept waiting longer than anyone else. By the end of 1993, more than 2,600 minors who had arrived in camps under the age of 16 had 'aged-out', putting them into the normal status determination procedures for adults.

international donors felt that UNHCR was not equipped to handle such a large and complex emergency.

In January 1982, the newly designated United Nations Border Relief Operation (UNBRO) took over the coordination of the relief operation. UNBRO was given a clear mission—to provide humanitarian relief to those who had fled to the 'no-man's-land' along the Thai–Cambodian border—but it had no explicit protection mandate, and no mandate to seek durable solutions for the population in its care.

In June 1982, the two Cambodian non-communist resistance factions fighting the Vietnamese occupation of their country joined with the forces of the Khmer Rouge who were also sheltering in the border camps to form a tripartite Coalition Government of Democratic Kampuchea (CGDK). Maintaining a seat in the UN General Assembly and a string of base camps along the Thai border, the CGDK applied steady political and military pressure on Phnom Penh throughout the decade, and the ensuing civil war brought new waves of violence into the camps.

Between 1982 and 1985, UNBRO staff assisted in more than 95 camp evacuations from the border area, 65 of them under shellfire.[26] A Vietnamese dry-season offensive in 1984–85 succeeded in driving most of the makeshift camps from the border area into Thai territory, although they remained under UNBRO care, administered by the CGDK, and closed to resettlement. Following the official closure of the border and of the holding centres to new arrivals in 1980, Khao-I-Dang became a kind of 'promised land' for many border Cambodians, a haven free of shelling and forced conscription, which held the possibility, however remote, of escape. Yet Khao I Dang had its own special protection problems. Would-be entrants faced bribery and abuse by smugglers and security guards just to get into the camp and, once inside, the 'illegals' often faced years of intimidation, exploitation, and risk of discovery before they were registered and given an opportunity to be interviewed for resettlement.

While UNHCR continued to administer Khao-I-Dang, it also continued its largely unfruitful efforts to negotiate organized, voluntary repatriation to Cambodia. As the resistance groups grew and as the conflict intensified, movement from the border area into Cambodia became increasingly difficult. One observer explained:

Not only did the Vietnamese and PRK [People's Republic of Kampuchea] government mine the Kampuchean side of the border but also, from the PRK's perspective, the people from the camps inevitably became associated with the resistance groups. The camp inhabitants therefore fear they would be deemed traitors and in risk of persecution if they did return. This changes their status from displaced people to refugees-sur-place . . . Correspondingly, the political-military groups have gained increasing control over the camp populations and the border entry posts to Kampuchea, making it very difficult for people to return to Kampuchea should they wish to do so.[27]

In September 1980, UNHCR had opened a small, two-person office in Phnom Penh, and had announced the establishment of a programme of humanitarian assistance for Cambodian returnees, then estimated at 300,000 (including 175,000

These Cambodian children at a camp in Aranyaprathet, Thailand, were among the tens of thousands who fled their country as Khmer Rouge soldiers emptied towns and cities at gunpoint. (UNHCR/Y. HARDY/1978)

returning from Thailand). The programme was to provide basic food assistance, seeds, tools, and household goods to returnees in five frontier provinces. This effort proved to be about a decade premature. Although talks con-tinued for many years, UNHCR was unable to find common ground between Bangkok and Phnom Penh, and organized returns from the Thai border camps did not take place. Between 1981 and 1988, only one Cambodian refugee officially returned from a UNHCR camp.[28]

Meeting in Paris in August 1989, the four rival factions of what had by then been renamed the State of Cambodia, failed to achieve any breakthroughs in their search for a comprehensive settlement.[29] They did, however, manage to agree on one thing: that the Cambodian refugees in Thailand and the Cambodians on the Thai border, who amounted to some 306,000 people, should be allowed to return home safely and voluntarily in the event of a peace agreement being reached. The collapse of the Paris meeting left that prospect in real doubt, however, while the withdrawal of the remaining 26,000 Vietnamese troops in September 1989 plunged Cambodia into renewed civil war. The border regions exploded in another round of displacement.

A UN-sponsored settlement, under which the United Nations was to provide an interim administration, was eventually signed in Paris in October 1991. This placed Cambodia under the control of a United Nations Transitional Authority in Cambodia (UNTAC) pending national elections [see Chapter 6]. The plan also required the factions to disarm and demobilize 70 per cent of their troops, release their political prisoners, open their 'zones' to international inspection and electoral registration, and permit all Cambodian refugees displaced in Thailand to return in time to register and vote. By the time that agreement was signed, the UNBRO border camps in Thailand held more than 353,000 refugees and another 180,000 Cambodians were displaced inside their own country. In the context of the peace settlement, UNHCR took over responsibility for the border camps from UNBRO from November 1991 and set in motion plans for repatriation.

From March 1992 to May 1993, UNHCR coordinated a repatriation effort that succeeded in closing the border camps and moving more than 360,000 people safely back to Cambodia in time to vote in the elections. On 3 March 1993, the last convoy of 199 returnees left Khao-I-Dang and the camp—first opened on 21 November 1979—was officially closed. In his speech at the closing ceremony, UNHCR's Special Envoy, Sergio Vieira de Mello, called Khao-I-Dang a 'powerful and tragic symbol' of the Cambodian exodus and the international humanitarian response. UNHCR's 'prime objective and eventual achievement', he said, was 'to create a camp that was neutral, where people of all political affiliations could seek refuge'. At the same time, Vieira de Mello commented, 'Khao-I-Dang also became a gateway for resettlement in third countries'.[30] From 1975 to 1992, more than 235,000 Cambodian refugees in Thailand were resettled overseas, including 150,000 in the United States. Most of them passed through the gates of Khao-I-Dang.

Laotian refugees in Thailand

In May 1975, when a communist victory in Laos was all but certain, US transport planes carried about 2,500 Hmong out of their mountain stronghold in Laos and into Thailand. A highland minority who had helped the US war effort in Laos, the Hmong had lost 20,000 soldiers in combat, 50,000 non-combatants had been killed or wounded, and 120,000 more had been displaced from their homes.[31] Many chose not to wait for a new political regime but fled across the Mekong River. By December 1975, when the Lao People's Democratic Republic was formally established, Laotian refugees in Thailand numbered 54,000, of whom all but 10,000 were Hmong.

A UNHCR official in Laos and Thailand offered this analysis of the Hmong flight from Laos: 'That the great majority of Hmong refugees fled because of a genuinely felt fear of reprisal or persecution from the new regime is not called into question . . . [but] there were additional economic reasons for the Hmong to leave Laos and to leave when they did.' Not only had the war removed large areas from cultivation through bombing and chemical defoliation but, as he explained:

A great many Hmong families came to rely increasingly on food drops by aircraft, handouts in the population centers, or the soldier's pay earned by adult males . . . When, in 1975, the alternative means of livelihood came to an abrupt end, tens of thousands of Hmong found themselves abruptly face to face not only with the fear of the enemy's revenge but also with a situation of accumulated resource scarcity . . . Had they remained in Laos, it is difficult to see how they could have avoided large-scale famine.[32]

During a visit to Laos in September 1975, High Commissioner Sadruddin Aga Khan had signed an agreement with the Laotian government 'to cooperate in supporting the Laotian refugees who want to go back to their native country as soon as possible'.[33] The following year, Laos reached agreement with the Thai government to accept the return of refugees, but despite UNHCR commitments of transportation and reintegration aid, no repatriation occurred until 1980 when 193 lowland Lao returned home.

UNHCR had opened a branch office in the Laotian capital, Vientiane, in October 1974. By the end of 1977, the office had helped thousands of people to go home and had provided them with food aid and agricultural equipment.[34] Following a visit by High Commissioner Poul Hartling in September 1978, however, UNHCR halted all further activities for displaced people inside Laos. Instead, it announced a 're-orientation of UNHCR's activities towards the provinces bordering Thailand, particularly in the southern part of the country . . . with a view to preventing the exodus of persons who might wish to leave Laos because of economic difficulties and chronic food shortages in some areas'.[35]

Indochinese arrivals by country or territory of first asylum, 1975–95

Figure 4.3

Country/territory of first asylum	1975–79	1980–84	1985–89	1990–95	Cumulative 1975–95
Vietnamese boat people					
Hong Kong	79,906	28,975	59,518	27,434	195,833
Indonesia	51,156	36,208	19,070	15,274	121,708
Japan	3,073	4,635	1,834	1,529	11,071
Korea, Republic of	409	318	621	0	1,348
Macau	4,333	2,777	17	1	7,128
Malaysia	124,103	76,205	52,860	1,327	254,495
Philippines	12,299	20,201	17,829	1,393	51,722
Singapore	7,858	19,868	4,578	153	32,457
Thailand	25,723	52,468	29,850	9,280	117,321
Other	2,566	340	321	0	3,227
Sub-total (boat people)	**311,426**	**241,995**	**186,498**	**56,391**	**796,310**
Thailand (overland)	**397,943**	**155,325**	**66,073**	**20,905**	**640,246**
Cambodians	171,933	47,984	12,811	4,670	237,398
Laotians	211,344	96,224	42,795	9,567	359,930
Vietnamese	14,666	11,117	10,467	6,668	42,918
Total (boat and land)	**709,369**	**397,320**	**252,571**	**77,296**	**1,436,556***

*There were also 2,163 Cambodians who arrived in Indonesia, Malaysia and the Philippines after 1975.

Although the exodus of lowland Lao had started slowly, by 1978, refugee camp records showed more than 48,000 arrivals in Thailand. Some Lao had fled due to fears of being incarcerated in re-education camps. Others had left because of the loss of political, economic and religious freedoms. For its part, UNHCR was concerned—and its concern was shared by Thai officials—that a significant portion of the lowland Lao outflow was being spurred by economic problems in Laos and the prospect of ready resettlement out of the camps just across the Mekong river.

In January 1981, Thailand opened a new camp for lowland Lao, Na Pho, and placed all new arrivals there; the camp provided only limited services, survival-level rations, and no access to resettlement.[36] The policy that Thailand referred to as 'humane deterrence'—keeping the borders open while closing the doors to resettlement and limiting camp amenities—seemed to have an effect on the lowland Lao exodus. Laotian resettlement drop-ped from over 75,000 in 1980 to about 9,000 in 1982. During this same period, lowland Lao refugee arrivals dropped from 29,000 to 3,200.

Resettlement of Indochinese refugees by destination, 1975–95

Figure 4.4

Resettlement country	Cambodians	Laotians	Vietnamese	Total 1975–95
Australia	16,308	10,239	110,996	137,543
Belgium	745	989	2,051	3,785
Canada	16,818	17,274	103,053	137,145
Denmark	31	12	4,682	4,725
Finland	37	6	1,859	1,902
France	34,364	34,236	27,071	95,671
Germany, FR	874	1,706	16,848	19,428
Japan	1,061	1,273	6,469	8,803
Netherlands	465	33	7,565	8,063
New Zealand	4,421	1,286	4,921	10,628
Norway	128	2	6,064	6,194
Sweden	19	26	6,009	6,054
Switzerland	1,638	593	6,239	8,470
United Kingdom	273	346	19,355	19,974
United States *	150,240	248,147	424,590	822,977
Others	8,063	4,688	7,070	19,821
Total	**235,485**	**320,856**	**754,842**	**1,311,183**

*Excludes arrivals under the Orderly Departure Programme (ODP).

UNHCR-assisted Cambodian, Laotian and Vietnamese refugee camps in Thailand, 1980s and 1990s   Map 4.2

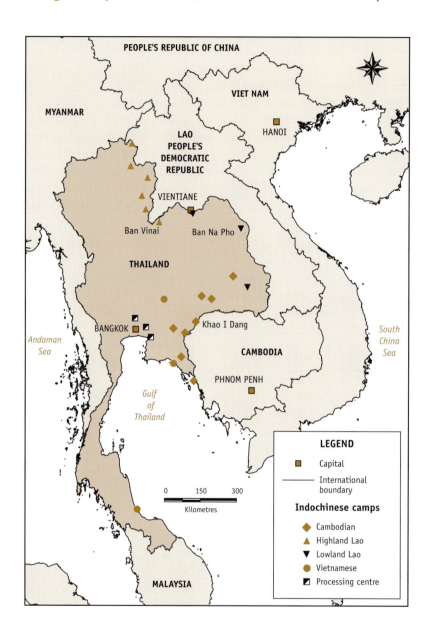

When Laotian arrivals climbed again in 1983 and in 1984, Thailand decided to try another approach. On 1 July 1985, the Thai government announced that it would institute a screening pro-cess at the border. Laotian arrivals were to present themselves at screening committee offices in any of the nine border provinces for interview by immigration officials. UNHCR legal officers were free to attend these interviews as observers. Those who were considered to be refugees were sent to Ban Vinai, the Hmong camp, or Na Pho, the camp for lowland Lao. For those whose applications were rejected, UNHCR was given an opportunity to appeal before they were detained pending return to Laos.

By the end of 1986, UNHCR reported that out of some 7,000 Laotians who had been interviewed, roughly 66 per cent had been approved as refugees. Although this exceeded many initial expectations, the figures showed that hardly any of the applicants were Hmong. Reports from the border indicated that, in fact, several hundred Hmong had been pushed back to Laos in 1986. By early 1988, the Thai government position toward the Hmong eased somewhat, influenced perhaps by a US commitment to raise resettlement numbers for the Hmong. From 1985 to 1989, Thai officials interviewed some 31,000 Laotians, of whom 90 per cent were given refugee status.

The Comprehensive Plan of Action called upon the governments of Thailand and Laos, together with UNHCR, to speed up negotiations aimed at 'maintaining safe arrival and access to the Lao screening process; and accelerating and simplifying the process for both the return of the screened-out and voluntary repatriation ... under safe, humane and UNHCR-monitored conditions'.[37] By the end of 1990, UNHCR and the Thai Ministry of the Interior had worked out new procedures consistent with those applied regionally to Vietnamese asylum seekers. UNHCR was permitted to observe interviews, to question the applicants themselves, and to appeal decisions of the Thai committee responsible for assessing claims. In all, from October 1989 to the end of 1996, a total of 10,005 Laotians were interviewed, of whom 49 per cent were given refugee status and 45 per cent were rejected, with the remainder pending or otherwise closed. One reason for the decline in the percentage of approvals was the fact that Thai immigration officers generally no longer considered the presence of close relatives in a resettlement country as sufficient grounds for approval.

By the end of 1993, all Laotian refugee camps had closed with the exception of Na Pho. UNHCR's main task on the Thai side of the border was to persuade people to return home and, on the Laotian side, to help them reintegrate once they did. Although the principal emphasis was on voluntary return, by the middle of 1991 the Laotian and Thai governments had agreed that 'those rejected in the screening process will be returned without the use of force in safety and dignity'.[38]

By the end of 1995, returns to Laos from Thailand totalled just over 24,000. Of those, more than 80 per cent had been granted refugee status in Thailand and thus were not obliged to return except voluntarily. Roughly 4,400 returnees (most of whom were Hmong) were rejected asylum seekers. Since 1980, it is estimated that somewhere between 12,000 and 20,000 Laotians may also have returned spontaneously from the camps in Thailand.

All returnees were given the same standard assistance package consisting of a cash grant equivalent to US$120 as well as an 18-month rice ration. Other standard assistance provided prior to departure from Thailand included agricultural and carpentry tools, vegetable seeds and mosquito nets. In addition to this, each returnee family going to a rural settlement site received a plot of land for a house, between one and two hectares of land for cultivation, and building materials. Most of the UNHCR-funded rural settlement sites were also provided with water supply systems, roads and primary schools. In 1996, UNHCR monitors reported that 'the physical security of returnees is not an issue in Laos. More frequently, returnees are concerned about re-establishing their lives and feeding their families.'[39]

Indochina as a turning point

In nearly a quarter of a century of displacement within and from Indochina, more than three million people fled their countries, of whom some 2.5 million found new homes elsewhere and half a million returned. In the course of this displacement, many lessons were learned with regard to international efforts to resolve refugee problems. On the positive side, it is possible to point to the extraordinary commitments from resettlement countries around the world, and to the fact that Cambodia, Laos and Viet Nam all eventually accepted repatriation and reintegration programmes. Innovative responses were also found in the Orderly Departure Programme and the anti-piracy and rescue-at-sea measures. Before the crisis, most countries in the region were not party to the 1951 UN Refugee Convention, but since then Cambodia, China, Japan, South Korea, Papua New Guinea and the Philippines have all become parties to the Convention.

On the negative side, there are the countless people who drowned at sea, or who lost their lives or suffered in other ways from pirate attacks, rape, shelling, pushbacks, and long-term detention in inhumane conditions. All too often, as High Commissioner Jean-Pierre Hocké noted in 1989, vigilance was not constant and international solidarity wavered or collapsed:

We are all painfully aware that what has been achieved in this spirit of international solidarity has required constant vigilance and ever renewed efforts in the face of the appalling tragedies and less spectacular human misery that have accompanied the Indo-Chinese refugee exodus. There have been occasions when the political will to provide asylum and durable solutions has faltered and even failed, resulting ... in the outright denial of asylum, including tragic 'push-offs' of refugee boats, in restriction of access by my Office to asylum-seekers, or in prolonged internment of persons of our concern under difficult conditions which fall below minimum accepted standards.[40]

The Indochinese refugee conference of 1979 witnessed an outpouring of international concern and commitment to refugee protection but it also gave rise to the concept of 'first asylum', whereby one country's promise of protection is purchased by another country's offer of resettlement. As one former UNHCR official noted, two concepts left behind from the Indochinese experience—international burden-sharing and temporary asylum—'proved a mixed legacy, both capable of being applied either to great humanitarian advantage or as an easy excuse to shift the responsibility and avoid the blame'.[41]

It has been suggested that the 1989 conference endorsing the Comprehensive Plan of Action represented not only a major policy change towards Vietnamese asylum seekers but a turning point in Western attitudes towards refugee issues. As the crises of the 1990s were to demonstrate all too clearly, Western countries were no longer prepared to make open-ended commitments to resettlement as a durable solution. Even within UNHCR, one 1994 assessment noted that 'the disenchantment with resettlement' brought on by the Indochinese experience, 'has had a negative effect on UNHCR's capacity to effectively perform resettlement functions'.[42]

From the vantage point of a new century, it may be possible to look back at UNHCR's experience with the Indochinese refugees and see that resettlement was not the problem. On its own, however, it was not the solution either. The legacy of the Indochinese refugee programme is that the international community and UNHCR stayed engaged over a long and challenging period to find a combination of solutions that eventually brought the crisis to a relatively humane end.

5 Proxy wars in Africa, Asia and Central America

The 1980s were characterized by heightened Cold War tensions and proxy wars in developing countries across the globe. During the decade, the superpowers intervened in local conflicts that might have been minor and short-lived, but which instead escalated and resulted in large-scale displacement. This chapter focuses on three regions where major refugee crises occurred: the Horn of Africa, Afghanistan and Central America. UNHCR played a major role in responding to each of these.

Although some of the conflicts described in this chapter began in the 1970s or earlier, the focus here is on the 1980s. In the Horn of Africa, a series of wars, exacerbated by famine, caused millions of people to flee their homes at different times. In Afghanistan, a major new conflict in a strategically important region compelled over six million people to seek refuge in neighbouring countries. In Central America, three separate wars led to the displacement of over two million people.

These refugee crises presented complex challenges to both host countries and the international community. For the first time, UNHCR found itself responding to multiple, large-scale refugee emergencies on three different continents simultaneously. UNHCR also had to work under the particular pressures resulting from the involvement of the superpowers. Virtually all of UNHCR's funding, and many of its staff, came from Western countries. Since many of the large refugee populations of the 1980s, including Afghans, Ethiopians, and Nicaraguans, were fleeing communist or socialist governments, these Western countries also had geopolitical interests in funding UNHCR programmes. Meanwhile, the Soviet bloc, which viewed the United Nations as essentially pro-Western, neither supported nor funded UNHCR.

With refugee crises erupting around the globe during the 1980s, UNHCR's budget increased dramatically. In 1975, there were 2.8 million refugees world-wide and UNHCR's budget stood at some US$76 million. By the end of the 1980s, the refugee population had grown to nearly 15 million, and UNHCR's budget had increased to more than US$580 million. During these years, UNHCR provided assistance on a much greater scale than ever before. One of the main challenges was that of managing large refugee camps. As had been the case in Indochina, the presence of armed elements in refugee camps was also a major concern to the organization.

The refugee movements described in this chapter were by no means the only ones to take place during the 1980s. Massive displacement also took place in a number of other places. For example, Sri Lankans fled to India, Ugandans fled to southern Sudan, Angolans fled to Zambia and Zaire, and Mozambican refugees fled to six neighbouring countries [see Box 5.2]. UNHCR was involved in providing protection and assistance to refugees in each of these cases.

Afghan refugees in the North West Frontier Province of Pakistan in the early 1980s. (M. KOBAYASHI/1983)

Refugee populations in Ethiopia, Kenya, Somalia and Sudan, 1982–99

Figure 5.1

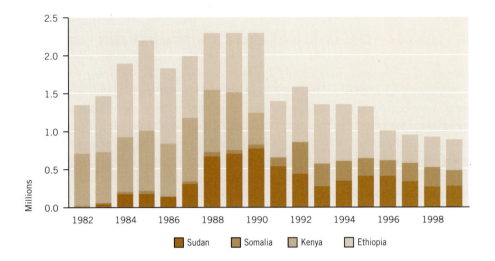

Sudan   Somalia   Kenya   Ethiopia

War and famine in the Horn of Africa

During the late 1970s and early 1980s, the Horn of Africa was the scene of numerous large-scale refugee movements. War, famine and mass displacement caught the world's attention, as the involvement of the superpowers fuelled the conflicts and magnified their consequences. Many Ethiopians, including people from Eritrea—then part of Ethiopia—sought refuge in Sudan, Somalia and Djibouti, and large numbers of Sudanese and Somalis sought refuge in Ethiopia.

A dramatic change in the superpower allegiances of Ethiopia and Somalia took place in the late 1970s. In Ethiopia, the consolidation of power by Lt.-Col. Mengistu Haile Mariam in 1977 resulted in the country seeking support from the Soviet Union and making a break with its traditional ally, the United States. As a result, the United States increased its backing of the governments in Sudan and Somalia. This had a significant impact on the conflicts in the region.

Ethiopian refugees in Somalia

Large-scale movements of refugees from Ethiopia into Somalia began at the end of the 1970s. Taking advantage of internal upheavals in Ethiopia, President Siad Barre of Somalia carried out an invasion of the Ogaden region of Ethiopia in 1977. Somali forces initially met with success, but when the Soviet Union switched its support to the Marxist regime of President Mengistu, his forces were able to repel the invasion. In early 1978, Somali troops were forced back across the border. Hundreds of thousands of ethnic Somalis in the Ethiopian Ogaden, fearing reprisals for involvement in the upsurge of violence that had preceded the Somali invasion, fled to Somalia. Another 45,000 went to neighbouring Djibouti.

The government of Somalia appealed to UNHCR for assistance in 1979. UNHCR helped the government establish and manage large refugee camps. In the short term, these camps helped to improve conditions for the refugees, many of whom were suffering from malnutrition and disease, but the problems inherent in large and overcrowded camps became increasingly apparent [see Box 5.1]. Camps grew so large that they became bigger than most cities in Somalia. The refugees, who were mainly nomadic people, found it difficult to adjust to sedentary life. In seeking to reduce the refugees' dependence on relief assistance, UNHCR initiated a number of agricultural projects. These had limited success, however, largely because of the scarcity of arable land and water.

UNHCR's relations with the Somali government were strained by a 'numbers game'. Initially, the Somali government claimed that there were 500,000 refugees in the country, while UNHCR estimated that there were only 80,000. After a second influx of refugees in 1981, the Somali government figure rose to two million, while UNHCR, other UN agencies and non-governmental organizations (NGOs) estimated the numbers of refugees to be between 450,000 and 620,000.[1] The entire population of the Ogaden region had previously been estimated to be well under one million.

Main refugee flows in northeast Africa during the 1980s   Map 5.1

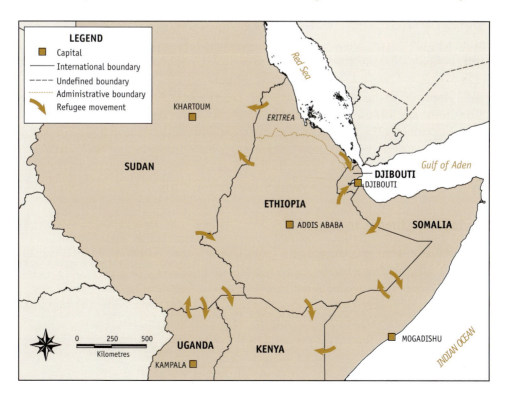

Box 5.1 Refugee camps and settlements

The vast refugee flows of the 1980s resulted in the growth of large camps and other kinds of organized settlements in host countries. In Africa in particular, the establishment of camps began to replace the previous practice of allowing refugees to settle amongst the local population.

For a number of years now, there has been widespread criticism of camps. UNHCR, in particular, has been held responsible both for the policy of establishing such camps and for the problems found in them. Critics argue that camps are harmful and unnecessary and that alternatives such as self-settlement (in which refugees live amongst the host community) should be pursued.[i]

The nature of camps

There is no clear definition of exactly what constitutes a 'refugee camp'. The term is used to describe human settlements which vary greatly in size and character. In general, refugee camps are enclosed areas, restricted to refugees and those assisting them, where protection and assistance is provided until it is safe for the refugees to return to their homelands or to be resettled elsewhere. Unlike other types of settlements, such as agricultural settlements or the 'refugee villages' seen in Pakistan in the 1980s and 1990s, refugee camps are not usually self-supporting.

Refugee camps are usually intended to be temporary, and are constructed accordingly. In many cases, however, they last for 10 years or more, creating new problems. Water and sewerage facilities often cannot cope with long-term usage, and housing plots become too small as families increase in size. In many

camps, firewood is inadequately supplied and refugees must forage outside the camps, causing deforestation and other environmental problems. As problems spill over from camps and affect the surrounding host communities, governments often impose restrictions on refugees, reducing their freedom to move and work outside the camps.

One of the most serious problems associated with many camps is the failure of local authorities to provide full protection for refugees, particularly since camps are often located in, or close to, conflict zones. In the long term, camps can become dangerous, crime-ridden places, beset by arms and drug smuggling and the presence of organized crime. Refugees in these camps often suffer domestic abuse and physical intimidation. Armed groups sometimes take control of camps or use them as bases, as in the case of the mujahedin in Pakistan, the 'contras' in Honduras and, more recently, the Interahamwe in eastern Zaire [see Box 10.1]. As camps lose their civilian character and become havens for armed groups, they become targets for attack by enemy forces. Camps have been bombed, shelled, raided for hostages, vehicles and supplies, and the scene of 'hot pursuit' by armed groups. Under such circumstances, host governments view them as increased security threats and impose greater restrictions on refugees.

Is self-settlement preferable?

Critics have accused UNHCR of favouring refugee camps over self-settlement, because camps provide the best means to manage refugees and facilitate repatriation. They argue that camps are harmful and unnecessary and that viable

alternatives can always be found. One such alternative is 'assisted self-settlement', whereby refugees are helped to settle amongst the local population. They claim that self-settled refugees enjoy better lives, are safer, freer, and live in more viable circumstances than those in camps or other organized settlements. The implicit assumption is that refugees would never choose to settle in a camp if they were given a choice.

On the face of it, it may seem obvious that no one would choose to live in a refugee camp when faced with the possibility of living elsewhere. The reality, however, is often more complex. General assumptions about better conditions for refugees outside camps have not been adequately substantiated by empirical research. It is by no means certain that self-settled refugees are generally safer or better off than those in camps. Depending on circumstances, refugees living outside camps can be subject to a range of security and economic problems ranging from threats by resentful local people, to attacks by rebel groups and forced recruitment into those groups. Self-settled refugees can be at risk of being rounded up by host authorities and relocated or forced into camps, as occurred in Karachi and Peshawar in Pakistan in the mid-1980s.

From a refugee's point of view, a camp may actually provide a safer and materially more secure option than self-settlement. Indeed, refugees and their leaders frequently organize themselves into camp-like settlements before UNHCR or any other humanitarian organization establishes an assistance programme. Nor should it be assumed that camps are always dreary, depressing places filled with dependent and passive victims.

On the contrary, refugee camps are often places of vibrant social and economic activity.

Most large camps become important zones of economic activity in the hosting area, with active markets, restaurants, and other facilities, which are run by refugees and attract locals from miles around.[ii] For example, Khao-I-Dang, a camp for Cambodian refugees on the Thai border, was renowned throughout much of the 1980s for its row of restaurants and for its thriving bicycle taxi service. A busy market was also established in the centre of the Rwandan refugee camp in Goma, eastern Zaire, from 1994 to 1997. The level of economic activity in this camp was illustrated by the fact that by late 1995 there were times when up to 20 cattle were slaughtered in the camp on a single day.

Although diseases such as cholera can spread easily in hastily constructed and overcrowded camps, in many cases—particularly after the initial emergency phase— refugees in camps receive significantly better health care, education and other services than people in the surrounding areas. As a result, humanitarian organizations working in camps are increasingly providing health, agricultural and education services not only to refugees but also to the local communities in these areas. This is not to suggest that camps are always an asset to the receiving region. Economic benefits can be offset by other problems, but these should be kept in perspective. The debate over the advantages and disadvantages of refugee camps should take place in the context of a clear understanding of how camps work, and the nature of their impact on the region.

UNHCR's official policy is to avoid the establishment of camps if viable alternatives are available. This is clearly stated in UNHCR's *Handbook for Emergencies*, and is one of the first rules for UNHCR emergency response teams. In many situations, it is the host government that insists on the establishment of camps, or the refugees themselves who congregate in large groups, forming settlements which eventually take the form of camps as international assistance enters the scene.

The preference of many host governments for camps rather than self-settlement is usually based on three factors: first, perceived security needs; second, the ability to organize repatriation; and third, the ability to attract international assistance through the creation of visible refugee settlements. In this respect, it is both legitimate and necessary to question the motivations of policymakers who insist on the establishment of camps, especially when opportunities for self-settlement exist. At the same time, and notwithstanding Article 26 of the 1951 UN Refugee Convention concerning refugees' rights to chose their place of residence and to freedom of movement, legal experts have recognized that host states do have the right to accommodate refugees in special camps or designated areas as long as minimum standards of treatment are respected. Given the political, economic and legal considerations which have underpinned the establishment of refugee camps, general arguments in favour of self-settlement are unlikely to have a significant impact on the policies of many refugee-hosting countries.

A blurred distinction

The debate over refugee camps has raised a number of important issues. In practice, however, refugee camps and self-settled refugees rarely form two clearly distinct categories. Apart from exceptions such as the detention camps in Hong Kong in the 1980s and early 1990s, most established camps do not confine refugees within their perimeters. On the contrary, in many situations refugees are able to move freely in and out of camps, to take advantage of wage-earning, trading or farming opportunities in the host country, or to visit their homelands, as many do prior to repatriation. Once displaced from their homes, refugees assess their prospects and spread their options between camps and the surrounding community. Some family members may live in camps while others take advantage of opportunities outside these camps. This means that the demarcation between camp communities and communities in the surrounding areas is often blurred.

In many ways, the debate between pro- and anti-camp advocates misses the point. Refugee camps are not inherently dangerous or destabilizing places, nor is self-settlement always the best option for refugees. The real challenge for host states, humanitarian organizations and policy makers is to ensure that refugees are able to enjoy safe, secure and dignified conditions of life, whether or not they live in a camp. Camps can serve their purpose well where they are prevented from becoming militarized, where the rule of law is maintained, where adequate health care, education and other essential services are provided, and where refugees have an opportunty to sustain themselves. It is to these ends that humanitarian efforts should be directed.

After UNHCR's attempts to conduct a credible census were thwarted, UN organizations agreed with the Somali government in 1982 on a 'planning figure' of 700,000 refugees. This remained the official refugee figure in Somalia until 1985, and all UNHCR assistance to the refugees was based on this figure. This was in spite of the fact that by 1984 UNHCR estimated that more than 300,000 of the refugees had repatriated to Ethiopia. Pressure from the United States, which had its own geopolitical interests in supporting Somalia at the time, was a factor in the continued acceptance by other Western donors of the Somali government's inflated figures.

The Somali government benefited in many ways from the international assistance which poured into the country during these years. Assistance given by organizations such as UNHCR and the World Food Programme (WFP) to meet the needs of the refugees was but one part of the overall assistance provided to the country. This assistance had a significant impact on Somalia's economy as a whole. According to one assessment, in the mid-1980s it represented at least a quarter of the country's gross national product.[2]

Between 1984 and 1986, there were further refugee influxes into Somalia. During the same period, a large number of refugees returned from Somalia to Ethiopia. By the late 1980s, however, increasing allegations of widespread human rights abuses being committed by the Somali government led to a dramatic reduction in US military assistance, and in 1989 this was halted completely. In August 1989, in an unprecedented action, UNHCR and WFP suspended assistance in northwest Somalia after the failure of repeated efforts to ensure that it was not diverted. Two years later, President Barre was overthrown and the country descended to a level of violence, famine and population displacement greater than anything it had experienced before [see Box 10.3].

Ethiopian refugees in Sudan

The first officially recognized refugees from Eritrea, which had been in a federation with Ethiopia but had been reduced to the status of a province in northern Ethiopia in 1962, arrived in Sudan as early as 1967.[3] They were fleeing the effects of an armed struggle for the right to self-determination which had been going on since the early 1960s. UNHCR assisted in establishing the first camp for these refugees in Sudan in 1970.

Large numbers of refugees also fled from other parts of Ethiopia to Sudan in the 1970s. The prolonged and bloody revolution which followed the overthrow of the autocratic Emperor Haile Selassie in 1974 was known at its peak as the 'red terror'. The left-wing military faction which seized power, known as the 'Derg', killed or imprisoned thousands of political opponents, labour activists and students, and caused a continuing exodus of refugees from the country.

By 1977, there were some 200,000 Eritrean refugees in Sudan. This number grew rapidly in 1978, when the Ethiopian government, now receiving massive Soviet aid and buoyed up by its recent victory over Somalia, launched a major offensive against the opposition forces in Eritrea. A mass exodus brought the total

These refugees in Sudan were among hundreds of thousands of Ethiopians who fled war and famine in their homeland in the mid-1980s. (UNHCR/M. VANAPPELGHEM/1985)

number of Ethiopian refugees in Sudan to over 400,000 by the end of that year, the majority of whom were from Eritrea.

Initially, the Sudanese government and the local people in the eastern part of the country welcomed the refugees. As the numbers grew, however, so did local resentment towards them. They began to be perceived as a threat to the stability of the eastern region. Fighting inside Eritrea had often taken place near the Sudanese border and had even spread to Sudanese soil.[4] With the country facing a growing economic crisis, exacerbated by a series of crop failures in eastern Sudan, the government requested UNHCR's assistance.

UNHCR worked closely with the Sudanese authorities in setting up refugee settlements. By 1984, the number of Ethiopian refugees had risen to some 500,000. Of these, around 128,000 were living in 23 refugee settlements. The remainder had settled spontaneously in towns, villages and the border area. UNHCR initially hoped that agricultural activities and opportunities for employment on large mechanized farms would enable the refugees to become self-sufficient. It soon became clear, however, that this would be difficult. A UNHCR report written at the time noted: 'Only a handful of settlements have access to sufficient land and water resources to make the concept of self-sufficiency realistic.'[5]

Box 5.2   Mozambican refugees in Malawi

During much of the 1980s, Mozambicans represented the world's third-largest refugee population after Palestinians and Afghans. They fled their country in the course of a devastating civil war which began in 1976 and which did not end until 1992. The consequences for neighbouring countries which received the vast majority of these refugees extended well beyond the provision of protection.

The Mozambican conflict began shortly after the country's independence in 1975. When Portugal hastily abandoned its African colonies following the fall of the military regime in Lisbon, the Mozambique Liberation Front (*Frente de Libertação de Moçambique*, or Frelimo), which had been waging a low-level guerrilla war against the Portuguese since 1964, assumed power in Mozambique. The conflict was between this Frelimo government and the Mozambique National Resistance (*Resistência Nacional Moçambicana*, or Renamo), an insurgent group established and supported by the white minority governments of Rhodesia and South Africa.

As the war continued, Renamo forces turned to increasingly ruthless tactics to control the population in their areas of operation. Wherever they went, they terrorized people with systematic killing, maiming, raping and pillaging. As they expanded the areas under their control, the number of Mozambicans fleeing escalated. Frelimo forces also resorted to increasingly brutal

measures, enabling Renamo to secure a degree of popular support.

The refugee crisis peaked in 1992, by which time some 1.7 million Mozambicans had become refugees in neighbouring countries and at least twice as many more had become internally displaced. Some of the areas deserted by the refugees were left virtually empty. For instance, in several districts of Mozambique's Tete province, as many as 90 per cent of all the inhabitants had fled. Apart from uprooting a total of some 5.7 million people, between 1976 and 1992 the conflict left more than one million Mozambicans dead and orphaned hundreds of thousands of children.

But Mozambicans were not the only ones to suffer the consequences of the conflict. A price was also paid by the people of the countries bordering Mozambique, which had to share their meagre resources, social services and sometimes their land with the refugees. These host countries were Malawi, South Africa, Swaziland, Tanzania, Zambia and Zimbabwe.

Malawi opens its doors

By far the most affected of these countries was Malawi, a small, impoverished, densely populated country which hosted the lion's share of those who fled Mozambique. At the height of the exodus there were as many as 1.1 million refugees, equivalent to 10 per cent of the Malawian population.

Malawi was ill-equipped to handle a major refugee influx. In the mid-1980s, Malawi was the world's sixth poorest country and one of Africa's least developed states. Fifty per cent of its children were undernourished and the country had the world's fourth highest infant mortality rate. Although refugees came to outnumber locals by as much as three to two in some areas, Malawi's welcome rarely wavered. Many of the early refugees, who were ethnically similar to Malawians, settled alongside the local population. Some were able to obtain land for agriculture, but others depended on international aid.

During the first decade of the conflict in Mozambique, the Malawian government, which provided covert support for Renamo, resisted international involvement with the refugees. It tried to provide for the refugees' needs through existing government structures and services, giving refugees access to local clinics, hospitals, and its limited social and welfare services. Then, in 1986, the same year that Malawi bowed to pressure from neighbouring governments to end its support for Renamo, Malawi recognized its inability to cope with the influx and asked UNHCR to help.

Initially, UNHCR sought to boost the government's efforts to aid the refugees through existing mechanisms. The UN World Food

Fighting between Ethiopian government forces and armed Eritrean opposition-groups, as well as between rival Eritrean factions, continued to produce a flow of refugees from Eritrea into Sudan. But another major crisis was looming, this time in the Tigray region of Ethiopia. This was to result in an even greater influx of Ethiopians into Sudan, putting further strain on the country and presenting UNHCR with one of its greatest challenges yet.

Programme (WFP) assisted by providing food aid. Even with this help, however, local institutions could not begin to meet both locals' and refugees' needs adequately. As refugee numbers mushroomed in 1987, Malawi asked UNHCR to establish refugee camps and instruc-ted all new refugees to move there. The govern-ment also barred local people from providing refugees with agricultural land. Eventually, more than two-thirds of the 1.1 million refugees who fled to Malawi settled in refugee camps.

Although housing refugees in camps made it easier for UNHCR, WFP and others to assist them, providing even basic care and maintenance remained a daunting task. Land-locked Malawi had a poor road system and lorries were scarce. Many of the camps were located in areas accessible only by dirt roads not suitable for heavy vehicles. The traffic severely damaged roads and bridges. Relief agencies leased many of the available lorries in Malawi for food distribution and this made it difficult for local farmers and merchants to transport their own goods. UNHCR and WFP had problems maintaining buffer stocks due to the poor transpor-tation system and inadequate storage facilities. The result was disruptions in food supply and a disturbing increase in malnutrition rates amongst the refugees.

Even though most refugees did not have access to land, they found

ways to generate income. More than 90 per cent of the refugees engaged in economic activities such as making and selling pots, pounding maize, rearing and selling domestic animals, and brewing beer. Many also sold or traded part of their rations in order to obtain necessities such as meat, fresh vegetables and soap. The poorest refugees, some of whom did not even have ration cards, survived by cutting trees for firewood. The large-scale cutting of trees inside Malawi led to such a high level of deforestation that Malawi's environment continues to be adversely affected.

The lack of overt conflict between the local people and the refugees was remarkable, given the length of time they stayed and the size of the refugee population. By 1992, however, the refugees' long stay in Malawi had begun to strain relations with the local population. Problems centred on the impact of their presence on the economy, environmental conse-quences such as deforestation, crime and other social problems. A drought that affected much of the region in 1992 and early 1993 exacerbated the situation. Although relief intended for the refugees was shared with drought-affected local people, theft at food storage warehouses and distribution centres increased. Wells in some refugee camps ran dry, leading to sanitation problems and an outbreak of cholera that spread to the local population.

Hidden costs

Such consequences represent the hidden costs borne by countries hosting large refugee populations, particularly when they are them-selves amongst the poorest countries in the world. Refugees can have a positive impact on host countries, but in some cases their presence can also have far-reaching detrimental conse-quences. The local economy and environment, as well as the local social and political balance, can all be affected. There can also be serious impli-cations for national, regional or international peace and security.

Development efforts in host countries can be undermined and distorted as the refugees' presence strains local supplies and facilities. Local authorities often find themselves obliged to divert funds from broader development projects in order to meet refugees' immediate needs for food, shelter and security. In Malawi, a World Bank-sponsored study found that, even taking into account the international aid provided through UNHCR, between 1988 and 1990 some US$25 million of public funds were spent on refugee-related assis-tance, having been diverted from other projects.

Famine in Ethiopia and new refugee flows

In 1984, a famine developed in Ethiopia that became one of the most widely publi-cized humanitarian crises of recent times. As one writer put it, 'the famine in northern Ethiopia, which became world news in 1984, was an earthquake in the humanitarian world'.[6] An estimated one million Ethiopians eventually died as a result.[7]

Although the famine was widely perceived as being drought-induced, the reality was far more complex. One analyst described it in the following terms:

Drought and harvest failure contributed to the famine but did not cause it. The economic and agricultural policies of the [Ethiopian] government also contributed, but were not central. The principal cause of the famine was the counter-insurgency campaign of the Ethiopian army and air force in Tigray and Wollo during 1980–85 . . . [which included] scorched earth tactics, the requisitioning of food by armies, blockades of food and people in sieges . . . and enforced rationing of food.[8]

The Ethiopian government allowed donor governments and international organizations to bring relief supplies into the country, but prevented them from assisting famine victims in areas under the control of the Eritrean and Tigrayan armed opposition groups. As a result, humanitarian organizations in Ethiopia were unable to assist people directly in the main famine-affected areas. From the early 1980s, a consortium of NGOs working from Sudan had begun trying to feed people in areas controlled by the armed opposition groups in Eritrea and Tigray. They delivered relief supplies to these areas in clandestine, night-time cross-border operations from Sudan. At the time, this was seen as an extremely radical form of humanitarian action.

The cross-border operation from Sudan was unable, however, to meet the needs of people in the famine-affected areas and hundreds of thousands of desperate people found themselves with no option but to move to government-controlled areas. Others resisted doing so, largely out of fear of being arrested or rounded up for forcible relocation by the Ethiopian government. The result was a mass exodus of Ethiopians mainly to Sudan, but also to Somalia and Djibouti.

Between October 1984 and March 1985, some 300,000 Ethiopian refugees arrived in Sudan. The majority of the refugees were from Tigray, and they left Ethiopia in a movement carefully organized by the Relief Society of Tigray (REST), which was essentially the civilian wing of the Tigray People's Liberation Front (TPLF). REST had announced that unless further food assistance was provided inside Tigray itself, it would not be able to retain its people there.

While some observers argued that these new arrivals were fleeing famine rather than conflict, UNHCR considered them refugees. The possibility of a significant influx had already been considered—and an alarm sounded—in late 1983. When it eventually occurred a year later, the scale and speed of the refugees' arrival in Sudan was much greater than expected. Many arrived in such poor physical condition that help came too late. Conditions in the refugee camps which were hastily established were initially poor, and death rates were high. Many died from malnutrition-related diseases, and severe outbreaks of measles killed many children.

At the same time as Ethiopians were entering Sudan from the Tigray region, famine—exacerbated by conflict—in the Eritrean region of Ethiopia caused a further influx of people into Sudan. These people arrived in the camps already accommodating Eritreans. Wad Sherife, a camp built to house 5,000 refugees, rapidly became home to 128,000, making it one of the largest refugee camps in the world.[9] UNHCR and its NGO partners struggled to accommodate the new arrivals in the camp, and to build the necessary additional warehouses, dispensaries and feeding centres.

UNHCR and other international humanitarian organizations, as well as governments and other donors, mobilized airlifts of food and supplies and sent medical teams and volunteers. In the West, musicians and other artists led by Bob Geldof spearheaded high profile fundraising efforts, including Live Aid and Band Aid, that raised millions of dollars for famine victims not only in Ethiopia and Sudan but all over sub-Saharan Africa. In 1985, donors gave UNHCR US$76 million for its programme in Sudan alone—an amount equal to the organization's entire global budget just 10 years earlier.[10]

In early 1986, UNHCR reported: 'International mobilization has produced results, and the situation [in Sudan] has improved considerably . . . The unbearable pictures of emaciated children and forlorn-looking men and women . . . already belong to the past.'[11] In May 1985, the rains had returned to Ethiopia and the TPLF encouraged its people to go home. By mid-1987, over 170,000 had returned. Unlike the Tigrayans, however, most of the Eritreans who had arrived in Sudan in 1984 and 1985 did not return. Rather, fighting and continued famine in Eritrea led to new influxes of Eritreans into Sudan.

During the 1980s, Ethiopia not only produced refugees but also hosted large numbers of refugees. From 1983, when war broke out again in southern Sudan between the Sudan People's Liberation Army (SPLA) and government forces, large numbers of people were displaced and by the end of the decade more than 350,000 southern Sudanese had fled to the Gambela region of Ethiopia. UNHCR assisted the Ethiopian government in meeting the needs of these refugees, though its access to these camps, which provided support for the SPLA, was often restricted. In 1987–88, some 365,000 Somalis also fled to Ethiopia to escape fighting between Somali government forces and rebels seeking independence for northwest Somalia. These refugees were accommodated in large camps in the Hartisheikh area. UNHCR coordinated international assistance to these camps.

The break-up of the Soviet Union and the end of the Cold War also signalled the end for President Mengistu's Marxist regime in Ethiopia. In May 1991, the EPLF captured the main Eritrean city of Asmara, ending the longest civil war in Africa and paving the way for Eritrean independence in 1993. Less than a week after the capture of Asmara, TPLF-led forces entered the Ethiopian capital Addis Ababa, the Ethiopian army collapsed, and President Mengistu was ousted.

Afghan refugees in Pakistan and Iran

Afghanistan—another of the world's poorest and least developed countries—also produced massive refugee movements during the 1980s. Although the conflicts which led to these movements had local roots, the enormous scale of the outflows was largely due to the substantial involvement of the superpowers in this strategically important region.

The crisis began in April 1978, when a group of urban intellectuals led by Nur Mohammad Taraki seized power and attempted to establish a communist state. They introduced wide-ranging social reforms which were resented by the deeply traditional rural populations they were intended to benefit. Opposition, both political and military, spread quickly. The regime, which received substantial military assistance from the Soviet Union, responded harshly. As one author wrote:

Religious, political, and intellectual elites were jailed or executed; ground attacks and aerial bombings destroyed villages and killed countless numbers of the rural population. It is estimated that between 50,000 and 100,000 people disappeared or were eliminated . . . from April 1978 to December 1979.[12]

Within months, Afghans began fleeing to neighbouring Pakistan and Iran. Despite pressure exerted by the Afghan and Soviet governments on Pakistan to expel the refugees, the government of Pakistan welcomed them.[13] By August 1978, some 3,000 had sought refuge in Pakistan; by early 1979, this figure had risen to over 20,000.

When the refugees first started arriving in Pakistan, UNHCR did not have an office in the country. The refugees turned to the United Nations Development Programme (UNDP) for help. UNDP in turn asked UNHCR for funds to provide temporary assistance to the neediest cases.[14] Then, in April 1979, the government of Pakistan formally requested UNHCR's assistance.[15] Following two assessment missions to Pakistan, UNHCR raised more than US$15 million to assist the refugees, and in October 1979 the organization opened an office in Islamabad.[16]

Meanwhile, in Afghanistan, the armed opposition was gaining ground against the communist government. In late December 1979, the Soviet Union, fearing the loss of an important ally on its southern border, invaded Afghanistan, triggering a massive exodus of refugees. Within weeks, 600,000 Afghans fled to Pakistan and Iran. Refugees continued to flee Afghanistan throughout the rest of the decade. By December 1990, UNHCR estimated that there were over 6.3 million Afghan refugees in neighbouring countries, including 3.3 million in Pakistan and three million in Iran. By this time, Afghans had come to constitute the largest refugee population in the world.

Disparities in assistance to refugees in Pakistan and Iran

The condition of the Afghan refugees in Pakistan contrasted greatly with that of the Afghan refugees in Iran. In Pakistan, the refugees were mostly ethnic Pashtuns, and they sought refuge mainly in Pashtun-dominated parts of Pakistan. More than 300 'refugee villages' were established by UNHCR, and the majority of the refugees lived in these villages. By contrast, in Iran, most of the Afghan refugees were ethnic Tajiks, Uzbeks and Hazaras, with only a small number of Pashtuns. Only relatively few of these refugees were accommodated in camps. Most spread out to towns and cities throughout the country, where they lived amongst the local community. Many were able to find work, not least because so many Iranian men were conscripted to fight in the war against Iraq which began in September 1980.

Main Afghan refugee flows, 1979–90   Map 5.2

The level of international assistance provided to the refugees in Pakistan and Iran also differed markedly. While donors contributed vast sums of money to assist Afghan refugees in Pakistan during the 1980s, they provided little for Afghans in Iran—even though the Afghan refugees in Iran comprised one of the world's largest refugee populations at the time.

Initially, the Iranian government refrained from asking for international assistance for the refugees. In view of the 1979 Islamic revolution, relations between the new Islamic government and Western states were strained to the limit. In addition, the assault on the US embassy in Teheran in November 1979, in which radical students seized dozens of US hostages, took place just one month before the Soviet invasion of Afghanistan. The resulting tension between Iran and the Western powers may well have been a factor in Iran's decision at the time not to seek international—or what it perceived as 'Western'—help.

The situation in Iran changed in 1980, largely as a result of the war with Iraq which began that year. This war generated a new influx of refugees, this time Shiite Iraqis, putting even more pressure on Iran. Two months later the Iranian government officially requested UNHCR assistance. Iran's deputy foreign minister wrote to High Commissioner Poul Hartling: 'We have received tens of thousands of refugees from those two countries and assisted them . . . through our own financial resources.' Adding that Iran did not have the resources to continue to assist the refugees adequately, the government asked UNHCR to 'set up a comprehensive humanitarian assistance programme for these innocent people who . . . should be cared for in the same manner as all other refugees'.[17]

International assistance to Iran was not forthcoming, however, and UNHCR wrestled with the disparity between the international response to the refugee crises in Pakistan and Iran. An internal UNHCR memorandum noted in June 1981: 'After one and a half years without external assistance and often without work, [Afghan refugees in Iran are] in very difficult circumstances . . . We can no longer close our eyes to the obvious needs of Afghan refugees in Iran who are in the same situation as those in Pakistan or India and who are *prima facie* [refugees] under our Mandate as confirmed by the Protection Division.'[18] Although UNHCR ultimately obtained some funds for Afghan refugees in Iran, the disparity in expenditures between Pakistan and Iran remained substantial throughout the 1980s and 1990s. Between 1979 and 1997, UNHCR spent more than US$1 billion on Afghan refugees in Pakistan, but only US$150 million on those in Iran.

In Pakistan, UNHCR, as well as other UN agencies, individual governments, and dozens of international NGOs, provided the refugees with food, water, health care, sanitation, and education. The proliferation of NGOs, which had begun in Southeast Asia in the 1970s, continued in Pakistan. By the late 1980s, there were over 100 international NGOs involved in the aid operation in Pakistan. They included many Muslim NGOs, which worked closely with UNHCR for the first time. UNHCR paid the salaries of more than 6,500 local staff, many of whom were employed by the Pakistani Commissariat for Afghan Refugees.[19]

For domestic political reasons, the Pakistan government would not give the refugees, who were mostly from rural areas, land for cultivation. The refugees were able to move freely around the country, however, and this helped many of them to find work. In the mid-1980s, UNHCR introduced a variety of programmes such as small-credit schemes, skills training, and construction projects, to provide employment and apprenticeships and to help the refugees become more self-sufficient. Many of these, however, were terminated at the insistence of the Pakistan government, which argued that since similar programmes were not available to local people, tensions could develop between local populations and the refugees.

From 1984, UNHCR and the World Bank set up a joint project in cooperation with the Pakistan government, known as the Income Generation Project for Refugee Areas. This programme, in which US$85 million was invested over the next 12 years, involved some 300 projects in three refugee-affected provinces. It included reafforestation, watershed management, irrigation, road repair and construction. The

Afghan refugee population by country of asylum, 1979–99

Figure 5.2

	Countries of asylum					
Year	Pakistan	Iran	India	Russian Fed.[a]	Other[b]	Total
1979	402,000	100,000	–	–	–	502,000
1980	1,428,000	300,000	–	–	–	1,728,000
1981	2,375,000	1,500,000	2,700	–	–	3,877,700
1982	2,877,000	1,500,000	3,400	–	–	4,380,400
1983	2,873,000	1,700,000	5,300	–	–	4,578,300
1984	2,500,000	1,800,000	5,900	–	–	4,305,900
1985	2,730,000	1,880,000	5,700	–	–	4,615,700
1986	2,878,000	2,190,000	5,500	–	–	5,073,500
1987	3,156,000	2,350,000	5,200	–	–	5,511,200
1988	3,255,000	2,350,000	4,900	–	–	5,609,900
1989	3,272,000	2,350,000	8,500	–	–	5,630,500
1990	3,253,000	3,061,000	11,900	–	–	6,325,900
1991	3,098,000	3,187,000	9,800	–	–	6,294,800
1992	1,627,000	2,901,000	11,000	8,800	3,000	4,550,800
1993	1,477,000	1,850,000	24,400	24,900	11,900	3,388,200
1994	1,053,000	1,623,000	22,400	28,300	12,300	2,739,000
1995	1,200,000	1,429,000	19,900	18,300	9,700	2,676,900
1996	1,200,000	1,415,000	18,600	20,400	10,700	2,664,700
1997	1,200,000	1,412,000	17,500	21,700	12,500	2,663,700
1998	1,200,000	1,401,000	16,100	8,700	8,400	2,634,200
1999	1,200,000	1,325,700	14,500	12,600	10,000	2,562,800

Notes:

As on 31 December of each given year.

[a] Asylum seekers registered with UNHCR only. By the end of 1999, an additional 100,000 Afghans were in need of protection according to UNHCR.

[b] Kazakhstan, Kyrgyzstan, Tajikistan, Turkmenistan and Uzbekistan.

programme was generally considered to have had a significant and positive impact.[20] Such projects, and the ability to work outside the refugee villages, helped many of the refugees to become self-sufficient by the late 1980s.

In Iran, a similar project was set up in the late 1980s in the South Khorasan rangeland. This time it was a joint project between UNHCR and the International Fund for Agricultural Development (IFAD), carried out in cooperation with the Iranian government. As with other projects in Iran, however, donors were less willing to provide funds for the project. Of the US$18 million initially requested by UNHCR and IFAD for this project, only a third was forthcoming during the project's first five years.

Another major difference between services provided to refugees in Pakistan and to those in Iran was in the field of education. In Pakistan, many boys received an education in UNHCR-funded schools in refugee villages, although fewer girls did so owing to discriminatory cultural practices which made it difficult for many of them to attend these schools. A significant number of boys also received an education in private *madrasas* (religious schools) with which UNHCR was not associated. In the mid-1990s, some of the boys who grew up as refugees in Pakistan, and who attended these *madrasas*, became leading members of the Taliban Islamic movement that seized power in Afghanistan. In Iran, by contrast, refugee children were enrolled in Iranian schools and girls had far greater access to education. During the 1990s, when repatriation to Afghanistan began in earnest, this access to education for girls was frequently cited by refugees as a reason for not wanting to return to Afghanistan, where such access was prohibited by the Taliban.

Security problems in Pakistan

Throughout the 1980s, the use of refugee villages in Pakistan as bases for the various Afghan Islamic armed resistance groups—known collectively as the *mujahedin*—was a major concern to UNHCR. The United States, its allies and various Islamic countries provided the *mujahedin* with vast amounts of military and financial assistance. The United States alone is estimated to have given them more than US$2 billion in aid between 1982 and 1991.[21] Since they supported the *mujahedin* in their fight against the Soviet-backed regime in Kabul, many donors were willing to turn a blind eye to the presence of armed fighters in refugee villages. They were also willing to tolerate substantial diversion of humanitarian aid for military purposes. This led some observers at the time to describe the refugee villages as 'refugee-warrior communities'.[22]

In 1984, as the security situation in many of the refugee villages deteriorated, UNHCR looked into ways of moving refugees away from the border, both to protect them from attack by Soviet or Afghan government forces, and to lessen the insurgents' ability to use refugee villages as bases. By this time, anti-aircraft weapons and other heavy weapons were a common feature in many of these refugee villages. In July 1984, the UNHCR Director of International Protection suggested that the organization terminate its assistance to villages which failed to take steps to prevent such militarization: 'The preservation of the civilian character of UNHCR-assisted refugee villages is essential to safeguard the non-political and humanitarian character of the Office . . . In cases where the necessary corrective action [to remove weapons] has not been taken, we would be in favour of the cessation of UNHCR assistance to the villages in question.'[23] He urged UNHCR staff on the ground to make 'every effort to encourage refugees . . . to move for their own safety to suitable alternative sites', but warned that it would be 'unwise and counterproductive to resort to any form of compulsion'.[24]

UNHCR's fears for the refugees' safety proved well founded. In mid-1984, Soviet and Afghan government forces conducted a number of cross-border attacks from Afghanistan into Pakistan in which many refugees were killed or injured. Further attacks in 1986 and 1987 killed hundreds more. Soviet and Afghan government forces also carried out attacks against Pakistani civilians, fanning tensions between local populations and refugees. In late 1986, apparently to appease angry local people, Pakistani authorities rounded up more than 50,000 Afghans who were living without permission in the city of Peshawar and returned them to their refugee villages.

Around the same time, the Pakistani authorities took other harsh measures to round up refugees, largely because of security concerns. In one incident, local authorities in Karachi, Pakistan's largest city, rounded up more than 18,500 Afghan refugees of ethnic Tajik, Uzbek, and Turkmen origin, destroyed their makeshift shelters, and removed them from the city. They were taken to a site some 10 kilometres away, where a new refugee village was established for them. At the time, UNHCR had denounced the way in which the refugees were treated, but the organization eventually provided over US$400,000 to help establish essential infrastructure for the village.

Meanwhile, nearer the border, UNHCR's concerns regarding the refugees' safety did not result in concrete steps to demilitarize the refugee villages. The *mujahedin* continued to move in and out of the villages throughout the 1980s. Soviet forces eventually withdrew from Afghanistan in 1989, but the war continued between the *mujahedin* and the communist regime in Kabul. After the *mujahedin* seized control in 1992, fighting continued in many parts of the country between various factions of the *mujahedin* itself. Many of these factions operated out of bases in Pakistan, and security problems continued in the refugee villages.

Mass displacement in Central America

During the 1980s, UNHCR became involved for the first time in Central America—the scene of three separate civil wars in Nicaragua, El Salvador and Guatemala. In each case, insurgency and counterinsurgency caused huge loss of life and large-scale displacement. Altogether, more than two million people in these countries were uprooted. For decades prior to the 1980s, violent struggles had taken place throughout the region, between the landless poor who wanted social and agrarian reform and the land-owning elites which were supported by the military. Successive US administrations had supported right-wing governments in the region in an effort to stop what they viewed as the spread of communism near US borders, and also to safeguard their economic interests in the region. The rebel movements which emerged in the region were influenced, and to some extent supported, by the communist regime in Cuba.

In Nicaragua, the United States had supported the Somoza regime for three generations. During the 1970s, political parties, students, labour unions, and many in the middle class and Roman Catholic church turned against the last of these dictators, Anastasio Somoza Debayle. The left-wing Sandinista National Liberation Front (*Frente Sandinista de Liberación Nacional*, or FSLN) made significant advances, and in July 1979, Somoza fled the country, leaving the Sandinistas in control.

Within weeks, many wealthy and middle class Nicaraguans, members of the Somoza government and thousands of the armed forces left the country. Meanwhile, most of the Nicaraguans who had previously gone into exile began returning home.[25] Some of the Nicaraguans who fled to Honduras formed an armed

Main refugee flows within Central America during the 1980s

Map 5.3

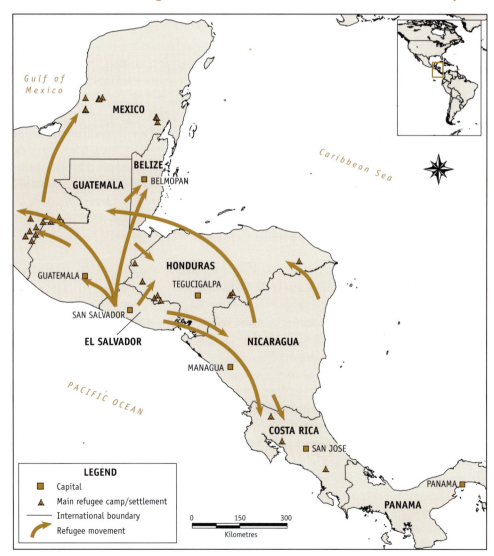

LEGEND
- Capital
- Main refugee camp/settlement
- International boundary
- Refugee movement

0   150   300
Kilometres

Box 5.3 | # The 1984 Cartagena Declaration

In November 1984, in response to the refugee crisis in Central America, a group of government representatives, academics and lawyers from Central America, Mexico and Panama met in Cartagena, Colombia, and adopted what became known as the Cartegena Declaration on Refugees.

The Cartagena Declaration builds on the 1951 UN Refugee Convention. Like the 1969 Refugee Convention of the Organization of African Unity, it broadens the definition of a refugee given in the 1951 UN Refugee Convention to include those persons who flee their country

> . . . because their lives, safety or freedom have been threatened by generalized violence, foreign aggression, internal conflicts, massive violation of human rights or other circumstances which have seriously disturbed public order.

Although the Declaration is not legally binding on states, it has repeatedly been endorsed by the General Assembly of the Organization of American States. Most states in Central and Latin America are party to the 1951 UN Refugee Convention or its Protocol, and most apply the Cartagena Declaration's broader definition of a refugee as a matter of practice. Some have incorporated this definition into their own national legislation.

opposition group known as the 'contras' (from the Spanish *contrarevolucionarios* or 'counter-revolutionaries'). Throughout the war waged during the 1980s, the United States, which viewed the Sandinista government in Nicaragua as a threat to its interests, provided considerable support to the contras.

In El Salvador, which had been plagued by frequent coups and political violence since independence, rebel groups, although fragmented, also asserted themselves during the 1970s. Often encouraged by clergy of the Roman Catholic Church, thousands of peasants joined organizations calling for agrarian reform and greater social justice. The government responded with increased repression and thousands of political killings took place.

Rather than quelling dissent, these attacks spurred greater support for the insurgents, particularly in rural areas. In January 1981, a wide range of opposition groups united to form the Farabundo Marti National Liberation Front (*Frente Farabundo Martí para la Liberación Nacional*, or FMLN). The FMLN established itself as a major military presence in many areas and became a serious political force both at home and abroad. In response, the United States increased military aid to the El Salvadoran government and became more directly involved in the Salvadoran armed forces' campaign against the FMLN. The conflict between the Salvadoran military and the FMLN continued throughout the 1980s.

In Guatemala also, insurgent groups rose up against the military regime in the 1970s. These groups enjoyed the support of much of the country's indigenous people

Main registered refugee populations in Central America and Mexico, 1980–99

Figure 5.3

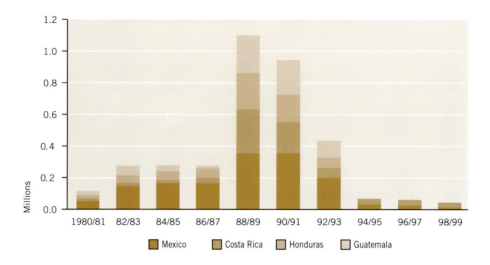

who, though comprising a majority of the population, were excluded from Guatemala's political and economic mainstream. In late 1981, the military initiated an 18-month counterinsurgency campaign that not only targeted the guerrillas but also indigenous communities, which it regarded as bases of rebel support. Tens of thousands of civilians, mostly indigenous people, were killed or disappeared.[26] At the peak of the violence, an estimated one million people were internally displaced as a result of this military campaign. Some months later, the various guerrilla groups united to form the Guatemalan National Revolutionary Unity (*Unidad Revolucionaria Nacional Guatemalteca*, or URNG). Despite popular support, the URNG was unable to mount a serious challenge to government troops. By 1983, the Guatemalan military had forced the URNG to retreat to remote mountain areas, where they remained until the beginning of peace talks later in the decade.

Most of the two million people uprooted as a result of these armed conflicts in Nicaragua, El Salvador and Guatemala remained internally displaced or became undocumented aliens in other Central or North American countries. These included Honduras, Mexico, Costa Rica, Belize and Panama, as well as the United States and Canada. Of those who fled their own country, only some 150,000 were recognized as refugees within Central America and Mexico. Of the hundreds of thousands who fled to the United States, only a relatively small number were recognized as refugees. The majority either did not have the opportunity to apply for refugee status or did not seek it for fear of deportation if it were denied.

Of the more than 500,000 Central Americans who fled to the United States, most did not receive protection as refugees. The US response to the Central American refugees was strongly influenced by political considerations.

Nicaraguans were generally welcomed and granted asylum, while a large number of Guatemalans and Salvadorans were denied asylum and deported, even though the United States did provide stays of deportation for some groups. Costa Rica, Honduras and Mexico also received several hundred thousand Central Americans, of whom only some 143,000 were recognized as refugees.[27] Two of the largest concentrations of officially recognized refugees were in Honduras and Mexico. In 1986, Honduras hosted some 68,000 refugees, including roughly 43,000 from Nicaragua, some 24,000 from El Salvador, and a small number from Guatemala, while Mexico hosted some 46,000 Guatemalan refugees and many more who were not formally registered.[28]

For UNHCR, efforts to provide protection and assistance to the two different groups of refugees in Honduras were constrained by Cold War politics and other political considerations. The Honduran government, which was dependent on US aid, welcomed the Nicaraguan refugees who were fleeing the Sandinista government, but was highly suspicious of the Salvadoran refugees. The unequal treatment by the Honduran authorities of these two groups of refugees posed serious challenges for UNHCR. Although most of the officially recognized refugees were sheltered in UNHCR-run camps, conditions in these camps varied widely. The Nicaraguan refugees were allowed to move in and out of their camps freely, while Salvadoran refugees were forced to stay in closed camps, guarded by Honduran armed forces.

Refugees by main region of asylum, 1975–2000*   Figure 5.4

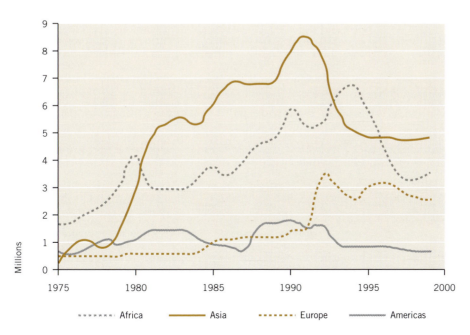

* Does not include Palestinian refugees assisted by the UN Relief and Works Agency for Palestine Refugees in the Near East (UNRWA).

Box 5.4   Chile under General Pinochet

Unlike most other Latin American countries, Chile had no tradition of military intervention in politics before 1973. It was regarded as one of the most stable democracies on the continent. On 11 September 1973, however, General Augusto Pinochet launched an armed attack against the democratically elected government of President Salvador Allende. The coup was swiftly followed by the suppression of legitimate political activity and the mass arrest of tens of thousands of supporters of the former socialist government. A 'state of siege' was declared throughout the country.

Torture, disappearances and killings were widespread, especially in the first few months of the military junta. Over 4,000 people are estimated to have been killed and some 60,000 arrested, although the majority of these were short-term detainees. Parliament was closed and purges were conducted of people suspected of left-wing sympathies. A UNHCR report at the time likened the situation to that of the fascist period in Europe in the 1930s.[iii]

Refugees already in Chile

For UNHCR, the Chilean coup and its aftermath presented considerable challenges. Chile was already home to many thousands of refugees and political exiles who had sought refuge in Chile in the preceding years. Their numbers were estimated by the Allende government in mid-1972 to be around 5,000. Many had come after Allende's election in 1970, either in flight from right-wing governments or in support of what was seen as a unique socialist experiment.

Two days after the coup, High Commissioner Sadruddin Aga Khan cabled the new Foreign Minister, Rear-Admiral Ismael Huerta Díaz, urging the government to honour its obligations under the 1951 UN Refugee Convention and its 1967 Protocol, which Allende's government had ratified in 1972.[iv] Had Chile not been party to these instruments, UNHCR's negotiations with the new government would almost certainly not have been so successful. On 20 September 1973, a UNHCR office was opened in the capital, Santiago.

Later the same month, the government allowed the creation of a National Committee for Aid to Refugees, (*Comité Nacional de Ayuda a los Refugiados,* or CONAR). The churches and voluntary agencies comprising CONAR set up 26 refugee reception centres, 15 in Santiago and 11 in the provinces. In these centres, 'mandate refugees' were assisted in putting their documents in order and arrangements were made for their transfer to countries of resettlement. By the end of September, 600 refugees had been registered at these centres and by 23 October their number had risen to 1,022.

Several hundred more refugees who were homeless were accommodated at different times in a house under the protection of the Swiss embassy, with the consent of the Chilean government. This *casa suiza* provided asylum to hundreds of UNHCR mandate refugees who had been released from detention and who were under expulsion orders pending resettlement abroad. Most were Brazilians, Uruguayans and Bolivians.

CONAR operated under the auspices of UNHCR, which offered it help in the resolution of refugee problems. By March 1974, out of the 3,574 people who had been registered with CONAR, 2,608 had been resettled in some 40 countries. This included 288 people who were repatriated to their own countries. In addition, some 1,500 had fled illegally to Peru and Argentina. Of CONAR's total expenditure of US$300,000 during this period, some US$215,000 was provided by UNHCR.

Exile of Chileans

From the outset, the Pinochet regime used exile as part of its strategy to redraw Chile's political map, thereby eliminating its previous political traditions. Such were the numbers arrested that the main football stadium in Santiago was turned into a massive makeshift detention centre.

Expulsions were conducted under Decree Law 81 of November 1973, which gave the regime virtually unconditional authority to expel citizens. From December 1974, detainees held under the state of siege and not yet sentenced were allowed to petition for their release on condition of immediate expulsion. In April 1975, Decree Law 504 extended the same policy to sentenced prisoners.

The Inter-governmental Committee for European Migration, the International Committee of the Red Cross and UNHCR played a major role, alongside local non-governmental organizations, in making it possible for thousands of Chileans to leave the country. UNHCR also received a great deal of support from other UN organizations, notably the International Labour Organization (ILO), the United Nations Development Programme (UNDP) and the United Nations Educational, Scientific and Cultural Organization (UNESCO). UNHCR established an eligibility determination procedure early in October 1973 to reach decisions on whether individuals had a well-founded fear of persecution in Chile, irrespective of whether this was their country of origin or simply their country of permanent residence. The quickest processing procedure possible was necessary for many refugees because they feared arrest or even death at the hands of the authorities.

As with the Hungarian exodus nearly two decades earlier, refugees were widely dispersed. Some 110 countries, from Iceland and Cyprus to Kenya and Cape Verde, resettled Chileans. Initially, many fled to other Latin American countries including Peru, Argentina and Brazil. Employment opportunities there were limited, however, and after the 1976 coup in Argentina, Chile's most immediate neighbour became especially unattractive. Other principal destinations for Chilean refugees were France, Sweden, Canada, Mexico, Australia and New Zealand.

UNHCR also appealed to Eastern European countries to resettle Chilean refugees. Around a thousand went spontaneously to the German Democratic Republic (East Germany) and a comparable number went to Romania with UNHCR's help. Smaller numbers went to other Eastern European countries including Bulgaria and Yugoslavia—the only Eastern bloc country with which UNHCR had until then had meaningful relations. UNHCR's appeal to these countries was a novelty at a time when the Soviet Union was still openly suspicious of the organization.

Diplomatic asylum

Many embassies in Santiago drew on the well-established Latin American practice of providing diplomatic protection to those on their premises. Within days of the coup, over 3,500 Chileans had sought asylum in embassies in Santiago, principally in those of Argentina, France, Italy, Mexico, the Netherlands, Panama, Sweden and Venezuela. In one case in December 1973, Harald Edelstam, the Swedish ambassador, was expelled from the country because of the particularly active role which he played in providing diplomatic asylum.

Using its 'good offices' role, UNHCR assisted these asylum seekers. By

mid-October, with UNHCR's assistance and with the agreement of the government, safe-conduct passes were accorded to 4,761 asylum seekers, the majority of whom were Chilean. By May 1974, some 8,000 such safe-conduct passes had been granted by the Foreign Ministry.[v]

Safe havens

Decree Law 1308 of 3 October 1973 brought about an important innovation in modern international practice on asylum: the creation within Chile of what were called 'safe havens' for foreign refugees, guaranteed by the Chilean government itself. In all there were six safe havens in the Santiago area. At first, these safe havens were respected by the regime, but a UNHCR cable at the end of 1973 noted that the law and order situation affecting refugees appeared extremely tense. It suggested that the junta might want to close the safe havens and insist on transit centres being established outside Chile.[vi] Ironically, this was also a demand of many of the refugees themselves.

In April 1974, the UNHCR office in Santiago estimated that there were still 15,000 people detained for political reasons throughout the country. Restrictions on civil and political liberties remained and there was a continuing absence of any meaningful legal process. It was under these conditions that all six safe havens continued to operate during most of 1974. A number of Chilean nationals waiting for resettlement were also lodged in a safe haven established under the protection of the UN flag by Decree Law 1698 of 17 October 1974. This decree specified that this centre could admit foreign refugees as well as relatives of Chilean refugees abroad who were awaiting family reunion. Chileans were allowed admission to this safe

haven only after receiving authorization from the Ministry of the Interior. The presence of Chilean nationals meant that UNHCR became increasingly involved in cases of family reunion, resettling the families of Chileans who had already found asylum abroad.

With the gradual departure of the refugees the number of safe havens dwindled. By the end of 1975, almost all the foreign refugees who could not remain in Chile had been satisfactorily resettled and in April 1976 the last remaining safe haven was closed.

A milestone for UNHCR

The UNHCR operation in Chile after 1973 was an important milestone in the history of the organization. It was UNHCR's first major operation in Latin America. There are no precise figures on the number of people who fled into exile in the years during which General Pinochet was head of state. The Inter-governmental Committee for European Migration alone enabled 20,000 people to flee by 1980. Other sources estimate the eventual total of those who fled the regime, whether voluntarily or as a result of expulsion, to be as many as 200,000.[vii]

Nicaraguan refugees in Honduras

Nicaraguan refugees had first started arriving in neighbouring Honduras in 1981. The majority of them (some 30,000) were indigenous Miskito people, fleeing both fighting between contra and Sandinista forces in their home areas and Sandinista attempts to move them. An estimated 14,000 of these Nicaraguan Miskitos lived in camps established by UNHCR. The remaining 8,000 Nicaraguan refugees were people of Spanish and mixed descent, known as 'ladinos'. These ladinos entered Honduras throughout the early 1980s. Many, like the Miskitos, were fleeing fighting between the contras and Sandinista forces. Others were contra recruits who settled in contra-run camps along the border.

UNHCR sought to maintain a clear division between the contra bases and the refugee communities by attempting to move refugees away from the border. It was well known, however, that contras were operating out of camps administered by UNHCR and the International Committee of the Red Cross, a situation one observer described as 'an instance of the most extreme use of refugees as policy objects'.[29] The presence of armed groups in the Nicaraguan refugee camps in Honduras, like that of Afghan armed groups in refugee villages in Pakistan, placed refugees at great risk. But with both the United States and Honduras supporting the contras, UNHCR found itself unable to prevent them operating from these camps. Meanwhile, a number of NGOs criticized UNHCR for not adequately protecting the refugees.

In 1987, refugee flows increased significantly, largely in response to a military recruitment drive by the Sandinista government. By December 1987, UNHCR had registered nearly 16,000 ladino refugees, roughly double the number registered at the end of 1986. In 1988, in the wake of the Iran-contra affair, the US Congress banned all aid to the contras. Without US assistance, the contras weakened and the conflict reached a stalemate. Later that year, the Sandinistas and the opposition, including the contras, began a 'national dialogue' that led to a series of agreements in 1989 aimed at ending the war.

Salvadoran refugees in Honduras

Salvadoran refugees first arrived in Honduras in 1980. Initially, the refugees settled without problems in various border communities, particularly in La Virtud. As more refugees arrived, however, the Honduran authorities sought to halt this spontaneous settlement. The Honduran government viewed the refugees as guerrilla collaborators and treated them with distrust and hostility. In May 1980, for example, Honduran troops turned back hundreds of refugees fleeing attack by the Salvadoran military. Many of those forced back were subsequently killed. Yet in spite of their poor reception, intensified fighting in El Salvador continued to force thousands of Salvadorans to flee to Honduras. By early 1981, the Salvadoran refugee population in Honduras had grown to 30,000.

The refugees did not find the safety they had hoped for when they fled to Honduras. According to a European nurse who worked in La Virtud: 'The Salvadoran military, by agreement with the Honduran soldiers at La Virtud, freely entered

Honduran territory. Some refugees disappeared, others were found dead, and others were arrested by the Honduran army.'[30] UNHCR issued a formal protest against the raids, as did senior members of the Church in the region, but this achieved little.

Then, in October 1981, the Honduran government announced that it planned to move the refugees in La Virtud to Mesa Grande, a site further from the border. The government's stated aim was to protect the refugees, which UNHCR supported. Some NGOs and other observers believed, however, that the government's real objectives were to prevent the refugees from assisting the Salvadoran guerrillas and to clear the border area so that the Honduran and Salvadoran militaries could operate there more freely. The refugees and most NGOs working at La Virtud opposed the planned move, arguing that this would put them even more at the mercy of the hostile Honduran military.

The situation came to a head on 16 November 1981, when Salvadoran paramilitaries and soldiers entered La Virtud and abducted a number of refugees. The Honduran government used the incursion as an excuse to proceed with the relocation immediately, even though preparations at Mesa Grande were incomplete. Despite the refugees' opposition and in spite of its own concerns, UNHCR found itself with little alternative but to assist with the move. Within five months, 7,500 refugees were relocated. Over 5,000 others returned to El Salvador rather than be moved to Mesa Grande. The relocation brought new problems. Many of the promised amenities never materialized and conditions for the refugees at Mesa Grande were far worse than they had been at La Virtud. As a result, the refugees' mistrust of both the Honduran authorities and of UNHCR increased.

The Honduran government's policy of keeping Salvadoran refugees in closed camps made it difficult for the refugees to achieve self-sufficiency. They were not allowed to seek employment outside the camps. They were also only allowed to farm within the confines of the camps, which limited the amount of food they could grow. In spite of this, the refugees were extremely resourceful. They planted their own vegetable gardens within the camp, which eventually provided all the camp's vegetable requirements. They also built fish ponds that provided tonnes of fish, raised pigs and chickens, and established workshops in which they produced most of their own clothes, shoes and hammocks.

In another controversial incident in 1983, the Honduran government told the Salvadoran refugees at the Colomoncagua camp, close to the Salvadoran border, that they would also have to relocate or be returned to El Salvador. UNHCR supported the proposed relocation but warned the Honduran government that it would oppose any attempt to repatriate these refugees forcibly to El Salvador.[31] Meanwhile, international NGOs supported the refugees' resistance to the move. In the end, the Honduran authorities backed down and the refugees were not forced to leave, but life in Colomoncagua remained tense and dangerous. From the beginning, there were many security problems at Colomoncagua, including violent attacks on refugees, sometimes in collaboration with members of the Salvadoran armed forces. A number of incidents also occurred involving conflicts between the refugees themselves, particularly when refugees sought to repatriate against the wishes of their leaders.

UNHCR was caught between conflicting pressures in the Salvadoran refugee camps. The Honduran and US governments wanted tighter control over the refugees' activities, while the refugees themselves, and most of the NGOs working in the camps, demanded greater freedom for the refugees. On a number of occasions, UNHCR staff in the camps were physically abused by the Honduran authorities.

UNHCR's relations with the NGOs working with Salvadoran refugees in Honduras were also strained. They often viewed UNHCR as being allied with the Honduran and US governments, which were generally hostile to the Salvadoran refugees. One UNHCR staff member wrote at the time: 'In no other country where I had previously worked was the international staff of voluntary agencies so hostile to UNHCR as in Mesa Grande and Colomoncagua.'[32]

Guatemalan refugees in Mexico

During the 1980s, Mexico—like Hon-duras—was not a signatory to either the 1951 UN Refugee Convention or its 1967 Protocol. When Guatemalans first started arriving in Mexico in large numbers in 1981, thousands were promptly deported. Following a series of international protests, however, the Mexican government established a registration process for Guatemalan refugees and allowed 46,000 to remain. These were amongst more than 200,000 Guatemalans who entered the country between 1981 and 1982. In 1982, UNHCR opened its first office in Mexico.

Many of those who were not registered had arrived in parts of Mexico to which Guatemalans had traditionally migrated in search of work, and where it was easy for them to blend in with the local and migrant work force. As many as 50,000 also made their way to the capital, Mexico City, where registration was not an option. Others arrived in Mexico after the government ended the registration process. All unregistered refugees lived in constant fear of deportation.

The registered refugees in Mexico were scattered in more than 50 camps in remote jungle areas in the impoverished state of Chiapas, bordering on Guatemala. Living conditions in the camps were desperately poor. From 1984, the Mexican government, aware of the poor conditions in these camps, adopted a policy to move the refugees from Chiapas to new settlements in the states of Campeche and Quintana Roo, on the Yucatan peninsula. Eventually some 18,000 refugees were moved. The government claimed, with some justification, that the move was necessary because the Guatemalan military had conducted several cross-border attacks on refugee sites. At the same time, the governor of Chiapas vehemently opposed the refugees' presence, while the Yucatan peninsula was an underdeveloped area where the refugees could assist development efforts.

Some 25,000 of the registered refugees in Chiapas resisted the relocation to Campeche and Quintana Roo, and remained in Chiapas. The Mexican government discouraged Mexican NGOs from assisting these refugees. The low wages they received for their labour and their lack of access to land and social services, made living conditions for these refugees extremely difficult, and in 1987 a number left the camps, some repatriating to Guatemala. Subsequently, however, the security situation and the living conditions for the refugees in Chiapas did improve somewhat.

From 1984, the Mexican government—in cooperation with UNHCR and NGOs—provided the refugees now settled in Campeche and Quintana Roo with land, shelter, food aid, and comprehensive social services. These settlements proved to be highly successful in terms of achieving self-sufficiency and local integration for refugees. Most of the refugees who moved to the settlements remained there permanently and the Mexican government eventually granted them citizenship.

Conflict resolution and repatriation

At the start of the 1980s, the Cold War was still firmly entrenched. By the end of the decade, both UNHCR and the global political landscape had changed dramatically. UNHCR had expanded significantly, not only in its staffing and budget levels, but also in terms of the scope of its activities. At the same time, many of the conflicts which had characterized the last decade of the Cold War were over or at least heading toward a resolution.

In the case of Afghanistan, Soviet troops withdrew from the country in 1989, shortly before the Soviet Union itself collapsed. The communist regime it left in place in Kabul fell to the mujahedin in 1992, eventually paving the way for the repatriation of some four million Afghans during the 1990s.

In Ethiopia, President Mengistu's government fell in 1991, leading to a period of relative calm in the country. Africa's longest ongoing civil war came to an end in 1991 and Eritrea formally obtained independence in 1993.

In Central America, the peace process which began in Esquipulas in 1987 crystallized the resolve of Central American leaders to bring an end to the conflicts in the region. In Nicaragua, a negotiated end to the conflict between the government and the contras began in 1989, and the following year the Sandinistas were voted out of office. In El Salvador and Guatemala, formal peace agreements were reached in 1992 and 1996 respectively, though many of the refugees returned home prior to these dates. At the beginning of the 1990s, the focus of UNHCR's activities therefore turned to repatriation.

6 Repatriation and peacebuilding in the early 1990s

As the 1980s drew to a close, the end of the Cold War created new opportunities for peace. Starved of superpower support, proxy wars that had raged in several countries around the world soon came to an end. In a number of these cases, the United Nations played a major role in brokering and consolidating peace accords by establishing large peacekeeping and peacebuilding operations.

In the early 1990s, there was palpable optimism that a more peaceful world order, characterized by international cooperation, the resolution of conflicts, and a dramatic reduction in the number of refugees and displaced persons, was within reach. Between 1988 and 1994, 21 new peacekeeping and peacebuilding operations were mounted by the United Nations, compared with only 13 peacekeeping operations in the previous 40 years. The new optimism was symbolized by UN Secretary-General Boutros Boutros Ghali's *Agenda for Peace* of June 1992, which envisaged a revitalized collective UN security system.

UNHCR played an important role in a number of UN peacebuilding operations, particularly in Namibia, Central America, Cambodia and Mozambique, which are the focus of this chapter. Each of these countries was the scene of protracted armed conflict during the Cold War years. In each case, peace agreements—reached through internationally mediated negotiations—resulted in large-scale repatriation movements. UNHCR's activities were integral to the broader UN peacebuilding operations in these countries. In each case, these operations involved the organization of elections and other measures aimed at assisting the transition from war to peace. They involved varying numbers of international monitors and civilian administrators, and in some cases peacekeeping forces and international civilian police.

In Namibia, UNHCR's involvement in the repatriation operation was short and limited. In Central America, Cambodia and Mozambique, however, the organization played a much greater role in assisting with the reintegration of the returning refugees. In each of these cases, UNHCR participated in a wide range of general rehabilitation programmes and in activities aimed at encouraging reconciliation. By assisting returning refugees and displaced people as part of a comprehensive programme, UNHCR and the international community sought to ensure their successful reintegration, thereby consolidating the peace process.

UNHCR's activities in each of these cases reflected a new, broader application of the organization's mandate. Except for the operation in Namibia, UNHCR's involvement did not end when the refugees crossed safely back over the border into their own countries. Rather, UNHCR remained actively involved in addressing the needs of returnees for longer periods than ever before, carrying out a wide range of protection and assistance activities to help these people to reintegrate and rebuild their lives.

A helicopter operating under the UN Transitional Authority in Cambodia arrives at Otaki reception centre for returning refugees, Battambang Province, Cambodia. (UNHCR/I. GUEST/1992)

The Namibian repatriation

Namibia's achievement of independence in 1990 was directly related both to the dismantling of apartheid in South Africa and to the end of the Cold War. The territory, which was known as South West Africa until 1968, had been controlled by South Africa since the end of the First World War. In 1966, the South West African People's Organization (SWAPO) began an armed struggle for independence, later establishing bases in Angola and Zambia. In 1978, the UN Security Council adopted Resolution 435, calling for the ending of South Africa's administration of Namibia, which had been ruled illegal in 1971, and for the territory's early independence following UN-monitored elections. It took more than a decade, however, for that resolution to be fully implemented.

The United States took the position that the independence of Namibia should be linked to a resolution of the civil war in neighbouring Angola, and the withdrawal of Cuban troops based there. It was not until December 1988 that South Africa, Angola and Cuba signed agreements to implement Resolution 435 and simultaneously to begin a phased withdrawal of Cuban troops from Angola. Two months later, the Security Council created the United Nations Transition Assistance Group (UNTAG), with a mandate which included monitoring the withdrawal of South African forces from Namibia and supervising the election of a constituent assembly.

Repatriation precedes elections

From the start, UNTAG considered that the return and peaceful reintegration of the Namibian refugees was a prerequisite for elections and for the successful transformation of Namibia into an independent, democratic country. UN Security Council Resolution 435 of 1978 eventually began to be implemented on 1 April 1989. Within less than a year of this date, over 43,000 Namibians had returned home from Zambia, Angola and a number of other countries.

The start of the organized repatriation had to be delayed while UNHCR, which facilitated the operation, held long and difficult negotiations with the South African government to secure a comprehensive amnesty for all returnees. Once the repatriation began, refugees were transported by air to the capital, Windhoek, and, between June and August, to more northerly entry points such as Grootfontein and Ondangwa. Three small entry points were also used for those arriving overland. From these points, the refugees were taken to five newly established reception centres where they were registered and given food, clothing, health care and basic household necessities. The returnees were then transported to their home destinations, primarily in the north of the country.

The operation suffered some major setbacks. Repatriation had to be delayed for one month when fully armed SWAPO forces marched into Namibia from their bases in Angola on 1 April 1989. Their apparent attempt to establish an armed, as well as a political, presence inside Namibia was thwarted by the remaining South African military units. Temporarily released from their barracks, the South African forces

Namibian refugees arrive back in Ovamboland, Namibia, after years in exile. (UNHCR/L. ASTRÖM/1989)

defeated and expelled the SWAPO troops. Another problem was that the South West African police, which included some notoriously violent 'counter-insurgency' elements, were still being deployed by the South African-controlled Administrator General during the repatriation. These elements, known as *Koevoets*, continued to operate illegally in the north, particularly in Ovamboland. They spread fear, impeded refugee returns and prompted the UN Secretary-General to issue a formal complaint in June 1989. UNHCR sent protection missions to the area to monitor the situation.[1]

UNHCR was criticized at the time for the high cost of the Namibian repatriation operation. More than US$36 million was spent on the return of just over 40,000 refugees. Almost half this amount was for the airlift operation to transport returning refugees and to deliver relief supplies. UNHCR considered this mode of transport essential, partly because it was unsafe to transit through southern Angola, and partly to make up for time lost due to the April incursion and delays caused by the lengthy negotiations to win full amnesties from South Africa for the returning refugees.

Despite the delays and setbacks, almost all the refugees were repatriated in time for the elections, which were held in November 1989. SWAPO won easily and formed the first independent government in Namibia. As had been the case in the repatriations to Algeria in 1962 and to Bangladesh in 1972, UNHCR limited its assistance to immediate needs for food and material and withdrew most of its staff after the returning refugees had been accompanied to their destinations. UNHCR considered its work done when it had completed the repatriation operation and resolved the amnesty question and other legal issues. The Council of Churches in Namibia, which was UNHCR's main implementing partner, established assistance centres throughout the country to receive returnees and to assist minors, the elderly and other vulnerable groups.

In 1990, a UN-led inter-agency mission found that the returning Namibians encountered serious difficulties in finding work, becoming self-sufficient, and achieving economic integration. This was particularly true of those who returned to the rural areas in the north of the country. Namibians who had returned in triumph felt abandoned by the international community.[2] The inter-agency mission recommended that assistance be made available to the Namibian returnees, but donors were reluctant to provide the necessary funding and few projects were actually put in place.

Meanwhile, some of the refugees had received advanced education while in places such as Eastern Europe or Cuba, and they brought back with them a variety of professional skills which eventually helped to build a stable and modestly prosperous new nation. A number of the returning refugees became leading members of the new government, including the new president, Sam Nujoma.

Namibia's attainment of independence proved to be the first of a series of post-Cold War achievements in which the UN system played a major role. In this case, UNHCR withdrew from the country soon after the main repatriation movements were over. In subsequent repatriation operations, UNHCR's involvement in assisting the reintegration of the returnees was to be much greater.

Repatriation in Central America

The civil conflicts that engulfed El Salvador, Guatemala and Nicaragua in the 1980s forced more than two million people to flee their homes. Of those who fled across international borders, fewer than 150,000 were officially recognized as refugees by host governments in the region [see Chapter 5]. The displaced found only relative safety in the countries or places to which they fled. Host governments became increasingly concerned about large refugee populations which could not easily be integrated and which they regarded as security threats. They were therefore eager for repatriation to take place.

With the proxy wars of the Cold War era coming to an end everywhere by the late 1980s, governments in Central America recognized a common interest in ending the three conflicts in El Salvador, Guatemala and Nicaragua. They organized two conferences in 1986 and 1987 in Esquipulas, Guatemala, and on 7

August 1987 a regional peace agreement was reached. The agreement, which became known as Esquipulas II, was signed by the presidents of Costa Rica, El Salvador, Guatemala, Honduras and Nicaragua. It set out a procedure for the establishment of a firm and lasting peace in Central America. In 1989, as the Cold War ended, external powers which had been involved in these conflicts—particularly the United States—were persuaded to support regional peace efforts. The 1989 International Conference on Central American Refugees (*Conferencia Internacional sobre Refugiados Centroamericanos*, or CIREFCA) also played an important role in addressing displacement problems. In addition, a number of initiatives taken by the refugees themselves helped to build peace in the region. First in El Salvador in the late 1980s and then in Guatemala in the early 1990s, refugees began organizing large-scale returns without waiting for official peace agreements to be signed.

In El Salvador, before the conclusion of the UN-brokered negotiations to end the conflict, Salvadoran refugees in Honduras announced that they would begin returning in organized groups. Although the government objected to their repatriation plans, it did not control the areas in which they proposed to settle, and the refugees began to repopulate areas which had been emptied as a result of the conflict. They returned regardless of the ongoing conflict, and settled in places of their own choice, despite their questionable claim to the land. They sought the support of UNHCR and other humanitarian organizations in organizing the repatriation, but since the refugees were going to areas where their safety could not be guaranteed, UNHCR was not willing to promote or facilitate the repatriation at that stage. By the mid-1990s, all of the registered Salvadoran refugees in neighbouring countries—some 32,000—had repatriated.

A number of Guatemalan refugees in Mexico followed the Salvadoran example. They repatriated in organized groups, having negotiated the conditions of their return with both the Guatemalan government and UNHCR. They continued to return from Mexico both before and after the full set of peace accords were finally concluded in 1996. The success of the repatriation and reintegration operation was constrained, however, by the shortage of available fertile land for the returnees. UNHCR involvement in the Guatemalan repatriation operation was strengthened by a high level of refugee participation in the process.

UNHCR established its first office in Guatemala in 1987. The extent of the assistance provided by UNHCR to the Guatemalan refugees was extremely high compared with other repatriation programmes. Significant efforts were put into working with refugee women and encouraging their participation in community structures. The programme to assist returnees in recovering identity papers and other personal documentation successfully built upon UNHCR's earlier experience in El Salvador. Between 1984 and June 1999, when the UNHCR-assisted repatriation programme ended, some 42,000 refugees repatriated from Mexico. A further 22,000, about half of whom were born in Mexico, had by this time accepted the Mexican government's offer to settle there permanently.[3]

Box 6.1 Protecting refugee children

War and displacement break down normal social structures and children are often amongst those who suffer most. For this reason, children have always been of particular concern to UNHCR and other humanitarian organizations working in emergency situations. About half the refugees and other people who have been assisted by UNHCR during its 50-year history have been below the age of 18.

Among the most vulnerable children are orphans and those separated from their families. When faced with war, families may send their children to distant countries to seek safety. In some cases, children are sent away to avoid conscription, to get an education, or to claim political asylum and pave the way for other family members to join them later [see Box 4.4]. As a result they are often at an increased risk of assault and exploitation.

These children's lives are often disrupted at a crucial stage in their physical development. Poor hygiene and insufficient food during the period of displacement frequently have a devastating impact on the mortality rates of the very young. Hastily constructed and overcrowded refugee settlements present further threats to health. In refugee situations, older children are often compelled to take on additional responsibilities within the family, as breadwinners or carers for incapacitated adults or younger siblings. At the same time, they are still developing their identity and learning skills, but they must do so divorced from their home communities and their familiar culture.

Up to 300,000 young people under the age of 18—some as young as seven or eight years old—are actively engaged in conflict around the world. Some are volunteers, but in countries such as Afghanistan and Sri Lanka, as well as several countries in Africa, children have been forced to take up arms. Refugee children are often at particular risk of such forced recruitment. Armed groups typically use children as porters, cooks, messengers, intelligence gatherers, or foot soldiers.

The participation of children and adolescents in education programmes is often cut short following displacement. In an emergency situation, the educational needs of refugee children are often not treated as a high priority and may suffer as a consequence of limited resources. Education and vocational training are crucial for children and adolescents, providing them with the skills required to live independent and productive lives. They are also an important protection mechanism against forced recruitment into armed forces and other forms of exploitation.

Recognizing children's needs

The 1989 UN Convention on the Rights of the Child, arguably the most comprehensive of all international human rights treaties, has been signed and ratified by every UN member state, except the United States and Somalia. For the purposes of the Convention, a child is defined as anyone 'below the age of eighteen years unless, under the law applicable to the child, majority is attained earlier' (Article 1). However, a lower age of 15 years is defined as the minimum age for recruitment into the armed forces (Article 38). An optional protocol under negotiation raises to 18 the age below which compulsory recruitment into the armed forces and participation in hostilities is prohibited. The 1990 African Charter on the Rights and Welfare of the Child, which entered into force in late 1999, already establishes 18 as the minimum age for all such recruitment and for participation in hostilities.

The protection of children in war-torn societies has been high on the UN agenda in recent years. In 1994, the UN Secretary-General appointed Graça Machel, widow of President Samora Machel of Mozambique, to conduct a study on the impact of armed conflict on children, and in 1997, the Secretary-General appointed a Special Representative for Children in Armed Conflict. Other international bodies have recently sought to protect children from the effects of armed conflict. The 1998 Rome Statute of the International Criminal Court considers it a war crime to conscript or enlist children under the age of 15 into national armed forces and use them in hostilities. In June 1999, the International Labour Organization approved Convention No. 182 on the Prohibition and Elimination of the Worst Forms of Child Labour, which includes a ban on the forced or compulsory recruitment of children for use in armed conflict. Most recently, the UN Secretary-General raised the minimum age for those participating in UN peacekeeping operations to 18.

Amongst UN organizations, the UN Children's Fund (UNICEF) has the lead role in assisting children. In addressing the special needs of displaced and refugee children, UNHCR cooperates closely with UNICEF, UNESCO andother specialist organizations, such as the International Save the Children Alliance. UNHCR's major concerns include child health, the special needs of adolescents and separated children, the prevention of sexual exploitation, the prevention of recruitment into the armed forces, and education for girls as well as boys. Although children are a category of particular concern to UNHCR, the programmes aimed at assisting and protecting them will only be effective if carried out as part of broader programmes aimed at addressing the needs of whole families and societies.

In Nicaragua, the situation was different. Here, it was only after the 1990 electoral defeat of the ruling Sandinista government that large-scale repatriation took place. Most of the 72,000 refugees, 350,000 internally displaced people and 30,000 former combatants returned to their homes in the early 1990s.

The Salvadoran and Guatemalan returns, which began before the formal peace agreements had been concluded, were different from most of the previous repatriation operations in which UNHCR had been involved, and led the organization to reconsider its traditional approaches to repatriation operations. It became necessary to define more clearly the organization's policies on when to promote and when to facilitate voluntary repatriation.

Reconstruction as a key component of peacebuilding

From 1989, UN Secretary-General Javier Pérez de Cuéllar played a key role in mediating between the two parties to the Salvadoran conflict. After an initial agreement on human rights was concluded in 1990, but before a ceasefire, both parties asked the Secretary-General to establish an observer mission. As a result, the UN Observer Mission in El Salvador (ONUSAL) was established by UN Security Council Resolution 693 of 20 May 1991, initially to monitor implementation of the agreement. A formal peace agreement was eventually concluded in January 1992. At the time, it was the most comprehensive document of its kind and was considered a major achievement for the United Nations as well as for the Salvadoran negotiating parties.

The Guatemalan accords, which in March 1994 agreed on a timetable and process to achieve peace, were drafted with even greater citizen participation. They built on the Salvadoran example, but provided a less specific agenda for compliance. In November that year, the UN Verification Mission in Guatemala (MINUGUA), established by UN General Assembly Resolution 48/267 of 19 September 1994, began its work in Guatemala. Initially, it monitored the general peace process in Guatemala, and from December 1996, when a final peace agreement was reached, it monitored the implementation of the various peace accords.[4]

As with subsequent UN peacebuilding operations in the 1990s, the UN operations in El Salvador and Guatemala went well beyond traditional peacekeeping functions by including programmes to strengthen local and national institutions, resolve questions of land distribution, and promote justice and human rights. This was carried out largely through cooperation with local non-governmental organizations (NGOs) and grassroots organizations.

Central American political leaders and opposition groups insisted that peace and development should go hand in hand, and sought a comprehensive plan for regional reconstruction. Major donors decided to channel funds through UNHCR and the United Nations Development Programme (UNDP), to implement a range of projects targeting all the war-affected groups. It was agreed that these funds should be used not to assist individual returnee families, but to support entire communities and affected areas. UNHCR and UNDP were to manage what became known as the

Salvadoran refugees dismantling their camp in Colomoncagua, Honduras, before repatriating. (UNHCR/D. BREGNARD/1990)

CIREFCA process, which proved to be one of the most important innovations to come from the region.

The CIREFCA process

The International Conference on Central American Refugees (*Conferencia Internacional sobre Refugiados Centroamericanos*, or CIREFCA) was held in May 1989. From then until the end of 1994, the CIREFCA process involved coordinated national, regional and international action to achieve lasting solutions to the problems of displacement in the region. The process was strongly supported by donors. For their part, local political leaders promised to link solutions for refugees, returnees and internally displaced people to national dialogue and reconciliation.

CIREFCA served as a forum in which the governments of Belize, Costa Rica, El Salvador, Guatemala, Honduras, Mexico and Nicaragua discussed their respective programmes and prepared projects, with the participation of NGOs, for presentation to international donor conferences. The programme was overseen by a combined

UNHCR–UNDP support unit. The CIREFCA framework promoted community-level projects, consensus-building among regional leaders, communication between governments and NGOs, and communication amongst the many different NGOs in the region.

The CIREFCA process enabled UNHCR to address the needs of returning refugees and displaced people in a more comprehensive manner than ever before. This was the first time that UNHCR and UNDP had worked closely together over a long period in the design and implementation of programmes. The different cultures, priorities and operational systems of the two organizations led to a number of difficulties. UNDP focused primarily on assisting governments in achieving long-term development goals, while UNHCR projects had until then been characterized by rapid implementation and shorter-term goals. In spite of what was at the time often a difficult relationship, UNHCR gained much from its experience of working in close cooperation with UNDP.[5]

Although the regional governments initially considered the CIREFCA process to involve only governments, UN organizations and other major donors, they gradually

UNHCR projects to assist the reintegration of returnees included the funding of small business ventures such as this carpentry workshop for returnees in Ixcan, Guatemala. (UNHCR/B. PRESS/1996)

Box 6.2   Linking relief and development

For many years, the linkage between emergency relief assistance and broader development assistance has been a cause of concern. In the late 1970s and 1980s, this concern focused on two main issues: first, the need to promote greater self-sufficiency for refugees in countries of asylum; and second, the need to address the social and environmental impact of large refugee populations on host countries. In the 1990s, the focus shifted to the reintegration of returning refugees and displaced people in countries making the transition from war to peace.

Gaps between emergency relief and long-term development assistance have often resulted from the institutional differences between organizations that provide emergency relief and those that foster development. Relief organizations must be able to respond quickly and must give priority to urgent needs. They usually rely heavily on international staff. Funding for emergency assistance is usually short-term and project-oriented. By contrast, development organizations usually rely on long-term strategies that can be conducted on a regional or national level. They are often absent during periods of conflict or political instability.

In practice, the transition from relief to development has often been difficult. On the one hand, projects initiated by relief agencies are often too small and too fragmented to lay the groundwork for sustainable, long-term development programmes. On the other hand, financial institutions and development organizations have their own priorities and are often unwilling to take on programmes in which they have had no formative role. Development organizations often lack the field experience and expertise necessary to assume responsibility for projects previously carried out by relief organizations. The success and sustainability of development programmes depend largely on the commitment of both the local population and the national government, which is often lacking in projects set up rapidly by relief organizations during the emergency phase.

In Africa, the initial impetus to limit the dependency of refugees on international assistance and to create situations of 'integrated development and self-reliance' came from a Pan-African conference on the situation of refugees in Africa, held in Arusha, Tanzania, in May 1979.[i] Two years later, the first International Conference on Assistance to Refugees in Africa (ICARA I) was held in Geneva. This conference focused on the linkages between UNHCR relief programmes for refugees and broader development programmes in refugee-hosting countries.

In 1984, a second international conference (ICARA II) attempted to get donors, international organizations and host governments to commit themselves to development-oriented approaches to refugee assistance. It was agreed that emphasis should be put on programmes aimed at achieving self-sufficiency and durable solutions for refugees. The initiatives agreed on at this conference were over-shadowed, however, by the magnitude of the new refugee crises in Africa at the time, many of which were exacerbated by severe drought. Progress was also hampered by host governments' insistence that funding for projects for non-nationals—including refugees—should be additional to resources dedicated to national development. This was known at the time as the question of 'additionality'. Limited commitments by the international community to certain refugee-hosting countries also stalled the process.

In Central America in the late 1980s and early 1990s, as various wars in the region ended and as large-scale repatriation began, it also became clear that sustainable peace was dependent upon the successful reintegration of returning refugees and displaced people. This, in turn, depended largely on the rehabilitation and reconstruction of infrastructure and institutions damaged by war. A series of development programmes was therefore launched to consolidate the peace, and UNHCR provided assistance not only to returning refugees and displaced people, but also to other war-affected populations. An International Conference on Central American Refugees (*Conferencia Internacional sobre Refugiados Centroamericanos*, or CIREFCA), held in Guatemala City in May 1989, launched several initiatives to bridge the gap between humanitarian assistance and longer-term development. The numerous quick impact projects (QIPs) implemented by organizations such as UNHCR played some part in consolidating peace in war-affected communities. On their own, however, these one-off, modestly funded micro-projects were unable successfully to bridge the gap between relief and development.

In 1999, UNHCR launched a new initiative, together with the Washington-based Brookings Institution, to study ways of bridging the gap between relief and development. The objective of the 'Brookings process' is to improve coordination and cooperation between relief and development organizations in efforts to achieve long-term, sustainable reintegration of returning refugees and displaced populations. Rather than relying on systems whereby responsibility for particular projects is handed over from relief organizations to development organizations at a particular point, this initiative attempts to ensure systematic cooperation and coordination between relief and development agencies from the beginning. The idea is for relief and development organizations to carry out joint analyses and needs assessments, and to prepare joint action plans and project evaluations.

Ultimately, the aim of the 'Brookings process' is to draw other international organizations, non-governmental organ-izations, and bilateral bodies into a more effective coalition of partners for reintegration and development. As one UN official put it: "'Relief' means saving lives, and "development" means saving livelihoods; both sets of activities need to take place simultaneously."[ii]

accepted the important role of local and international NGOs. Their eventual cooperation with these NGOs was no small achievement, given their initial animosity towards them.

Among the CIREFCA initiatives, the most innovative and influential in future repatriation operations were the quick impact projects. It was in Nicaragua that they were first implemented on a large scale. They were micro-projects, often involving the rehabilitation of clinics, schools and water systems, or aimed at creating income-generating opportunities. They required a modest injection of funds and a great deal of community involvement. These projects addressed urgent needs identified by community members, and were carried out in communities with large numbers of recent returnees. They encouraged people to share ideas, skills and resources and helped reduce tensions between former adversaries. Ultimately, these projects were seen not only as innovative but also as essential to successful reintegration and reconciliation.

Quick impact projects were subsequently implemented in Cambodia, Mozambique and other returnee situations. In 1995, High Commissioner Sadako Ogata described them as bringing rapid and tangible benefits to local communities and returnees alike, while at the same time she warned that the impact of such projects would be limited if insufficient efforts were made to sustain them.[6] Indeed, while they succeeded in attracting donor support and in helping communities in the immediate post-conflict phase, the lack of donor interest beyond the initial phase and limited local government commitment to incorporate these projects into national development strategies, rendered many of the projects largely unsustainable.

Following this Central American experience, it became increasingly clear to UNHCR and other humanitarian organizations that peace and development in post-conflict situations cannot be achieved solely by initiating modest, short-term projects for vulnerable groups. Nor can such projects address the structural problems that often give rise to conflicts in the first place, such as weak governance structures, the inability or unwillingness to redirect national resources, and lack of income-generating opportunities. In Central America, efforts to achieve sustainable reintegration continue to this day. Quick impact projects are no longer visible in the region, but the lasting impact of the CIREFCA process remains evident in the strength and effectiveness of community groups and local NGOs throughout Central America.

The Cambodian repatriation

The 1991 Cambodian peace accords were another example of the dramatic shift in geopolitics that followed the end of the Cold War. Vietnamese forces withdrew from Cambodia in 1989 as Soviet assistance to Viet Nam dried up. Regional leaders soon sought an end to the fighting and a peace process was begun with the full involvement of the UN Security Council and substantial international support. For the first time, the four Cambodian armed factions which had been involved in the conflict agreed to cooperate in the pursuit of peace.

The Paris Peace Agreements were concluded on 23 October 1991 at an international conference.[7] Under these agreements, all parties agreed to give the United Nations primary responsibility for overseeing Cambodia's transition to democracy. This resulted in the creation of the UN Transitional Authority in Cambodia (UNTAC), authorized under UN Security Council Resolution 745 of 28 February 1992. The signing of the peace agreements and the creation of UNTAC signalled that the time had come to encourage refugee repatriation. It was widely agreed that the refugees' return was essential to the success of the peace agreements and the impending national elections, planned for May 1993. Before the conclusion of the agreements, extensive consultations with UNHCR took place on matters relating to repatriation.

UNTAC faced enormous challenges. After 22 years of war, Cambodia's infrastructure had been all but completely destroyed. Most of its political, social and judicial institutions were neither viable nor legitimate. The majority of the people with the skills needed to rebuild the country had either been killed or had fled. On paper at least, UNTAC's powers and responsibilities exceeded those of all earlier UN peacekeeping operations. In addition to demilitarization and demobilization of the armed factions, UNTAC had responsibility for ensuring 'a neutral political environment'. This entailed managing the civil administration and supervising the parties' compliance with the peace agreement, pending the election of a new government. At the time, UNTAC was the largest and costliest UN mission ever mounted. It eventually cost US$1.7 billion and at its height had a staff of 22,000. This included over 15,000 peacekeepers and some 3,600 civilian police from more than 40 countries.[8]

Repatriation as part of the peace plan

UNHCR had been in Cambodia helping to resettle spontaneous returnees well before the arrival in March 1992 of Yasushi Akashi, the head of UNTAC and Special Representative of the Secretary-General. The organization had first opened an office in the Cambodian capital, Phnom Penh, in 1980. In 1989, as the political situation in started to improve, UNHCR had started planning for repatriation. The Paris Peace Agreements formalized the process by calling on UNHCR to act as lead agency for the repatriation operation and to assume primary responsibility for the reintegration of returning refugees and displaced people. Following the precedent set in Namibia, the peace agreements anticipated that the refugees would return to Cambodia from the camps on the Thai border in time for the national elections in May 1993.[9]

Formally, the repatriation operation constituted one of the seven components of UNTAC, and Sergio Vieira de Mello, the UNHCR Special Envoy who directed the repatriation operation, also reported to Akashi. The other six components dealt with military issues, civilian police, elections, human rights, rehabilitation and civil administration. In practice, every component of UNTAC had a role to play in the repatriation and reintegration process. Most importantly, the UN presence was needed to prevent continuing internal conflict from endangering the lives of returning refugees and displaced people.

As in so many other cases, the repatriation took place much more quickly than had been expected. The UN Advance Mission in Cambodia (UNAMIC), which preceded the deployment of UNTAC, coordinated with UNHCR to establish repatriation routes, reception centres and resettlement areas, and was instrumental in assisting the first returning convoys. Much of the early work had to be carried out on an *ad hoc* and emergency basis with whatever resources were available on the ground. UNHCR's presence in the country before the peace accord was concluded enabled the organization to play an important role during this initial period.

Between March 1992 and April 1993, more than 360,000 Cambodians returned. Although the overwhelming majority returned from Thailand, some 2,000 also repatriated from Indonesia, Viet Nam and Malaysia.[10] The repatriation operation was a logistically complicated and costly one, given the devastated infrastructure, the presence of land mines, the absence of reliable data about conditions in the countryside, continuing distrust among the different political factions, and frequent ceasefire violations. In addition, the heavy monsoon rains transformed many of the roads used in the repatriation operation into mudbaths, and extensive use had to be made of railways and waterways. Nearly 100,000 Cambodians returned by train, especially to the capital and the eastern provinces.

Before the Cambodians began their journey back from the camps in Thailand, UNHCR staff made efforts to ensure that they would be able to choose their own destinations. This was relatively straightforward in Khao I Dang camp, which was managed by UNHCR, but was more problematic in some of the border camps which were still under the control of the Khmer Rouge. UNHCR also sought assurances that it would have full access to returnees living in zones within Cambodia controlled by the Khmer Rouge. Despite persistent efforts to maintain a dialogue with their representatives, UNHCR had difficulty monitoring the situation of returnees in these zones.

UNHCR also sought guarantees from the Cambodian authorities that they would not carry out reprisals against people returning from camps known to have been used as bases for attacks on government forces. After some delay, the Cambodian authorities committed themselves to ensuring that there would be no such reprisals. The military, police and human rights component of UNTAC assisted in monitoring this, and there were few incidents of harassment of returnees by the Cambodian government.[11]

In its preparations for the safe return of the refugees and displaced people, UNHCR had identified five essential preconditions: peace and security; provision of adequate agricultural land by the government of Cambodia; de-mining of settlements; repair of key repatriation roads and bridges; and strong funding support from donor countries. In the event, as the scale of the undertaking became apparent, these preconditions were often met only in part.[12]

A particular problem in ensuring safe return concerned the huge number of land mines and unexploded ordnance in the country. De-mining and mine awareness operations were slow to be set up and landmines remained a constant threat. As one UNHCR representative stated in late 1991: 'The only de-mining going on now is when people tread on them.'[13] Indeed, landmines continued to be laid, and even when the de-mining operations got underway, there was initially evidence that landmines were being laid more quickly than they were being removed. By the May 1993 elections, UNTAC's small Mine Clearance Training Unit had cleared around 15,000 mines and other unexploded ordnance, out of over eight million mines estimated to be scattered around the country.[14]

From June 1992, UNHCR began to implement a number of quick impact projects in areas with large numbers of returnees. By the end of 1994, UNHCR had provided US$9.5 million for around 80 projects including the repair or recon-struction of tertiary roads, bridges, hospitals, dispensaries and schools. These community-based projects proved far more difficult to implement than had been the case in Central America, as local NGOs and grassroots organizations in Cambodia were far less developed and there were only minimal local adminis-trative and social structures. This problem was addressed to some extent by close cooperation between UNHCR and UNDP, which led to the establishment of the Cambodian Repatriation and Resettlement operation (CARERE). Under this operation, UNDP progressively assumed responsibility for reintegration efforts as UNHCR phased out its activities.[15]

Access to land

The question of the returnees' access to land for settlement and cultivation proved to be a complex one, and UNHCR had to adjust its policy on the matter as events unfolded. Initially, UNHCR told the refugees in the Thai camps that they could select destinations in rural areas and that they would receive two hectares of arable land, in addition to assistance packages containing basic household and agricultural items.

Most of them chose land in the northwest, near the border, which they knew to be fertile, but initial assessments of available land proved unreliable, not least because of the large number of landmines. UNHCR eventually concluded that there was simply not enough unutilized and suitable land in the country—let alone in the desired northwestern provinces—for its plan to be viable.[16]

This miscalculation was illustrative of the larger problems facing the peace-keeping mission. Cambodia had been cut off from the outside world for so long that major initiatives were based largely on out-of-date or inaccurate data. Relying on data produced in a 1989 survey, UNHCR policy-makers in Geneva and Bangkok were unaware of subsequent economic changes in the country that had affected land values and availability.[17]

In May 1992, UNHCR presented the returnees with several new options, including that of receiving agricultural land but not necessarily in their area of choice, and the option of receiving a cash grant and other material assistance. In the end, about 85 per cent of Cambodian families opted for the cash grant, a food allocation and a household/agricultural kit. UNHCR was criticized at the time for having initially raised false expectations among the refugees that they would automatically receive land upon their return. At first, the Cambodian authorities were concerned about the effects that the cash grant would have. They feared that returnees with cash in hand would flock to already crowded urban centres, but their concerns proved unfounded. Most returnees settled with surviving relatives, largely in rural areas.

The 1993 elections and subsequent developments

The deadline of the May 1993 elections exerted considerable pressure on the repatriation operation. Virtually all of the refugees repatriated in advance of the elections, leading the commander of the military component of UNTAC to describe the repatriation operation as 'astonishingly successful'.[18] UNTAC failed, however, to achieve one of its principal objectives: the disarming and demobilization of the military factions. The Khmer Rouge, which had led the genocidal regime of the 1970s, withdrew from the demobilization agreements and remained in armed strongholds with a sizeable number of Cambodians brought in from the border camps. Sporadic fighting between government forces and the Khmer Rouge took place throughout the period of UNTAC's presence in Cambodia, resulting in the renewed displacement of several thousand people, many of whom were recent returnees.[19] UNTAC's efforts to create a civilian police force and an effective civil administration also foundered.

Despite the prevailing security situation and widespread fears that the elections would be disrupted, the May 1993 elections were remarkably free of violence. In the elections, the United National Front for an Independent, Peaceful and Cooperative Cambodia (Funcinpec), led by Prince Ranariddh, secured the largest share of the seats. Although the Cambodian People's Party, led by Hun Sen at first contested the result, it later joined a coalition government with Funcinpec, which was co-headed by Prince Ranariddh and Hun Sen as first and second prime ministers. Almost the entire staff of UNTAC departed within a few months of the elections, and UNHCR began scaling down its operations soon after.

The exodus of thousands of international staff over such a short period raised concerns about the still unfulfilled conditions of the peace accords. In particular, the failure of the factions to disarm contributed to continuing violence and further displacement both within Cambodia and to neighbouring countries. In July 1997, Hun Sen seized power. A year later, his party secured victory in a general election which was alleged by opposition parties to have involved widespread fraud. Although the Khmer Rouge leader, Pol Pot, died in April 1998, and some Khmer Rouge leaders have been arrested, many others have been given amnesties. Since then, however, an agreement has been reached between the Cambodian government and the United Nations on the composition of a tribunal to try the Khmer Rouge leadership.

The Mozambican repatriation

Soon after the Cambodian repatriation, another major repatriation operation began, this time in Mozambique. The large-scale return of Mozambican refugees followed a peace agreement which brought to an end more than three decades of armed conflict in the country. Between 1964 and 1975, the conflict had consisted of a struggle for independence from Portugal by the the Mozambique Liberation Front (*Frente de Libertação de Moçambique*, or Frelimo). After independence was achieved in 1975, war broke out again, this time between Frelimo and the opposition forces of the Mozambique National Resistance (*Resistência Nacional Moçambicana*, or Renamo).

It was largely the dire economic conditions in the country that led the Frelimo government to start abandoning its socialist economic policies in the 1980s. South Africa's withdrawal of support to Renamo at the beginning of the 1990s had also deprived the resistance group of essential support. But it was poverty, above all, that drove the parties to the negotiating table. A severe drought that began in 1992 worsened the already dismal conditions and made it impossible for the government or Renamo to continue to support their armies. Beginning in May 1991, the two factions began negotiations which eventually led to the signing of the General Peace Agreement for Mozambique in October 1992. By that time, much of the country's infrastructure had been destroyed and more than a third of the population had been uprooted at least once. Out of a population of 16 million, more than 1.7 million people had sought refuge in neighbouring countries, some four million had been internally displaced, and at least a million people had been killed.[20]

Repatriation from six countries

By far the largest number of Mozambican refugees—some 1.3 million—were living in Malawi, where most of them had been living in camps since the early 1980s [see Box 5.2]. More than 400,000 others were in South Africa, Swaziland, Tanzania, Zambia and Zimbabwe.

As with the repatriation operation in Cambodia, UNHCR operated within the framework of a wider UN peacekeeping and peacebuilding operation. The UN Operation in Mozambique (ONUMOZ) was established in December 1992 and comprised some 7,500 troops, police and civilian observers. It included an Office for Humanitarian Assistance Coordination, which was responsible for coordinating and monitoring humanitarian assistance, including the reintegration of refugees and internally displaced people.

Repatriation to Mozambique, 1992–94   Map 6.1

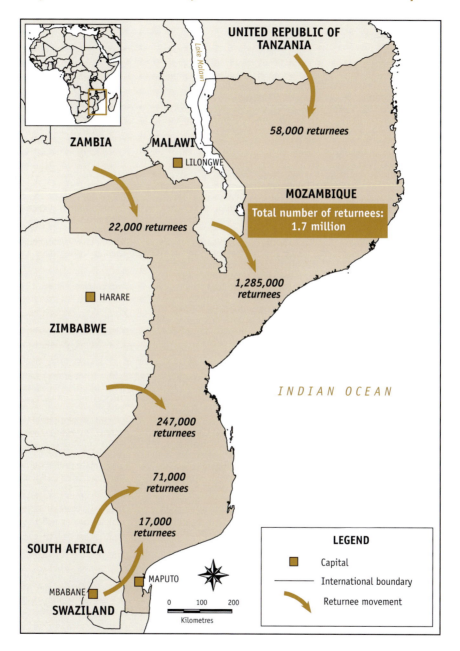

UNITED REPUBLIC OF TANZANIA

Lake Malawi

58,000 returnees

ZAMBIA   MALAWI

■ LILONGWE

MOZAMBIQUE

**Total number of returnees:
1.7 million**

22,000 returnees

1,285,000
returnees

■ HARARE

ZIMBABWE

INDIAN OCEAN

247,000
returnees

71,000
returnees

17,000
returnees

SOUTH AFRICA

MBABANE ■

■ MAPUTO

SWAZILAND

0   100   200
Kilometres

LEGEND

■ Capital

—— International boundary

➤ Returnee movement

Once again, the refugees began repatriating of their own accord even before the peace agreement was signed. The bulk of returns were spontaneous, especially from Malawi, where most refugees had easy access to Mozambique from the camps. Organized transport was provided only for vulnerable groups of refugees, such as unaccompanied children, female-headed households, the elderly, and those travelling

Box 6.3   Human rights and refugees

Violations of internationally recognized human rights are a prime cause of forced displacement. This is so whether people flee persecution directed at them as individuals, or whether they flee *en masse*. In some cases, forced displacement of particular groups of civilians is a specific aim of parties to a conflict. In other cases, factors such as acute poverty and social discrimination—often on racial or ethnic lines—lie at the heart of the problem. Violations of basic economic, social and cultural rights often lead to political instability and violence, which in turn can cause forced displacement. There is a logical connection, therefore, between human rights and refugee protection. As High Commissioner Sadako Ogata put it, 'human rights concerns go to the essence of the cause of refugee movements as well as to the precepts of refugee protection and the solution of refugee problems'.[iii]

Human rights standards

The legal foundation for the link between human rights and refugee protection is found, amongst other places, in Article 14 of the 1948 Universal Declaration of Human Rights, which affirms 'the right of everyone to seek and enjoy in other countries asylum from persecution'. In searching for a definition of the word 'persecution', it is important to start with the human rights standards contained in the three instruments known collectively as the UN Bill of Rights—the Universal Declaration, the 1966 International Covenant on Civil and Political Rights, and the 1966 International Covenant on Economic, Social and Cultural Rights.

Particular categories of refugees and displaced people, such as women and children, also receive special attention through human rights treaties such as the 1979 UN Convention on the Elimination of All Forms of Discrimination against Women and the 1989 UN Convention on the Rights the Child. The 'best interests' principle is of special importance to displaced children, as it pervades all procedures and decisions concerning children, irrespective of their migration status.

The right to be free from torture and cruel treatment is another fundamental right protected by treaties such as the 1984 UN Convention Against Torture and Other Cruel, Inhuman or Degrading Treatment or Punishment, and the 1950 European Convention for the Protection of Human Rights and Fundamental Freedoms. This right also involves a prohibition against forced return of refugees (*refoulement*) and has been shown to apply to asylum seekers who might otherwise face deportation to places where they fear torture. This right is increasingly being used to protect refugees from *refoulement* in circum-stances where national asylum procedures have not proved effective.

Human rights standards also provide an important yardstick for determining the proper treatment of refugees and asylum seekers when they reach a country of asylum. Traditional refugee law, including the 1951 UN Refugee Convention, gives no specific guidance to states on the standards of reception they are expected to provide to asylum seekers. Human rights standards have been particularly helpful in areas that affect the quality of life of refugees and asylum seekers in host countries. This includes issues such as health, housing, education, freedom of movement, detention and family reunification.

Human rights standards also help to define the conditions for the safe and dignified return of refugees and displaced people to their countries or places of origin. Civil, political, economic and social rights provide a principled and objective framework within which return, reintegration, reconciliation and reconstruction activities can take place. For example, a key priority for returnees is often to recover their property, and particularly their homes.

Monitoring, supervision and enforcement mechanisms

In recent decades, the proliferation of human rights standards has been accompanied by a broad range of mechanisms that monitor, supervise and, on occasion, enforce these standards. At the international level, compliance is monitored by UN treaty bodies, such as the committees established under the six main human rights treaties, and by non-treaty-based bodies, such as the UN Commission on Human Rights, whose work often has a direct impact on refugee protection. With their extensive field presence, organizations such as UNHCR have a responsibility to cooperate with these bodies, subject to considerations of security and confidentiality.

Since its creation in 1993, the Office of the UN High Commissioner for Human Rights has emphasized the importance of national human rights structures. It has actively promoted the creation of national human rights bodies that support and implement international standards. These national institutions are becoming increasingly important partners for UNHCR in the promotion and protection of refugee rights. For example, national human rights commissions and independent ombudsmen often have power to investigate and enquire into human rights violations that affect refugees and asylum seekers, such as the legality and conditions of detention. Efforts to strengthen independent judicial bodies and the rule of law are also critical activities at the national level that ensure basic rights of refugees are respected.

Humanitarian organizations and human rights bodies have distinct yet complementary areas of expertise. As UN Secretary-General Kofi Annan stated in 1997, 'human rights are integral to the promotion of peace and security, economic prosperity and social equity'. He emphasized that 'a major task for the United Nations, therefore, is to enhance its human rights programme and fully integrate it into the broad range of the Organization's activities'.[iv]

long distances.[21] Direct assistance with departure, transport and reception was provided to 380,000 refugees (22 per cent of the total), a number comparable with the large-scale repatriation of Cambodian refugees in 1992–93 from camps on the Thai border.[22] The vast majority of the refugees returned to Mozambique well before the elections which were held in October 1994.

Reintegration and reconstruction

The reintegration programmes for returnees which were carried out by UNHCR and other international organizations in Mozambique were even more ambitious than those which had been carried out in Central America and Cambodia. Of the total UNHCR funding of US$145 million for the Mozambican operation, some US$100 million was spent on reintegration projects. Moreover, the reintegration programme provided assistance to four times as many people as were directly assisted by UNHCR during the actual repatriation.[23]

Protecting the returnees in Mozambique proved easier than in Cambodia. In the latter, sporadic fighting continued even after the peace agreements were signed, and the United Nations failed to demobilize and disarm the Khmer Rouge. By contrast, in Mozambique almost all fighting ended after the peace accords were signed. There were only a few isolated ceasefire violations and these were handled successfully through a ceasefire commission. Unlike Cambodia, the cooperation of all parties was ultimately secured in Mozambique, even though Renamo withdrew from the ceasefire super-vision and control commission for sev-eral months in 1993. Although demobilization was delayed, it was eventually achieved with con-siderable success in Mozambique. Even in areas where supporters of both the previous warring parties settled, there were few security incidents. The peace agreement provided for a general

Estimated annual refugee returns worldwide, 1975–99

Figure 6.1

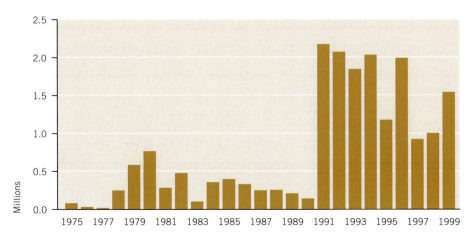

amnesty and did not seek to punish war crimes committed against the civilian population. Com-munities employed their own traditional means to seek justice and reconciliation, rather than relying on international intervention.

UNHCR's field presence proved vital when the ONUMOZ mission left in December 1994. Following its departure, UNHCR, UNDP and the World Bank worked closely together to design complementary programmes. UNHCR also collaborated with UN mine clearance operations but soon shifted its focus to promoting mine awareness, because of the slow progress in clearing mines.[24] The repatriation operation officially ended in July 1996, and UNHCR retained 20 field offices in Mozambique until the end of the year.

International organizations, including UNHCR, assisted with the rehabilitation of schools, clinics, wells, roads and other infrastructure throughout the country. More than 1,500 quick impact projects were initiated. Funding from donors was readily available and there were numerous agencies involved in the reconstruction work. The reintegration programme helped stabilize and strengthen communities that had been torn apart during the war. As in Central America, the contacts which were made amongst former adversaries as a result of these quick impact projects helped reduce tensions and build stability.

Aldo Ajello, the UN Secretary-General's Special Representative in Mozambique, attributed the success of the ONUMOZ operation largely to three main factors: first, the new opportunities which had opened up as a result of the end of the Cold War and the breakdown of apartheid in South Africa; second, the strong will of the Mozambican people to build peace; and third, the fact that the international community had been willing to commit substantial funds and other resources from the moment the peace agreement was signed.[25]

Changing approaches to repatriation and reintegration

During the 1990s, it became increasingly clear that in post-conflict situations, refugees often go back to situations of fragile peace where tensions remain high, where there is still chronic political instability and where the infrastructure is devastated. Such countries are often precariously perched between the prospect of continued peace and a return to war. In such situations, the prevention of renewed fighting and further refugee flight depends largely on efforts made by local, regional and international actors to ensure durable peace.

In the few years between the refugee returns to Namibia in 1989 and the returns to Mozambique in 1993–94, UNHCR's role in repatriation operations changed profoundly. In previous decades, UNHCR's involvement in repatriation operations was generally short-term and small-scale and the organization focused primarily on ensuring that refugees returned safely. The repatriation operations in Central America, Cambodia and Mozambique involved a new and broader approach. In each case, UNHCR played a major role in UN peacebuilding operations, and humanitarian activities were integrated into a wider strategic and political framework aimed at ensuring reconciliation, reintegration and reconstruction.

It also became increasingly clear during the 1990s that peacebuilding efforts need to be sustained over time if they are to be effective in helping societies overcome the animosities, trauma and despair engendered by years of war and exile. During the optimistic years of the early 1990s, donors contributed generously to UN peace-keeping and peacebuilding efforts. In subsequent years, however, they often proved unwilling to sustain such funding levels over long periods. It proved particularly difficult to gain the necessary donor support for programmes in countries of little strategic importance, particularly as the spotlight of the international media moved away. As early as 1993, financial support for UNHCR was already falling far short of expected needs. This problem was to continue throughout the rest of the decade.

7 Asylum in the industrialized world

The 1951 UN Refugee Convention was primarily drawn up in response to the mass displacement in Europe at the end of the Second World War. Half a century later, it is in Europe, and in the world's other industrialized countries, that the institution of asylum is facing some of its greatest challenges. Anxious to protect their borders from unwanted immigration, and suspicious of the motivations of many of those seeking asylum, governments of industrialized countries have adopted a range of new measures to control and restrict access to their territory. For refugees fleeing persecution, these measures have in many cases severely affected their ability to gain access to asylum procedures and safety.

This chapter examines refugee policy developments in Europe, North America, Australia, New Zealand and Japan. The first section assesses European countries' approaches to refugee protection, focusing on developments during the 1980s and 1990s. These include efforts to combat illegal migration and their consequences for refugees and asylum seekers, moves to harmonize asylum policies within the European Union, and responses to the massive displacement resulting from war in the Balkans. It also traces the transformation since 1989 of countries in Central and Eastern Europe from refugee-producing to refugee-receiving countries.

The second and third sections describe how in the United States, Canada and Australia, which are all traditional countries of immigration, government-supported resettlement programmes have offered millions of refugees a new start since the end of the Second World War. These sections examine how, in spite of the hospitality shown to refugees through these programmes, political interests have repeatedly threatened to undermine governments' obligations towards asylum seekers. In both North America and Australia, government policies have increasingly been influenced by the need to respond to growing numbers of asylum seekers arriving spontaneously.

One of the main challenges now faced by all industrialized states in meeting their obligations towards refugees is that of dealing with the phenomenon of 'mixed flows' of refugees and other migrants, and the related phenomenon of 'mixed-motive migration'. Many people leave their home countries for a combination of political, economic and other reasons.[1] This mixture of motives is one factor creating a perception of widespread abuse of asylum systems, which is often manipulated by politicians and the media.

In addition, the illegal trafficking and smuggling of people is increasingly becoming a complicating feature of the migration landscape. With regular arrival routes closed, many refugees are turning to smugglers to reach safety, in spite of the dangers and the financial costs involved. Asylum seekers who resort to human smugglers seriously compromise their claims in the eyes of many states. When

An asylum seeker from Nigeria being interviewed at the Krome detention centre in Miami, United States.
(UNHCR/B. PRESS/1999)

combined with the increased tendency of states to detain asylum seekers, the effect is to stigmatize further asylum seekers in the public mind as criminals.

States have legitimate interests in controlling access to their territory, but they also have international legal obligations to provide protection to those fleeing persecution. Industrialized states have particular responsibilities in matters of refugee protection. Not only were they instrumental in drafting the major international refugee and human rights instruments half a century ago, but more importantly, the example they set will inevitably influence the way in which refugees are treated by other states in the years ahead.

The evolution of asylum policy in Europe

At the end of the Second World War, Europe faced a massive humanitarian challenge. While the continent struggled to rebuild its shattered infrastructure and economy, over 40 million displaced people needed to be repatriated or resettled. In addition, in 1956, some 200,000 people fled following the Soviet crushing of the Hungarian uprising, and in 1968 a smaller number left Czechoslovakia after the Soviet suppression of the 'Prague spring'. While the 1951 UN Refugee Convention provided the international legal framework for the protection of these refugees, asylum in Europe—and indeed in the West in general—also had an ideological tinge. It reflected a broad political commitment to take in refugees from communist countries.

Refugees from other continents first began arriving in Europe in large numbers during the 1970s. They included refugees fleeing from Latin America as a result of the military coups in Chile and Uruguay in 1973, and then in Argentina in 1976. Refugees from these countries found refuge in both Western and Eastern Europe [see Box 5.4]. Also, although the majority of refugees fleeing from countries in Indochina after 1975 were resettled in North America, some 230,000 were resettled in Western Europe.

By the 1980s, increasing numbers of people from all over the world were fleeing directly to Europe. Unlike the organized resettlement of Indochinese refugees from countries of first asylum, these were unplanned movements. Spontaneous arrivals of asylum seekers had been rising since the early 1970s, and in the mid-1980s they began to cause serious concern. The number of asylum seekers in Western Europe increased from under 70,000 in 1983 to over 200,000 in 1989. This increase was linked to the number of internal conflicts and serious human rights violations in Africa, Asia, Latin America and the Middle East. It was also due to changes in immigration policy during the economic recession which followed the steep increase in oil prices in the 1970s. No longer in need of migrant workers, many European countries ceased to encourage labour migration, although family reunion continued. As a result, at least some would-be migrants turned to the asylum channel. Improved communications, easier access to air transport and growing numbers of people seeking better economic and social opportunities world-wide were other important factors.[2]

These new, non-European asylum seekers rarely fitted the Cold War mould. Tamil asylum seekers from Sri Lanka were among the first groups to arrive independently in large numbers, and they raised particular problems for European states during the 1980s. They included people fleeing for a variety of reasons, including persecution and the indiscriminate effects of an ill-understood civil war.[3] Their arrival generated fierce debate about states' obligations towards people who travel half-way around the world to seek asylum, when they might have found an alternative closer to home—in this case in Tamil Nadu in India. Many European governments suspected, often unfairly, that the primary motivation of these asylum seekers was economic. Most European governments imposed visa requirements on Sri Lankan nationals as a result. There was great controversy, however, over proposals to return the Tamil asylum seekers to a place still riven with fierce civil war.

Set against the number of refugees in the developing world, the proportion arriving in Western Europe was still modest. But the case-by-case determination of refugee status required by European asylum procedures, and the need to provide at least minimal social assistance to the asylum seekers, meant that the administrative

Asylum applications submitted in Europe, North America, Australia and New Zealand, 1980–2000

Figure 7.1

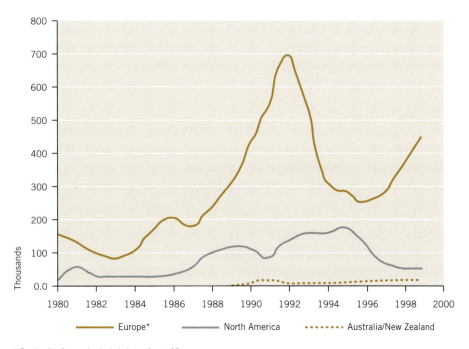

* For details of countries included, see Annex 10.
Source: Governments.

and financial burden escalated. According to one estimate, the total cost of administering asylum procedures and providing social welfare benefits to refugee claimants in 13 of the major industrialized states rose from around US$500 million in 1983 to around US$7 billion in 1990.[4] The latter figure represented over 12 times the global UNHCR budget that year.

Asylum after the fall of the Berlin Wall

The fall of the Berlin Wall in November 1989 put the international refugee protection system in Western Europe under even more serious pressure than had been the case during the 1980s. Suddenly, people from the former communist bloc were free to leave their countries. There were concerns about uncontrollable floods of people pouring into Western Europe. The chaotic exodus from Albania to Italy during the 1990s—particularly in 1991 and 1997—and the mass arrival of refugees from the former Yugoslavia from 1992 brought home to Western European governments the fact that they were not immune from forced population movements originating in their immediate vicinity.

Asylum applications in Western Europe peaked at nearly 700,000 in 1992. As a result of its liberal asylum laws and its geographic position, the Federal Republic of Germany received by far the largest proportion of them—over 60 per cent that year, nearly half of whom were Romanians and Bulgarians. Most did not have a well-founded fear of persecution, but were anxious to exercise their new-found freedom of movement. They quickly learned that the right to leave one's country is not automatically matched by a right to enter another country.

A new defensiveness appeared in Western European countries' asylum policies. Receiving states were not prepared for such large numbers. Existing capacity was quickly overwhelmed, and states proved unwilling to commit resources commensurate with the scale of the problem. At the same time, tens of thousands of asylum seekers also arrived from countries outside Europe, including Afghanistan, Angola, Ghana, Iran, Iraq, Nigeria, Pakistan, Somalia, Sri Lanka, Viet Nam and Zaire.

The prevailing refugee policy framework, with its emphasis on assessment of each individual claim, appeared increasingly ill-equipped to cope. In 1992, High Commissioner Sadako Ogata voiced her concern about the future of refugee protection: 'As we move into the 1990s there is no doubt that Europe is at a crossroads. Will Europe turn its back on those who are forced to move, or will it strengthen its long tradition of safeguarding the rights of the oppressed and the uprooted? Will Europe build new walls, knowing that walls did not stop those who were fleeing totalitarian persecution in the past?'[5]

It was in this context that European governments decided to deal with the large-scale influx of asylum seekers from the wars in the former Yugoslavia by establishing temporary protection regimes. In the Federal Republic of Germany, which hosted the largest numbers of refugees from the region, the government tried in vain to persuade other European states to engage in 'burden-sharing' as a complement to temporary protection regimes. Then, in 1993, Germany amended its constitution to

Box 7.1 European Union asylum policy

Attempts by member states of the European Union (EU) to create an 'ever closer union' have included moves to harmonize their policies on immigration and asylum. The documents outlined below are a combination of binding conventions and non-binding inter-governmental agreements to which most, but not always all, member states are party.

1986 Single European Act

This committed European Community member states to creating a single internal market by the end of 1992. Although this has been achieved for goods, services and capital, free movement of people has proved more elusive.

1990 Dublin Convention

This established common criteria for EU member states to determine the state responsible for examining an asylum request. It seeks to put an end to the practice of asylum seekers moving or being moved from country to country with their claim either being assessed several times or not at all. It entered into force for all 15 EU member states on 1 September 1997, although states began to implement it well before then.

1990 Schengen Convention

This seeks to reinforce external border controls to permit free movement within participating states. It includes provisions to strengthen police and judicial cooperation and to introduce common visa policies and carrier sanctions. It followed the similar 1985 Schengen Agreement between six EU member states. The Convention came into force on 1 September 1993 and began to be implemented in individual states from March 1995. All EU member states except Denmark, Ireland and the United Kingdom are parties.

1992 Treaty on European Union

This treaty—also known as the Maastricht Treaty—established the European Union. It incorporated existing European Community issues and increased inter-governmental cooperation on issues including 'justice and home affairs'. This includes measures to harmonize asylum and immigration policies and the introduction of the concept of EU citizenship. It came into force on 1 November 1993.

1992 London Resolutions

European Community ministers responsible for immigration approved three resolutions in London in 1992. They defined 'manifestly unfounded' asylum applications, host (or safe) third countries which asylum seekers transited and to which they can be returned, and countries where there is generally no serious risk of persecution. These concepts were aimed at accelerating procedures to assess asylum claims. The resolutions are not binding, but they have been applied in EU member states and further afield.

Other EU Council resolutions and recommendations

During the 1990s, the EU Council of Ministers approved a series of resolutions, recommendations and joint positions, which are also not legally binding. Among the instruments adopted are two recommendations on readmission agreements, approved in 1994 and 1995. These established a model agreement for returning asylum seekers whose applications for asylum had been rejected or deemed unfounded. Between 1993 and 1996, a series of 'burden-sharing' measures set out principles of solidarity in situations of large-scale influx. In June 1995, the Council of Ministers approved a resolution on minimum guarantees for asylum procedures, outlining procedural rights and obligations. In March 1996, a Joint Position was agreed on the harmonized application of the definition of the term 'refugee'. Many of these measures have been described by critics as representing harmonization on the basis of a lowest common denominator.

1997 Treaty of Amsterdam

This includes a commitment by member states to develop common immigration and asylum policies within five years. Until then, decision-making will continue to be on an inter-governmental basis, thus allowing some states, such as those party to the Schengen Convention, to opt for closer co-operation even if others do not wish to do so. After five years, the development of common asylum policies will come under the Council of Ministers' normal decision-making procedures, where unanimity is not always required. The European Parliament has acquired a limited consultative role in developing these policies, while the European Court of Justice is permitted to issue preliminary rulings and to act as a last court of appeal in interpreting the relevant EU treaty provisions. The treaty came into effect on 1 May 1999.

1999 European Council meeting in Tampere

In October 1999, EU heads of state and government meeting in Tampere, Finland, reaffirmed the importance they attached 'to absolute respect of the right to seek asylum'.[i] They 'agreed to work towards establishing a Common European Asylum System, based on the full and inclusive application of the [1951 UN Refugee] Convention, thus ensuring that nobody is sent back to persecution, i.e. maintaining the principle of *non-refoulement*'. This common European asylum system was initially to include 'a clear and workable determination of the State responsible for the examination of an asylum application, common standards for a fair and efficient asylum procedure, common minimum conditions of reception of asylum seekers, and the approximation of rules on the recognition and content of the refugee status'. Subsequently, 'measures on subsidiary forms of protection offering an appropriate status to any person in need of such protection' were to be agreed.

remove its unqualified guarantee of a right to asylum, prompting the development of new policies aimed at both limiting the admission of asylum seekers and facilitating their return to countries through which they passed. Other governments across Europe introduced similar restrictive measures, based on three resolutions approved by European Community ministers responsible for immigration in December 1992 [see Box 7.1].

As channels for legal entry began to close, asylum seekers, along with other migrants, turned increasingly to smugglers and traffickers to reach Western Europe. Many used false documents or destroyed their papers *en route*. This, in turn, reinforced public scepticism about the real motives of asylum seekers. In an effort to counter the growing hostility toward asylum seekers, support groups made efforts to promote more positive images of refugees and to seek public support for refugee protection. Throughout this period, these advocacy groups were reluctant to acknowledge the need for unsuccessful asylum seekers to be returned to their countries of origin—a factor which helped to polarize the debate on asylum issues. At the same time, certain political parties and elements of the media often appeared to be more concerned with playing to racist and xenophobic, anti-immigrant sentiments in an effort to win votes or boost sales. In October 1998, for example, one local newspaper in the United Kingdom, the *Dover Express*, went as far as to describe asylum seekers as 'human sewage'.[6]

Main country/territory of origin of asylum seekers in Western Europe, 1990–99*

Figure 7.2

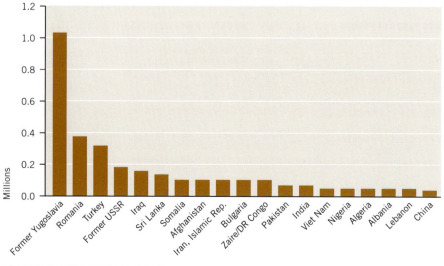

* For details of countries included, see Annex 11.

'Fortress Europe'

The new, restrictive policies introduced in Western Europe, which were aimed at combating illegal immigration and abuse of asylum systems, shifted the balance between refugee protection and immigration control. The term 'fortress Europe' became a shorthand for this phenomenon.

Four types of measures were taken to tackle the 'mixed flows' of irregular migrants and refugees with which European countries were confronted. These measures tended to affect both groups indiscriminately and had the effect of making it more difficult for people seeking protection to reach a country where they could ask for it. UNHCR warned as early as 1986: 'Piecemeal restrictive measures, unilaterally adopted, cannot suffice. Their consequence, more often than not, is to shift rather than lift the burden and to set in motion a self-defeating chain of events . . . In the longer term they cannot fail to bring about a general lowering of accepted international standards.'[7]

First, countries sought to adopt 'non-arrival' policies aimed at preventing improperly documented aliens, who included potential asylum seekers, from reaching Europe. Visa requirements and 'carrier sanctions'—fines against transport companies for bringing in passengers without proper documentation—became widespread. Some countries began to post immigration liaison officers abroad to 'intercept' improperly documented migrants and to prevent them from travelling to these countries.

Second, for those asylum seekers who managed to arrive at the borders despite these efforts, 'diversion' policies were designed, shifting to other countries the responsibility for assessing asylum seekers' claims and providing protection. This approach was made possible not least by the emergence of Central European countries as places where refugees could, at least in theory, find protection. After 1989, most of these countries rapidly acceded to the 1951 UN Refugee Convention and, during the 1990s, UNHCR, the Council of Europe and other agencies, and Western European governments devoted considerable effort to building the capacity of these countries to cope with asylum seekers and refugees.

As a result, Western European governments drew up lists of 'safe third countries' to the east of the European Union, creating a kind of 'buffer zone'.[8] They concluded re-admission agreements on the return of illegal entrants with Central and Eastern European and other governments, and began sending asylum seekers back to 'safe' countries through which they had travelled. These agreements rarely contained any particular guarantees for asylum seekers. They created a risk of 'chain deportations', whereby asylum seekers could be passed from one state to another, without an assurance that their request for protection would eventually be examined. UNHCR described this practice as 'clearly contrary to basic protection principles' and as not providing sufficient protection against *refoulement*.[9] Not surprisingly, the Central and Eastern European countries, with the encouragement of their neighbours to the west, themselves introduced similar controls to reduce the number of arrivals.

Third, governments increasingly opted for a restrictive application of the 1951 UN Refugee Convention in an effort to exclude certain categories of claimants from the scope of the refugee definition. In some countries this continues to result in situations where people who have suffered persecution at the hands of 'non-state agents' are not considered to be refugees, and are often offered a lesser form of protection with fewer rights and benefits [see Box 7.2]. As a result of this and other factors, the proportion of applicants recognized as refugees under the Convention has declined. Many of those denied refugee status are given the possibility of remaining in the countries where they applied for asylum, but with a lesser status than formal refugee status granted under the 1951 Convention. Examples include "B' status', 'humanitarian status' and 'exceptional leave to remain'.[10] Thus, their need for protection is acknowledged, but the receiving countries' obligations—especially with regard to family reunification and the issuing of Convention travel documents—are kept to a minimum. The multiplicity of statuses gave rise to considerable confusion in the public mind about who is a 'real' refugee.

Finally, various 'deterrent' measures were introduced, including the increasingly widespread automatic detention of asylum seekers, the denial of social assistance, and the restriction of access to employment.[11] In addition, restrictions were placed on the right of refugees already in the country to bring their family members to join them.

Searching for a common European Union policy

Western European countries' efforts to adapt their asylum and immigration policies coincided with efforts to achieve closer economic and political integration through the creation of a single European market. This involved the removal of all internal barriers to commerce and the free movement of people within the European Community, which became the European Union when the Maastricht Treaty on European Union entered into force in 1993. The wish to remove obstacles to trade and other flows within the European Union went in parallel with the desire to maintain control over the movement of people from non-member countries. At the same time, governments feared that freedom of movement within the European Union would create numerous new problems in the immigration and asylum arena. The result was a complex and protracted process, as the 12—and later 15—member states of the European Union tried to 'harmonize' their policies relating to border controls, immigration and asylum [see Box 7.1].[12]

Much of the immigration and asylum-related activity during the 1990s focused on coordinating and tightening member states' admission policies. The 1990 Schengen Convention included provisions for reinforced police and judicial cooperation, common visa policies, and the strengthening of carrier sanctions. The 1990 Dublin Convention listed criteria to determine, among contracting parties, which member state was responsible for examining an asylum request. It was designed to prevent asylum seekers from 'shopping around' for the 'best' country to hear their claim, and to solve the problem of asylum seekers for whom no country was willing to take responsibility, a phenomenon known as 'refugees in orbit'.

Box 7.2   Non-state agents of persecution

Picture yourself in a village where government troops and rebels harass you, demand food, beat up your family and threaten to kill you or cut off your hands. You decide to flee from an intolerable situation and request asylum in another country. When you describe your plight to an immigration officer, you explain that the most serious threats and harassment came from the rebels. The immigration officer looks gravely at you and says that you are not a real refugee because it was not the government forces that persecuted you, but an armed group which is not an instrument of the state. Of course, you could not care less whether you are tortured by one or the other. But some countries do. They do not recognize as refugees people who are persecuted by so-called 'non-state agents'.

The 1951 UN Refugee Convention provides protection against persecution. Persecution is not defined, nor is anything said about the perpetrators of such persecution. This has led to much debate about the extent of the Convention's protection. When one speaks of persecution, one often thinks of sinister state services, the use of torture by police officers, or soldiers oppressing civilians. At the time of the Holocaust, an entire state machinery was engaged in the persecution of particular people. When the drafters of the Convention formulated the definition of a 'refugee', they were no doubt thinking primarily of persecution by state services.

One of the main purposes of the 1951 UN Refugee Convention is to prevent people from being returned to places where they may suffer serious violations of human rights or persecution. It does not say that a state must be responsible for the persecution. Any group which holds substantial power in a country can persecute. UNHCR has therefore con-

sistently advanced the view that the Convention applies to any person who has a well-founded fear of persecution, regardless of who is responsible for the persecution. UNHCR's position is shared by the overwhelming majority of the states party to the Convention. In some countries, however, claims to refugee status will fail if the feared persecution emanates from non-state actors and the government of the country of origin is unable or unwilling to provide protection. This minority view is held by France, Germany, Italy and Switzerland.

Other international human rights treaties, such as the 1984 Convention Against Torture and Other Cruel, Inhuman or Degrading Treatment or Punishment and the 1950 European Convention for the Protection of Human Rights and Fundamental Freedoms, make no distinction between the state and other actors who are responsible for torture or other inhuman or degrading treatment. A person should be protected against such treatment regardless of who is the perpetrator.

The power of enforcement through police and armed forces no longer rests exclusively with states. A country like Somalia does not have a government with firm control over its territory and its people; indeed, it has no government that enjoys international recognition. Instead, it has fiefdoms where armed bands and warlords control different stretches of land. The dominant political and military power in Afghanistan, the Taliban, is not recognized by some other countries as a legitimate state agent. In countries such as Angola, Colombia and Sri Lanka, groups other than the government exercise power over entire regions.

Persecution is not the exclusive domain of the state, or even of non-governmental armed groups. It can

also be perpetrated by a sect, a clan, or a family. Traditional customs may amount to persecution. If the government is unable or unwilling to suppress such customs, people may be forced to flee their country to save their life, liberty or physical integrity. In 1985, the UNHCR Executive Committee recognized that the vulnerable situation of women frequently exposes them to physical violence, sexual abuse and discrimination. It agreed that women who face harsh or inhuman treatment because they have transgressed the social mores of the society in which they live may be included under the terms of the 1951 UN Refugee Convention.

An example of gender-based persecution is the case of two Pakistani women who claimed refugee status in the United Kingdom on the grounds that they were maltreated to the point of being persecuted by their husbands. According to the House of Lords, the highest panel of judges in the United Kingdom, they were refugees under the Convention since the government of Pakistan was unwilling to do anything to protect them due to the fact that they were women.[ii]

Societies which discriminate against women or homosexuals may condone persecution on the grounds of sex or sexual orientation. Some societies permit, even encourage, female genital mutilation. For certain women or girls, this custom may amount to persecution. If they refuse to submit to the custom and, by doing so, 'transgress the social mores', will the state step in to protect them? In the absence of state protection, their only way to avoid serious harm is to flee their country and become refugees.

While the Schengen and Dublin Conventions are binding on states which have ratified them, other harmonization activities have taken place outside a binding framework in a far from transparent inter-governmental process. Even so, agreement among European Union countries more often than not could only be reached at the level of the lowest common denominator. In one of the most crucial discussions, European Union governments sought to reach agreement on how to interpret the refugee definition given in the 1951 UN Refugee Convention. Largely because of Germany's narrow interpretation of the definition, and France's desire to limit its obligations *vis-à-vis* Algerians fleeing their country, the European Union's March 1996 Joint Position on a harmonized application of the definition of the term 'refugee' takes a restrictive approach, regarding persecution as being 'generally' at the hands of the state.[13] As a result, the treatment of persons fleeing persecution perpetrated by non-state actors continues to differ from one state to another. Indeed, there has been considerable variation among member states in their implementation of supposedly harmonized policies on asylum.[14]

Within the European Union, some countries receive significantly higher numbers of asylum applications than others. Having taken in 350,000 Bosnians in the early

Central European asylum applications, 1990–99*

Figure 7.3

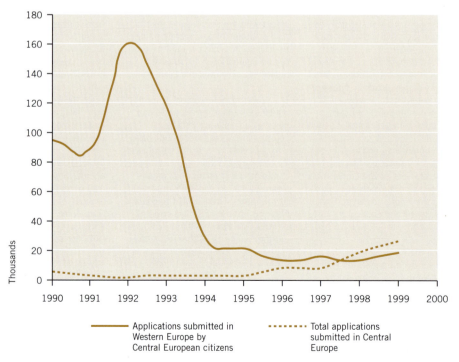

Legend:
— Applications submitted in Western Europe by Central European citizens
····· Total applications submitted in Central Europe

* Western Europe comprises the European Union, Norway and Switzerland. Central Europe comprises Bulgaria, Czech Republic, Hungary, Poland, Romania and Slovakia.
Source: Governments.

1990s, the German government pushed hard for some kind of burden-sharing arrangement. In 1995, the European Union adopted a non-binding Resolution on burden-sharing with regard to the admission and residence of displaced persons on a temporary basis.[15] The mass outflow of refugees from Bosnia and Herzegovina in the mid-1990s and from Kosovo in the late 1990s meant that the issue of burden-sharing was a prominent issue in Europe throughout the decade. It remains a contentious one. Germany's share of Western Europe's asylum applications nevertheless declined from 63 per cent at the beginning of the 1990s to 23 per cent in 1999.

The process of harmonizing asylum policies in Europe continues. UNHCR has endorsed these efforts where they have been aimed at making asylum systems fairer, more efficient and more predictable, not only for the benefit of governments but also for refugees and asylum seekers themselves. In many cases, however, it is the standard of the lowest common denominator which has prevailed, resulting in diminished rather than enhanced protection for refugees.

Temporary protection and the former Yugoslavia

Until the 1990s, it was generally assumed that when individuals were recognized as refugees in Europe, they would be able to remain in their country of asylum indefinitely. During the conflict in the former Yugoslavia, however, a new approach to asylum was introduced whereby states offered temporary protection to people fleeing the conflict, meaning that they would be expected to return once they conflict was over. UNHCR endorses temporary protection as an emergency response to an

Annual number of asylum seekers granted asylum in Europe, 1990–99
Figure 7.4

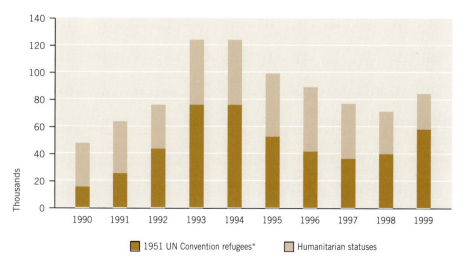

* 1999 figure excludes Austria and France. For further details and explanations, see Annex 10.
Source: Governments.

Box 7.3

Funding trends

Global government spending on humanitarian assistance has increased steadily in volume over the last 50 years. It rose dramatically in the early 1990s, peaking at US$5.7 billion in 1994. As a share of gross domestic product (GDP), however, humanitarian assistance dropped between 1990 and 1998 from 0.03 per cent to 0.02 per cent, or 20 cents out of each US$1,000.[iii]

The proportion of official development assistance (ODA) allocated by governments to humanitarian assistance, as opposed to long-term development, also grew significantly in the early 1990s. At its height, in 1994, it represented 10 per cent of total ODA. The proportion fell in the latter part of the decade, however, dropping to around six per cent of total ODA by 1998.[iv]

While the total volume of government funding for humanitarian operations has increased, the proportion of this channelled through international organizations such as UNHCR, as opposed to that given directly to governments of recipient countries, or channelled through non-governmental organizations in the donor's own country, has decreased. Increasingly, governments are giving priority to bilateral funding arrangements rather than multilateral assistance.

UNHCR expenditure and funding sources

UNHCR's budget has risen dramatically over the 50 years of its existence, as the extent and scope of the organization's work has expanded. From a budget of only US$300,000 in 1951, annual expenditure grew to around US$100 million in the mid-1970s. Two significant increases then took place in the late 1970s and early 1990s.

The first major increase was between 1978 and 1980, when expenditure more than tripled, from US$145 million to US$510 million.

This was at the time of the major refugee emergencies in Indochina. The second, equally large increase, was between 1990 and 1993, when expenditure more than doubled, from US$564 million to US$1.3 billion. This increase was mainly because of the large repatriation operations at the beginning of the decade and the major relief operations in northern Iraq and the former Yugoslavia. Expenditure subsequently dropped to US$887 million in 1998, and then rose to just over US$1 billion in 1999 as a result of the Kosovo crisis. None of these figures take into account contributions of goods such as tents and medicines, or assistance with transportation and other services. If these were taken into account, the figures would be significantly higher.

UNHCR's relative spending in different regions has reflected the changing geographical focus and operational scope of the organization. In the early 1960s, more than half of UNHCR's expenditure was on

Contributions to UNHCR as a percentage of GDP by major donors, 1999*　　Figure 7.5

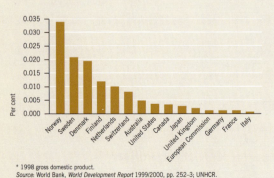

* 1998 gross domestic product.
Source: World Bank, *World Development Report* 1999/2000, pp. 252–3; UNHCR.

Top 15 contributors to UNHCR, 1980–99　　Figure 7.6

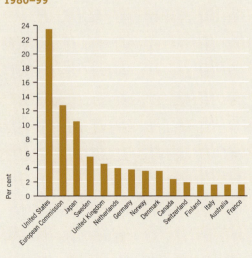

programmes for European refugees still remaining from the Second World War. Less than a decade later, European spending accounted for only seven per cent of the total budget. By 1999, UNHCR had programmes in over 100 countries. In the 1990s, UNHCR spent an average of US$40 to US$50 per year for each 'person of concern'—whether refugee, asylum seeker, returnee, internally dis- placed person or other—although there were significant disparities in per capita expenditure from region to region.

UNHCR's main source of funding has always been voluntary contributions, mainly from governments. During the 1990s, an average of less than three per cent of the organization's total annual income came from the UN regular budget. Most government funding comes from a small number of key industrialized states. In 1999, for example, North America, Japan and western European countries accounted for 97 per cent of

all government contributions to UNHCR.

Increasingly, donor countries tend to earmark funds pledged to UNHCR for particular countries, programmes or projects, depending on their national priorities. In 1999, only 20 per cent of contributions were not earmarked, significantly reducing the organization's flexibility to use funds where they are most needed. In 1999, UNHCR received just over 90 per cent of the funds requested for programmes in the former Yugoslavia, while it received only around 60 per cent of those requested for some of its programmes in Africa. Indeed, the international community spent some US$120 per person of concern to UNHCR in the former Yugoslavia during 1999, which was more than three times the amount spent in West Africa (about US$35 per person). Even after taking into account the different costs due to climatic differences, the disparity remains great.

Like other humanitarian organizations, UNHCR is attempting to broaden its donor base. For instance, UNHCR is encouraging the private sector to donate funds for humanitarian programmes and to participate in post-conflict reconstruction. In 1999, in response largely to events in Kosovo and East Timor, UNHCR received an estimated US$30 million in contri-butions from the general public, foundations, corporations and non-governmental organizations. In some cases, companies have offered their services free of charge in refugee emergencies. During the Kosovo crisis, for example, Microsoft provided UNHCR with computer equipment and software that was used to register the refugees. In approaching commercial corporations and the private sector in general, UNHCR has emphasized its belief that meeting the basic needs of refugees and displaced persons is a global responsibility.

UNHCR expenditure, 1950–2000* **Figure 7.7**

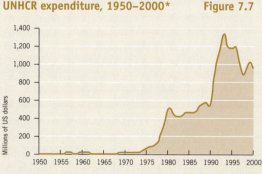

* This includes United Nations regular budget, general programmes and special programmes. Projected figure for 2000.

UNHCR expenditure by region, 1990–2000* **Figure 7.8**

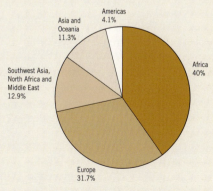

* Actual expenditure for 1990–99 and projections for 2000.

overwhelming situation, where there are self-evident protection needs and where there is little or no possibility of determining such needs on an individual basis in the short term. The organization considers that the purpose of temporary protection is to ensure immediate access to safety and the protection of basic human rights, including protection from *refoulement*, in countries directly affected by a large-scale influx. Temporary protection may also serve to enhance prospects for a coherent regional response, beyond the immediately affected areas.[16]

In 1992, UNHCR called on states to offer at least temporary protection to the hundreds of thousands of people fleeing the conflict in the former Yugoslavia. Reaction to UNHCR's appeal varied. As the exodus continued, tensions over the reception of the refugees in Western Europe grew. In 1993, European Union governments were the first to suggest the creation of 'safe areas' in Bosnia and Herzegovina. They agreed that protection and assistance 'should wherever possible be provided in the region of origin' and that 'displaced persons should be helped to remain in safe areas situated as close as possible to their homes'.[17] The massacres which later took place, when Bosnian Serb forces overran the 'safe areas' of Srebrenica and Zepa in 1995, showed just how precarious this approach can be.[18]

When temporary protection was offered in Western Europe to refugees from the former Yugoslavia, it was not without problems.[19] Questions were raised regarding the entitlements of people who had been granted temporary protection, as well as the extent of receiving states' responsibilities towards the refugees once the war was over. Even before the ink was dry on the December 1995 Dayton Peace Agreement, a vigorous debate was under way about return. Should it be voluntary or enforced? What constituted return 'in safety and dignity'? Should refugees be required to return if they could not go back to their home areas but would have to settle in another part of the country? The controversy intensified in 1996, when it became clear that large-scale, voluntary returns were not likely to take place quickly.

When open conflict erupted in Kosovo in both 1998 and 1999, European governments were at first reluctant to repeat the temporary protection experiment. They continued to channel asylum seekers from Kosovo into regular status determination procedures, as had been the case throughout the 1990s. The numbers rose rapidly from early 1999, and when the NATO bombing of the Federal Republic of Yugoslavia began on 24 March 1999, a mass exodus of Kosovo Albanians to Albania and the former Yugoslav Republic of Macedonia began. Fears mounted of a new, uncontrollable flow of refugees from the Balkans.

In an effort to keep the door of the former Yugoslav Republic of Macedonia open to the fleeing Kosovo Albanians, and thereby to preserve asylum in the region for the majority of the refugees, a Humanitarian Evacuation Programme was launched, in which UNHCR played a leading role. During May and June 1999, approximately 92,000 Kosovo Albanian refugees were flown out of the former Yugoslav Republic of Macedonia to more than two dozen receiving countries. Although the majority returned home by the end of the year, this particular example of international burden sharing appears likely to remain the exception rather than the rule.

Albanians on the quayside of the port of Brindisi, southern Italy. Thousands of Albanians fled the political upheavals in their country in the early 1990s. (ASSOCIATED PRESS/1991)

The Treaty of Amsterdam and beyond

Despite the resources devoted to border control measures, the enforcement approach to migration and asylum has not solved the problem of large numbers of migrants entering Europe in an irregular manner. Instead, it has tended to drive both migrants and asylum seekers into the hands of smugglers and traffickers, compounding the problems for governments and often putting the individuals themselves at great risk.[20]

In their attempt to control this complex issue, European Union governments have taken further measures to strengthen their harmonization efforts. The Treaty of Amsterdam, which was signed in 1997 and which came into force in May 1999, represents a milestone in the development of a European Union asylum policy. It sets out an agenda to move asylum matters over a five-year period from an area where they are subject to inter-governmental agreement by the member states to one where policy development and decision-taking clearly fall within the competence of the European Union institutions. This development should allow UNHCR and other organizations to work more closely and systematically with the institutions of the European Union, including the European Commission, which under the Treaty has greater powers to initiate common asylum policy measures.

At the same time, however, governments' frustration over their inability to control migration has led to some radical proposals, such as the one contained in a 'migration strategy' paper prepared during the second half of 1998 under the aegis of the Austrian presidency of the European Union. In addition to proposing a 'defence line' to protect Europe from illegal migrants seeking employment or asylum, the strategy paper called for the 1951 UN Refugee Convention to be amended or replaced altogether. The implication was that the Convention was to blame for the inability of governments to curb unwanted migration—a purpose for which it was never designed. Widespread criticism of the paper prompted its withdrawal, but similar rumblings have been heard elsewhere in Europe and as far afield as Australia.

In contrast to these developments, the heads of state and government of the European Union, meeting in October 1999 in Tampere, Finland, reaffirmed their 'absolute respect of the right to seek asylum', the need for common policies which 'offer guarantees to those who seek protection in or access to the European Union', and their commitment to establish a common European asylum system 'based on the full and inclusive application of the Geneva [Refugee] Convention'.[21] European leaders outlined a range of measures to be taken, ranging from common minimum conditions of reception of asylum seekers to measures on subsidiary forms of protection and temporary protection. They included a 'comprehensive approach to migration addressing political, human rights and development issues in countries and regions of origin and transit'. The challenge now is to ensure that these assurances are translated into reality—a difficult task given the range of measures which the same governments

Asylum applications submitted in main receiving industrialized states, 1980–99* Figure 7.9

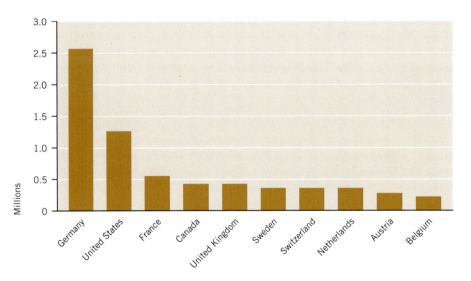

* Applications to the United Kingdom and United States include joint applications for more than one person.
Applications to all other countries are for one person only.
Source: Governments.

have introduced to prevent asylum seekers from gaining access to their territory. UNHCR has urged European countries 'to ensure that policies and practices designed to control irregular immigration do not jeopardize the rights of refugees and asylum seekers'.[22]

In parallel with these developments, the Council of Europe, whose membership includes the vast majority of European states, not just the 15 European Union member states, has worked to strengthen the protection of refugee rights as basic human rights. In 1991, the European Court of Human Rights clearly established the principle that asylum seekers should not be returned to a country where they would be exposed to the danger of torture or ill-treatment.[23] Provisions of the 1950 European Convention for the Protection of Human Rights and Fundamental Freedoms, regarding issues such as detention, the right to family life and the right to effective remedy, have also been shown to apply to asylum seekers and refugees. As such, the work of the Council of Europe underpins and complements that of the European Union and also enhances the rights of refugees and asylum seekers across the continent.

Another key factor in the future of refugee protection in Europe will be the ability of countries in Central and Eastern Europe to respond to requests for protection. In the decade since the end of the Cold War, many of these countries have made huge strides in establishing their own asylum systems and are now no longer simply countries through which asylum seekers pass. In 1999, for example, Hungary received more asylum applications than Denmark and Finland combined [see also Figure 7.3].

Number of asylum applications per 1,000 inhabitants submitted in main receiving industrialized states, 1999*

Figure 7.10

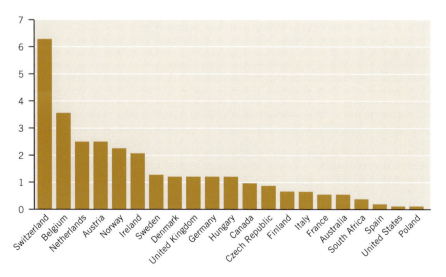

* Applications to the United Kingdom and United States include joint applications for more than one person. Applications to all other countries are for one person only. Industrialized countries receiving 2,500 or more asylum applications during 1999. For details and explanations, see Annex 10.

Political map of Europe, 1999

Map 7.1

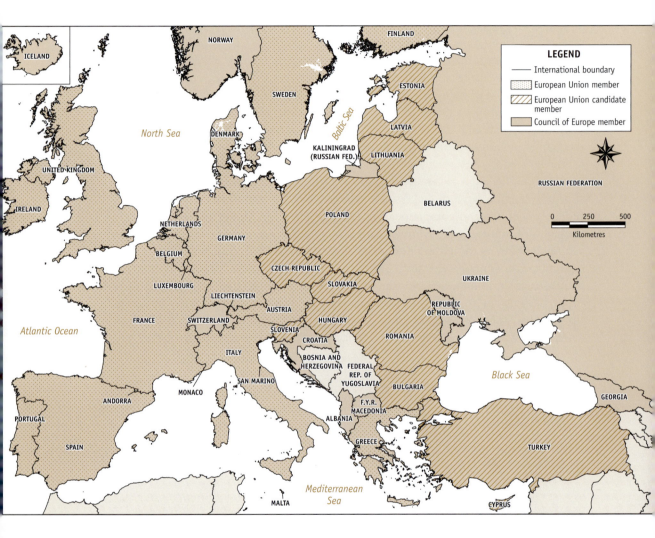

At the end of the 1990s, Europe again stood at a crossroads. In the years ahead, changing demographic trends may make governments more receptive towards immigration. Some analysts maintain that as a result of low birth rates and ageing populations, significant numbers of immigrants would be needed over the next half-century, just to keep the ratio of retired people to active workers at current levels. A recent report by the United Nations Population Division estimated that, at current birth and death rates, an average of 1.4 million immigrants per year would be needed in the European Union between 1995 and 2050, for it to keep the ratio of the working population to the non-working population constant at the 1995 level. The report also mentions that, according to recent national estimates, net migration into the European Union amounted to an average of 857,000 people per year from 1990 to 1998.[24]

If governments react by significantly easing restrictions on legal immigration, they may discover that this takes some of the pressure off the asylum channel, and public and political support for the institution of asylum could be strengthened. Alternatively, an increase in immigration may lead to more irregular migration. Nevertheless, if migration possibilities remain elusive, there is every reason to expect that both asylum seekers and migrants will continue to crowd the asylum process, and the institution of asylum will remain under strain. The changing dynamics of the migration debate may well determine the future of refugee protection in Europe.

Resettlement and asylum in North America

Unlike Europe, the United States and Canada are traditional countries of immigration. As such, they are accustomed to planning for the arrival of newcomers, and to integrating them into their societies. Refugees have long been regarded as one category of immigrants, and many of those displaced by the Second World War found new homes in North America in the framework of ongoing immigration programmes. Both countries have long had well-defined refugee intakes and, in both, the government and the voluntary sector work closely together to resettle refugees.

During the Cold War years, both the United States and Canada welcomed refugees from the communist bloc. But their geographical location, flanked by the Pacific and Atlantic Oceans, meant that it was not until the 1980s that asylum seekers—as opposed to refugees selected for resettlement—began to arrive spontaneously and in large numbers in North America. Systems designed to deal with relatively small numbers of individual asylum applications could not respond to the demand, and calls for change came from many quarters. Like their European counterparts, both the United States and Canada have struggled to find the right balance between refugee protection and immigration control, with the added challenge of having to strike the right balance between the resettlement of refugees and the admission of immigrants.

US policy towards refugees during the Cold War

Between 1975 and 1999, the United States offered permanent resettlement to more than two million refugees, including some 1.3 million Indochinese. During this period, the United States accepted more refugees for resettlement than the rest of the world put together. Throughout the Cold War years, the political value of accepting refugees from communism guaranteed European refugees a warm welcome. Despite being a key UNHCR supporter, the United States never acceded to the 1951 UN Refugee Convention, although in 1968 it acceded to its 1967 Protocol, thereby agreeing to accept most of the obligations of the 1951 Convention. From the late 1950s, US law defined a refugee as a person fleeing communism or a Middle East country, and refugee policy was almost entirely dictated by foreign policy interests.[25]

The effect was that these people were assured protection in the United States, while others were not assured the same protection.

From the mid-1970s, the United States began to resettle large numbers of Vietnamese refugees. This resettlement programme had its roots in a sense of obligation toward former allies in Southeast Asia and in the fear that the refugee flows could destabilize the remaining non-communist countries in the region. In addition, when there was a foreign policy interest to do so, the United States admitted people as refugees directly from their countries of origin. These 'in-country' processing arrangements were used, for example, to resettle Jews and dissidents from the Soviet Union, those seeking refuge from the regimes of Nicolae Ceausescu in Romania and Fidel Castro in Cuba, as well as Vietnamese resettled under the UNHCR-sponsored Orderly Departure Programme.

In the late 1970s, members of Congress joined forces with refugee advocates in the non-governmental sector to bring about a reform of US refugee policy. The administration of President Jimmy Carter, keen to highlight human rights promotion as a centrepiece of its foreign policy, responded positively. In 1979, a new Office of the US Coordinator for Refugee Affairs was created, and the following year the 1980 Refugee Act incorporated the 1951 UN Refugee Convention definition and introduced a statutory asylum procedure. The new law did not, however, remove refugee policy entirely from presidential control. It allowed the executive branch considerable latitude in shaping refugee policy, which was often harnessed to foreign policy objectives.

A case in point concerns Salvadoran and Guatemalan asylum seekers in the 1980s. The United States denied the asylum claims of the overwhelming majority of asylum seekers from these two countries. This was at a time when the US government was accepting large numbers of refugees who were fleeing the left-wing Sandinista government in Nicaragua. US officials maintained that they were not discriminating against Salvadoran and Guatemalan nationals. Rather, they said that most of them did not qualify as refugees either because they had migrated for economic reasons or, even if their reasons were not economic, they had not suffered or did not fear individual persecution. Refugee advocates suggested that the denial of asylum was due to the fact that they were fleeing right-wing governments supported by the United States. In 1985, advocacy groups challenged the US government's treatment of Salvadoran and Guatemalan asylum seekers in the courts, alleging bias in the US determination of these claims. In 1990, the government agreed to settle the case, and to review the claims of all asylum seekers from these two countries denied asylum between 1980 and 1990.[26]

Similar allegations of bias have been raised regarding the differing treatment of Haitian and Cuban asylum seekers. For the first 25 years after Fidel Castro came to power in Cuba in 1959, the United States had an open-door policy towards asylum seekers from Cuba. This policy was severely tested in 1980, when Castro relaxed exit restrictions and over 125,000 Cubans (including over 8,000 criminals and psychiatric patients) set sail for Florida in the 'Mariel boatlift'. Despite the controversy which this provoked, most were allowed to remain. Yet during that same period, Haitians were interdicted at sea, denied asylum in the United States, and sent back to Haiti [see Box 7.2]. While the government maintained that many Haitians were fleeing for economic reasons, refugee advocates remained critical of the US government's actions.

Emigration pressures continued to rise in Cuba, especially after the dissolution of the former Soviet Union, its principal ally, in 1991. As economic and social conditions deteriorated in Cuba, the numbers of Cubans attempting to reach the United States continued to rise. Amidst growing anti-immigrant sentiment in the United States, a new exodus of Cubans began in the early 1990s. More than 35,000 'rafters' were picked up by the US Coast Guard in mid-1994. The administration of President Bill Clinton decided to interdict the Cubans and detain them at the US naval base in Guantánamo, Cuba, and other locations in the region. To halt the flow, the US government reached a controversial agreement with Cuba in September 1994, in which Cuba reverted to its previous policy whereby Cuban citizens required a permit to leave the country, which government authorities could issue or not at their discretion.[27] For its part, the US government promised to admit 20,000 Cubans each year through other immigration admission channels.

Proportion of asylum seekers recognized as refugees or granted humanitarian status, 1990–2000

Figure 7.11

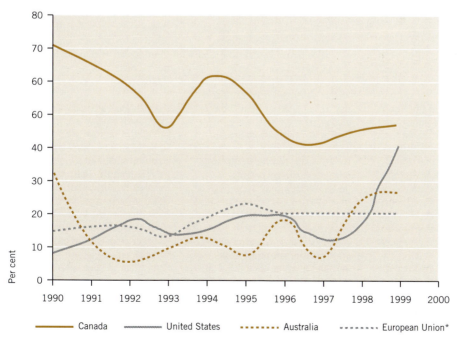

* 1999 figure excludes Austria, France and Luxembourg. For further details and explanations, see Annex 10.

Box 7.4   Haitian asylum seekers

Since the 1970s, successive US governments' treatment of migrants arriving by boat has severely restricted Haitians' access to asylum procedures. US government statistics show that between 1981 and 1991, over 22,000 Haitians were interdicted at sea, and that only 28 of these were allowed into the United States to pursue asylum claims.

UNHCR, other humanitarian organizations and advocacy groups have repeatedly argued that the United States' interdiction and return of Haitian asylum seekers—without the implementation of appropriate procedures to identify those with a well-founded fear of persecution—could lead to forcible return to an unsafe place (*refoulement*), which is prohibited under Article 33 of the 1951 UN Refugee Convention. In the early 1990s, advocacy groups in the United States challenged the government's interdiction policy in the federal courts, and the issue was appealed to the highest US court, the Supreme Court.
In 1993, the Supreme Court ruled that the United States' obligation under Article 33 did not apply outside US territory, where the Haitians were interdicted.[v] By contrast, UNHCR maintains that the principle of *non-refoulement* applies wherever states may act.[vi] In 1997, the Organization of American States' Inter-American Commission on Human Rights contradicted the US Supreme Court's position, declaring that the guarantees under Article 33 also apply outside national borders.[vii]

Some advocacy groups have argued that because of its leading role in international affairs, the US government's actions towards Haitians have contributed to the undermining of the principle of asylum elsewhere around the globe. They argue that if the world's richest nation can turn asylum seekers away, then poor nations ill-equipped to handle large refugee influxes should be able to do so too. During the 1980s, while the United States supported UNHCR's efforts to prevent countries in Southeast Asia from forcibly returning Vietnamese boat people, at least one of the governments responsible for doing so countered that what it was doing was no different from what the United States was doing to Haitians.

Double standards

Throughout the 1960s and 1970s, there was great disparity in the way in which US authorities treated asylum seekers from Cuba and Haiti. Critics argue that the US government treated Cubans as refugees because they were fleeing a communist government, while it viewed Haitians as economic migrants, despite manifest evidence of widespread persecution in Haiti. It is often pointed out, particularly by African-American political leaders, that those arriving from Cuba were predominantly white, while those from Haiti were mainly black.

For 30 years, two harsh dictators ruled Haiti: first, François Duvalier—known as 'Papa Doc'—from 1957 to 1971, and then his son Jean-Claude Duvalier—known as 'Baby Doc'—from 1971 to 1986. The country's first democratically-elected president, former priest Jean-Bertrand Aristide, took office in February 1991, but was ousted seven months later by a military coup. In July 1993, the military leaders, in the face of international sanctions and pressure, agreed to step down but did not. They remained in power until late 1994, when the United States intervened and restored the Aristide government.

Haitians fleeing political repression, widespread human rights violations, and deteriorating economic conditions had started reaching Florida by boat in the early 1970s. Many sought asylum, though most applications were denied. Others were absorbed into Miami's growing Haitian community.

In 1978, the US government began carrying out the 'Haitian Program', aimed at deterring Haitian asylum seekers and migrants from entering the United States. Critics saw this as a programme to deny Haitians fair hearings and hasten their deportation. Indeed, US courts halted the programme in 1979 and ordered new hearings for rejected Haitian asylum seekers still in the United States.

Haitian boat arrivals increased in 1979 and accelerated dramatically in 1980, the same year that more than 125,000 Cubans arrived in the United States during the 'Mariel boatlift'. Immediately afterwards, many Haitians benefited from pressure on the US government to treat Haitians and Cubans equally and equitably. Haitian arrivals were awarded a special 'entrant' status, permitting them to stay while their status was resolved, but, unlike the Cubans, barring them from applying for permanent residence.

The interdiction programme

In late 1981, the new administration of President Ronald Reagan took a series of steps that paved the way for the interdiction of Haitians on the high seas. The US government agreed with the Haitian authorities in Port-au-Prince that it would return Haitians who left illegally. President Reagan ordered the US Coast Guard to interdict vessels that might be carrying undocumented aliens to the United States. If it determined that the passengers were seeking to enter the United States without documentation from a country with which the United States had an agreement to return illegal migrants, the Coast Guard was to return them to that country. Haiti was the only country with which the United States had such an agreement at the time.

The Reagan administration instructed the Coast Guard not to return people who might be refugees. Yet the procedures that it put in place to identify potential refugees aboard Coast Guard boats were such that it was extremely difficult for anyone to qualify for entry into the United States to apply for asylum.

Following the September 1991 coup that ousted President Aristide, the United States temporarily halted the interdiction programme. The programme was restarted a month later, but this time, instead of returning interdicted Haitians to Haiti, they were taken for 'screening' to the US naval base in Guantánamo, Cuba. According to some US non-governmental organizations and at least one US federal judge, Haitians at the Guantánamo base were kept in prison-like conditions.[viii] US government statistics indicate that some 10,500 of the 34,000 Haitians interdicted after the 1991 coup were found to have a credible fear of persecution and were allowed to enter the United States to apply for asylum. Although only a minority actually received asylum, most were ultimately able to remain in the United States legally.

In May 1992, President George Bush again ordered that all interdicted Haitians be returned to Haiti, this time without even the cursory refugee screening that was previously in place. Although Bill Clinton criticized the Bush policy as 'cruel' while running for office, once elected president he continued it. The policy did not deter Haitians from fleeing, however, and in 1992 the Coast Guard interdicted 31,400 Haitians. While this number fell to 2,400 the following year, it shot up again to 25,000 in 1994, before falling to an average of 1,150 over the next five years.

In June 1994, President Clinton instituted a new and short-lived procedure for interdicted Haitians. The United States carried out full refugee determination procedures on board the USNS *Comfort*, anchored off the coast of Jamaica. Those granted refugee status were resettled in the United States; those rejected were returned to Haiti. A record number of those processed on the *Comfort* were granted refugee status. The number of Haitians picked up and awaiting refugee interviews grew so rapidly— the Coast Guard picked up 3,247 on one day in July—that the United States ended the on-board processing. It then sent those still on the *Comfort* and all newly interdicted Haitians to Guantánamo. The US authorities told the Haitians they could remain there as long as it was unsafe for them to return to Haiti, but added that none would be permitted to enter the United States. As a result, the Coast Guard took more than 21,000 Haitians to Guantánamo. Although by the end of the operation most were repatriated, some were allowed to enter the United States.

In September 1994, a US-dominated multinational force arrived in Haiti and the Haitian military junta finally resigned. President Aristide returned to Haiti, followed almost immediately by a majority of the Haitians in Guantánamo who repatriated voluntarily. In December, the US government told the 4,500 Haitians still in Guantánamo that it was safe to return to Haiti. Several hundred returned voluntarily, but 4,000 who refused were returned against their will.

In October 1998, the US Congress passed the Haitian Refugee Immigration Fairness Act, which allowed Haitians, who arrived in the United States before 31 December 1995 and who had applied for asylum before then, to apply for permanent residence. The policy of interdiction at sea remains in force, however, preventing the majority of those leaving Haiti from ever reaching US shores.

Recent developments in US law and practice

At the beginning of the 1990s, the US Immigration and Naturalization Service established a new system to determine asylum claims. The changes were designed to address concerns that asylum determinations were often made by immigration officers un-trained in refugee law and interviewing techniques, who in many cases relied more heavily on foreign policy-related US State Department recommendations than on the applicant's own testimony and relevant legal standards. The reforms included the formation of a specially trained corps of asylum officers, and the establishment of a documentation centre to provide objective information on conditions in countries of origin.

The new procedures, as well as changes in the criteria for adjudicating asylum claims, promised to make the process fairer. For instance, the consistent and credible testimony of an applicant could be considered sufficient proof of fear of persecution, even without documentary corroboration. However, asylum applicants often still lacked legal representation or qualified interpreters.[28]

Also in 1990, the US Congress amended immigration and nationality legislation to introduce a temporary protected status (TPS). The Attorney General was given the discretion to provide temporary protection to nationals of countries experiencing ongoing conflict or natural disasters. TPS differed from temporary protection as developed in Europe, in that it was not related to situations of mass influx and did not prevent an individual from pursuing an asylum claim (as was the case in some European countries). It gave authorization to find employment, and it precluded deportation. The new status provided at least temporary refuge to people who might otherwise be returned to danger. Some observers expressed concern, however, that it might be used to deny full refugee status to nationals of certain countries or that it would undermine the traditionally permanent nature of US protection. Historically, virtually all those to whom the United States granted asylum or resettlement became eligible for permanent residence, and later for citizenship.

In the early 1990s, anti-immigrant sentiment spread in the United States, driven in part by a weak economy in certain regions and a growing number of undocumented migrants arriving in search of work. At the same time, as in other industrialized countries, the number of asylum applications filed in the United States rose significantly, from 20,000 in 1985 to 148,000 in 1995. These included both valid claims and claims lodged by people looking for alternative immigration channels. Right-wing politicians opposed to large-scale immigration fuelled public fears by blaming immigrants and refugees for a host of economic and social problems.

The anti-immigrant sentiment was reflected in a 1994 debate in California over a measure called 'Proposition 187', which sought to make undocumented migrants ineligible for most social services and to bar their children from public education. Although Proposition 187 dealt with undocumented migrants rather than refugees, it sparked a nationwide debate on immigration in general. The Proposition was passed, though local courts later declared most of its provisions unconstitutional.

Two years later, in 1996, Congress passed the Illegal Immigration Reform and Immigrant Responsibility Act (IIRIRA). The Act was primarily aimed at limiting illegal immigration and abuse of the asylum procedure, but in the process it also fundamentally changed the way in which the US government responded to asylum seekers and what rights they were accorded.[29] It authorized 'expedited removals', whereby immigration officers can order that an alien arriving without proper documents be removed from the United States 'without further hearing or review'. An exception is made for people who indicate an intention to apply for asylum. In such a case, the immigration officer has to refer the case to an asylum officer. If the asylum officer determines that the person has a 'credible fear' of persecution, the person is then allowed to apply for asylum. Failure to demonstrate such a 'credible fear' before the asylum officer or, upon review, an immigration judge, makes the person subject to deportation. The 1996 law thus created a new legal standard for screening asylum seekers arriving at US borders to determine whether they should be admitted to the asylum procedure.[30]

The 1996 legislation also barred certain categories of people from the asylum procedure. Advocacy groups were particularly concerned that it barred people with convictions for 'aggravated felonies' from asylum. Even minor offences, committed years earlier, such as shoplifting, could bar an individual from access to protection. UNHCR and other groups urged that the nature of the crime committed and the danger the individual might pose to the community in the country of asylum should always be balanced against the severity of the persecution feared in the country of origin.

The new law also provided that, while asylum seekers were being screened for admittance to the asylum procedure, they would remain in detention. When Immigration and Naturalization Service detention facilities were unable to accommodate the significantly increased number of detainees, many were held in prisons alongside criminal offenders. Finally, the Act amended the definition of a refugee specifically to include individuals fleeing coercive population control programmes.

There were certain exceptions to some of the Act's more drastic provisions, but UNHCR and other organizations warned that the 1996 legislation could result in the refoulement of refugees, particularly if they had committed crimes. Indeed, asylum seekers increasingly had to resort to provisions of the 1984 UN Convention Against Torture and Other Cruel, Inhuman or Degrading Treatment which were implemented in US law from 1998. These forbid the return of anyone to a country where there are substantial grounds for believing they would be subjected to torture, and contain no exception for those convicted of crimes. By the end of 1999, Congress was considering legislation to address some of the concerns relating to the 1996 law, particularly with regard to expedited removal and the detention of asylum seekers.

Canadian policies towards refugees

Like the United States, Canada is a country founded on immigration, and the resettlement of refugees is an integral part of Canada's immigration policy. Although immigration was initially restricted mainly to people of European origin, in 1962 this policy was revised to include nationals of all states. This provided new opportunities for the resettlement of refugees in Canada.

Between the end of the Second World War and the early 1970s, Canada took in significant numbers of refugees, including people resettled from Europe after 1945, Hungarian refugees in 1956–57, and Czech refugees who fled in 1968. In 1972, Canada accepted over 6,000 Ugandan Asians expelled by President Idi Amin and, following the 1973 coup in Chile, Canada resettled a similar number of Chilean refugees. Other refugees were admitted on an *ad hoc*, individual basis during this period. Then, in the two decades after 1975, Canada accepted over 200,000 refugees from Indochina, this being the second largest number after the United States. Together with the earlier refugee movements, these new arrivals made it clear that the former, case-by-case approach to refugee admission had to be replaced by a more systematic one.

A new Immigration Act was passed in 1976. It set out a refugee status determination procedure and for the first time a broader framework for Canada's refugee policy. Like the United States four years later, the Act incorporated the 1951 UN Refugee Convention definition of a refugee. It affirmed Canada's commitment to the 'displaced and the persecuted', and identified refugees as a distinct class of people to be selected and admitted separately from immigrants. The Act provided for new, flexible arrangements for the private sponsorship of refugees to be resettled in Canada. It also allowed the government to designate special classes of refugees apart from Convention refugees, thereby giving Canada the scope to help specific groups on its own terms.

During the 1980s, Canada offered resettlement to an average of 21,000 refugees each year. This included refugees who were government-sponsored, meaning that the state assumed responsibility for the costs associated with their resettlement, as well as people who were sponsored privately by churches and other local organizations. As in the United States, cooperation between government agencies and non-governmental groups is a feature of refugee resettlement in Canada. Between 1989 and 1998, resettlement admissions fell from 35,000 to under 9,000. In 1999, however, they rose to 17,000 because of the humanitarian evacuation programme for refugees from Kosovo.

By the late 1980s, the steady arrival of asylum seekers in Canada made it clear that the in-country refugee status determination process needed to be reformed. It was an onerous procedure with a serious flaw: at no point during the process was the individual asylum seeker given a chance to be heard by the decision-makers. A landmark decision of the Canadian Supreme Court in 1985 ruled that fundamental justice required that the credibility of asylum seekers be determined on the basis of a hearing.[31] As a result, an Immigration and Refugee Board, including a Convention refugee determination division to hear asylum seekers' claims, was established in 1989.

The new structure was set up partly in response to public pressure, which had mounted in 1986 when 155 Sri Lankan asylum seekers were rescued at sea off the coast of Newfoundland, and in 1987 when a boatload of Sikhs arrived in Nova Scotia. The Canadian government did not want normal immigration channels to be circumvented, and feared abuse of the country's liberal asylum process, particularly as its neighbour to the south tightened its own system.

Since then, the Canadian government has introduced other restrictive measures, but the country has nevertheless often taken the lead in matters of refugee protection. For instance, Canada was the first country to introduce a 'fast track' in its asylum procedure for applicants who are clearly in need of protection—a procedure now also adopted with some variations in Australia. Also, in 1993, Canada's Immigration and Refugee Board published ground-breaking guidelines on women refugee claimants fearing gender-related persecution.

Asylum policies in Australia, New Zealand and Japan

Like the United States and Canada, immigration has been integral to the development of Australia and New Zealand. Both were significant destinations for refugees after the end of the Second World War, and most came from Europe. In the 25 years after 1945, over 350,000 refugees resettled in Australia, not counting thousands of others who arrived under family reunion or other immigration channels. In addition, some 7,000 resettled in New Zealand.

Australia only ended its 'White Australia' immigration policy in 1973. Since then, political upheavals in the Asia–Pacific region have made countries in this region the prime source of refugees in both Australia and New Zealand. From 1975, Australia accepted the largest number of Indochinese refugees for resettlement after the United States and Canada. This amounted to over 185,000, of whom well over half

Refugees resettled in industrialized states, 1981–99*   **Figure 7.12**

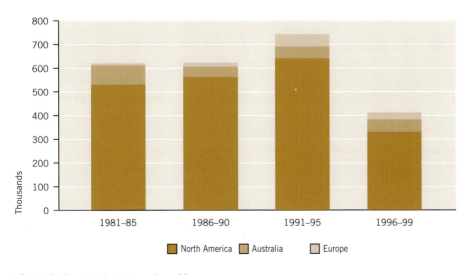

* For details of countries included, see Annex 10.
Source: Governments.

were Vietnamese boat people. New Zealand resettled 13,000 during the same period. In addition to those who were resettled, some boat people managed to make the long sea journey between southern Viet Nam and Australia's northern port of Darwin. The first small boat landed in 1976, and dozens more followed. The need for a process to handle asylum applications was evident.

In 1978, for the first time, the Australian government set up a refugee status determination committee to assess applications for refugee status. Throughout the 1980s, the number of applicants remained low. After the events in Tiananmen Square in Beijing in 1989, however, numbers started to rise since many Chinese students already in Australia sought to remain. In 1992, the refugee status determination committee was replaced by a new system, under which a protection unit within the Department of Immigration and Multicultural Affairs made a first instance decision on applications and a refugee review tribunal heard appeals.

Particular controversy has surrounded Australia's policy of mandatory detention of all unauthorized arrivals. No exception is made for asylum seekers. Australia has a universal visa policy, requiring a visa of all foreign travellers other than citizens of New Zealand. Many are detained in the controversial detention centres at Port Headland, Curtin and Woomera, in the remote northwest of the country.

In mid-1999, Australia joined other industrialized states in introducing legislation on temporary protection. New temporary safe haven visas were intended to provide greater flexibility in dealing with large-scale displacement and were granted to several thousand Kosovo Albanians and Timorese that year. Beneficiaries of this temporary safe haven are barred from applying for asylum unless the minister decides otherwise, leaving the duration and quality of protection to ministerial discretion rather than a reviewable procedure. During 1999, there was an increasing number of illegal arrivals by boat in Australia. In response, the government introduced new legislation on the reception and treatment of asylum seekers who arrive illegally in the country. A 'regional cooperation agreement' with Indonesia was also concluded, which provides for the interception, detention and screening of third country nationals transiting Indonesia en route to Australia.

New Zealand is one of just a dozen countries world-wide with an established refugee resettlement programme. Its annual quota of 750 places puts New Zealand's intake, on a per capita basis, on a par with Canada's. Although geography has kept New Zealand relatively shielded from the spontaneous movements of asylum seekers which have put other industrialized countries under such pressure, the number rose steadily throughout the 1990s, reaching nearly 3,000 a year in 1998.

Of the major industrialized countries, Japan, which has been a party to the 1951 UN Refugee Convention since 1981, has received by far the smallest number of asylum applications. The country's ethnic and cultural homogeneity has been sustained by strict controls on population movement and immigration, although over 10,000 Indochinese refugees have been resettled or allowed to remain in Japan since 1975. In the 10 years from 1990 to 1999, only 1,100 people applied for asylum in Japan. A strict time limit for making an application for asylum and an unusually high standard of proof meant that between 1990 and 1997, fewer than four per cent of these were recognized as refugees under the Convention. In 1998 and 1999, more asylum determinations were made than in the preceding decade, and the acceptance rate rose to over seven per cent in 1999, while an increasing number of rejected asylum seekers were allowed to remain on humanitarian grounds. Outside its borders, the Japanese government's commitment to refugees is reflected in its strong support for UNHCR's programmes.

Preserving the right to seek asylum

The legislative changes to asylum systems in industrialized states in the last two decades have largely been built around the control of irregular migration. Concerns about mass outflows of people from war-torn regions and about trafficking and smuggling of people have also contributed to the introduction of tighter control measures. In most cases these changes, which have been accompanied by a range of new border control measures, have failed to recognize adequately that some people have a real need to seek protection from persecution. Preserving the right to seek asylum in industrialized states which have sophisticated and costly legal systems and border control mechanisms remains a major challenge for the 21st century.

Policies of deterrence have also contributed to a blurring of the already problematic distinction between refugees and economic migrants, and have stigmatized refugees as people trying to circumvent the law. Once refugees reach safety, they are sometimes detained for prolonged periods. This is a serious concern in many countries, especially when separated and unaccompanied children and family groups are held in detention. Equally, in the area of family reunification, practices in a number of countries have made it virtually impossible for family members to be reunited. This has had a negative impact both on their capacity to adjust to their new situations in the short term, and on their longer-term integration prospects. Apart from preserving the right to seek asylum, the challenge is therefore also to ensure that states respect basic human rights principles.

Managing mixed flows of refugees and other migrants is a complex problem to which there are no easy answers. Ultimately, the systems developed by countries in the industrialized world depend on changes in the dynamics of international migration, including the numbers of refugees and other migrants seeking to enter these countries, and the methods used to gain entry. This in turn depends on the measures taken by governments and international organizations to address the causes of refugee flight and other migratory flows. If the disparity between the world's wealthiest and poorest countries continues to grow, as it has done in the last 50 years, and if countries outside the industrialized world are not sufficiently encouraged and supported in providing protection and assistance to refugees in their regions, the numbers of people seeking new lives in the world's wealthiest states will remain high. Regional approaches to migration and asylum, such as those adopted in Europe, have their value, but they may prove to be counter-productive if they undermine global approaches to these issues.

8 Displacement in the former Soviet region

The dissolution of the Soviet Union in December 1991 unleashed massive population movements in the countries that subsequently formed the new Commonwealth of Independent States (CIS). Inter-ethnic disputes and unresolved conflicts came to the surface and were played out with devastating consequences.

The erection of new national boundaries left millions of Russians and others outside their 'homelands'. Many of these people sought to repatriate, and complex questions of citizenship arose. Some of the peoples who had been deported in the 1940s were finally able to return to their original homelands, and new influxes of refugees and asylum seekers arrived from further afield. It has been estimated that during the decade up to nine million people were on the move, largely as a result of the political upheavals, making this the largest movement of people in the region since 1945.[1]

In the first half of the decade, hundreds of thousands of people were uprooted by inter-ethnic and separatist conflict in the South Caucasus. This included the Armenian–Azerbaijani conflict over Nagorno-Karabakh, and the conflicts in the Georgian autonomous territories of Abkhazia and South Ossetia. At the same time, civil war in Tajikistan caused hundreds of thousands of people to flee their homes. The North Caucasus also became the scene of large-scale forced displacement. In 1992, tens of thousands of Ingush were expelled from North Ossetia to neighbouring Ingushetia. Subsequently, there was large-scale displacement in and around Chechnya, first in 1994–95 and then again from September 1999. In addition, throughout the decade, large numbers of people, in particular ethnic Russians outside the Russian Federation, found themselves 'aliens' in various parts of the former Soviet Union and left those areas for places where they felt that they were safer or had better prospects.

Complex interconnections between forced displacement and mass migration became increasingly evident. To clarify these issues, a major international conference was convened in 1996 by UNHCR, in cooperation with the International Organization for Migration (IOM) and the Organization for Security and Cooperation in Europe (OSCE). These organizations worked closely with the governments of CIS countries to identify displacement problems needing to be resolved, to establish common terminology, and to develop a common strategy. In addition to widely used terms such as 'refugees' and 'internally displaced persons', new categories were developed to describe the different movements of people specific to the region. These included 'formerly deported peoples', 'repatriants', and 'involuntarily relocating persons'.

UNHCR faced many challenges in setting up programmes in the region, particularly in the territory of the Russian Federation—a permanent member of the UN Security Council. It was a highly politicized environment, not least because the Soviet

For lack of more suitable shelters, many Azerbaijanis displaced in the early 1990s as a result of the Nagorno-Karabakh dispute have lived for years in disused railway carriages. (UNHCR/A. HOLLMANN/1999)

Union had been largely hostile towards UNHCR. This chapter describes the processes through which UNHCR came to establish a presence in the region, and how it developed a comprehensive approach, including capacity-building activities designed to help prevent further forced displacement.

The Soviet legacy

In the early 1920s, the Soviet Union became the successor to the ethnically hetero-geneous empire of the tsars. It was the massive outflow of refugees from the former Russian Empire which, in 1921, led the League of Nations to appoint Fridtjof Nansen as its High Commissioner to deal with this huge displacement problem. Missions such as those undertaken by Nansen's representatives in 1923 to assess the conditions of returnees in southern Russia were not to be repeated in this region until the final days of the Soviet Union's existence.

The Soviet Union sought to forge individuals, peoples and society in accordance with its all-embracing communist ideology. The transfer and mixing of peoples—whether voluntary or involuntary—became a standard means to a utopian end. Tens of millions were uprooted. This was compounded by the massive displacements caused by the Second World War. Stalin's forced transfers of entire nations in the 1930s and 1940s provided classic examples of 'ethnic cleansing' long before the term was coined.[2] The stimulation of population movements in the name of political and economic goals continued under his successors.

When in the second half of the 1980s political controls gradually began to be relaxed, the ethnic and nationalist tensions and aspirations that had been suppressed and largely concealed in the Soviet Union were released. The political unravelling of the Soviet system was therefore accompanied by 'ethnic unmixing' and the assertion of claims to sovereignty in disputed territories.[3]

One of the first indications of Moscow's declining control was the beginning, in early 1988, of the Armenian–Azerbaijani conflict. This was over the contested territory of Nagorno-Karabakh, situated in Azerbaijan but with an Armenian majority seeking unification with Armenia. The flight of Armenians from Azerbaijan, and vice versa, produced the first waves of *bezhentsi* (the Russian catch-all term for both refugees and internally displaced) used by the Soviet media and the public.[4] In June 1989, there was another explosion of inter-ethnic violence in the Uzbekistani section of Central Asia's main fault line, the Fergana Valley, when the local population drove out tens of thousands of Meskhetians. These so-called 'immigrants' had been deported en masse during the Stalin era from southern Georgia and forced to settle in Central Asia.[5]

Such dramatic examples of inter-ethnic clashes and ethnic expulsions fuelled fears, both within and outside the Soviet Union, that its dissolution would unleash greater violence and bloodshed and generate mass flows of refugees, internally displaced people and migrants. Certainly, the results of the last Soviet census

Soviet mass deportations of the 1940s

Figure 8.1

Poles/Jews (1940–41)	380,000
Volga Germans (Sept. 1941)	366,000
Chechens (Feb. 1944)	362,000
Meskhetians (Nov. 1944)	200,000
Crimean Tatars (May 1944)	183,000
Koreans (1937)	172,000
Ingush (Feb. 1944)	134,000
Kalmyks (Dec. 1943)	92,000
Karachai (Nov. 1943)	68,000
Poles (1936)	60,000
Finns (St Petersburg region, 1942)	45,000
Balkars (April 1944)	37,000
Moldovans (1949)	36,000
Black Sea Greeks (1949)	36,000
Other Soviet Germans (1941–52)	843,000
Other Crimean groups (1944)	45,000
Other Black Sea groups (1949)	22,000
Other N. Caucasus groups (1943–44)	8,000
Total	**3,089,000**

Source: UNHCR (Public Information Section), *Commonwealth of Independent States conference on refugees and migrants*, 30–31 May 1996.
Note: All statistics on the original deportations, with the exception of the Meskhetians, are provided by A. Blum of the Institut National d'Etudes Démographiques in Paris. Historical details were supplied by Blum or taken from *Les peuples déportés d'Union Soviétique* by J.-J. Marie. Population transfers (amounting to several million people) linked to collectivization and the Gulag labour camps rather than the 'special settlers regime', are not included. Further large-scale deportations took place from the Baltic states, Moldova and the Ukraine from 1944 until 1953.

conducted in 1989 seemed to underscore this potential. They indicated how large a number of people risked being viewed as aliens, if independent states were to emerge. Depending on what definition of a homeland was used, between 54 million and 65 million people (roughly a fifth of the Soviet population of 285 million) lived outside their national-administrative units. Of these, some 25.3 million were Russians who, as the predominant nation accounting for around half the total Soviet population, had been accustomed to feeling at home anywhere in the Soviet Union.[6]

Establishing a UNHCR presence in the region

At the beginning of the 1990s, the continuing economic decline and resurgence of nationalism in the Soviet Union raised widespread fears that a 'tidal wave' of

Soviet migrants could move westward. In Western Europe the asylum system was already under pressure. In Central Europe, which itself had only recently emerged from the Soviet sphere of influence, an asylum regime had barely begun to be established. UNHCR, which was gradually establishing a presence there, saw a clear need to bolster fledgling refugee protection mechanisms and thereby to strengthen the expanding European edifice as a whole.

For many years the Soviet Union had viewed UNHCR with suspicion, regarding the organization as an instrument of the Cold War. However, in the second half of the 1980s, after the new Soviet leader Mikhail Gorbachev inaugurated his policies of *perestroika* (restructuring) and *glasnost* (openness), the Soviet attitude towards the organization began to change. Faced with such challenges as resolving the conflicts in Cambodia and Afghanistan, both of which entailed the return of large numbers of refugees, the Soviet leadership increasingly recognized the usefulness of cooperation with UNHCR.

It was not only foreign policy exigencies that prompted the Soviet Union to develop cooperation with UNHCR. New domestic problems connected with internal forced displacement were also a determining factor. After decades of pervasive regimentation at home and tight controls over external contacts, the Soviet Union was not in a position to deal with either the large-scale displacement generated by ethnic conflicts on its territory or the appearance of increasing numbers of foreign asylum seekers in the capital, Moscow.

As they began to address these problems at the practical level, the Soviet authorities recognized the need to integrate the country into the international refugee protection system and began to look to UNHCR for assistance and guidance. In September 1990, the Soviet Union sent an observer delegation to UNHCR's annual Executive Committee meeting in Geneva. This delegation informed the High Commissioner, Thorvald Stoltenberg, that the Soviet government intended to accede to the 1951 UN Refugee Convention and that new legislation was being prepared on managing migration and dealing with 'an estimated 600,000 internally displaced'.[7]

UNHCR was initially reluctant to become involved in the Soviet Union. The scale and complexity of the displacement problems were daunting and those who had been uprooted were internally displaced people who did not necessarily appear to fall within the organization's mandate. In addition, UNHCR faced funding constraints. The rapid pace of change in the Soviet Union, however, led UNHCR to review its approach. During 1991, burgeoning bilateral contacts resulted in the first UNHCR missions to the Soviet Union, as a result of which an informal understanding on the desirability of establishing a continuing presence was reached. An internal UNHCR strategy paper on 'the disintegrating USSR', prepared in September 1991, advised that, 'given the uniquely historical dimension of the change, this office should be pragmatic rather than formalistic and—in its field—be pro-active rather than reactive'.[8]

Box 8.1 Statelessness and disputed citizenship

After the dissolution of the Soviet Union and Czechoslovakia and the break-up of Yugoslavia, millions of people needed to confirm a new citizenship status. Was a former Czechoslovak citizen now Czech or Slovak? Was someone born in Belgrade, raised in Sarajevo, now married to someone from Zagreb and living in Ljubliana, a Yugoslav, Bosnian, Croat or Slovene citizen? New states emerging from these dissolutions established their own criteria for citizenship. In some cases, people who did not meet those criteria became 'stateless'; in other cases they failed to acquire citizenship where they lived.

These questions are by no means confined to Europe, nor does statelessness result only from the dissolution of states. Sometimes it can result from flaws in legislation and procedures governing marriage and the registration of births. In other cases, discriminatory policies targeted at minorities or other groups or individuals lead to statelessness. In some instances, governments have passed citizenship laws which have had the effect of marginalizing whole sections of society. Individuals affected by problems of statelessness or unclear citizenship often lack a clear legal status and therefore have difficulties contracting marriages, sending children to school, working, travelling or owning property. The result is that statelessness is often a cause of population displacement.

It is not possible to provide a list of the world's stateless people because unclear citizenship or nationality is more often than not disputed. Every country is affected to some degree because all countries have laws to determine who is a citizen and who is not, and approaches are not always harmonized between states.

The political changes in Europe during the 1990s illustrated the problems which can arise when conflicts on nationality status occur. When the Baltic states regained independence, their nationality laws excluded hundreds of thousands of ethnic Russians who had lived there for decades. When many Crimean Tatars returned to Ukraine, their families having been deported from there by Stalin in the 1940s, some arrived after the termination date for automatic access to Ukrainian citizenship, creating difficulties in finding jobs and housing. Yugoslavia's violent break-up displaced over four million people, and many records needed to trace citizenship were destroyed, creating numerous problems. When Czechoslovakia broke into two republics, many living on the Czech side were attributed Slovak citizenship, making them foreigners in their place of habitual residence.

In Asia, the Biharis (non-Bengali Muslims who moved from India to what was East Pakistan in the late 1940s) considered themselves to be Pakistani nationals and refused to take Bangladeshi nationality when Bangladesh gained independence in 1971. The government of Pakistan has since been reluctant to 'repatriate' them, and over 200,000 are still in camps in Bangladesh. In Myanmar, restrictive nationality laws continue to prevent many residents, such as the Rohingyas, from being considered as nationals. In Bhutan, citizenship laws adopted in the 1980s effectively excluded many ethnic Nepalis from Bhutanese nationality. Some 100,000 ethnic Nepalis from Bhutan are still living in camps in Nepal.

In Africa, some 75,000 people were expelled from Mauritania as a result of inter-ethnic clashes in 1989–90. Although most have since returned, around 30,000 remain in Senegal, their claims to citizenship challenged by the Mauritanian authorities. In Zaire, following legislation passed in 1981, thousands of Banyarwanda people de jure lost their citizenship. In Ethiopia, as a result of the war with Eritrea which started in 1998, the authorities expelled 68,000 people to Eritrea for being nationals of an enemy state. Although both countries issued papers to these people, as of December 1999 neither was willing to accept full responsibility for them as citizens.

In the Middle East, more than 120,000 Kurds who have lived in northeastern Syria all their lives have not been able to acquire citizenship.

In Kuwait, up to 250,000 Bidoons have long lived as a minority without an effective nationality. Many were forced out of Kuwait during the 1991 Gulf crisis and now live in Iraq and other Gulf countries. Finally, although Palestinians may not be considered as stateless since a Palestinian state has technically existed since the approval of UN General Assembly Resolution 181 (1947), some three million have been unable to return to their homes and their legal status has constantly been disputed by the Israeli government.

A link exists between statelessness and potential refugee flows, though clearly not every stateless person is a refugee. UNHCR promotes accession to and implementation of the 1954 Convention Relating to the Status of Stateless Persons and the 1961 Convention on the Reduction of Statelessness. These instruments provide a legal framework for avoiding and reducing cases of statelessness and resolving conflicts between states.

In 1995, UNHCR's Executive Committee and, subsequently, the UN General Assembly requested that UNHCR apply its expertise to the problem of statelessness. Since then, the organization has become increasingly involved in promoting the prevention and reduction of statelessness by disseminating information, training government officials, and encouraging cooperation amongst other organizations working on related issues. UNHCR has encouraged states to set up national structures so that stateless people can seek representation and has, where appropriate, worked with states to establish procedures to allow stateless people to acquire citizenship. Some states have made significant progress in recent years in addressing problems arising from statelessness and disputed citizenship. Thus far, however, problems have been tackled on a case-by-case basis. Instances of inadvertent loss of nationality, as well as those of discrimination leading to loss of nationality and expulsion, continue and are often a root cause of refugee flows. The challenge is to establish a harmonized international framework for acknowledging and responding systematically to statelessness problems.

The Commonwealth of Independent States and neighbouring countries, 1999   Map 8.1

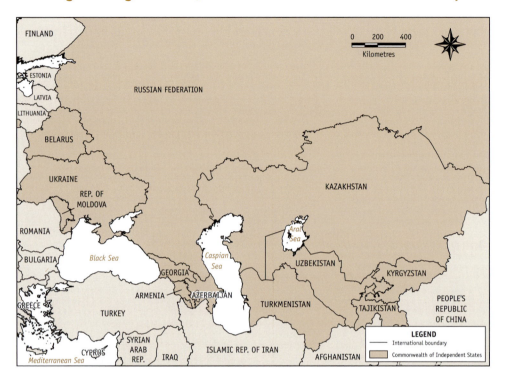

The concept of preventive protection

In September 1991, the new High Commissioner, Sadako Ogata, approved in principle the opening of a regional office in Moscow. The following month, UNHCR organized its first training activity in Moscow on emergency preparedness. Building on experience gained in Central Europe, UNHCR sought to pursue a policy which would strengthen its operational capacity and enable it to play a preventive and early warning role. [9]

In early December, UNHCR sent a mission to the region to 'determine . . . [its] ongoing presence in the USSR'. These officials ended up witnessing the dissolution of the Soviet Union and the birth of the CIS on 8 December 1991. The conclusions of this landmark mission helped shape UNHCR's approach to the post-Soviet region. They emphasized that 'the classic approach of reacting to events *ex post facto* and with traditional mandate measures exclusively within the country of asylum is likely to prove inadequate'. Drawing on lessons 'from current UNHCR experience in ethnic conflict situations such as Sri Lanka and Yugoslavia', the mission recommended 'a primarily protection/preventive role, with the accent on early warning and pragmatic measures to reduce pressures on affected populations to move out'. It also recommended the establishment of an 'ongoing presence' in the Transcaucasus (hereafter referred to as the South Caucasus) and Central Asia.[10]

During the first months of 1992, UNHCR sent fact-finding missions to most of the newly independent states that had emerged in Eastern Europe, the South Caucasus and Central Asia, thereby establishing direct ties with the new governments. In March, the High Commissioner convened a meeting to develop a UNHCR strategy for the post-Soviet region. It agreed on the need for more systematic measures to provide legal advice and support to strengthen the capacities of governments and non-governmental organizations (NGOs) to deal with issues related to forced displacement. It also endorsed the overall concept of 'preventive protection'. In the context of the CIS, this was to involve establishing a presence, monitoring and early warning, setting the tone of international humanitarian standards, training initiatives, and public information efforts to promote human rights with special regard to minorities and displaced persons.[11]

Building new partnerships

The emerging strategy recognized what had been apparent from the very outset of UNHCR's involvement in this region, namely the need for close cooperation with other relevant agencies and organizations of the UN system, as well as with the IOM.[12] During this initial period, UNHCR worked with the Russian Red Cross and Médecins Sans Frontières in providing assistance to asylum seekers in Moscow. It fielded joint fact-finding missions with the UN Children's Fund (UNICEF) and the World Food Programme (WFP), and disseminated human rights documentation from stocks of the UN Centre for Human Rights.

However, it became clear that in addressing the refugee and broader forced migration challenges in the CIS and Central Europe, UNHCR would also need to establish partnerships with other important international actors which had an interest in these issues. These included in particular the Council of Europe and the Conference on Security and Cooperation in Europe (CSCE)—predecessor to the OSCE.

On the occasion of a CSCE 'human dimensions conference' held in Moscow in September 1991, the High Commissioner pointed out the complementarity of UNHCR and CSCE concerns. She suggested the question of dislocated populations be placed on the CSCE agenda and called for more direct dialogue between CSCE member states and UNHCR.[13] This and subsequent initiatives proved effective and helped focus attention on refugee and migration issues. Indeed, at a further CSCE meeting in Helsinki in June 1992, 10 states, including the Russian Federation and Kyrgyzstan from the CIS, submitted a draft resolution expressing concern at 'the aggravation of the problem of refugees and displaced persons'. In it they declared that 'displacement is often a result of violations of the existing commitments under the CSCE human dimension . . . and is thus of direct and legitimate concern to all participating States and does not belong exclusively to the internal affairs of the State concerned'. [14]

UNHCR came to be seen as having an important role within, or alongside, the CSCE process. UNHCR's participation in a CSCE-led mission to Nagorno-Karabakh in

March 1992 was the first practical experience of interaction between the United Nations and the CSCE generally, and between UNHCR and CSCE in particular. [15]

When, later on, UNHCR began operating in the South Caucasus, it was to become increasingly involved in broader peacemaking efforts led by the United Nations or the OSCE. Among these were the OSCE 'Minsk Group' consultations on Nagorno-Karabakh, the UN-sponsored negotiations between Georgia and Abkhazia, and the OSCE-led reconciliation process for Georgia and South Ossetia. In Tajikistan, UNHCR also cooperated closely with OSCE in organizing the repatriation programme.

Conflicts in the South Caucasus and Tajikistan

The struggle between Armenia and Azerbaijan over Nagorno-Karabakh, which had intensified at the end of the 1980s, was only one of several conflicts that escalated into war soon after the dissolution of the Soviet Union in December 1991. In Georgia, the armed confrontation which had begun in 1989 with the South Ossetians, who were demanding independence, worsened until an uneasy ceasefire was arranged in May 1992. Within weeks of this, a new conflict broke out in Georgia, this time in the autonomous territory of Abkhazia. In Moldova, a brief but fierce bout of fighting broke out in early 1992 between Moldovan forces and those of the self-proclaimed 'Transdniester Republic'. In Central Asia, a bloody civil war began in Tajikistan in May 1992.

During the second half of 1992, the number of people displaced by these conflicts rose dramatically. By this time, the need for emergency humanitarian assistance was widely acknowledged and UNHCR put aside many of its early reservations about becoming involved on the ground. The difficulty now, as UNHCR's representative in the region put it, was 'to get around donor compassion fatigue'. In August he argued in a policy paper that 'even if it may be currently obsessed with Yugoslavia, the international community cannot, on reflection, further ignore the situation in the Transcaucasus'.[16] UNHCR subsequently played a key role, together with the UN Department of Humanitarian Affairs (which later became the Office for the Coordination of Humanitarian Affairs), in initiating a programme of international humanitarian relief.

The conflict between Armenia and Azerbaijan over Nagorno-Karabakh

Even before the dissolution of the Soviet Union, fighting over Nagorno-Karabakh had uprooted some 300,000 Armenians and 350,000 Azerbaijanis. Armenia's declaration of independence in October 1991 and the dissolution of the Soviet Union less than two months later both led to an escalation in the fighting and to further displacement. By August 1993, Nagorno-Karabakh and Armenian forces controlled some 20 per cent of Azerbaijan territory and had established two 'corridors' linking the enclave with Armenia.

This ethnic Azerbaijani widow, displaced as a result of the conflict between Armenia and Azerbaijan, has been living in a disused gas container for more than 10 years. (UNHCR/A. HOLLMANN/1999)

In the context of this continuing violence, UNHCR was reluctant to initiate a large-scale humanitarian operation on its own. Instead, UNHCR decided to deploy and test its newly created emergency response capacity. On 3 December 1992, UNHCR emergency teams arrived in the Armenian and Azerbaijani capitals, Yerevan and Baku.

By the time a ceasefire was eventually arranged in May 1994, more than half a million Azerbaijanis had been forcibly displaced from large areas of Azerbaijan by Karabakh Armenian forces. While the ceasefire has held, a political settlement has remained elusive and most of those who were uprooted have remained hostages of a frozen conflict. Despite the political deadlock, UNHCR has worked in close partnership with the World Bank, the UN Development Programme (UNDP) and NGOs in assisting the Azerbaijani government in the rehabilitation and reconstruction of areas to which uprooted populations have been able to return in safety.

Conflicts in the Georgian territories of Abkhazia and South Ossetia

In Georgia, the populations of the autonomous territories of South Ossetia and Abkhazia both began to press for secession as early as 1989. The original inhabitants of Ossetia, the northern part of which now lies in the Russian Federation, accounted for two-thirds of the region's population in 1979. South Ossetians favoured greater autonomy and unification with North Ossetia and were disliked by Georgians for

Box 8.2   Non-governmental organizations

The term 'non-governmental organization' (NGO) applies to a wide range of bodies which are non-commercial in nature. It includes, in particular, humanitarian organizations and human rights monitoring and advocacy organizations. Since its inception, UNHCR has worked with a large number of NGOs. They include inter-national NGOs, which operate in many different countries, national NGOs, which operate only in their own country, and some large, decen-tralized NGO 'families', such as CARE International, World Vision Inter-national, Oxfam, and the Save the Children Alliance.

These organizations engage in a broad spectrum of activities, including emergency relief work, long-term development, and human rights monitoring and advocacy. High Commissioner Sadako Ogata has described NGOs as 'an important democratizing factor in the United Nations international spectrum'.[i] The growing international recognition of their important contributions is also illustrated by the fact that the 1999 Nobel Peace Prize went to Médecins Sans Frontières.

Accurate global statistics on the number of NGOs and resources channelled through them are hard to obtain. Some obser-vers estimate the total funding channelled through NGOs worldwide to be in excess of US$8.5 billion a year.[ii] In emergencies in particular, the proportion of overseas development assistance being channelled through NGOs has increased dramatically in the past 15 years.

UNHCR has worked closely with NGOs since its inception. Indeed, the organization's Statute expressly provides that UNHCR should administer assistance to refugees through private as well as public agencies. During its early years, partly because of the limited funds at its own disposal, UNHCR functioned primarily as a coordinating and supervisory body. During this period, NGOs became important partners for UNHCR. At the time of the large-scale refugee influxes in Africa in the 1960s, UNHCR and NGOs developed a new, more dynamic working relationship, operating in particular through the International Council of Voluntary Agencies (ICVA), an NGO umbrella organization founded in 1962, which continues to play an important role.

In the 1970s, the number of NGOs began to grow and they became UNHCR's main implementing partners in all aspects of the organization's work. By the end of the 1970s, for example, 37 different NGOs were working in Khao I Dang, a Cambodian refugee camp in Thailand. Throughout the 1980s, NGOs continued to proliferate during the major refugee emergencies in the Horn of Africa, Asia and Central America. By the late 1980s, over 100 international NGOs were working in the Afghan refugee camps and settlements in Pakistan.

The 1990s saw the biggest increase in the number of NGOs, their size, operational capabilities and resources. In 1994, there were estimated to be over 100 NGOs operating in the Rwandan camps in what was then Zaire, 150 in Mozambique, 170 in Rwanda, and some 250 in Bosnia and Herzegovina. The Kosovo crisis in 1999 again confirmed the number and diversity NGOs able to access public and private sources.

It is governments, rather than individual donors, that are most responsible for the recent increase in NGO funding. In 1970, public-sector funding accounted for a mere 1.5 per cent of NGO budgets. By the mid-1990s, it had risen to 40 per cent and was still increasing.[iii] This increase in funding from governments and UN sources has led some observers to question whether a number of these organizations should indeed still be called non-governmental organizations. In many of their projects, NGOs essentially act as subcontractors for governments or the United Nations. Conversely, however, in many cases NGOs act as outspoken critics of both governments and UN organizations.

Increasingly, governments are funding national NGOs, undercutting the traditional intermediary role of inter-national NGOs. Many of these national NGOs are small. Some are community-based organizations with only a few staff and operating only in one small town or village. There has been a pro-liferation of such NGOs. For example, by 1999 there were over 200 different national NGOs working in Afghanistan alone.

UNHCR has established increasingly close working partnerships with national NGOs. During the Bosnian crisis, more than 90 per cent of UNHCR's humanitarian assistance was distributed by local organizations like Merhamet, CARITAS and local Red Cross branches. By 1999, 395 national NGOs were working in partnership with UNHCR—three times the number five years earlier. In 1999, these national NGOs implemented nearly 20 per cent of UNHCR's projects. They play an important role in the creation of local civil society and invariably remain long after international humanitarian organizations have left.

Since 1994, UNHCR–NGO cooperation and consultation has expanded through what is known as the Partnership in Action (PARinAC) process. UNHCR and NGOs hold regular meetings in most countries where they operate. These help build partnership structures and allow NGOs to participate in UNHCR's own policy development and planning. The PARinAC process has proved particularly useful in sudden, large-scale refugee emergencies.

The importance of NGOs to UNHCR is illustrated by the fact that in 1999, UNHCR channelled US$295 million through 544 NGO implemen-ting partners. Some 50 per cent of all UNHCR programmes are now implemented by international NGOs, 34 of these NGOs receiving more than US$2 million each in 1999.

The Humanitarian Charter and the Minimum Standards in Disaster Response, known as the Sphere Project, aims to increase the effectiveness of humanitarian assistance, and to make humanitarian agencies more accountable. Launched in 1997, this principled and practical framework for humanitarian action is the result of the combined efforts of over 200 organizations, including NGOs, the International Red Cross and Red Crescent Movement, academic institutions, the United Nations (including UNHCR), and government agencies.

their traditionally pro-Russian stance. The Abkhazians, a largely Muslim people, had enjoyed virtual sovereignty within Georgia in the 1920s. Under Stalin, however, Georgians were settled in the area and, by 1989, Abkhazians comprised only 18 per cent of the population, while Georgians accounted for nearly half.

Fighting in South Ossetia broke out in 1989 between Ossetians and local Georgians. Despite the presence of Soviet and then Georgian troops, a successful ceasefire agreement was not reached until May 1992. By this time, some 50,000 Ossetians had fled across the border to North Ossetia in the Russian Federation, while an estimated 23,000 Georgians had been chased out of South Ossetia into Georgia proper.

Just as one conflict ended in Georgia, another started. Fighting broke out in Abkhazia in mid-1992 when the republic declared its independence, and 2,000 Georgian troops were sent in to restore order. Over the next year-and-a-half, this conflict resulted in the displacement and expulsion of an estimated 250,000 Georgians from Abkhazia.

In July 1993, a ceasefire was agreed, and the following month the UN Security Council decided to establish a small UN Observer Mission in Georgia (UNOMIG). This was the United Nations' first such mission in the former Soviet Union. At first, the ceasefire faltered, but by December UN-sponsored talks resulted in a memorandum of understanding between the two sides and the inclusion of peace-keeping personnel in UNOMIG. As the situation began to stabilize, UNHCR, which had opened an office in the Georgian capital, Tiblisi, in June 1993, became actively involved with the Georgian and Abkhaz sides and the Russian Federation in negoti-ating a quadripartite agreement on the voluntary return of refugees and displaced people. An agreement was eventually signed in Moscow in April 1994, providing for a 2,500-strong CIS peacekeeping force comprising mainly Russian troops, and giving UNHCR the task of overseeing the return process.

Though not without its flaws, the quadripartite agreement appeared to represent a bold but credible attempt to reverse what had amounted to the expulsion of an entire population on ethnic grounds. However, the implementation of the agreement was subsequently obstructed by the insistence of the Abkhaz side that the issue of Abkhazia's political status be settled in advance of repatriation. UNHCR was thus compelled to suspend its return programme.

Despite the continuation of UN-sponsored proximity talks and other negotiations, the overall situation remained volatile. Tens of thousands of displaced Georgians returned spontaneously to the Gali district, which lies closest to Georgia proper, despite the threat of land mines and other dangers. The lack of security guarantees in an area which was not under government control made UNHCR reluctant to promote or facilitate voluntary repatriation to Abkhazia. Instead, it negotiated with both the Abkhaz and Georgian sides in an effort to reach the returnees in the Gali zone, as well as victims of conflict in other parts of Abkhazia, mainly in the regional capital, Sukhumi. UNHCR subsequently provided those who had spontaneously returned to Gali with building materials, seeds and diesel fuel to assist reconstruction, while similar assistance was provided in other parts of Abkhazia.

In May 1998, fighting between Georgian partisans and Abkhaz militia flared up again in the Gali district, marking a major setback for local and international peace-making efforts. As a result, some 40,000 of the original 50,000 returnees were again displaced, and many of the houses and schools rehabilitated by UNHCR were looted and burned down.

Efforts to achieve a peaceful resolution of the conflict between Georgia and South Ossetia were more fruitful. The political impasse which had prevailed since May 1992 was broken in February 1997 at a meeting in Vladikavkaz in North Ossetia. A joint control commission, operating under the aegis of the OSCE, adopted three decisions, including one on the voluntary repatriation of refugees and displaced people. UNHCR established a presence in Tskhinvali, South Ossetia, and set up a modest assistance programme there, primarily providing construction materials to returnees whose homes had been destroyed or damaged during the conflict. This cooperation between UNHCR and OSCE in assisting with the resolution of the Georgian–Ossetian conflict was extended in 1998 to include the Council of Europe in a joint effort to strengthen the Georgian government's capacity to establish a judicial and legal process to facilitate the return of property to victims of the conflict.

Civil war in Tajikistan

Civil war broke out in Tajikistan in May 1992, less than six months after the break-up of the Soviet Union. The conflict revolved around political, ethnic or clan, and, to a lesser extent, ideological issues. The Uzbek, Khojandi and Kulyabi groups, which had traditionally wielded political and economic power during the Soviet era, were challenged by marginalized groups from other regions (Garm and the Pamiris) with an anti-communist, pro-Islamic and nationalist agenda. Russian troops, which had remained in the country following the break-up of the Soviet Union, assisted the government in bringing the fighting under control and in preventing rebel forces from entering the country through its southern border. Within months, the fighting had caused some 600,000 people to flee their homes. Of these, around 60,000 Tajiks fled south to Afghanistan, while many other ethnic Russians, Uzbeks and Tajiks fled to other parts of the CIS and beyond.

While an integrated UN approach to the conflict in Tajikistan was being worked out, UNHCR provided emergency assistance to Tajik refugees in northern Afghanistan. Then, in January 1993, a UNHCR team arrived in the Tajik capital, Dushanbe. In the same month, a small UN Mission of Observers to Tajikistan (UNMOT), established by the UN Security Council, was deployed. Over the next few months, UNHCR staff found themselves operating in an extremely volatile environment. During this time, they conducted difficult, though ultimately successful, negotiations with the warlords responsible for the expulsions to win the confidence of all parties and create the necessary conditions for the return of the refugees and displaced people.

Former refugee children who have returned to Khatlon Province, Tajikistan, attend classes outdoors because their school was destroyed during the war. (UNHCR/A. HOLLMANN/1995)

The civil war effectively ended in early 1993, although some insurgency activity continued to destabilize the country after that. From April 1993, UNHCR, working together with other UN agencies and NGOs and with the support of the government of Tajikistan, helped to organize the repatriation of refugees and the return of those who had been internally displaced. To achieve this, UNHCR established an extensive field presence to monitor returns and provide protection. UNHCR, together with its partners, provided the returnees with assistance in reconstructing their destroyed homes and vital infrastructure.

By mid-1995, the majority of the internally displaced as well as some 40,000 refugees had returned and nearly 19,000 shelters had been rebuilt. UNHCR handed over its monitoring activities to the OSCE. Then, in June 1997, a new UN-sponsored peace agreement signed in Moscow resulted in further repatriation. Over the following two years, another 17,000 Tajiks returned, while UNHCR also implemented income-generation, crop and education programmes to facilitate the reintegration of the returnees in the south of the country. Since then, Tajikistan has succumbed to more bouts of fighting, which have resulted in further internal displacement. Although the opposition has been brought into the government, the political situation remains tense.

New challenges in CIS countries

In the years following the dissolution of the Soviet Union, the newly established states grappled with the need to establish appropriate legal and administrative procedures to cope with complex refugee and migration-related issues. Between 1992 and 1993, most of the CIS countries either introduced temporary refugee legislation or adopted refugee laws. In February 1993, the Russian Federation and Azerbaijan became the first of the CIS countries to accede to the 1951 UN Refugee Convention and 1967 Protocol, to be followed by Armenia and Tajikistan by the end of the year.

Increasingly, however, it became clear that the CIS states were preoccupied primarily with their own displaced populations and were reluctant to assume responsibilities for dealing with classic refugee issues. UNHCR faced considerable difficulties in promoting the internationally accepted idea of asylum, including the introduction of fair and reliable status determination procedures and the acceptance of a uniform definition of a refugee.

In 1991–92, UNHCR and its NGO partners were faced with the dilemma of how to respond to the needs of asylum seekers stranded in Moscow airport and of some 10,000 non-CIS asylum seekers. The latter were mostly Afghans, Somalis, Iraqis and Ethiopians, and were mostly in the Russian capital. UNHCR's representative in Moscow reported in January 1993 that 'refugees/asylum seekers are not welcome; as far as Russia is concerned they are in transit and assisting them here would create a pull factor'.[17] He added that Russia did not even have the financial means to look after its own displaced, the 1992 budget of the Federal Migration Service being US$3 million for one million displaced people. Other CIS countries faced similar problems. UNHCR therefore began providing assistance to the most vulnerable refugees and asylum seekers, surveyed the needs of stranded Afghans in Russia, and launched public awareness activities.

A further complication was the confusion in terminology and concepts in some of the CIS countries. In particular, Russia and some other countries introduced the term 'forced migrant' into their legislation to describe Russians and russophones who were repatriating from former Soviet republics that had now become independent countries. This legislation obfuscated the internationally recognized refugee definition and reinforced the distinction between refugees from within the CIS and those from outside the CIS. It often resulted in discrimination against the latter.[18]

Russian 'forced migrants' and other population movements

For Russia, the key migration management issue was thus the mass inflow of Russians and russophones. Many of these people felt stranded and discriminated against in the new states. This was particularly the case in Central Asia and the Baltic states. The whole question became highly politicized. The issue of millions of repatriants weighed on national pride, while the protection of the rights of Russians in the 'near abroad' featured prominently in Russia's foreign policy.

A 'repatriation' movement from the Central Asian republics had actually been under way during the last decade of Soviet rule, but now the volume and political visibility of these flows suddenly increased. Between 1992 and 1996, approximately three million people migrated to Russia, although barely a million of them were registered with the authorities. This was the largest single population movement within the CIS region in the post-Soviet period.

Russia labelled those Russian citizens or would-be citizens who were arriving from the former Soviet republics 'forced migrants'. Other CIS countries countered that this definition was politically judgemental. They maintained that what was happening was a form of post-imperial relocation which did not affect only Russians. Rather, they argued that many of those on the move were returning to their ancestral homeland on a voluntary basis for cultural, social or economic motives. To add to the confusion, the term 'forced migrant', was also applied to those who were internally displaced.

There were other large-scale displacement and migration problems facing the CIS states. These included the movement of people such as the Crimean Tatars, who had been deported in the 1940s and until the collapse of the Soviet Union had been prevented from returning to their homeland. There were flows of ethnic repatriates to their titular states, such as ethnic Kazaks returning to Kazakhstan from Mongolia, Tajikistan and Afghanistan. There was also resettlement induced by environmental

'Forced migrants' registered in the Russian Federation by previous place of residence, 1993-98* (Total = 978,000)

Figure 8.2

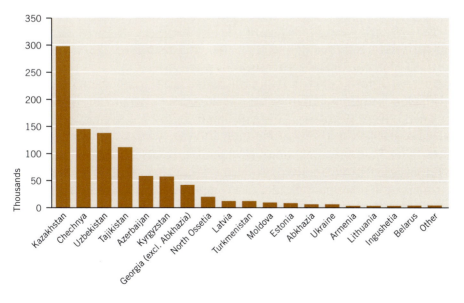

*The total number of registered and unregistered 'forced migrants' who arrived in the Russian Federation during the 1990s is estimated to be over three million.
Source: Russian Federal Migration Service.

disaster and, increasingly, a westward flow of illegal migrants using the CIS countries as a transit corridor to Western Europe. In addition, within the CIS, millions of people sought work in other states. This labour migration, especially from countries affected by war, was generally of an unregulated nature.

To tackle these issues, the CIS states worked together, both on a bilateral and sub-regional basis, and within the CIS framework. As early as October 1992, 10 CIS states signed an agreement concerning formerly deported peoples in Bishkek, Kyrgyzstan.[19] A year later, nine CIS countries also signed an agreement on assistance to refugees and forced migrants. This agreement gave definitions of a 'refugee' and 'forced migrant' that were wider than the 1951 UN Refugee Convention and included those who had fled from conflict. It considered a refugee to be someone who was not a national of the country of asylum, whereas a 'forced migrant' was.[20]

These and similar CIS agreements from this period appeared to represent sound initiatives, but in practice they remained only on paper. This was not only because of lack of funding but also, more importantly, because of enduring tensions within the CIS between states such as Russia, which favoured greater integration, and states such as Ukraine, Azerbaijan, Moldova and Georgia, which opposed the CIS's transformation into a supra-state structure. Increasingly, therefore, the need was recognized for some form of neutral framework within which displacement and migration problems could be addressed by CIS countries.

The CIS conference

In a move to draw international attention to the problem of 'forced migrants', the Russian authorities turned to the UN General Assembly. In December 1993, the General Assembly approved a resolution, sponsored by the Russian Federation, to hold a UN conference on 'the problems of refugees, returnees, displaced persons and migrants'.[21] Two months later, Russian Foreign Minister Andrei Kozyrev officially requested the High Commissioner to convene a conference. [22]

UNHCR initially responded cautiously, being well aware of the politically sensitive nature of the proposal and the financial and operational implications. Increasingly, however, it also recognized the limitations of a piecemeal approach to the problems of this vast region, and that an effective and relevant framework for action could not, in this non-traditional environment, be based solely on an asylum-centred strategy. UNHCR decided to dovetail CIS initiatives with its own evolving strategic thinking and promote the idea of a comprehensive multilateral approach to the region's problems. In this, the organization drew on its experience gained in the CIREFCA process in Central America more than a decade earlier.

During discussions held in Moscow in May 1994, the Russian Federation agreed to the broad approach proposed by UNHCR. Other CIS countries and affected states and organizations were then invited to participate. UNHCR, IOM and the OSCE, represented by its Office for Democratic Institutions and Human Rights (ODIHR), agreed to organize this ambitious multilateral endeavour jointly. In December 1994, a new General Assembly resolution reinforced support for the initiative. [23]

The intense preparatory work lasted almost two years and consolidated agreement to address current and potential displacement problems within an international forum for cooperation and dialogue. Through a series of sub-regional meetings, the CIS states were encouraged to identify the problems and needs in their countries more clearly. A first meeting of experts in May 1995 agreed to recognize a broad range of displaced populations as relevant to the conference.[24]

The CIS conference was finally convened in Geneva on 30–31 May 1996. The full name was 'Regional Conference to Address the Problems of Refugees, Displaced Persons, Other Forms of Involuntary Displacement and Returnees in the Countries of the Commonwealth of Independent States and Relevant Neighbouring States'. In searching for a strategy to address humanitarian problems and to bolster regional stability, the conference had an underlying political dimension which integrated displacement and migration issues with security concerns. It therefore represented the nearest the international community got to addressing directly, albeit under a humanitarian aegis, some of the most acute problems resulting from the dissolution of the Soviet Union.

Participants reviewed the population movements taking place in the region and went on to establish clearer definitions of the different categories of people involved. These included refugees, internally displaced persons, repatriants and formerly deported peoples, as well as ecological, labour and transit migrants. Instead of the term 'forced migrant', the neutral term 'involuntarily relocating persons' was devised.[25] Clarifying these definitional issues represented both the starting point and the key achievement of the conference. Identifying the type of movement involved helped depoliticize the issues. The conference adopted a Programme of Action which, on the basis of agreed principles, set out a comprehensive and integrated strategy to address migration and displacement issues. In doing so, it sought to prevent the emergence of situations which would create further involuntary displacement.[26]

Follow-up to the CIS conference

The CIS conference process helped bring the countries concerned into the mainstream of international norms and practices relating to refugees and displaced populations, and to focus the attention of donors on the region. Its Programme of Action subsequently provided the impetus for the adoption of new legislation in practically all fields, including human rights and refugee law.

The conference helped UNHCR refine and energize its activities in the region by allowing it to extend its activities to a broader range of displaced populations. UNHCR has since opened offices in all CIS countries. It has also worked closely with governments to develop and implement asylum and citizenship legislation which conforms to international standards. In Central Asia, UNHCR helped establish the Bishkek Migration Management Centre to provide training, research and inter-regional dialogue on refugee and migration issues in the area. More generally, it has provided training programmes not only on refugee law issues, but also on issues concerning human rights, humanitarian affairs, migration and aliens law, and emergency preparedness.

Together with its partners, UNHCR actively promoted the recognition of the role of NGOs in civil society and the establishment of a legal framework defining their status. The Council of Europe gradually assumed the lead role in the process of providing a normative framework on NGO legislation. Through an NGO fund established in 1997, UNHCR provided small grants to local NGOs to strengthen their capacity to address migration and refugee issues.

In the context of the follow-up process, UNHCR and its partners, particularly the OSCE High Commissioner on National Minorities and the Council of Europe, sought to address the crucial but politically sensitive issues of statelessness [see box 8.1] and that of the Soviet institution of residence permits (*propiska*), which restricted freedom of movement and choice of residence. Although some of the CIS countries formally abolished the *propiska* system, in practice it has more often than not been perpetuated tacitly or under another name.

Formerly deported peoples

Among the peoples deported by Stalin in the 1940s, the Crimean Tatars, the Meskhetians and the Volga Germans were not allowed to return in substantial numbers until the late 1980s, when controls within the Soviet Union began to loosen. Volga Germans were allowed to emigrate to the Federal Republic of Germany under the provisions of the German constitution. Some 850,000 went to Germany between 1992 and 1999, while only a few thousand returned to the Volga region during this period.

In the case of the Crimean Tatars, some 250,000 returned to the Crimea in Ukraine between 1988 and 1999. A similar number are estimated to remain outside the Crimea, mainly in Uzbekistan. The Crimean Tatars' return has caused tensions with residents of the peninsula which have been exacerbated by economic difficulties affecting the whole population. Returning Tatars also had problems acquiring Ukrainian citizenship and in finding housing, which led them to set up squatter settlements.

In 1997, the Ukrainian government asked for international assistance in reintegrating the Tatars. At the same time, mediation by UNHCR and the OSCE High Commissioner on National Minorities enabled the Ukrainian and Uzbekistan governments to conclude an accord facilitating returning Tatars' acquisition of Ukrainian citizenship. UNHCR also carried out a public awareness campaign in Ukraine on the issue of the Tatars. By the end of 1999, the problem of statelessness among formerly deported people in Crimea was largely resolved.

The question of the Meskhetians was more complex. This disparate Turkic group from southwestern Georgia did not acquire a clear national identity until after their deportation in the 1940s. Unlike the other groups, they were never accused of collaboration with the invading Nazi forces. However, the strategic importance of the area near the Turkish border from which they were deported led the Soviet authorities to prevent their return. In the late 1980s, communal violence in the area where they had settled (the Fergana Valley between Uzbekistan and Kyrgyzstan) forced around 90,000 of them to flee. More than half of them went to Azerbaijan. Since then, Meskhetians have continued to encounter problems of status, citizenship and integration in several CIS countries.

In September 1998, all of the parties involved were brought together for informal consultations for the first time. The meeting in The Hague was organized by the OSCE High Commissioner on National Minorities in cooperation with UNHCR and the Open Society Institute's forced migration projects.[27] Subsequently, other actors including the Council of Europe have also become involved. The Council of Europe included the gradual repatriation of those Meskhetians who wanted to go to Georgia as one of the conditions for the latter's accession to the organization in April 1999.

Conflict in the North Caucasus

The first inter-ethnic fighting on the territory of the Russian Federation took place in the North Caucasus in October and November 1992, within a year of the dissolution of the Soviet Union. Longstanding tensions between the Ingush, a formerly deported people, and the North Ossetians, flared into violence, forcing between 40,000 and 50,000 Ingush to flee the disputed Prigorodny District of North Ossetia for the neighbouring autonomous republic of Ingushetia. In October 1994, the Russian authorities invited UNHCR to investigate the situation in the area. However, shortly after the fact-finding mission left, a full-scale military conflict erupted in neighbouring Chechnya.

War in Chechnya

Chechnya declared its independence in November 1991, after which some 150,000 non-Chechens left, largely to other parts of the Russian Federation. Fighting erupted in late 1993, when opponents of the rebel Chechen government launched the first of a series of unsuccessful offensives. In December 1994, Russian forces intervened directly against the breakaway republic, dramatically altering the political and security situation in the area. Bombing and artillery attacks destroyed large parts of the capital, Grozny, and surrounding villages, forcing over 250,000 people out of a total Chechen population of 700,000 to flee their homes. These people fled into Ingushetia, Daghestan and North Ossetia, as well as to other parts of Chechnya.

The Russian government invited UNHCR to provide humanitarian assistance to the displaced at the end of December 1994, not long after the entry of the Russian troops. With the agreement of the UN Secretary-General that it work with this huge new caseload of internally displaced people, UNHCR launched its first emergency humanitarian assistance operation in the Russian Federation. This assistance in the North Caucasus was provided in cooperation with the Russian Ministry of Emergencies, the International Committee of the Red Cross (ICRC), other UN

Main population displacements in the Caucasus region during the 1990s

Map 8.2

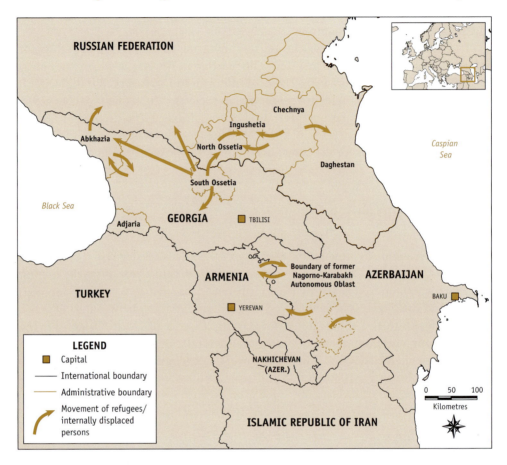

agencies and NGOs. Largely as a result of this operation, social and ethnic tensions resulting from the mass influx were contained, preventing destabilization in Ingushetia and Daghestan and the spread of the military conflict from Chechnya.

A ceasefire was eventually secured in August 1996. This provided for the withdrawal of Russian troops but did not resolve the question of Chechnya's status. Over the next year, many of the displaced returned to their homes in Chechnya, allowing the UN inter-agency emergency operation in the region to be phased down. Attention reverted once again to the issue of the repatriation of internally displaced Ingush people to the Prigorodny District.[28]

The situation in Chechnya remained volatile, however. Kidnappings and killings were widespread. In December 1996, six ICRC staff members were brutally assassinated as they slept in the hospital where they worked. In North Ossetia, Vincent Cochetel, head of UNHCR's Field Office in Vladikavkaz, was kidnapped in January 1998, taken to Chechnya and not freed there until 11 months later. The security risks to humanitarian workers prompted UNHCR to redeploy its staff from Vladikavkaz to Stavropol, 300 km to the northwest, in early 1999.

Continuing tensions in the region obliged UNHCR to abandon plans to promote return. In 1997, UNHCR provided assistance to over 90,000 internally displaced people from Chechnya who were living in neighbouring Russian republics and in Georgia. Cross-border assistance was also provided to displaced people in Chechnya itself. In addition, over 35,000 people uprooted from the Prigorodny District of North Ossetia, who were still living in Ingushetia, were assisted. In North Ossetia, UNHCR began organizing the repatriation of 29,000 registered refugees to South Ossetia and Georgia proper.

Armed hostilities broke out again in Chechnya in the second half of 1999. At first, fighting in neighbouring Daghestan between Chechen armed groups and Russian forces obliged about 30,000 people to flee. Then, in October, a new war between Russian forces and forces of the secessionist republic broke out. Once again over 200,000 people fled into neighbouring republics, particularly Ingushetia, and several thousand escaped across the international border into Georgia. UNHCR and other humanitarian organizations provided food and emergency supplies to these people, many of whom were sheltered in camps, and sought to ensure protection of their basic human rights.

Families in Chechnya mourn their dead after their houses were destroyed by aerial bombardment.
(UNHCR/L. VAN DER STOCKT/1995)

Box 8.3

Armed attacks on humanitarian personnel

The dangers faced by humanitarian personnel are not new. In July 1964, François Preziosi, a UNHCR official working in the Rwandan refugee camps in what was then the Republic of the Congo, described some of these dangers in one of his field reports: 'If I seem to take some risks by going frequently to the front lines, it is not out of pure curiosity, but to be able, when the time is ripe, to intervene and try to prevent any inconsiderate action against the refugees both in the field and in the resettlement centers. To be able to do this I have to become a familiar sight among the officers and soldiers and therefore to visit them frequently.'[iv] Six weeks later, on 18 August 1964, Preziosi and an official working for the International Labour Organization were murdered at the Mwamba refugee camp, in the Kivu area of eastern Congo, while trying to protect Rwandan refugees.

Humanitarian personnel have regularly found themselves working in life-threatening situations all over the world. Until the end of the Cold War, however, UNHCR and most other humanitarian organizations largely avoided operating inside active war zones. Only the International Committee of the Red Cross (ICRC) and a handful of non-governmental organizations (NGOs), such as Médecins Sans Frontières, routinely operated in the midst of conflict.

Increased dangers

Throughout the 1990s, humanitarian organizations—including UNHCR—have become increasingly active in situations of ongoing armed conflict, and the number of humanitarian

personnel injured or killed in the line of duty has grown accordingly. In many cases, humanitarian personnel are victims of landmines or are threatened by indiscriminate attacks on civilian areas. During the war in Bosnia and Herzegovina, for example, over 40 humanitarian workers from different organizations were killed and many others were injured by shelling or sniper attacks, particularly in Sarajevo, where in early 1994 the city was the target of 1,200 shells every day.[v] At that time, and for the first time in its history, UNHCR routinely used armoured vehicles and staff were provided with bullet-proof vests.

Humanitarian organizations operating in conflict situations have attempted to distinguish themselves by using white vehicles, clearly marked with flags and logos, to avoid being attacked. But in many cases this has not provided sufficient protection. In places of random violence, where criminality is rife, where warlords and local commanders are accountable to no one but themselves, where checkpoints are manned by drunken soldiers or by child soldiers who carry guns bigger than themselves, no one is safe. On the contrary, aid organizations, with shiny white four-wheel drive vehicles, bristling with radio antennae and other sophisticated and expensive equipment, are often prime targets.[vi]

But humanitarian personnel are not only exposed to criminality and random violence. The presence of humanitarian organizations is often resented by one or more of the warring parties, and this resentment can develop into a particular kind of threat. Relief operations in

situations of on-going armed conflict are often perceived by warring parties as posing obstacles to their military, political or strategic goals. Humanitarian personnel may be suspected of passing on secret or sensitive information, or they may become unwanted witnesses to crimes that the warring parties would like to conceal. Combatants sometimes try to remove or deter actual or potential witnesses to human rights abuses and other violations of international law by creating an environment in which it is unsafe for humanitarian staff to operate. Organizations that operate on both sides of a front-line may also be resented for providing assistance to the 'enemy'. In many situations, locally recruited humanitarian personnel find themselves at even greater risk than international staff largely because of their local, religious or ethnic ties.

Direct attacks

Attacks on humanitarian personnel have become disturbingly commonplace. In February 1993, Reinout Wanrooy, a UNHCR staff member working in Afghanistan, was travelling on the road from Peshawar to Jalalabad with two UN colleagues and two Afghan drivers. As they neared Jalalabad, three unidentified gunmen in a pick-up truck overtook them and started shooting at the two clearly marked UN vehicles. After forcing the UN cars to a halt, the gunmen jumped out and opened fire on their victims at point-blank range. Three men died instantly and one of the Afghan drivers was fatally wounded and died later in hospital. Wanrooy managed to escape by jumping from the car and running as fast as he could, dodging a hail of gunfire.

Numerous other aid workers, from different organizations, have lost their lives in similar situations. At least 23 people working for the Red Cross movement have been killed since 1996 in the Great Lakes region of Africa alone. The brutal assassination of six ICRC staff members in Chechnya in December 1996 was particularly alarming. Mostly doctors and nurses, they were all shot as they lay in their beds in the hospital where they worked. In Burundi in the same year, three ICRC workers were assassinated in another chilling, premeditated attack. Dozens of other aid workers have lost their lives in direct attacks, caught in cross-fire from small arms or indiscriminate shelling, in planes that were shot down, or because of landmines. Many more have been injured or have suffered, and continue to suffer, the effects of trauma.

Aid workers have also increasingly been taken hostage. One such victim was Vincent Cochetel, head of UNHCR's office in Vladikavkaz, in the Russian Federation, who was overseeing a programme to help tens of thousands of people displaced by the conflicts in Chechnya, Ossetia and Ingushetia. In January 1998, as he unlocked the door to his seventh floor apartment, three masked gunmen forced him to kneel on the floor and a gun was jammed into his neck. For the next 317 days he was held prisoner in Chechnya in appalling conditions. He was stuffed into the boot of a car for three days, regularly beaten,

manacled in cellars and subjected to mock executions, before his eventual release there.

Between 1 January 1992 and 31 December 1999, 184 UN international and local staff members lost their lives in the line of duty. Most were engaged in humanitarian operations. During the same period, there were over 60 incidents of taking UN staff hostage, more than half of these involving humanitarian personnel. Since the beginning of the 1990s, 15 UNHCR staff members have been killed in deliberate, premeditated armed attacks; some were shot in the head at close range. If the death and injury of NGO staff are also taken into account, these grim statistics are significantly higher.

Safety measures

Before the conflict in the former Yugoslavia, UNHCR employed only one person, on a part-time basis, to advise on issues related to staff security. In 1992, UNHCR initiated an entirely new security system, involving the employment of specialist advisors on security, a training programme for staff members and improved coordination both within the United Nations and with NGOs. By the end of the decade, UNHCR was employing 21 field safety advisors in 15 countries in Africa, Asia and Europe. These security officers provide support and advice to UNHCR staff on security issues, monitor the local security situation, liaise with relevant local authorities, other UN agencies, NGOs and embassies, and provide on-the-spot training on how to minimize risks and respond to threats and attacks.

In places such as northern Iraq, Somalia, the Balkans, East Timor and Liberia, UN peacekeeping forces or other international or regional security forces have been deployed to enhance security for humanitarian personnel and to improve access to vulnerable populations. They escort relief convoys, clear land mines, rehabilitate roads and bridges, and manage airports. In many other places, however, governments have been less willing to commit troops or other resources to improve security for humanitarian personnel. In some of the most dangerous places in the world, far from the spotlight of the international media, many unarmed humanitarian workers continue to work on their own, risking their lives in an attempt to protect and assist others.

Refugees and IDPs in the Commonwealth of Independent States, 1999

Figure 8.3

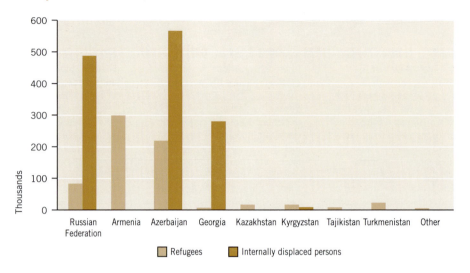

The second Chechen crisis became highly politicized internationally. No Western country disputed the right of the Russian Federation to carry out what the government maintained was an anti-terrorist campaign on its own territory. Many countries, however, criticized the means used and the disproportionate force unleashed against the civilian population by the Russian military.

The challenges ahead

The dissolution of the Soviet Union unleashed a host of latent inter-ethnic antagonisms and nationalist and secessionist aspirations in the region. Many of the conflicts that broke out in the late 1980s and early 1990s remain unresolved, leaving thousands of people still internally displaced. Most of these people have been unable either to return to their homes in safety or integrate satisfactorily in the places to which they fled. Some borders are still disputed, complicating the state-building process. The dead-locked peace processes in the South Caucasus and the continuing situations of neither war nor peace have created additional anguish and uncertainty for those concerned. Although a settlement was reached in Tajikistan, peace there remains fragile. There are also tensions in other parts of Central Asia. In Chechnya, fighting continues and much of the infrastructure and housing has been destroyed. The capital, Grozny, has become the scene of destruction on a scale not seen in Europe since the Second World War. Thousands remain displaced in Chechnya, Ingushetia and Daghestan, with an uncertain future.

Over the last decade, many CIS countries have made significant progress in developing migration and refugee legislation and most of them have now acceded to the

1951 UN Refugee Convention. However, implementation of the principles of refugee protection remain problematic, and the asylum system in the region is still inchoate and fragmented. The widespread use of the 'safe third country' notion and the existence of re-admission agreements without adequate guarantees for the protection of refugees have perpetuated serious gaps in the emerging regional and broader international asylum system.

For many citizens of CIS countries, the concept of providing asylum to refugees from outside the CIS is still a difficult one to digest. In a climate of acute socio-economic stress, xenophobia has flourished rather than been tempered. Among the general public, distrust has also grown between Slavic and Caucasian peoples within the CIS, exacerbated by the Chechen war and perceptions of a terrorist threat. In this respect, NGOs can play a vital role in promoting tolerance rather than xenophobia and in helping to build confidence among communities recovering from conflict. The NGO sector has been boosted greatly by the CIS conference process, but more needs to be done to create an environment in which NGOs can operate effectively.

In addition to the many challenges within the former Soviet region, the European Union's expanding and increasingly restrictive asylum and border-control systems are perceived by CIS countries as assigning them the role of being a barrier for illegal migration to the west. The governments of the CIS countries maintain that western and central European countries should take an integral European view of the problem. They argue that these countries should assist them both in establishing fair and effective asylum systems, and in combating illegal and transit migration, which is also a major concern in the region.

9 War and humanitarian action: Iraq and the Balkans

The 1990s presented humanitarian organizations with a range of fundamentally new challenges. In the changed political environment of the post-Cold War era, not only UNHCR, but a wide spectrum of humanitarian organizations and other international actors began operating in war-torn countries and regions to a greater extent than ever before. There was a dramatic increase in intervention by multinational military forces in internal wars, and the media—particularly in the form of live television reports—played a key role in driving international responses to humanitarian crises around the world.

The mass outflow of Kurds from northern Iraq following the Gulf War in 1991 posed a particular challenge for UNHCR. Turkey refused to grant the Kurds asylum, and US-led coalition forces therefore established a 'safe haven' for them inside northern Iraq. UNHCR participated in this operation, which involved working closely with coalition military forces. It was UNHCR's first major emergency relief operation in the post-Cold War era and it proved to be a watershed for the organization.

The large-scale population movements in the Balkan region which began later the same year as Yugoslavia disintegrated, resulted in a series of even more complex international relief operations, in which UNHCR played a leading role. Again, the organization worked in close cooperation with multinational military forces in dangerous and highly politicized environments. In Bosnia and Herzegovina, for the first time in its history, UNHCR mounted a relief operation in the midst of an ongoing war, in an attempt to assist not only refugees, but also internally displaced people and other war-affected populations.

In the course of these and other operations during the 1990s, UNHCR faced two main challenges. First, the attempt to assist civilians in the midst of armed conflict proved vastly more difficult than assisting refugees in countries of asylum. Gaining access to vulnerable populations often proved to be a complex problem, and security was a major concern, not only for the people being assisted, but also for humanitarian personnel. To continue to be seen as impartial was hard if not impossible. Second, the large number of international actors involved in responding to humanitarian crises led to the need for improved cooperation between them. New relationships were established, not only with multinational military forces and other humanitarian organizations, but also with a range of other actors including regional security organizations, human rights organizations, war crimes investigators, development organizations, peace negotiators and the media.

This chapter describes the difficulties and dilemmas which confronted UNHCR and other humanitarian organizations in these operations. For example, when should protecting people in conflict situations in their home countries be given priority

A relative waits for news as a Bosnian government soldier reads the names of men in Srebrenica known to have survived when the enclave fell to Bosnian Serb forces in 1995. (UNHCR/R. LEMOYNE/1995)

over protection through asylum? What kind of relationships should humanitarian organizations establish with warring parties which are responsible for the direct targeting of civilians? How can humanitarian organizations prevent relief supplies from being diverted to local military forces, thereby fuelling and sometimes prolonging war? How can humanitarian organizations preserve their impartiality when their aims are contrary to those of one or more of the warring parties, and particularly when working in close cooperation with international military forces?

The Kurdish crisis in northern Iraq

In March 1991, after Iraqi forces had been driven out of Kuwait by the US-led Coalition Task Force, disaffected groups within Iraq launched a rebellion in both the north and the south of the country. President Saddam Hussein's military forces responded quickly and severely, and the consequences for Iraqi civilians were devastating. In the face of a military campaign directed against them by the Iraqi army, over 450,000 mainly Kurdish people fled to the Turkish frontier within the space of a week. Between then and mid-April, another 1.3 million Kurds fled to Iran. In addition, some 70,000 Iraqis—mostly Shiites—fled their homes in the south of Iraq. In anticipation of possible refugee outflows, UNHCR had previously pre-positioned relief goods for an estimated 35,000 people in Iran and 20,000 people in Turkey, but the scale and pace of these movements exceeded all predictions.

As the refugees poured into Iran, the Iranian government requested UNHCR assistance. According to Iranian government figures, Iran was already host to over two million refugees, including 1.4 million Afghans and 600,000 Iraqi refugees displaced during the Iran–Iraq war. With this new influx, Iran became the country with the largest refugee population in the world. UNHCR assisted the Iranian authorities to respond to the influx and to manage the refugee camps.

The relief operation in Turkey was much more complicated. The Turkish government, which itself faced a significant Kurdish insurrection in southeastern Anatolia, closed its border with Iraq to prevent the Iraqi Kurds from entering, arguing that they would destabilize the country. Several hundred thousand Kurds were therefore stranded in inhospitable, snow-covered mountain passes along the Iraqi–Turkish border.

Television crews, fresh from covering the Gulf War, captured the suffering of the Kurds exposed to extreme temperatures and the lack of food and shelter. They put further pressure on UNHCR and governments to mount an international emergency relief operation. Rarely had a humanitarian crisis received such intensive media coverage.

The relief operation on the Iraqi–Turkish border was initially dominated by the US military and other coalition forces. They played a major role in organizing and carrying out the distribution of emergency supplies. But in spite of all the available military hardware and personnel, there were serious logistical problems in distributing assistance to populations in dozens of inaccessible mountain locations.

The response of Western states to Turkey's refusal to grant asylum to the Iraqi Kurds was muted. Some diplomatic representations were made but these were neither intense nor sustained. Key states were primarily concerned about the need for the North Atlantic Treaty Organization (NATO) to maintain the use of air bases in Turkey, and were therefore reluctant to criticize the Turkish government for closing its border. In addition, suggestions that large refugee camps for Iraqi Kurds in Turkey would create a Palestinian-type situation tended to silence Western governments' appeals for Turkey to grant them asylum.[1]

Establishing a 'safe haven'

As televised images of desperate Kurds trapped on the mountains continued to pour in, international pressure to find a solution mounted. At the beginning of April 1991, President Turgut Özal of Turkey broached the idea of a 'safe haven' for the Kurds inside northern Iraq. After some deliberation, on 5 April the UN Security Council adopted Resolution 688. This insisted that 'Iraq allow immediate access by international human- itarian organizations to all those in need of assistance' and authorized the Secretary- General to 'use all resources at his disposal' to address 'the critical needs of the refugees and displaced Iraqi populations'. It was on the basis of this resolution and in the context of the aftermath of the wider Gulf crisis that the US-led joint task force justified the launch of Operation Provide Comfort to establish a 'security zone' in northern Iraq.

On 10 April, members of the task force declared a no-fly zone in northern Iraq, and assumed the leadership of the relief effort. On 16 April, US President George Bush announced that coalition forces would move into northern Iraq to establish camps for the Kurds. Although President Bush promised to 'protect' the Kurds, the US adminis- tration was wary of recommitting its troops to a hostile environment and was careful to place time limits on the US military role.[2] The aim was to enable a quick return of the Kurds to northern Iraq and then to turn the operation over to the United Nations.

The motives of Western states in launching Operation Provide Comfort clearly went beyond immediate humanitarian concerns, and included a wish to accom- modate Turkey, an important ally. Their strategy had the advantage of providing a short-term solution for the Iraqi Kurds, which improved their security, while at the same time avoiding any suggestion that this might lead to full independence. This was a solution that NATO countries were to apply again, with some variations, in Kosovo at the end of the decade.

The Iraqi government also wanted the United Nations to take over the operation rapidly from the coalition forces. The result was that on 18 April the Iraqi government and the United Nations signed a Memorandum of Understanding setting out terms for a humanitarian operation aimed at enabling the displaced to return. Former High Commissioner Sadruddin Aga Khan, who was at that time the UN Secretary-General's Executive Delegate for the crisis, played a key role in these discussions with the Iraqi government.

Within the United Nations, it was suggested that UNHCR should lead the humani- tarian operation. There was initially some resistance to this from UNHCR, however, as it

Box 9.1 Internally displaced persons

International concern for the plight of internally displaced persons gained new urgency during the 1990s. This was partly because of the scale of displacement caused by new internal armed conflicts during the decade, and partly because of the greater scope for involvement in areas of ongoing conflict in the changed political environment of the post-Cold War era.

When the international legal and institutional regime to protect refugees was set up 50 years ago, it did not include internally displaced persons. In keeping with traditional notions of sovereignty, internally displaced persons were seen as falling under the domestic jurisdiction of the state concerned. The result is that the response of the international community to the problem of internal displacement has been inconsistent, and large numbers of internally displaced persons have remained without effective protection or assistance.

The extent of internal displacement

For many years, the issue of internal dis-placement did not feature prominently on the international agenda, although the Inter-national Committee of the Red Cross had traditionally assisted internally displaced persons in the course of protecting victims of armed conflict. In the 1990s, the number of internally displaced persons increased dramatically. Although precise figures are difficult to ascertain, in 1999 it was estimated that there were some 20 to 25 million internally displaced persons—forced from their homes by conflict and human rights violations—in at least 40 countries [see Figure 9.1].

More than half of the world's internally displaced are in Africa. In Sudan alone, the long-running civil war has uprooted four million people, while equally brutal and sometimes genocidal conflicts have displaced large numbers of people within Angola, Burundi, the Democratic Republic of the Congo, Rwanda and Sierra Leone. In Asia, there are some five million internally displaced persons, in particular in Afghanistan,

Azerbaijan, Indonesia, Iraq, Myanmar and Sri Lanka. Armed conflicts in Europe, such as those in the former Yugoslavia, Cyprus, Georgia, the Russian Federation and Turkey, have displaced another five million people. In the Americas, some two million people are internally displaced, the majority of whom are in Colombia.

In July 1992, Francis Deng was appointed as the Representative of the UN Secretary-General on Internally Displaced Persons. In Deng's view, internally displaced persons easily fall into 'a vacuum of responsibility' within the state. The authorities concerned see them as 'the enemy', rather than as 'their people' who require protection and assistance. Gaining access to the displaced in such circumstances is often fraught with danger. Each side fears that humanitarian aid will fortify the other and thereby seeks to obstruct assistance to the other side. Assistance may even be used as a weapon in the struggle. Access is further complicated by the fact that internally displaced people do not always congregate in easily reachable camps or settlements, but sometimes disperse to avoid identification. Many merge into urban slums where gaining access may require programmes that extend to the entire community; or they may be mixed in with other war-affected populations. Even the task of assessing their numbers is thus more contentious than with refugees.

Since the internally displaced sometimes seem indistinguishable from others in need around them, the question often arises as to whether they should be identified as a special category or subsumed under the broad rubric of vulnerable people. Internally displaced people often have particular needs resulting from their displacement. They may have limited or no access to land, no stable emp-loyment prospects, and inadequate documentation, and they may remain vulnerable to acts of violence such as forcible relocation, forced conscription and sexual assault. During return and reintegration, those who have been

displaced internally may also have distinct protection needs.

Internal displacement disrupts not only the lives of the individuals and families concerned but whole communities and societies. Both the areas left behind and the areas to which the displaced flee can suffer extensive damage. Socioeconomic systems and community structures can break down and impede reconstruction and development for decades. Conflict and displacement also spill over borders into neighbouring countries, upsetting regional stability. That is why Secretary-General Kofi Annan has underscored the compelling need for the international community to strengthen its support for national efforts to assist and protect all displaced populations.

The Guiding Principles

In 1998, Francis Deng presented the Guiding Principles on Internal Displacement to the UN Commission on Human Rights. These identify the specific needs of internally displaced persons together with the obligations of governments, insurgent groups, international organizations and non-governmental organizations (NGOs) towards these populations. Based on international human rights law, human-itarian law and analogous refugee law, the Guiding Principles, which UNHCR and a number of other humanitarian organizations helped draft, gather into one document the various provisions of existing international law applicable to internally displaced persons.

The Guiding Principles address grey areas and perceived 'gaps' in the law by making explicit many of the provisions which were previously only implicit. For example, they emphasize that internally displaced persons may not be forcibly returned to conditions of danger, they set out special pro-tection measures for women and children, and provide that displaced persons are entitled to compensation or reparation for lost property and possessions. They also assert a right *not* to be displaced, specify the grounds and conditions under which displacement is unlawful, and set out minimum guarantees to be upheld when displacement does occur. Although not a binding legal document as such, the Guiding Principles have gained considerable recognition and standing in a relatively short time, and are widely disseminated and promoted by the United Nations, regional bodies and NGOs.

Coordination of international action

During the 1990s, humanitarian organizations, human rights organizations and development agencies have focused increasingly on the problem of internal displacement. Attempts by the international community to address problems of internal displacement have, however, repeatedly been constrained by issues of national sovereignty, and by security problems and lack of access. They have also been constrained by definitional problems and difficulties of identifying displaced persons in need of protection and assistance.

In spite of the increased awareness of the problem of internal displacement, the international response has remained selective, uneven, and in many cases inadequate. Within the United Nations, moves to remedy this situation have focused on strengthening cooperation amongst the various agencies involved with the displaced, as set out in the Secretary-General's 1997 UN reform programme.[i] In their book *Masses in Flight*, Francis Deng and Roberta Cohen call for more effective divisions of labour in the field to address the needs of internally displaced persons, so that the response is more targeted.[ii] They argue that greater attention should be paid to protecting the physical safety and human rights of the internally displaced.

UNHCR's role

UNHCR was set up in 1950 to protect and assist refugees who had crossed international borders in search of safety. Although the organization's

involvement with the internally displaced goes back to the 1960s, during the 1990s the scale and scope of its activities on behalf of the internally displaced increased dramatically. By 1999, UNHCR was providing protection and assistance to some five million internally displaced persons, covering a range of operations from Colombia to Kosovo and the Caucasus.[iii]

While UNHCR's Statute makes no reference to internally displaced persons, it recognizes in Article 9 that the High Commissioner may, in addition to the work with refugees, 'engage in such activities . . . as the General Assembly may determine, within the limits of the resources placed at his [or her] disposal'. Based on this Article, and over a period of several decades, a series of UN General Assembly resolutions has acknowledged UNHCR's particular humanitarian expertise and encouraged its involvement in situations of internal displacement. In particular, UN General Assembly Resolution 48/116 (1993) set out important criteria to guide UNHCR's decision on when to become involved in protecting and assisting internally displaced persons. These resolutions, together with Article 9 of the Statute, provide the legal basis for UNHCR's interest in and action on behalf of internally displaced persons.

UNHCR considers it has particular responsibilities when the links between refugee problems and internal displacement are strong, and when problems relating to the protection of internally displaced persons require the organization's special expertise. In some situations it is difficult to draw a meaningful distinction between the internally displaced, refugees, returnees and other vulnerable war-affected people in the same area. In such cases, it is often necessary to adopt a broad, comprehensive approach towards all those affected in the community.

An important consideration for UNHCR, when becoming involved with internally displaced persons, is the impact this involvement may have on

refugee protection and the institution of asylum. There can be both positive and negative consequences of UNHCR's involvement. Countries of asylum may be more inclined to maintain their asylum policies if something is done to alleviate the suffering of the internally displaced, to reduce their compulsion to seek asylum, and to create conditions conducive to their return. On the other hand, UNHCR's activities for the internally displaced may be misinterpreted as obviating the need for international protection and asylum. Critics have also argued that a blurring of the distinction between refugees, who enjoy additional rights under international refugee law, and internally displaced persons will undermine the protection of refugees themselves.

Largest IDP populations, 1999	**Figure 9.1**
Country	Millions
Sudan	4.0
Angola	1.5–2.0
Colombia	1.8
Myanmar	0.5–1.0
Turkey	0.5–1.0
Iraq	0.9
Bosnia & Herzegovina	0.8
Burundi	0.8
Congo, Dem. Rep. of	0.8
Russian Federation	0.8
Afghanistan	0.5–0.8
Rwanda	0.6
Yugoslavia, FR	0.6
Azerbaijan	0.6
Sri Lanka	0.6
India	0.5
Congo, Rep. of	0.5
Sierra Leone	0.5

Source: US Committee for Refugees, *World Refugee Survey 2000*, Washington DC, 2000.

was argued that the establishment of a safe haven would essentially be a substitute for asylum. The presence of UNHCR inside Iraq could potentially be used by neighbouring countries as a pretext for denying asylum to refugees, which would set a dangerous precedent. UNHCR was also concerned about the safety of Kurds returning to northern Iraq. The Iraqi government had not provided any guarantees for their security. It had agreed to allow a 500-strong UN guard contingent to operate in conjunction with the humanitarian operation, but many in UNHCR doubted that this would be sufficient to ensure the safety of the returning Kurds. It had been agreed that the guards would be mandated and equipped to protect the staff, equipment and supplies of an inter-agency humanitarian programme in Iraq, but not the Kurds themselves.

The action of US, British, French and other forces to establish the security zone was swift and decisive. It was also of limited scope and duration, which in itself generated some tension. The military commanders wanted to hand over the relief operation to UNHCR quickly. They argued that once a humanitarian presence was established in northern Iraq, with UN guards to protect humanitarian personnel, the security issue would be resolved. UNHCR, however, was hesitant about establishing a relief operation in northern Iraq in a situation where the security of the returning Iraqi Kurdish population could not be guaranteed. UNHCR therefore argued for a more gradual transition.[3]

Return and reconstruction

To encourage return, the coalition forces presented the concept of the UN guards to the Kurds as a genuine safeguard, and distributed hundreds of thousands of leaflets announcing that it was safe to go back.[4] Following this, the desperate Kurds, blocked in the cold mountain passes on the Turkish border, soon started to return.

As they began moving *en masse* back into Iraq, UNHCR's immediate dilemma was resolved. As one official of the organization put it, 'UNHCR had an obligation to follow the returnees'.[5] Having received a request from the Secretary-General to assist displaced people in all parts of Iraq, the organization agreed to take the lead role. On 6 May 1991, High Commissioner Ogata advised her staff that 'UNHCR should assume overall responsibility for protection and assistance on the border and for voluntary repatriation from the border area'.[6]

In the first two weeks, nearly 200,000 refugees returned to Iraq. During this time, the relief operation continued to be dominated by the US military and other coalition forces. At its height, the operation involved some 200 aircraft and more than 20,000 military personnel. Emergency relief was also provided by over 50 international humanitarian organizations and some 30 governments.

Never before had humanitarian organizations worked together with the military in such a concerted manner. The large number of humanitarian organizations and military contingents involved, and their lack of experience in working together, created serious problems of coordination. But important lessons were learned, opening up new channels of communication between the military and humanitarian organizations.

The United States maintained 5,000 troops in Turkey and coalition aircraft continued to patrol the no-fly zone over northern Iraq. Yet UNHCR remained concerned about the safety of the Kurds. In a letter to the UN Secretary-General on 17 May 1991, High Commissioner Ogata expressed her 'continued concern' for the security of the returnees. She explained that 'nothing short of a negotiated settlement' accompanied by 'international guarantees' could offer a lasting solution to the plight of the Kurds.[7]

In early June 1991, the last of the mountain camps on the Turkish border were closed. By this time, some 600,000 of the refugees who had fled to Iran three months before had also returned. In a race against the oncoming winter, UNHCR initiated a massive shelter programme. Between August and November, some 1,600 trucks crossed the border from Turkey to Iraq to deliver around 30,000 tonnes of construction material to 500,000 people. Most of this consisted of roof beams and corrugated iron, which Kurds used to carry out reconstruction work on their houses, schools, clinics and other infrastructure in more than 1,500 villages. These were among thousands of villages which had been destroyed by the Iraqi government.[8]

In June 1992, once the initial emergency phase was over and as the focus shifted to longer-term reconstruction work, UNHCR handed over control of the relief operation to other UN agencies. Subsequent assessments of the poorly coordinated response of the international humanitarian community during the initial emergency phase of the Kurdish crisis led governments and humanitarian organizations alike to call for improved coordination amongst the different humanitarian organizations, and between these organizations and the military. An important role was envisaged for the new UN Department of Humanitarian Affairs (DHA), which was set up to coordinate UN responses to humanitarian emergencies on the basis of General Assembly Resolution 46/182 of 19 December 1991. At the beginning of 1998, DHA became the Office for the Coordination of Humanitarian Affairs (OCHA).

The establishment of the safe haven in northern Iraq has often been regarded as a success, particularly since it allowed the return of hundreds of thousands of Iraqi Kurds to their homes. Initially, however, economic conditions in the zone were hard. It suffered from a double economic embargo—UN sanctions against Iraq as a whole, and an internal embargo imposed by the Iraqi government. In the following years, security problems continued in the zone, both as a result of power struggles between the rival Kurdish factions and because of military incursions from outside.[9] There was violence in 1996, for instance, when Iraqi government forces briefly surrounded the city of Irbil. The zone also experienced incursions by Iranian military forces and, on a far larger scale, Turkish military forces, which on a number of occasions attacked places suspected of harbouring members of the Kurdistan Workers' Party (PKK). In a major attack in March 1995, Turkey sent 35,000 troops into the zone. In spite of these problems, rehabilitation and reconstruction work continued throughout the decade, and economic and security conditions in northern Iraq gradually improved.

The safe haven in northern Iraq in 1991 was initially hailed by some as reflecting a 'new world order'. Under this new order, intervention by a united international community would ensure that the protection of people from gross violations of human rights would take precedence over the principle of sovereignty.

However, subsequent use of the safe haven concept and other attempts at protecting and assisting civilians in situations of ongoing armed conflict, in places such as Bosnia and Herzegovina, Somalia, Rwanda and Kosovo, were to lead to sober reassessments.

War in Croatia and in Bosnia and Herzegovina

Almost immediately after the exodus of Kurds from northern Iraq in 1991, UNHCR was faced with another massive humanitarian emergency, this time in the Balkans.[10] The violent break-up of the Socialist Federal Republic of Yugoslavia, which began in June 1991 when Slovenia and Croatia both declared independence, resulted in the largest refugee crisis in Europe since the Second World War. Fighting first broke out in Slovenia, but this was limited and lasted only a few days. The first major outbreak of violence was in Croatia, which had a minority population of over half a million Serbs. Following Croatia's declaration of independence, the Yugoslav army and Serb paramilitaries rapidly seized control of a third of Croatian territory. It was in Croatia that the violent and pernicious phenomenon which euphemistically became known as 'ethnic cleansing' first became evident. At first, thousands of Croats were expelled from areas which fell under Serb control. Subsequently, thousands of Serbs were forced from their homes by Croatian forces. In Croatia, in 1991 alone, some 20,000 people were killed, more than 200,000 refugees fled the country, and some 350,000 became internally displaced.

In 1992, the war spread to neighbouring Bosnia and Herzegovina, with even more devastating consequences. Bosnia and Herzegovina was the most ethnically mixed of all the republics of the former Yugoslavia. According to a 1991 Yugoslav population census, the three main groups in Bosnia and Herzegovina were Muslims (44 per cent) Serbs (31 per cent) and Croats (17 per cent).[11] When Bosnia and Herzegovina declared its independence in March 1992, the government of Serbia, led by President Slobodan Milosevic, vowed to fight on behalf of the Serb minority population there. Within days, Serbian paramilitary forces moved into the eastern part of the republic and began killing or expelling Muslim and Croat residents. At about the same time, Serb forces from the Yugoslav army took to the hills surrounding the Bosnian capital Sarajevo and began attacking it with artillery. By the end of April 1992, 95 per cent of the Muslim and Croat populations in the major towns and cities of eastern Bosnia had been forced from their homes and Sarajevo was under daily bombardment. By mid-June, Serb forces controlled two-thirds of Bosnia and Herzegovina and approximately one million people had fled their homes.

In the early stages of the war, Muslims and Croats in Bosnia and Herzegovina fought together against the Bosnian Serbs, but in early 1993, fighting broke out between Bosnian Croats and Bosnian Muslims. Another round of 'ethnic cleansing' began, this time in central Bosnia. Bosnian Croat forces, backed by Croatia, attempted to create an ethnically pure swathe of territory adjoining Croatia. Although tensions between them continued, fighting between Bosnian Croat forces and the mainly

The relentless shelling of Sarajevo during the Bosnian War caused massive destruction.
(UNHCR/A. HOLLMANN/1966.)

Muslim Bosnian government forces came to an end in March 1994, with the signing of the Washington Agreement and the creation of a Muslim–Croat Federation.

By the time the war ended in December 1995, over half the 4.4 million people of Bosnia and Herzegovina were displaced. An estimated 1.3 million were internally displaced and some 500,000 were refugees in neighbouring countries. In addition, around 700,000 had become refugees in Western Europe, of whom some 345,000 were in the Federal Republic of Germany.

The humanitarian 'fig leaf'

These massive population movements and the extensive media coverage of the horrors of the war prompted one of the largest international relief operations ever mounted. In October 1991, in the midst of the population displacement taking place in Croatia, the Yugoslav authorities requested UNHCR's assistance. Then, in November, UN Secretary-General Javier Pérez de Cuéllar formally requested High

Commissioner Sadako Ogata to consider lending her 'good offices' to bring relief to needy internally displaced people affected by the conflict and to coordinate humanitarian action in the region.[12] Following an investigative mission to the region, UNHCR accepted the role and officially took the lead in coordinating the humanitarian assistance of the UN system in the region in November 1991.[13]

UNHCR set up relief operations in all the republics of the former Yugoslavia, but the organization faced its greatest challenges in Bosnia and Herzegovina. When the International Committee of the Red Cross (ICRC) withdrew temporarily from Sarajevo in May 1992 following the fatal shooting of one of its delegates, UNHCR's role in Sarajevo, in particular, became pivotal. UNHCR began delivering thousands of tonnes of relief supplies by air to Sarajevo, and by road to destinations throughout the country. For the first time in its history, UNHCR coordinated—in the midst of an ongoing war—a large-scale relief operation to assist not only refugees and internally displaced people, but also hundreds of thousands of other war-affected civilians.[14]

Unable to agree on how to end the conflict, the international community focused much of its energy on supporting the humanitarian relief operation led by UNHCR. Governments offered large amounts of funding for the relief operation, but were able to find a consensus on little else. The humanitarian operation increasingly became a 'fig leaf' and the only visible response of the international community to the war. As François Fouinat, Coordinator of the UNHCR Task Force for the former Yugoslavia, stated in October 1993, 'it is not simply that the UN's humanitarian efforts have become politicized; it is rather that we have been transformed into the only manifestation of international political will'.[15]

The high priority given to the humanitarian operation meant that UNHCR also played an important role in international political negotiations concerning the war. High Commissioner Ogata frequently briefed the UN Security Council on the humanitarian situation on the ground. Also, as chair of the Humanitarian Issues Working Group of the International Conference on the Former Yugoslavia, she regularly met international peace negotiators, leaders of the parties to the conflict and government delegations.

A key element of the international response was the deployment of UN peacekeepers. The UN Protection Force (UNPROFOR), which established a sectoral headquarters in Sarajevo in February 1992, was initially deployed to monitor the ceasefire in Croatia. When the war spread, successive UN Security Council resolutions gave UNPROFOR the additional mandate of creating conditions for the effective delivery of humanitarian aid in Bosnia and Herzegovina.[16] UNPROFOR was initially successful, in June 1992, in obtaining control of Sarajevo airport which, for the remainder of the war, was of critical importance in facilitating the delivery of relief supplies to the besieged population of Sarajevo. Although UNPROFOR's mandate was subsequently expanded to include deterring attacks on 'safe areas' and other tasks, ensuring access for humanitarian supplies remained a central part of its mandate throughout the war. By 1995, there were over 30,000 UNPROFOR troops in Bosnia and Herzegovina.

A UNHCR convoy, escorted by UNPROFOR troops, travelling between Zepce and Zavidovici in central Bosnia.
(UNHCR/S. FOA/1994)

Confronting 'ethnic cleansing'

While UNHCR and other humanitarian organizations were able to deliver large quantities of humanitarian supplies during the war, they were much less successful in protecting civilians from 'ethnic cleansing'. UNHCR personnel intervened on numerous occasions with local authorities to try to prevent expulsions and evictions from taking place, particularly in places like Banja Luka, where UNHCR had an office only a few streets away from places where people were being forced from their homes at gunpoint. But on the whole UNHCR was powerless to prevent the killings, beatings, rape, detention, expulsions and evictions of civilians. In many situations, the most UNHCR personnel could do was to report on the atrocities they witnessed. These reports, while inadequate on their own, provided vital information to the outside world. They were particularly important since journalists, like UNPROFOR, had no access to large parts of Bosnian Serb territory for most of the war. Often, especially on the Bosnian Serb side, ICRC and UNHCR were the only international organizations present to bear witness to the atrocities.

These reports, and public denunciations made by UNHCR officials against those responsible for committing atrocities, strained relations with the parties to the conflict, often resulting in threats against UNHCR staff and travel restrictions. The resulting dilemma for UNHCR staff was clear: it was difficult to cooperate with local authorities in carrying out assistance programmes, while at the same time condemning them for human rights abuses. In some cases, UNHCR was criticized for not speaking out more openly than it did.

Another difficult choice which UNHCR had to make was whether or not to assist in evacuating vulnerable civilians. Initially, UNHCR resisted evacuating civilians, but as it became apparent that the alternative for many was detention camps where they were often beaten, raped, tortured or killed, the organization began evacuating civilians whose lives were under threat. Such evacuations, however, led to an outpouring of criticism that UNHCR was facilitating 'ethnic cleansing'. In November 1992, High Commissioner Ogata described the predicament as follows:

In the context of a conflict which has as its very objective the displacement of people, we find ourselves confronted with a major dilemma. To what extent do we persuade people to remain where they are, when that could well jeopardize their lives and liberties? On the other hand, if we help them to move, do we not become an accomplice to 'ethnic cleansing'?[17]

The UNHCR Special Envoy for the former Yugoslavia, José-Maria Mendiluce, was even more blunt: 'We denounce ethnic cleansing', he said, 'but with thousands of women and children at risk who want desperately to be evacuated, it is my responsibility to help them, to save their lives. I cannot enter any philosophical or theoretical debate now . . .'[18]

In addition to assisting people within Croatia and Bosnia and Herzegovina, UNHCR urged states in the region and in Western Europe to grant 'temporary protection' to the substantial numbers of people escaping from the escalating war in the former Yugoslavia. Together these states opened their borders to hundreds of thousands of people, but some critics argued that the granting of a lesser 'temporarily protected' status rather than full refugee status weakened the international refugee protection system [see Chapter 7].

The creation of 'safe areas'

As 'ethnic cleansing' continued to produce waves of refugees and internally displaced people, the international community looked for new ways of protecting civilians to avoid the outflows. At the beginning of 1993, a critical situation developed in eastern Bosnia, which had largely been emptied of non-Serbs, except for three small pockets of territory around Srebrenica, Zepa and Gorazde. These enclaves were crowded with Muslims, many of whom had fled there from the surrounding countryside. They were defended by poorly armed Bosnian government soldiers and surrounded by Bosnian Serb forces. A UNHCR field report written on 19 February 1993 described the situation in Srebrenica as follows: 'Every day people are dying of hunger and exhaustion. The

Areas of control in Croatia and Bosnia and Herzegovina, April 1995

Map 9.1

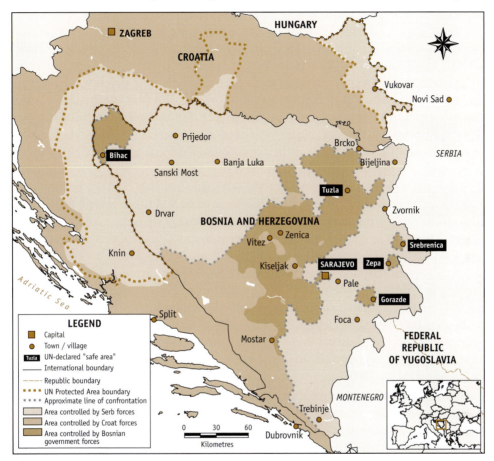

medical situation could not be more critical. People who are wounded are taken to the hospital where they die from simple injuries because of the lack of medical supplies'.[19]

The situation in Srebrenica became increasingly intolerable and on 2 April 1993, High Commissioner Ogata wrote to UN Secretary-General Boutros Boutros-Ghali warning that current efforts to address the increasing human suffering were 'totally inadequate', and stressing the need for 'more drastic action' to ensure the survival of the population in Srebrenica. In her letter, she urged that UNPROFOR peacekeepers be permitted to use force to protect the population of Srebrenica, or that UNHCR be permitted to organize a mass evacuation.[20]

Fourteen days later, after Bosnian Serb shelling had killed 56 people during a UNHCR-organized evacuation from Srebrenica, the Security Council adopted Resolution 819, declaring the enclave to be a UN-protected 'safe area' and, amongst other things, calling on UNPROFOR to increase its presence there. Three weeks later, the Security Council adopted Resolution 824, also declaring Sarajevo, Tuzla, Zepa, Gorazde and Bihac to be safe areas.

The safe areas were established without the consent of the parties to the conflict and without the provision of any credible military deterrent. Although the UN Secretary-General had warned that an additional 34,000 troops would be required 'to obtain deterrence through strength', governments were not willing to provide this number of troops and the Security Council therefore adopted an alternative 'light option' in which only 7,500 peacekeepers were to be deployed for this task. UNPROFOR troops were permitted to use force only in self-defence, and not in defence of the civilians they had been sent to protect. This was eventually to prove entirely inadequate. As UN Secretary-General Kofi Annan later acknowledged, the areas designated by the UN Security Council as safe areas were in fact 'neither protected areas nor safe havens in the sense of international humanitarian law, nor safe areas in any militarily meaningful sense'.[21]

Since the safe areas contained not only civilians but also Bosnian government troops, the Bosnian Serb forces considered them to be legitimate targets in the war. They often shelled them and subjected them to sniper fire. On many occasions, attacks carried out by Bosnian Serb forces were in response to attacks made out of the safe areas by Bosnian government troops. The Bosnian Serb authorities denied the people living in the safe areas freedom of movement through Serb-controlled territory, and frequently prevented humanitarian organizations such as UNHCR from reaching them. The safe areas became crowded—predominantly Muslim—ghettos. While they provided some refuge for vulnerable civilians, they also became areas of confinement where civilians were trapped: in essence, open detention centres. Meanwhile, as the international community focused on the safe areas, little attention was given to the plight of any remaining non-Serbs living in Serb-held territory. As a result these people became even more vulnerable to 'ethnic cleansing'.

As had been the case in northern Iraq, governments had mixed motives in promoting the concept of safe areas. Throughout the war, it remained unclear whether the primary aim of the safe areas was to protect territory or people.[22] This ambiguity led to misunderstandings and created many false expectations. As UN Secretary-General Kofi Annan acknowledged in November 1999 in a highly critical report on the United Nations' role in Srebrenica, by failing to admit that declaring particular places to be safe areas entailed a significant commitment to their defence, the UN Security Council resolutions in effect created a false sense of security. The report stressed:

When the international community makes a solemn promise to safeguard and protect innocent civilians from massacre, then it must be willing to back its promise with the necessary means. Otherwise, it is surely better not to raise hopes and expectations in the first place, and not to impede whatever capability they may be able to muster in their own defence.[23]

On 11 July 1995, the Bosnian Serb army overran Srebrenica, taking hundreds of Dutch peacekeepers hostage and forcing some 40,000 people to flee. Meanwhile some 7,000 people, virtually all of them men or boys and virtually all Muslims, were killed by Bosnian Serb forces in the largest massacre in Europe since the Second World War. Judge Riad of the International Criminal Tribunal for the former

Yugoslavia described what happened as 'scenes from hell, written on the darkest pages of human history'.[24] Days after the fall of Srebrenica, Serb forces overran Zepa, another so-called safe area.

Distributing emergency relief supplies

The humanitarian relief operation in Bosnia and Herzegovina was unprecedented in its scale, scope and complexity. Between 1992 and 1995, UNHCR coordinated a massive logistical operation in which some 950,000 tonnes of humanitarian relief supplies were delivered to various destinations in Bosnia and Herzegovina. By 1995, UNHCR was providing humanitarian supplies for some 2.7 million beneficiaries. This consisted mostly of food provided by the UN World Food Programme (WFP).

In delivering relief supplies, UNHCR cooperated closely not only with WFP but also with other UN agencies such as the Food and Agriculture Organization (FAO), the UN Children's Fund (UNICEF), and the World Health Organization (WHO), as well as with international and local non-governmental organizations (NGOs) which operated under the UNHCR 'umbrella'. Most of these organizations relied heavily on UNHCR for official UN accreditation, which was required by the parties to the conflict and without which it was virtually impossible for them to operate.

UNHCR's 'lead agency' role involved a wide range of responsibilities. At its height, there were over 3,000 humanitarian personnel from over 250 organizations carrying UNHCR identification cards, and there were over 2,000 vehicles in Bosnia and Herzegovina with UNHCR registration plates. The UNHCR convoy operation comprised over 250 trucks, with convoy teams provided by, or through, the governments of Denmark, Norway, Sweden, the United Kingdom, Germany and the Russian Federation. In addition, over 20 states participated in the UNHCR airlift operation into Sarajevo, and some 18,000 tonnes of humanitarian supplies were airdropped into inaccessible places such as Konjic, Gorazde, Maglaj, Srebrenica, Tesanj and Zepa. Supplies were dropped at night from high altitude, in order to reduce the risk of attack on the aircraft.

The humanitarian operation was hampered throughout the war by security problems, lack of cooperation from the parties to the conflict and logistical difficulties. Humanitarian personnel were constantly exposed to indiscriminate shelling, sniping and land mines, and were sometimes specifically targeted. They came to rely heavily on UNPROFOR for information on security issues, armed escorts, transportation in armoured vehicles, and logistical support. They also used bullet-proof vests and armoured vehicles to an extent never seen before in any major humanitarian operation. In spite of this protection, in the course of the war, over 50 personnel involved in the UNHCR-led operation lost their lives and hundreds more were injured. In addition, 117 UNPROFOR soldiers lost their lives.[25]

In most cases, humanitarian supplies were handed over by UNHCR to local authorities, who were responsible for their distribution. In spite of efforts to ensure that they were not diverted, there was inevitably some diversion of supplies to military forces and to the black market. Such diversion often led to criticism that the humanitarian operation was fuelling the war.

In May 1992, the Secretary-General had stated that 'the delivery of relief must be seen by all parties as a neutral humanitarian act'.[26] It was clear from very early on, however, that this would not be the case. The humanitarian operation was subject to constant obstructionism from the parties to the conflict, particularly from the Bosnian Serbs, who controlled access to besieged Bosnian government enclaves, and the Bosnian Croats, who controlled access to central Bosnia.

At one stage in 1992, a UNHCR convoy had to negotiate its way through 90 roadblocks to get from Zagreb, the Croatian capital, to Sarajevo. Following extensive negotiations with the parties to the conflict, many of these roadblocks were subsequently removed, but they were replaced by a series of bureaucratic hurdles. Written clearances containing numerous details had to be obtained from local authorities up to two weeks in advance, before convoys could travel. In practice, the system proved to be a convenient way for local authorities to control and restrict access to enemy territory without overtly prohibiting it. All kinds of delaying tactics were used, and endless excuses were found for refusing to grant clearances.

In many cases, the parties to the conflict denied clearances for UNHCR convoys to transit through areas under their control to enemy territory unless there was an increase in the percentage of supplies sent to areas under their own control. Lengthy negotiations ensued, during which time convoys were often blocked for weeks or months at a time. UNHCR officials on the ground spent much of the war negotiating humanitarian access. Some of the local civilian authorities who were ostensibly UNHCR's counterparts, such as the Commissioners for Humanitarian Aid on the Bosnian Serb side, were in fact directly responsible for ensuring that humanitarian aid did not reach civilians in enemy territory. This was clearly illustrated at a meeting which took place between UNHCR and Serb civilian authorities on 2 July 1995. At this meeting, Nikola Koljevic, President of the Coordinating Board for Humanitarian Assistance (and Vice-President of the self-proclaimed Republika Srpska), explained his constant obstructionism by saying that if he allowed Muslims to be fed he would be indicted as a war criminal by his own regime.[27]

UNPROFOR's role in the humanitarian operation

UNPROFOR's primary mandate in Bosnia and Herzegovina was to assist UNHCR by creating conditions for the effective delivery of humanitarian assistance. UNPROFOR had, however, no significant presence in, and only limited access through, Bosnian Serb-controlled areas. In carrying out its mandate, UNPROFOR concentrated on establishing reliable land supply routes and air corridors, and on enhancing security for humanitarian personnel. UNPROFOR engineers succeeded in opening up and maintaining key land routes in Bosnian government-held territory, and in maintaining the runway and vital facilities at Sarajevo airport. An inevitable problem, however, was that heavy dependence on particular routes made it easy for the parties to the conflict to block these routes whenever they wanted.[28]

Although UNPROFOR did much to improve security for humanitarian personnel, there were times when its presence appeared to do the opposite. The Bosnian Serbs, in particular, were often extremely hostile to UNPROFOR. On some occasions, UNHCR convoy teams complained that the presence of UNPROFOR escorts had the effect of drawing fire on to them, and that they would have been safer with no military escort.

One of UNPROFOR's main roles in assisting the humanitarian operation was that of providing 'passive protection' for convoys. This consisted of UNPROFOR armoured personnel carriers escorting convoys through dangerous front-line areas. The principle was that if a convoy came under fire, civilian personnel would be able to shelter in the armoured vehicles. In some cases, UNPROFOR escort vehicles also fired back when convoys came under attack. The use of military escorts for humanitarian convoys was an innovation for UNHCR and, at the time, provoked much criticism from some critics who considered that the impartiality of humanitarian action was being undermined. By contrast, throughout the war, ICRC operated without military escorts. The system nevertheless enabled UNHCR to deliver large quantities of emergency supplies and to cross active front-lines, even during some of the worst fighting. More than 80 per cent of the emergency supplies distributed to civilians in Bosnia and Herzegovina during the war were delivered by UNHCR.

UNPROFOR troops provided vital security and logistical support for the humanitarian operation, but they were able to do little to improve access to areas which required movement through territory controlled by Bosnian Serb forces. Operating on the basis of consent—in accordance with traditional peacekeeping principles—UNPROFOR depended on the Bosnian Serb authorities for authorization to travel through their territory. Yet the Bosnian Serbs viewed UNPROFOR more consistently as a hostile force than did the other parties to the conflict. The result was that on some routes, the movement of UNPROFOR vehicles was not approved for months at a time. Indeed, in places such as Gorazde and Bihac, UNPROFOR troops themselves sometimes ran out of fresh food as they were unable to get the necessary authorizations for their own resupply convoys. On a number of such occasions, UNHCR provided them with food, thereby providing a lifeline for the very force that had been sent to support the humanitarian operation.

The siege of Sarajevo and the humanitarian airlift

For much of the war, the international community focused its attention on the Bosnian capital, Sarajevo. The city was surrounded by Bosnian Serb artillery and snipers, and often went for months at a time without adequate water, electricity or gas supplies. As Bosnian Serb forces laid siege to the city, often killing civilians who were shopping in the market place or waiting in queues for bread or water, UNHCR struggled to deliver food and other relief supplies.

Between 3 July 1992 and 9 January 1996, UNHCR coordinated what became the longest-running humanitarian airlift in history, surpassing the duration of the 1948–49 Berlin airlift. Most of the aircraft were lent by Canada, France, Germany, the United Kingdom and the United States, but more than 20 countries participated. Altogether some 160,000 tonnes of food, medicines and other goods were delivered to Sarajevo in over 12,000 flights. The airlift was also used to evacuate more than 1,100 civilians in need of medical care.

The airlift was affected not only by bureaucratic obstacles but also by constant security threats. Both sides, but particularly Bosnian Serb forces, fired at aircraft using the airport. There were more than 270 serious security incidents, which in many cases forced UNHCR temporarily to suspend the airlift. The worst such incident took place on 3 September 1992, when a surface-to-air missile downed an Italian Air Force G-222 cargo plane, killing all four of the crew on board. Responsibility for this attack was never established.

On many occasions, Bosnian Serb inspectors, whose presence at the airport was a Bosnian Serb condition for the airlift, refused to allow particular items to be off-loaded from UNHCR planes. Items had to be flown back to Croatia, Italy or Germany at great cost. At other times, Bosnian Serb forces, which controlled access by road to the airport, refused to allow humanitarian supplies to leave the airport. Thus, as thousands of civilians went hungry in the capital, hundreds of tonnes of food rotted on the airport tarmac. Some items, including pipes and water pumping equipment, generators and other items urgently needed for the repair of vital utilities in the city, were blocked at the airport for almost the entire war. At the same time, medical evacuations of seriously ill or wounded civilians were often prevented.

Events leading to the Dayton Peace Agreement

In early 1995, there was a new wave of 'ethnic cleansing' by the Bosnian Serbs in western Bosnia, particularly in the Banja Luka area, which the UNHCR spokesman at the time labelled the Bosnian 'heart of darkness'. In May, the United Nations' credibility in Bosnia and Herzegovina was further tarnished when hundreds of UNPROFOR soldiers were taken hostage by the Bosnian Serbs following airstrikes carried out by NATO at UNPROFOR's request. Some of the hostages were chained by the Bosnian Serbs to potential air-strike targets as 'human shields', and television images of them were broadcast across the world.

Then in mid-1995 a number of events dramatically changed the dynamics of the war. In July, the Bosnian Serb army overran the safe areas of Srebrenica and Zepa. In early August, the Croatian army launched 'Operation Storm', a massive military offensive involving more than 100,000 troops, in which it overran all Serb-controlled areas in the western and southern Krajina region of Croatia. As a result, some 200,000 Serb civilians fled, the majority of them going to the Federal Republic of Yugoslavia, while smaller numbers remained in Serb-controlled parts of Bosnia and Herzegovina. Then, on 28 August 1995, Bosnian Serb forces fired a shell into a busy market place in Sarajevo, killing 37 people and injuring dozens more. NATO responded by launching a two-week intensive air campaign against Bosnian Serb targets. Bolstered by the air strikes, Croatian and Bosnian government forces mounted a joint offensive in Bosnia and Herzegovina to recapture Serb-held territory, taking back a third of the territory held by Bosnian Serb forces. Aware that they were losing territory by the day, Bosnian Serb officials accepted a ceasefire and agreed to attend peace talks in Dayton, Ohio.

The Dayton Peace Agreement which resulted from these talks was signed in Paris on 14 December 1995 by the presidents of the Republic of Bosnia and Herzegovina,

Main displaced populations from the former Yugoslavia, December 1995

Map 9.2

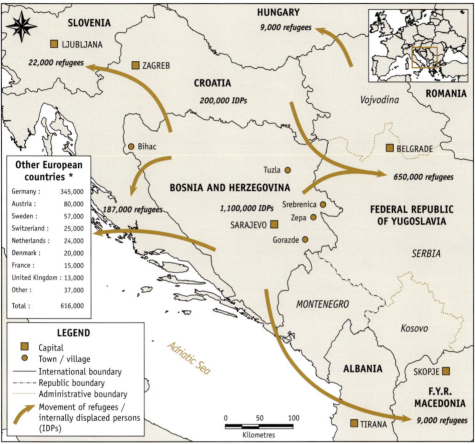

SLOVENIA
■ LJUBLJANA
22,000 refugees

HUNGARY
9,000 refugees

■ ZAGREB

CROATIA
200,000 IDPs

● Bihac

Vojvodina

ROMANIA

■ BELGRADE

Tuzla ●

BOSNIA AND HERZEGOVINA

Srebrenica ●
187,000 refugees   **1,100,000 IDPs**   Zepa ●
SARAJEVO ■
Gorazde ●

650,000 refugees

FEDERAL REPUBLIC OF YUGOSLAVIA

SERBIA

MONTENEGRO

Kosovo

Adriatic Sea

ALBANIA   SKOPJE ■

F.Y.R. MACEDONIA

■ TIRANA   *9,000 refugees*

Other European countries *

Germany :	345,000
Austria :	80,000
Sweden :	57,000
Switzerland :	25,000
Netherlands :	24,000
Denmark :	20,000
France :	15,000
United Kingdom :	13,000
Other :	37,000
Total :	616,000

LEGEND
■ Capital
● Town / village
— International boundary
–·–·– Republic boundary
·········· Administrative boundary
➔ Movement of refugees / internally displaced persons (IDPs)

0   50   100
Kilometres

* The figures for other European countries are from Sept. 1996 and are based on information made available to UNHCR by governments (Humanitarian Issues Working Group, HIWG96/6, 11 Dec. 1996).

the Republic of Croatia, and the Federal Republic of Yugoslavia. Although the agreement keeps Bosnia and Herzegovina united as a single state, it recognizes two entities: Republika Srpska and the Muslim–Croat Federation.

The agreement contained detailed provisions for demilitarization of the former parties to the conflict and for the replacement of UNPROFOR by a 60,000-strong NATO-led Implementation Force (IFOR). Less attention, however, was given to the implementation of the civilian aspects of the peace agreement. Annex VII of the agreement called on UNHCR 'to develop in close consultation with asylum countries and the parties a repatriation plan that will allow for an early, peaceful, orderly and phased return of refugees and displaced persons'. Although the peace agreement stated that 'all refugees and displaced persons have the right freely to return to their homes of origin', it made no provisions to enforce such returns. Rather, it relied on the former parties to the conflict voluntarily to create an environment in which refugees could return 'in safety, without risk of harassment, intimidation, persecution, or discrimination'.[29]

Destruction caused by the fighting in Ilidza, Sarajevo. The large number of landmines posed a major threat to people returning to their homes after the war. (UNHCR/R. LEMOYNE/1996)

The military provisions of the agreement were successfully implemented and there have been no clashes between the military forces of either side since the agreement was signed. On the civilian side, however, the agreement left the nationalist leaders in power on both sides, undermining, among other things, prospects for reconciliation amongst the different ethnic groups and the possibility for displaced people and refugees to return to the areas from which they were 'ethnically cleansed' during the war. With its limited provisions for policing, reconstruction and reconciliation, High Commissioner Ogata pointed out in 1997 that the agreement left humanitarian actors like UNHCR 'to grapple with essentially political issues'.[30]

Repatriation and continued ethnic separation

The reluctance of the NATO-led multinational military force to get involved in potentially dangerous policing activities, in order to prevent civil disturbances and to maintain public order in Bosnia and Herzegovina in the post-Dayton period, was evident from the start. This was clearly illustrated in early 1996, when Bosnian Serb police, paramilitaries and extremists pressured some 60,000 fellow Serbs to leave the

Sarajevo suburbs as they reverted to the control of the Muslim-Croat Federation. Armed groups of Serb agitators torched buildings in full view of heavily armed—but completely passive—IFOR personnel.[31]

The lack of public order in Bosnia and Herzegovina, and particularly the lack of effective security for ethnic minorities, prevented any significant reversal of the 'ethnic cleansing' which took place during the war. Local political leaders on both sides repeatedly blocked returns by relocating members of their own ethnic group into available housing space and creating a climate of fear and intimidation for minorities. Although some 395,000 of the refugees who fled Bosnia and Herzegovina during the war returned to the country by December 1999, the majority of them did not return to their original homes. Instead, most of them relocated to new areas where their own ethnic group was in the majority. At the end of 1999, some 800,000 people in Bosnia and Herzegovina remained displaced and unable to return to their former homes.

UNHCR and other humanitarian organizations have made strenuous efforts to encourage reconciliation, and to facilitate voluntary returns of refugees and displaced people to their original homes, even where this involves returning to areas which have become dominated by another ethnic group. UNHCR has set up a number of bus lines travelling between the two entities in Bosnia and Herzegovina, and has facilitated group visits of refugees and displaced people to places of origin. UNHCR also set up an 'Open Cities' project, whereby donors were encouraged to invest in cities, which allowed minority groups to return. But there is a limit to how much can be done by humanitarian organizations. As High Commissioner Ogata concluded in her statement to the Peace Implementation Council conference in 1998:

The fundamental prerequisite for return—significant and lasting changes in the circumstances that drove people from their homes—still has not occurred. UNHCR's leading role in return was predicated on the political constraints being removed. They are still there. We have identified them but, as a humanitarian organization, cannot remove them.[32]

Even if small numbers of people have returned to areas where they now form part of an ethnic minority, there has been minimal progress in rebuilding genuinely multi-ethnic societies in either Croatia or Bosnia and Herzegovina. The prospects for large-scale returns to areas now dominated by another ethnic group remain bleak. By the end of 1999, more than four years after the fighting in Croatia and Bosnia and Herzegovina ended, fewer than 10 per cent of the total of around 300,000 Serbs who fled from Croatia between 1991 and 1995 had returned to their homes. Similarly, fewer than five per cent of the 650,000 Muslims and Croats who were expelled by the Serbs from western Bosnia and Herzegovina had returned to their former homes, and fewer than one per cent of those who were expelled by the Serbs from eastern Bosnia had returned.[33]

Of the few who have returned to areas where they now form part of a minority ethnic group, many are people who have returned to areas near the inter-entity boundary line, which is closely monitored by the NATO-led military force, and many are elderly people, who are not considered by the local authorities to pose any real

The 1995 Dayton Agreement for Bosnia and Herzegovina   Map 9.3

threat. Moreover, some of those who have returned have done so with the intention of making arrangements to exchange their property. The process of ethnic separation, which began during the war, has continued by other means in the post-war period.

While the total number of returns to areas dominated by another ethnic group remained low, UNHCR and other observers noted a substantial increase in the number of 'minority returns' in both Croatia and Bosnia and Herzegovina during the first few months of 2000.[34] This increase was ascribed to impatience amongst refugees and displaced people, a change in the psychology of the majority and minority populations, a change of government in Croatia following the death of President Franjo Tudjman in December 1999, new Bosnian government policies, and measures taken by the Office of the High Representative—which oversees the civilian implementation of the Dayton Agreement—to remove obstructionist officials and to implement property laws.

The return process is a regional one, involving all the countries of former Yugoslavia. UNHCR has consistently emphasized that for the return process to be sustained, the international community will need to continue to commit considerable resources to building peace in the region. Since the war ended, UNHCR has cooperated closely with the Office of the High Representative in Bosnia and Herzegovina, the NATO-led military force, the UN International Police Task Force, the Organization for Security and Cooperation in Europe (OSCE), the World Bank and numerous other local and international organizations, to assist in the process of return, reconstruction and reconciliation. The Stability Pact for South Eastern Europe, initiated by the European Union in June 1999, has also reaffirmed a commitment to support democratic political processes and to promote multi-ethnic societies in the region.

The Kosovo crisis

As the war in Bosnia and Herzegovina ended, elsewhere in the Balkans another crisis was looming. Kosovo had a long history of human rights abuses. From 1989, when Kosovo's autonomous status within Serbia was partially revoked, the majority of Kosovo Albanians had been living in an apartheid-like situation in which they were denied access to jobs and services, and were unable to exercise basic rights. As a result, the Kosovo Albanians, who comprised about 90 per cent of the population of Kosovo, established parallel systems for almost every aspect of daily life, including employment, health and education. Between 1989 and the beginning of 1998, an estimated 350,000 Kosovo Albanians left the province at one stage or another, most of them going to countries in Western Europe.

The long-simmering crisis took on a new dimension in February 1998. The Serbian security forces intensified operations against Kosovo Albanians suspected of involvement with the Kosovo Liberation Army (KLA). As security deteriorated, some 20,000 people fled over the mountains to Albania in May–June 1998. Others made their way to Montenegro, as well as to Italy, Switzerland, Germany and other parts of Western Europe. Over the following months, the clashes escalated, and by September there were an estimated 175,000 internally displaced people in Kosovo. UNHCR set up a large operation to assist these internally displaced people and others affected by the conflict.

Increased international pressure after the adoption of UN Security Council Resolution 1199 in September 1998 led the Yugoslav authorities to agree to a ceasefire and a partial troop withdrawal from Kosovo. An international verification mission under the auspices of the OSCE was deployed to verify compliance with the agreement. A temporary calm followed, but isolated ceasefire violations continued, and by the end of 1998 the ceasefire was unravelling. In mid-January 1999, 45 Kosovo Albanians were massacred by Serb forces in Racak. These developments gave fresh impetus to efforts to end the conflict, which culminated in peace negotiations in Rambouillet, France, in February 1999.

Although further fighting and displacement continued throughout the Rambouillet talks, Western governments were optimistic about prospects for peace and called on UNHCR to plan for the return of refugees and displaced people. But the peace talks collapsed on 19 March, and on 24 March, without authorization from the UN Security Council, NATO commenced an air campaign against the Federal Republic of Yugoslavia, including attacks on targets in Kosovo. Since the campaign was justified principally in terms of stopping actual and potential killings and expulsions of Kosovo Albanians by Serbian forces, it was often referred to as NATO's 'humanitarian war'.[35] The nomenclature could not conceal, however, that the air strikes resulted in an even larger humanitarian crisis, at least in the short term.

The influx into Albania and the former Yugoslav Republic of Macedonia

When the air strikes began, there were already an estimated 260,000 internally displaced people within Kosovo. In addition, outside Kosovo, there were some 70,000 Kosovo Albanian refugees and displaced people in the region and over 100,000 refugees and asylum seekers in Western Europe and further afield.

The NATO air campaign triggered an escalation of violence on the ground. Local fighting between the KLA and Yugoslav forces continued, while Yugoslav armed forces and police, as well as paramilitary forces and local Serbs, carried out a brutal campaign of 'ethnic cleansing', which included organized mass deportations to neighbouring states.[36] Thousands of Kosovo Albanians were killed and some 800,000 fled or were expelled from Kosovo after the start of the air campaign. Of these, some 426,000 fled to Albania, some 228,000 to the former Yugoslav Republic of Macedonia (FYR Macedonia), and some 45,000 to Montenegro.[37] In addition, large numbers of people were internally displaced within Kosovo by the end of the 78-day air campaign.

Responding to a refugee crisis of this size in such a highly charged political environment was a huge challenge. Over the previous years and months, UNHCR—in cooperation with other UN agencies and NGOs—had made contingency plans for an exodus of up to 100,000 people. But no one had anticipated the scale and rapidity of the exodus that eventually took place. The influx overwhelmed the response capacity of the host governments and humanitarian organizations. UNHCR, in particular, was strongly criticized by some donors and NGOs for its lack of preparedness and its management of the crisis in the initial phase.[38]

In FYR Macedonia, the authorities temporarily closed the border at the beginning of April 1999, denying entry to tens of thousands of Kosovo Albanians in a situation reminiscent of the Turkish response to Iraqi Kurds in 1991. Facing tensions related to its own ethnic Albanian minority, the Macedonian government feared that a large influx of Kosovo Albanians would destabilize the country. To reduce the number of refugees on its territory, the government requested that a system of international burden-sharing be put in place, involving the evacuation or transfer of some of the refugees to third countries. NATO needed the Macedonian government's consent for its continued presence on Macedonian territory, and this gave the Macedonian government considerable leverage over the governments of NATO member states.

The relief operation became even more politicized as NATO military forces became involved in assisting the refugees. The international media continued to

Displaced populations from Kosovo in neighbouring countries/territories, mid-June 1999

Map 9.4

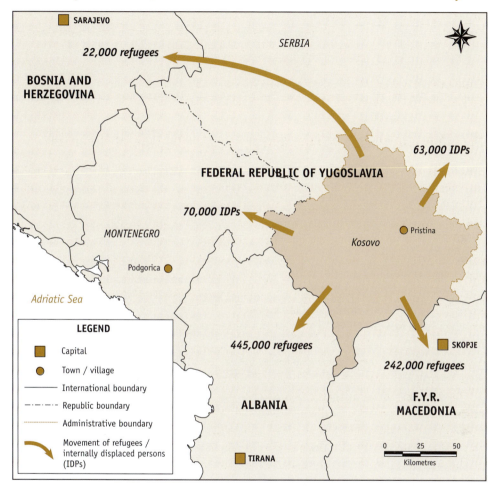

SARAJEVO

SERBIA

22,000 refugees

BOSNIA AND HERZEGOVINA

FEDERAL REPUBLIC OF YUGOSLAVIA

63,000 IDPs

70,000 IDPs

MONTENEGRO

Kosovo

Pristina

Podgorica

Adriatic Sea

LEGEND

■ Capital

● Town / village

— International boundary

–·–·– Republic boundary

·········· Administrative boundary

➤ Movement of refugees / internally displaced persons (IDPs)

445,000 refugees

SKOPJE

242,000 refugees

ALBANIA

F.Y.R. MACEDONIA

0   25   50
Kilometres

TIRANA

provide dramatic images of desperate refugees flooding into Albania or stranded on the Macedonian border. It became increasingly clear that, in the short term, the air campaign had led to more rather than less violence against Kosovo Albanians. In response, NATO increasingly turned its attention to the plight of the refugees. On 2 April, NATO Secretary-General Javier Solana wrote to High Commissioner Ogata offering to support UNHCR in the humanitarian relief operation. The High Commissioner accepted this offer in a letter sent the following day which outlined the main areas where services were needed. This included management of the airlift operation to bring in relief supplies to Albania and FYR Macedonia, assistance with transportation, and logistical support in setting up refugee camps.[39]

UNHCR's acceptance of NATO's offer of assistance helped to provide an urgently needed solution for the 65,000 Kosovo Albanians stranded on the Macedonian border. Immediate camp construction and a subsequent evacuation programme to

Box 9.2 East Timor: the cost of independence

East Timor's long struggle for independence came to a head in 1999, when the local population overwhelmingly supported independence in a referendum organized and supervised by the United Nations. Immediately after the result of the referendum was announced, Indonesian security forces and anti-independence militia instigated a campaign of violence, looting and arson against the civilian population. This led to a mass outflow of people from East to West Timor and resulted in large-scale displacement within East Timor itself. For UNHCR, providing protection and assistance to refugees in West Timor involved delicate interactions with anti-independence militia groups which, to a large extent, controlled the refugee camps.

The status of East Timor, the eastern half of an island in the eastern Indonesian archipelago, has long been in dispute. For 450 years, it was Portugal's most distant and neglected colony. In 1960, as other colonies were gaining independence, the UN General Assembly placed East Timor on the international agenda by adding the colony to its list of 'non-self-governing territories'.

The downfall of the Caetano regime in Portugal in April 1974 opened the way for East Timor to become independent under the leftist Revolutionary Front for an Independent East Timor (*Frente Revolucionária do Timor-Leste Independente*, or Fretilin). However, rather than let this happen, the staunchly anti-communist regime of General Suharto in Indonesia backed a coup against Fretilin. When this attempt failed, he launched a full-scale invasion in December 1975 and annexed the territory as Indonesia's 27th province in July 1976.

The Indonesian occupation

The Indonesian armed forces' occupation of East Timor gave rise to serious and widespread human rights abuses. Out of a pre-1975 population of around 700,000, over 170,000 East Timorese civilians are estimated to have died in the first six years of military rule.[iv] Both the UN Security Council and General Assembly repeatedly refused to recognize the occupation and called for Indonesia's withdrawal, but to no avail. General Suharto's Western allies, particularly the United States, saw the regime as a vital strategic bulwark in Southeast Asia, and Western powers sold the Indonesian government sophisticated counter-insurgency weaponry.

For years, East Timor's status remained in dispute. Was it Indonesia's 27th province? Or was it still a non-self-governing territory that had yet to exercise its right of self-determination? Between November 1982 and May 1998, successive UN Secretaries-General held regular talks with the Indonesian and Portuguese governments on East Timor, but made no real progress. Apart from Australia, no major Western country gave de jure recognition to Indonesia's July 1976 annexation.

As the Cold War ended, East Timor's position began to change. Foreign journalists gained greater access to the territory and provided vivid accounts of the brutality of the occupation. Western photographers captured the image of Indonesian troops gunning down over 250 mourners at a cemetery in East Timor's capital, Díli, in November 1991. These pictures, flashed around the world, gave the lie to the government's assurances that the East Timorese people had accepted Indonesian integration. The regime was dealt a further diplomatic blow when the 1996 Nobel Peace Prize was awarded to East Timor's Roman Catholic Bishop, Carlos Belo, and to José Ramos Horta, chief spokesman of the East Timorese resistance abroad. By the time General Suharto was forced to resign in May 1998, in the midst of an economic crisis and general political discontent, Indonesia's hold on East Timor was becoming more tenuous.

The 1999 referendum and its aftermath

The new government of President B.J. Habibie moved quickly to resolve the East Timorese problem. In May 1999, Indonesia and Portugal agreed to give the UN Secretary-General responsibility for conducting a 'popular consultation' on whether the local population favoured limited autonomy or full independence. In June 1999, the Security Council established the UN Advisory Mission in East Timor (UNAMET) to oversee the referendum and subsequent transition towards autonomy or full independence. However, the Indonesian government insisted that it retain responsibility for security in the run-up to the vote and during any transition period.

Despite the tense situation and ambitious timetable, UNAMET succeeded in registering 451,792 potential voters out of an East Timorese population of over 800,000. On 30 August, over 98 per cent of those registered went to the polls. Of these, 78.5 per cent rejected the autonomy proposal in favour of independence. As soon as the result was announced on 4 September, murder, rape, looting and arson by anti-independence militia groups and the security forces erupted.

It is not possible to know how many people were killed at this time, but UN civilian police had by late 1999 received reports of over 1,000 extra-judicial killings. The Special Rapporteur of the UN Commission on Human Rights reported in late 1999 that over 100 bodies had been unearthed, although local non-governmental organizations reported a higher death toll.[v] The territory's infrastructure was destroyed. Under diplomatic pressure from the international community, the Indonesian government agreed to allow an Australian-led multinational military force to intervene. On 20 September, the International Force in East Timor (INTERFET) began deployment in East Timor. Within 32 days, INTERFET had secured the whole of the territory and the East Timor enclave of Oecussi (Ambeno) in West Timor.

On 19 October, Indonesia's supreme constitutional body, the Indonesian People's Consultative Assembly, formally recognized the independence vote. Within a week, the UN Security Council established the UN Transitional Administration in East Timor (UNTAET) to provide security and oversee the territory's transition to independence.

Protecting the displaced

The violence in East Timor in the period leading up to and in the days after the referendum resulted in the displacement of some 500,000 people. An estimated 250,000 became internally displaced in East Timor, while some 290,000 fled to West Timor.

Most of the internally displaced stayed in mountain hideouts or resistance-controlled areas between 4 September and the full deployment of INTERFET in mid-October. INTERFET troops helped humanitarian organizations provide emergency relief to those remaining in Díli. As INTERFET secured more territory, relief supplies were distributed to other major towns. Some assistance was air-dropped into inaccessible areas. By late October, most of those who had been internally displaced

had returned to their homes. UNHCR assumed the lead role in providing long-term assistance to returnees.

Most of those who fled to West Timor ended up in hastily constructed camps near the West Timor capital, Kupang, or the border town of Atambua. These refugees were at the mercy of anti-independence militia groups, who restricted international agencies' access to the camps. Conditions in the camps were poor. Food, water, sanitation and health care were all in short supply. The monsoon in November 1999 further exacerbated the appalling living conditions and led to an increase in illness and deaths from waterborne diseases.

UNHCR organized the repatriation of refugees to East Timor. Those who chose to repatriate, however, were at risk from the anti-independence militias. Suspected pro-independence supporters were stripped of their personal belongings. Some were raped or killed. At first, UNHCR staff had to go into the camps with fully armed military and police escorts to remove those who said they wished to repatriate. Eventually, access to the camps improved, though security problems continued. Many militia members' families were unwilling to return; others who wished to return were unable to do so because of continued intimidation by militia groups.

The first voluntary repatriation flights were organized by UNHCR on 8 October, but most people were too intimidated by the militia to take advantage of them. From 21 October, ships leased by UNHCR ferried over 2,000 people a week back to East Timor in an operation subsequently assisted by the International Organization for Migration (IOM). By the end of 1999, over 130,000 people had returned voluntarily, 85,000 of them under organized return programmes. But militia members

were still present in the camps and discouraged returns through a sustained campaign about conditions and alleged atrocities in East Timor.

Over 150,000 people remained in the camps in West Timor at the end of 1999. An estimated 50,000 of these were ex-civil servants and locally recruited members of the Indonesian army or police and their families. Many of these are likely to opt to remain in Indonesia. But many former militia members will probably try to return to East Timor. Others who remained were refugees who may have been 'held hostage' and prevented from returning. Given the pressures exerted on refugees in the camps, there was no reliable way of assessing the attitudes of most of the East Timorese still in West Timor. Some of those who returned were attacked and harassed for their presumed support of the anti-independence militia. UNHCR and other humanitarian organizations continue to assist with reintegration efforts in East Timor. Such efforts form an essential part of the process of rebuilding East Timorese society.

East Timor and region, 1999 Map 9.5

Some 65,000 Kosovo Albanian refugees were trapped for several days in this no-man's land before border guards from the former Yugoslav Republic of Macedonia allowed them to enter the country. (UNHCR/H.J. DAVIES/1999)

third countries were the 'package' needed to secure the Macedonian government's agreement to admit the refugees.

NATO's participation in the establishment of refugee camps set a precedent. UNHCR was criticized by some observers for its close cooperation with NATO on the grounds that, since NATO was a party to the conflict, the involvement of its military forces in setting up camps for the refugees challenged the impartiality of the humanitarian operation. But, as had been the case in northern Iraq in 1991, the military appeared to be better placed than any other actor to provide the logistical support and security necessary to bring the humanitarian crisis under control.

The other part of the package which was agreed to ensure that FYR Macedonia kept its border open was a 'humanitarian evacuation programme'. The initiative was launched at the insistence of the Macedonian government, strongly supported by the United States. It was implemented by UNHCR, in cooperation with the International Organization for Migration. Under the programme, refugees were transferred from FYR Macedonia to third countries. The programme represented a new variation of burden-sharing. It was understood as a short-term solution only. The ambiguity of the legal status and rights of those evacuated under the programme resulted in different governments applying their own standards to issues such as the right to family reunion. UNHCR insisted that the evacuation should be voluntary, should respect family unity and should give priority to those who were particularly vulnerable. But deciding which refugees were in greatest need, which countries were the most appropriate destinations, and registering and tracking them as they moved—with few or no documents—was a difficult task.

By the end of the emergency, almost 96,000 refugees had benefited from the programme in 28 host countries. The largest numbers went to Germany (14,700), the United States (9,700) and Turkey (8,300), while France, Norway, Italy, Canada and Austria each took more than 5,000 refugees. In addition, several thousand refugees were transferred on buses from FYR Macedonia to Albania.

In Albania and FYR Macedonia, donor governments contributed generously to the relief operation. Indeed, there was a great disparity between the amounts of funding and resources provided by donors for this operation and those provided for new refugee emergencies in Africa at the same time. The enormous publicity being given to the relief operation in the Balkans by the international media meant that political considerations dictated the way in which assistance was provided. As one UNHCR official working there at the time explained: 'Being there and being seen to be dealing directly with refugees became almost a necessity for many different actors. The more it seemed that bombing had no effect except to push refugees out, the more governments felt obliged to be seen to be caring for the refugees.'[40] The result was that, rather than providing multilateral assistance through organizations such as UNHCR, governments channelled unprecedented amounts of funding through their own national NGOs, or directly to the Albanian and Macedonian governments.

This presented a major challenge to UNHCR in carrying out its lead agency role. Some camps were set up and used before UNHCR was even informed of their existence. Standards of bilateral assistance varied widely, and for many actors visibility often seemed more important than impact and coordination. High Commissioner Ogata urged governments not to weaken the action of international humanitarian organizations such as UNHCR by by-passing them. She also emphasized the importance of multilateral assistance in guaranteeing impartiality, since such assistance is 'aimed at people and is not based on the interests of states'.[41]

Rebuilding Kosovo

On 9 June 1999, the Federal Republic of Yugoslavia formally accepted a peace plan requiring the withdrawal of all Serb forces from Kosovo, the safe and free return of all refugees and displaced people, and the establishment of a UN mission which was

Box 9.3 International criminal justice

During the 1990s, for the first time since the Nuremberg and Tokyo trials of the late 1940s, the international community established a series of international tribunals in order to bring to justice those responsible for violations of international humanitarian and human rights law. The ad hoc international tribunals for the former Yugoslavia and for Rwanda, established in 1993 and 1994 respectively, were followed at the end of the decade by an agreement to set up an International Criminal Court.

By putting an end to cultures of impunity, international criminal justice can curtail the gross violations of human rights which often give rise to forced displacement. International criminal justice can also play a vital part in enabling refugees and displaced people to return to their homes in post-conflict situations. Justice is a part of national reconciliation, and without it peace is less likely to take hold and the danger of renewed conflict remains.

International tribunals

Since its establishment in May 1993, the International Criminal Tribunal for the former Yugoslavia (ICTY) has worked to ensure that there is no impunity for those responsible for war crimes and crimes against humanity in the former Yugoslavia. The Tribunal's work forms an integral part of the slow process of reconciliation that is a prerequisite for lasting peace in the region.

ICTY has publicly indicted more than 90 people, but its work has been hampered by obstruction from some of the governments concerned. Nearly a third of those who have been publicly indicted remain at large, including Yugoslav President Slobodan Milosevic and the Bosnian Serb leader Radovan Karadzic. The cases of many of the accused are still at the pre-trial stage. As of the end

of 1999, eight people had been found guilty of violations of the laws or customs of war, of grave breaches of the 1949 Geneva Conventions on the laws of warfare, or of crimes against humanity. They were sentenced to terms of up to 40 years' imprisonment.

The International Criminal Tribunal for Rwanda (ICTR) was established in November 1994 in an attempt to bring to justice the perpetrators of the 1994 genocide in Rwanda. Its task has proved extremely difficult. By November 1999, ICTR had completed just four full trials and two cases related to guilty pleas. Only five individuals had been convicted. They were sentenced to prison terms ranging from 15 years to life.

For all its procedural problems and failures, the Tribunal's fundamental contribution to international justice and the development of international criminal law should not be underestimated. The 1998 sentencing of a former Rwandan mayor involved not only a groundbreaking application of the 1948 Convention on the Prevention and Punishment of the Crime of Genocide, but also set an important precedent concerning the interpretation of acts of sexual violence and rape when committed in armed conflict.

Where similar crimes have been committed in other countries, however, the international community has not demonstrated the same resolve. In Cambodia, for instance, more than a million people were killed by the Khmer Rouge in the 1970s. Only now is there some prospect of legal action against those responsible. More recently, some of the most heinous crimes against civilians were committed in Sierra Leone, including the deliberate mutilation of babies and young children. Yet the 1999 peace agreement in Sierra Leone gave a

sweeping amnesty for all these crimes. In order to combat impunity without resorting to criminal justice, some states have taken other measures such as the establishment of 'truth and reconciliation' commissions. In many other countries which have suffered tremendous civilian losses in brutal and long-running conflicts, there has been neither criminal prosecution nor other such alternatives.

Towards an International Criminal Court

These broader concerns were in part addressed by the conclusion in July 1998 of longstanding deliberations on the establishment of an International Criminal Court. A truly universal regime for the exercise of international criminal justice would have a deterrent effect on the perpetrators of such crimes, and thereby help to prevent situations that create refugee flows.

In an inter-agency statement issued in May 1999, UNHCR and other humanitarian agencies encouraged all states to sign and ratify the Rome Statute of the Court as soon as possible, in order to bring to justice those responsible for serious violations of international humanitarian and human rights law. The agencies also called upon states to live up to their responsibility to protect civilian populations, which have become deliberate targets in an increasing number of conflicts.

By the end of 1999, six states had ratified the Criminal Court's Statute. For it to enter into force, 60 ratifications are required. Meanwhile, lengthy discussions are continuing in New York to define in detail the crimes covered by the Statute and the rules of procedure for the Court.

authorized under UN Security Council Resolution 1244. On 12 June, a NATO-led Kosovo Force (KFOR), which included Russian troops, began deploying in Kosovo.

The refugees started returning immediately. Within three weeks, 500,000 people had returned and, by the end of 1999, more than 820,000 Kosovo Albanians had returned (including people who had left before 24 March). Those returning went back to a society without a functioning civil administration, police force, or any legal or judicial system, and where there had been massive destruction of property. Returnees also faced danger from landmines, booby traps and unexploded ordnance.

With tens of thousands of homes destroyed or badly damaged in Kosovo, UNHCR and other humanitarian organizations immediately set up a large-scale

A Swiss helicopter transporting humanitarian supplies for UNHCR to Kukes in northern Albania. The supplies were part of a US donation channelled through the World Food Programme. (UNHCR/U. MEISSNER/1999)

rehabilitation programme. Providing material assistance to the returning Kosovo Albanians, however, represented only one of the many challenges of building peace in Kosovo. The whole society was severely traumatized by the war and the events of the previous years, and the security situation in Kosovo remained volatile. The funds allocated to NATO's air campaign had been massive, but post-war investment—both politically and economically—once again proved minimal by comparison.

A United Nations Interim Administration Mission in Kosovo (UNMIK) was entrusted by the UN Security Council to provide an interim civilian administration. It was to be responsible for everything from social welfare and housing to law and order. Added to years of neglect, the damage caused by the war required urgent reconstruction in all key sectors: power and water, health and education, factories and small businesses, agriculture and communications.

Apart from the enormity of the reconstruction task, however, the greatest challenge faced by KFOR and the UN-led mission proved to be that of protecting the remaining Serbs, Roma (gypsies) and other minorities in Kosovo. As the refugees and displaced people flooded back, Kosovo Albanians attacked and intimidated Serbs and other minority groups suspected of perpetrating atrocities against them or of collaborating in doing so. Within three months, up to 200,000 Serbs and other minorities left Kosovo in a process dubbed 'reverse ethnic cleansing'. In spite of the emphasis which had been placed by NATO governments on the need to preserve multi-ethnicity in Kosovo, and the commitments of the Kosovo Albanian leadership to this end, the province has become deeply divided between Kosovo Albanian areas and pockets of territory still inhabited by Serbs and Roma. Since June 1999, UNHCR and other humanitarian organizations have carried out a number of activities, in cooperation with KFOR and UNMIK, aimed at protecting and assisting Serbs and other minorities in Kosovo.

Meanwhile, the flight of Serbs from Kosovo to other parts of the Federal Republic of Yugoslavia has put a further strain on a country already suffering from the prolonged effects of international sanctions and aerial bombardment. Even before this latest influx, the Federal Republic of Yugoslavia was hosting over 500,000 refugees from Croatia and Bosnia and Herzegovina, making it the largest refugee-hosting country in the region.

Limits of humanitarian action in times of war

During the last decade of the 20th century, humanitarian organizations operating in war-torn countries saved thousands of lives and did much to mitigate human suffering. One of the central lessons of the decade, however, was that in conflict situations humanitarian action can easily be manipulated by warring parties, and it can have the unintended consequence of strengthening the positions of authorities responsible for human rights violations. Also, relief supplies provided by humanitarian organizations can feed into war economies, helping to sustain and prolong war.

Important lessons have also been learned in the last decade concerning the use of military forces to protect civilian victims of war. In a highly critical report to the UN General Assembly on the fall of Srebrenica, submitted in November 1999, Secretary-General Kofi Annan summed up the most significant of these:

The cardinal lesson of Srebrenica is that a deliberate and systematic attempt to terrorize, expel or murder an entire people must be met decisively with all necessary means, and with the political will to carry the policy through to its logical conclusion. In the Balkans, in this decade, this lesson has had to be learned not once, but twice. In both instances, in Bosnia and in Kosovo, the international community tried to reach a negotiated settlement with an unscrupulous and murderous regime. In both instances it required the use of force to bring a halt to the planned and systematic killing and expulsion of civilians.[42]

All too often during the 1990s, humanitarian organizations such as UNHCR were left to deal with problems which were essentially political in nature. In each case, the limits of humanitarian action were clearly demonstrated. As High Commissioner Ogata emphasized with growing insistence throughout the decade, emergency relief operations should not be treated as a substitute for timely and firm political action to address the root causes of conflict.[43]

10 The Rwandan genocide and its aftermath

Ethnic tensions and armed conflict in the Great Lakes region of Central Africa have been the cause of repeated instances of human displacement. The pattern of events in the last 50 years is rooted in a long history of violence, but it is also a story of missed opportunities, on the part of both local actors and the international community in general. Failure to pursue just solutions to old grievances has in all too many cases, years or decades later, led to a recurrence of violence and to bloodletting on an even greater scale than before.

The legacy of the 1959–63 crisis in Rwanda (described in Chapter 2) was the presence of Tutsi refugees in all neighbouring countries. Denied the possibility of repatriation for the next three decades, they nevertheless maintained links with the Tutsi in Rwanda. In the late 1980s, Tutsi exiles in Uganda, who had joined Yoweri Museveni's National Resistance Army (NRA) to fight against the regime of Milton Obote, and who had come to form part of the Ugandan national armed forces when the NRA came to power, began to plot a military comeback, creating the Rwandan Patriotic Front (*Front patriotique rwandais*, or RPF).

The RPF attacked Rwanda in 1990. The ensuing armed conflict and internal political pressure led to the power-sharing Arusha Agreement of August 1993, but the accord was never effectively implemented. Tensions between the Hutu and Tutsi increased sharply following the assassination of the President of Burundi, Melchior Ndadaye, a Hutu, in October 1993. This resulted in mass killings of Tutsi in Burundi, and then mass killings of Hutu. The subsequent death of President Juvenal Habyarimana of Rwanda and President Cyprien Ntaryamira of Burundi in an unexplained crash as their plane approached the Rwandan capital Kigali on 6 April 1994, was used by Hutu extremists as the occasion to seize power in Rwanda and to attack the Tutsi population and Hutu moderates.

Approximately 800,000 people were killed between April and July 1994 in the genocide which followed. Although a multinational UN peacekeeping force, the United Nations Assistance Mission to Rwanda (UNAMIR), had been deployed in Rwanda in October 1993 with a limited mandate to help the parties implement the Arusha Agreement, the bulk of this force withdrew soon after the outbreak of violence. This failure by the United Nations and the international community to protect the civilian population from genocide was examined and acknowledged in a UN report published in December 1999.[1]

RPF forces in Rwanda quickly gained control of Kigali and, in a matter of weeks, most of the country. It was now the turn of the Hutu to flee. Over two million did so, taking refuge in the same countries to which they had forced the Tutsi to flee over 30 years earlier. In the absence of concerted action by the international community at

Rwandan refugees fleeing to Goma, eastern Zaire. These refugees were among some 1.2 million Rwandans who fled to Zaire between April and August 1994. (UNHCR/J. STJERNEKLAR/1994)

the political level, and in the face of ruthless manipulation of refugee populations by combatants, UNHCR and other humanitarian organizations faced some of their most difficult dilemmas.

The Rwandan genocide set in train a series of events that are still in the process of unfolding. They included not only the exodus of Rwandan Hutu from the country, but also the collapse of the regime of President Mobutu Sese Seko and continuing civil war in Zaire (which was renamed the Democratic Republic of the Congo in May 1997). This war came to involve many other African states, most of them militarily, and became linked to other ongoing wars in Angola, Burundi and Sudan.

The mass exodus from Rwanda

The 1994 genocide and the later removal of the genocidal government the same year by the RPF provoked a mass exodus of over two million people from the country.[2] But the exodus was far from spontaneous. It was partly motivated by a desire to escape renewed fighting and partly by fear of vengeance on the part of the advancing RPF. It was also the product of a carefully orchestrated panic organized by the collapsing regime, in the hope of emptying the country and of taking with it the largest possible share of the population as a human shield. By late August 1994, UNHCR estimated that there were over two million refugees in neighbouring countries, including some 1.2 million in Zaire, 580,000 in Tanzania, 270,000 in Burundi and 10,000 in Uganda.[3]

The large camps in Goma, in the Kivu provinces in eastern Zaire, were close to the Rwandan border. They rapidly became the main base for the defeated Rwandan armed forces (*Forces armées rwandaises*, or FAR) and members of the Hutu militia group, the Interahamwe. Collectively, these groups were often referred to as the *génocidaires*. They also became the main base for military activity against the new government in Kigali. From the start, the refugees became political hostages of the former government of Rwanda and its army, the ex-FAR. The latter's control of the camps, particularly those around Goma, was undisguised. This created serious security problems for the refugees themselves and it raised difficult dilemmas for UNHCR in its attempt to ensure their effective protection.

By the end of 1994, the human toll of the crisis in Rwanda was in the millions. In addition to the 800,000 victims of the genocide and the two million refugees outside Rwanda, some 1.5 million people were internally displaced. Out of a population of seven million, over half had been directly affected. The stage was set for a new phase of the Rwandan tragedy.

The refugee camps, especially those in eastern Zaire, were initially in complete disarray. In July 1994, High Commissioner Sadako Ogata described the situation in these terms:

With the rocky volcanic topography and already dense population, the surrounding area is almost totally inadequate for the development of sites to accommodate the refugees. Water resources are severely deficient and local infrastructure with the capacity of supporting a major humanitarian operation is virtually non-existent.[4]

In July 1994, cholera and other diseases broke out, killing tens of thousands before being brought under control.[5] The Goma camps suffered most. About one million refugees lived there, initially in three large settlements. There were many other problems. The Zairean central government's authority in eastern Zaire, far from the capital Kinshasa, was weak. The Rwandan *génocidaires* had allies in the local administration in the Kivus and ex-FAR officers established effective control of the camps. Relief workers were in no position to confront them. Tents at Goma were grouped by *secteur*, *commune*, *sous-préfecture* and *préfecture*, in a mirror image of the administrative organization of the country the refugees had just left. The presence of the former leaders of Rwanda amounted to a government in exile. High-ranking officers from the ex-FAR were eventually moved to a separate camp, and rank and

Following the genocide in Rwanda in 1994, an estimated 250,000 Rwandans swept into Tanzania over a period of 24 hours. (UNHCR/P. MOUMTZIS/1994)

| Box 10.1 | # The problem of militarized refugee camps |

In 1994–96, the domination of the Rwandan refugee camps in eastern Zaire by armed Hutu groups (Interahamwe) drew the attention of the international community to the problem of militarized refugee camps. The presence of armed elements in refugee camps, however, is not a new phenomenon. Numerous other examples can be cited.

During the 1970s, the camps for South African refugees in Mozambique and Tanzania were controlled by members of the military wing of the African National Congress and the Pan-Africanist Congress, and were consequently subject to raids and aerial bombardment by South African armed forces. Similarly, in Angola, Namibian refugee camps run by the Namibian liberation movement, the South West Africa People's Organization, were attacked by the South African air force. In Zambia and Mozambique, camps for refugees from the war in what was then Rhodesia were controlled by the Zimbabwean liberation movements and were attacked by Rhodesian government forces.

During the 1980s, there were many other examples of camps in which armed elements could not easily be distinguished from the civilian population. In the early 1980s, Cambodians fleeing the civil war and the invasion by Viet Nam fled to border camps controlled by the Khmer Rouge and other armed factions. Because of military activities on the Thai border, the camps had to be relocated numerous times, creating additional problems for international organizations attempting to assist refugees in these camps. In Pakistan during the

mid-1980s, Afghan refugee villages near the border harboured tanks and heavy artillery, as well as Mujahedin fighters actively engaged in conflict with the Russian-backed regime in Afghanistan. In southwestern Ethiopia, southern Sudanese rebels used refugee camps as rear bases. In Honduras, Salvadoran guerrillas operated out of refugee camps and Nicaraguan 'contras' also operated from areas in which refugees were settled.

Throughout the 1990s, the problem of the militarization of refugee camps continued in various parts of the world. In West Africa, for example, refugee settlement areas were often a focus for militia recruitment, and the movement of militias between Sierra Leone and Liberia often exacerbated conflicts in both countries and affected the security of the refugee population. In 1998–99, refugee settlements and camps in Albania were used as staging posts by the Kosovo Liberation Army. In West Timor, camps for refugees fleeing the violence in East Timor provided safe haven for armed militias. In Burundi, rebel groups have used refugee-populated areas in Tanzania as recruitment grounds and as conduits for resources.

In each of these cases, the presence of armed elements amongst refugee populations has exposed civilians to increased risks. It has made them vulnerable to intimidation, harassment and forced recruitment by armed groups. It has also exposed them to armed attacks on refugee camps and settlements by enemy forces, the mining of areas in which they live, infiltration by enemy forces, kidnappings and

assassinations. The presence of armed elements in camps has also created security problems for relief workers and has undermined the credibility of humanitarian organizations such as UNHCR.

Ensuring the safety of refugees

Faced with this problem, UNHCR has made increasing efforts over the years to find ways of ensuring the civilian and humanitarian nature of refugee camps. But the problem is a complex one, and UNHCR has neither the mandate nor the capacity to carry out the demili-tarization of refugee camps and settlements.

Under international refugee law, responsibility for ensuring the security of refugee camps rests in the first instance with the host government. In many cases, however, governments prove unable or unwilling to prevent militarization. Although in some cases initial screening and disarming of incoming refugees is carried out at border crossing points by host authorities, this is not always effective and in situations of mass influx it is often not possible. Furthermore, unless combatants are willing to yield their weapons, it is almost impossible for unarmed border officials or UNHCR protection officers to disarm them.

Once armed combatants are mixed with civilian refugee populations, screening and separating them out is notoriously difficult. Where there is resistance to demilitarization, to achieve this may require the inter-vention of a heavily armed military force. Yet even well-trained and equipped military forces often re-fuse to take on this task, as was illustrated in the camps for Rwandan refugees in eastern Zaire, where UNHCR, through the UN Secretary-General, repeatedly asked states to assist in separating armed elements from the civilian population. No government was willing to send external military or police forces to assist with this task. As a result, UNHCR eventually paid and equipped a special Zairean Contingent, recruited from among the Zairean presidential guard, to establish some law and order in the camps.

Article II.6 of the 1969 Refugee Convention of the Organization of African Unity (OAU) states: 'For reasons of security, countries of asylum shall, as far as possible, settle refugees at a reasonable distance from the frontier of their country of origin' [see Box 2.3]. Although the actual distance is not specified in the OAU Refugee Convention, and although the 1951 UN Refugee Convention includes no provisions concerning the distance of refugee camps from borders, UNHCR has on many occasions sought to ensure that refugee camps are located at a 'reasonable distance' from international borders. This, however, can be difficult to achieve for a number of reasons. Refugees spontaneously establish camps close to borders to make it easier for them to return or to monitor the situation in their home region. They are liable to be reluctant to be moved. Relocation is a complex and expensive operation. And host governments often prefer to keep camps close to the border in the hope of eventually encouraging return.

It has been argued that militarized camps should be removed from the protected category of 'refugee camps', and that UNHCR should withdraw services from them. But this is a difficult decision to make when such camps continue to house substantial numbers of *bona fide* refugees. UNHCR has often avoided operating in particular camps because of their militarized nature. In other situations, such as the Goma camps for Rwandans in eastern Zaire, UNHCR maintained a presence in spite of the militarization, as it considered that a withdrawal would put the refugees at even greater risk.

During the last few years, UNHCR has made various innovative attempts to improve security in refugee camps and settlements and to ensure their civilian nature. For example, in 1999 in the Kosovo Albanian camps in the former Yugoslav Republic of Macedonia, UNHCR arranged for the deployment of international police advisers to improve security and law enforcement in the camps. Also, in 1998 in the Burundian refugee camps in Tanzania, UNHCR started supporting some 270 Tanzanian police officers whose task is to enhance security for the refugees and to assist in ensuring the civilian and humanitarian character of the camps.

In line with these new initiatives, High Commissioner Sadako Ogata recently proposed a 'ladder of options' for addressing security problems in camps, including 'soft', 'medium' and 'hard' options. These include measures aimed at ensuring law and order such as programmes to train and build the capacity of national police to handle refugee camp security, the deployment of international police advisers, and as a last resort, the deployment of military forces. But the success of all such attempts to improve the situation depends on the political will of states, particularly the host state and other states in the region. Unless host governments and other actors take active steps to prevent the militarization of refugee camps, the problem will persist and the safety of refugees will continue to be jeopardized.

Rwandan and Burundian refugee populations, 1993–99

Figure 10.1

	Rwandan refugee population						
Country of asylum	1993	1994	1995	1996	1997	1998	1999
Burundi	245,500	278,100	153,000	720	2,000	2,000	1,300
DR of Congo (ex–Zaire)	53,500	1,252,800	1,100,600	423,600	37,000	35,000	33,000
Tanzania	51,900	626,200	548,000	20,000	410	4,800	20,100
Uganda	97,000	97,000	6,500	11,200	12,200	7,500	8,000
Total	447,900	2,254,100	1,808,100	455,520	51,610	49,300	62,400

	Burundian refugee population						
Country of asylum	1993	1994	1995	1996	1997	1998	1999
DR of Congo (ex–Zaire)	176,400	180,100	117,900	30,200	47,000	20,000	19,200
Rwanda	250,000	6,000	3,200	9,600	6,900	1,400	1,400
Tanzania	444,900	202,700	227,200	385,500	459,400	473,800	499,000
Total	871,300	388,800	348,300	425,300	513,300	495,200	519,600

Note: As on 31 December of each given year.

file were persuaded to shed their uniforms, but the population was still clearly under their control and the control of the Interahamwe. In South Kivu, the physical situation of the refugees was better: they were fewer in number and the camps were smaller, but these camps were alsoinfiltrated by armed elements. Only in Tanzania did the authorities manage to disarm them and gain a modicum of control over the camps.

In the early days of the refugee crisis, relief workers found themselves cooperating with these military authorities and the Interahamwe militia leaders. The administrative structure they had established was the quickest and seemingly most effective way to distribute relief items. This distribution system was changed as soon as possible to ensure that food and other relief items were distributed directly to the refugees, but the criticism that the *génocidaires* were using humanitarian agencies to strengthen their position vis-à-vis the refugee population was a valid one.

The camp leaders had control over the distribution of food and other relief supplies in the early days. It soon became evident, however, that relief items were not their main source of support. More substantial resources were acquired through their control of the economy of the camps, running retail businesses and levying taxes on the camp population, especially on refugee employees of humanitarian agencies, who earned regular salaries. The camps at Goma thus became a microcosm of Rwanda before 1994, and a significant military threat to the new government in Rwanda itself. The leaders had also brought with them most of the contents of the Bank of Rwanda and much of the public transport fleet.

In late August, High Commissioner Ogata wrote to the UN Secretary-General asking for a number of emergency measures, as the Zairean authorities had failed to take appropriate action. These measures included four key elements: first, to 'totally disarm the ex-FAR troops, collect all arms and military equipment and gather them in a secure place far from the border'; second, to 'isolate and neutralize civilian leaders'; third, to 'set up a mechanism for dealing with perpetrators of crime'; and fourth, to 'ensure maintenance of law and order in the camps through the deployment of police'.[6] But members of the Security Council and other states failed to support such measures, and humanitarian organizations working in the camps remained powerless. A further catastrophe was in the making.

The indecisive international response

Rwanda's new government was extremely critical of the situation in the camps and repeatedly requested the immediate repatriation of the refugees or their removal away from the border area deeper into Zaire. But this was more easily said than done. There was widespread opposition to their presence among Zaireans, and in the increasingly unstable political atmosphere in Zaire, such opposition could result in violence at any time. In a memorandum addressed to UNHCR soon after the exodus, Zairean opposition political forces threatened violence. The refugees, they asserted,

have destroyed our food reserves, destroyed our fields, our cattle, our natural parks, caused famine and spread epidemics and . . . benefit from food aid while we get nothing. They sell or give weapons to their fellow countrymen, commit murders both of Tutsi and of local Zaireans . . . They must be disarmed, counted, subjected to Zairean laws and finally repatriated.[7]

Rwandan refugees in the Great Lakes region, end-August 1994 — Figure 10.2

Location	
Northern Burundi	270,000
Western Tanzania	577,000
Southwestern Uganda	10,000
Zaire (Goma)	850,000
Zaire (Bukavu)	332,000
Zaire (Uvira)	62,000
Total	**2,101,000**

For the shaky government in Kinshasa, however, the refugees were a potential proxy force, useful to help reassert control of the eastern provinces. For President Mobutu, the refugee issue deflected attention from his government's mismanagement of the country and thereby offered a chance to regain the international stature he had lost since the end of the Cold War.

Western donor countries involved in the effort to assist the refugees were divided. Delegations to Kinshasa routinely demanded that President Mobutu negotiate with the various forces involved, but there was no clarity about who should be involved in the negotiations or what should be negotiated. Lip-service was paid to the idea of repatriation of the refugees, but no donor government supported it sufficiently strongly to take the political risk necessary to force the issue through. Western

Kibeho camp for displaced Rwandan Hutu in southwestern Rwanda, which was to be the scene of mass killings in April 1995. (S. SALGADO/1994)

Box 10.2 **Refugees and the AIDS pandemic**

At the end of 1999, there were an estimated 32 million adults around the world with the HIV virus or with AIDS. In addition, there were some 11 million children who had either lost both parents to AIDS, or who had become infected with the HIV virus themselves. AIDS has contributed to political and socioeconomic crises in many developing countries. The issue is now amongst the most urgent topics on the United Nations' agenda, and has even been discussed by the UN Security Council.

UN Secretary-General Kofi Annan has described the impact of AIDS in Africa as 'no less destructive than that of war itself'. Though it knows no borders, AIDS has taken a part-icularly devastating toll on Africa. Sub-Saharan Africa, home to just 10 per cent of the world's population, contains nearly 70 per cent of the world's HIV-positive population. In some of these countries one in four of the population is infected.

Forced population movements often place people at greater risk to HIV transmission. HIV can spread fast where there is poverty, powerlessness, lawlessness and social instability— conditions that often give rise to or accompany forced displacement. Rape and other forms of sexual and gender-related violence perpetrated by soldiers or paramilitary forces often become weapons of war and a tactic to terrorize.

In responding to refugee health needs, UNHCR and its partners have increasingly attempted to adopt comprehensive approaches which address reproductive health issues including HIV/AIDS prevention and care. The 1994 refugee crisis in the Great Lakes region of Africa helped to raise awareness amongst the inter-national community about the need to address the issue of AIDS preven-tion and care. This involved a large-scale movement of people with a high rate of HIV infection seeking refuge in countries also plagued with AIDS.

Strategies to reduce transmission of the HIV virus are well known, yet they are notoriously difficult to implement, as they touch on sensitive and private aspects of life as well as cultural beliefs and behaviour. They include good hygiene, safe blood transfusions, access to condoms, prevention and treatment of sexually transmitted diseases, and the provision of culturally sensitive and well-targeted education and information.

Throughout the 1990s, major initiatives were launched to put reproductive health and HIV/AIDS high on the global agenda. Spear-headed by the UN International Conference on Population and Development in Cairo in 1994, the international community has come to recognize reproductive health care as a basic right, even though there remains controversy over the forms that this care should take. The conference agreed that such health care should 'be provided to all, including migrants and refugees, with full respect to their various religious and ethical values and cultural backgrounds while conforming with universally recognized inter-national human rights'. In 1995, the Fourth World Conference on Women in Beijing further stressed the right of women to have control over and decide freely and responsibly on matters related to their sexuality without being subject to coercion, discrimination or violence.

The United Nations Programme on AIDS (UNAIDS) was established in 1996 to coordinate the UN approach to the AIDS pandemic, document its evolution, and promote a cost-effective universal response. UN humanitarian organizations, non-governmental organizations, and some governments have also worked together to strengthen reproductive health services to refugees and refugee-like communities. The 1999 inter-agency field manual, *Reproductive Health in Refugee Situations*, and the development of

reproductive health kits by the United Nations Population Fund (UNFPA) are some of the results of this process.

While there may be clear strategies to reduce HIV transmission, there are a number of major hurdles to overcome before effective HIV/AIDS prevention and care programmes can be put in place. In many places where refugees live, especially in Africa, national AIDS control programmes are under-developed. Local populations have only limited access to basic primary health care and most people have no access at all to effective but extremely costly HIV/AIDS-related drugs. Providing services for refugees and not for the local population can do little to prevent the pandemic from spreading.

An effective response to the complex nature of HIV and AIDS requires human, material and financial res-ources as well as technical cap-abilities which many humanitarian organizations have not yet been able to develop. It also calls for a multi-sectoral approach encompassing not only health but also social and economic issues, human rights and legal matters. Women, including refugee women, are often particularly exposed to the threat of HIV/AIDS and in many cases they do not have the means to influence the behaviour of their partners due to cultural and other attitudes and practices.

The stigma which is so often attached to AIDS can affect both the willing-ness of those affected by it to seek care and the willingness of local authorities to extend the necessary support to them. Refugees, who fall into a distinct category and whose presence is sometimes resented by local people, can easily find them-selves discriminated against because of a stereotypical perception that 'refugees bring AIDS'. It is a matter of particular concern to UNHCR that refugees are sometimes refused resettlement or denied asylum or repatriation because of their HIV status.

guilt about UN inaction in the face of the genocide complicated established political and economic interests in the region. The result was incoherence at policy level.

The Zairean government, nominally responsible for the welfare of the refugees, was showing signs of imminent collapse. Members of the government contradicted one another. The new Rwandan government was also giving mixed signals. Officially, government representatives insisted on the desirability of an early return, but initiatives by humanitarian organizations to accelerate this were invariably frustrated.

For UNHCR, there were urgent practical problems, but the solution to these was frustrated at every point by the growing military instability in the region. Goma was becoming not so much a place of refuge as a low-intensity war zone. One UNHCR field officer wrote from Goma: 'Neither our mandate nor the means at our disposal match the requirements needed to address the regional crisis.'[8]

The escalation of the conflict in eastern Zaire

From early 1995, Rwandan military groups in eastern Zaire, mostly ex-FAR, mounted a series of cross-border attacks into Rwanda. The RPA then launched a series of counter-raids into Zaire, attacking Birava camp on 11 April and Mugunga on 26 April 1995, killing 33 people. UNHCR found itself at the centre of a conflict between the two Rwandan armies. In Zaire, President Mobutu was supporting the rearmament and retraining of the ex-FAR. Cheap light weaponry from the former communist countries of Eastern Europe also contributed to the rearmament of the former génocidaires.[9] The ex-FAR and militia were increasingly in a position to use the camps as recruitment grounds and rear bases for infiltration into Rwanda.

In Rwanda, meanwhile, the political situation had deteriorated. At Kibeho camp in southwestern Rwanda, thousands of internally displaced Hutu were killed by RPF forces in April 1995. Between July and August 1994, the Kibeho camp had been part of a 'humanitarian protection zone' established by a French-led multinational military force under 'Operation Turquoise', which was authorized by the UN Security Council.[10] By August 1995, the RPF had marginalized the more independent members of the Rwandan cabinet, and Prime Minister Faustin Twagiramungu, Interior Minister Seth Sendashonga and Justice Minister Alphonse-Marie Nkubito were forced to resign. The main concern of the new cabinet was the military threat posed by ex-FAR forces operating from the Zairean refugee camps.

UNHCR made repeated calls for measures to be taken by the Security Council to ensure the civilian and humanitarian nature of the refugee camps. The High Commissioner requested 'a multinational contingent composed of police/gendarmes from French-speaking African countries and perhaps Canada, logistical support in transport and equipment from non-African countries and financial support from other countries'.[11] But this was not forthcoming. Most donor countries were alarmed at the instability in the region and the high costs of troop deployment. Indecisiveness within the Security Council further prevented any serious tackling of the issue.

UNHCR fell back on the resources of the host country. A specially recruited force, the Zairean Contingent for the Security of the Camps, was established. It was made up of

1,500 men of President Mobutu's 'Division spéciale présidentielle', who were paid and re-equipped by UNHCR. The force had international advisers from the Netherlands and from several West African countries. It started operating in early 1995 and worked reasonably well, to the surprise of some sceptical observers. Although its mandate did not extend to border security, it brought a modicum of law and order to the camps, and went some way towards undermining the authority of the refugee leadership, thus increasing refugees' freedom to opt for return.

After a good beginning, however, the Zairean Contingent eventually proved to be poorly disciplined. It was directly accountable to President Mobutu, through his Minister of Defence, and not to the Prime Minister, so that it became a factor in the widening political divide in Zaire. It was soon drawn into the endemic corruption of the administration in the Kivus and other parts of Zaire. In early 1996, High Commissioner Ogata wrote to Zairean Prime Minister Kengo Wa Dondo:

I would like to renew my demands for ending the impunity of the camps. The various measures taken by your government should be actually enforced and Zairean law and order should prevail. All this of course in full co-operation with UNHCR and with the Zairean Contingent for the Security of the Camps.[12]

As before, the lack of concerted international diplomatic support meant that President Mobutu was able to continue to play a double game, publicly accepting UNHCR's concerns about growing violence in the border zones and privately tolerating or even supporting it. But President Mobutu himself had miscalculated; he was to be the next victim of the forces unleashed in the east.

The failure of repatriation

Repatriation from Zaire to Rwanda began rapidly, with over 200,000 refugees going back between July 1994 and January 1995 from the Goma area.[13] Smaller but still significant numbers were also coming back from south Kivu, Tanzania and Burundi. Deteriorating security conditions in the camps undoubtedly contributed to the refugees' desire to return. But the situation was deteriorating in Rwanda as well, and by early 1995 the repatriation movement had 'ground to a halt'.[14] An inquiry commissioned by UNHCR to test the feasibility of repatriation had already given warning in mid-1994 of killings and other human rights violations committed in Rwanda by elements of the RPF. After informing the Rwandan government of its findings, UNHCR stopped facilitating the repatriation programme. The massacre which took place in April 1995 at Kibeho camp in southwestern Rwanda strengthened the opposition of those opposed to repatriation. After this incident, repatriation stopped completely.

Later in 1995, with the situation in Rwanda more stable, UNHCR resumed repatriation efforts, but the attitude of all parties concerning the return of refugees was ambiguous. This was clearly demonstrated when the Zairean government tried to trigger a return movement by forcibly closing one camp in August 1995. In this case, some 15,000 refugees were put on rented trucks and forcibly returned to

Box 10.3 Somalia: from exodus to diaspora

The Somali Republic, which gained independence in 1960, was built upon far from secure foundations. Clan allegiances had long posed problems for the development of an effective form of civil government. After President Siad Barre's defeat by Ethiopia in the Ogaden war of 1977, rival clan families in Somalia were systematically marginalized and exploited by Barre's ruling clan alliance. By 1988, resistance from the Isaq Somali National Movement (SNM) in the northwest met with the full force of the state.

The first major refugee exodus from Somalia after the Ogaden war occurred when government forces bombed Hargeisa and Burao in the northwest of the country in 1988. Refugee flows to Ethiopia amounted to some 365,000, while some 60,000 people became internally displaced. Around 50,000 people are estimated to have been killed by government troops.

Temporarily defeated, the SNM was later to form an alliance with the Hawiye-based United Somali Congress (USC) and the smaller Somali Patriotic Movement (SPM). This loose alliance overthrew the government of President Barre in January 1991. The alliance was, however, unable to retain control of the country and instead fell apart, precipitating a major humanitarian emergency. The opposition was clan-based, but clan rivalries were exacerbated by the competition amongst militia leaders for power and resources.

Clan reprisals became the order of the day as Mogadishu fell to the USC. Internal factionalism and the ongoing war with Barre's forces resulted in intensified conflict.

The attacks on areas occupied by the Digil and Rahanweyn clan families, in addition to the wholesale slaughter of minority populations in the coastal areas, resulted in massive internal displacement. Clan members sought out 'clan homelands', displacing more people. Drought and famine brought further disruption and by mid-1992 some two million people had been uprooted as a result of the conflict. They included some 400,000 who went to Ethiopia and over 200,000 who went to Kenya.

International intervention

The response of the international community to the worsening crisis in Somalia was slow to gather momentum. Hundreds of thousands of Somalis died of starvation and disease, or as a result of fighting, before the first UN peacekeeping forces arrived in April 1992, as part of the United Nations Operation in Somalia (UNOSOM I).[i] Initially, the mandate of the UNOSOM force was limited to overseeing a ceasefire between the warring factions.

The steady deterioration in the humanitarian situation led US President George Bush to decide in December 1992 to deploy 28,000 US troops as part of what was to become a 37,000-strong, US-led Unified Task Force (UNITAF). UNITAF's 'Operation Restore Hope', was authorized under UN Security Council Resolution 794 of 3 December 1992. It was authorized without any invitation from the warring parties. The humanitarian impulse of ensuring that food supplies reached the victims of famine was an important part of the operation, but the lack of clear strategy dogged the intervention

from the outset. The humanitarian operation became more compromised as attempts were made to disarm the rival Somali factions.

In May 1993, UNITAF was replaced by UNOSOM II and the US commander handed over responsibility for the operation to a UN commander. The UNOSOM II force was larger and had a broader mandate than the original UNOSOM, which had remained in Somalia throughout. UNOSOM II launched a programme of national reconstruction in Somalia. The 28,000-strong UN peacekeeping force came from 27 different countries and had a budget of US$1.6 billion. Unprecedented in size and scope, the force included 17,700 US troops not under direct UN command.

The sudden shift in the UN's role from providing humanitarian relief to attempts at nation-building succeeded only in alienating Somalia's warlords. A series of open clashes with General Mohamed Farah Aidid's powerful Hawiye clan faction culminated in the shooting down of two US helicopters in October 1993. The death of 18 US soldiers and the spectacle the body of a dead US soldier being hauled through the streets of Mogadishu rapidly led to a decision by the Clinton administration to withdraw US troops from Somalia. All US and European military personnel left Somalia by March 1994 and all remaining UN troops departed by the end of March 1995.

During the worst moment of the crisis in Somalia, only the International Committee of the Red Cross and a small number of non-governmental organizations (NGOs) remained in the country. However, with the presence of international troops, UN agencies such as the World Food Programme and the UN Children's Fund (UNICEF) played a major role in delivering relief supplies, together with large numbers of NGOs. In spite of the presence of international military forces, security remained a serious problem, and many humanitarian personnel were killed or injured. Humanitarian personnel had to be escorted by local militia groups acting as armed guards to carry out their duties.

In response to the humanitarian crisis in Somalia, UNHCR began a series of cross-border operations from Kenya in September 1992. Launched at the request of the UN Secretary-General, these operations were intended to stabilize population movements inside Somalia. After the deployment of UNITAF in December 1992, 'preventive zones' were established in southern Somalia to assist people in specific areas where they might otherwise be forced to flee because of famine. As well as providing food and relief within Somalia, the cross-border operations were intended to begin rehabilitation of the infrastructure and thus enable the voluntary return of the refugees in camps in Kenya, who by the end of 1992 numbered more than 285,000.

The mobile phone society

The civil war in Somalia created a large Somali diaspora. Refugees fleeing the country added to the Somali migrant workers already living in the Gulf and Western Europe before 1988. In addition to refugees who fled to Yemen, Djibouti and Libya, there are now established communities of Somalis living in North America and Europe. The former colonial link between the United Kingdom and the northern part of Somalia, now known as Somaliland (formerly the British Protectorate of Somaliland), means that there are now settled communities of Somalis in many major UK cities.

Communication between members of the Somali diaspora has been facilitated by mobile phones, the Internet and e-mail. This has been a key factor in enabling Somalis, and indeed other refugee groups, to maintain links with family members overseas. The proliferating network of telephone companies throughout Somalia—there are now at least eight—has been encouraged by joint ventures involving local residents and Somalis in the diaspora. The growing telephone system allows for family ties to be maintained and is also central to the steady flow of remittances which has kept Somalia's economy from collapse in recent years.

The strong clan system, which divided Somalis and led to the deaths of hundreds of thousands of people during the 1990s, also proved to be a source of unity and strength. The compelling nature of these clan ties prompted the development of an international banking system of remittance agencies. At present, most Somalis in the diaspora continue to use fax machines to transfer remittances, but e-mail is now also increasingly being used. A remittance given to a local clan banker in London, for example, will result in the equivalent amount being transferred to family members in Somalia within 24 hours. The sending of goods in kind and the transfer of cash carried by hand on regular flights from Jeddah and Dubai are other favoured methods of transferring remittances. The current value of remittances is placed at several hundred million US dollars a year and significantly outstrips livestock as a source of foreign exchange.[ii]

One remittance agency has a website which allows people to replay Somali language news reports by the British Broadcasting Corporation, the major source of news for Somalis in the diaspora. In a world made smaller by the impact of information technology, the creation of numerous websites has enabled Somalis to explore their changing perceptions of home and the new demands and possibilities of life in the diaspora. At the same time, e-mail and mobile phones have helped Somalis in the diaspora and at home to maintain links, and have gone some way towards enabling them to remain united as one society.

Rwanda. As a result of international pressure, the Zairean authorities rapidly put an end to the operation.

UNHCR tried various means to loosen the grip of the refugee leadership. Information campaigns and family visits into Rwanda were organized. Negotiations were held with the Rwandan authorities to open additional border crossing points to facilitate the movement of the refugees from the camps. Camp businesses were temporarily closed by the Zairean Contingent to try and undermine the power of the refugee leaders. Repatriation convoys were organized on a daily basis to pick up and escort refugees volunteering to return. But all these initiatives were ineffective as a result of the combination of opposition from Zairean or Rwandan authorities and lack of support from the international community, particularly governments of the main donor countries and front-line countries.

Within UNHCR and the humanitarian community in general, there was considerable uncertainty on the issue of repatriation. The traditional principle that all refugees should be given the opportunity of a voluntary return, on the basis of individual informed choices, was difficult to put into practice. The reality was that most of the refugees had been coerced into exile by their leaders. Many of them were more like hostages than refugees. This was a different type of human displacement, in which the concept of voluntary return, and the very meaning of the word 'refugee', had been twisted into new and complex realities, which could not easily be tackled through traditional approaches.[15]

Flight from the refugee camps

North and South Kivu, the two eastern Zairean provinces where the refugees had found shelter, had for a long time been hotbeds of opposition to the regime of President Mobutu, who now attempted to use ethnic rivalries to his advantage. The Kivus had a large ethnic Banyarwanda population (both Tutsi and Hutu) which he had used in the past against other indigenous groups.[16] The resulting ethnic tension was exacerbated when new legislation was passed by the Zairean parliament in 1981, resulting in the *de jure* loss of citizenship by thousands of Banyarwanda people. Even in 1993, before the Rwandan genocide, there was fighting between Banyarwanda and other groups when the authorities tried to organize a census of 'foreigners'. The influx of Rwandan refugees during the summer of 1994 had a disastrous effect on the fragile balance in the Kivus as the political wing of the Hutu refugees brought with them their violent ethnic prejudices.

By early 1995, violence in the Kivus had been rekindled, particularly in North Kivu, where the Goma camps were situated. This time it was not limited to the local population. General Augustin Bizimungu, the chief of staff of the ex-FAR, was attempting to carve out a territory in the Kivus from which he could operate against Rwanda, and against the Zairean Tutsi communities in the Kivus. He recruited some of the Zairean armed forces (*Forces armées zaïroises*, or FAZ), who, being unpaid and poorly commanded, became little more than soldiers of fortune. A conflict developed which included on one side the ex-FAR, their FAZ allies and some anti-government local militias known as Mayi Mayi, and on the other side the Zairean Tutsi population. The latter were the weaker from the military point of view and many Tutsi were killed or forced to flee.

Between November 1995 and February 1996, about 37,000 Tutsi left for Rwanda, half of them Zairean Tutsi driven out by the conflict in the Masisi area in North Kivu, and the other half refugees from the earlier 1959 exile. The government of Rwanda immediately asked UNHCR to open refugee camps on the Rwandan side of the border. It was a paradoxical situation since many of the 'refugees' arriving in Rwanda were originally from Rwanda. Having wanted to achieve a successful repatriation to Rwanda rather than the creation of additional camps on the Rwanda side of the border, it was with extreme reluctance that UNHCR opened two camps in Rwanda.[17] To make matters worse, these Tutsi refugee camps were only a few kilometres from the border and were close to the camps at Goma.

High Commissioner Ogata once again sought international assistance in improving the security situation. 'The recent influx from Masisi to Rwanda now stands at 9,000 persons' she wrote in May 1996 to UN Secretary-General Boutros-Ghali. 'The international community should consider urgent measures to prevent a further deterioration in the security situation . . . Renewed efforts to relocate the camps away from the border should be undertaken.'[18] Even the Zairean government began to see that intervention in Kivu ethnic politics had created a situation that was running out of control, but it was too late. The crisis was about to engulf the whole sub-region.

The conflict spreads

By mid-1996, the situation in the Great Lakes region was extremely tense. In Burundi, there was escalating tension between the Tutsi and Hutu. In October 1993, the democratically elected Hutu president, Melchior Ndadaye, had been murdered by Tutsi soldiers. This had led to an outburst of violence in which thousands of people—both Tutsi and Hutu—were killed. It had also led to the flight, mainly to Rwanda, of about 700,000 Hutus, some of whom later became active in the Rwandan genocide. On 26 July 1996, former president Major Pierre Buyoya, a Tutsi, overthrew the weak civilian administration led by President Sylvestre Ntibantunganya. For some it was seen as an attempt to reimpose state control, but for others this was just another military coup. The neighbouring countries convened an emergency meeting and declared an economic embargo against Burundi.

Elsewhere in the region, relations between Uganda and Sudan were deteriorating. Kampala accused Khartoum of arming guerrilla groups and encouraging them to attack Uganda both from Sudan and (with support from Kinshasa) from northeastern Zaire.

Box 10.4 # War and displacement in West Africa

During the 1990s, West Africa became the scene of violent wars that uprooted millions of people. The two main conflicts, largely internal but fuelled by external funds, weapons, and interests, were in Liberia and Sierra Leone. These conflicts sent nearly one million refugees into neighbouring countries, primarily into Guinea and Côte d'Ivoire. A smaller conflict in Senegal and an army mutiny in Guinea-Bissau in 1998 also produced some 200,000 refugees.

By the end of the decade, more than a third of Africa's refugees and displaced people were in West Africa. Most of these people were displaced within their own countries. Many of those who did cross international borders remained within a few kilometres of the border. As a result, even those who fled to what they hoped would be safer ground remained vulnerable to attack. UNHCR had to move several camps in Guinea further from the border to protect the camp's residents. Staff of humanitarian organizations that came to the aid of the refugees and displaced also found themselves at great risk. Many were threatened, several were abducted, property was stolen, and on a number of occasions humanitarian workers had to be evacuated for their own safety.

When Liberians first fled into Guinea and Côte d'Ivoire, local people opened their homes to them. In those early stages, relatively few refugees were accommodated in camps. When Sierra Leoneans began fleeing into Guinea, some also moved into the homes of local people, but the absorption capacity was soon exhausted and many moved into camps. Both countries offered considerable hospi-tality to large refugee populations throughout the 1990s. At one point in late 1996, Guinea was hosting some 650,000 refugees from Liberia and Sierra Leone. Today, Guinea still hosts over 500,000 refugees. Côte d'Ivoire hosted between 175,000 and 360,000 refugees every year between 1990

and 1997, and still hosted around 138,000 in 1999.

The wars in West Africa during the 1990s have had a number of different dimensions, including ethnic tensions, struggles for resources, and uprisings of disaffected youths. Focusing on ethnic tensions, some observers point out that in Liberia the rebel forces initially had an ethnic character, even though they drew in participants from a wide cross-section of Liberian youth. In Senegal, the Casamance separatists were often portrayed as a movement of the Jola people, but not all Jola were separatists and not all separatists were Jola.

Other observers have characterized these wars as being primarily struggles for control over timber and diamond resources. In Liberia, clandestine logging was a mainstay of the rebels, much of the timber ending up in France. In Sierra Leone, rebel forces depended largely on the diamond trade for purchasing weapons, and both the government and rebels turned to international mining and security companies for support.Others claim that the common thread in the three conflicts was not ethnic tensions or competition over resources, but rather the impact of corruption and state recession on marginalized and vulnerable youths.[iii] The prolonged struggle in Casamance, where there was little in the way of timber or minerals, is sometimes cited as an example.

Liberia

The conflict that affected Liberia throughout the 1990s began in December 1989 between forces of the National Patriotic Front of Liberia (NPFL), who were mostly ethnic Gio and Mano, and forces loyal to President Samuel Doe, who were mostly ethnic Krahn people. The conflict was characterized by massacres of civilians, mutilations, widespread destruction of property,

and the recruitment of large numbers of child soldiers who were often made to kill to prove their loyalty. During eight years of terror, more than 150,000 Liberians were killed and half of all Liberians fled their homes. Of the more than 1.7 million uprooted, approximately 40 per cent fled to neighbouring countries and almost all the remainder were internally displaced.

In 1990, in an attempt to restore order, the Economic Community of West African States (ECOWAS) sent a force into Liberia, the ECOWAS Military Observer Group (ECOMOG). ECOMOG gained control of the capital, Monrovia, but 95 per cent of the country remained in rebel hands. Other armed factions emerged, further exacerbating the conflict. There were 11 such factions by 1994. The conflict became one of the most destructive, intractable, and yet least publicized civil wars anywhere in the world.

Even in Monrovia, civilians were not safe. Continued fighting for control of the city repeatedly displaced people sheltering there. In April 1996, fighting among the various three armed factions seeking control over the city left 3,500 dead. More than 350,000 civilians, including displaced people in Monrovia, fled the city. Among them were at least 2,000 Liberians who fled by sea aboard the *Bulk Challenge*, and 400 others who fled on the *Zolotista*. Both ships sailed from port to port along the West African coast seeking safe haven for the refugees aboard. At each port, they were turned back. Ghana finally permitted the *Bulk Challenge* to land after reports that many of those aboard were gravely ill. The *Zolotista* and its passengers were obliged to return to Monrovia after three weeks at sea.

After the violence in 1996, the warring factions signed an important peace agreement. Unlike the many previous agreements, this one held. In 1997, in an internationally supervised poll, NPFL leader Charles

Taylor was elected president. Although there were no other major military confrontations between 1997 and the end of 1999, the political and security situation in Liberia remained volatile.

Sierra Leone

In Sierra Leone, an insurgency by the Revolutionary United Front (RUF) began with a cross-border incursion from Liberia in March 1991. The RUF had close connections with Charles Taylor's NPFL, as well as political and economic backing from Libya and Burkina Faso. An ECOMOG force was sent to Sierra Leone to assist the government, but the violence continued, uprooting more than a million people over the next three years. By 1994, the RUF had weakened, but violence against civilians continued unabated, primarily at the hands of disaffected current or former government soldiers.

In 1995, the government hired a South African mercenary force that helped restore some order, and in early 1996 elections were held. Voters elected a civilian, Ahmed Tejan Kabbah, as president. Finally, the government and RUF signed a peace accord, and hundreds of thousands of displaced people returned home.

But peace proved elusive. In May 1997, frustrated members of the military joined forces with the RUF, to oust Kabbah and establish an Armed Forces Revolutionary Council (AFRC). Fighting between ECOMOG and AFRC forces displaced thousands more in 1997, but ended when the two sides agreed a new peace agreement in late 1997 that called for the restoration of Kabbah and provided a role for the RUF's imprisoned leader, Foday Sankoh. During 1998, heavy fighting once again displaced large numbers of civilians and by the end of the year, over one million Sierra Leoneans remained uprooted, including some 400,000 in neighbouring countries.

In July 1999, the government and rebels met in Lomé, Togo, and signed another agreement aimed at ending hostilities. The agreement called on both sides to share power and provided an amnesty for those who had committed atrocities against civilians. ECOMOG was replaced in October 1999 by an 11,000-strong UN peacekeeping force, whose main task was to oversee the demobilization of former combatants and to create a secure environment for the return of refugees and displaced people to their homes. By the end of the year, the situation in Sierra Leone remained precarious, with ceasefire violations, continued human rights abuses, and limited demobilization of soldiers. Despite the amnesty, there are constant reminders of the many atrocities which took place during the 1990s. The large-scale forced recruitment of children which took place during the war, and the gruesome mutilation of civilians which was a particular characteristic of the war, have resulted in a deeply traumatized society.

Populations of refugees and internally displaced persons in West Africa, 1994

Map 10.1

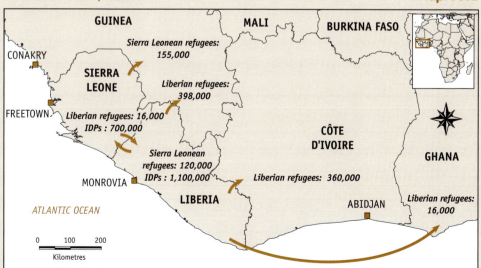

Source: IDP figures from US Committee for Refugees.

Finally, in eastern Zaire, the conflict in North Kivu was spreading to South Kivu. There, the Banyamulenge, a Zairean Tutsi group, also faced problems resulting from changes made in 1981 to Zaire's citizenship laws. Whipped into a nationalist frenzy by local politicians acting on President Mobutu's behalf, armed elements attacked the Banyamulenge and by mid-September groups of refugees started to arrive at the Rwandan border post of Cyangugu. There were also revenge attacks by Banyamulenge militias against a variety of civilian and military targets in South Kivu. There were reports that soldiers of the Rwandan Patriotic Army (RPA) had entered Zaire from Rwanda and were fighting alongside the Banyamulenge militia and other armed opposition groups which had by then launched a rebellion against the regime of President Mobutu.

A year later, Rwandan Vice-President Paul Kagame confirmed reports that the Rwandan government had provided key support to the Banyamulenge and other Zairean opposition groups in their rebellion. Rwanda's justification for attacking Zairean territory and targeting the refugee camps in North and South Kivu was the need to put an end to armed incursions by Hutu extremists based in the refugee camps.

The already difficult position of UNHCR and other humanitarian organizations in the Kivus became more difficult still. Rarely, if ever, had humanitarian organizations become so clearly identifiable with the primary military objective of a war—the dismantling of refugee camps which they had built and supported for the past two years. This was further complicated by the presence of the Zairean Contingent, which UNHCR paid to maintain law and order in the camps, but which—being a Zairean military force—attempted to fight the rebels. Resistance to military advances by the rebel forces, heavily backed by the Rwandan government, also came from the ex-FAR.

UNHCR was therefore portrayed by the Rwandan government and its allies as supporting not so much the refugees, but the *génocidaires* and their sponsor, the regime of President Mobutu. The refugees also criticized UNHCR, and when the High Commissioner exhorted Rwandans caught in the conflict to return to Rwanda, extremist groups accused UNHCR of collaborating with the attackers. The Zairean government even accused UNHCR of having taken part in what they described as the 'invasion' of South Kivu.

UNHCR and other humanitarian organizations thus found themselves in a situation which was not only politically extremely difficult, but also increasingly dangerous. The argument that humanitarian aid in the absence of political action can prolong, and sometimes exacerbate, armed conflict was given force by the events in eastern Zaire. As High Commissioner Sadako Ogata stated at the beginning of October 1996:

The link between refugee problems and peace and security is perhaps nowhere more evident than in the Great Lakes region in Africa . . . Probably never before has my Office found its humanitarian concerns in the midst of such a lethal quagmire of political and security interests. While our humanitarian assistance and protection serve an innocent, silent majority of needy and anxious refugees, they also serve the militants who have an interest in maintaining the *status quo*. This cannot go on.[19]

Attacks on the Goma refugee camps

The armed forces operating against the Rwandan (and Burundian) refugee camps in South Kivu were at first difficult to identify. They were initially all referred to as Banyamulenge. But after mid-October, mention was increasingly made of the Alliance of Democratic Forces for the Liberation of Zaire/Congo (*Alliance des forces démocratiques pour la libération du Zaïre/Congo*, or AFDL/ZC), a name which implied a native Zairean participation in the new war and a wider political agenda.

But, even if there were a wider agenda, the refugee camps were the initial target. The first ones to be attacked were those to the south, in the Uvira area, which hosted the bulk of the Burundian refugees. These camps had been infiltrated by the Forces for the Defence of Democracy (*Forces de défense de la démocratie*, or FDD), who were Hutu guerrillas fighting the government of President Buyoya, who had seized power in mid-1996. In October 1996, the camps were overrun with surprising ease and the refugees were quickly herded across the border into Burundi. The FDD suffered heavy losses in the process. These attacks assisted President Buyoya in Burundi at a critical juncture. The attack on Uvira forced UNHCR and its partner agencies to suspend their operations; expatriate staff were evacuated, leaving behind their Zairean colleagues and tens of thousands of refugees. UNHCR premises were looted and vandalized.

After the main attack in Uvira, the surviving Rwandan refugees were swept northwards towards Bukavu. By then Bukavu itself had come under attack. The last international aid workers were evacuated from Bukavu during heavy fighting on 29 October, when UNHCR and its partner agencies suspended their operations. Again the Rwandan refugees were forced to leave, moving either westwards or northwards, in an attempt to link up with the main body of refugees in the Goma area.

But North Kivu was also unsafe. The rebellion was spreading with great speed, taking Zaireans and international observers alike by surprise. Rebel forces attacked two of the camps north of Goma—Katale and Kahindo—and hundreds of thousands of people were forced to flee towards the two last bastions of safety, the camps at Mugunga and Kibumba. A few days later, Kibumba was the object of a direct attack, and over 200,000 refugees fled towards Goma town and Mugunga. On 31 October, Goma town itself came under attack. On 2 November, UNHCR staff and other humanitarian staff remaining in Goma were evacuated across the border to nearby Rwanda, under RPA protection.[20]

These events amounted to a dramatic failure by the international community of refugee protection. They also represented one of the most serious crises in UNHCR's history. In the space of a few days, UNHCR and its partner agencies had been obliged to abandon hundreds of thousands of refugees in a situation of intensifying conflict. They were cut off from the only remaining refugee camp and had lost touch with the majority of refugees now moving in disorder across the Kivus. The plight of these refugees, many of whom were fleeing through the dense rainforests of eastern Zaire, demanded urgent action. As in 1994, UNHCR requested an international force to protect humanitarian access to refugees. But if mobilizing such a force had been difficult in 1994, it was now almost impossible.

The refugees, whether they liked it or not, were under the complete control of armed elements. The difficulties and contradictions of past years had reached a peak. Once more, a protracted discussion on whether or not to send a multinational force, and on what it should do, took place in Western capitals, but nothing happened on the ground.

While the suspension of humanitarian operations had been a dramatic one, UNHCR and its partner agencies were able to resume some activities only a few days later. With the rebel forces, now known as the AFDL, occupying most of the eastern Kivus, the United Nations started negotiating the resumption of humanitarian activities in the areas under AFDL control. A UN delegation met in Goma with the AFDL leader, Laurent-Désiré Kabila, who was later to become president of the Democratic Republic of the Congo. The AFDL, adopting a tactic which was to be used over and over again in the following months, announced that it would allow UNHCR to have access to refugees, while in reality it limited access to areas that had come under its control. Invariably, UNHCR only gained access after suspected armed elements had been killed. Often refugees were also killed in the process.

On 12–13 November, the camp of Mugunga was bombarded by the RPA. Refugees tried to flee west, further into Zaire. Some managed to do so, but most were blocked by rebel forces. The only way to safety was the road leading back to Rwanda. Large numbers started to stream across the border. Meanwhile, UNHCR had been authorized by the AFDL to resume activities in Goma. All its staff could do, however, was to watch hundreds of thousands of people walk in eerie silence back to the country from where—under a different kind of pressure, but equally unwillingly—they had fled in a mass exodus just over two years earlier.

Repatriation from Tanzania to Rwanda

The situation in the Rwandan refugee camps in Tanzania had always been less tense than in the camps in Zaire. The grip of the former regime over the refugee population was weaker, the ex-FAR troops did not have the same military presence, and the attitude of the Tanzanian authorities was much more resolute and transparent than that of the Zairean government. A Tripartite Agreement on Voluntary Repatriation had been signed on 12 April 1995 between Rwanda, Tanzania and UNHCR. But repatriation had nevertheless been extremely limited: 6,427 people in 1995 and 3,445 in 1996, out of a refugee population of around 480,000 in the camps.

The presence of this large number of refugees in western Tanzania had resulted in various problems, including deforestation, theft and occasional violence. The massive forced repatriation which occurred in Zaire in November 1996, was therefore taken by the Tanzanian authorities as a clear signal. President Benjamin Mkapa declared: 'Repatriation of the refugees is now much more feasible.'[21] The next day Colonel Magere, the permanent secretary of the Ministry of Home Affairs, met with the UNHCR Representative and told him: 'Following the mass return from eastern Zaire and the developments which have taken place, the Rwandese refugees in Tanzania have no longer any legitimate reason to continue to refuse to return to Rwanda.'[22]

UNHCR officials in Tanzania argued that safe repatriation to Rwanda was possible, and claimed that many refugees were willing to repatriate but were being prevented from doing so by their leaders. These leaders, they argued, many of whom were *génocidaires*, were effectively holding the majority of the refugees as hostages, to provide a cover for themselves. UNHCR therefore decided to take action to undermine the leadership by publicly calling for the refugees to repatriate.[23] On 6 December 1996, the Tanzanian government and UNHCR issued a joint statement to all Rwandan refugees in Tanzania.[24] It stated that the Tanzanian government had decided, following recent commitments made by the Rwandan government, that all Rwandan refugees 'can now return to their country in safety' and that all the refugees 'are expected to return home by 31 December 1996'. It then stated: 'The Tanzanian Government and UNHCR, therefore, urges that all refugees make preparations to return before that date'. Rather than repatriating, however, on 12 December refugee leaders decided to move the refugees further east into Tanzania. The Tanzanian government immediately took action to prevent this movement and deployed troops to redirect the refugees across the border into Rwanda.

The mass return of refugees from Tanzania to Rwanda in December 1996. (UNHCR/R. CHALASANI/1996)

Box 10.5 Western Sahara: refugees in the desert

The boundaries of what was once known as Spanish Sahara were drawn in four Franco-Spanish agreements between 1900 and 1912, at a time when most of Morocco became a French protectorate. Spanish Sahara remained under Spanish rule until 1975, when the colonial authorities evacuated the territory in response to political developments in Spain, growing resistance to colonialism amongst a large part of the local population, and pressure from independent Morocco. In November, the Madrid Accords between Spain, Morocco and Mauritania split the colony into northern and southern zones, which were ceded to Morocco and Mauritania respectively. It was at this time that the colony became known as Western Sahara. In the following months, thousands of troops and civilians from both countries poured into the newly acquired territory and thousands of inhabitants of Western Sahara left.

During the last years of Spanish rule, an anti-colonial movement had developed around a military and political organization founded in 1973 by a group of students: the *Frente Popular para la Liberación de Saguia el-Hamra y de Río de Oro*, better known as the Polisario Front. The unexpected agree-ment between Spain, Morocco and Mauritania in 1975 provoked renewed support for this organization, which already received military training and equip-ment from Libya and, increasingly, from Algeria. With the support of the Algerian government, those refugees who managed to flee Western Sahara were settled in four refugee camps to the south of Tindouf, an arid and rocky region in southwestern Algeria. It was from these camps that the Polisario Front proclaimed the independence of the Sahrawi Arab Democratic Republic (SADR) and established a government in exile

in February 1976. When Mauritania renounced its territorial claims in August 1979, Morocco moved to occupy the southern sector and has asserted administrative control since then. The Moroccan and Polisario armies continued a bitter war until a settlement plan was agreed by both parties with UN mediation and approved by the Security Council in April 1991. Under the plan, they implemented a formal ceasefire from September and agreed to hold a referendum under the auspices of the United Nations. This would give the Sahrawi people the opportunity to choose between integration with Morocco and independence.

The complex process of establishing the electorate for this referendum has been carried out by the United Nations Mission for the Referendum in Western Sahara (MINURSO), which was set up in April 1991. The task of identifying Sahrawis among a population scattered throughout the region has been repeatedly delayed by disagreements between the Moroccan government and the Polisario Front as to who is eligible. Both sides believe the composition of the electorate will determine the outcome of the referendum. By December 1999, more than five years after the voter registration process began, and after interviewing 198,500 applicants, of whom just over 86,000 were deemed eligible to vote, MINURSO had still not completed its task. It has become embroiled in a difficult and delicate phase of appeal hearings launched by some two thirds of those denied registration.

In anticipation of the referendum, UNHCR has been preparing for the voluntary repatriation of those refugees who have the right to vote and their immediate families—some 120,000 people in all. The over-

whelming majority of the refugees have consistently said they wish to return to the part of Western Sahara east of a 2,500 km long wall of sand—the berm—erected by Moroccan forces, regardless of which part of the territory they originally came from. In an attempt to build confi-dence, UNHCR has tried to promote family visits across the border. But the refugees themselves are concerned for their security if they are to return to the western part of the territory.

Western Sahara remains divided into two zones either side of the berm. Polisario forces control a sizeable part of the interior and up to the eastern borders with Algeria and Mauritania. Morocco maintains control over the coastal areas, including the so-called 'useful triangle' in the north between Laayoune, Smara and the vast phosphate reserves in Boucraa. While the boundaries of these zones have barely altered over the last decade, much has changed within them. Morocco has considerably improved the basic and industrial infrastructure in Laayoune and, to a lesser extent, in the rest of the 'useful triangle'.

The refugee camps

In 1975, the largest proportion of the refugees fled to the harsh desert area around Tindouf, about 500 kilometres east of Laayoune and 50 kilometres from the border with Western Sahara. By the end of 1976, some 50,000 Sahrawis were reported to be living in settlements there. Three refugee camps were established over an area of a few hundred square kilometres, which the Algerian government temporarily ceded to the SADR. Later, a fourth camp was established. The refugees in these camps received humanitarian assistance from the Algerian government, the Red Cresent and UNHCR. At their peak, the camps accommodated some 165,000 people, according to estimates by the Algerian government.

During the military conflict, most of the men from the camps joined the growing and increasingly well-equipped Polisario army. The women ran the camps. Over the past 25 years, hospitals, schools, workshops and ministries have been built amongst the tents that are the refugees' homes.

Today, the refugees are largely dependent upon international assistance. This is provided by the European Community Humanitarian Office (ECHO), the Algerian government, the World Food Programme and UNHCR, as well as various European non-governmental organizations and bilateral sources. Nonetheless, standards of nutrition, hygiene and medical care have been deteriorating steadily over the years. Malnutrition and illness amongst children are on the rise and the quality of drinking water is poor. Refugees have access to primary and secondary education in the camps and some have found opportunities to continue their studies abroad. Every year, a few thousand refugees spend their summer holidays in Europe, particularly in Spain, as guests of sympathetic families. In addition to the refugees in these camps, at the end of 1999 there were estimated to be around 26,400 Sahrawis in Mauritania and over 800 who had become students in Cuba.

Over the years, the Polisario Front has maintained close links with the Sahrawi refugees. The organization has set up a wide network of representatives. Most live in Europe, particularly in Italy and Spain. Other representatives, scattered throughout the world, establish and maintain networks of assistance for the refugees and support for the Sahrawi struggle for independence.

Despite the Sahrawis' considerable success in promoting projects to improve social welfare in the camps, some refugees have left the camps in search of work. Many refugees have joined their relatives in Mauritania, Algeria, and even Morocco. Some of those remaining in the camps migrate seasonally, leaving the Tindouf during the hot summer months for places like the Canary Islands, mainland Spain or further afield.

But most Sahrawi refugees still live in the camps or visit them frequently. Many have been increa-singly active in social and economic relations with Sahrawi communities as far away as the Mauritanian cities of Nouadhibou and Nouakchott, in the Canary Islands and mainland Spain. These activities now account for a significant part of the economy of the camps.

More than 25 years have elapsed since the Sahrawi refugee population dispersed and it is almost nine years since the referendum was first supposed to take place. It has still not been decided when the referendum will take place and there are no enforcement mechanisms in place for the implementation of the referendum results. As such, the future of Western Sahara, described by some as 'Africa's last colony', remains uncertain.

Western Sahara, 1999   Map 10.2

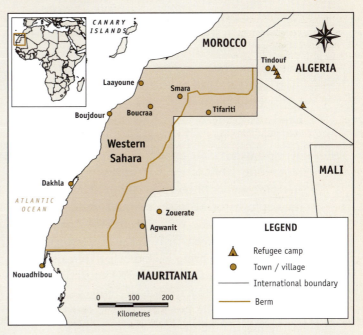

The Tanzanian forced repatriation differed greatly from the violent events that had occurred in Zaire, where thousands had been killed and where refugees had been forced to flee into an active war zone. But it caused much controversy. Although UNHCR had never endorsed any proposal to return the refugees by force, the organization was strongly criticized by Amnesty International, Human Rights Watch and other human rights organizations for its role in this repatriation operation, most notably for the joint statement calling for the refugees to return in less than a month.[25]

Searching for lost refugees in Zaire

In Zaire, the AFDL and its Rwandan allies had launched a military campaign. This eventually took them across the whole country to Kinshasa, which they entered on 17 May 1997, unseating President Mobutu and taking over the government. Meanwhile, in the forests of Zaire, an unknown number of Rwandan Hutu refugees were moving in desperate circumstances. A battle of numbers broke out. In November 1996, a rough head count which had been carried out at the repatriation point between Goma and Gisenyi indicated that a total of 380,000 returnees had crossed during the initial, massive movement following the fall of Mugunga.[26] Returns through Cyangugu and stragglers coming in through Gisenyi in the next few days were thought to have added at least another 100,000. This brought the figure to about 500,000. But a rough estimate was all that was possible.

UNHCR staff agreed with the Rwandan government to use a figure of 600,000 returnees, although they believed that this figure was probably too high. The authorities in Kigali, backed by some Western governments, then insisted that UNHCR's figures for the inhabitants of the camps in Zaire (about 1.1 million) had been vastly overestimated. They now declared, with the backing of the AFDL, that most refugees had returned and that very few—except armed elements with reasons to hide in the forests—remained in Zaire. Meanwhile, UNHCR and other humanitarian agencies claimed that hundreds of thousands had not yet returned.

The refugee figures became a hotly debated political issue internationally. The deployment of a multinational force had finally been approved by Security Council Resolution 1080 of 15 November 1996, but this presupposed the existence of a sizeable number of refugees still in Zaire. A number of governments did not favour the deployment because it would undeniably expose their soldiers to risks. The AFDL, backed by Rwanda, rejected the idea of a multinational force entirely, fearing that its advance westwards to Kinshasa would be blocked. The AFDL said that it did not need help to bring back the 'few' remaining refugees.

On 21 November 1996, a UN spokesperson in New York announced, referring to UNHCR data, that there were 'still 746,000 refugees in Zaire and the problem is not resolved'. The Rwandan government issued a communiqué on the same day saying that 'the numbers of Rwandan refugees given by international organizations are totally incorrect and misleading' and that people trekking west 'could be

Zaireans or Burundians'. The US ambassador to Rwanda said that there were 'only tens to twenties of thousands of refugees still in Zaire rather than the vast numbers proffered', while the French newspaper *Le Monde* stated in its 23 November issue that there were still 800,000 left. These estimates were difficult to verify. Political interests dictated the figures.[27]

Lieutenant-General Maurice Baril, who had been appointed to head the multinational force in eastern Zaire in mid-November, declared on 21 November 1996: 'The situation is unclear, with refugee estimates varying from 100,000 to 500,000 . . . It will be necessary to be better informed about conditions on the ground to study the military choices which could be made.'[28] In Goma and Bukavu, and later in Uvira, UNHCR was involved in strenuous efforts to locate dispersed refugees, setting up information systems and collection points, and transporting back to Rwanda those wanting to return, which was virtually all of them. UNHCR regularly provided information to those planning the multinational force, but international attention was on the wane again. By the end of the year, the embryonic force headquartered in Uganda was withdrawn. Once again, as had been the case in the Kivu camps, humanitarian agencies were left to operate without much international support.

The UNHCR search and rescue operation

From the beginning, despite statements to the contrary by the AFDL and the Rwandan government, it was clear that many of the refugees driven from the camps in Zaire were stranded in the remote areas stretching west of Goma and Bukavu, deep in Zaire. Hundreds of thousands of Rwandans remained in Zaire. Most fled westwards, simultaneously protected and compelled by the remnants of the ex-FAR. Some groups halted in remote areas and remained in hiding. Others formed strongholds of resistance in places such as Masisi. As the advance of the ADFL and its allies towards Kinshasa became a rout, the fleeing Rwandans became the rebels' principal target, the FAZ having all but dissolved and the only effective resistance being put up by the ex-FAR.

Thousands of fleeing Rwandans perished. The exact number will never be known. Rumours of massacres by the rebels had been rife since the beginning, but were hard to confirm. In November, journalists published the first accounts of killings of refugees. Later, more precise accounts were supplied by non-governmental organizations (NGOs) and human rights groups. UNHCR and other humanitarian organizations which had information about the fate of the refugees were divided over speaking out because of the risk this could pose to their ability to continue the rescue operation. In early December 1996, UNHCR participated in a joint UN mission to Tingi-Tingi, where large numbers of refugees had begun arriving. A second large group was found in Shabunda, further south.

Humanitarian organizations depended on the rebels for access to the refugees and this access was largely subordinated to strategic considerations. After lengthy and painstaking negotiations with the AFDL authorities, UNHCR and its partner agencies set up a number of collection points for refugees. There was a risk,

Rwandan and Burundian refugee movements, 1994–99   Map 10.3

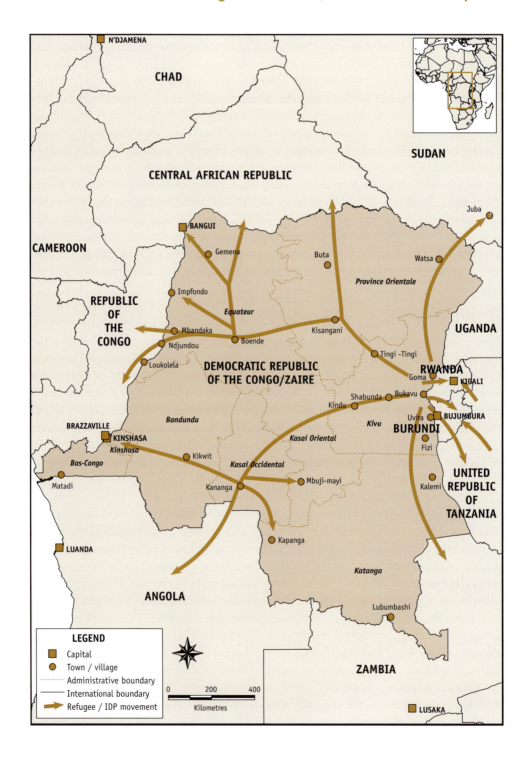

however, that collection points would be used by AFDL authorities to identify and round-up refugees in remote areas. Those who managed to make it to these collection points emerged from the forest in very poor physical condition, terrified both of what they were leaving behind—their earlier captors, the *génocidaires* and their latest custodians, the rebels—and of what awaited them in Rwanda. UNHCR was permitted access to refugees only after the fighting was over.

A turning-point in the war was the fall of the militarized Rwandan Hutu camp at Tingi-Tingi in March 1997. For the rebels, this opened the route to Kisangani, the largest Zairean city between the Kivus and Kinshasa. The events that took place in Kisangani in 1997 provide an example of the relation between the war and the search and rescue operation. In April, UNHCR reached a large pocket of about 80,000 fleeing refugees before the advancing AFDL reached them. UNHCR helped them settle in two encampments south of Kisangani. When the rebels gained control of the area, just as a UNHCR airlift to take the refugees back to Rwanda was about to begin, they denied UNHCR access to the refugees, attacked the camps, and killed any men they suspected of belonging to the armed opposition. In the process, by design or not, many refugees were killed. The location of mass graves was kept off limits to humanitarian organizations.

For those Rwandans it did manage to reach, UNHCR could only offer the option of a return to an uncertain and dangerous situation in Rwanda. Staying in Zaire meant almost certain death. In the circumstances, it was not possible to offer the refugees any other choice. Faced with this dilemma, UNHCR contemplated withdrawing, but the imperative to save lives prevailed. The rescue operation continued until September 1997. UNHCR arranged for the transportation of these refugees by truck or by plane back to Rwanda. Eventually, over 260,000 Rwandans were rescued in this way, some 60,000 of them being flown back to Rwanda in a UNHCR airlift. The organization subsequently mounted a large reintegration operation in Rwanda to assist the hundreds of thousands of returnees.

The Rwandan Hutu diaspora

Many of the Rwandans who were not repatriated and who did not die in their great move westwards, ended up at the other end of the continent, as far away as Angola and Congo-Brazzaville. Some reached the Atlantic Ocean, having trekked for well over 2,000 kilometres. Many among them were the remnants of the FAR and the Hutu militias that the AFDL and its allies had tried to destroy during their attack on the camps in Kivu, and throughout the war. They had weapons and arrived in better physical shape than the ordinary refugees. They could walk more easily and commandeer vehicles, which gave them privileged access to food supplies.

When the rescue operation finished, UNHCR attempted to interview these remaining Rwandans to separate the refugees from the *génocidaires*. Once more, this proved virtually impossible. By 1997, the fate of the refugees had become so entwined with that of the armed elements amongst them that a separation was quite impractical. In 1999, UNHCR resumed the repatriation of Rwandan refugees who had managed to survive and who had remained in the eastern part of the Democratic Republic of the Congo. More than 35,000 returned that year. The Rwandan armed groups which remained outside Rwanda became a lesser, though continuing, threat to Rwanda. Many followed the example of the members of other defeated armies in central Africa and became 'lost soldiers'. Some found their way into other conflicts, for example in Angola or Congo-Brazzaville. Many continued to fight in the new Democratic Republic of the Congo, where war broke out again in 1998.[29]

A new phase in the Congolese war

In August 1998, it became apparent that the Rwandan and Ugandan governments no longer supported President Kabila of the Democratic Republic of the Congo. The coalition of African countries that had hitherto supported him had split into two: the first group, led by Angola and Zimbabwe, still supported him, while the second, led by Rwanda and Uganda, now wanted to see him overthrown. The crisis that originally had its epicentre in Rwanda and Burundi was transforming itself into a broader conflict centred on the Democratic Republic of the Congo. This new war had its roots in the Congolese civil war that had brought down President Mobutu and in the unresolved tensions in the wider Great Lakes region. Since Mobutu's downfall, the war has evolved into a struggle for control of the country and its rich natural resources. It has involved the armies of six countries and several other non-state armed groups. The price in human suffering continues to mount. The number of displaced people was estimated to be more than one million by the end of 1999.

This new phase of the war confirms previous tendencies in international involvement in the region. African countries bordering the Democratic Republic of the Congo, and some others, have not hesitated to intervene to defend their strategic interests. Meanwhile, in stark contrast to the crises in Kosovo and East Timor in 1999, the wider international community has been reluctant to intervene. The failure to halt the genocide in Rwanda in 1994, the failure to prevent the militarization of the refugee camps at Goma in 1994–96, and the failure to monitor effectively the dispersal of the Rwandan Hutu refugees driven into Zaire and to protect and assist them, have shown that if civil conflict and forced human displacement are not addressed promptly, the longer-term consequences can be catastrophic.

The April 1994 genocide is the defining moment in the recent history of the region. It could have been prevented. The fact that it occurred was the culmination of decades of missed opportunities. Worse still, its consequences have still not been dealt with adequately and have led to the deaths of tens, perhaps hundreds of thousands, more people—whether by the gun, by disease or by starvation during the fighting in 1996–97. President Mobutu has gone, but the Democratic Republic of the Congo is not a fully functioning state. The status and nationality of the Banyarwanda in the Kivu region remain unresolved. The security situation in Rwanda remains volatile, as it does in Burundi. The antagonism between Hutu and Tutsi endures.

In central Africa, humanitarian organizations have been caught up in long-term political processes involving a high degree of violence and coercion. The pattern of conflict and the consequent movement of people is something such organizations cannot effectively predict or control. In dealing with the effects of violence, organizations such as UNHCR have been forced to negotiate with armed groups that show a high degree of political sophistication and a capacity for ruthless manipulation of the populations under their control. Often humanitarian organizations have found themselves on the front line of conflict while the rest of the international community has held back. Only an international response which is better orchestrated and brings the process of peacekeeping and diplomatic pressure into the same frame as humanitarian assistance, can hope to improve the flawed record of the last decade.

11 The changing dynamics of displacement

The dynamics of displacement have changed greatly over the half-century of UNHCR's existence. So too, have international responses to the problem of forced displacement. UNHCR's early development took place in the tense climate of the Cold War, when the organization focused on refugees in Europe. UNHCR then played a key role during the decolonization process, not least because of the wave of international solidarity with refugees from wars of national liberation. In the 1970s and 1980s, the political and military stalemate between the superpowers diverted their mutual hostility into immensely destructive proxy wars which created millions of refugees. The scale and scope of UNHCR's operations increased dramatically as it attempted to meet the needs of many of these refugees, some of whose terms of exile stretched into decades.

The end of bipolar confrontation at the beginning of the 1990s again profoundly altered the universe in which UNHCR operated. The proxy wars ended, although several of them took on lives of their own without superpower patronage. External intervention in a conflict became less risky, since it no longer threatened major retaliation from a superpower sponsor. In many cases, the ideological motivation for conflict diminished. Often, it was replaced by identity-based conflicts built around religion, ethnicity, nationality, race, clan, language or region. Many of these conflicts were sustained by the economic interests of one or more of the warring parties.

More often than not, these conflicts took place within national boundaries, rather than across them. In many cases, they were complicated by the involvement of people of similar ethnicity or religion in other countries, including refugees and politically active diasporas further afield. Since these conflicts were no longer connected to an epic geopolitical struggle, many of the people who were driven by violence and persecution to flee their homes were marginalized by powerful states which no longer found their vital national interests at stake. UNHCR's role and responsibilities in responding to such crises developed considerably throughout the 1990s. They will no doubt continue to do so as the organization attempts to respond to the challenges of the 21st century.

The challenge of globalization

The far-reaching political consequences of the end of the Cold War added to the impact of another transformation which took shape in the 20th century and which is sweeping forward into the 21st. This complex set of technological, institutional, organizational, cultural and social changes are grouped together under the rubric of 'globalization'. The economic manifestations of globalization are a vast increase in

Refugees returning to East Timor from West Timor in October 1999. (UNHCR/M. KOBAYASHI/1999)

the speed and a decrease in the cost of transactions—particularly those involving money and information—with a resulting escalation in the volume and value of all kinds of exchanges. The cultural and social manifestations are an explosion of cheap and instant communication and some convergence of the values and expectations held by people everywhere. The spread of democratic aspirations and Disney animations are equally products of globalization.

The globalization process challenges the sanctity of national boundaries, and this has implications for refugee protection. The current structure of refugee protection was designed in and for a state-centric system. Under the terms of the 1951 UN Refugee Convention, a refugee is a person who cannot avail himself or herself of the protection of his or her own state, and who has crossed an international boundary marking the limits of the sovereign territory of that state. One is forced to question the relevance of notions such as sovereignty and national frontiers as states lose much of their ability to control what crosses their borders as well as what goes on within them.

Goods and capital now circulate with greater ease than ever before, and business personnel, tourists and students constantly move across increasingly invisible borders. In contrast, governments are still determined to control unwanted movements of people. Stringent measures to keep out unauthorized entrants often prevent people in need of protection from reaching a country where they may seek safety.

Globalization has many other consequences, both positive and negative. Although almost every part of the world has been affected by globalization, its impact has been extremely uneven. The rapid changes associated with the expansion of the global market economy have exacerbated the inequality between the world's wealthiest and poorest states. This has implications for global migration. It has also led to the increased marginalization of particular groups in industrialized states, a rise in anti-immigrant sentiment and growing hostility towards asylum seekers.

Among the most successful organizations in adapting to globalization and making the most of its potential are organized crime syndicates. The anonymity of electronic financial transactions, declining regulation, and the hugely increased volumes of trade and travel facilitate transnational criminal activity. Their revenues, whether from the cocaine trade in the Americas or the diamond trade in West Africa, are fuelling conflicts that produce millions of refugees and internally displaced people. These sophisticated networks have also been quick to realize the profit potential in human trafficking and migrant smuggling and have created a global 'service industry' to move people to countries they are not authorized to enter. A report commissioned by UNHCR and released in July 2000 shows that the very successes of measures to prevent unauthorized immigration to Europe—such as strict visa policies, carrier sanctions, readmission treaties and the like—push refugees desperate to escape persecution into the hands of human smugglers.[1]

The changing nature of conflict

When UNHCR was founded in 1950, the European refugees on which it focused its efforts were mainly people fleeing actual or feared persecution from totalitarian governments—people displaced by fascism and those seeking to escape Stalinism. Political repression and massive human rights violations are still significant elements in today's displacements. But for the majority of today's refugees, armed conflict—which often involves persecution and other human rights abuses against civilians—is the major source of threat. Many of the armed conflicts of the post-Cold War period have proved particularly dangerous for civilians, as shown by the scale of displacement and the high ratio of civilian to military casualties—more than 9:1 in some cases.

The devastating civilian toll of recent wars has prompted much discussion of the changing nature of armed conflict in the post-Cold War period. In fact, the targeting of civilian populations is not a new phenomenon in the longer perspective of human history. The Thirty Years War, which ended with the 1648 Treaty of Westphalia establishing the modern nation-state system, was a conflict which was one of the most brutally destructive of civilian life, property and social organization that Europe has known. As Norman Davies describes it, by the time it ended 'Germany lay desolate. The population had fallen from 21 million to perhaps 13 million. Between a third and a half of the people were dead. Whole cities, like Magdeburg, stood in ruins. Whole districts lay stripped of their inhabitants, their livestock, their supplies. Trade had virtually ceased. A whole generation of pillage, famine, disease, and social disruption had wreaked havoc . . .'[2] Variations of this scenario have been played out in numerous places across the globe for centuries.

What distinguished the 1990s from earlier decades was the weakening of central governments in countries that had been shored up by superpower support, and the consequent proliferation of identity-based conflicts, many of which have engaged whole societies in violence. The easy availability and growing power of sophisticated light weaponry has increased the destructiveness of even relatively low-intensity conflict. Insurgent forces now fund many of their efforts by exploiting natural resources in areas under their control, often in collaboration with international criminal organizations. The commercial potential of lucrative, lawless, globalized trade often eclipses whatever political or ideological agenda might originally have propelled them into taking up arms. The profits to be derived from war economies often become the main force perpetuating conflict—and an extremely difficult one to reverse.

Significant progress has been made since the end of the Second World War in defining the laws of war. The four Geneva Conventions of 1949, which form the basis of international humanitarian law, have been ratified by virtually every state across the globe, illustrating the importance attached to this body of law. In addition, 150 states have ratified either one of both of the two 1977 Additional Protocols to the Geneva Conventions. In spite of this, wars in which disciplined, well-provisioned armies fight each other and try to avoid damage to civilian people and property while permitting the sick and wounded to be treated, still appear to be the exception rather than the rule.

In the post-Cold War period, civil wars and communal conflicts have involved wide-scale, deliberate targeting of civilian populations. The violence of these wars is often viciously gender-specific. Women are systematically raped and young men are

Major refugee populations worldwide, 1999 Map 11.1

Algeria
There are some 165,000 refugees from Western Sahara, according to estimates by the Algerian government, who are living in camps in the Tindouf region of southwestern Algeria.

Armenia and Azerbaijan
As a result of the conflict between Armenia and Azerbaijan in the early 1990s, there are nearly 300,000 Azerbaijani refugees in Armenia and nearly 190,000 Armenian refugees in Azerbaijan. Armenia hosts more refugees per capita than any other country in the world.

China
There are over 290,000 recognized refugees in China, virtually all of whom are from Viet Nam. Most are ethnic Chinese who have been in China since 1979.

Democratic Republic of the Congo
As well as generating over 250,000 refugees, the Democratic Republic of the Congo hosts some 285,000 refugees from neighbouring countries. These include, amongst others, some 150,000 Angolans, 68,000 Sudanese, 33,000 Rwandans, 19,000 Burundians and 12,000 from the Republic of the Congo.

Ethiopia
Ethiopia hosts nearly 260,000 refugees, including over 180,000 Somalis, some 70,000 Sudanese, and around 5,000 Kenyan refugees.

Federal Republic of Germany
The German government estimates that it hosts almost one million refugees – the largest number of refugees of any country in Western Europe. However, not all of these have been granted Convention refugee status. Most of those who have arrived over the past 10 years have come from the former Yugoslavia, Turkey, Iraq and Iran.

Guinea and Côte d'Ivoire
Despite being one of the poorest countries in Africa, Guinea continues to host some 370,000 refugees from Sierra Leone and some 130,000 from Liberia. Côte d'Ivoire hosts some 136,000 Liberian refugees.

India
India accommodates a large and varied refugee population including around 100,000 Tibetans, 66,000 Sri Lankans, 15,000 Bhutanese and 14,000 Afghans. Like other countries in the region, India is not party to the 1951 UN Refugee Convention or the 1967 Protocol and does not give UNHCR access to all the refugees on its territory.

Indonesia
As a result of the violence which erupted at the time of the vote for independence in East Timor in 1999, some 280,000 people fled from East Timor to West Timor, in Indonesia. Although many subsequently returned, some 163,000 refugees remained in Indonesia in December 1999.

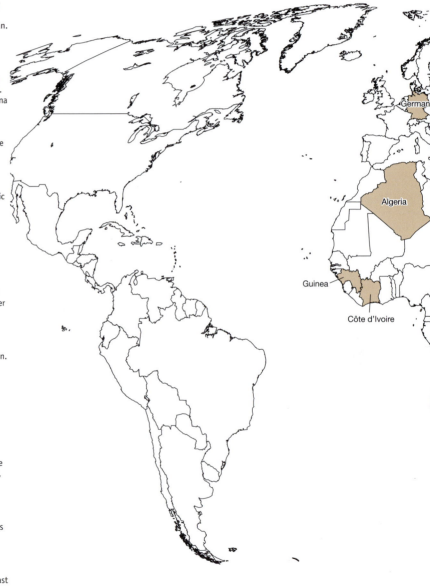

Note:
The countries selected are representative, not exhaustive.
The boundaries shown on this map are those used by the UN Cartographic Section, New York.

Iran and Pakistan

Iran and Pakistan continue to host the largest refugee population for which UNHCR has responsibility – the Afghans. From a peak of 6.2 million in 1990, there are now over 2.5 million Afghan refugees. This includes 1.3 million in Iran and 1.2 million in Pakistan. There are also over 500,000 Iraqi refugees in Iran which, with a total of over 1.8 million refugees, hosts the largest number of refugees in the world.

Kenya and Uganda

Kenya hosts some 224,000 refugees. The largest groups are Somalis (some 140,000) and Sudanese (some 64,000). Uganda hosts nearly 220,000 refugees, including some 200,000 Sudanese.

Nepal

There are over 100,000 Bhutanese refugees in Nepal. Many have been there for more than a decade. Nepal is also host to some 20,000 Tibetans.

The Palestinians

The Palestinians are the world's largest refugee population and over the past 50 years have spread all over the world. Some 3.6 million remain concentrated in Jordan, Syria, Lebanon, Gaza and the West Bank. The UN Relief and Works Agency (UNRWA) has responsibility for providing assistance to these refugees.

Sudan

Sudan hosts over 390,000 refugees, including over 340,000 Eritreans and some 35,000 Ethiopians. Most of the Eritrean refugees have been in Sudan since before Eritrea gained independence in 1993. Sudan has also produced some 475,000 refugees as a result of its long-running civil war, most of whom are in Uganda, Ethiopia, the Democratic Republic of the Congo and Kenya.

United Republic of Tanzania

With a total of over 620,000 refugees, Tanzania hosts the largest refugee population in Africa. This refugee population comprises some 500,000 Burundians, nearly 100,000 from the Democratic Republic of Congo and some 20,000 Rwandans.

Thailand

Thailand hosts nearly 100,000 refugees from Myanmar. Although Thailand does not regard these people officially as refugees, it does permit UNHCR and other humanitarian organizations to assist them.

Federal Republic of Yugoslavia

The Federal Republic of Yugoslavia hosts some 500,000 refugees, the largest refugee population in the region. The refugee population includes around 300,000 Croatian refugees and some 200,000 refugees from Bosnia and Herzegovina.

Zambia

Zambia hosts over 160,000 Angolan refugees. It also hosts some 36,000 refugees from the Democratic Republic of the Congo.

the targets of mass murder or forcible conscription. Child soldiers are also a common feature. The spread of terror through the practice of conspicuous atrocity continues to be used in many wars, the systematic amputations carried out in Sierra Leone by forces of the Revolutionary United Front being one of the most recent examples. Humanitarian organizations such as UNHCR have little influence over the perpetrators of such atrocities. Negotiating with them is distasteful at best, and raises real ethical dilemmas. Other states are often unwilling to intervene militarily, leaving humanitarian organizations to operate on their own in a desperate vacuum.

The growing complexity of population movements

People who flee their home countries out of a fear of persecution join a larger stream of migrants who leave in search of opportunities for work, education, reunification with family members, or for other reasons. It has been estimated that at the end of the 20th century some 150 million people were living outside the country of their birth, amounting to about 2.5 per cent of the world's population, or one out of every 40 people.[3] Of these, about 15 million, or 10 per cent, are refugees.

Many states have adopted explicit immigration laws and policies under which immigrants are admitted from three different 'streams': for family reunification; for employment, education or investment-related ends; and for humanitarian reasons. While the categories are neatly distinguished on paper, in reality the boundaries between them are far from clear and the connections between them are many. A member of a persecuted minority, having made the wrenching decision to leave her home, opts to seek asylum in an affluent country where the chances of being able to support herself are better. Does this make her an economic migrant? A political dissident in an authoritarian country receives death threats and tries to join his brother who emigrated to Canada. A case of refugee resettlement or family reunification? A computer programmer in a strict Islamic state joins a sect regarded as heretical, and then accepts a job offer in Europe. A refugee or a labour migrant? An indigenous subsistence farmer, after the third time his community is attacked by right-wing paramilitaries, slips across a border to the north and finds work in the fields. Refugee or illegal immigrant?

Modern states, in exercising their fiercely defended sovereign right to determine who may or may not enter their territory, have to make these judgement calls every day. The only part of the immigration flow over which governments have surrendered some discretion is the humanitarian stream, in that parties to the 1951 UN Refugee Convention or its 1967 Protocol obligate themselves not to return refugees to a country where they are likely to face persecution. Pressure on the asylum systems of advanced industrialized countries has grown as some have narrowed or closed off other channels of legal immigration. European states, for example, have virtually ended official programmes of labour migration, despite a sharp decline in the native-born workforce. Attempts by non-refugees to use the asylum channel to gain a legal foothold in industrialized countries are a real—though often exaggerated—fact of life.

Preoccupation with immigration control is a comparatively recent development in historical terms. Until roughly the time of the First World War, except for a few countries such as Japan, states placed no serious constraints on the movement of people across their borders. The early attempts that were made to control movements in Europe were aimed at preventing departures, especially of people with acquired skills and able bodies. As one author has observed:

The creation of the modern passport system, and the use of similar systems in the interior of a variety of countries . . . signaled the dawn of a new era in human affairs, in which individual states and the international state system as a whole successfully monopolized the legitimate authority to permit movement within and across their jurisdictions.[4]

Over the past decade, many states have experienced increased immigration pressure, not least because of technological advances which have facilitated travel. Rising xenophobia in some places, and states' fears of losing control over entry to their territory, have led them to adopt increasingly stringent measures to prevent unauthorized migration. This has been the case not only in Europe and North America. Almost any country that has prospered relative to the states around it has found that one reward of success is increasing immigration pressure. Regional power-houses such as Thailand, Malaysia, South Africa or Mexico have found themselves struggling to deal with unauthorized entry from their poorer, and often troubled, neighbours.

No state has yet succeeded in developing deterrent strategies for undocumented immigrants that manage to differentiate fairly and effectively between people with well-founded fears of persecution and those with economic or other motivations for seeking entry. The same measures that make it difficult for an unauthorized migrant to gain access to the job markets of a 'land of opportunity' make it difficult for a refugee to gain access to the territory of a potential asylum country and to asylum procedures. UNHCR has repeatedly expressed its concern about indiscriminate barriers to entry, since even an asylum system which functions well cannot protect people who are unable to reach the country concerned. The result is that some refugees resort to the dangerous and costly services of human smugglers and traffickers to circumvent the high barriers—some physical, some administrative—that separate them from safety.

As the recognized categories of migrants overlap and blur, the needs of other groups of uprooted people are being acknowledged. Their relationship with established mechanisms and institutions of international protection and assistance are uncertain, even though many of them have the same humanitarian needs as refugees. A 1996 conference addressing migration and displacement in the Commonwealth of Independent States, for example, drew international attention to no fewer than nine categories of uprooted people in the former Soviet Union: refugees, people in refugee-like situations, internally displaced people, repatriants, formerly deported peoples, transit migrants, illegal migrants, ecological migrants and involuntarily relocating persons.

The category of 'internally displaced people' attracted substantial attention worldwide in the late 1990s, partly because of the enormous growth in their numbers during the decade and partly because of their particular vulnerability. The Secretary-

General's Representative on Internally Displaced Persons, Francis Deng, has focused attention on their needs and has issued a set of 'Guiding Principles' for protecting and assisting them. Even so, the internally displaced have neither a binding legal instrument like the 1951 UN Refuge Convention nor a specifically mandated institution like UNHCR responsible for their protection.[5]

In January 2000, the US ambassador to the United Nations, Richard Holbrooke, argued that there is no meaningful difference between a refugee and someone who is internally displaced. He made an impassioned plea that policy makers should 'not let bureaucratic euphemisms and acronyms allow us to ignore these people'.[6] UNHCR has in fact often taken responsibility for assisting internally displaced people, when requested to do so by the UN Secretary-General or the General Assembly, and with the consent of the host government. By 1999, the organization was assisting some five million internally displaced people in Africa, the Balkans, the former Soviet region, Colombia, Sri Lanka and other locations.

Some observers see a danger in obscuring the distinction between refugees and internally displaced people. Refugees, defined in the 1951 UN Refugee Convention as people who are outside their countries of origin, are the bearers of certain rights under international law. Most importantly, states have obligations under the Convention not to return them forcibly to a place where they have a well-founded fear of persecution. In an international system still organized around sovereign states, there is a world of difference between being within the jurisdiction of the state where persecution takes place and being outside it. Conflating refugees and the internally displaced would, in the eyes of some observers, eradicate this vital distinction and the protection that flows from it.[7] Others also point out that such a solution fails to address the needs of all civilian victims of armed conflict, whether or not they are displaced.

The changing nature of humanitarian action

Humanitarian action has grown over the course of the last half-century into an increasingly costly and complex undertaking. The cast of characters has expanded to include a plethora of actors, from United Nations agencies to small local non-governmental organizations (NGOs), from national military forces to private contractors, from religious organizations to professional associations. They differ profoundly in their resources, mandates, philosophies and capabilities. Coordinating the efforts of disparate actors is a challenge in high-profile humanitarian crises. It has been a particular challenge for UNHCR, which has often been called on by the UN Secretary-General to act as the lead UN agency in humanitarian emergencies.

Armed conflict is now the driving force behind most refugee flows, and the challenges of operating in the midst of ongoing violence are commonly encountered by UNHCR and other humanitarian organizations in their daily operations. Refugee movements are no longer side effects of conflict, but in many cases are central to the objectives and tactics of war. Humanitarian assistance to refugees, as a result, is no longer necessarily seen as a neutral act apart from and above the dynamics of conflict.

UNHCR and other humanitarian actors are increasingly perceived by parties to a conflict as taking sides, particularly where one party is a more obvious perpetrator of atrocities which produce displacement.

In violent and politicized settings, UNHCR faces excruciating dilemmas in its mission to protect refugees, sustain them, and find solutions to their displacement. During the Bosnian war, for example, it was feared that the removal of endangered minorities to safety would abet 'ethnic cleansing'. In the former Yugoslav Republic of Macedonia in 1999, it was feared that humanitarian evacuation could undermine the principle of first asylum. In the Rwandan refugee crisis of 1994–96, many critics called upon UNHCR to withdraw from the refugee camps in eastern Zaire and Tanzania, arguing that the organization was feeding those who were responsible for the genocide, and that it was fuelling further conflict. In places such as Angola and Somalia, meeting the extortionate demands of armed elements was frequently the price of access to people in need. UNHCR has dealt with such dilemmas again and again in its history, and particularly in the past decade. In practice, applying the principles of refugee protection is much more difficult than upholding them in the abstract. In some situations, there may indeed be no satisfactory options available, and humanitarian actors must choose whether to do nothing or to pursue the least harmful option.

Critics have also increasingly drawn attention to the potential dangers of providing relief. Humanitarian assistance can inadvertently prolong conflict, sustain the perpetrators of human rights violations, and undermine local institutions of self-reliance. And yet the price of suspending assistance to avoid these unintended consequences may be paid in the suffering and death of innocent people. UNHCR is increasingly called upon to make fine judgements about when it is appropriate to continue operating in less than ideal circumstances, and when persevering in the attempt to do so may actually contribute to the suffering of the intended beneficiaries in the long run. These are inherently political decisions.

The visibility of refugee crises has changed radically in the information age. Mass displacement and other disasters are today routinely played out in 'real time' on the television screens and, increasingly, on the websites of the world. Much has been made of the 'CNN effect' in shaping public opinion and, through it, driving the policy response to refugee crises.[8] The hugely increased public awareness that comes with media exposure generates support for humanitarian action, but the media is selective in its approach and neglects some emergencies. Where there is substantial media coverage, this puts humanitarian agencies under increased pressure. The effect may be salutary. Public criticism of slow or inadequate responses has prompted UNHCR and other humanitarian organizations to re-evaluate and reform their emergency response procedures, set new standards for assistance, and improve coordination mechanisms. But the pressure to be visible in high-profile emergencies has also spurred unproductive competition among agencies and has short-circuited careful planning in some instances. Working with the media to enhance the protection of refugees and the internally displaced has now become an essential element of humanitarian action.

UNHCR's changing role

The preceding chapters have traced the evolution of UNHCR through some of its most formative episodes. Each crisis drew new responses from the international community and new roles for UNHCR and its partners. UNHCR broke from its early focus on individual refugees when its services were called upon during the mass flight of Hungarians from their country in 1956. It then broke from its Eurocentrism in the 1960s, at the time of the wars of independence in Africa. The negotiation of the 1967 Protocol to the 1951 UN Refugee Convention put the stamp of permanence on this departure from the founding framework.

UNHCR first played a larger coordinating role, within the UN system and beyond, during the South Asian crisis of the early 1970s, which created independent Bangladesh. It greatly expanded the scope of its activities in Indochina, building and managing refugee camps for Cambodians, Laotians and Vietnamese, and assisting with the resettlement of some two million Indochinese people—mostly from Viet Nam—in the United States and elsewhere.

UNHCR's role and responsibilities then increased again in the 1980s, as a result of simultaneous crises in Indochina, the Horn of Africa, Central America and Afghanistan. At the end of the Cold War, as many conflicts came to an end, UNHCR took on not only the physical repatriation of refugees but also the much more complex task of trying to ensure that this solution would indeed be durable. More and more people from conflict zones in Africa, Asia and Latin America sought asylum in Europe and North America during the 1980s, putting pressure on existing asylum systems and prompting governments to introduce increasingly restrictive measures aimed at deterring entry. As a result, UNHCR found itself confronting the states that were its major donors and political supporters.

The early 1990s saw a breakthrough in UNHCR's relations with the successor states of the former Soviet Union, which through most of its history had been hostile to UNHCR. UNHCR opened offices throughout this vast region to assist governments and people confronting the immense complexity of migration flows and forced displacement. The major crises of the mid-1990s—in northern Iraq, the former Yugoslavia and Rwanda—forced UNHCR to operate on an unprecedented scale and in the midst of armed conflict.

This 50-year trajectory has taken UNHCR far beyond what its founders envisaged. The organization started out as a small and modestly funded organization, with limited responsibilities and a focus on Europe. Today it employs over 5,000 people in some 120 countries, and has a budget of around US$1 billion a year, which it spends in the pursuit of a complex and sometimes bewildering menu of tasks. Still, its size and operational capacity are small compared to the needs it seeks to address. Today UNHCR is dealing with greatly expanded categories of people, some of whom have protection needs that differ from those of refugees—for example, stateless people and those whose citizenship and nationality is disputed. Others, including many internally displaced people, inhabit regions where there is no competent authority to protect them.

The road ahead

To address the contemporary challenges facing refugees and other displaced people, UNHCR has formed new kinds of strategic partnerships, with human rights organizations, military forces, the private sector, and a range of other actors. It has become involved in a number of activities which might previously have been considered beyond its mandate: environmental protection, mine clearance, community development projects, and anti-racism campaigns—to name but a few. What these activities have in common is that they aim to ensure that whatever solutions UNHCR helps refugees and other displaced people to find are indeed durable. But there is still much work to do to make these wide-ranging partnerships more effective and to improve coordination mechanisms.

UNHCR has long been concerned with the discontinuity between emergency relief and longer-term development assistance. Poverty, particularly in places where there are wide discrepancies in living standards, is fertile ground for conflict and displacement. Refugees and internally displaced people who return to their homes in post-conflict situations often suffer greatly from the lack of resources to re-establish a sustainable livelihood. This in turn can provoke the recurrence of conflict and renewed displacement of people. UNHCR is therefore working with the World Bank, key donor governments, and other UN agencies to bridge the institutional and funding gaps between emergency relief and longer-term development efforts.

But physical and economic reconstruction is not the only element needed to fill the gap between emergency and development assistance. The international community also needs to make more systematic and substantial efforts to strengthen democratic institutions and to ensure good governance in countries making the transition from war to peace. Helping weak states strengthen their institutions as quickly as possible is a crucial factor in ensuring the protection of returnees and in establishing lasting peace. In many situations the first priority should be to strengthen the law enforcement capacity of the police and the judiciary.

UNHCR has become increasingly involved in efforts to build peace in countries which have been affected by war or communal violence. In its earliest days, UNHCR's activities ceased when refugees were resettled in new countries or when they repatriated. By contrast, in recent years it has been deeply involved in a number of peace negotiations. For instance, it participated in the extensive consultations which led to the Paris Peace Agreements for Cambodia in 1991, where repatriation was recognized as an essential element of the settlement; it played an important part in the International Conference on the Former Yugoslavia during the conflict there; and it advised on repatriation issues when the Dayton Peace Agreement was drawn up in 1995. As High Commissioner Sadako Ogata has pointed out: 'Peace processes do not end with peace agreements. In the best circumstances, they start there.'[9]

Another important component of human security is the successful coexistence of people who must reconstitute communities that have been deeply divided by violent civil conflict. This is a critical issue for refugees and internally displaced people when they return to their homes. Few goals are more difficult. Encouraging and assisting divided communities to live together and opening the path to their reconciliation may be one of the most crucial challenges for humanitarian organizations in the 21st century.

A continuing challenge in the years ahead will also be that of finding ways to ensure the security of refugees, the internally displaced and other people of concern. Areas populated by refugees or internally displaced people are typically prone to high levels of insecurity. Beyond the crime and violence associated with large, poor, dense settlements in which normal social structures have been disrupted, refugee settlements often become militarized owing to the presence of combatants intermingled with civilians. Rebel movements, host country governments, and other states often manipulate these populations for political and military gain, drawing them into dangerous confrontations. In some cases, the displaced are themselves willing participants in ongoing conflicts, compromising the neutrality of their places of refuge. In others, they are virtual hostages. Pervasive insecurity affects the displaced, the communities they enter, and the staff of humanitarian agencies who work to provide assistance and protection.

States are becoming increasingly reluctant to send in their own military forces to provide security to humanitarian operations, not only because they are financially and politically costly, but also because they have on a number of occasions proved to be blunt and ineffective instruments for the purpose. UNHCR—together with the UN Department of Peacekeeping Operations, governments, regional organizations and other humanitarian organizations—has therefore been examining alternative mechanisms for improving security. Between large-scale military intervention and inaction, an expanded range of options is being developed, including the deployment of public security experts, the strengthening of local policing in host countries, and the provision of support to regional security organizations.

Ensuring the security of humanitarian personnel in conflict situations has also become a major challenge. Increasingly, they have become victims of direct attacks, with frequent examples of assault, murder and kidnapping. Managing the risks to staff and determining the acceptable threshold of risk will be an ever-present challenge for humanitarian organizations in volatile regions.

Fifty years of humanitarian action have demonstrated time and time again that humanitarian organizations alone cannot resolve the fundamental social, economic and political problems that lead to displacement. They have also demonstrated that unresolved displacement may fatally complicate the resolution of wars and the stability of peace. UNHCR's mandate to seek durable solutions for refugees is embedded in the larger framework of human security. Not only does insecurity impel people to flee in search of refuge, but the persistence of conflict and displacement has weakened the commitment of many states to uphold internationally agreed principles of refugee protection.

The decline in the willingness of states to provide asylum is a major challenge for people fleeing their countries in search of safety and for organizations attempting to assist them. In a world where serious human rights abuses cannot always be prevented, it is important to ensure that those who have to flee are able to find safety.

Asylum must be upheld as a fundamental instrument of protection. Access to asylum therefore remains a primary goal of UNHCR's strategy for international protection. One of the main challenges now is to frame concerns for the protection of refugees more firmly within the wider framework of the complex migration challenges facing states, and to promote responses that take into account the links between migration and asylum.

Under the existing terms of international law, and based primarily on the 1951 UN Refugee Convention, an important distinction is still made between refugees who cross international borders and people who remain displaced within their own countries. While UNHCR's mandate to provide protection and solutions for refugees has not changed over the last 50 years, its involvement with the internally displaced has grown considerably. The extent to which UNHCR is called upon to assume further responsibilities in relation to the internally displaced will be a key issue in the future development of the organization.

International responses to the problem of forced displacement have evolved steadily over the last 50 years, and they will continue to evolve. Year by year, the legal framework and institutional arrangements for protecting and assisting refugees and other displaced people have also developed, and they will also continue to do so. It is our collective responsibility now to learn from the lessons of the past in developing new mechanisms for responding effectively to the challenges of the future. Meeting the needs of the world's displaced people—both refugees and the internally displaced—is much more complex than simply providing short-term security and assistance. It is about addressing the persecution, violence and conflict which bring about displacement in the first place. It is about recognizing the human rights of all men, women and children to enjoy peace, security and dignity without having to flee their homes. This is the task ahead for governments, international organizations and the people of the world in the new millennium.

Endnotes

Many of the documents cited in the book are drawn from the UNHCR archives. These references give the author, recipient (if appropriate), the title or subject of document, date, file, unit, and fonds and series number (e.g. F/HCR 11.2).

Introduction

1 E. Hobsbawm, *On History*, Abacus, London, 1998, p. 353.
2 See UNHCR, *The State of the World's Refugees: In Search of Solutions*, Oxford University Press, Oxford, 1995, pp. 30–55.
3 L.W. Holborn, *Refugees: A Problem of our Time: The Work of the United Nations High Commissioner for Refugees, 1951–1972*, 2 vols, Methuen, Scarecrow Press, NJ, 1975.

Chapter 1

1 E. Hobsbawm, *The Age of Extremes: The Short Twentieth Century*, Michael Joseph, London, 1994, pp. 50–2; L.W. Holborn, *Refugees: A Problem of our Time: The Work of the United Nations High Commissioner for Refugees, 1951–1972*, 2 vols, Scarecrow Press, Methuen NJ, 1975, p. 23; G. Loescher, *Beyond Charity: International Cooperation and the Global Refugee Crisis*, Oxford University Press, Oxford, 1993, pp. 46–54; M.R. Marrus, *The Unwanted: European Refugees in the Twentieth Century*, Oxford University Press, Oxford, 1985, pp. 296–345; J.G. Stoessinger, *The Refugee and the World Community*, University of Minnesota Press, Minneapolis, 1956, pp. 45–8.
2 Ibid.
3 Holborn, *Refugees*, p. 24.
4 Marrus, *The Unwanted*, p. 321.
5 See in general, Loescher, *Beyond Charity*, pp. 47–9.
6 IRO Constitution, Article 2(1)(a); Annex, Article 1c.
7 UNGA Res. (8/1), para. (c)(ii), 12 Feb. 1946.
8 B. Harrell-Bond, 'Repatriation: Under What Conditions is it the Most Desirable Solution for Refugees? An Agenda for Research', *African Studies Review*, vol. 32, no. 1, 1988.
9 L.W. Holborn, *The International Refugee Organization: A Specialized Agency of the United Nations, Its History and Work 1946–1952*, Oxford University Press, Oxford, 1956, p. 200; Holborn, *Refugees*, p. 40.
10 UNGA Res. 319 (IV), 3 Dec. 1949.
11 G. Loescher, 'American Foreign Policy, International Politics and the Early Development of UNHCR', paper presented at conference on 'The Uprooted: Forced Migration as an International Problem in the Post-War Era', Lund, 19–21 Aug. 1988, pp. 2–3.

12 G.J.L. Coles, 'Conflict and Humanitarian Action: An Overview', paper prepared for UNHCR Division of International Protection, Geneva, 29 Nov. 1993, pp. 8, 15–16.
13 Ibid.; M. Cutts, 'Politics and Humanitarianism', *Refugee Survey Quarterly*, vol. 17, no. 1, 1998.
14 Prince Sadruddin Aga Khan, Deputy High Commissioner, speech to Norwegian Refugee Council, 19 May 1965.
15 G. S. Goodwin-Gill, *The Refugee in International Law*, 2nd edn, Oxford University Press, Oxford, 1996, p. 118.
16 American Council of Voluntary Agencies for Foreign Service, 'Report of Fact Finding Committee of the Committee on Migration and Refugee Problems on the Hungarian Refugee Program', New York, 1958.
17 J. Furlow, 'Revolution and Refugees: The Hungarian Revolution of 1956', *The Fletcher Forum of World Affairs*, vol. 20, no. 2, 1996, pp. 107–8.
18 Oral history interview with A. Lindt, 4 Feb. 1998, F/HCR 36.1.
19 Ibid.
20 High Commissioner, 'HC's Report from Yugoslavia, No. 1', memo, 15 April 1953, 1/7/5 YUG, HC Missions, F/HCR 11.1.
21 For figures see UNREF Executive Committee, 'Report and Further Recommendations of the Problem of Hungarian Refugees', UN Doc. A/AC.79/73, 8 May 1957, Tables I and IV.
22 R.A. Saager to High Commissioner, memo, 19 March 1957, 1/7/5 YUG, HC Missions, F/HCR 11.1.
23 P. Weis to M. Pagès, 'Eligibility of Refugees from Hungary', memo, 9 Jan. 1957, 6/1/HUN, F/HCR 11.1.
24 UNGA Res. 1006(ES-11) and 1129(XI), 9 and 21 Nov. 1956.
25 UNHCR Branch Office for Austria to High Commissioner, Geneva, 'Eligibility Procedure and Screening of New Arrivals', memo, 20 Nov. 1956, 22/1/AUS, F/HCR 11.1.
26 American Council of Voluntary Agencies, 'Report on the Hungarian Refugee Problem', New York, 1958.
27 Holborn, *Refugees*, pp. 395–7; *Manchester Guardian*, 29 Nov. 1956.
28 Coles, 'Approaching the Refugee Problem Today', unpublished manuscript, Venice, Nov. 1987, p. 7.
29 Lindt interview; see also G.J.L. Coles, 'Solutions to the Problem of Refugees and the Protection of Refugees', background report for UNHCR, Geneva, 1989.
30 P. Weis, 'Notes Taken on Meeting Held at International Committee of the Red Cross Concerning the Question

of Repatriation of Hungarian Refugee Children', 13
Dec. 1956, 6/9 HUN/AUS, F/HCR 11.1; P. Weis, to M.
Pagès, 'Status of Hungarian Refugee Children', memo,
10 Jan. 1957, 6/9 HUN, ibid. See also A. Schnitzer,
'Some Aspects of the Legal Situation of Unaccompanied
Hungarian Children', Opinion submitted to the UN
High Commissioner for Refugees, 8 May 1959, ibid.

31 Executive Committee of the High Commissioner's
Programme, 'Progress Report on Programme for New
Hungarian Refugees as of 31 December 1960', UN
Doc. A/AC.96/112, 19 April 1961, p. 1.

32 UNGA Res. 1166(XII), 26 Nov. 1957.

33 UNGA Res. 1167(XII), 26 Nov. 1957.

Chapter 1 boxes

i C. Skran, 'Profiles of the First Two High Commissioners',
Journal of Refugee Studies, vol. 1, nos. 3–4, 1988.

ii The report was subsequently published as E. Hambro,
The Problem of Chinese Refugees in Hong Kong, Leyden, 1955.

iii UNGA Res. 1167(XII), 26 Nov. 1957.

Chapter 2

1 On the use of torture see H. Alleg, La Question, Paris, 1958;
translated as The Question, London, 1958; C. Moorehead,
Dunant's Dream: War, Switzerland and the History of the Red Cross,
HarperCollins, London, 1998, pp. 585–94. Oral history
interview with A. Lindt, 4 Feb. 1998, F/HCR 36.1.

2 J.D.R. Kelly to the High Commissioner, 'Visit to Eastern
Border Area', memo, 28 July 1962, 13/1/31 ALG,
F/HCR 11.1.

3 P. Weis, 'Note on Algeria', 2 Aug. 1957,
PW/PR/HCR/ISSN/18, Paul Weis archive, Refugee
Studies Centre, University of Oxford.

4 President Bourguiba to A. Lindt, letter, 31 May 1957,
13/1/31 TUN, F/HCR 11.1.

5 L.W. Holborn, Refugees: A Problem of our Time: The Work of the
United Nations High Commissioner for Refugees, 1951–1972, 2
vols, Methuen, Scarecrow Press, NJ, 1975, pp. 1006–7.

6 A. Lindt to J. Foster Dulles, letter, 20 Sept. 1957,
13/1/31 TUN, F/HCR 11.1. See also A. Lindt to J.W.
Hanes, Deputy Assistant Secretary for International
Organizations, US Department of State, letter, 7 Oct.
1958; Lindt to R. McCollum, Bureau of Security and
Consular Affairs, letter, 29 Oct. 1958, ibid.

7 D.J. Walton, UNHCR Representative for Morocco, 'High
Commissioner's Visit – General', 21 Dec. 1959, 1/7/5
TUN/MOR, F/HCR 11.1.

8 See e.g. A.R. Zolberg et al., Escape from Violence: Conflict and the
Refugee Crisis in the Developing World, Oxford University Press,
Oxford, 1989; C. Ruthström-Ruin, Beyond Europe: The
Globalization of Refugee Aid, Lund University Press, Lund,
1993, pp. 117–20.

9 Horne, A Savage War of Peace: Algeria 1954–1962, Faber and
Faber, London, 1969, pp. 249–50, 265–9.

10 Walton, 'Rations for Combatants', memo, 1 Feb. 1961,
13/1/31 MOR, F/HCR 11.1.

11 Walton to UNHCR HQ, 'Distribution of Rations to
Refugees who May be Mobilized or Trained for Warlike
Activities', memo, 25 Feb. 1961, ibid.

12 GA Res. 1672(XVI), 18 Dec. 1961.

13 Walton, 'Visit of Deputy High Commissioner', memo, 5
April 1962, 1/7/43 Missions—Deputy High
Commissioner, F/HCR 11.1.

14 Walton to UNHCR HQ, 'Report on Activities of Tripartite
Commission for Morocco', memo, 28 July 1962,
13/1/31 MOR, F/HCR 11.1.

15 Zolberg, Escape from Violence, p. 234; Moorhead, Dunant's
Dream, pp. 593–4.

16 F. Schnyder to U Thant, letter, 3 Oct. 1962, 13/1/31
ALG, F/HCR 11.1.

17 Interview with Lindt, 4 Feb. 1998, F/HCR 36.1.

18 The Belgian colony of the Republic of the Congo was
often referred to at the time as Congo-Leopoldville. This
was to distinguish it from the country on the west bank
of the Congo River bearing the same name, which was
often referred to as Congo-Brazzaville. The former was
renamed the Democratic Republic of the Congo in
1964, and then the Republic of Zaire in 1971. It reverted to the Democratic Republic of the Congo in 1997.

19 A. Destexhe, L'humanitaire impossible ou deux siècles d'ambiguité,
Armand Colin, Paris, 1993, ch. 5; Moorhead, Dunant's
Dream, pp. 614–27.

20 G. Prunier, The Rwanda Crisis 1959–1994: History of a Genocide,
Hurst & Co, London, 1995; R. van der Meeren, 'Three
Decades in Exile: Rwandan Refugees 1960–1990', Journal
of Refugee Studies, vol. 9, no. 3, 1966 pp. 252–67; R.
Lemarchand, 'The Apocalypse in Rwanda. Ethnic
Conflict: The New World Order', Cultural Survival Quarterly,
summer/fall, 1994, pp. 29–33; B. Anderson, Imagined
Communities, Verso, London, 1983.

21 UN Trusteeship Commission Report, March 1961.

22 O. Gobius to High Commissioner, memo, 5 April 1962,
15/BUR/RWA, F/HCR 11.1.

23 President Nyerere to High Commissioner Sadruddin Aga
Khan, letter, 20 Feb. 1963, 15/81/TAN, F/HCR 11.1.

24 High Commissioner to UN General Assembly, 'Report
on the Situation of Refugees from Rwanda', 13 Feb.
1963, UN Doc. A/AC.96/190.

25 J. Cuénod, Burundi Regional Delegate to High
Commissioner, 'Subversive Activities Amongst Rwandese
Refugees in Burundi', memo, 6 Nov. 1964,
15/BUR/RWA, F/HCR 11.1.

26 R. Lemarchand, Selective Genocide in Burundi, Minority Rights
Group, report no. 20, London, July 1974.

27 R. Dayal, Special Representative of the Secretary-General
to Dag Hammarskjöld, 'Report on the Kasai Refugees,
Republic of the Congo', n.d., enclosed in O. Gobius to T.
Jamieson, memo, 13 Jan. 1961, 15/78 'Situation in the
Congo', F/HCR 11.1.

28 G. Streijffert, Assistant Chief Delegate of the League of Red
Cross Societies, Delegation to the Congo, 'Report on a
Joint Fact-Finding and Operational Planning Mission to
Kivu Province', 3 March 1962, 15/81 KIVU, F/HCR 11.1.

29 F. Preziosi, 'Situation in North Kivu', memo, 21 Oct.
1963, ibid.

30 R. Bunche, UN Under Secretary-General for Political
Affairs, to High Commissioner for Refugees, letter, 8
Sept. 1964, ibid.

31 It was finally withdrawn only in 1966. UNHCR, 'Note
sur la protection au Congo (Leopoldville)', 20 June
1966, 6/1 PROTECTION CONGO, F/HCR 11.1.

32 F.P. Hordijk to High Commissioner, 'Report on the First Moves of Refugees from Central Kivu to Tanganyika via Goma', memo, 20 Nov. 1964, 15/81 KIVU, F/HCR 11.1.

33 Cited by R. Lemarchand, *Rwanda and Burundi*, Pall Mall Press, London, 1970, p. 215.

34 R. Gorgé, UNHCR Principal Legal Adviser and Political Adviser, to M. Dorsinville, Officer-in-Charge ONUC, 'Report on Joint Congolese–UN Commission set up to Investigate Refugee Situation in North Kivu', 9 Dec. 1963, enclosed in H.H. Schindler to High Commissioner, memo, 11 Dec 1963, F/HCR 11.1.

35 Appendix to UNGA Res. 429(V), 14 Dec. 1950, GAOR, Fifth Session, Supplement No. 20 (A/1775); Holborn, *Refugees*, pp. 177–82.

36 R. Greenfield, 'The OAU and Africa's Refugees', in El-Ayouty and I.W. Zartman (eds), *The OAU after Twenty Years*, Praeger, New York, 1984, p. 212; G. Loescher, *Beyond Charity: International Cooperation and the Global Refugee Crisis*, Oxford University Press, Oxford, 1996, p. 80; Holborn, *Refugees*, pp. 183–94.

Chapter 3

1 L. Lifschultz, *Bangladesh: The Unfinished Revolution*, Zed Press, London, 1979; T. Maniruzzaman, *The Bangladesh Revolution and its Aftermath*, Bangladesh Books International, Dhaka, 1980.

2 A. Mascarenhas, *The Rape of Bangladesh*, Vikas, New Delhi, 1971; contemporary newspaper reports such as S. Schanberg, 'In Dacca, Troops Use Artillery to Halt Revolt', *New York Times*, 28 March 1971.

3 UNHCR, *A Story of Anguish and Action: The United Nations Focal Point for Assistance to Refugees from East Bengal in India*, Geneva, Nov. 1972, p. 9.

4 Branch Office New York to UNHCR HQ, cable, 24 April 1971, 1.IND.PAK, F/HCR 11.1. See Statement by Ambassador Sen, Permanent Representative of India to the UN, Economic and Social Committee, ECOSOC, Agenda 5(a), Report, Commission on Human Rights, 17 May 1971.

5 High Commissioner Sadruddin Aga Khan to U Nyun and others, cable, 5 May 1971, 1.IND.PAK, F/HCR 11.1.

6 C. Mace, Deputy High Commissioner to UNHCR HQ, cable from Calcutta, 15 May 1971, ibid.

7 UNHCR, *Anguish and Action*, p. 18.

8 R.E. Sisson and L.E. Rose, *War and Secession: Pakistan, India and the Creation of Bangladesh*, University of California Press, Berkeley CA, 1990, pp. 152–3.

9 Ibid., p. 206.

10 UNHCR, *Anguish and Action*, p. 19.

11 Ibid., p. 27.

12 Ibid., p. 30.

13 'UN Secretary General's Appeal for Assistance to East Bengal on June 17, 1971', 11 Aug. 1972, UN Doc. A/8662/Add.3, p. 7.

14 Items 250, 8 June 1971, and G. Jaeger, Director of Asia Bureau, to High Commissioner, memo, 22 June 1971, both 1.IND.PAK, F/HCR 11.1.

15 High Commissioner Sadruddin Aga Khan to P. Hoffman, Administrator, UNDP, cable, 21 May 1971, 1/6/5 IND, F/HCR 11.1.

16 Sisson and Rose, *War and Secession*, p. 189. For the views of the High Commissioner see 'Record of Press Conference of UN High Commissioner for Refugees, UN, New York, 23 June 1971', in Indian Ministry of External Affairs, *Bangladesh Documents*, New Delhi, 1971–73, vol. 1, pp. 628–32; C. Mace, Deputy High Commissioner, to U Thant, Secretary-General, cable, 8 June 1971, 1.IND.PAK, F/HCR 11.1.

17 Sisson and Rose, *War and Secession*, p. 190. See also *New York Times*, 19 Nov. 1971.

18 Government of India, reply to UN Secretary-General's *Aide Mémoire*, 2 Aug. 1971, *Bangladesh Documents*, vol. 1, pp. 660–3.

19 H. Zaheer, *The Separation of East Pakistan: The Rise and Realization of Bengali Muslim Nationalism*, Oxford University Press, Oxford, 1994, ch. 11; UN Office of Public Information, *Yearbook of the United Nations 1971*, vol. 25, New York, 1974.

20 On J. Kelly's role see M. Sayle, 'How Dacca Fell: The Inside Story', *Observer*, 19 Dec. 1971; oral history interview with J. Kelly, 1 April 1998, F/HCR 11.1.

21 UNHCR, *Anguish and Action*, p. 74.

22 Ibid., p. 79.

23 G.J.L. Coles, 'Solutions to the Problem of Refugees and the Protection of Refugees: A Background Study', paper prepared for roundtable on durable solutions and the protection of refugees convened by UNHCR and the International Institute of Humanitarian Law, 1989.

24 UNHCR, *Airlift: The Sub-continent Repatriation Operation, September 1973–June 1974*, Geneva, 1975, p. 7.

25 UNHCR headquarters to UNHCR Branch Office, Dacca, cable with text of press release, 29 Jan. 1974, 1/9/1/SCSU/BGD, F/HCR 11.1.

26 UNHCR Branch Office, Dacca, to UNHCR headquarters, cable, 12 March 1974, ibid.

27 F.L. Pijnacker Hordijk, UNHCR representative in India to I. Singh, Deputy Secretary, Indian Ministry of External Affairs, New Delhi, 'Sub-continental Repatriation Operation', letter, 10 July 1974, 1/9/1 SCSU/IND, F/HCR 11.1; R. McAlpine, chargé de mission, UNHCR Dhaka, to Pijnacker Hordijk, 'Sub-continent Repatriation 1973/74', letter, 28 Nov. 1979, 120.GEN Statistics, F/HCR 11.2; UNHCR, *Airlift*, p. 18.

28 UNHCR Branch Office, Dacca, to UNHCR HQ, cable, 16 Feb. 1974, 1/9/1/SCSU/PAK, F/HCR 11.1.

29 M. Weiner, 'Rejected Peoples and Unwanted Migrants in South Asia', *Economic and Political Weekly*, 21 Aug. 1993, p. 1739.

30 A.R. Zolberg et al., *Escape from Violence: Conflict and the Refugee Crisis in the Developing World*, Oxford University Press, Oxford, 1989, p. 145; M. Nur Khan, 'Biharis in Bangladesh: Forgotten Pakistani Citizens', in T.K. Bose and R. Manchanda (eds), *States, Citizens and Outsiders: The Uprooted Peoples of South Asia*, South Asia Forum for Human Rights, Kathmandu, 1997; S. Sen, 'Stateless Refugees and the Right to Return: The Bihari Refugees of South Asia', *International Journal of Refugee Law*, part 1, vol. 11, no. 4, part 2, vol.12, no.1.

31 C.R. Abrar, *A Forsaken Minority: Stateless Persons of the Bihari Community in Bangladesh*, Refugee and Migratory Movements Research Unit, Jan. 1999, p. 13; K.M. Rahman, 'Bihari Refugees in Bangladesh: On the Way to Integration', *South Asian Refugee Watch*, vol. 1, no. 1, July 1999, p. 29.

Chapter 3 boxes

i C. Furer-Haimendorf, *The Renaissance of Tibetan Civilization*, Synergetic Press, Tennessee, 1990.

ii Human Rights Watch, *The Rohingya Muslims: Ending a Cycle of Exodus?*, New York, Sept. 1996; Amnesty International, *Myanmar/Bangladesh: Rohingyas—The Search for Safety*, London, Sept. 1997. On the other hand, UNHCR's presence in Rakhine state and its role in helping to create and ensure situations conducive to the return of the Rohingyas were welcomed by the UN Commission for Human Rights Special Rapporteur on the situation in Myanmar, in his reports for 1995 and 1996. See UN Docs. E/CN.4/1995/65, 12 Jan. 1995, and E/CN.4/1996/65, 5 Feb. 1996.

Chapter 4

1 This chapter draws extensively on W.C. Robinson, *Terms of Refuge: The Indochinese Exodus and the International Response*, Zed Books, London, 1998. UNHCR facilitated the author's research and gave full access to relevant UNHCR documents.

2 L.A. Wiesner, *Victims and Survivors: Displaced Persons and Other War Victims in Viet-Nam, 1954–1975*, Westport Press, New York, 1988; A.R. Zolberg et al., *Escape from Violence: Conflict and the Refugee Crisis in the Developing World*, Oxford University Press, Oxford, 1989, pp. 160–70.

3 High Commissioner for Refugees Sadruddin Aga Khan, 'Statement to the Twenty-fifth Session of the Inter-governmental Committee for European Migration', 10 May 1966.

4 Zolberg, *Escape from Violence*, p. 163.

5 'Statement of the United Nations High Commissioner for Refugees to the Third Committee, 17 Nov. 1975.'

6 'Report of the United Nations High Commissioner for Refugees, General Assembly, Thirty-Fifth Session', Supplement No. 12, A/35/12, 1980.

7 UNHCR Regional Office Malaysia to UNHCR HQ, cable, 13 Nov. 1978.

8 UNHCR HQ to Regional Office Malaysia, cable, 14 Nov. 1978.

9 'Joint Communiqué Issued at the Twelfth ASEAN Ministerial Meeting, Bali, Indonesia, 28–30 June 1979', in Thai Ministry of Foreign Affairs, *Documents on the Kampuchean Problem: 1979–1985*, Bangkok, 1985, p. 78.

10 On the Geneva conference see UNHCR, 'Meeting on Refugees and Displaced Persons in Southeast Asia, Convened by the Secretary-General of the United Nations at Geneva on 20 and 21 July 1979, and Subsequent Developments', 7 Nov. 1979.

11 UNHCR, 'Note by the High Commissioner for the Meeting on Refugees and Displaced Persons in Southeast Asia', 9 July 1979.

12 Robinson, *Terms of Refuge*, p. 128.

13 D. de Haan, Deputy High Commissioner to UN Headquarters New York, 'Procedures for Orderly Departure from Vietnam', note, 15 June 1979, 100.ORD.SRV GEN, F/HCR 11.2. See also J. Kumin, 'Orderly Departure from Viet Nam: A Humanitarian Alternative?', Ph.D. thesis, Fletcher School of Law and Diplomacy, Medford, MA, 1987, copy in UNHCR Centre for Documentation on Refugees.

14 B. Wain, *The Refused: The Agony of the Indochina Refugees*, Dow Jones Publishing Co., Hong Kong, 1981, p. 83.

15 UNHCR Press Release, 'UNHCR Expresses Grave Concern at Continuing Plight of Refugees in Distress at Sea', 14 Nov. 1983.

16 Robinson, *Terms of Refuge*, p. 193.

17 For further discussion, see A. Casella, 'The Refugees from Vietnam: Rethinking the Issue', *The World Today*, Aug.–Sept. 1989.

18 UNHCR Information Bulletin, 'The Comprehensive Plan of Action', Aug. 1995.

19 V. Muntarbhorn, 'Displaced Persons in Thailand: Legal and National Policy Issues in Perspective', *Chulalongkorn Law Review*, vol. 1, Chulalongkorn University, Bangkok, 1982, p. 14.

20 Although the two names, Cambodia and Kampuchea, came to have political and ideological overtones, they derive from the same Khmer word, *kambuja*, and are essentially interchangeable.

21 B. Kiernan, *How Pol Pot Came to Power*, Verso, London, 1985, pp. 415–16.

22 See W.C. Robinson, *Double Vision: A History of Cambodian Refugees in Thailand*, Chulalongkorn University, Institute of Asian Studies, Bangkok, July 1996.

23 D. McNamara, 'The Politics of Humanitarianism' (unpublished manuscript), 1986, Section V, p. 21. See also W. Shawcross, *The Quality of Mercy: Cambodia, Holocaust and Modern Conscience*, André Deutsch, London, 1984.

24 Thai Ministry of the Interior, *An Instrument of Foreign Policy: Indochinese Displaced Persons*, Department of Local Administration, Bangkok, 1981, p. 41.

25 J. Rogge, 'Return to Cambodia', in F.C. Cuny, B.N. Stein and P. Reid (eds), *Repatriation During Conflict in Africa and Asia*, Center for the Study of Societies in Crisis, Dallas, 1992, p. 144.

26 Office of the Special Representative of the Secretary-General of the United Nations for Coordination of Cambodian Humanitarian Assistance Programmes (OSRSG), *Cambodian Humanitarian Assistance and the United Nations, 1979–1991*, UN, Bangkok, 1992, p. 42.

27 J. Reynell, *Political Pawns: Refugees on the Thai-Kampuchean Border*, Refugee Studies Programme, Oxford, 1989, p. 42.

28 Robinson, *Double Vision*, p. 137.

29 The four political factions were the State of Cambodia (SOC) based in Phnom Penh under Prime Minister Hun Sen, and the three resistance factions which made up the Coalition Government of Democratic Kampuchea (CGDK). The CGDK comprised the United National Front for an Independent, Neutral, Peaceful and Cooperative Cambodia (FUNCINPEC) led by Prince Norodom Sihanouk; the Khmer People's National Liberation Front (KPNLF) headed by former Prime Minister Son Sann; and the Party of Democratic Kampuchea, more commonly known as the Khmer Rouge, led by Pol Pot.

30 Statement by S. Vieira de Mello at the closure of Khao-I-Dang, 3 March 1993.

31 Robinson, *Terms of Refuge*, p. 13.

32 R. Cooper, 'The Hmong of Laos: Economic Factors in Refugee Exodus and Return', in G.L. Hendricks, B.T. Downing, and A.S. Deinard (eds), *The Hmong in Transition*, Center for Migration Studies, New York, 1986, pp. 23–40.

33 Cited in a 25 Oct. 1975 press release by the Thai Ministry of Foreign Affairs.
34 UNHCR, 'Report on UNHCR Activities in the LPDR in 1977', Feb. 1978.
35 UNHCR, 'Report on UNHCR Activities in the LPDR in 1979', Feb. 1980.
36 See J.A. Hafner, 'Lowland Lao and Hmong Refugees in Thailand: The Plight of Those Left Behind', *Disasters*, vol. 9, no. 2, 1985, p. 83; M. Lacey, 'A Case Study in International Refugee Policy: Lowland Lao Refugees', *People in Upheaval*, Center for Migration Studies, New York, 1987, p. 24.
37 'Draft Declaration and Comprehensive Plan of Action', approved by the preparatory meeting for the International Conference on Indochinese Refugees, 8 March 1989.
38 UNHCR, 'Outline of the Plan for a Phased Repatriation and Reintegration of Laotians in Thailand', Fourth Session of the Tripartite Meeting, 27–29 June 1991, p. 5.
39 UNHCR Information Bulletin, 'Laos', April 1996.
40 High Commissioner for Refugees, J.-P. Hocké, statement to International Conference on Indochinese Refugees, Geneva, 13 June 1989.
41 A. Simmance, 'The International Response to the Indo-Chinese Refugee Crisis', paper presented at international seminar on the Indochinese Exodus and the International Response, Tokyo, Japan, 27–28 Oct. 1995.
42 UNHCR, 'Resettlement in the 1990s: A Review of Policy and Practice', evaluation summary prepared by the Inspection and Evaluation Service for the Formal Consultations on Resettlement, Geneva, 12–14 Oct. 1994, p. 1.

Chapter 4 boxes

i High Commissioner, 'Note for the Meeting on Refugees and Displaced Persons in Southeast Asia', July 1979.
ii High Commissioner J.-P. Hocké, statement to International Conference on Indochinese Refugees, Geneva, 13 June 1989.
iii Draft Declaration and Comprehensive Plan of Action, approved by preparatory meeting for the International Conference on Indochinese Refugees, 8 March 1989.
iv Ibid.
v H.Kamm, 'Vietnam's Refugees Sail into Heart of Darkness', *New York Times*, 4 July 1984.
vi US Committee for Refugees, *World Refugee Survey*, Washington DC, 1977.
vii W.C. Robinson, *Terms of Refuge: The Indochinese Exodus and the International Response*, Zed Books, London, 1998, table, p. 295.
viii E. Ressler, 'Analysis and Recommendations for the Care of the Unaccompanied Khmer Children in the Holding Centers in Thailand', Interagency Study Group, Bangkok, Dec. 1980.

Chapter 5

1 A. Zolberg and A. Callamard, 'Displacement-Generating Conflicts and International Assistance in the Horn of Africa', paper presented at joint ILO–UNHCR meeting on international aid as a means to reduce the need for emigration, Geneva, 1992, p. 7.
2 J. Crisp and N. Cater, 'The Human Consequences of Conflict in the Horn of Africa: Refugees, Asylum and the Politics of Assistance', paper presented at regional security conference, Cairo, 27–30 May 1990, p. 6.
3 A. Karadawi, *Refugee Policy in Sudan 1967–1984*, Berghahn Books, New York, 1999.
4 R. Ek and A. Karadawi, 'Implications of Refugee Flows on Political Stability in the Sudan', *Ambio*, vol. 20, no. 5, Aug. 1991, pp. 196–203; J.R. Rogge, *Too Many, Too Long: Sudan's Twenty-Year Refugee Dilemma*, Rowman and Allenheld, New Jersey, 1985.
5 P. Vigne, 'Eastern Sudan: Refugee Agriculture Programme, Bread Basket or Basket Case?', *Refugees*, no. 27, March 1986, p. 30.
6 A. de Waal, *Famine Crimes: Politics and the Disaster Relief Industry in Africa*, African Rights, London, and James Currey, Oxford, 1997, p. 106.
7 H.A. Ruiz, *Behind the Headlines: Refugees in the Horn of Africa*, US Committee for Refugees, Washington DC, 1989, p. 17.
8 De Waal, *Famine Crimes*, pp. 115–17.
9 A. Billard, 'Eastern Sudan: Huge Efforts Paying Off', *Refugees*, no. 27, March 1986, p. 21.
10 Ibid., p. 22.
11 Ibid., pp. 19–20.
12 L. Dupree and N. Hatch Dupree, 'Afghan Refugees in Pakistan', *1987 World Refugee Survey*, US Committee for Refugees, Washington DC, 1988, p. 17.
13 M. Priestly, UNDP Representative in Islamabad, to J. Cuenod, UNHCR Assistance Division, Geneva, letter, 2 Aug. 1979, 100/PAK/AFG, F/HCR 11.2.
14 H. C. von Sponek, Resident Representative a.i. Islamabad, to High Commissioner P. Hartling, 3 Aug. 1978, and von Sponek to F. J. Homann-Herimberg, cable, 16 Aug. 1978, both in 100/PAK/AFG, F/HCR 11.2.
15 J.K.A. Marker, Ambassador of Pakistan in Geneva, to High Commissioner Hartling, letter, 10 Apr. 1979, 100/PAK/AFG, F/HCR 11.2.
16 UN Information Centre for Pakistan, News Release 22/79, 25 Oct. 1979, 100/PAK/AFG, F/HCR 11.2.
17 K. Khoda Panahi, Foreign Minister of Iran, to High Commissioner Hartling, letter, 29 Nov. 1980, 010/IRN, F/HCR 11.2.
18 R. Yazgi, Chief of the Middle East and North Africa Section, to High Commissioner Hartling, memo, 26 June 1981, 100/IRN/AFG, F/HCR 11.2.
19 S. Lamb, 'Afghans in Pakistan: The Target of Blame, the Beneficiaries of Hospitality', *Refugees*, no. 41, May 1987, p. 20.
20 UNHCR Programme and Technical Support Section Mission Report 96/28, 'Evaluation of the Income Generation Project for Refugee Areas (IGPRA)', 1996, F/HCR 18.1.
21 H. Ruiz, *Left Out in the Cold: The Perilous Homecoming of Afghan Refugees*, US Committee for Refugees, Washington DC, 1992, p. 4.
22 A.R. Zolberg et al., *Escape from Violence: Conflict and the Refugee Crisis in the Developing World*, Oxford University Press, Oxford, 1989, p. 154.
23 M. Moussalli, UNHCR Director of International Protection, to G. Walzer, UNHCR Chief of Mission Islamabad, memo, 3 July 1984, 100/PAK/AFG, F/HCR 11.2.
24 Ibid.

25 P. Sargisson, UNHCR Regional Representative for Northern Latin America, to UNHCR HQ, cable, 10 March 1980, 600.HON, F/HCR 11.2; Deputy High Commissioner D.S. de Haan to C. Lopez Contreras, Minister of External Relations of Honduras, 16 Aug. 1979, 600/HON, F/HCR 11.2.

26 J. Hampton (ed.), *Internally Displaced People: A Global Survey*, Norwegian Refugee Council and Earthscan, London, 1998, p. 103.

27 Zolberg, *Escape from Violence*, p. 212.

28 UNHCR Statistical Unit, Geneva.

29 Zolberg, *Escape from Violence*, p. 218.

30 R. Camarda et al., *Forced to Move: Salvadoran Refugees in Mexico*, Solidarity Publications, San Francisco, CA, 1985, p. 26.

31 J. Henkel, Washington Liaison Office of UNHCR, to High Commissioner Hartling, 28 March 1984, enclosing 'Media Backgrounder: UNHCR and the Relocation of Salvadoran and Guatemalan Refugees in Honduras', 100/HON/SAL, F/HCR 11.2. See also UNHCR Tegucigalpa to UNHCR Geneva, cable, 8 June 1984, 600/HON, F/HCR 11.2.

32 B. Thiesbrummel, 'Report on My Mission in Honduras (August–December 1983)', Item 965, 600/HON, F/HCR 11.2.

Chapter 5 boxes

i See, for example, B. Harrell-Bond, *Imposing Aid: Emergency Assistance to Refugees*, Oxford University Press, Oxford, 1986; articles on 'People in Camps', *Forced Migration Review*, no. 2, Aug. 1998; J. Crisp and K. Jacobsen, 'Refugee Camps Reconsidered', *Forced Migration Review*, no. 3, Dec. 1998, pp. 27–30 and response on p. 31.

ii M. Cutts, 'Surviving in Refugee Camps', in International Committee of the Red Cross, *Forum: War, Money and Survival*, Geneva, Feb. 2000.

iii E. Schlatter, chargé de mission, 'Report on UNHCR Operation to Chile, 19 October 1973–29 March 1974', 1/CHL/GEN F/HCR 11.1. See also generally G. Perkins, to UNHCR HQ, 'The UNHCR in Latin America—A Post-Chile Analysis', 31 Jan. 1974, enclosed in G. Perkins to G. Koulischer, 12 Feb. 1974, 600/LAM, F/HCR 11.2.

iv High Commissioner Prince Sadruddin Aga Khan to Minister for Foreign Affairs, Santiago, Chile, cable, 13 Sept. 1973, 1/CHL/GEN, F/HCR 11.1.

v D.S. Blanchard, UNHCR acting chief of mission, Santiago, to UNHCR Regional Representative for Latin America, Buenos Aires, 'Report on the Operation in Chile—1 April–24 May 1974', 24 May 1974, 100/CHL/GEN, F/HCR 11.2.

vi G. Koulischer, UNHCR New York, to UNHCR HQ, cable, 23 Dec. 1973, 600/CHL F/HCR 11.2.

vii A.R. Zolberg et al., *Escape from Violence: Conflict and the Refugee Crisis in the Developing World*, Oxford University Press, Oxford, 1989, pp. 199–200.

Chapter 6

1 F. Hampson, *Nurturing Peace: Why Peace Settlements Succeed or Fail*, US Institute for Peace, Washington DC, 1996, pp. 75 and 77; A. O. Akiwmi, Senior Legal Adviser for Africa, to M. Goulding, UN Under Secretary-General, July 6, 1989, enclosing 'Mission Report to Angola and Namibia, 14-28 June 1989', Records relating to Protection, Geographical File, Namibia II, F/HCR 17.

2 R. Preston, 'Returning Exiles in Namibia Since Independence', in T. Allen and H. Morsink (eds), *When Refugees Go Home: African Experiences*, UN Research Institute for Social Development (UNRISD), Africa World Press, James Currey, London, 1994.

3 See generally, P. Worby, 'Lessons learned from UNHCR's Involvement in the Guatemala Refugee Repatriation and Reintegration Programmes (1987–1999)', report sponsored by UNHCR Regional Bureau for the Americas and Evaluation and Policy Analysis Unit, Geneva, Dec. 1999.

4 See also UNGA Res. 51/198, 27 March 1997.

5 G. Perez del Castillo and M. Fahlen, 'CIREFCA: An Opportunity and Challenge for Inter-agency Cooperation', Joint UNDP/UNHCR Review, May 1995.

6 High Commissioner S. Ogata, speech at Sophia University, Tokyo, 1995.

7 These and other relevant UN documents are reproduced in United Nations, *The United Nations and Cambodia 1991–1995*, UN Blue Book Series, Department of Public Information, New York, 1995.

8 M. Berdal and M. Leifer, 'Cambodia', in J. Mayall (ed.), *The New Interventionism 1991–1994: United Nations Experience in Cambodia, Former Yugoslavia and Somalia*, Cambridge University Press, Cambridge, 1996, p. 36.

9 See generally S. Heder and J. Ledgerwood, *Propaganda, Politics, and Violence in Cambodia: Democratic Transition under United Nations Peace-Keeping*, Armouk, New York, 1996; M.W. Doyle, *Peacebuilding in Cambodia*, International Peace Academy, New York, 1996; M.W. Doyle, *UN Peacekeeping in Cambodia: UNTAC's Civil Mandate*, International Peace Academy, Boulder CO, 1995.

10 Secretary-General, 'Fourth Progress Report of the Secretary-General on UNTAC', UN Doc. S/25719, 3 May 1993, para. 89, UN Blue Book on Cambodia, p. 285.

11 D. McNamara, 'UN Peacekeeping and Human Rights in Cambodia: A Critical Evaluation', paper prepared for a meeting on UN Peacekeeping and Human Rights, Aspen Institute, Colorado, Aug. 1994, p. 12. McNamara, a UNHCR staff member, headed the human rights component of UNTAC on secondment from UNHCR.

12 UNHCR, 'Summary of Revised Operations Plan (Cambodia Portion)', 7 Nov. 1991. See also W.C. Robinson, *Terms of Refuge: The Indochinese Exodus and the International Response*, Zed Books, London, 1998, p. 239.

13 Berdal and Leifer, 'Cambodia', p. 48.

14 Ibid., W.C. Robinson, et al. *Rupture and Return: Repatriation, Displacement and Reintegration in Battambang Province Cambodia*, Indochinese Refugee Information Center, Chulalongkorn University, Bangkok, 1994, p. 11; Secretary-General, 'Fourth Progress Report of the Secretary-General on UNTAC', UN Doc. S/25719, 3 May 1993, paras. 88–94, reproduced in UN Blue Book on Cambodia, p. 296.

15 UNHCR (J. Crisp and A. Mayne), 'Review of the Cambodian Repatriation Operation', Eval/CAM/13,

Sept. 1993 (hereinafter, UNHCR, 'Evaluation').

16 See Asia Watch, *Political Control, Human Rights, and the UN Mission in Cambodia*, Human Rights Watch, Sept. 1992; UNHCR, 'Evaluation'; UNHCR, *Bulletin: Repatriation Operation, Cambodia*, 3 Aug. 1992; W. Blatter, Director of the Regional Bureau for Asia and Oceania, to S. Ducasse, Chargé de Mission, Phnom Penh, letter, 19 Aug. 1993, A004/PNP/276, F/HCR 15, Records of the Assistant High Commissioner, Sub-Fonds 1, Cambodia, Chronological File June–October 1993.

17 UNHCR, 'Evaluation', paras. 151–4. UNHCR undertook a satellite land survey instead of a field survey, which compounded the miscalculations, according to the evaluation report, paras. 167–8. See also Robinson, *Rupture and Return*, p. 10.

18 Lt.-Gen. J. Sanderson, 'UNTAC: Successes and Failures', in H. Smith (ed.), *International Peacekeeping: Building on the Cambodian Experience*, Australian Defence Studies Centre, Canberra, 1994, p. 23.

19 P. Utting, 'Linking Peace to Reconstruction', in P. Utting (ed.), *Between Hope and Insecurity: The Social Consequences of the Cambodian Peace Process*, UNRISD, Geneva, 1994, p. 4.

20 See generally, United Nations, *The United Nations and Mozambique, 1992–1995*, UN Blue Book Series, Department of Public Information, New York, vol. 5, 1995.

21 Lawyers' Committee for Human Rights, *African Exodus: Refugee Crisis, Human Rights and the 1969 OAU Convention*, New York, July 1995.

22 UNHCR, *Mozambique: An Account from a Lessons Learned Seminar on Reintegration*, Geneva, 24–26 June 1996, para. 7.

23 UNHCR, 'Rebuilding a War-Torn Society: A Review of the UNHCR Reintegration Programme for Mozambican Returnees, July 1996', *Refugee Survey Quarterly*, vol. 16, no. 2, p. 24.

24 R. Eaton et al., *Mozambique, The Development of Indigenous Mine Action Capacities*, UN Department of Humanitarian Affairs, New York, 1997.

25 A. Ajello in *Winning the Peace: Concept and Lessons Learned of Post-Conflict Peacebuilding*, international workshop, Berlin, 4–6 July 1996, Stiftung Wissenschaft und Politik, Ebenhausen, pp. 13–16.

Chapter 6 boxes

i UN Doc. A/AC.96/INF 158, recommendation 10.1.

ii H. Cholmondeley, cited in *Winning the Peace: Concept and Lessons Learned of Post-Conflict Peacebuilding*, international workshop, Berlin, 4–6 July 1996, Stiftung Wissenschaft und Politik, Ebenhausen, p. 24.

iii High Commissioner S. Ogata, Address to UN Commission on Human Rights, 7 Feb. 1995.

iv UN Secretary-General, 'Renewing the United Nations: A Programme for Reform', 14 July 1997, UN Doc. A/51/950, part 1, section B, paras. 78–9.

Chapter 7

1 S. Collinson, 'Globalization and the Dynamics of International Migration: Implications for the Refugee Regime', UNHCR Working Paper no. 1, Geneva, May 1999.

2 D. Joly, *Haven or Hell? Asylum Policies and Refugees in Europe*, Macmillan, London, 1996; S. Collinson, *Europe and International Migration*, 2nd edn, Pinter and Royal Institute of International Affairs, London, 1994.

3 See N. Chandrahasan, 'A Precarious Refuge: A Study of the Reception of Tamil Asylum Seekers into Europe, North America and India', *Harvard Human Rights Yearbook*, vol. 2, 1989; US Committee for Refugees, *Time for Decision: Sri Lankan Tamils in the West*, Washington DC, 1985.

4 UNHCR, *The State of the World's Refugees: In Search of Solutions*, Oxford University Press, Oxford, 1995, p. 199.

5 High Commissioner S. Ogata, statement to international conference on 'Fortress Europe? Refugees and Migrants: Their Human Rights and Dignity', Akademie Graz, Austria, 23 May 1992.

6 Editorial, 'We Want to Wash Dross Down Drain', *Dover Express*, 1 Oct. 1998.

7 UNHCR, 'Note submitted by the High Commissioner for the Consultations with Concerned Governments', Geneva, Dec. 1986.

8 European Council on Refugees and Exiles, *Safe Third Countries: Myths and Realities*, ECRE, London, 1996; R. Byrne and A. Shacknove, 'The Safe Country Notion in European Asylum Law', *Harvard Human Rights Law Journal*, vol. 9, spring 1996; Danish Refugee Council, *'Safe Third Country' Policies in European Countries*, Copenhagen, 1997.

9 UNHCR, *Note on International Protection*, 1999, para. 19.

10 B.S. Chimni, 'Globalisation, Humanitarianism and the Erosion of Refugee Protection', Working Paper no. 3, Refugee Studies Centre, Oxford, Feb. 2000, pp. 11–12.

11 F. Liebaut and J. Hughes (eds), *Detention of Asylum Seekers in Europe: Analysis and Perspectives*, Kluwer Law International, The Hague, 1998; UNHCR Standing Committee of the Executive Committee, 'Detention of Asylum-seekers and Refugees: The Framework, the Problem and Recommended Practice', UN Doc. EC/49/SC/CRP.13, 4 June 1999.

12 E. Guild and J. Niessen, *The Developing Immigration and Asylum Policies of the European Union*, Kluwer Law International, The Hague, 1996; D. Papademetriou, *Coming Together or Pulling Apart? The European Union's Struggle with Immigration and Asylum*, Carnegie Endowment for International Peace, Washington DC, 1996; J. van der Klaauw, 'Refugee Protection in Western Europe: A UNHCR perspective', in J.-Y. Carlier and D. Vanheule (eds), *Europe and Refugees: A Challenge?*, Kluwer Law International, The Hague, 1997; F. Nicholson and P. Twomey (eds), *Refugee Rights and Realities: Evolving International Concepts and Regimes*, Cambridge University Press, Cambridge 1999, part 4, 'The European Regime'.

13 *Official Journal of the European Communities*, 1996, L63/2.

14 S. Peers, '"Mind the Gap!"' Ineffective Member State Implementation of European Union Asylum Measures', Immigration Law Practitioners' Association/British Refugee Council, London, May 1998.

15 *Official Journal of the European Communities*, 1995, C262.

16 UNHCR, 'Report of the United Nations High Commissioner for Refugees', GAOR, 48th Session, Supplement No. 12 (A/48/12), 1994, para. 24; UNHCR, *A Comprehensive Response to the Humanitarian Crisis in the Former Yugoslavia*, Geneva, 24 July 1992; W. Kälin,

Towards a Concept of Temporary Protection, unpublished study commissioned by UNHCR, 1996.

17 Resolution on certain common guidelines as regards the admission of particularly vulnerable persons from the former Yugoslavia, Council of Immigration Ministers, 1–2 June 1993.

18 United Nations, 'The Fall of Srebrenica, Report of the Secretary-General Pursuant to General Assembly Resolution 53/55', UN Doc. A/54/549, 15 Nov. 1999.

19 IGC (Intergovernmental Consultations) Secretariat, *Report on Temporary Protection in States in Europe, North America and Australia*, Geneva, 1995; UNHCR/Humanitarian Issues Working Group of the International Conference on the Former Yugoslavia, *Survey on the Implementation of Temporary Protection*, Geneva, March 1995.

20 J. Harding, *The Uninvited: Refugees at the Rich Man's Gate*, Profile Books, London, 2000; J. Morrison, *The Cost of Survival: The Trafficking of Refugees to the UK*, British Refugee Council, London, 1998.

21 Conclusions of the Presidency, Tampere European Council, 15–16 Oct. 1999.

22 UNHCR, Press Release, 8 Oct. 1999.

23 *Cruz Varas v. Sweden*, 20 March 1991, European Court of Human Rights, Series A, no. 201; *Vilvarajah v. United Kingdom*, 30 Oct. 1991, Series A, no. 215; N. Mole, *Problems Raised by Certain Aspects of the Present Situation of Refugees from the Standpoint of the European Convention on Human Rights*, Human Rights Files no. 9, rev., Council of Europe, Strasbourg, 1997, update forthcoming 2000; R. Plender and N. Mole, 'Beyond the Geneva Convention: Constructing a *de facto* Right of Asylum from International Human Rights Instruments', in Nicholson and Twomey, *Refugee Rights and Realities*, pp. 81–105.

24 UN Population Division, Department of Economic and Social Affairs, *Replacement Migration: Is it a Solution to Declining and Aging Populations?*, UN Secretariat, New York, March 2000, pp. 85–7. See also, 'Europe's Immigrants: A Continent on the Move', *Economist*, 6 May 2000; Harding, *The Uninvited*, pp. 90–102.

25 G. Rystad, 'Victims of Oppression or Ideological Weapons? Aspects of US Refugee Policy in the Postwar Era', in G. Rystad (ed.), *The Uprooted: Forced Migration as an International Problem in the Post-War Era*, Lund University Press, Lund, 1990, p. 209.

26 *American Baptist Churches v. Thornburgh*, 760 F.Supp. 796 (N.D. Cal. 1991). See also US Committee for Refugees, *Refugee Reports*, vol. 12, no. 1, 29 Jan. 1991. See also N. Zucker and N. Flink Zucker, *Desperate Crossings: Seeking Refuge in America*, M.E. Sharpe, Inc., New York, 1996.

27 Commission on Human Rights, 'Cuba: Report on the Human Rights Situation', E/CN.4/1995/52, 11 Jan. 1995, paras 34 and 41.

28 Lawyers' Committee for Human Rights, *Uncertain Haven: Refugee Protection on the Fortieth Anniversary of the 1951 United Nations Refugee Convention*, New York, 1991.

29 US Committee for Refugees, *World Refugee Survey 1997*, Washington DC, 1997. See also M.J. McBride, 'The Evolution of US Immigration and Refugee Policy: Public Opinion, Domestic Politics and UNHCR', UNHCR Working Paper no. 3, Geneva, May 1999.

30 Lawyers' Committee for Human Rights, *Slamming the 'Golden Door': A Year of Expedited Removal*, LCHR, New York, April 1998.

31 *Singh et al v. Canada (Minister of Employment and Immigration)*, [1985] 1 Supreme Court Reports 1997.

Chapter 7 boxes

i Tampere European Council, 'Presidency Conclusions', 15–16 Oct. 1999.

ii *Islam v. Secretary of State for the Home Department and Regina v. Immigration Appeal Tribunal and Another Ex Parte Shah*, House of Lords judgement, 25 March 1999, [1999] 2 WLR 1015, [1999] Imm AR 283.

iii Inter-Agency Standing Committee, 'Global Humanitarian Assistance 2000', 23rd meeting, draft final report, March 2000.

iv Development Assistance Committee, 1999 *Development Cooperation Report*, Organization for Economic Cooperation and Development, Paris, 2000, Table 19; Earthscan, *The Reality of Aid*, annual publication, London.

v *Sale v. Haitian Centers Council, Inc., et al.*, 113 S. Ct. 2549 (1993); See also 'Cases and Comment', *International Journal of Refugee Law*, vol. 6, no. 1, 1994, pp. 69–84.

vi Brief of the Office of the United Nations High Commissioner for Refugees as *amicus curiae* in Haitian interdiction case, 1993, see *International Journal of Refugee Law*, vol. 6, no. 1, 1994, pp. 85–102 at p. 97.

vii *Haitian Refugee Cases*, Case no. 10.675, Inter-American Commission on Human Rights, OEA/Ser/L/V/II.93, Doc. 36, 17 Oct. 1996; *International Human Rights Reports*, vol. 5, 1998, pp. 120–65.

viii *Haitian Centers Council, Inc. v. Sale*, 8 June 1993, 823 F. Supp. 1028, 1042.

Chapter 8

1 UNHCR, Public Information Section, 'CIS Conference on Refugees and Migrants', 30–31 May 1996, Geneva, p. 3.

2 See R. Conquest, *The Nation Killers: The Soviet Deportation of Nations*, Macmillan, London, 1970; A.M. Nekrich, *The Punished Peoples: The Deportation and Fate of Soviet Minorities at the End of the Second World War*, W.W. Norton and Co., New York, 1978; J.-J. Marie, *Les peuples déportés d'Union Soviétique*, Editions Complexe, Brussels, 1995.

3 R. Brubaker, 'Aftermaths of Empire and the Unmixing of Peoples: Historical and Comparative Perspectives', *Ethnic and Racial Studies*, vol. 18, no. 2, April 1995, pp. 189–218; B. Nahaylo and V. Swoboda, *Soviet Disunion: A History of the Nationalities Problem in the USSR*, Hamish Hamilton, London, 1990.

4 Human Rights Watch/Helsinki, *Bloodshed in the Caucasus: Escalation of the Armed Conflict in Nagorno-Karabakh*, Human Rights Watch, New York, 1992.

5 See N. F. Bugai, *Turki iz Meskhetii: dolgii put k reabilitatsii* [*Turks from Meskhetia: the Long Road to Rehabilitation*], Ross, Moscow, 1994, pp. 131–5; H. Carrrere d'Encausse, *The End of the Soviet Empire: The Triumph of the Nations*, Basic Books, New York, 1992, pp. 98–9, 103–4.

6 Gosudarstvennyi komitet SSSR po statistike [USSR State Committee for Statistics], *Natsionalnyi sostav naseleniia: Chast II* [*The National Composition of the Population: Part II*], Moscow,

1989, pp. 3–5.

7 A.-M. Demmer, Director, UNHCR Regional Bureau for Europe and North America, 'Meeting of the Delegation of the USSR to ExCom with the High Commissioner, 17.09.90', Note for the File, 18 Oct. 1990, 010.RUS, F/HCR 11.3.

8 A. Verwey, Deputy Director, UNHCR Regional Bureau for Europe and North America, 'UNHCR and the Disintegrating USSR', Note for File, 15 Sept. 1991, Russia Development, 1988-06/93, F/HCR 19.4.

9 UNHCR Regional Bureau for Europe and North America, 'UNHCR Strategy for the Commonwealth of Independent States', paper prepared for a meeting chaired in UNHCR HQ by the High Commissioner, 5 March 1992, Russia Development, 1988-06/93, F/HCR 19.4.

10 W.D. Clarance, 'Report on Mission to the Soviet Union 5–18 December 1991', Note for the File, 9 Jan. 1992, 010.RUS, F/HCR 11.3.

11 O. Andrysek, Head of Desk IV, UNHCR Regional Bureau for Europe and North America, 'Note for the File', 12 March 1992, 600.CIS, F/HCR 11.3; UNHCR Regional Bureau for Europe and North America, 'UNHCR Strategy for the Commonwealth of Independent States'.

12 Andrysek, 'Note for the File', 12 March 1992, 600.CIS, F/HCR 11.3. See also 'The Commonwealth of Independent States: UNHCR's Approach and Involvement', paper prepared for meeting of the Inter-governmental Consultations in Geneva on 26 Feb. 1992, Russia Development, 1988-06/93, F/HCR 19.4.

13 High Commissioner S. Ogata, to B. Pankin, Foreign Minster of the Soviet Union, letter, 26 Sept. 1991, CSCE.General, F/HCR 17.

14 D. Petrasek, Amnesty International, to E. Feller, Division of International Protection, fax, 12 June 1992, enclosing Delegation of the Russian Federation and those of Albania, Austria, Bulgaria, Greece, Kyrgyszstan, Romania, Slovenia, Switzerland and Yugoslavia to the CSCE Helsinki Follow-up Meeting 1992, proposal on 'Refugees and Displaced Persons', CSCE/HM/WG3/17, Helsinki, 5 June 1992, CSCE.General, F/HCR 17.

15 Dienstbier, CSCE Chairman in Office, to High Commissioner Ogata, letter, 24 April 1992, CSCE.General, F/HCR 17.

16 W. D. Clarance, UNHCR Regional Office, Moscow, 'CIS: Some Realities and Responsibilities', paper, 14 Aug. 1992, CIS, F/HCR 19.4.

17 A. Akiwumi, UNHCR Moscow, to UNHCR HQ, 'Project Proposal 1993—Interim Response', fax, 22 Jan. 1993, 600.CIS, F/HCR 11.3.

18 Secretariat of the CIS Conference, 'Note on the Concept of the "Forced Migrant"', working paper, Sept. 1995, reproduced in UNHCR, IOM, OSCE, 'The CIS Conference on Refugees and Migrants', European Series, vol. 2, no. 1, Jan. 1996, pp. 161–6. See also V. Tishkov (ed.), Migratsii i novye diaspory v post-Sovetskih gosudarstvakh [Migrations and New Diasporas in post-Soviet States], Aviaizdat, Moscow, 1996; V. Tishkov (ed.), Vynyzhdennye migranty: Intergatsiya i vozvraschenie [Forced

Migrants: Integration or Return], Aviaizdat, Moscow, 1997.

19 Agreement on Questions Relating to the Restitution of the Rights of Deported Individuals, National Minorities and Peoples. See 'The CIS Conference on Refugees and Migrants', European Series, vol. 2, no. 1, Jan. 1996, pp. 167–70.

20 This document and other CIS refugee and migration-related agreements, together with relevant legislation from the various CIS countries, are compiled in V. Mukomel and E. Pain (eds.), Bezhentsy I vynuzhdennye pereselentsi v gosudarstvakh SNG [Refugees and Forced Migrants in the States of the CIS], Centre for Ethnopolitical and Regional Research, Moscow, 1995. See also R. Plender, Basic Documents on International Migration Law, 2nd edn, Kluwer Law International, The Hague, 1997, p. 882.

21 UN Doc. GA/RES/48/113, 20 Dec. 1993.

22 A. Kozyrev, Foreign Minister of the Russian Federation, to High Commissioner Ogata, letter, Feb. 1994.

23 UN Doc. GA/RES/49/173, 23 Dec. 1994.

24 'Summary of the First Meeting of Experts, Geneva, 18–19 May 1995', in UNHCR, CIS Conference on Refugees and Migrants, pp. 51–8.

25 See C. Messina, 'Refugee Definitions in the Countries of the Commonwealth of Independent States', in F. Nicholson and P. Twomey (eds), Refugee Rights and Realities; Evolving International Concepts and Regimes, Cambridge University Press, Cambridge, 1999, pp. 136–50.

26 UNHCR, IOM, OSCE, 'Report of the Regional Conference to address the problems of refugees, displaced persons, other forms of involuntary dis-placement and returnees in the countries of the Commonwealth of Independent States and relevant neighbouring States', Geneva, 30–31 May 1996.

27 'Document of the Hague Meeting on the Issues Relating to the Meskhetian Turks,' in UNHCR, Bureau for Europe, 'Report on the Consultation on the Meskhetian Turk Issue, The Hague, 7–10 September 1998', Nov. 1998.

28 L. Funch Hansen and H. Krag, 'On the Situation in the Prigorodny District', consultants' report for UNHCR Bureau for Europe, Geneva, Oct. 1997–April 1998.

Chapter 8 boxes

i High Commissioner S. Ogata, 'Statement to the Partnership in Action global conference', June 1994.

ii J. Bennett and S. Gibbs, NGO Funding Strategies, International NGO Training and Research Centre (INTRAC)/ICVA, Oxford, 1996.

iii P. Ryder, Funding Trends and Implications: Donors, NGOs and Emergencies, INTRAC, Oxford, 1996, p. 7.

iv F. Preziosi, UNHCR chargé de mission Bukavu, Kivu, to High Commissioner, 'Situation in Central Kivu', memo, 1 July 1964, 15/81 KIVU, F/HCR 11.1.

v M. Rose, 'Field Coordination of UN Humanitarian Assistance, Bosnia, 1994', in J. Whitman and D. Pocock (eds), After Rwanda: The Coordination of United Nations Humanitarian Assistance, Macmillan, Basingstoke, 1996, p. 158.

vi M. Cutts, 'Prime Targets', The World Today, Aug.–Sept. 1998, pp. 220–1.

Chapter 9

1 E. Morris: 'The Limits of Mercy: Ethnopolitical Conflict and Humanitarian Action', Center for International Studies, Massachusetts Institute of Technology, 1995, p. 54.

2 *New York Times*, 17 April 1991.

3 N. Morris, A. Witschi-Cestari, 'Meetings at US European Command', mission report, Stuttgart, 3 May 1991.

4 A. Roberts, *Humanitarian Action in War: Aid, Protection and Impartiality in a Policy Vacuum*, Adelphi Paper 305, International Institute for Strategic Studies/Oxford University Press, Dec. 1996, p. 41.

5 C. Faubert, 'Repatriation in Situations of Armed Conflicts—The Case of Northern Iraq', UNHCR, 20 Feb. 1992.

6 High Commissioner S. Ogata, memo to staff, 6 May 1991.

7 High Commissioner Ogata to Secretary-General J. Pérez de Cuéllar, letter, 17 May 1991.

8 D. McDowall, *The Kurds: A Nation Denied*, Minority Rights Publications, London, 1992.

9 D. Keen, 'The Kurds in Iraq: How Safe is Their Haven Now?', Save the Children, London, 1993.

10 See generally N. Malcolm, *Bosnia: A Short History*, 2nd edn, Papermac, London, 1996; L. Silber and A. Little, *The Death of Yugoslavia*, Penguin Group and BBC Worldwide Ltd, London, 1995; M. Glenny, *The Balkans 1804–1999: Nationalism, War and the Great Powers*, Granta Publications, London, 1999.

11 The majority of those who did not identify themselves as Croats, Muslims or Serbs identified as Yugoslav.

12 High Commissioner Ogata to Secretary-General Pérez de Cuéllar, letter, 14 Nov. 1991.

13 Secretary-General, 'Report of the Secretary-General Pursuant to Security Council Resolution 721(1991)', 11 Dec. 1991, UN Doc. S/23280.

14 S. Ogata, 'UNHCR in the Balkans: Humanitarian Action in the Midst of War', in W. Biermann and M. Vadset (eds), *UN Peacekeeping in Trouble: Lessons Learned from the Former Yugoslavia*, Ashgate, Aldershot, UK, 1998, p. 186; L. Minear et al., *Humanitarian Action in the Former Yugoslavia: The UN's Role 1991–1993*, Thomas J. Watson Jr Institute for International Studies and Refugee Policy Group, Occasional Paper no. 18, Brown University, Providence, RI, 1994.

15 Interview with F. Fouinat, Coordinator, UNHCR Task Force for the former Yugoslavia, Oct. 1993, cited in Minear et al., *Humanitarian Action in the Former Yugoslavia*, p. 7; See also S.A. Cunliffe and M. Pugh, 'The Politicization of UNHCR in the Former Yugoslavia', *Journal of Refugee Studies*, vol. 10, no. 2, 1997, p. 134.

16 Key UN Security Council resolutions included Resolutions 758 (8 June 1992), 770 (13 Aug. 1992), and 776 (14 Sept. 1992).

17 High Commissioner Ogata, 'Refugees: A Humanitarian Strategy', statement at the Royal Institute for International Relations, Brussels, 25 Nov. 1991.

18 Interview with J.M. Mendiluce, April 1993. See also Silber and Little, *The Death of Yugoslavia*, pp. 296–7.

19 UNHCR situation report, Srebrenica, 19 Feb. 1993,
'BH West', Records of the Senior External Affairs Officer, F/HCR31/1.

20 High Commissioner Ogata to Secretary-General Boutros-Ghali, letter, 2 April 1993, UN Doc. S/25519.

21 United Nations, 'The Fall of Srebrenica, Report of the Secretary-General Pursuant to General Assembly Resolution 53/55', UN Doc. A/54/549, 15 Nov. 1999 (hereafter 'UN Srebrenica Report') para. 499.

22 W. Van Hovell, 'New Concepts of Protection in Conflict: 'Safe Keeping' Interventions in Iraq, Bosnia and Rwanda', internal UNHCR research paper, July 1995. See also K. Landgren, 'Safety Zones and International Protection: A Dark Grey Area', *International Journal of Refugee Law*, vol. 7, no. 3, pp. 436–58.

23 UN Srebrenica Report, para. 502.

24 UN Srebrenica Report, para. 9. See also, D. Rohde, *Endgame: The Betrayal and Fall of Srebrenica, Europe's Worst Masscre since World War II*, Farra, Straus, Giroux, 1998.

25 UN Srebrenica Report, para. 3.

26 UN Secretary-General, 'Further Report Pursuant to Security Council Resolution 749 (1992)', UN Doc. S/23900, 12 May 1992.

27 M. Cutts, 'The Humanitarian Operation in Bosnia, 1992–95: Dilemmas of Negotiation Humanitarian Access', UNHCR Working Paper no. 8, Geneva, May 1999.

28 C. Thornberry, 'Peacekeepers, Humanitarian Aid and Civil Conflicts', in J. Whitman and D. Pocock (eds), *After Rwanda: The Coordination of United Nations Humanitarian Assistance*, Macmillan, Basingstoke, 1996, pp. 226–44.

29 Dayton Peace Agreement, Annex VII, Article I.2.

30 High Commissioner Ogata, 'Peace, Security and Humanitarian Action', Alistair Buchan Memorial Lecture at the International Institute of Strategic Studies, London, 3 April 1997.

31 J. Sharp, 'Dayton Report Card', *International Security*, vol. 22. no. 3, pp. 101–37.

32 High Commissioner Ogata, statement to Peace Implementation Council, Madrid, 15 Dec. 1998.

33 For a description of the return process between 1996 and 1999, see also the following reports by the International Crisis Group, 'Going Nowhere Fast: Refugees and Displaced Persons in Bosnia and Herzegovina', 1 May 1997, 'Minority Returns or Mass Relocation', 14 May 1998, and 'Preventing Minority Return in Bosnia and Herzegovina: The Anatomy of Hate and Fear', 2 Aug. 1999.

34 International Crisis Group, 'Bosnia's Refugee Logjam Breaks: Is the International Community Ready?', Balkans Report no. 95, 30 May 2000.

35 A. Roberts, 'NATO's Humanitarian War', *Survival*, vol. 41, no. 3, 1999.

36 OSCE Office of Democratic Institutions and Human Rights, *Kosovo/Kosova, As Seen As Told: an Analysis of the Human Rights Findings of the OSCE Kosovo Verification Mission, October 1998 to June 1999*, vol. 1, OSCE/ODIHR, Warsaw, Nov. 1999.

37 These figures are for those who fled between 24 March, when the NATO air campaign began, and 12 June 1999.

38 A. Suhrke et. al, *The Kosovo Refugee Crisis: An Independent Evaluation of UNHCR's Preparedness and Emergency Response*, Geneva, Feb. 2000, available on <http://www.unhcr.ch> .

39 High Commissioner Ogata and NATO Secretary-General, correspondence, 2 and 3 April 1999.

40 Interview in Dec. 1999 with I. Khan, former UNHCR Emergency Coordinator in FYR Macedonia.

41 High Commissioner Ogata, Introductory Remarks, Colloquium on the Global Refugee Crisis—A Challenge for the 21st Century, Brussels, 20 May 1999.

42 UN Srebrenica Report, para. 502.

43 See, for example, High Commissioner Ogata, 'Half a Century on the Humanitarian Frontlines', lecture, Graduate Institute for International Studies, Geneva, 25 Nov. 1999.

Chapter 9 boxes

i Secretary-General, 'Renewing the United Nations: A Programme for Reform', 14 July 1997, UN Doc. A/51/950.

ii R. Cohen and F.M. Deng, *Masses in Flight: The Global Crisis of Internal Displacement*, Brookings Institution, Washington DC, 1998.

iii UNHCR, 'Internally Displaced Persons: The Role of the United Nations High Commissioner for Refugees', 6 March 2000.

iv G. Defert, *Timor-est—Le génocide oublié: Droit d'un peuple et raisons d'état*, Harmattan, Paris, 1992, pp. 147–51, fig. 5.

v General Assembly, 'Situation of Human Rights in East Timor', Note by the Secretary-General, UN Doc. A/54/660, 10 Dec. 1999, para. 37.

Chapter 10

1 United Nations, 'Report of the Independent Inquiry into the Actions of the United Nations during the 1994 Genocide in Rwanda', New York, 15 Dec. 1999, available on <http://www.un.org/News/ossg/rwanda_report.htm>.

2 See in general, G. Prunier, *The Rwanda Crisis: History of a Genocide*, Hurst and Co., London, 1995; G. Prunier, 'The Geopolitical Situation in the Great Lakes Area in Light of the Kivu Crisis', *Refugee Survey Quarterly*, vol. 16, no. 1, 1997, pp. 1–25; African Rights, *Rwanda: Death, Despair and Defiance*, African Rights, London, 1994; Human Rights Watch Africa, *Leave None to Tell the Story*, Human Rights Watch, New York, 1999; P. Gourevitch, *We Wish To Inform You That Tomorrow We Will Be Killed With Our Families*, Picador, New York, 1999.

3 UNHCR, Special Unit for Rwanda and Burundi, information meeting, Geneva, 16 Nov. 1994.

4 High Commissioner S. Ogata to UN Secretary-General B. Boutros-Ghali, letter, 18 July 1994, High Commissioner's private archive.

5 Joint Evaluation of Emergency Assistance to Rwanda, *The International Response to Conflict and Genocide: Lessons from the Rwanda Experience, Study 3: Humanitarian Aid and Effects*, Copenhagen, March 1996, pp. 68–86.

6 High Commissioner Ogata to UN Secretary-General Boutros-Ghali, letter, 30 Aug. 1994, High Commissioner's private archive.

7 Zairean political parties (UDPS, PDSC) to UNHCR, memo, 28 Oct. 1994.

8 J. Boutroue to K. Morjane, letter, 21 Nov. 1994.

9 Human Rights Watch Arms Project, *Rwanda/Zaire: Rearming with Impunity—International Support for the Perpetrators of the Rwandan Genocide*, Human Rights Watch, New York, May 1995.

10 See generally, United Nations, 'Report of the Independent Inquiry'; Human Rights Watch, *Leave None to Tell*, pp. 668–91; African Rights, *Rwanda: Death, Despair and Defiance*, pp. 1138–54; Commission de la Défense nationale et des forces armées et Commission des affaires étrangères de l'Assemblée nationale française, 'Les opérations militaires menées par la France, d'autres pays et l'ONU au Rwanda entre 1990 et 1994', Paris, 15 Dec. 1998, available on <http://www.assembleenationale.fr/9/9recherche.html>.

11 High Commissioner Ogata to UN Secretary-General Boutros-Ghali, letter, 24 Oct. 1994, High Commissioner's private archive.

12 High Commissioner Ogata to Prime Minister of Zaire Kengo Wa Dondo, letter, 12 April 1996.

13 UNHCR, 'Goma Situation Report no. 19, 15 Jan./15 Feb. 1995', 20 Feb. 1995, OPS 16 COD, 'Sitrep Zaire: Bukavu, Goma, Uvira, août 1994–juillet 1996', F/HCR 19/7.

14 UNHCR, 'Goma Situation Report no. 22', 19 April 1995, loc. cit.

15 J. Boutroue, 'Missed Opportunities: The Role of the International Community in the Return of the Rwandan Refugees from Eastern Zaire', Working Paper, no. 1, Inter-University Committee on International Migration, Massachusetts Institute of Technology, Center for International Studies, Cambridge MA, June 1998, p. 19; S. Lautze, B.D. Jones and M. Duffield, 'Strategic Humanitarian Coordination in the Great Lakes Region, 1996–97: An Independent Assessment', UNHCR, Geneva, March 1998.

16 See J.C. Willame, *Banyarwanda et Banyamulenge*, Editions L'Harmattan/CEDAF, Paris/Brussels, 1997.

17 A. Liria-Franch to K. Morjane/W.R. Urasa, fax, 12 April 1996, 1996 Rwanda Masisi 1, F/HCR 19/7.

18 High Commissioner Ogata, to UN Secretary-General Boutros-Ghali, letter, 9 May 1996, 1996 Rwanda Masisi 1, F/HCR 19/7.

19 High Commissioner Ogata, opening statement, UNHCR Executive Committee, 47th session, Geneva, 7 Oct. 1996, ExCom 1 Aug. 1994–Dec. 1997, F/HCR 19/7 or UN Doc. A/AC.96/878, Annex II.

20 D. McNamara, Director, UNHCR Division of International Protection, 'Statement to Subcommittee on International Operations and Human Rights of US House of Representatives Committee on International Relations, hearing on "Rwanda: Genocide and the Continuing Cycle of Violence"', 5 May 1998, Director's Chron. 1998, F/HCR 17.

21 *The Guardian* (Dar es Salaam), 26 Nov. 1996.

22 A. Sokiri, UNHCR Representative in Dar es Salaam, to S. Vieira de Mello, Assistant High Commissioner, et al., 27 Nov. 1996, enclosing 'Note for the File: Meeting with Col. Magere', Rwanda 1994–96 REP.TAN 1, F/HCR 19/7.

23 S. Vieira de Mello, 'The Humanitarian Situation in the Great Lakes Region', speaking notes for statement to Standing Committee of Executive Committee, 30 Jan. 1997, EXCOM 1 Aug. 1994–Dec. 1997, F/HCR 19/7.

24 UNHCR, 'Message to all Rwandese Refugees in Tanzania from the Government of the United Republic of Tanzania and the Office of the United Nations High Commissioner for Refugees', 5 Dec. 1996, transmitted by L. Kotsalainen, Deputy Representative, Tanzania, to S. Vieira de Mello et al., UNHCR HQ, fax, MAHIGA–TANZANIA–3, F/HCR 19/7.

25 Amnesty International, 'Rwanda: Human Rights Overlooked in Mass Repatriation', International Secretariat, London, 14 Jan. 1997; Amnesty International, 'Tanzania: Refugees Should Not be Returned to Near Certain Death', news release, London, 20 Jan. 1997; Amnesty International, 'Great Lakes Region: Still in Need of Protection— Repatriation, Refoulement and the Safety of Refugees and the Internally Displaced', London, 24 Jan. 1997; Human Rights Watch, 'Uncertain Refuge: International Failures to Protect Refugees', New York, April 1997, p. 4; Human Rights Watch, 'Tanzania: In the Name of Security—Forced Round-ups of Refugees in Tanzania', New York, July 1999.

26 Integrated Regional Information Network (IRIN), Information Bulletin, no. 29, 18 Nov. 1996.

27 UN Department of Humanitarian Affairs, Integrated Regional Information Network, 'IRIN Update 50 on Eastern Zaire', 6 Dec. 1996.

28 C. Correy, US Information Agency dispatch, 22 Nov. 1996.

29 F. Reyntjens, La guerre des Grands Lacs, Harmattan, Paris, 1999; J.-C. Willame, L'odyssée Kabila, Karthala, Paris, 1999.

Chapter 10 boxes

i United Nations, Department of Public Information, 'Mission Backgrounder', United Nations Operation in Somalia I, 21 March 1997. See also M. Sahnoun, Somalia: The Missed Opportunities, United States Institute of Peace, Washington DC, 1994; I. Lewis and J. Mayall, 'Somalia', in J. Mayall (ed.), The New Interventionism 1991–1994: United Nations Experience in Cambodia, Former Yugoslavia and Somalia, Cambridge University Press, Cambridge, 1996, pp. 108–9.

ii Economist, 28 Aug. 1999.

iii P. Richards, Fighting for the Rain Forest: War, Youth and Resources in Sierra Leone, James Currey, Oxford, 1996.

Chapter 11

1 J. Morrison, 'The Trafficking and Smuggling of Refugees: The End Game in European Asylum policy?', report for UNHCR Evaluation and Policy Analysis Unit, Geneva, July 2000, available on <http://www.unhcr.ch>.

2 N. Davies, Europe: A History, Oxford University Press, Oxford, 1996, pp. 565 and 568.

3 J. Harding, The Uninvited: Refugees at the Rich Man's Gate, Profile Books, London, 2000, p. 7.

4 J. Torpey, The Invention of the Passport, Cambridge University Press, Cambridge, 2000, p. 9.

5 UNHCR, 'Internally Displaced Persons: The Role of the United Nations High Commissioner for Refugees', 6 March 2000.

6 R. Holbrooke, speech to Cardoza Law School, New York, 28 March 2000.

7 G.S. Goodwin-Gill, 'UNHCR and Internal Displacement: Stepping into a Legal and Political Minefield', US Committee for Refugees, World Refugee Survey 2000, Washington DC, 2000, pp. 25–31.

8 The term 'CNN effect' refers to the growing power of television stations such as the Cable News Network (CNN) to dictate policy agendas.

9 High Commissioner S. Ogata, 'On the Humanitarian Frontlines: Refugee Problems Between Changing Wars and Fragile Peace', lecture at the University of California at Berkeley, 17 March 1999.

Annexes

Technical notes on statistical information

Most countries have adopted the refugee definition contained in the 1951 UN Refugee Convention, but there are important national differences in refugee registration and determination. In the industrialized countries, where UNHCR usually relies on data provided by the authorities, information on the determination of individual asylum requests is the main source of statistical information. In much of the developing world, however, refugees are often accepted on a group basis. In such cases, rather than individual screening, maintaining a credible refugee registration for the provision of material assistance becomes a priority. These registers, often maintained by UNHCR at the request of the host government, are an important source of refugee data in developing countries. While subject to double registration, refugee registers are often verified and supplemented with information from health records and surveys.

In recent years, UNHCR's involvement with persons who have not crossed an international border, such as internally displaced persons, those threatened with displacement as a result of armed conflict and refugees who have returned home ("returnees") has increased. In view of this, and taking into consideration the complexity and variation in legal distinctions made by industrialized states between the various statuses granted to refugees ("refugee status", "humanitarian status", "temporary protection", "provisional admission", etc.), the term "refugees and others of concern to UNHCR" has been adopted to reflect the various categories of persons with whom UNHCR is concerned. Palestinian refugees who come under the mandate of the United Nations Relief and Works Agency for Palestine Refugees in the Near East (UNRWA) are, however, not included in the statistics.

While efforts have been made to make the statistics as comprehensive as possible, some populations and movements may remain unrecorded, because UNHCR is not directly involved, because records are lacking, etc. In particular, precise figures on refugee returns and on those who are internally displaced are difficult to obtain due to unregistered movements and lack of access to those people. The return data presented in Annexes 1 and 9 mostly reflect arrivals rather than departures.

For industrialized countries which do not keep track of recognized refugees, UNHCR has adopted a simple method to estimate the refugee population, based on recent arrivals of refugees and/or recognition of refugees, including those allowed to remain on humanitarian grounds. For Australia, Canada, New Zealand and the United States, recent refugee population estimates are based on the number of resettled refugees and recognized refugees over a five-year period. For Austria, Denmark, Finland, Ireland, Japan, the Netherlands, Norway, Portugal, Spain, Sweden and the United Kingdom, a 10-year period has been applied, taking into account the longer period it takes to naturalize refugees in these countries. The method of estimation for some of the earlier data could not be established (see Annexes 3, 4 and 5). In Annex 6, the origin of refugees in these countries is estimated using data of recently recognized refugees.

The regional classification adopted in the annexes is that of the Population Division of the United Nations Secretariat. Asia includes much of the "Middle East" (though not North Africa), as well as Turkey. Annex 1 shows the precise classification of countries by region. In the tables, figures below 1,000 are rounded to the nearest 10, whereas figures of 1,000 and above are rounded to the nearest 100. A dash (-) indicates that the value is zero, rounded to zero or not applicable. Two dots (..) indicate that the value is not available.

Much of the historical data presented here is based on archival material and has not been published before. More recent data is available in UNHCR's Statistical Overview, published annually since 1994 (see: http://www.unhcr.ch/statist/main.htm).

States party to the 1951 UN Refugee Convention, the 1967 Protocol, the 1969 OAU Refugee Convention and members of UNHCR's Executive Committee (EXCOM), as on 31 December 1999

United Nations member states	1951 UN Refugee Convention[a]	1967 Protocol[b]	1969 OAU Refugee Convention[c]	UNHCR's EXCOM members[d]
Afghanistan				
Albania	1992	1992		
Algeria	1963	1967	1974	1963
Andorra				
Angola	1981	1981	1981	
Antigua and Barbuda	1995	1995		
Argentina	1961	1967		1979
Armenia	1993	1993		
Australia	1973	1973		1951
Austria	1954	1973		1951
Azerbaijan	1993	1993		
Bahamas	1993	1993		
Bahrain				
Bangladesh				1995
Barbados				
Belarus				
Belgium	1953	1969		1951
Belize	1990	1990		
Benin	1962	1970	1973	
Bhutan				
Bolivia	1982	1982		
Bosnia and Herzegovina	1993	1993		
Botswana	1969	1969	1995	
Brazil	1960	1972		1951
Brunei Darussalam				
Bulgaria	1993	1993		
Burkina Faso	1980	1980	1974	
Burundi	1963	1971	1975	
Cambodia	1992	1992		
Cameroon	1961	1967	1985	
Canada	1969	1969		1957
Cape Verde		1987	1989	
Central African Republic	1962	1967	1970	
Chad	1981	1981	1981	
Chile[e]	1972	1972		
China	1982	1982		1958
Colombia	1961	1980		1955
Comoros				
Congo	1962	1970	1971	
Costa Rica	1978	1978		
Côte d'Ivoire[e]	1961	1970	1998	
Croatia	1992	1992		
Cuba				
Cyprus	1963	1968		
Czech Republic	1993	1993		

United Nations member states	1951 UN Refugee Convention[a]	1967 Protocol[b]	1969 OAU Refugee Convention[c]	UNHCR's EXCOM members[d]
Democratic People's Rep. of Korea				
Democratic Republic of the Congo	1965	1975	1973	1979
Denmark	1952	1968		1951
Djibouti	1977	1977		
Dominica	1994	1994		
Dominican Republic	1978	1978		
Ecuador	1955	1969		
Egypt	1981	1981	1980	
El Salvador	1983	1983		
Equatorial Guinea	1986	1986	1980	
Eritrea				
Estonia	1997	1997		
Ethiopia	1969	1969	1973	1993
Fiji	1972	1972		
Finland	1968	1968		1979
France	1954	1971		1951
FYR of Macedonia	1994	1994		
Gabon	1964	1973	1986	
Gambia	1966	1967	1980	
Georgia	1999	1999		
Germany, FR	1969	1969		1951
Ghana	1963	1968	1975	
Greece	1960	1968		1955
Grenada				
Guatemala	1983	1983		
Guinea	1965	1968	1972	
Guinea–Bissau	1976	1976	1989	
Guyana				
Haiti	1984	1984		
Holy See[f]	1956	1967		1951
Honduras	1992	1992		
Hungary	1989	1989		1993
Iceland	1955	1968		
India				1995
Indonesia				
Iran, Islamic Republic of	1976	1976		1955
Iraq				
Ireland	1956	1968		1996
Israel	1954	1968		1951
Italy	1954	1972		1951
Jamaica	1964	1980		
Japan	1981	1982		1979
Jordan				
Kazakhstan	1999	1999		
Kenya	1966	1981	1992	
Kiribati				
Kuwait				
Kyrgyzstan	1996	1996		
Lao People's Democratic Republic				
Latvia	1997	1997		
Lebanon				1963
Lesotho	1981	1981	1988	1979

United Nations member states	1951 UN Refugee Convention[a]	1967 Protocol[b]	1969 OAU Refugee Convention[c]	UNHCR's EXCOM members[d]
Liberia	1964	1980	1971	
Libyan Arab Jamahiriya			1981	
Liechtenstein	1957	1968		
Lithuania	1997	1997		
Luxembourg	1953	1971		
Madagascar	1967			1963
Malawi	1987	1987	1987	
Malaysia				
Maldives				
Mali	1973	1973	1981	
Malta	1971	1971		
Marshall Islands				
Mauritania	1987	1987	1972	
Mauritius				
Mexico[g]				
Micronesia (Federated States of)				
Monaco	1954			
Mongolia				
Morocco	1956	1971	1974[h]	1979
Mozambique	1983	1989	1989	1999
Myanmar				
Namibia	1995			1982
Nauru				
Nepal				
Netherlands	1968	1968		1955
New Zealand	1960	1973		
Nicaragua	1980	1980		1979
Niger	1961	1970	1971	
Nigeria	1967	1968	1986	1963
Norway	1953	1967		1955
Oman				
Pakistan				1988
Palau				
Panama	1978	1978		
Papua New Guinea	1986	1986		
Paraguay	1970	1970		
Peru	1964	1983		
Philippines	1981	1981		1991
Poland	1991	1991		1997
Portugal	1976	1976		
Qatar				
Republic of Korea[e]	1992	1992		
Republic of Moldova				
Romania	1991	1991		
Russian Federation	1993	1993		1995
Rwanda	1980	1980	1979	
Saint Kitts and Nevis				
Saint Lucia				
Saint Vincent and the Grenadines	1993			
Samoa	1988	1994		
San Marino				
São Tomé and Príncipe	1978	1978		

United Nations member states	1951 UN Refugee Convention[a]	1967 Protocol[b]	1969 OAU Refugee Convention[c]	UNHCR's EXCOM members[d]
Saudi Arabia				
Senegal	1963	1967	1971	
Seychelles	1980	1980	1980	
Sierra Leone	1981	1981	1987	
Singapore				
Slovakia	1993	1993		
Slovenia	1992	1992		
Solomon Islands	1995	1995		
Somalia	1978	1978		1988
South Africa	1996	1996	1995	1997
Spain	1978	1978		1994
Sri Lanka				
Sudan	1974	1974	1972	1979
Suriname	1978	1978		
Swaziland		1969	1989	
Sweden	1954	1967		1958
Switzerland[f]	1955	1968		1951
Syrian Arab Republic				
Tajikistan	1993	1993		
Thailand				1979
Togo	1962	1969	1970	
Tonga				
Trinidad and Tobago				
Tunisia	1957	1968	1989	1958
Turkey	1962	1968		1951
Turkmenistan	1998	1998		
Tuvalu[f]	1986	1986		
Uganda	1976	1976	1987	1967
Ukraine				
United Arab Emirates				
United Kingdom	1968	1968		1951
United Republic of Tanzania	1964	1968	1975	1963
United States of America		1968		1951
Uruguay	1970	1970		
Uzbekistan				
Vanuatu				
Venezuela		1986		1951
Viet Nam				
Yemen	1980	1980		
Yugoslavia, Federal Republic of	1959	1968		1958
Zambia	1969	1969	1973	
Zimbabwe	1981	1981	1985	
Total	134	134	45	54

[a] Year of ratification, accession and/or succession to the 1951 UN Refugee Convention.

[b] Year of accession and/or succession to the 1967 Protocol.

[c] Year of ratification of the 1969 Refugee Convention of the Organization of African Unity (OAU).

[d] Refers to Executive Committee of the High Commissioner's Programme.

[e] On 17 Dec. 1999 the UN General Assembly passed Resolution 54/143 allowing for Chile, Côte d'Ivoire and Republic of Korea to become members of UNHCR's Executive Committee.

[f] Not member states of the United Nations.

[g] On 31 Dec. 1999 Mexico was not party to the 1951 UN Refugee Convention or its 1967 Protocol. In June 2000, howerver, it acceded to both instruments.

[h] Morocco withdrew from the OAU and its obligations in 1984.

Situation as on 31 Dec. 1999.

Number of refugees and others of concern to UNHCR, 31 December 1999

Region and country/ territory of asylum/residence	Refugees[a]	Asylum seekers[b]	Returned refugees[c]	Internally displaced	Others of concern[d] Returned IDPs	Various	Total population of concern
Burundi	22,100	510	36,000	50,000	50,000	10,600	169,210
Comores	10	–	–	–	–	–	10
Djibouti	23,300	410	–	–	–	–	23,710
Eritrea	3,000	–	7,800	–	–	–	10,800
Ethiopia	257,700	2,000	14,700	–	–	–	274,400
Kenya	223,700	5,800	–	–	–	–	229,500
Madagascar	30	–	–	–	–	–	30
Malawi	1,700	1,300	–	–	–	–	3,000
Mauritius	40	–	–	–	–	–	40
Mozambique	220	1,200	–	–	–	–	1,420
Rwanda	34,400	1,800	49,100	–	626,100	–	711,400
Somalia	130	–	77,400	–	–	–	77,530
Uganda	218,200	180	1,200	–	–	–	219,580
United Rep. of Tanzania	622,200	12,300	–	–	–	–	634,500
Zambia	206,400	180	–	–	–	–	206,580
Zimbabwe	2,000	40	–	–	–	–	2,040
Eastern Africa sub-total	**1,615,130**	**25,720**	**186,200**	**50,000**	**676,100**	**10,600**	**2,563,750**
Angola	13,100	930	41,100	–	–	–	55,130
Cameroon	49,200	740	–	–	–	–	49,940
Central African Rep.	49,300	1,300	–	–	–	–	50,600
Chad	23,500	570	2,300	–	–	–	26,370
Congo	39,900	220	77,200	–	–	–	117,320
Dem. Rep. of the Congo	285,200	170	79,800	–	–	–	365,170
Gabon	15,100	2,100	–	–	–	–	17,200
Middle Africa sub-total	**475,300**	**6,030**	**200,400**	**–**	**–**	**–**	**681,730**
Algeria	165,200	–	–	–	–	–	165,200
Egypt	6,600	4,600	–	–	–	–	11,200
Libyan Arab Jamahiriya	10,500	220	–	–	–	–	10,720
Morocco	900	–	–	–	–	–	900
Sudan	391,000	–	250	–	–	–	391,250
Tunisia	450	20	–	–	–	–	470
Northern Africa sub-total	**574,650**	**4,840**	**250**	**–**	**–**	**–**	**579,740**
Botswana	1,300	180	–	–	–	–	1,480
Namibia	7,400	340	1,400	–	–	–	9,140
South Africa	14,500	17,300	–	–	–	–	31,800
Swaziland	620	50	–	–	–	–	670
Southern Africa sub-total	**23,820**	**17,870**	**1,400**	**–**	**–**	**–**	**43,090**
Benin	3,700	1,600	–	–	–	–	5,300
Burkina Faso	680	280	–	–	–	–	960
Côte d'Ivoire	138,400	660	–	–	–	–	139,060
Gambia	17,200	–	–	–	–	–	17,200
Ghana	13,300	480	1,100	–	–	–	14,880
Guinea	501,500	430	–	–	–	–	501,930
Guinea–Bissau	7,100	–	5,300	–	265,000	–	277,400
Liberia	96,300	30	296,900	212,900	–	–	606,130
Mali	8,300	610	31,900	–	–	–	40,810
Mauritania	220	30	7,000	–	–	26,400	33,650
Niger	350	–	3,800	–	–	–	4,150
Nigeria	6,900	–	–	–	–	–	6,900
Senegal	21,500	2,100	430	–	–	–	24,030

Region and country/ territory of asylum/residence	Refugees[a]	Asylum seekers[b]	Returned refugees[c]	Others of concern[d] Internally displaced	Returned IDPs	Various	Total population of concern
Sierra Leone	6,600	30	198,100	500,000	–	–	704,730
Togo	12,100	280	–	–	–	–	12,380
Western Africa sub-total	**834,150**	**6,530**	**544,530**	**712,900**	**265,000**	**26,400**	**2,389,510**
Africa total	**3,523,050**	**60,990**	**932,780**	**762,900**	**941,100**	**37,000**	**6,257,820**
China	293,300	10	–	–	–	–	293,310
Hong Kong, China	970	–	–	–	–	–	970
Japan[e]	4,200	300	–	–	–	–	4,500
Rep. of Korea	10	10	–	–	–	–	20
Eastern Asia sub-total	**298,480**	**320**	**–**	**–**	**–**	**–**	**298,800**
Afghanistan	–	10	359,800	258,600	10,000	–	628,410
Bangladesh	22,200	10	13,400	–	–	–	35,610
India	180,000	20	–	–	–	–	180,020
Islamic Rep. of Iran	1,835,700	–	–	–	–	–	1,835,700
Kazakhstan	14,800	–	25,200	–	–	–	40,000
Kyrgyzstan	10,800	180	1,200	5,600	–	–	17,780
Nepal	127,900	20	–	–	–	–	127,920
Pakistan	1,202,000	460	–	–	–	–	1,202,460
Sri Lanka	20	–	160	612,500	–	–	612,680
Tajikistan	4,500	2,200	8,400	–	–	–	15,100
Turkmenistan	18,500	820	–	–	–	–	19,320
Uzbekistan	1,000	260	–	–	–	–	1,260
South–central Asia sub-total	**3,417,420**	**3,980**	**408,160**	**876,700**	**10,000**	**–**	**4,716,260**
Cambodia	20	50	53,700	–	–	–	53,770
East Timor	–	–	127,500	–	–	–	127,500
Indonesia	162,500	20	–	–	–	–	162,520
Lao People's Dem. Rep.	–	–	1,400	–	–	–	1,400
Malaysia	50,500	30	–	–	–	–	50,530
Myanmar	–	–	1,200	–	–	–	1,200
Philippines	170	–	–	–	–	–	170
Singapore	–	–	–	–	–	–	–
Thailand	100,100	580	–	–	–	40	100,720
Viet Nam[f]	15,000	–	160	–	–	–	15,160
South–eastern Asia sub-total	**328,290**	**680**	**183,960**	**–**	**–**	**40**	**512,970**
Armenia	296,200	10	–	–	–	–	296,210
Azerbaijan	221,600	350	–	569,600	–	–	791,550
Cyprus	120	210	390	–	–	–	720
Georgia	5,200	–	1,800	278,500	600	110	286,210
Iraq	128,900	280	32,700	–	–	–	161,880
Israel	130	240	–	–	–	–	370
Jordan	1,000	4,300	–	–	–	–	5,300
Kuwait	4,300	60	–	–	–	138,100	142,460
Lebanon	4,200	3,300	–	–	–	–	7,500
Qatar	10	–	–	–	–	–	10
Saudi Arabia	5,600	140	–	–	–	–	5,740
Syrian Arab Rep.	6,500	5,000	–	–	–	2,100	13,600
Turkey	2,800	5,100	730	–	–	–	8,630
United Arab Emirates	500	340	–	–	–	–	840
Yemen	60,500	340	–	–	–	9,000	69,840
Western Asia sub-total	**737,560**	**19,670**	**35,620**	**848,100**	**600**	**149,310**	**1,790,860**
Asia total	**4,781,750**	**24,650**	**627,740**	**1,724,800**	**10,600**	**149,350**	**7,318,890**
Belarus	260	16,400	–	–	–	160,000	176,660
Bulgaria	540	1,600	–	–	–	–	2,140
Czech Rep.	1,200	1,400	–	–	–	2,300	4,900

Region and country/ territory of asylum/residence	Refugees[a]	Asylum seekers[b]	Returned refugees[c]	Others of concern[d] Internally displaced	Returned IDPs	Various	Total population of concern
Hungary	5,000	2,600	–	–	–	–	7,600
Poland	950	–	–	–	–	–	950
Rep. of Moldova	10	220	–	–	–	–	230
Romania	1,200	50	–	–	–	–	1,250
Russian Federation	80,100	16,000	–	498,400	64,500	845,300	1,504,300
Slovakia	440	330	–	–	–	–	770
Ukraine	2,700	300	–	–	–	260,000	263,000
Eastern Europe sub-total	**92,400**	**38,900**	**–**	**498,400**	**64,500**	**1,267,600**	**1,961,800**
Denmark[e]	69,000	–	–	–	–	–	69,000
Estonia	–	30	–	–	–	–	30
Finland[e]	12,800	–	–	–	–	–	12,800
Iceland	350	10	–	–	–	–	360
Ireland[e]	1,100	9,800	–	–	–	–	10,900
Latvia	10	–	–	–	–	–	10
Lithuania	40	50	–	–	–	–	90
Norway[e]	47,900	–	–	–	–	–	47,900
Sweden[e]	159,500	7,900	–	–	–	–	167,400
United Kingdom[e,g]	132,700	129,000	–	–	–	–	261,700
Northern Europe sub-total	**423,400**	**146,790**	**–**	**–**	**–**	**–**	**570,190**
Albania	3,900	20	–	–	–	–	3,920
Bosnia and Herzegovina	65,600	20	161,100	809,500	73,000	–	1,109,220
Croatia	28,400	30	33,600	50,300	70,300	–	182,630
FYR Macedonia	21,200	–	–	–	–	–	21,200
Greece	3,500	–	–	–	–	–	3,500
Italy	22,900	5,000	–	–	–	–	27,900
Malta	270	–	–	–	–	–	270
Portugal[e]	380	–	–	–	–	–	380
Slovenia	4,400	610	–	–	–	11,300	16,310
Spain[e]	6,400	3,300	–	–	–	–	9,700
Yugoslavia, Federal Rep. of	500,700	30	755,500	234,900	168,900	–	1,660,030
Southern Europe sub-total	**657,650**	**9,010**	**950,200**	**1,094,700**	**312,200**	**11,300**	**3,035,060**
Austria	80,300	5,500	–	–	–	–	85,800
Belgium	36,100	23,100	–	–	–	–	59,200
France	140,200	–	–	–	–	–	140,200
Germany[h]	975,500	264,000	–	–	–	–	1,239,500
Liechtenstein	–	–	–	–	–	–	–
Luxembourg	700	–	–	–	–	–	700
Netherlands[e]	129,100	–	–	–	–	–	129,100
Switzerland	82,300	45,400	–	–	–	–	127,700
Western Europe sub-total	**1,444,200**	**338,000**	**–**	**–**	**–**	**–**	**1,782,200**
Europe total	**2,617,650**	**532,700**	**950,200**	**1,593,100**	**376,700**	**1,278,900**	**7,349,250**
Bahamas	100	–	–	–	–	–	100
Cuba	970	10	–	–	–	–	980
Dominican Rep.	630	10	–	–	–	–	640
Jamaica	40	–	–	–	–	–	40
Caribbean sub-total	**1,740**	**20**	**–**	**–**	**–**	**–**	**1,760**
Belize	2,900	–	–	–	–	20,000	22,900
Costa Rica	22,900	30	–	–	–	–	22,930
El Salvador	20	–	–	–	–	–	20
Guatemala	730	10	5,900	–	–	–	6,640
Honduras	10	–	–	–	–	–	10
Mexico	24,000	–	–	–	–	–	24,000
Nicaragua	470	10	70	–	–	–	550
Panama	1,300	60	–	–	–	–	1,360

Region and country/ territory of asylum/residence	Refugees[a]	Asylum seekers[b]	Returned refugees[c]	Internally displaced	Others of concern[d] Returned IDPs	Various	Total population of concern
Central America sub-total	**52,330**	**110**	**5,970**	**–**	**–**	**20,000**	**78,410**
Argentina	2,300	960	–	–	–	–	3,260
Bolivia	350	10	–	–	–	–	360
Brazil	2,500	370	–	–	–	–	2,870
Chile	320	50	–	–	–	–	370
Colombia	230	10	–	–	–	–	240
Ecuador	310	–	–	–	–	1,200	1,510
Paraguay	20	–	–	–	–	–	20
Peru	700	–	–	–	–	–	700
Uruguay	90	–	–	–	–	–	90
Venezuela	190	–	–	–	–	–	190
South America sub-total	**7,010**	**1,400**	**–**	**–**	**–**	**1,200**	**9,610**
Latin America and Caribbean total	**61,080**	**1,530**	**5,970**	**–**	**–**	**21,200**	**89,780**
Canada[i]	136,600	24,700	–	–	–	–	161,300
United States[ij]	513,000	580,900	–	–	–	–	1,093,900
North America total	**649,600**	**605,600**	**–**	**–**	**–**	**–**	**1,255,200**
Australia[i]	59,700	–	–	–	–	–	59,700
New Zealand[i]	4,800	–	–	–	–	–	4,800
Australia–New Zealand sub-total	**64,500**	**–**	**–**	**–**	**–**	**–**	**64,500**
Papua New Guinea	–	–	–	–	–	–	–
Solomon Islands	–	–	–	–	–	–	–
Melanesia sub-total	**–**	**–**	**–**	**–**	**–**	**–**	**–**
Oceania total	**64,500**	**–**	**–**	**–**	**–**	**–**	**64,500**
Grand total	**11,697,630**	**1,225,470**	**2,516,690**	**4,080,800**	**1,328,400**	**1,486,450**	**22,335,440**

Notes:

[a] Refugees: persons recognized as refugees under the 1951 UN Refugee Convention, the 1969 OAU Refugee Convention, in accordance with the UNHCR Statute, persons granted a humanitarian status and those granted temporary protection.

[b] Asylum seekers: persons whose application for refugee status is pending in the asylum procedure or who are otherwise registered as asylum seekers.

[c] Returned refugees: refugees who have returned to their place of origin and who remain of concern to UNHCR for a maximum period of two years.

[d] Others of concern: certain specific group of persons not coming within the ordinary mandate of UNHCR.

– Internally displaced persons (IDPs): persons who are displaced within their country and to whom UNHCR extends protection and/or assistance in pursuance to a special request by a competent organ of the United Nations.

– Returned IDPs: IDPs of concern to UNHCR who have returned to their place of origin and who remain of concern to UNHCR for a maximum period of two years.

[e] Number of refugees estimated by UNHCR, based on the arrival of refugees and/or recognition of asylum seekers as refugees over the past 10 years.

[f] In this case, the returned refugees also include returned rejected asylum seekers.

[g] Asylum seekers: number of pending applications in first instance (102,900) multiplied by the average number of persons per case (1.25).

[h] Asylum seekers: cases pending in all instances (Source: Central Aliens Register).

[i] Number of refugees estimated by UNHCR, based on the arrival of refugees and/or recognition of asylum seekers as refugees over the past 5 years.

[j] Asylum seekers: number of pending cases in first instance (342,000) and in review (59,000) multiplied by the average number of persons per case (1.45).

Refugee population figures for Austria, France, Luxembourg, Portugal and Romania refer to 1998, those for Belgium refer to 1995.

See technical notes for further explanations and data limitations.

Source: Governments, UNHCR

Estimated number of refugees by region, 1950–99

Region	1950	1951	1952	1953	1954	1955	1956	1957	1958	1959
Africa	..	5,000	2,900	2,800	5,400	–	–	–	3,700	3,700
Asia	..	41,500	16,000	18,000	40,500	20,100	18,200	14,900	12,200	10,000
Europe	..	1,221,200	1,128,200	1,067,500	975,800	917,900	991,000	904,800	871,400	839,200
Latin America/Caribbean	..	120,000	120,000	120,000	120,000	120,000	120,000	120,000	120,000	120,000
North America	..	518,500	654,800	607,000	575,800	552,600	517,500	546,300	546,900	547,900
Oceania	..	180,000	–	–	–	–	–	–	–	–
Various/unknown	..	30,000	31,000	32,000	32,000	33,000	31,000	27,000	23,000	26,200
Total	..	2,116,200	1,952,900	1,847,300	1,749,500	1,643,600	1,677,700	1,613,000	1,577,200	1,547,000

Region	1960	1961	1962	1963	1964	1965	1966	1967	1968	1969
Africa	9,000	6,500	7,100	6,000	1,269,600	1,407,800	1,408,100	164,000	174,000	167,900
Asia	9,000	6,500	7,100	6,000	1,267,300	1,407,800	1,408,100	164,000	173,300	167,300
Europe	804,200	775,800	753,100	710,600	706,500	738,400	684,900	641,500	633,500	639,500
Latin America/Caribbean	120,000	120,000	120,000	120,000	120,000	125,000	125,100	115,000	110,000	106,000
North America	548,600	544,500	512,300	510,900	510,200	520,000	510,200	490,000	516,000	519,300
Oceania	–	–	–	–	–	40,000	40,000	47,000	45,000	44,000
Various/unknown	25,200	23,000	19,500	3,600	–	130,000	6,000	54,000	12,000	79,000
Total	1,516,000	1,476,300	1,419,100	1,357,100	3,873,600	4,368,900	4,182,500	1,675,500	2,461,100	2,461,100

Region	1970	1971	1972	1973	1974	1975	1976	1977	1978	1979
Africa	998,100	991,900	1,088,300	1,012,200	1,108,600	1,616,700	1,716,100	2,105,000	2,416,400	3,062,100
Asia	158,900	203,400	208,700	102,000	75,300	90,600	802,200	991,500	723,300	1,451,500
Europe	645,700	617,500	592,200	567,900	553,500	546,700	550,000	550,600	516,000	558,500
Latin America/Caribbean	110,000	209,900	103,800	108,000	119,700	148,000	112,000	110,600	324,400	117,000
North America	518,500	547,200	550,900	543,400	541,400	546,300	527,400	714,200	765,300	791,900
Oceania	44,000	38,000	38,000	38,000	38,000	38,000	50,000	50,000	315,000	315,000
Various/unknown	5,000	143,000	151,000	–	24,100	5,000	–	8,900	9,300	2,100
Total	2,480,200	2,750,900	2,732,900	2,371,500	2,460,600	2,991,400	3,757,700	4,530,800	5,069,700	6,298,100

Region	1980	1981	1982	1983	1984	1985	1986	1987	1988	1989
Africa	4,153,600	3,026,000	2,951,900	2,907,000	3,408,100	3,713,500	3,469,100	3,981,000	4,590,900	4,811,600
Asia	2,728,100	4,677,900	5,298,000	5,525,200	5,320,200	5,986,700	6,769,200	6,784,300	6,771,300	6,819,100
Europe	574,300	587,900	569,900	621,300	676,200	1,032,100	1,119,200	1,173,100	1,203,100	1,213,300
Latin America/Caribbean	178,700	405,800	345,400	353,800	369,900	334,300	339,000	338,600	1,198,200	1,203,900
North America	941,700	1,099,400	1,107,600	1,120,900	736,500	579,700	491,100	463,200	486,900	543,200
Oceania	315,000	327,800	329,800	328,800	104,500	105,400	101,600	101,400	104,400	110,300
Various/unknown	2,600	70,100	70,000	70,000	70,000	65,500	300,000	227,000	200	200
Total	8,894,000	10,194,900	10,672,600	10,927,200	10,685,400	11,817,200	12,589,200	13,068,700	14,355,000	14,701,600

Region	1990	1991	1992	1993	1994	1995	1996	1997	1998	1999
Africa	5,891,400	5,277,700	5,384,700	6,444,000	6,752,200	5,692,100	4,341,500	3,481,400	3,270,900	3,523,100
Asia	7,943,800	8,518,700	7,736,700	5,818,600	5,015,200	4,819,900	4,813,900	4,733,000	4,747,300	4,781,800
Europe	1,468,400	1,564,400	3,446,200	3,061,600	2,555,300	3,095,000	3,173,100	2,945,900	2,667,700	2,617,700
Latin America/Caribbean	1,197,400	899,400	885,800	125,000	109,000	127,700	87,600	83,200	74,200	61,100
North America	617,600	683,700	763,800	806,500	795,500	771,300	737,500	687,500	659,700	649,600
Oceania	109,700	76,000	73,800	62,300	64,200	67,600	75,000	72,900	74,300	64,500
Various/unknown	200	2,000	15,500	–	–	–	–	–	–	–
Total	17,228,500	17,022,000	18,306,400	16,317,900	15,291,400	14,573,600	13,228,500	12,003,900	11,494,200	11,697,800

Notes:
As on 31 December of each given year.
Due to the general lack of comparable data on refugee populations in Europe, North America and Oceania, most figures for these regions have been estimated by UNHCR based on the arrival of refugees and/or recognition of asylum seekers as refugees. Consequently, regional totals for some years may differ from estimates provided by UNHCR earlier.
See technical notes for further explanations and data limitations.

Refugee populations by main country of asylum, 1980–99 (in thousands)

Country of asylum	1980	1981	1982	1983	1984	1985	1986	1987	1988	1989
Algeria	52.0	167.0	167.0	167.0	167.0	174.2	167.2	167.0	170.0	169.1
Angola	75.0	91.7	96.3	96.3	92.3	91.5	92.3	91.2	90.4	12.9
Armenia	–	–	–	–	–	–	–	–	–	–
Australia[a]	304.0	317.0	317.0	317.0	89.0	89.0	85.9	87.6	91.0	97.9
Austria[b]	15.5	17.9	35.0	37.3	39.1	40.5	41.2	41.2	39.8	39.4
Azerbaijan	–	–	–	–	–	–	–	–	–	–
Bangladesh	–	–	–	–	–	–	–	–	–	–
Benin	–	–	–	0.1	0.8	3.7	3.7	3.1	1.2	0.9
Burundi	234.6	234.6	253.2	253.8	273.8	267.4	267.5	267.5	267.5	267.5
Cameroon	128.0	172.7	36.8	4.2	13.7	35.2	53.6	59.2	51.2	48.6
Canada[c]	0.1	0.1	0.1	0.1	0.1	0.1	0.1	0.1	0.1	0.1
China	263.0	265.0	272.1	276.6	279.8	279.7	285.8	280.6	284.3	284.3
Costa Rica	10.1	15.0	16.4	16.9	16.9	24.0	31.2	31.6	278.8	278.8
Côte d'Ivoire	–	–	–	0.5	0.7	0.8	0.9	0.8	0.8	0.5
Croatia	–	–	–	–	–	–	–	–	–	–
Djibouti	45.3	31.8	34.2	29.2	16.8	17.3	16.7	13.1	1.3	31.4
DR Congo (ex–Zaire)	611.1	576.7	497.6	303.5	337.3	283.0	301.2	320.0	340.7	340.7
Ethiopia	10.9	5.5	5.6	31.4	180.5	180.4	132.4	310.5	679.5	710.2
France	150.0	150.0	150.0	161.2	167.3	174.2	180.3	179.3	184.4	188.3
Germany, FR[d]	94.0	100.0	100.0	115.0	126.6	475.0	547.9	596.2	610.2	628.5
Ghana	–	–	0.1	0.1	0.1	0.1	0.2	0.2	0.1	0.1
Guatemala	4.1	100.0	70.0	70.0	70.0	12.0	12.0	12.0	223.1	223.1
Guinea	–	–	–	–	–	–	–	–	–	–
Honduras	25.0	28.0	32.2	39.7	49.2	60.0	68.0	63.0	237.1	237.2
India	–	3.5	5.0	6.9	7.2	6.7	6.4	6.7	6.6	9.5
Indonesia	8.5	14.9	13.2	10.1	9.5	8.2	4.0	2.5	2.4	1.0
Iran, Islamic Rep.	300.0	1,565.0	1,700.1	1,900.1	2,000.0	2,300.0	2,590.0	2,760.0	2,850.0	2,850.0
Iraq	0.4	1.2	1.2	1.2	1.2	83.2	111.0	1.0	–	–
Italy	14.0	13.5	13.6	14.2	15.1	15.2	15.5	10.6	11.0	11.4
Kenya	3.5	3.4	4.8	6.8	8.1	8.8	8.0	10.2	12.8	12.7
Kuwait	5.0	2.0	2.2	2.2	2.8	2.3	–	–	–	0.2
Liberia	–	–	–	0.1	0.3	0.2	0.3	0.2	0.1	0.3
Malawi	–	–	–	–	–	–	100.0	401.6	628.1	822.5
Malaysia	104.0	103.3	99.2	110.7	109.1	105.3	99.0	99.4	104.6	110.5
Mauritania	–	–	–	–	–	–	–	0.1	–	15.0
Mexico	44.0	150.0	167.8	170.0	175.0	175.0	175.1	177.1	356.4	356.5
Nepal	–	–	–	–	–	–	–	–	0.1	0.1
Netherlands[e]	12.0	13.0	14.0	14.5	15.0	15.5	16.0	24.0	26.0	27.2
Nigeria	100.0	89.6	5.2	4.6	4.6	5.9	4.8	5.1	5.2	3.8
Pakistan	1,428.2	2,375.3	2,877.5	2,901.4	2,500.0	2,732.4	2,882.1	3,159.0	3,257.6	3,275.7
Russian Federation	–	–	–	–	–	–	–	–	–	–
Rwanda	10.5	18.2	62.0	49.5	48.9	20.1	19.4	19.5	22.2	23.3
Saudi Arabia	100.0	65.0	59.0	59.0	105.5	130.0	202.1	–	–	–
Sierra Leone	–	–	0.1	0.2	0.2	0.2	0.2	0.1	0.1	–
Somalia	2,000.0	700.0	700.0	700.0	701.3	812.0	700.0	840.1	834.0	769.6
Sudan	493.0	553.0	637.0	690.0	971.0	1,164.0	974.2	807.1	745.0	767.7
Sweden[f]	20.0	20.0	20.0	43.0	90.6	90.6	120.0	130.0	139.8	139.8
Switzerland[g]	32.0	40.0	33.4	32.3	31.2	30.7	31.3	31.7	31.9	36.8
Tanzania, United Rep.	159.6	164.2	160.0	180.1	179.9	214.5	223.5	266.2	265.2	265.1
Thailand	261.4	193.0	169.0	144.3	128.5	130.4	119.9	112.7	107.8	99.9
Uganda	113.0	113.0	113.0	133.0	151.0	151.0	144.1	87.7	103.1	130.0
United Kingdom[h]	148.0	146.0	143.0	140.0	135.0	135.0	100.0	100.0	101.3	39.2
USA[a]	849.0	1,003.0	1,000.0	1,000.0	623.5	487.5	392.3	358.4	370.4	407.5
Yemen[i]	15.6	1.0	1.4	3.7	4.3	5.0	105.0	73.0	78.2	80.1
Yugoslavia, Fed. Rep.	2.0	1.9	2.0	2.0	3.2	3.5	2.2	1.4	0.9	1.0
Zambia	36.4	40.6	89.1	103.0	96.5	103.8	138.3	144.1	143.6	· 137.2
Zimbabwe	0.1	5.1	20.2	50.4	50.5	62.8	65.2	123.6	174.5	175.4

Country of asylum	1990	1991	1992	1993	1994	1995	1996	1997	1998	1999
Algeria	169.1	169.1	219.3	219.1	219.1	206.8	190.3	170.7	165.2	165.2
Angola	11.6	11.0	11.0	10.9	10.7	10.9	9.4	9.4	10.6	13.1
Armenia	–	–	300.0	340.7	304.0	218.0	219.0	219.0	310.0	296.2
Australia[a]	97.9	53.1	49.8	50.6	52.1	54.3	59.0	60.2	61.8	59.7
Austria[b]	34.9	34.5	62.4	57.7	40.7	34.4	89.1	84.4	79.9	80.3
Azerbaijan	–	–	246.0	230.0	231.6	233.7	233.0	233.7	221.6	221.6
Bangladesh	–	40.3	245.0	199.0	116.2	51.1	30.7	21.6	22.3	22.2
Benin	0.5	0.5	0.3	156.2	70.4	23.5	6.0	2.9	2.9	3.7
Burundi	268.4	270.1	271.7	271.9	300.3	173.0	20.7	22.0	25.1	22.1
Cameroon	49.9	45.2	42.2	44.0	44.0	45.9	46.4	47.1	47.7	49.2
Canada[c]	154.8	170.9	183.7	183.2	164.3	151.0	138.7	133.6	135.7	136.6
China	287.2	288.9	288.1	288.2	287.1	288.3	290.1	291.5	292.3	293.3
Costa Rica	276.2	117.5	114.4	24.8	24.6	24.2	23.2	23.1	23.0	22.9
Côte d'Ivoire	272.3	230.3	174.1	251.7	360.1	297.9	327.7	208.5	119.9	138.4
Croatia	–	–	648.0	280.0	183.6	188.6	165.4	68.9	29.0	28.4
Djibouti	70.2	96.1	28.0	34.1	33.4	25.7	25.1	23.6	23.6	23.3
DR Congo (ex-Zaire)	416.4	483.0	391.1	572.1	1,724.4	1,433.8	676.0	297.5	240.3	285.2
Ethiopia	772.8	527.0	431.8	247.6	348.1	393.5	390.5	323.1	262.0	257.7
France	193.2	170.0	182.6	183.0	152.3	170.2	151.3	147.3	140.2	140.2
Germany, FR[d]	816.0	821.5	1,236.0	1,418.0	1,354.6	1,267.9	1,266.0	1,049.0	949.2	975.5
Ghana	8.1	8.1	12.1	150.1	113.7	89.2	35.6	22.9	14.6	13.3
Guatemala	223.4	223.2	222.9	4.7	4.7	1.5	1.6	1.5	0.8	0.7
Guinea	325.0	548.0	478.5	577.2	553.2	633.0	663.9	435.3	413.7	501.5
Honduras	237.1	102.0	100.3	0.1	0.1	0.1	0.1	–	–	–
India	12.7	210.6	258.4	260.3	258.3	274.1	233.4	223.1	185.5	180.0
Indonesia	20.6	18.7	15.6	2.4	0.1	–	0.1	–	0.1	162.5
Iran, Islamic Rep.	4,174.4	4,405.0	4,150.7	2,495.0	2,236.4	2,024.5	2,030.4	1,982.6	1,931.3	1,835.7
Iraq	0.9	88.0	95.0	108.1	119.6	123.3	113.0	104.0	104.1	128.9
Italy	11.7	12.2	12.4	12.4	12.5	80.0	71.6	73.4	68.3	22.9
Kenya	14.4	120.2	401.9	301.6	252.4	239.5	223.6	232.1	238.2	223.7
Kuwait	–	125.0	124.9	24.0	30.0	30.0	3.8	3.8	4.2	4.3
Liberia	–	–	100.0	150.2	120.2	120.0	120.1	126.9	103.1	96.3
Malawi	926.7	981.8	1,058.5	713.6	90.2	1.0	1.3	0.3	0.4	1.7
Malaysia	14.9	13.9	10.3	0.9	5.3	0.2	0.2	5.3	50.6	50.5
Mauritania	20.4	35.2	37.5	46.7	82.2	40.4	15.9	0.0	0.0	0.0
Mexico	356.4	360.2	361.0	52.0	47.4	39.6	34.6	31.9	28.3	24.5
Nepal	0.1	9.6	75.5	85.3	103.3	124.8	126.8	129.2	126.1	127.9
Netherlands[e]	15.1	18.3	29.8	44.2	62.8	80.8	103.5	119.0	131.8	129.1
Nigeria	3.6	3.6	4.8	4.8	6.0	8.1	8.5	9.0	7.9	6.9
Pakistan	3,185.3	3,099.9	1,629.2	1,479.5	1,055.4	1,202.7	1,202.7	1,202.7	1,202.5	1,202.0
Russian Federation	–	–	17.1	44.7	50.2	42.3	205.5	237.7	128.6	80.1
Rwanda	23.6	34.0	25.2	277.0	6.0	7.8	25.3	34.2	33.4	34.4
Saudi Arabia	–	33.1	28.7	24.0	18.0	13.3	9.9	5.8	5.5	5.6
Sierra Leone	125.8	28.0	5.9	15.8	15.9	4.7	13.5	13.0	9.9	6.6
Somalia	460.0	–	0.5	0.3	0.4	0.6	0.7	0.6	0.3	0.1
Sudan	780.0	729.2	725.6	745.2	727.2	558.2	393.9	374.4	391.5	391.0
Sweden[f]	183.4	238.4	324.5	257.0	186.1	189.9	191.2	186.7	178.8	159.5
Switzerland[g]	40.9	45.6	51.9	56.6	75.3	82.9	84.4	83.2	81.9	111.6
Tanzania, United Rep.	265.2	288.1	292.1	564.5	883.3	829.7	498.7	570.4	543.9	622.2
Thailand	99.8	88.2	63.6	104.4	100.8	101.4	108.0	169.2	138.3	100.1
Uganda	142.4	162.5	196.3	286.5	286.5	229.4	264.3	188.5	204.5	218.2
United Kingdom[h]	43.7	43.4	64.8	80.3	85.1	90.5	97.5	105.3	116.1	132.7
USA[a]	462.9	512.8	580.1	623.2	631.3	620.3	598.8	553.9	524.1	513.0

Country of asylum	1990	1991	1992	1993	1994	1995	1996	1997	1998	1999
Yemen[i]	3.0	30.0	59.7	53.8	13.6	40.3	53.5	38.5	61.4	60.5
Yugoslavia, Fed. Rep.	0.9	0.5	516.5	479.1	195.5	650.0	563.2	550.1	502.0	500.7
Zambia	138.0	140.7	142.1	141.1	141.1	130.6	131.1	165.1	168.6	206.4
Zimbabwe	182.7	197.6	237.7	100.5	2.2	0.4	0.6	0.8	0.8	2.0

Notes:

This table includes countries with 75,000 or more refugees in at least one year during 1980–99. As on 31 December of each given year.

[a]The 1984–99 figures have been estimated by UNHCR, based on the arrival of refugees and/or recognition of asylum seekers as refugees over a 5 year period. The method of estimation prior to 1984 is unknown.

[b]Number of refugees estimated by UNHCR, based on the arrival of refugees and/or recognition of asylum seekers as refugees over a 10 year period, refugees benefiting from the Temporary Protection Scheme and refugees provided with a regular aliens residence permit.

[c]Number of refugees estimated by UNHCR, based on the arrival of refugees and/or recognition of asylum seekers as refugees over a 5 year period.

[d]The 1980–84 figures include "persons granted asylum and refugees recognized abroad", "quota refugees" and "homeless foreigners" while the 1985–99 figures include the additional categories "family members of persons granted asylum", "civil war refugees from Bosnia and Herzegovina" and "de facto refugees" (*Source*: Central Aliens Register).

[e]The 1990–99 figures have been estimated by UNHCR, based on the arrival of refugees and/or recognition of asylum seekers as refugees over a 10 year period. The method of estimation prior to 1990 is unknown.

[f]The 1994–99 figures have been estimated by UNHCR, based on the arrival of refugees and/or recognition of asylum seekers as refugees over a 10 year period. The method of estimation prior to 1994 is unknown.

[g]The 1980–84 figures include "recognized refugees" only, while the 1985–99 figures include the additional categories "temporary admission" granted during, after or without procedure and humanitarian and other comparable regulations.

[h]The 1989–99 figures have been estimated by UNHCR, based on the arrival of refugees and/or recognition of asylum seekers as refugees over a 10 year period. The method of estimation prior to 1989 is unknown.

[i]The 1980–89 figures are for the Yemen Arab Republic and People's Democratic Republic of Yemen combined. Those from 1990 onwards are for the united Republic of Yemen.

See technical notes for further explanations and data limitations.

Largest refugee populations by origin, 1980–99 (in thousands)

Origin	1980	1981	1982	1983	1984	1985	1986	1987	1988	1989
Afghanistan	1,734.7	3,879.5	4,487.7	4,712.2	4,417.1	4,652.6	5,093.7	5,511.2	5,609.3	5,630.8
Angola	449.0	457.1	465.9	298.1	357.8	317.4	355.4	391.7	407.3	408.4
Armenia	0.3	0.3	0.7	0.3	0.3	0.3	0.5	0.2	0.3	–
Azerbaijan	–	–	–	–	–	–	–	–	–	–
Bhutan	–	–	–	–	–	–	–	–	–	–
Bosnia and Herzegovina	–	–	–	–	–	–	–	–	–	–
Burundi	169.8	183.0	176.3	176.6	182.9	199.8	210.6	186.9	190.2	191.4
Cambodia	192.7	134.9	123.2	90.9	72.3	67.3	54.7	48.4	44.5	40.4
Chad	221.0	234.3	17.0	16.7	181.3	212.2	170.1	146.9	130.8	125.9
China	–	–	–	–	–	–	–	–	–	–
Croatia	–	–	–	–	–	–	–	–	–	–
DR Congo (ex–Zaire)	116.8	119.0	92.5	101.6	94.5	86.4	96.6	69.4	103.4	100.5
East Timor	–	–	–	–	–	–	–	–	–	–
El Salvador	91.6	304.8	242.4	244.6	243.0	180.6	171.8	167.6	165.3	38.6
Eritrea	0.4	1.4	1.4	1.2	1.2	1.2	–	–	–	–
Ethiopia	2,567.4	1,362.3	1,333.9	1,350.7	1,545.4	1,748.5	1,533.7	1,486.7	1,501.0	1,462.4
Iran, Islamic Rep.	–	0.7	2.3	5.0	3.9	86.6	85.8	8.5	9.5	5.4
Iraq	31.0	66.4	103.6	103.5	101.4	401.2	400.4	410.4	505.9	504.1
Lao People's Dem. Rep.	105.2	89.9	80.5	84.9	86.6	99.2	91.1	78.8	80.0	72.5
Liberia	–	–	–	–	–	–	–	–	–	–
Mali	–	–	–	–	–	–	–	–	–	–
Mauritania	–	–	–	–	–	–	–	–	–	48.2
Mozambique	0.1	5.2	20.2	50.2	51.2	72.3	193.6	635.0	921.2	1,120.7
Myanmar	–	–	–	–	–	–	–	–	–	–
Namibia	55.6	74.5	75.2	75.1	77.6	76.9	77.0	75.7	76.5	3.7
Nicaragua	1.0	2.5	19.0	23.5	35.0	52.7	67.6	68.5	77.4	84.3
Palestinians	–	–	9.8	9.1	–	31.6	52.7	2.0	5.0	4.1
Philippines	90.0	90.0	90.0	100.0	100.0	90.0	90.0	90.0	90.0	90.0
Rwanda	286.7	277.0	328.0	321.8	357.1	376.5	371.9	353.4	327.5	319.5
Sierra Leone	–	–	–	–	–	–	–	–	–	–
Somalia	–	–	–	–	–	–	–	60.0	350.7	325.6
Sri Lanka	–	–	–	–	–	0.2	0.3	0.2	0.1	0.1
Sudan	10.9	5.4	5.4	31.0	180.1	180.9	132.8	253.2	347.2	438.7
Togo	–	–	–	–	–	–	–	–	–	–
Turkey	–	–	0.3	0.5	1.0	0.8	0.9	1.1	–	1.5
Uganda	224.3	176.7	271.3	315.3	294.0	306.0	238.6	111.0	21.0	19.7
Viet Nam	344.5	310.1	322.8	325.6	321.3	318.2	318.0	316.5	317.4	326.2
Western Sahara	50.0	165.0	165.0	165.0	165.0	165.0	165.0	165.0	165.0	167.2
Yemen	15.0	–	–	–	–	–	100.0	70.0	77.0	77.0
Yugoslavia, FR	–	–	–	–	–	–	–	–	–	–

Origin	1990	1991	1992	1993	1994	1995	1996	1997	1998	1999
Afghanistan	6,326.4	6,294.8	4,550.6	3,388.2	2,745.2	2,681.7	2,673.2	2,650.4	2,633.9	2,562.0
Angola	407.5	381.3	300.1	325.6	283.9	246.2	248.9	265.7	315.9	350.7
Armenia	–	–	195.0	195.1	201.5	198.6	198.7	201.2	190.2	190.3
Azerbaijan	–	–	300.0	328.0	299.0	200.3	210.9	234.2	328.5	13.2
Bhutan	–	9.5	75.4	85.3	103.3	104.7	106.8	108.7	105.7	107.6
Bosnia and Herzegovina	–	–	436.9	579.3	321.2	468.2	893.6	706.5	471.6	382.9
Burundi	191.6	223.9	184.1	871.3	389.2	349.8	427.5	517.6	500.0	524.4
Cambodia	38.1	36.8	24.0	7.7	6.9	60.1	59.7	100.7	73.1	38.6
Chad	184.8	72.3	66.4	212.9	211.9	59.7	58.4	54.9	59.3	58.2
China	–	–	80.0	109.1	109.2	118.0	118.0	118.5	118.5	120.1
Croatia	–	–	168.6	151.2	78.3	242.9	305.6	342.1	334.6	340.3
DR Congo (ex–Zaire)	67.0	65.3	80.4	74.7	71.6	86.2	154.3	168.7	152.4	249.3
East Timor	–	–	–	–	–	–	–	–	–	162.5
El Salvador	27.1	29.6	27.2	22.6	16.7	13.5	13.9	13.5	9.6	9.6
Eritrea	–	500.6	503.2	427.2	422.4	285.7	330.9	318.2	345.4	345.6
Ethiopia	1,324.8	225.9	282.1	219.8	188.1	66.0	73.0	64.1	53.2	53.7
Iran, Islamic Rep.	2.9	56.8	56.2	49.6	50.0	46.4	70.1	59.0	52.2	54.2
Iraq	1,116.9	1,305.2	1,322.7	740.0	702.1	628.0	654.5	631.6	590.8	572.1
Lao People's Dem. Rep.	71.3	61.4	43.4	29.3	14.1	23.1	19.6	16.4	13.5	15.5
Liberia	735.6	673.3	519.8	701.8	794.2	740.0	778.1	487.0	258.7	285.0
Mali	–	14.7	71.2	98.6	172.7	77.1	55.1	10.4	3.6	0.3
Mauritania	66.0	79.9	79.6	67.9	68.0	83.9	82.3	68.9	67.8	27.7
Mozambique	1,248.0	1,316.6	1,344.9	1,309.2	234.5	125.5	34.6	33.6	–	–
Myanmar	–	40.0	245.0	281.3	203.9	146.3	135.1	132.3	129.6	127.8
Namibia	0.5	0.2	–	0.1	0.1	–	–	–	1.9	0.7
Nicaragua	36.9	31.6	31.0	23.4	22.9	20.8	20.1	19.8	18.9	18.6
Palestinians [a]	4.0	59.6	89.0	74.7	75.3	65.1	74.0	71.1	72.8	100.5
Philippines	–	–	–	–	–	–	–	–	45.1	45.1
Rwanda	361.3	431.2	434.7	450.4	2,257.0	1,818.4	467.7	66.0	73.4	84.3
Sierra Leone	–	142.6	253.6	311.1	275.1	379.1	374.4	328.4	411.0	487.2
Somalia	455.2	720.8	788.2	516.6	535.9	579.3	573.0	525.4	480.8	451.5
Sri Lanka	–	200.0	113.4	76.8	77.3	71.4	79.5	93.7	87.3	93.4
Sudan	523.8	195.9	266.9	391.4	398.6	436.5	464.0	351.7	374.2	467.7
Togo	–	–	0.1	291.0	167.7	92.9	25.2	6.6	2.7	2.7
Turkey	–	–	–	5.5	16.9	32.9	41.6	38.3	32.7	36.9
Uganda	56.4	36.8	28.5	28.4	26.0	18.8	23.8	50.9	9.0	10.3
Viet Nam	343.6	325.5	322.0	307.6	300.4	342.5	329.2	320.2	315.7	326.3
Western Sahara	165.0	165.0	165.0	165.0	166.5	165.0	166.3	166.1	166.0	165.9
Yemen	–	–	–	–	–	0.2	0.9	1.3	1.4	1.5
Yugoslavia, FR	–	43.0	418.6	48.8	38.5	46.9	76.8	79.9	100.2	112.6

Notes:

The table shows the origin for refugee populations of 75,000 or more in at least one year during 1980–99.

As on 31 December of each given year.

The origin of refugees is not available for a number of, mostly industrialized, states.

[a] Does not include Palestinian refugees assisted by the UN Relief and Works Agency for Palestine Refugees in the Near East (UNRWA).

See technical notes for further explanations and data limitations.

Refugee populations by origin and country/ territory of asylum, 31 December 1999

Origin	Country/territory of asylum	Number	Origin	Country/territory of asylum	Number
Afghanistan		**2,601,400**	**Cambodia**		**38,600**
	Iran	1,325,700		France*	21,400
	Pakistan	1,200,000		Viet Nam	15,000
	Netherlands*	20,300		Other	2,200
	Germany*	16,600			
	India	14,500	**Chad**		**57,900**
	Tajikistan	4,500		Cameroon	44,600
	United Kingdom*	3,500		Sudan	4,400
	Denmark*	2,300		Central African Rep.	3,500
	Kazakhstan	2,300		Nigeria	3,200
	Other	11,700		Other	2,200
Angola		**349,600**	**China**		**107,600**
	Zambia	163,100		India	98,000
	Dem. Rep. of Congo	150,000		USA**	3,800
	Congo	20,600		Netherlands*	2,100
	Namibia	7,000		Other	3,700
	South Africa	3,800	**Congo**		**26,200**
	Other	5,100		Gabon	12,200
				Dem. Rep. of Congo	11,800
Armenia		**189,700**		Other	2,200
	Azerbaijan	188,400			
	Other	1,300	**Croatia**		**343,400**
				Yugoslavia, Fed. Rep.	298,000
Azerbaijan		**310,700**		Bosnia and H.	39,600
	Armenia	296,200		Croatia	2,800
	Russian Federation	12,900		Other	3,000
	Other	1,600			
			Democratic Rep. of Congo		**252,400**
Bhutan		**107,600**		Tanzania, United Rep.	98,500
	Nepal	107,600		Zambia	36,400
				Rwanda	33,000
Bosnia and Herzegovina		**472,700**		Burundi	20,800
	Yugoslavia, Fed. Rep.	198,200		Angola	12,800
	Austria	66,700		Congo	12,400
	Germany*	50,000		Central African Rep.	9,500
	Sweden*	52,800		Uganda	8,000
	Denmark*	27,300		France*	5,200
	Croatia	25,000		South Africa	4,100
	Netherlands*	23,900		Canada**	2,300
	Norway*	14,300		Other	9,400
	Switzerland	7,300			
	Slovenia	3,100	**East Timor**		**162,500**
	Other	4,100		Indonesia	162,500
Burundi		**524,700**	**Eritrea**		**345,500**
	Tanzania, United Rep.	499,000		Sudan	342,100
	Dem. Rep. of Congo	19,200		Yemen	2,500
	Other	6,500		Other	900

Origin	Country/territory of asylum	Number	Origin	Country/territory of asylum	Number
Ethiopia		**59,500**	**Myanmar**		**127,800**
	Sudan	35,400		Thailand	99,700
	Kenya	4,800		Bangladesh	22,100
	United Kingdom*	4,300		Malaysia	5,100
	Sweden*	3,300		Other	900
	Yemen	2,400			
	Netherlands*	2,000	**Palestinians**		**104,300**
	USA**	2,000		Iraq	90,000
	Other	5,300		Libyan Arab Jamah.	7,600
				Denmark*	3,900
Georgia		**28,400**		Kuwait	2,200
	Russian Federation	28,000		Other	600
	Other	400			
			Philippines		**45,100**
Guatemala		**23,100**		Malaysia	45,100
	Mexico	22,300			
	Other	800	**Russian Federation**	22,400	
				Kazakhstan	7,000
Iran, Islamic Republic of		**90,900**		Georgia	5,200
	Iraq	26,500		USA**	2,700
	Germany*	19,100		Other	7,500
	Sweden*	11,000			
	Netherlands*	9,700	**Rwanda**		**84,800**
	Canada**	4,700		Dem. Rep. of Congo	33,000
	Norway*	3,800		Tanzania, United Rep.	20,100
	Denmark*	2,800		Uganda	8,000
	France*	2,800		Congo	6,500
	United Kingdom *	2,400		Zambia	4,200
	Other	8,100		Kenya	2,900
				Belgium*	2,100
Iraq		**639,300**		Other	8,000
	Iran, Islamic Rep.	510,000			
	Germany*	34,500	**Sierra Leone**		**487,200**
	Sweden*	24,000		Guinea	370,600
	Netherlands*	22,900		Liberia	96,300
	Denmark*	10,500		Gambia	12,000
	United Kingdom*	5,700		Other	8,300
	Saudi Arabia	5,400			
	Norway*	4,800	**Somalia**		**496,200**
	Syrian Arab Rep.	3,400		Ethiopia	180,900
	USA**	2,600		Kenya	141,100
	Lebanon	2,500		Yemen	55,200
	Other	13,000		Djibouti	21,600
				Netherlands*	18,500
Liberia		**288,400**		United Kingdom*	18,100
	Côte d'Ivoire	135,600		Denmark*	9,600
	Guinea	129,100		Sweden*	7,700
	Ghana	10,400		USA**	5,200
	Sierra Leone	6,600		South Africa	4,700
	USA**	2,500		Canada**	4,000
	Other	4,200		Norway*	3,600
				Tanzania, United Rep.	3,300
Mauritania		**29,200**		Libyan Arab Jamah.	2,900
	Senegal	20,000		Egypt	2,600
	Mali	6,100		Finland*	2,400
	Other	3,100		Switzerland	2,400

Origin	Country/territory of asylum	Number	Origin	Country/territory of asylum	Number
Somalia continued			Turkey continued	Sweden*	2,400
	Eritrea	2,300		Other	400
	Other	10,100			
Sri Lanka		120,700	Uzbekistan		44,300
	India	66,400		Azerbaijan	33,200
	France*	15,900		Russian Federation	11,000
	Canada**	9,700		Other	100
	Germany*	9,200			
	United Kingdom*	8,300	Viet Nam		326,300
	Switzerland	4,300		China	293,200
	Norway*	2,300		France*	15,700
	Netherlands*	2,100		Belgium*	3,100
	Other	2,500		Japan	3,100
				Switzerland	3,100
Sudan		474,700		Sweden*	2,400
	Uganda	200,600		Other	5,700
	Ethiopia	70,300			
	Dem. Rep. of Congo	68,000	Western Sahara		165,900
	Kenya	64,300		Algeria	165,000
	Central African Rep.	35,500		Other	900
	Chad	23,300			
	Egypt	2,600	Yugoslavia, Fed. Rep.		153,400
	Netherlands*	2,300		Sweden*	29,200
	United Kingdom *	2,000		Bosnia and H.	26,100
	Other	5,800		FYR Macedonia	21,000
				Germany*	21,000
Tajikistan		44,900		Norway*	10,400
	Turkmenistan	17,000		Netherlands*	7,000
	Russian Federation	12,300		France*	5,600
	Kyrgyzstan	10,100		United Kingdom*	4,400
	Kazakhstan	5,400		Italy	4,100
	Other	100		USA**	4,100
				Albania	3,900
Turkey		71,700		Croatia	3,400
	Germany*	40,800		Switzerland	4,500
	France*	11,900		Denmark*	3,100
	Iraq	11,200		Finland*	2,200
	Switzerland	5,000		Other	3,400

Notes:

The table shows the origin for refugee populations of 20,000 and more only. Countries of asylum are listed if they host 2,000 refugees or more from that country/territory of origin.

*Number of refugees estimated by UNHCR, based on the arrival of refugees and/or recognition of asylum seekers as refugees over the past 10 years. These estimates exclude resettled refugees.

**Number of refugees estimated by UNHCR, based on the arrival of refugees and/or recognition of asylum seekers as refugees over the past 5 years. These estimates exclude resettled refugees.

This table includes estimates on recognized asylum seekers as refugees in industrialized states. As a result, the totals by origin differ from those provided in Annex 5 as well as from estimates in other UNHCR documents.

See technical notes for further explanations and data limitations.

Source: Governments, UNHCR

Refugees per 1,000 inhabitants: top 40 countries as on 31 December 1999

Country of asylum/residence	Refugees per 1,000 inhabitants	Country of asylum/residence	Refugees per 1,000 inhabitants
Armenia	84.2	FYR Macedonia	10.5
Guinea	67.5	Norway	10.3
Yugoslavia, Federal Republic of	47.1	Uganda	10.0
Djibouti	36.5	Austria	9.8
Liberia	32.7	Côte d'Ivoire	9.4
Azerbaijan	28.7	Netherlands	8.2
Iran, Islamic Republic of	27.1	Pakistan	7.7
Zambia	22.5	Kenya	7.4
Tanzania, United Republic of	18.6	Croatia	6.3
Sweden	17.5	Guinea–Bissau	5.9
Bosnia and Herzegovina	16.5	Costa Rica	5.7
Central African Republic	13.6	Iraq	5.6
Congo	13.6	Democratic Republic of the Congo	5.5
Sudan	13.3	Nepal	5.3
Gambia	13.2	Algeria	5.2
Denmark	13.0	Rwanda	4.4
Gabon	12.3	Canada	4.4
Belize	12.0	Namibia	4.3
Germany	11.9	Turkmenistan	4.1
Switzerland	11.1	Ethiopia	4.1

Note: See technical notes for explanations and data limitations.

Source: United Nations, Department of Economic and Social Affairs, *World Population Prospects: The 1998 Revision*, New York, 1999; UNHCR

Number of refugees in the Great Lakes region of Africa, 1960–99

Country	1960	1961	1962	1963	1964	1965	1966	1967	1968	1969
Burundi	..	30,000	30,000	34,000	78,000	65,000	79,000	79,000	72,000	46,200
DR Congo (ex–Zaire)	..	203,000	223,000	237,000	236,000	265,000	357,100	434,100	475,400	496,300
Rwanda	..	–	–	–	–	3,000	300	–	–	–
Uganda	..	52,000	52,000	59,000	113,000	137,400	156,000	162,800	175,700	177,300
United Rep. of Tanzania	..	12,000	12,000	12,000	25,000	29,000	34,000	39,800	46,000	54,600
Total	..	297,000	317,000	342,000	452,000	499,400	626,400	715,700	769,100	774,400

Country	1970	1971	1972	1973	1974	1975	1976	1977	1978	1979
Burundi	38,800	33,000	43,400	49,000	48,500	49,500	49,500	50,000	50,300	50,500
DR Congo (ex–Zaire)	489,000	474,300	495,300	460,100	503,300	510,000	515,000	530,300	653,000	710,500
Rwanda	–	–	4,000	6,500	6,000	7,400	7,500	7,500	7,600	7,900
Uganda	179,800	180,900	166,600	113,900	118,500	112,600	112,900	113,600	113,700	112,700
United Rep. of Tanzania	71,500	71,200	165,000	180,900	193,200	171,200	154,000	164,600	161,000	160,800
Total	779,100	759,400	874,300	810,400	869,500	850,700	838,900	866,000	985,600	1,042,400

Country	1980	1981	1982	1983	1984	1985	1986	1987	1988	1989
Burundi	234,600	234,600	253,200	253,800	273,800	267,400	267,500	267,500	267,500	267,500
DR Congo (ex–Zaire)	611,100	576,700	497,600	303,500	337,300	283,000	301,200	320,000	340,700	340,700
Rwanda	10,500	18,200	62,000	49,500	48,900	20,100	19,400	19,500	22,200	23,300
Uganda	113,000	113,000	113,000	133,000	151,000	151,000	144,100	87,700	103,100	130,000
United Rep. of Tanzania	159,600	164,200	160,000	180,100	179,900	214,500	223,500	266,200	265,200	265,100
Total	1,128,800	1,106,700	1,085,800	919,900	990,900	936,000	955,700	960,900	998,700	1,026,600

Country	1990	1991	1992	1993	1994	1995	1996	1997	1998	1999
Burundi	268,400	270,100	271,700	271,900	300,300	173,000	20,700	22,000	25,100	22,100
DR Congo (ex–Zaire)	416,400	483,000	391,100	572,100	1,724,400	1,433,800	676,000	297,500	240,300	285,200
Rwanda	23,600	34,000	25,200	277,000	6,000	7,800	25,300	34,200	33,400	34,400
Uganda	145,700	162,500	196,300	286,500	286,500	229,400	264,300	188,500	204,500	218,200
United Rep. of Tanzania	265,200	288,100	292,100	564,500	883,300	829,700	498,700	570,400	543,900	622,200
Total	1,119,300	1,237,700	1,176,400	1,972,000	3,200,500	2,673,700	1,485,000	1,112,600	1,047,200	1,182,100

Note: As on 31 December of each given year.

See technical notes for explanations and data limitations.

Asylum applications and refugee admissions to industrialized states, 1990–99

Country	1990	1991	1992	1993	1994	1995	1996	1997	1998	1999	Total
Australia[a]											
Asylum applications	12,100	16,700	6,100	7,200	6,300	7,600	9,800	9,300	8,200	9,500	92,800
1951 Conventions status	90	190	610	990	1,000	680	1,400	1,000	2,500	1,900	10,400
Humanitarian status	-	-	-	-	-	-	-	-	-	-	-
Total recognition rate	31.8	11.4	5.8	9.9	13.3	9.1	18.1	6.6	23.8	26.4	14.6
Resettlement arrivals	12,000	7,800	7,200	10,900	11,400	13,600	11,300	8,000	11,100	8,300	101,600
Austria											
Asylum applications	22,800	27,300	16,200	4,700	5,100	5,900	7,000	6,700	13,800	20,100	129,600
1951 Convention status	860	2,500	2,300	1,200	680	990	720	640	500	..	10,400
Humanitarian status	-	-	-	-	-	-	-	-	-	-	-
Total recognition rate	6.8	12.5	9.8	7.8	7.5	13.0	8.2	8.1	5.3	..	9.1
Resettlement arrivals	-	-	-	-	-	-	-	-	-	-	-
Belgium											
Asylum applications	13,000	15,200	17,600	26,900	14,400	11,400	12,400	11,800	22,000	35,800	180,500
1951 Convention status	530	620	900	1,100	1,600	1,400	1,700	1,900	1,700	1,500	13,000
Humanitarian status	-	-	-	-	-	-	-	-	-	-	-
Total recognition rate	30.3	22.1	19.4	21.8	24.0	24.6	22.5	19.7	24.6	31.2	24.8
Resettlement arrivals	-	-	-	-	-	-	-	-	-	-	-
Bulgaria											
Asylum applications	-	-	-	-	-	520	300	430	830	1,300	3,400
1951 Convention status	-	-	-	-	-	50	150	130	90	180	600
Humanitarian status	-	-	-	-	-	20	10	*	10	380	420
Total recognition rate	-	-	-	-	-	70.8	49.8	47.6	22.0	37.8	39.3
Resettlement arrivals	-	-	-	-	-	-	-	-	-	-	-
Canada											
Asylum applications	36,700	32,300	37,700	20,300	22,000	26,100	26,100	22,600	23,800	30,100	277,700
1951 Convention status	10,700	19,400	17,400	14,100	15,200	9,600	9,500	10,000	12,900	13,000	131,800
Humanitarian status	-	-	-	-	-	-	-	-	-	-	-
Total recognition rate	70.5	64.6	57.0	46.2	60.7	55.9	43.8	40.2	43.8	46.4	52.1
Resettlement arrivals	35,200	27,300	15,700	15,500	12,400	12,700	12,200	21,700	20,500	9,800	183,000
Czech Republic											
Asylum applications	1,800	2,000	820	2,200	1,200	1,400	2,200	2,100	4,100	8,500	26,300
1951 Convention status	30	780	250	240	120	60	160	100	80	80	1,900
Humanitarian status	-	-	-	-	-	-	-	-	-	-	-
Total recognition rate	100.0	99.9	96.6	95.7	40.5	74.7	87.1	3.9	2.8	0.9	11.1
Resettlement arrivals	-	-	-	-	-	-	-	-	-	-	-
Denmark											
Asylum applications	5,300	4,600	13,900	14,300	6,700	5,100	5,900	5,100	5,700	6,500	73,100
1951 Convention status	700	990	760	650	680	5,000	1,400	980	1,100	1,100	13,400
Humanitarian status	1,600	2,200	2,500	2,300	1,700	14,900	6,800	4,500	3,200	2,600	42,300
Total recognition rate	-	-	-	-	-	86.7	81.7	58.3	54.5	51.8	72.4
Resettlement arrivals	750	860	550	3,200	3,800	2,000	600	500	450	520	13,300
Finland											
Asylum applications	2,700	2,100	3,600	2,000	840	850	710	970	1,300	3,100	18,200
1951 Convention status	20	20	30	20	30	10	10	10	10	30	190
Humanitarian status	140	1,700	700	2,100	390	230	340	290	380	470	6,700
Total recognition rate	32.1	73.3	35.1	59.6	45.6	46.8	58.6	52.1	44.1	18.2	47.3
Resettlement arrivals	640	460	670	590	650	640	840	630	300	540	6,000

Country	1990	1991	1992	1993	1994	1995	1996	1997	1998	1999	Total
France											
Asylum applications	54,800	47,400	28,900	27,600	26,000	20,200	17,400	21,400	22,400	30,800	296,900
1951 Convention status	13,500	15,500	10,300	9,900	7,000	4,500	4,300	4,100	4,000	-	73,100
Humanitarian status	-	-	-	-	-	-	-	-	-	-	-
Total recognition rate	15.4	19.7	28.0	27.9	23.7	15.6	19.6	17.0	17.5	-	20.0
Resettlement arrivals	-	-	-	-	-	-	-	-	-	-	-
Germany											
Asylum applications	193,100	256,100	438,200	322,600	127,200	127,900	116,400	104,400	98,600	95,100	1,879,600
1951 Convention status[b]	6,500	11,600	9,200	16,400	25,600	23,500	24,100	18,200	11,300	10,300	156,700
Humanitarian status	-	-	-	-	-	3,600	2,100	2,800	2,500	2,100	13,100
Total recognition rate[c]	4.4	6.9	4.2	3.2	7.5	13.5	13.5	12.3	9.4	9.1	7.6
Resettlement arrivals	-	-	-	-	-	-	-	-	-	-	-
Greece											
Asylum applications	6,200	2,700	1,900	810	1,300	1,300	1,600	4,400	3,000	1,500	24,700
1951 Convention status[d]	1,100	330	200	40	90	200	230	220	440	150	3,000
Humanitarian status	-	-	-	-	-	-	70	90	290	420	870
Total recognition rate	19.4	4.5	5.7	5.3	11.9	16.1	15.7	12.9	17.4	26.5	12.9
Resettlement arrivals	-	-	-	-	-	-	-	-	-	-	-
Hungary[d]											
Asylum applications	4,000	1,300	860	730	440	590	670	1,100	7,400	11,500	28,600
1951 Convention status	2,600	450	490	400	250	180	170	160	440	310	5,500
Humanitarian status	-	-	-	-	-	-	-	-	230	1,800	2,000
Total recognition rate	89.0	45.4	46.8	46.1	27.4	31.9	23.3	11.7	14.0	18.3	29.2
Resettlement arrivals	-	-	-	-	-	-	-	-	-	-	-
Ireland											
Asylum applications	-	30	40	90	360	420	1,200	3,900	4,600	7,700	18,300
1951 Convention status	-	-	-	-	-	20	40	210	170	510	950
Humanitarian status	-	-	-	-	10	10	10	120	30	40	220
Total recognition rate	-	-	-	-	25.0	34.8	56.8	52.3	12.0	9.2	13.9
Resettlement arrivals	-	-	-	-	-	-	-	-	-	-	-
Italy											
Asylum applications	4,800	26,500	6,000	1,600	1,800	1,700	680	1,900	7,100	33,400	85,500
1951 Convention status[d]	820	800	340	130	300	290	170	350	1,000	810	5,000
Humanitarian status	-	-	-	-	-	-	-	-	-	860	860
Total recognition rate	59.5	4.9	4.8	8.8	17.7	16.6	24.8	21.0	29.6	20.0	13.4
Resettlement arrivals	-	-	-	-	-	-	-	-	-	-	-
Japan											
Asylum applications	30	40	70	50	70	50	150	240	130	220	1,100
1951 Convention status	*	*	*	10	*	*	*	*	20	30	60
Humanitarian status	-	-	-	-	-	-	-	-	-	30	30
Total recognition rate	5.4	5.3	6.5	10.9	2.0	1.8	2.0	0.9	4.3	26.8	10.4
Resettlement arrivals	320	370	410	300	170	90	*	*	10	*	1,700
Netherlands											
Asylum applications	21,200	21,600	20,300	35,400	52,600	29,300	22,200	34,400	45,200	39,300	321,500
1951 Convention status	690	780	4,900	10,300	6,700	8,000	8,800	6,600	2,400	1,500	50,700
Humanitarian status	860	1,900	6,900	4,700	12,700	10,500	14,800	10,400	12,700	8,000	83,500
Total recognition rate	10.9	10.7	23.0	35.2	33.2	32.2	28.1	34.6	31.6	15.6	27.3
Resettlement arrivals	700	590	640	660	550	610	620	190	540	20	5,100
New Zealand[a]											
Asylum applications	-	1,200	320	380	450	710	1,300	1,600	2,900	2,100	11,000
1951 Convention status	-	160	150	50	50	80	90	100	240	360	1,300
Humanitarian status	-	-	-	-	-	-	-	-	-	-	-
Total recognition rate	-	49.1	15.1	4.6	15.0	25.9	13.3	16.9	12.9	16.2	15.4
Resettlement arrivals	810	680	620	410	740	820	780	530	680	1,100	7,200

Country	1990	1991	1992	1993	1994	1995	1996	1997	1998	1999	Total
Norway											
Asylum applications	4,000	4,600	5,200	12,900	3,400	1,500	1,800	2,300	8,400	10,200	54,300
1951 Convention status	130	120	140	50	20	30	10	90	110	180	880
Humanitarian status	1,500	1,900	2,000	8,000	6,300	2,600	1,500	1,100	2,100	3,000	30,000
Total recognition rate	28.3	34.4	29.9	53.7	48.7	52.3	38.6	29.7	39.9	33.3	41.4
Resettlement arrivals	970	1,100	2,000	1,500	690	1,600	790	1,300	1,100	1,500	12,600
Poland											
Asylum applications	-	-	-	820	600	840	3,200	3,500	3,400	3,000	15,400
1951 Convention status	-	-	-	60	400	110	130	150	60	50	960
Humanitarian status	-	-	-	-	-	-	-	-	-	-	-
Total recognition rate	-	-	-	14.1	41.7	14.4	6.3	3.8	1.9	1.4	6.7
Resettlement arrivals	-	-	-	-	-	-	-	-	-	-	-
Portugal											
Asylum applications	80	260	690	2,100	770	450	270	250	340	270	5,500
1951 Convention status	10	30	20	80	30	50	10	*	*	20	250
Humanitarian status	-	-	-	-	-	-	-	-	-	50	50
Total recognition rate	18.0	12.2	3.7	11.7	6.8	8.7	22.8	7.2	12.5	14.8	8.4
Resettlement arrivals	-	-	-	-	-	-	-	-	-	-	-
Romania											
Asylum applications	-	-	-	-	-	-	590	1,400	1,200	1,700	4,900
1951 Convention status	-	-	-	-	-	-	90	80	180	250	600
Humanitarian status	-	-	-	-	-	-	-	-	100	370	470
Total recognition rate	-	-	-	-	-	-	13.3	21.6	10.5	26.4	17.6
Resettlement arrivals	-	-	-	-	-	-	-	-	-	-	-
Slovak Republic											
Asylum applications	-	-	90	100	140	360	420	650	510	1,300	3,600
1951 Convention status	-	-	60	40	50	70	130	70	50	30	500
Humanitarian status	-	-	-	-	-	-	-	-	-	-	-
Total recognition rate	-	-	100.0	45.8	35.8	21.1	33.4	9.4	15.9	2.2	15.5
Resettlement arrivals	-	-	-	-	-	-	-	-	-	-	-
Slovenia											
Asylum applications	-	-	-	-	-	-	40	70	500	870	1,500
1951 Convention status	-	-	-	-	-	*	-	-	*	-	*
Humanitarian status	-	-	-	-	-	-	-	-	30	10	40
Total recognition rate	-	-	-	-	-	100.0	-	-	15.0	1.3	4.1
Resettlement arrivals	-	-	-	-	-	-	-	-	-	-	-
South Africa											
Asylum applications	-	-	-	-	-	-	16,000	15,600	15,000	13,200	59,800
1951 Convention status	-	-	-	-	-	-	3,300	3,500	1,700	6,200	14,700
Humanitarian status	-	-	-	-	-	-	-	-	-	-	-
Total recognition rate	-	-	-	-	-	-	35.7	52.3	10.2	38.5	30.5
Resettlement arrivals	-	-	-	-	-	-	-	-	-	-	-
Spain											
Asylum applications	8,600	8,100	11,700	12,600	12,000	5,700	4,700	5,000	6,700	8,400	83,500
1951 Convention status	490	560	260	1,300	630	460	240	160	240	290	4,600
Humanitarian status	-	-	-	-	-	230	190	200	730	470	1,800
Total recognition rate	14.1	9.2	2.4	7.3	4.9	10.3	9.1	7.2	15.8	11.0	8.0
Resettlement arrivals	-	-	-	-	-	-	-	-	-	-	-
Sweden											
Asylum applications	29,400	27,400	84,000	37,600	18,600	9,000	5,800	9,700	12,800	11,200	245,500
1951 Convention status	2,200	1,400	620	1,000	790	150	130	1,300	1,100	330	9,000
Humanitarian status	9,200	15,500	8,800	34,500	36,700	3,500	3,100	7,100	6,000	2,600	127,000
Total recognition rate	41.7	45.4	28.3	41.5	69.0	37.6	43.1	58.2	49.8	31.6	46.4
Resettlement arrivals	1,500	1,700	3,400	940	7,400	2,000	1,600	1,200	1,100	550	21,400

Country	1990	1991	1992	1993	1994	1995	1996	1997	1998	1999	Total
Switzerland											
Asylum applications	35,800	41,600	18,000	24,700	16,100	17,000	18,000	24,000	41,300	46,100	282,600
1951 Convention status	880	1,200	1,400	3,800	2,900	2,700	2,300	2,600	2,000	2,100	21,900
Humanitarian status	130	940	6,700	12,200	13,800	11,900	8,200	6,000	7,000	22,800	89,700
Total recognition rate	6.1	5.6	21.9	54.2	66.7	75.8	50.4	36.5	36.8	52.7	39.7
Resettlement arrivals	-	-	-	-	-	-	-	-	-	-	-
United Kingdom[e]											
Asylum applications	26,200	44,800	24,600	22,400	32,800	44,000	29,600	32,500	46,000	71,100	374,000
1951 Convention status	920	510	1,100	1,600	830	1,300	2,200	4,000	5,300	7,100	24,900
Humanitarian status	2,400	2,200	15,300	11,100	3,700	4,400	5,100	3,100	3,900	13,300	64,500
Total recognition rate	82.5	44.4	47.1	54.3	21.4	21.1	18.7	19.7	29.3	61.7	34.9
Resettlement arrivals	650	490	620	510	260	70	20	-	*	-	2,600
United States[aef]											
Asylum applications	73,600	56,300	104,000	143,100	144,600	149,100	107,100	52,200	35,900	31,700	897,600
1951 Convention status	4,200	2,100	3,900	5,000	8,100	12,500	13,500	9,900	9,900	13,200	82,300
Humanitarian status	-	-	-	-	-	-	-	-	-	-	-
Total recognition rate[c]	8.6	12.7	17.8	14.6	15.2	19.6	20.3	13.2	20.8	40.3	17.9
Resettlement arrivals[g]	122,300	112,800	132,200	119,500	112,700	99,500	75,700	70,100	76,600	85,000	1,006,400

Notes:

Asylum applications: generally excludes 're-opened' applications. Figures generally reflect the number of persons who applied for asylum.

1951 Convention status: Where the asylum procedure includes an administrative review or appeal process, a positive outcome of such decisions is generally included. Figures generally exclude resettled refugees.

Humanitarian status: includes all non-Convention statuses granted (i.e. 'temporary admission status', 'provisional residence permit', 'exceptional leave to remain', etc.), but excludes persons whose deportation has been temporarily suspended.

Total recognition rate: number of refugees granted 1951 Convention and/or humanitarian status divided by the total number of decisions taken.

Resettlement arrivals: Figures may include persons who do not meet the international refugee definition and generally exclude family reunification.

* Value is below 5.

[a] Data refers to fiscal year.

[b] Including 're-opened' applications.

[c] Excluding decisions in administrative review.

[d] Includes applications/refugee determination under the UNHCR Mandate.

[e] Number of cases.

[f] Data provided by the United States Immigration and Naturalization Service (INS).

[g] Including family reunification.

See technical notes for further explanations and data limitations.

Source: Governments

Main country/territory of origin of asylum seekers in Western Europe, 1990–99[a]

Origin	1990	1991	1992	1993	1994	1995	1996	1997	1998	1999	Total
Former Yugoslavia	33,200	115,500	235,300	177,900	81,000	71,200	47,200	59,500	104,600	118,400	1,043,800
Romania	62,100	61,700	116,000	86,100	21,100	13,600	8,600	9,500	7,500	6,000	392,200
Turkey	48,800	45,500	37,100	25,500	26,100	41,400	38,300	32,900	20,900	19,400	335,900
Former USSR	4,800	10,300	16,400	28,300	16,300	18,100	20,800	23,100	21,400	37,100	196,600
Iraq	7,400	9,000	10,700	9,800	10,000	15,100	22,600	35,800	33,300	31,100	184,800
Sri Lanka	19,300	23,700	16,800	12,600	12,900	12,700	12,400	13,000	11,100	11,400	145,900
Somalia	12,200	11,100	14,600	13,300	12,400	11,800	7,500	8,500	11,900	14,000	117,300
Afghanistan	8,900	8,500	7,500	7,800	9,200	11,300	11,500	14,700	15,400	18,500	113,300
Iran, Islamic Rep.	18,300	15,300	7,800	7,100	12,000	10,000	10,000	8,300	8,100	11,900	108,800
Bulgaria	13,000	16,900	33,800	25,100	5,200	3,500	2,900	3,200	1,400	1,300	106,300
Dem. Rep. of the Congo	11,800	17,600	17,800	11,700	8,800	7,700	7,700	7,700	6,600	6,800	104,200
Pakistan	10,400	13,700	9,600	6,600	6,000	9,800	7,600	7,800	6,000	7,100	84,600
India	11,900	11,700	9,600	9,300	6,000	9,000	7,100	5,600	4,100	5,200	79,500
Viet Nam	13,400	11,600	13,700	12,400	4,100	3,700	2,800	3,500	3,500	2,900	71,600
Nigeria	8,100	12,400	12,700	4,300	6,300	8,900	6,300	4,500	3,600	2,500	69,600
Algeria	1,600	2,000	9,000	13,900	7,600	8,500	5,100	6,300	7,500	7,400	68,900
Albania	4,400	26,300	7,300	6,500	1,900	1,300	1,500	7,700	6,500	3,400	66,800
Lebanon	29,700	8,200	7,400	3,900	2,600	2,700	2,400	2,200	1,400	1,500	62,000
China	2,600	5,300	5,400	7,600	4,500	3,900	4,300	6,900	6,000	10,700	57,200
Ghana	9,400	11,100	10,500	5,500	3,100	3,200	1,600	1,400	800	800	47,400
Angola	9,700	11,200	2,200	4,000	4,900	3,100	2,500	1,900	2,000	4,100	45,600
Poland	16,600	7,500	6,400	3,300	1,400	1,700	1,500	1,100	1,700	2,300	43,500
Ethiopia	8,900	7,600	3,400	2,400	2,800	2,500	2,200	2,000	1,500	1,700	35,000
Syrian Arab Republic	6,700	2,900	2,200	1,700	1,600	2,100	3,100	3,000	3,200	4,100	30,600
Bangladesh	2,900	4,300	4,200	2,500	2,400	2,800	2,800	3,500	2,200	2,700	30,300
Liberia	1,400	4,500	6,900	4,700	2,000	2,200	3,000	1,800	700	500	27,700
Togo	500	3,200	4,700	4,300	5,000	1,800	1,700	2,500	1,100	1,300	26,100
Palestinians	7,300	2,800	3,800	2,600	1,800	500	600	400	100	300	20,200
Other/unknown	39,100	44,900	52,000	45,000	39,500	35,800	30,600	34,600	40,200	78,300	440,000
Total	**424,400**	**526,300**	**684,800**	**545,700**	**318,500**	**319,900**	**276,200**	**312,900**	**334,300**	**412,700**	**4,155,700**

Note:

[a]Countries included are Austria, Belgium, Denmark, Finland, France, Germany, Greece, Italy, Netherlands, Norway, Spain, Sweden, Switzerland, United Kingdom (number of cases).

See technical notes for explanations and data limitations.

Source: Governments

UN High Commissioners for Refugees, 1951–2000

Gerrit Jan van Heuven Goedhart (Netherlands) 1951–56

Before his appointment as the first United Nations High Commissioner for Refugees, Gerrit van Heuven Goedhart was a lawyer and journalist. During the Second World War, he was active in the Dutch resistance and its government-in-exile in London. As High Commissioner, van Heuven Goedhart put much of his energy into securing funds for the estimated 2.2 million refugees still displaced after the Second World War. By the time of his sudden death in 1956, he had put UNHCR on a much sounder financial footing than five years earlier. He shifted the focus of the organization's work from resettlement abroad to local integration within Europe, and his achievements on behalf of refugees were acknowledged in 1954, when UNHCR was awarded the Nobel Peace Prize.

Auguste R. Lindt (Switzerland) 1956–60

Auguste Lindt worked as a foreign correspondent for various European newspapers in the 1930s and served in the neutral Swiss army during the Second World War. Moving into the diplomatic field, he chaired the UNICEF Executive Committee, and from 1953 he served as Switzerland's observer to the United Nations. Almost immediately after his appointment as High Commissioner, he mobilized support for some 200,000 Hungarians who fled to Austria and Yugoslavia as a result of the Soviet suppression of the 1956 Hungarian uprising. Soon after this, he initiated an assistance programme for some 260,000 Algerians who had fled to Tunisia and Morocco during the Algerian war of independence. Lindt's diplomatic handling of these sensitive situations did much to ensure states' acceptance of UNHCR as an organization with worldwide responsibilities.

Félix Schnyder (Switzerland) 1960–65

Like his predecessor, Félix Schnyder was a Swiss diplomat who chaired the UNICEF Executive Board and served as Switzerland's observer to the United Nations before he was appointed High Commissioner. Schnyder oversaw the repatriation of Algerian refugees from Tunisia and Morocco, an operation which marked the first of UNHCR's many involvements in large repatriation and reintegration operations. He also secured General Assembly support for UNHCR's increased use of its 'good offices' role to mediate between governments in refugee crises globally, in particular in assisting Rwandan refugees in the Great Lakes region. In expanding UNHCR's activities in Africa, he helped to ensure further international recognition of the global character of the refugee problem. He played an important role in initiating the process which led to the adoption of the 1967 Protocol.

Sadruddin Aga Khan (Iran) 1965–77

Prince Sadruddin Aga Khan worked for UNHCR before becoming High Commissioner. He led missions to the Middle East and Asia and served as Deputy High Commissioner from 1962 to 1966. By the time he was appointed High Commissioner, UNHCR's expenditure in Africa and Asia exceeded that in Europe, marking a definitive shift from Europe to the developing world. He strengthened the organization's relations with African governments and helped to improve inter-agency cooperation within the United Nations to address problems of mass displacement in sub-Saharan Africa and Asia. He played a key role during the Bangladesh refugee crisis in 1971 and in assisting Asians expelled from Uganda in 1972.

Poul Hartling (Denmark) 1978–85

Poul Hartling served first as foreign minister and then as prime minister of Denmark before becoming High Commissioner in 1978. During his eight years in office, refugee problems became highly politicized with an intensification of the Cold War. The sustained mass exodus in Indochina and the large-scale international response thrust the organization into a lead role in a complex, highly politicized and large-scale humanitarian operation. During his time as High Commissioner, the organization set up other large-scale emergency relief operations in the Horn of Africa and Central America, and for Afghan refugees in Asia. UNHCR was awarded the Nobel Peace Prize for a second time in 1981, largely because of its key role in helping to manage the Vietnamese refugee crisis.

Jean-Pierre Hocké (Switzerland) 1986–89

Jean-Pierre Hocké served as Director of Operations for the International Committee of the Red Cross before his appointment as High Commissioner. During his term in office, the Indochinese refugee crisis continued. The Comprehensive Plan of Action, launched during his time as High Commissioner, instituted regional refugee status determination procedures and provided for the voluntary return of Vietnamese refugees. Hocké also played a key role in launching the 'CIREFCA process' in Central America, to consolidate peace in the region by extending assistance not only to returnees but also more broadly to war-affected populations. During his period in office, UNHCR played an important role in establishing and managing large camps for Ethiopian refugees in Sudan and for Somali refugees in Ethiopia.

Thorvald Stoltenberg (Norway) Jan. 1990–Nov. 1990

Thorvald Stoltenberg was Norwegian foreign minister before his appointment as High Commissioner. His short term of office marked the beginning of UNHCR's increased involvement in large-scale United Nations peacebuilding operations. While High Commissioner, he oversaw several ongoing repatriation operations, particularly in Central America. He resigned in November 1990 to return to his previous position as Norwegian foreign minister. In May 1993, at the height of the Bosnian war, he returned to the United Nations as the Secretary-General's Special Representative to the Former Yugoslavia.

Sadako Ogata (Japan) 1990–2000

Before her appointment as High Commissioner, Sadako Ogata was Dean of the Faculty of Foreign Studies at Sophia University, Tokyo. While in academia, she also held positions in the United Nations, chairing the UNICEF Executive Board in 1978–79, and serving on the UN Commission on Human Rights and as the Commission's independent expert on the human rights situation in Burma (now Myanmar). As High Commissioner she oversaw large-scale emergency operations in northern Iraq, Bosnia and Herzegovina, Kosovo, and the Great Lakes region of Africa. UNHCR's budget and staff more than doubled during her time in office, and the organization became increasingly involved in assisting internally displaced people and other vulnerable civilians in conflict situations. Emphasizing the link between refugees and international security, she strengthened UNHCR's relations with the UN Security Council.

Further reading

Much of the information in this book is drawn from unpublished UNHCR documents and reports. The book has also made extensive use of the documentation available on *RefWorld*, the UNHCR CD-ROM (for details see below). The following bibliography identifies some of the most accessible and useful literature on the issues examined in the book. Additional sources are also cited in the endnotes to each chapter. The inclusion of any item in this bibliography does not imply its endorsement by UNHCR.

Aasland, A., 'Russians Outside Russia: The New Russian Diaspora', in G. Smith (ed.), *The Nationalities Question in the Post-Soviet States*, Longman, London, 1996

Adelman, H., *Refugee Policy: Canada and the United States*, York Lanes Press, Toronto, 1991

African Rights, *Rwanda: Death, Despair and Defiance*, African Rights, London, 1994

Aga Khan, S., *Legal Problems Related to Refugees and Displaced Persons*, Academy of International Law, The Hague, 1976

Aga Khan, S., 'Study on Human Rights and Massive Exoduses', ECOSOC Doc. E/CN 4/1503, 1981

Allen, T. (ed.), *In Search of Cool Ground: War, Flight and Homecoming in Northeast Africa*, United Nations Research Institute for Social Development, Africa World Press and James Currey, London, 1996

Allen T. and Morsink, H. (eds.), *When Refugees Go Home: African Experiences*, James Currey, London, 1994

Amnesty International, 'Great Lakes Region: Still in Need of Protection: Repatriation, *Refoulement* and the Safety of Refugees and the Internally Displaced', report no. AFR02/07/97, London, 1997

Amnesty International, *Refugees: Human Rights Have No Borders*, London, 1997

Amnesty International and International Service for Human Rights, *The UN and Refugees' Human Rights*, London, 1997

Anderson, E., 'The Role of Asylum States in Promoting Safe and Peaceful Repatriation under the Dayton Agreement', *European Journal of International Law*, vol. 7, no. 2, 1996

Anderson, M., 'Do No Harm: Supporting Local Capacities for Peace through Aid', Local Capacities for Peace Project, Cambridge, 1996

Anderson, M., *Frontiers: Territory and State Formation in the Modern World*, Polity Press, Cambridge, UK, 1996

Arzt, D., *Refugees Into Citizens: Palestinians and the end of the Arab/Israeli Conflict*, Council on Foreign Relations, New York, 1997

Ball, N., *Making Peace Work: The Role of the International Development Community*, Overseas Development Council, Washington DC, 1996

Barber, B., 'Feeding Refugees, or War?', *Foreign Affairs*, vol. 76, no. 4, 1997

Barutciski, M., 'The Reinforcement of Non-admission Policies and the Subversion of UNHCR: Displacement and Internal Assistance in Bosnia-Herzegovina (1992–94)', *Journal of Refugee Studies*, vol. 8, no. 1/2, 1996

Bascom, J., *Losing Place: Refugee Populations and Rural Transformations in East Africa*, Berghahn Books, Providence RI, 1996

Batchelor, C., 'Stateless Persons: Some Gaps in International Protection', *International Journal of Refugee Law*, vol. 7, no. 2, 1995

Biermann, W. and Vadset, M. (eds.), *UN Peacekeeping in Trouble: Lessons Learned from the Former Yugoslavia*, Ashgate Publishing, Aldershot, UK, 1999

Black, R. and Koser, K. (eds.), *The End of the Refugee Cycle? Refugee Repatriation and Reconstruction*, Berghahn Books, Oxford, 1998

Black, R., *Refugees, Environment and Development*, Longman, New York, 1998

Booth, K., 'Human Wrongs and International Relations', *International Affairs*, vol. 71, no. 1, 1995

Bose, T. and Manchanda, R., *States, Citizens and Outsiders: The Uprooted Peoples of South Asia*, South Asia Forum for Human Rights, Kathmandu, 1997

Brown, M. (ed.), *The International Dimensions of Internal Conflict*, MIT Press, Cambridge MA, 1996

Brunner, G., *Nationality Problems and Minority Conflicts in Eastern Europe*, Bertelsman Foundation, Guetersloh, 1996

Bush, K., 'Rocks and Hard Places: Bad Governance, Human Rights Abuse and Population Displacement', *Canadian Foreign Policy*, vol. 4, no. 1, 1996

Byrne, R. and Shacknove, A., 'The Safe Country Notion in European Asylum Law', *Harvard Human Rights Journal*, vol. 9, spring 1996

Cahill, K. (ed.), *A Framework for Survival: Health, Human Rights, and Humanitarian Assistance in Conflicts and Disasters*, Council on Foreign Relations/BasicBooks, New York, 1993

Carlier, J.-Y. and Vanheule, D. (eds.), *Europe and Refugees: A Challenge?*, Kluwer Law International, The Hague, 1997

Carlier, J.-Y. et al (eds.), *Who is a Refugee? A Comparative Case Law Study*, Kluwer Law International, The Hague, 1997

Childers, E. and Urquhart, B., *Strengthening International Responses to Humanitarian Emergencies*, Ford Foundation, New York, 1991

Chimni, B.S., 'The Incarceration of Victims: Deconstructing Safety Zones', in N. Al-Naumi and R. Meese (eds.), *International Legal Issues Arising under the United Nations Decade of International Law*, Martinus Nijhoff, The Hague, 1995

Chimni, B.S., 'From Resettlement to Involuntary Repatriation: Towards a Critical History of Durable Solutions', UNHCR Working Paper no. 2, Geneva, May 1999

Chimni, B.S. (ed.), *International Refugee Law: A Reader*, Sage Publications, New Delhi, 2000

Cohen, Roberta and Deng, F., *Masses in Flight: The Global Crisis of Internal Displacement*, Brookings Institution, Washington DC, 1998

Cohen, Roberta and Deng, F. (eds.), *The Foresaken People: Case Studies of the Internally Displaced*, Brookings Institution, Washington DC, 1998

Cohen, Robin (ed.), *The Cambridge Survey of World Migration*, Cambridge University Press, Cambridge, 1995

Cohen, Robin, 'Diasporas and the Nation State: From Victims to Challengers', *International Affairs*, vol. 72, no. 3, 1996

Cohen, Robin, *Global Diasporas: An Introduction*, University College London, London, 1997

Coles, G.J.L., 'Solutions to the Problems of Refugees and the Protection of Refugees: A Background Study', UNHCR, Geneva, 1989

Coles, G.J.L., 'Conflict and Humanitarian Action: An Overview', UNHCR, Geneva, Nov. 1993

Coles, G.J.L., 'UNHCR and the Political Dimensions of Protection', UNHCR, Geneva, Aug. 1995

Coletta, N. et al, *The Transition from War to Peace in Sub-Saharan Africa*, World Bank, Washington DC, 1996

Collinson, S., *Europe and International Migration*, 2nd edn, Pinter and Royal Institute of International Affairs, London, 1994

Collinson, S., 'Globalization and the Dynamics of International Migration: Implications for the Refugee Regime', UNHCR Working Paper no. 1, Geneva, May 1999

The Commission on Global Governance, *Our Global Neighbourhood*, Oxford University Press, Oxford, 1995

Crisp, J., 'Meeting the Needs and Realizing the Rights of Refugee Children and Adolescents: From Policy to Practice', *Refugee Survey Quarterly*, vol. 15, no. 3, 1996

Crisp, J., 'Who has Counted the Refugees? UNHCR and the Politics of Numbers', UNHCR Working Paper no. 12, Geneva, June 1999

Crisp, J., 'Africa's Refugees: Patterns, Problems and Policy Challenges', *Journal of Contemporary African Studies*, vol. 18, no. 2, 2000

Curtis, P., 'Urban Household Coping Strategies During War: Bosnia-Hercegovina', *Disasters*, vol. 19, no. 1, 1995

Cutts, M., 'Politics and Humanitarianism', *Refugee Survey Quarterly*, vol. 17, no. 1, 1998

Daoust, I. and Folkelius, K., 'UNHCR Symposium on Gender-Based Persecution', *International Journal of Refugee Law*, vol. 8, no. 1/2, 1996

de Waal, A., *Famine Crimes: Politics and the Disaster Relief Industry in Africa*, James Currey, Oxford, 1997

Deng, F., 'Dealing with the Displaced: A Challenge to the International Community', *Global Governance*, vol. 1, no. 1, 1995

Dowty, A. and Loescher, G., 'Refugee Flows as Grounds for International Action', *International Security*, vol. 21, no. 1, 1996

Doyle, M., *UN Peacekeeping in Cambodia: UNTAC's Civil Mandate*, Lynne Rienner, Boulder CO, 1995

Duffield, M., 'Aid Policy and Post-Modern Conflict: A Critical Review', Occasional Paper no. 19, Birmingham University, UK, 1998

Durch, W. (ed.), *The Evolution of UN Peacekeeping: Case Studies and Comparative Analysis*, Macmillan Press, London, 1993

European Council on Refugees and Exiles, *Safe Third Countries: Myths and Realities*, ECRE, London, 1996

Ferris, E., 'After the Wars are Over: Reconstruction and Repatriation', Working Paper no. 10, Migration Policy in Global Perspective Series, International Center for Migration, Ethnicity and Citizenship, New School for Social Research, New York, 1997

Fitzpatrick, J., 'Temporary Protection of Refugees: Elements of a Formalized Regime', *American Journal of International Law*, vol. 94, No. 2, 2000

Forbes Martin, S., *Refugee Women*, Zed Books, London, 1992

Forbes Martin, S., 'Forced Migration and the Evolving Humanitarian Regime', UNHCR Working Paper no. 20, Geneva, July 2000

Forsythe, D., 'The International Committee of the Red Cross and Humanitarian Assistance: A Policy Analysis', *International Review of the Red Cross*, no. 314, 1996

Franco, L., 'An Examination of Safety Zones for Internally Displaced Persons as a Contribution Toward Prevention and Solution of Refugee Problems', in N. Al-Naumi and R. Meese (eds.), *International Legal Issues Arising Under the United Nations Decade of International Law*, Martinus Nijhoff, The Hague, 1995

Frelick, B., 'Preventive Diplomacy' and the Right to Seek Asylum', *International Journal of Refugee Law*, vol. 4, no. 4, 1992

Frelick, B., 'Unsafe Havens: Reassessing Security in Refugee Crises', *Harvard International Review*, Spring 1997

Gibney, Mark, *Open Borders, Closed Societies: The Ethical and Political Issues*, Greenwood Press, New York, 1988

Gibney, Matthew, J., 'The Responsibilities of Liberal Democratic States to Refugees', *American Political Science Review*, March 1999

Goodwin-Gill, G.S., *International Law and the Movement of Persons Between States*, Clarendon Press, Oxford, 1978

Goodwin-Gill, G.S., *The Refugee in International Law*, 2nd edn, Clarendon Press, Oxford, 1996

Goodwin-Gill, G.S., 'Refugee Identity and Protection's Fading Prospect', in Nicholson, F. and Twomey, P. (eds.), *Refugee Rights and Realities: Evolving International Concepts and Regimes*, Cambridge University Press, Cambridge, 1999

Gordenker, L., *Refugees in International Politics*, Croom Helm, Sydney, 1987

Gowlland-Debbas, V., *The Problem of Refugees in the Light of Contemporary International Law*, Martinus Nijhoff, The Hague, 1996

Grahl-Madsen, A., *The Status of Refugees in International Law*, vols. 1 and 2, Sijthoff, Leyden, 1966, 1972

Grant, B., *The Boat People: An 'Age' Investigation*, Penguin Books, Harmondsworth, 1979

Guild, E. and Niessen, J., *The Developing Immigration and Asylum Policies of the European Union*, Kluwer Law International, The Hague, 1996

Hampson, F.O., *Nurturing Peace: Why Peace Settlements Succeed or Fail*, US Institute of Peace, Washington DC, 1996

Hampton, J. (ed.), *Internally Displaced People: A Global Survey*, Norwegian Refugee Council and Earthscan Publications, London, 1998

Harding, J., *The Uninvited: Refugees at the Rich Man's Gate*, Profile Books/London Review of Books, London, 2000

Harrell-Bond, B., *Imposing Aid: Emergency Assistance to Refugees*, Oxford University Press, Oxford, 1986

Hathaway, J., *The Law of Refugee Status*, Butterworths, Markham, Ontario, 1991

Hathaway, J., 'New Directions to Avoid Hard Problems: The Distortion of the Palliative Role of Refugee Protection', *Journal of Refugee Studies*, vol. 8, no. 3, 1995

Hathaway, J. (ed.), *Reconceiving International Refugee Law*, Martinus Nijhoff, The Hague, 1997

Helton, A.S., 'The CIS Migration Conference: A Chance to Prevent and Ameliorate Forced Movements of People in the Former Soviet Union', *International Journal of Refugee Law*, vol. 8, no. 1/2, 1996

Helton, A.S. and Jacobs, E, 'What is Forced Migration?' *Georgetown Immigration Law Journal*, vol. 13, no. 4, 1999

Henkin, Alice N. (ed.), *Honoring Human Rights and Keeping the Peace: Lessons from El Salvador, Cambodia, and Haiti*, The Aspen Institute, 1995

Hoffmann, S., 'The Politics and Ethics of Military Intervention', *Survival*, vol. 37, no. 4, 1995–96

Holborn, L.W., *The International Refugee Organization: A Specialized Agency of the United Nations, Its History and Work 1946–1952*, Oxford University Press, Oxford, 1956

Holborn, L.W., *Refugees: A Problem of Our Time: The Work of the United Nations High Commissioner for Refugees, 1951–1972*, 2 vols., Scarecrow Press, Methuen NJ, 1975

Hollingworth, L., *Merry Christmas, Mr Larry*, Heinemann, London, 1966

Human Rights Watch, 'Discussion Paper: Protection in the Decade of Voluntary Repatriation', New York, 1996

Human Rights Watch, 'Uncertain Refuge: International Failures to Protect Refugees', report no. 9/1(G), New York, 1997

Human Rights Watch/Africa, *Leave None to Tell the Story*, New York, 1999

Independent Commission on International Humanitarian Issues, *Refugees: Dynamics of Displacement*, Zed Books, London, 1986

International Journal of Refugee Law, special issue on OAU/UNHCR symposium on refugees and the problems of forced population displacements in Africa, 4 vols. OECD, Summer 1995

Ignatieff, M., *Virtual War: Kosovo and Beyond*, Chatto Bodley Head and Cape, London, 2000

Ignatieff, M., *The Warrior's Honour: Ethnic War And the Modern Conscience*, Metropolitan Books, New York, 1997

Indra, D. (ed.), *Engendering Forced Migration: Theory and Practice*, Berghahn Books, Oxford, 1998

Jackson, I., *The Refugee Concept in Group Situations*, Kluwer Law International, The Hague, 1999

Joint Evaluation of Emergency Assistance to Rwanda, *The International Response to Conflict and Genocide: Lessons from the Rwanda Experience*, 4 vols, Copenhagen, March 1996

Joly, D., *Haven or Hell? Asylum Policies and Refugees in Europe*, Macmillan, London, 1996

Kaldor, M. and Vashee, B., *New Wars: Restructuring the Global Military Sector*, UNU/WIDER, London, 1997

Kälin, W., *Guiding Principles on Internal Displacement: Annotations*, Studies in Transnational Legal Policy no. 32, American Society of International Law, Washington DC, 2000

Karadawi, A., *Refugee Policy in Sudan 1967–1984*, Berghahn Books, New York, 1999

Keen, D., 'The Economic Functions of Violence in Civil Wars', Adelphi Paper no. 320, International Institute for Strategic Studies/Oxford University Press, London, 1998

Keen, D., *Refugees: Rationing the Right to Life: The Crisis in Emergency Relief*, Zed Books, London, 1992

Khan, I., 'UNHCR's Mandate Relating to Statelessness and UNHCR's Preventive Strategy', *Austrian Journal of Public and International Law*, vol. 49, no. 1, 1995

Kibreab, G., 'Environmental Causes and Impact of Refugee Movements: A Critique of the Current Debate', *Disasters*, vol. 21, no. 1, 1997

Korn, D., *Exodus Within Borders: An Introduction to the Crisis of Internal Displacement*, Brookings Institution, Washington DC, 1998

Kourula, P., *Broadening the Edges: Refugee Definition and International Protection Revisited*, Martinus Nijhoff, The Hague, 1997

Kumar, K. (ed.), *Rebuilding Societies After Civil War: Critical Roles for International Assistance*, Lynne Rienner, Boulder CO, 1997

Landgren, K., 'Safety Zones and International Protection: A Dark Grey Area', *International Journal of Refugee Law*, vol. 7, no. 3, 1995

Larkin, M.A., Cuny, F.C. and Stein, B.N., *Repatriation under Conflict in Central America*, CIPRA and Intertect, Washington DC, 1991

Lavoyer, P., 'Refugees and Internally Displaced Persons: International Humanitarian Law and the Role of the ICRC', *International Review of the Red Cross*, no. 305, 1995

Lawyers' Committee for Human Rights, *Uncertain Haven: Refugee Protection on the Fortieth Anniversary of the 1951 United Nations Refugee Convention*, LCHR, New York, 1991

Lawyers' Committee for Human Rights, *African Exodus: Refugee Crisis, Human Rights and the 1969 OAU Convention*, LCHR, New York, 1995

Lawyers' Committee for Human Rights, *Slamming the 'Golden Door': A Year of Expedited Removal*, LCHR, New York, April 1998

Loescher, G., *Refugees and International Relations*, Clarendon Press, Oxford, 1989

Loescher, G., *Beyond Charity: International Cooperation and the Global Refugee Crisis*, Oxford University Press, Oxford, 1993

Loescher, G. and Scanlan, J.A., *Calculated Kindness: Refugees and America's Half-Open Door, 1945–Present*, Free Press, Macmillan, New York, 1986

Macalister-Smith, P. and Alfredsson, G. (eds.), *The Land Beyond: Collected Essays on Refugee Law and Policy by Atle Grahl-Madsen*, Kluwer Law International, The Hague, 2000

Macrae, J. and Zwi, A. (eds.), *War and Hunger: Rethinking International Responses to Complex Emergencies*, Zed Books, London, 1995

McNamara, D., 'The Protection of Refugees and the Responsibility of States: Engagement or Abdication', *Harvard Human Rights Journal*, vol. 11, spring 1998

Malkki, L., *Purity and Exile: Violence, Memory and National Cosmology among Hutu Refugees in Tanzania*, University of Chicago Press, Chicago IL, 1995

Marrus, M., *The Unwanted: European Refugees in the Twentieth Century*, Oxford University Press, New York, 1985

Mayall, J. (ed.), *The New Interventionism 1991–1994: United Nations Experience in Cambodia, Former Yugoslavia and Somalia*, Cambridge University Press, Cambridge, 1996

McDowell, C., *A Tamil Diaspora: Sri Lankan Migration, Settlement and Politics in Switzerland*, Berghahn Books, Providence RI, 1997

Médécins Sans Frontières, *World in Crisis: The Politics of Survival at the End of the 20th Century*, Routledge, London, 1997

Meron, T., 'Answering for War Crimes: Lessons from the Balkans', *Foreign Affairs*, vol. 76, no. 1, 1997

Minear, L. and Weiss, T., *Humanitarian Action in Times of War: A Handbook for Practitioners*, Lynne Rienner, Boulder CO, 1993

Minear, L. and Weiss, T., *Mercy Under Fire: War and the Global Humanitarian Community*, Westview, Boulder CO, 1995

Mooney, E., 'Presence *ergo* Protection? UNPROFOR, UNHCR and ICRC in Croatia, and Bosnia and Herzegovina', *International Journal of Refugee Law*, vol. 7 no. 3, 1995

Moore, J. (ed.), *Hard Choices: Moral Dilemmas in Humanitarian Intervention*, Rowman and Littlefield, Oxford, 1998

Moorehead, C., *Dunant's Dream: War, Switzerland and the History of the Red Cross*, HarperCollins, London, 1998

Morris, E., 'The Limits of Mercy: Ethnopolitical Conflict and Humanitarian Action', Center for International Studies, Massachusetts Institute of Technology, 1995

Morris, N., 'Protection Dilemmas and UNHCR's Response: A Personal View from Within UNHCR', *International Journal of Refugee Law*, vol 9, no. 3, 1997

Morrison, J., *The Cost of Survival: The Trafficking of Refugees to the UK*, Refugee Council, London, July 1998

Morrison, J., 'The Trafficking and Smuggling of Refugees: The End Game in European Asylum Policy?', report for UNHCR Evaluation and Policy Analysis Unit, Geneva, July 2000

Muni, S.D. and Lok Raj Baral (eds.), *Refugees and Regional Security in South Asia*, Regional Centre for Strategic Studies, Konark Publishers PVT, Colombo, 1996

Nahajlo, B., 'Forcible Population Transfers, Deportations and Ethnic Cleansing in the CIS: Problems in Search of Responses', *Refugee Survey Quarterly*, vol. 16, no. 3, 1997

Nash, A. (ed.), *Human Rights and the Protection of Refugees under International Law*, Canadian Human Rights Foundation, Quebec, 1988

Newland, K., *US Refugee Policy: Dilemmas and Directions*, Carnegie Endowment for International Peace, Washington DC, 1995

Nicholson, F. and Twomey, P. (eds.), *Refugee Rights and Realities: Evolving International Concepts and Regimes*, Cambridge University Press, Cambridge, 1999

Ogata, S., 'Prevention, Protection and Solution: Elaborating a Post-Cold War Refugee Strategy', *The Brown Journal of World Affairs*, Brown University, vol. 1, no. 2, 1994

Ogata, S., 'The Evolution of UNHCR', *Journal of International Affairs*, Columbia University, vol. 47, no. 2, 1994

Ogata, S., 'UNHCR in the Balkans', in Biermann, W. and Vadset, M. (eds.), *UN Peacekeeping in Trouble: Lessons Learned from the Former Yugoslavia*, Ashgate Publishing, Aldershot, UK, 1999

Omaar, R. and de Waal, A., 'Humanitarianism Unbound? Current Dilemmas Facing Multi-Mandate Relief Operations in Political Emergencies', Discussion Paper no. 5, African Rights, London, Nov. 1994

Open Society Institute (Forced Migration Projects), *Roma and Forced Migration: An Annotated Bibliography*, New York, 1997

Papademetriou, D., *Coming Together or Pulling Apart? The European Union's Struggle with Immigration and Asylum*, Carnegie Endowment for International Peace, Washington DC, 1996

Plaut, W., *Asylum: A Moral Dilemma*, Praeger, CT, 1995

Plender, R., *Basic Documents on International Migration Law*, 2nd edn., Kluwer Law International, The Hague, 1997

Posen, B., 'Military Responses to Refugee Disasters', *International Security*, vol. 21, no. 1, 1996

Pottier, J., 'Relief and Repatriation: Views by Rwandan Refugees, Lessons for Humanitarian Aid Workers', *African Affairs*, vol. 95, no. 380, 1996

Preeg, E., *The Haitian Dilemma: A Case Study in Demographics, Development and US Foreign Policy*, Westview Press, Boulder CO, 1996

Prendergast, J., *Frontline Diplomacy: Humanitarian Aid and Conflict in Africa*, Lynne Rienner, Boulder CO, 1996

Prunier, G., *The Rwanda Crisis: History of a Genocide*, Hurst, London, 1995

Pugh, M., 'Military Intervention and Humanitarian Action: Trends and Issues', *Disasters*, vol. 22, no. 4, 1998

Raoul Wallenberg Institute, *Temporary Protection: Problems and Prospects*, report no. 22, Lund, 1996

Reynell, J., *Political Pawns: Refugees on the Thai-Kampuchean Border*, Refugee Studies Programme, Oxford, 1989

Richards, P., *Fighting for the Rain Forest: War, Youth and Resources in Sierra Leone*, James Currey, London, 1996

Rieff, D., 'The Humanitarian Trap', *World Policy Journal*, vol. 10, no. 4, 1995/96

Roberts, A., *Humanitarian Action in War: Aid, Protection and Impartiality in a Policy Vacuum*, Adelphi Paper no. 305, International Institute for Strategic Studies/Oxford University Press, London, 1996

Roberts, A. and Kingsbury, B. (eds.), *United Nations, Divided World: The UN's Role in International Relations*, Clarendon Press, Oxford, 1993

Robinson, N., *Convention Relating to the Status of Refugees: Its History, Contents and Interpretation*, Institute of Jewish Affairs, 1955

Robinson, W.C., *Terms of Refuge: The Indochinese Exodus and the International Response*, Zed Books, London, 1998

Rogers, R. and Copeland, E., *Forced Migration: Policy Issues in the Post-Cold War World*, Fletcher School of Law and Diplomacy, Tufts University, Medford MA, 1993

Rohde, D., *A Safe Area: Srebrenica: Europe's Worst Massacre Since the Second World War*, Simon and Schuster, New York, 1997

Rotberg, R. and Weiss, T. (eds.), *From Massacres to Genocide: The Media, Public Policy and Humanitarian Crises*, Brookings Institution/World Peace Foundation, Cambridge MA, 1996

Rubin, B. R., *The Fragmentation of Afghanistan: State Formation and Collapse in the International System*, Yale University Press, New Haven CT, 1995

Ruthstrom-Ruin, C., *Beyond Europe: The Globalization of Refugee Aid*, Lund University Press, Lund, 1993

Rystad, G., (ed.), *The Uprooted: Forced Migration as an International Problem in the Post-War Era*, Lund University Press, Lund, 1990

Salomon, K., *Refugees in the Cold War: Toward a New International Refugee Regime in the Early Postwar Era*, Lund University Press, Lund, 1991

Shacknove, A., 'From Asylum to Containment', *International Journal of Refugee Law*, vol. 5 no. 4, 1993

Shawcross, W., *The Quality of Mercy: Cambodia, Holocaust and Modern Conscience*, André Deutsch, London, and Simon and Schuster, New York, 1984

Shawcross, W., *Deliver Us From Evil: Peacekeepers, Warlords and a World of Endless Conflict*, Simon and Schuster, New York, 2000

Skran, C., *Refugees in Inter-War Europe: The Emergence of a Regime*, Clarendon Press, Oxford, 1995

Slim, H., 'Doing the Right Thing: Relief Agencies, Moral Dilemmas and Moral Responsibility in Political Emergencies and War', *Studies on Emergency and Disaster Relief no. 6*, Nordiska Afrikainstitutet, Uppsala, 1997

Smillie, I., 'Relief and Development: The Struggle for Synergy', Occasional Paper no. 33, Thomas J. Watson Jr Institute, Providence RI, 1998

Sorensen, G., 'Individual Security and National Security: The State Remains the Principal Problem', *Security Dialogue*, vol. 27, no. 4, 1996

Stein, B.N., Cuny, F.C. and Reed, P. (eds.), *Refugee Repatriation During Conflict*, Center for the Study of Societies in Crisis, Dallas TX, 1995

Suhrke, A. et al, 'The Kosovo Refugee Crisis: An Independent Evaluation of UNHCR's Emergency Preparedness and Response', UNHCR, Geneva, 2000

Teitelbaum, M. and Weiner, M. (eds.), *Threatened Peoples, Threatened Borders: World Migration and US Policy*, W.W. Norton, New York, 1995

Tishkov, V., *Ethnicity, Nationalism and Conflict in and after the Soviet Union: The Mind Aflame*, United Nations Institute for Social Development, International Peace Research Institute and Sage Publications, London, 1997

Tuitt, P., *False Images: The Law's Construction of the Refugee*, Pluto Press, London, 1996

Türk, V., 'The Role of UNHCR in the Development of International Refugee Law' in Nicholson, F. and Twomey, P. (eds.), *Refugee Rights and Realities: Evolving International Concepts and Regimes*, Cambridge University Press, Cambridge, 1999

UNHCR (Office of the United Nations High Commissioner for Refugees), *A Mandate to Protect and Assist Refugees*, Geneva, 1971

UNHCR, *Handbook on Procedures and Criteria for Determining Refugee Status*, Geneva, 1979

UNHCR, *Images of Exile: 1951–1991*, Geneva, 1991

UNHCR, *The State of the World's Refugees: The Challenge of Protection*, Penguin Books, London, 1993

UNHCR, *UNHCR's Operational Experience with Internally Displaced Persons*, Geneva, September 1994

UNHCR, *Collection of International Instruments and other Legal Texts Concerning Refugees and Displaced Persons*, 2 vols, 2nd edn, Geneva, 1995

UNHCR, 'An Overview of Protection Issues in Western Europe: Legislative Trends and Positions Taken by UNHCR', *European Series*, no. 3, 1995

UNHCR, *The State of the World's Refugees: In Search of Solutions*, Oxford University Press, Oxford, 1995

UNHCR, *International Thesaurus of Refugee Terminology*, United Nations, New York and Geneva, 1996

UNHCR, *The State of the World's Refugees: A Humanitarian Agenda*, Oxford University Press, Oxford, 1997

UNHCR, *Handbook for Emergencies*, Geneva, 1999

UNHCR, *Protecting Refugees: A Field Guide for NGOs*, Geneva, 1999

UNHCR, 'Internally Displaced Persons: The Role of the United Nations High Commissioner for Refugees', Position Paper, Geneva, March 2000

United Nations, 'The Fall of Srebrenica, Report of the Secretary-General Pursuant to General Assembly Resolution 53/55', UN Doc. A/54/549, 15 Nov. 1999

United Nations, 'Report of the Independent Inquiry into the Actions of the United Nations during the 1994 Genocide in Rwanda', New York, 15 Dec. 1999

Van Hear, N., *New Diasporas: The Mass Exodus, Dispersal and Regrouping of Migrant Communities*, University College London Press, London, 1998

Vernant, J., *The Refugee in the Post-War World*, Yale Press, New Haven CT, 1953

Wain, B., *The Refused: The Agony of the Indochina Refugees*, Simon and Schuster, New York, 1981

Walker, P., 'Whose Disaster is it Anyway? Rights, Responsibilities and Standards in Crisis', *Journal of Humanitarian Assistance*, Aug. 1996, website: http://www.jha.ac//articles/a009.htm

Waters, T., 'The Coming Rwandan Demographic Crisis: Or Why Current Repatriation Policies Will Not Solve Tanzania's (or Zaire's) Refugee Problems', *Journal of Humanitarian Assistance*, July 1997, website: http://www.jha.ac//articles/a013.htm

Weiner, M., 'Bad Neighbors, Bad Neighbourhoods: An Enquiry into the Causes of Refugee Flows', *International Security*, vol. 21, no. 1, 1996

Weiner, M., 'The Clash of Norms: Dilemmas in Refugee Policies', *Journal of Refugee Studies*, vol. 11, no. 4, 1998

Weiner, M., *The Global Migration Crisis: Challenge to States and to Human Rights*, Harper Collins, New York, 1995

Weiner, M. and Munz, M., 'Migrants, Refugees and Foreign Policy: Prevention and Intervention Strategies', *Third World Quarterly*, vol. 18, no. 1, 1997

Weis, P., 'The 1967 Protocol Relating to the Status of Refugees and Some Questions of the Law of Treaties', *British Yearbook of International Law*, vol. 23, 1967

Weiss, T. and Minear, L. (eds.), *Humanitarianism Across Borders: Sustaining Civilians in Times of War*, Lynne Rienner, Boulder CO, 1993

Weiss, T. et al, *The United Nations and Changing World Politics*, Westview Press, Boulder CO, 1994

Weiss, T. and Collins, C., *Humanitarian Challenges and Intervention: World Politics and the Dilemmas of Help*, Westview Press, Boulder CO, 1996

Whitman, J. and Pocock, D. (eds.), *After Rwanda: The Coordination of the United Nations Humanitarian Assistance*, Macmillan Press, London, 1996

Wiesner, L.A., *Victims and Survivors: Displaced Persons and Other War Victims in Viet-Nam 1954–1975*, Westport Press, New York, 1988

Xenos, N., 'Refugees: The Modern Political Condition', in M. J. Shapiro and H. R. Alker (eds.), *Challenging Boundaries: Global Flows: Territorial Identities*, University of Minnesota Press, Minneapolis, 1996

Zieck, M., 'UNHCR and Voluntary Repatriation: A Legal Analysis', University of Amsterdam (doctoral thesis), Amsterdam, 1997

Zolberg, A., 'The Unmixing of Peoples in the Post-communist World', occasional paper, International Center for Migration, Ethnicity and Citizenship, New School for Social Research, New York, 1997

Zolberg, A.R., Suhrke, A. and Aguayo, S., *Escape from Violence: Conflict and the Refugee Crisis in the Developing World*, Oxford University Press, Oxford, 1989

Zucker, N.L. and Zucker, N.F., *Desperate Crossings: Seeking Refuge in America*, M.E. Sharpe, Armonk NY, 1996

Periodicals

Amnesty International Report, published annually by Amnesty International, London

In Defense of the Alien, published annually by the Center for Migration Studies, New York

Forced Migration Review, published quarterly by the Refugee Studies Centre, Oxford, in collaboration with the Norwegian Refugee Council/Global IDP Project, Geneva

International Journal of Refugee Law, published quarterly by Oxford University Press

International Migration, published quarterly by the International Organization for Migration

International Migration Review, published quarterly by the Center for Migration Studies, New York

International Review of the Red Cross, published six times a year by the International Committee of the Red Cross and Red Crescent Societies

Journal of Refugee Studies, published quarterly by Oxford University Press

Refuge, published six times a year by the Centre for Refugee Studies, York University, Toronto

Refugee Survey Quarterly, published quarterly by Oxford University Press

Refugees magazine, published quarterly by UNHCR, Geneva

World Disaster Report, published annually by the International Federation of Red Cross and Red Crescent Societies

World Refugee Survey, published annually by the US Committee for Refugees, Washington DC

World Report, published annually by Human Rights Watch, New York

Selected websites

United Nations sites:

UNHCR:
http://www.unhcr.ch

UNHCR *RefWorld*:
http://www.unhcr.ch/refworld/welcome.htm

United Nations:
http://www.un.org

UN Office for the High Commissioner for Human Rights:
http://www.unhchr.ch

UN ReliefWeb:
http://www.reliefweb.int/

Other sites:

Amnesty International:
http://www.amnesty.org/

Centre for Refugee Studies, York University, Toronto:
http://www.yorku.ca/crs/

European Council on Refugees and Exiles:
http://www.ecre.org/

Global IDP Survey:
http://www.nrc.no/idp.htm

Human Rights Internet:
http://www.hri.ca

Human Rights Watch:
http://www.hrw.org

InterAction:
http://www.interaction.org

International Association for the Study of Forced Migration:
http://141.13.240.13/~ba6ef3/iasfm.htm

International Committee of the Red Cross:
http://www.icrc.org/

International Crisis Group:
http://www.intl-crisis-group.org/

International Federation of Red Cross and Red Crescent Societies:
http://www.ifrc.org/

International Organization for Migration:
http://www.iom.int/

Jesuit Refugee Service:
http://www.JesRef.org/

Journal of Humanitarian Assistance:
http://www.jha.ac/

Lawyers' Committee for Human Rights:
http://www.lchr.org/

Migration and Ethnic Relations:
http://www.ercomer.org/wwwvl/

OneWorld:
http://www.oneworld.org/index.html

Palestinian refugees:
http://www.Palestine-net.com/palestine.html

Refugee Studies Centre, University of Oxford:
http://www.qeh.ox.ac.uk/rsp/

Refugees International:
http://www.refintl.org/

US Committee for Refugees:
http://www.refugees.org

RefWorld: UNHCR's CD-ROM

RefWorld is a reference tool designed to meet the information needs of those interested in the problem of forced displacement: governments, judicial authorities, international organizations, voluntary agencies, academic institutions and legal counsel. This CD-ROM is a collection of full-text databases, updated twice a year. It provides access to the most comprehensive refugee-related information available, drawn from the most current and reliable sources.

The information available on *RefWorld* includes data on conditions in refugees' countries of origin; national legislation; jurisprudence; international treaties and documents on human rights and refugee law; UN General Assembly and Security Council documents; documents emanating from the UN Commission on Human Rights and its Sub-Commission; official UNHCR documents; an extensive reference library including training manuals; refugee statistics; and the library catalogue of UNHCR's Centre for Documentation and Research.

RefWorld is available on an annual subscription basis for US$250. Multiple subscriptions can be ordered at a reduced rate of $125 per year. Network licence agreements based on concurrent use are also available upon request. For more information contact the UNHCR Centre for Documentation and Research, CP 2500, CH-1211 Geneva 2, Switzerland. Fax: (41-22) 739-7367; e-mail: <cdr@unchr.ch>.

Index

Abkhazia 9, 185, 192–6, 199
Ad Hoc Committee on Statelessness
  and Related Problems 30–1
Adoula, C. 50
Afghanistan/Afghans 7, 105, 112,131,
  138, 158, 160, 163, 215, 248,
  278–9, 284
  and former Soviet region 188, 194,
  196, 198–9, 206
  in Pakistan and Iran 116–20, 212
African Charter on the Rights and
  Welfare of the Child (1991) 138
African National Congress (ANC) 248
Aga Khan, S. 42, 55, 126, 213, 326
  and Bangladesh 62, 65–8, 73, 76
  and Vietnam and Laos 81–2, 97–8
Aidid, M.F. 256
AIDS 11, 253
airlifts
  Balkans 220, 225–8
  Bangladesh 60, 70, 72, 74
  of Rwandans 51, 271
Ajello, A. 152
Akashi, Y. 144
Albania 158, 160, 169
  and Kosovo Albanian refugees 10,
  233–9, 241, 248
Algeria/Algerians 6, 35, 37–44, 136,
  160, 164, 266–7, 278
Allende, S. 7, 126
Alliance of Democratic Forces for the
  Liberation of Zaire/Congo
  (AFDL) 263–4, 268–9, 271
Amin, I. 6, 69, 77, 180
Angola/Angolans 44, 71, 105, 134–5,
  158, 163, 214–16, 246, 248,
  271–2, 278, 283
Annan, K. 150, 214–15, 224, 236,
  243, 253
Anti-piracy 7, 79, 86–7, 102
Arab-Israeli Six Day War (1967) 21
Arafat, Y. 21
Argentina 7, 126–7, 156
Aristide, J.-B. 176–7
Armed Forces Revolutionary Council
  (AFRC), Sierra Leone 261
Armée de libération nationale (ALN), Algeria
  38–9, 41, 43
Armenia/Armenians 1, 9, 15, 185–6,
  193, 198, 208, 279
Asians, Ugandan 6, 69, 180
Association of Southeast Asian Nations
  (ASEAN) 83–6

asylum
  first asylum concept 85, 88–9, 98,
  102, 156, 283
  manifestly-unfounded asylum
  applications 159
  right to seek 8, 25, 150, 159–60,
  170, 183, 287
Australia 8, 17, 28, 32, 69, 86, 99,
  127, 155, 166, 170–1, 175,
  181–2, 236–7
Austria 14, 18, 22, 69, 165, 170–1,
  175, 239
  and Hungarian crisis 26–9, 31–2, 34
Awami League 60, 67
Azerbaijan/Azerbaijanis 185–6,
  198–200, 203, 208, 214–15, 278

Baltic states 14, 187, 189, 198
Band Aid 115
Bangladesh Red Cross 71
Bangladesh/Bangladeshis 6, 59–77,
  136, 189, 284
Banyamulenge 262–3
Banyarwanda 189, 258, 273
Baril, M. 269
Barre, S. 106, 110, 256
Belarus/Belorussians 13, 28, 199
Belgium 46–9, 52, 69, 99, 170–1
Belize 124, 140
Belo, C. 236
Bengal/Bengalis 62, 65–6
  see also East Bengal, West Bengal
Berlin blockade (1948–49) 18, 227
Bhutan/Bhutanese 63, 189, 278–9
Bhutto, Z.A. 60
Biafra 46–7
Bidoons 189
Bihac (Bosnia and Herzegovina) 223,
  227
Bihar/Biharis 65, 73–6, 189
Bizimungu, A. 258–9
Black Sea Greeks 187
boat people
  Haitian 174–7
  Vietnamese 7, 79, 82–90, 94, 98,
  176, 182
Bolivians 126
Bosnia and Herzegovina 1, 9, 164–5,
  168, 194, 206, 211, 215, 218–33,
  242–3, 279
Botswana 44
Bourguiba, H. 39, 41
Boutros-Ghali, B. 133, 135, 138,

223–4, 226
Brazil/Brazilians 126–7
British Broadcasting Corporation (BBC)
  257
British Voluntary Society for Aid to
  Hungarians 30
Brookings Institution 142
Buddhists 75, 92
Bukavu (Zaire/DRC) 50–1, 251, 263,
  269
Bulganin, N. 29
Bulgaria/Bulgarians 15, 76, 127, 158,
  160
Bulk Challenge 260
Bunche, R. 50
Burden-sharing 102, 158–9, 165, 168,
  234, 239
Burkina Faso 261
Burma 6, 59, 71, 75, 77
  see also Myanmar
Burundi/Burundians 11, 44, 47, 49,
  51, 207, 214–15, 278
  and Rwanda 245–6, 249–51, 255,
  259, 263, 273
Bush, G. 177, 213, 256
Buyoya, P. 259, 263

Caetano, M. 236
Cambodia/Cambodians 6–8, 71, 79,
  81, 85, 88, 94–9, 102, 109, 188,
  240, 248, 284
  repatriation and peacebuilding 133,
  143, 146–8, 151
  in Thailand 91–7, 100
Cambodian People's Party 147
Cambodian Repatriation and
  Resettlement operation (CARERE)
  146
camps, see refugee camps
Canada 17, 29, 32, 43, 69, 86, 99,
  124, 127, 155, 166, 170–1, 173,
  175, 179–81, 227, 239, 254
Canary Islands 267
Cape Verde 53, 127
CARE (Cooperative Action for
  American Relief Everywhere) 30,
  194
CARITAS 194
carrier sanctions 159, 162
Cartagena Declaration (1984) 123
Carter, J. 174
Casamance 260
Castro, F. 174

Caucasus 9, 185, 187, 191–6, 203–6, 208, 209, 215
Ceausescu, N. 174
Central African Republic 44, 46
Chechnya/Chechens 1, 9, 185, 187, 199, 203–9
children 3, 112, 114–15, 149–50, 214, 222, 224, 240, 253, 267
  child soldiers 138, 206, 260–1, 280
  unaccompanied/separated 8, 34, 93, 94, 136
Chile/Chileans 7, 29, 32, 126–7, 156, 180
China/Chinese 13, 18–19, 63, 68, 160, 182, 278
  refugees in Hong Kong 5, 33, 35, 59
  and Viet Nam 79, 81–2, 88, 102
cholera 64–5, 109, 113, 247
Church World Service 30
CIREFCA (International Conference on Central American Refugees) 137, 140–3, 200
CIS, see Commonwealth of Independent States
citizenship 74–6, 159, 178, 258, 262, 284
  in former Soviet Union 185, 189, 203
Clinton, B. 175, 177, 256
CNN effect 283
Cochetel, V. 204, 207
Cohen, R. 215
Colombia 123, 163, 214–15, 282
Comfort, USNS 177
Commonwealth of Independent States (CIS) 185, 190–1, 195–6, 198–203, 208–9, 281
Communist Party of the Soviet Union 26, 31
Comprehensive Plan of Action (CPA) 79, 84–5, 87–9, 91, 94, 101–3
Conference on Jewish Material Claims against Germany 28
Conference on Security and Cooperation in Europe (CSCE) 191–2
  see also Organization for Security and Cooperation in Europe (OSCE)
Congo, Democratic Republic of (formerly Zaire) 11, 44–5, 47–8, 51, 71, 105, 108–9, 158, 160, 189, 194, 206, 214–15, 278–9, 283
  and Rwanda 6, 245–51, 254–5, 258–9, 262–4, 268, 271–3
Congo, Republic of (Congo Brazzaville) 44, 49, 215, 271–2, 278
contras 108, 123, 128, 248
Convention Against Torture and Other Cruel, Inhuman or Degrading Treatment or Punishment (1984) 150, 163, 179

Convention Concerning the Status of Refugees from Germany (1938) 25
Convention Governing the Specific Aspects of Refuge Problems in Africa (1969) 37, 55–7, 123, 249
Convention on the Elimination of All Forms of Discrimination against Women (1979) 150
Convention on the Prevention and Punishment of the Crime of Genocide (1948) 240
Convention on the Reduction of Statelessness (1961) 189
Convention on the Rights of the Child (1989) 138, 150
Convention Relating to the International Status of Refugees (1933) 25
Convention Relating to the Status of Refugees (1951) 2, 5–8, 37, 56–7, 75, 109, 150, 170, 249, 276, 279–80, 282, 287
  and Central America 123, 126, 130
  and Indochina 83, 85, 91, 102
  and industrialized world's asylum policy 155–6, 159, 161
  and Second World War aftermath 13, 20, 23–6, 29–31
  Article (33) 23, 25, 53, 176
  Conference of Plenipotentiaries (1951) 5
  refugee definition 162–5, 170, 173–4, 180–2, 198–200, 209
Convention Relating to the Status of Stateless Persons (1954) 189
Costa Rica 124–5, 137, 140
Côte d'Ivoire 47, 260, 278
Council of Churches 136
Council of Europe 161, 171–2, 191, 196, 202–3
Crimean Tatars 187, 189, 199, 202
Croatia/Croats 218–33, 242, 279
Cuba/Cubans 52, 121, 134, 136, 174–6, 267
Cyprus 127, 214
Czech Republic 164, 171
Czechoslovakia/Czechs 13, 19, 28, 32, 156, 180, 189

Daghestan 203–5, 208
Dalai Lama 63
Dayton Peace Agreement (1995), Bosnia and Herzegovina 9, 168, 228–30, 232, 285
Declaration of Principles on Palestinian self-rule in the Occupied Territories (1993) 21
decolonization 5–6, 37–57, 275
Deng, F. 214–15, 282
Denmark 29, 69, 99, 159, 166, 171, 225
development assistance 139–43, 166, 285

DISERO (Disembarkation Resettlement Offers) 87
Djibouti 106–7, 114, 257
Doe, S. 260
Dominican Republic 32
Dublin Convention (1990) 159, 162, 164
Dulles, J.F. 40
durable solutions 37, 52, 84, 91, 95, 102–3, 142, 286
Duvalier, F. 176
Duvalier, J–C. 176

East Bengal 70
East Timor 11, 167, 207, 236–7, 248, 278
Economic Community of West African States (ECOWAS) 260
  Military Observer Group (ECOMOG) 260–1
economic migrants 8, 155, 157, 175–6, 281
Edelstam, H. 127
Egypt 21, 44
Eisenhower, D.D. 29
El Salvador/Salvadorans 8, 121–5, 128–30, 131, 136–7, 139–40, 174, 248
environmental issues 108, 113, 142
Equatorial Guinea 47
Eritrea/Eritreans 7, 46, 106, 110–15, 131, 189, 279
Esquipulas (Central American peace process) 131, 136–7
Estonia/Estonians 13, 199
Ethiopia/Ethiopians 7, 44, 46, 105–15, 131, 189, 198, 248, 256, 278–9
ethnic cleansing 9–10, 186, 218, 221–4, 228, 230–1, 234, 242, 283
European Commission 169
European Community (EC) 91, 159–60, 162, 166
European Community Humanitarian Office (ECHO) 267
European Convention for the Protection of Human Rights and Fundamental Freedoms (1950) 150, 163, 171
European Court of Human Rights 171
European Court of Justice 159
European Parliament 159
European Union (EU) 155, 159, 161–5, 168–9, 170, 172, 175, 209
Ewe refugees 44
Executive Committee of the High Commissioner's Programme (EXCOM) 2, 31, 34, 35, 163, 188–9

family reunification 8, 94, 127, 150, 156, 162, 183, 239, 280

Farabundo Martí National Liberation Front (FMLN) 123
Fergana Valley (Uzbekistan–Kyrgyzstan)186, 203
Finland/Finns 99, 166, 171, 187
forced migrants (former Soviet region) 198–201
Forces armées rwandaises (FAR), 'ex-FAR' 246–7, 251, 254, 258–9, 262–4, 269–71
Forces armées zaïroises (FAZ) 259, 269
Ford Foundation 22, 33
formerly deported peoples 202–3
Fouinat, F. 220
France 6, 29, 32, 38–44, 46, 80, 86, 99, 127, 216, 227, 239, 254, 260, 266
    asylum policy 163–6, 170–1, 175
Frelimo (Mozambique)112, 148
Front de libération nationale (FLN), Algeria 38, 41
Funcinpec (Cambodia) 147

Gabon 47
Gandhi, I. 64–5, 67–8
de Gaulle, C. 38, 43
Gaza Strip 20–1, 279
Geldof, B. 115
General Assembly *see* United Nations
Geneva Conventions (1949) 84–5, 240, 277
génocidaires (Rwanda) 246–7, 250, 254, 262, 265, 271
genocide 240
    Rwanda 11, 47, 52, 245–6, 254, 258–9, 272–3
Georgia 9, 185, 192–6, 199–200, 203–5, 208, 214
Germany, Democratic Republic of 18, 73, 127
Germany, Federal Republic of 1, 13–14, 17–18, 22, 28, 32, 99, 160, 163–6, 170–1, 187, 202, 278
    refugees from Iraq and Balkans 158, 219, 225, 227–8, 233, 239
Ghana 44, 158, 260
globalization 11, 275–6
Goma camps 50–1, 109, 245–51, 254–5, 258–9, 268–9
Gorazde (Bosnia and Herzegovina) 222–3, 225, 227
Gorbachev, M. 188
Graeco-Turkish war (1922) 15
Great Lakes region 37, 44, 47–52, 207, 245–73
Greece/Greeks 13, 15, 22, 24, 76, 187
Grozny (Chechnya) 203, 208
Guantánamo, Cuba 175, 177
Guatemala/Guatemalans 8, 121–5, 130–1, 136–7, 139–41, 174
Guatemalan National Revolutionary Unity (URNG) 124

Guiding Principles on Internal Displacement (1998) 214–15, 282
Guinea 260, 278
Guinea-Bissau 44, 71, 260
Gulf War (1991) 9, 189, 211–12
gypsies (Roma) 28, 242

Habibie, B.J. 236
Habyarimana, J. 245
Hai Hong 82
Haile Selassie 110
Haiti/Haitians 174–7
harkis (France) 43
Hartling, P. 84, 86–7, 98, 118, 327
Hassan II, King 41
van Heuven Goedhart, G.J. 22, 26, 29–30, 33, 326
Hindus 59, 69
HIV infection 11, 253
Hmong 97, 101
Hobsbawm, E. 1
Hocké, J.-P. 84, 102, 327
Holborn, L. 5
Holbrooke, R. 282
Honduras 108, 122, 124–5, 137, 140, 248
Hong Kong 33, 41, 81, 85, 88–9, 98, 109
Horta, J.R. 236
host third country, *see* safe third country
Huerta Diaz, I. 126
human shields 11, 228
humanitarian
    evacuation programme 10–11, 168, 238–9
    status 162, 165, 175
Humanitarian Charter 194
Hun Sen 147
Hungary/Hungarians 5, 13, 26–35, 156, 164, 171, 180, 284
Hussein, S. 212
Hutus 47–8, 52, 245–8, 252–4, 258–9, 262–3, 268, 271–3

Iceland 32, 127
Ile de Lumière 87
Implementation Force (IFOR) 229, 231
India/Indians 6, 19, 105, 119, 157, 160, 189, 215, 278
    Bangladeshi crisis 59–62, 65–70, 73, 76
    Tibetans in 4, 63
Indian Red Cross 66, 71
Indochina/Indochinese 6–7, 38, 77, 79–103, 156, 166, 173, 180, 284
Indonesia 59, 83–9, 98, 145, 182, 214, 236–7, 278
Ingushetia/Ingush 185, 187, 199, 203–5, 207–8
Interahamwe 108, 246, 248, 250
interdiction policy (USA) 176–7

Intergovernmental Committee for European Migration (ICEM) 22, 31, 69, 126–7
internally displaced persons (IDPs), *see especially* 214–15, 281–2
International Committee of the Red Cross (ICRC) 15, 19, 26, 34, 214, 256
    Africa 38, 42, 47
    Balkans 220, 222, 227
    Bangladesh 69, 73
    Central America 126, 128
    Indochina 92–3
    Soviet Union, former 194, 203–4, 206–7
International Conference on Central American Refugees (CIREFCA) 137, 140–3, 200
International Conference on the Former Yugoslavia 285
International Conferences on Assistance to Refugees in Africa (ICARA I and II) 142
International Council of Voluntary Agencies (ICVA) 194
International Court of Justice 55
International Covenant on Civil and Political Rights (1966) 150
International Covenant on Economic, Social and Cultural Rights (1966) 150
International Criminal Court 138, 240
international criminal justice 11, 138, 224–5, 240
International Criminal Tribunal for Rwanda (ICTR) 240
International Criminal Tribunal for the former Yugoslavia (ICTY) 224–5, 240
International Force in East Timor (INTERFET) 237
International Fund for Agricultural Development (IFAD) 119–20
International Labour Organization (ILO) 15, 51, 126, 138, 206
International Organization for Migration (IOM) 22, 69, 185, 191, 200, 237–9
International Refugee Organization (IRO) 5, 13, 16–19
International Save the Children Alliance 138
intifada 21
Iran 7, 119, 158, 160, 217, 278–9
Iran–Iraq war (1980–88) 118, 212
Iraq/Iraqis 1, 278–9, 284
    asylum in industrialized countries 158, 160, 166
    Kurdish crisis 212–18
    and Soviet Union 189, 198, 207
Ireland 32, 159, 171
Israel 17, 20–1, 43
Israeli Occupied Territories 21

Italy 14, 18, 22, 46, 69, 127, 158, 163, 166, 169, 171, 228, 233, 239, 267

Jamieson, T. 49, 62, 70
Japan 8, 13, 155, 166–7, 182–3, 281
and Indochinese refugees 89, 98–9, 102, 182
Jews 15, 29, 174, 187
Jola people 260
Jordan 20–1, 279

Kabbah, A.T. 261
Kabila, L.-D. 264, 272
Kádár, J. 29, 32
Kagame, P. 262
Kalmyks 187
Kampuchea see Cambodia
Kap Anamur 87
Karadzic, R. 240
Katanga 50, 52
Kazakhstan/Kazaks 119, 199, 208
Kelly, J. 68
Kenya/Kenyans 69, 106, 127, 256–7, 278–9
Khan, A. 60
Khan, Y. 60, 67
Khao-I-Dang 93, 97, 109, 145, 194
Khmer Rouge 7, 81, 92–6, 145–8, 151, 240, 248
Khrushchev, N. 26, 29
Kibeho camp 252, 254–5
Kigali 49, 245–6, 268
Kinshasa 247, 252, 259, 268–9, 271
Kinyarwanda speakers 51–2
Kivu provinces 48–52, 206, 246–7, 250, 255, 258–9, 262–4, 271–3
Koljevic, N. 226
Korean War (1950–53) 18, 22
Kosovo 1, 10, 165–8, 180, 182, 215, 233–43, 249
Kosovo Force (KFOR) 241
Kosovo Liberation Army (KLA) 233–4, 248
Kozyrev, A. 200
Kurds 9, 189, 211–18
Kuwait 189, 212
Kyrgyzstan 119, 191, 199–200, 203, 208

ladinos 128
landmines 42, 146, 206–7, 230, 241
Laos/Laotians 6–7, 79–82, 85, 92, 97–102, 284
Latvia/Latvians 13, 199
League of Nations 1, 5, 15, 20–2, 30, 47, 186
League of Red Cross Societies 26, 30, 40–2
Lebanon 20–1, 160, 279
Liberia 44, 207, 248, 260, 278
Libya 257, 261, 266
Lindt, A. 47, 326

and Algeria 39–40, 43
and Hungary 26, 29–30, 32, 34–5
Lithuania/Lithuanians 13, 199
Live Aid 115
London Resolutions (1992) 159, 160
Luxembourg 175

Maastricht Treaty (1992) 159, 162
Macau 89, 98
McDonald, J. 15, 22
Mace, C. 62, 64
Macedonia, former Yugoslav Republic of 10, 168, 234–9, 249, 283
Machel, G. 138
Machel, S. 138
Madagascar 53
Magere, Colonel 264
Malawi 112–13, 148–9
Malaysia 59, 82–5, 88–9, 98, 145, 281
Malik, A.M. 67
Malta 69
manifestly-unfounded asylum applications 159
Mao Zedong 18
Marie, J.-J. 187
Mariel boatlift 174, 176
Mauritania 189, 266–7
Mayi Mayi 259
Médecins Sans Frontières 194, 206
Mendiluce, J.-M. 222
Mengistu H.M. 106, 115, 131
Merhamet 194
Meskhetians 186–7, 202–3
Mexico 123–5, 127, 130, 137, 140, 281
Microsoft 167
Milosevic, S. 218, 240
Minimum Standards in Disaster Response 194
Minsk Group 192
Miskito people 128
Mkapa, B. 264
Mobutu Sese Seko 51–2, 246, 252, 254–5, 258, 262, 268, 272–3
Moldova/Moldovans 187, 192, 199–200
Monaco 53
Mongolia 199
Montenegro 233–4
Morice Line 40
Morocco 6, 35, 37–8, 39–41, 266–7
Moscow 26, 186, 188, 190–1, 197, 198
Moussalli, M. 86
Mozambique Liberation Front (Frelimo) 112, 148
Mozambique National Resistance (Renamo) 112, 148, 151
Mozambique/Mozambicans 8, 44, 54, 71, 105, 112–13, 133, 143, 151–2, 194, 248
mujahedin 7, 108, 120–1, 131, 248
Mukhti Bahini (Bangladesh) 67–8

Mulele, P. 50
Museveni, Y. 245
Muslim-Croat Federation 219, 229, 231
Muslims 195
and Balkans 218, 222, 224, 226, 231
and Bangladesh 59–60, 69, 74–5
Mutesa II, King 50
Myanmar 75, 189, 214–15, 279
see also Burma

Nagorno-Karabakh 9, 185–6, 191–3
Nagy, I. 26–7
Namibia 8, 44, 53, 133–5, 144, 152, 248
Nansen, F. 5, 15, 22, 186
Nansen International Office 15
National Committee for Aid to Refugees (CONAR), Chile 126
National Patriotic Front of Liberia (NFPL) 260–1
National Resistance Army (NRA), Uganda 245
nationality see citizenship
NATO (North Atlantic Treaty Organization) 10, 18, 213
and Balkans 168, 228, 230–1, 233–5, 238, 241, 242
Nazism 15, 28
Ndadaye, M. 245, 259
Nepal/Nepalis 63, 74, 189, 279
Netherlands 69, 99, 127, 166, 170–1, 224, 255
New Caledonia 32
New Delhi Agreement (1973) 73–4
New Zealand 8, 69, 99, 127, 155, 181–2
Ngendandumwe, P. 49
Nicaragua/Nicaraguans 105, 121–5, 128, 131, 174, 136–7, 139–40, 143, 248
Nigeria/Nigerians 46–7, 71, 158, 160
Nkubito, A.-M. 254
Nobel Peace Prize 15, 236, 326, 327
non-governmental organizations (NGOs), see especially 194
non-refoulement 2, 25, 57, 84, 92, 150, 159, 161, 168, 176, 179
non-state agents of persecution 162–4
North Ossetia 185, 196, 199, 203, 205, 207
Norway 29, 69, 99, 164, 166, 171, 225, 239
Ntaryamira, C. 245
Ntibantunganya, S. 259
Nujoma, S. 136
Nuremberg laws 15
Nyerere, J. 49

Obote, M. 50, 69, 245
Office for Democratic Institutions and Human Rights (ODIHR) 200

Office for the Coordination of Humanitarian Affairs (OCHA) 192, 217
Ogaden region 106–7, 256
Ogata, S. 143, 150, 158, 190, 194, 249, 285, 327
  and Balkans 220, 222–3, 230–1, 235, 239, 243
  and Kurds 216–17
  and Rwandan crisis 246–7, 251, 255, 259, 262
Open Cities project 231
Open Society Institute 203
Operation Provide Comfort (northern Iraq) 213
Operation Restore Hope (Somalia) 256
Operation Storm (Croatia) 228
Operation Turquoise (Rwanda) 254
Orderly Departure Programme (ODP) 79, 84, 89–91, 99, 102, 174
Orderly Return Programme 85
Organization for Security and Cooperation in Europe (OSCE) 185, 191–2, 197, 200, 202–3, 233
  see also Conference on Security and Cooperation in Europe (CSCE)
Organization of African Unity (OAU) 6, 55
  Refugee Convention (1969) 37, 55–7, 123, 249
Organization of American States 123, 176
Oxfam 194
Özal, T. 213

Pakistan/Pakistanis 6–7, 19, 189, 194, 248, 279
  and Afghan refugees 108, 116–21
  and Bangladesh 59, 67–9, 73, 76
  and Europe 158, 160, 163
Palestinian National Authority 21
Palestinians 1, 4, 15, 20–1, 112, 125, 189, 279
Pan-Africanist Congress 248
Panama 123–4, 127
Papua New Guinea 102
Paraguay 32
Partnership in Action (PARinAC) 194
peacekeeping and peacebuilding 8, 133, 139–40, 143, 152–3, 220, 227, 256, 261
Pérez de Cuéllar, J. 21, 139, 213, 216, 219
persecution 158, 176–7, 179, 183
  gender-related 181, 253, 277
  by non-state agents 162–4
  social group 23
Peru 126–7
Philippines 59, 81, 83–6, 89, 98, 102
Pijnacker Hordijk, F.L. 60–1
Pinochet, A. 126–7
piracy 7, 79, 86–7, 102

Pol Pot 92, 147
Poland/Poles 13, 26, 28, 164, 171, 187
Polisario Front (Western Sahara) 266–7
Portugal 44, 46, 112, 148
Potsdam conference (1945) 14
Prague spring (1968) 156
Preziosi, F. 50–2, 206
Protocol Relating to the Status of Refugees (1967) 6, 23, 25, 37, 53–5, 57, 83, 173, 198, 279–80, 284
  and Central America 123, 126, 130
pushbacks (Indochina) 83–4, 86–8, 92, 102

quick impact projects (QIPs) 142–3

Rabin, Y. 21
Racak (Kosovo) 233
Rahman, M. 60, 67, 73
Rambouillet talks (on Kosovo, 1999) 233–4
Ranariddh, Prince 147
Read, J. 39
re-admission agreements 161, 209
Reagan, R. 177
Red Crescent Movement 40, 194, 267
Red Cross 29, 194, 207
  see also International Committee of the Red Cross
Redd Barna 94
refoulement, see non-refoulement
refugee
  camps, see especially 108–9
  militarized camps 11, 105, 120–1, 248–9, 271–2
  definition 15, 20, 23–4, 30–1, 53–6, 123, 159, 162–4, 173–4, 179–80, 198–201
  status 20, 23–6, 30–1, 53–5, 83–5, 101, 124, 162, 175–6
regroupement (Algeria) 38–9
Relief Society of Tigray (REST) 114
Renamo (Mozambique) 112, 148, 151
rescue-at-sea 7, 79, 84, 86–7, 102
Rescue-at-Sea Resettlement Offers (RASRO) 87
Revolutionary Front for an Independent East Timor (Fretilin) 236
Revolutionary United Front (RUF), Sierra Leone 261, 280
Rhodesia, see Zimbabwe
Riad, Judge 224–5
Rohingyas 6, 71, 75, 77, 189
Roma (gypsies) 28, 242
Roman Catholic Church 47, 80, 122–3, 129
Romania/Romanians 158, 160, 164
Rome Statute of the International Criminal Court 240
Rørholt, A. 39

Russian Federation/Russians 119, 185–95, 192–7, 196, 198–200, 203, 204–5, 203–6, 207–8, 214–15, 225, 241
Rwandan Patriotic Army (RPA) 254, 262–4
Rwandan Patriotic Front (RPF) 245–6, 255
Rwanda/Rwandans 1, 6, 11, 109, 194, 206, 214–15, 240, 245–73, 278–9, 283–4
  1959–63 crisis 44, 47–52, 245

safe areas 9, 92–3, 127, 168, 211, 222–5
safe havens
  Chile 127
  northern Iraq 9, 213, 216–18
safe third countries 161, 209
Sahrawi Arab Democratic Republic (SADR) 266–7
St Vincent and the Grenadines 53
Sandinista National Liberal Front (FSLN) 122–3, 125, 128, 131, 139, 174
Sankoh, F. 261
Sarajevo (Bosnia and Herzegovina) 206, 218, 223, 225, 230–1
  airlift 220, 225–8
Save the Children Alliance 194
Schengen Agreement (1985) 159
Schengen Convention (1990) 159, 162, 164
Schnyder, F. 40–1, 43, 49–50, 54, 326
Security Council, see United Nations Security Council
Sen, S. 62
Sendashonga, S. 254
Senegal 189, 260
Serbia, see Yugoslavia, Federal Republic of
Serbs 10, 28, 218, 225, 233–4, 239, 242
Shaba 50
Shiites 118, 212
Sierra Leone 214–15, 240, 248, 260–1, 278, 280
Sikhs 69, 180
Singapore 81, 83–4, 88–9, 98
Single European Act (1986) 159
Sino-Indian border war (1962) 63
Sino-Japanese War (1937–45) 33
Slovakia/Slovaks 28, 164
Slovenia 218
Smith, I. 45
Solana, J. 235
Somali National Movement (SNM) 256
Somali Patriotic Movement (SPM) 256
Somalia/Somalis 11, 106, 114, 138, 198, 207, 256–7, 278–9, 283
  asylum in industrialized world 158, 160, 163
Somaliland 257
Somoza Debayle, A. 121–2

South Africa/South Africans 28, 32, 44, 112, 134–5, 148, 152, 171, 248, 261, 281
South Korea/Koreans 2, 18, 22, 98, 102, 187
South Ossetia 9, 185, 192–6, 205, 207
South West Africa 44, 134–5
South West Africa People's Organization (SWAPO) 134–5, 248
Soviet Union 9, 13–16, 19, 24, 43, 73, 143, 174–5, 186–92, 281–2, 284
  and Cold War politics 105–6, 110, 115–17, 121, 127, 131
  and Hungary 5, 13, 26–35, 156
  and Indochina 79, 81
  mass displacement after dissolution 185–209
  see also Commonwealth of Independent States; Russian Federation
Spain 15, 43, 46, 69, 171, 266–7
Spanish Sahara, see Western Sahara
Sphere Project 194
Srebrenica (Bosnia and Herzegovina) 9, 168, 222–5, 228, 243
Sri Lanka/Sri Lankans 105, 138, 214–15, 278, 282
  asylum in industrialized world 157–8, 160, 163, 180
Stability Pact for South Eastern Europe (1999) 233
Stalin, J. 9, 13–14, 26, 29, 186, 189, 195, 202
statelessness 3–4, 30–1, 69, 76, 189, 202, 284
Stoltenberg, T. 188, 191, 200, 327
Sudan People's Liberation Army (SPLA) 115
Sudan/Sudanese 44–6, 71, 105–6, 114–15, 214–15, 246, 259, 278–9
Suharto, General 236
Swaziland 53, 112, 148
Sweden 29–30, 69, 99, 127, 166, 170–1, 225
Switzerland 32, 39–40, 62, 69, 99, 163–4, 166, 170–1, 233
Syria 20–1, 189, 279

Taiwan 33
Tajikistan/Tajiks 9, 116, 119–21, 185, 192, 196–9, 208
Taliban 120, 163
Tamil Nadu 157
Tampere European Council 159, 170
Tanganyika, see Tanzania
Tanzania 11, 37, 112, 142, 148, 279, 283
  and Rwanda 44, 49–52, 54, 246–51, 255, 264–8

Taraki, N.M. 116
Taylor, C. 260–1
Television, impact of 1, 47, 211–13, 228, 283
temporary protected status (TPS) 178
temporary protection 165–8, 170, 178, 222
Thailand 7, 71, 81, 83–5, 87–9, 95–6, 98–9, 109, 279, 281
  open door policy 92–3
  repatriation and peacebuilding 144–6, 151
Tiananmen Square 182
Tibet/Tibetans 4–6, 63, 77, 278–9
Tigray People's Liberation Front (TPLF) 114–15
Tigray/Tigrayans 112, 114–15
Tito, J.B. 29–30
Togo 44, 261
torture 38, 45, 126, 150, 163, 222
  and asylum 171, 179
trafficking and smuggling of people 8, 155, 160, 169, 183, 276, 281
Transcaucasus, see Caucasus
Transdniester Republic 192
Treaty of Amsterdam (1997) 159, 169–73
Treaty of Peace and Friendship (India and Soviet Union, 1971) 68
Treaty of Westphalia (1648) 277
Treaty on European Union (1992) 159, 162
Tudjman, F. 232
Tunisia 6, 35, 37–41
Turkey/Turks 9, 15, 24, 76, 160, 278
  and Kurds 211–17, 239
Turkmenistan/Turkmen 119, 121, 199, 208
Tutsis 47–52, 245, 251, 258–9, 262, 273
Tuzla (Bosnia and Herzegovina) 223
Twagiramungu, F. 254

U Thant 6, 43, 50, 62, 65, 68
Uganda/Ugandans 11, 44, 49–51, 77, 105, 279
  Asians 6, 69, 180
  and Rwanda 245–6, 250–1, 259, 269, 272
Ukraine/Ukrainians 13–14, 28, 187, 189, 199–200, 202
UNHCR (United Nations High Commissioner for Refugees)
  budget 22, 65, 105, 115, 131, 158, 166–7
  establishment 18–24
  Executive Committee 2, 31, 34, 35, 163, 188–9
  Focal Point 6, 62, 73, 76
  good offices function 44, 53, 127, 220
  lead agency role 6, 7, 76, 79, 93, 144, 168, 211, 213, 216, 220,

225, 231, 237, 239, 282, 284
  mandate 2, 3, 34, 39, 43, 85, 118, 126, 133, 188, 190, 248, 254, 286
  Statute 3, 19–20, 31, 39, 53, 194, 214–5
United Kingdom 20, 29, 32–3, 45, 85, 69, 73, 75, 99, 216, 225, 227, 257
  asylum policy 159–60, 163, 166, 170–1
United Nations (UN)
  Advance Mission in Cambodia (UNAMIC) 145
  Advisory Mission to East Timor (UNAMET) 236
  Assistance Mission to Rwanda (UNAMIR) 245
  Border Relief Operation (UNBRO) 95–7
  Centre for Human Rights 191
  Charter 19
  Children's Fund (UNICEF) 47, 64, 93, 138, 225, 257
  Commission on Human Rights (UNCHR) 150, 214, 236
  Conciliation Commission for Palestine 20
  Department of Humanitarian Affairs (DHA) 192, 217
  Department of Peacekeeping Operations 286
  Development Programme (UNDP) 116, 126, 139, 141, 146, 152, 193
  East Pakistan Relief Operation 71
  Educational, Scientific and Cultural Organization (UNESCO) 126, 138
  Food and Agriculture Organization (FAO) 225
  General Assembly 3, 95, 139, 282; and Africa 41–2, 44, 49, 53; and Balkans 236, 243; and former Soviet Union 189, 200; Kurds in Iraq 215, 217; Second World War aftermath 16, 19–20, 22, 29, 33, 35
  High Commissioner for Refugees, see UNHCR
  Interim Administration Mission in Kosovo (UNMIK) 242
  International Conference on Population and Development (Cairo, 1994) 253
  International Police Task Force (Bosnia and Herzegovina) 233
  Korean Reconstruction Agency (UNKRA) 22
  Mission for the Referendum in Western Sahara (MINURSO) 266
  Mission of Observers to Tajikistan (UNMOT) 196

Observer Mission in El Salvador (ONUSAL) 139
Observer Mission in Georgia (UNOMIG) 195
Operation in Mozambique (ONMOZ) 148, 152
Operation in the Congo (ONUC) 52
Operation in Somalia (UNOSOM I and II) 256
Population Division 172
Population Fund (UNFPA) 253
Programme on AIDS (UNAIDS) 253
Protection Force (UNPROFOR) 220–8
Refugee Fund (UNREF) 22, 31
Relief and Rehabilitation Administration (UNRRA) 5, 13–16
Relief and Works Agency for Palestine Refugees in the Near East (UNRWA) 4, 20–2, 125, 279
Relief for Palestine Refugees (UNRPR) 20
Security Council 16, 39, 68, 134, 139, 144, 213; and Balkans 220, 223–4, 233–4, 236–7, 241–2; and former Soviet Union 185, 195–6; and Rwanda 251, 253–4, 256, 266, 268
Standing Inter-Agency Consultative Unit 66
Transition Assistance Group (UNTAG) 134
Transitional Administration in East Timor (UNTAET) 237
Transitional Authority in Cambodia (UNTAC) 96, 144–7
Unified Task Force (UNITAF) 256–7
Verification Mission in Guatemala (MINUGUA) 139
World Food Programme (WFP) 110, 113, 191, 225, 241, 257, 267
World Health Organization (WHO) 64, 225
United Somali Congress (USC) 256
United States 7, 16–19, 21–2, 24, 29, 32, 34–5, 68–9, 117, 134, 137–8, 155, 166, 170–1, 173, 175–7, 180, 284
 and Balkans 227, 236, 239, 241
 and Cold War politics 106, 110, 120–1, 123–5, 128, 130
 and decolonization in Africa 38, 40, 44, 53, 55
 and Indochinese 79, 81, 86–7, 91, 99, 101
 and Iraq 9, 212–13, 216
 Coast Guard 175, 177
 Congress 24, 128, 178–9
 Escapee Program 22, 31
 interdiction 176–7

Universal Declaration of Human Rights (1948) 24, 150
Uruguay/Uruguayans 126, 156
Uzbekistan/Uzbeks 116, 119, 121, 186, 196, 199, 202–3

Venezuela 53, 127
Vieira de Mello, S. 97, 144
Viet Nam/Vietnamese 6, 38, 79–92, 99, 102–3, 143–5, 158–60, 248, 278, 284
 see also boat people
visa requirements 86, 157, 159, 161–2, 182
Volga Germans 187, 202

Wa Dondo, K 255
Waldheim, K. 73, 76, 84, 86
war crimes 1, 138, 151, 211, 226, 240
Warsaw Pact 27
Weis, P. 30–1, 39, 62
West Bank 20–1, 279
West Bengal 63–5
West Timor 236–7, 248, 278
Western Sahara 266–7, 278
women 3, 87, 115, 120, 181, 277, 280
 gender-related persecution 163
 Iraq and Balkans 214, 222
 repatriation and peacebuilding 137–8, 149–50
World Conference on Women (Beijing, 1995) 253
World Bank 113, 118, 152, 193, 233, 285
World Refugee Year (1959/60) 33, 35
World Vision International 194

Yalta conference (1945) 14
Yemen 257
Yugoslav Red Cross 30
Yugoslavia, Federal Republic of 10, 215, 218, 228–9, 234, 239, 242, 279
 and Hungary 26, 29–30, 34–5
 former Yugoslavia 9, 37, 43, 127, 158, 160, 166–7, 211, 214, 218–35, 238–43, 278, 284

Zaire see Congo, Democratic Republic of
Zairean Contingent 254–5, 258, 262
Zambia 44–6, 105, 112, 134, 148, 248, 279
Zepa (Bosnia and Herzegovina) 9, 168, 222–3, 225, 228
Zimbabwe African National Union (ZANU) 45
Zimbabwe African People's Union (ZAPU) 45
Zimbabwe 44–5, 112, 148, 272
Zolotista 260